T0351800

Housing and the Financial Crisis

A National Bureau of
Economic Research
Conference Report

Housing and the
Financial Crisis

Edited by   **Edward L. Glaeser and Todd Sinai**

The University of Chicago Press

Chicago and London

EDWARD L. GLAESER is the Fred and Eleanor Glimp Professor of
Economics at Harvard University and a research associate and director
of the Urban Economics Working Group at the National Bureau of
Economic Research. TODD SINAI is associate professor of real estate
and business economics and public policy at the Wharton School at the
University of Pennsylvania and a research associate of the National
Bureau of Economic Research.

The University of Chicago Press, Chicago 60637
The University of Chicago Press, Ltd., London
© 2013 by the National Bureau of Economic Research
All rights reserved. Published 2013.
Printed in the United States of America

22 21 20 19 18 17 16 15 14 13   1 2 3 4 5
ISBN-13: 978-0-226-03058-6 (cloth)
ISBN-13: 978-0-226-03061-6 (e-book)

Library of Congress Cataloging-in-Publication Data

Housing and the financial crisis / edited by Edward L. Glaeser and
    Todd Sinai.
        pages ; cm. — (National Bureau of Economic Research
    conference report)
        Includes bibliographical references and index.
        ISBN 978-0-226-03058-6 (alk. paper) — ISBN 978-0-226-03061-6
    (e-book)   1. Housing—United States—Finance—Congresses.
    2. Financial crises—United States—History—21st century—
    Congresses.   3. Global Financial Crisis, 2008–2009—Congresses.
    I. Glaeser, Edward L. (Edward Ludwig), 1967–   II. Sinai, Todd
    M. (Todd Michael)   III. Series: National Bureau of Economic
    Research conference report.
    HD7293.Z9H678 2013
    332.10973—dc23
                                                            2012041286

♾ This paper meets the requirements of ANSI/NISO Z39.48-1992
(Permanence of Paper).

Relation of the Directors to the
Work and Publications of the
National Bureau of Economic Research

1. The object of the NBER is to ascertain and present to the economics profession, and to the public more generally, important economic facts and their interpretation in a scientific manner without policy recommendations. The Board of Directors is charged with the responsibility of ensuring that the work of the NBER is carried on in strict conformity with this object.

2. The President shall establish an internal review process to ensure that book manuscripts proposed for publication DO NOT contain policy recommendations. This shall apply both to the proceedings of conferences and to manuscripts by a single author or by one or more co-authors but shall not apply to authors of comments at NBER conferences who are not NBER affiliates.

3. No book manuscript reporting research shall be published by the NBER until the President has sent to each member of the Board a notice that a manuscript is recommended for publication and that in the President's opinion it is suitable for publication in accordance with the above principles of the NBER. Such notification will include a table of contents and an abstract or summary of the manuscript's content, a list of contributors if applicable, and a response form for use by Directors who desire a copy of the manuscript for review. Each manuscript shall contain a summary drawing attention to the nature and treatment of the problem studied and the main conclusions reached.

4. No volume shall be published until forty-five days have elapsed from the above notification of intention to publish it. During this period a copy shall be sent to any Director requesting it, and if any Director objects to publication on the grounds that the manuscript contains policy recommendations, the objection will be presented to the author(s) or editor(s). In case of dispute, all members of the Board shall be notified, and the President shall appoint an ad hoc committee of the Board to decide the matter; thirty days additional shall be granted for this purpose.

5. The President shall present annually to the Board a report describing the internal manuscript review process, any objections made by Directors before publication or by anyone after publication, any disputes about such matters, and how they were handled.

6. Publications of the NBER issued for informational purposes concerning the work of the Bureau, or issued to inform the public of the activities at the Bureau, including but not limited to the NBER Digest and Reporter, shall be consistent with the object stated in paragraph 1. They shall contain a specific disclaimer noting that they have not passed through the review procedures required in this resolution. The Executive Committee of the Board is charged with the review of all such publications from time to time.

7. NBER working papers and manuscripts distributed on the Bureau's web site are not deemed to be publications for the purpose of this resolution, but they shall be consistent with the object stated in paragraph 1. Working papers shall contain a specific disclaimer noting that they have not passed through the review procedures required in this resolution. The NBER's web site shall contain a similar disclaimer. The President shall establish an internal review process to ensure that the working papers and the web site do not contain policy recommendations, and shall report annually to the Board on this process and any concerns raised in connection with it.

8. Unless otherwise determined by the Board or exempted by the terms of paragraphs 6 and 7, a copy of this resolution shall be printed in each NBER publication as described in paragraph 2 above.

Contents

Preface   ix

Postmortem for a Housing Crash   1
Edward L. Glaeser and Todd Sinai

1.   **House Price Moments in Boom-Bust Cycles**   19
Todd Sinai

2.   **The Supply Side of the Housing Boom and Bust
of the 2000s**   69
Andrew Haughwout, Richard W. Peach, John Sporn,
and Joseph Tracy

3.   **A Spatial Look at Housing Boom and Bust Cycles**   105
David Genesove and Lu Han

4.   **Mortgage Financing in the Housing Boom and Bust**   143
Benjamin J. Keys, Tomasz Piskorski, Amit Seru, and
Vikrant Vig

5.   **A New Look at Second Liens**   205
Donghoon Lee, Christopher Mayer,
and Joseph Tracy

6.   **International Capital Flows and House Prices:
Theory and Evidence**   235
Jack Favilukis, David Kohn, Sydney C. Ludvigson,
and Stijn Van Nieuwerburgh

7.   **Can Cheap Credit Explain the Housing Boom?**   301
            Edward L. Glaeser, Joshua D. Gottlieb,
            and Joseph Gyourko

8.   **The Future of the Government-Sponsored**
            Enterprises: The Role for Government in the US
            Mortgage Market   361
            Dwight Jaffee and John M. Quigley

            Contributors   419
            Author Index   421
            Subject Index   427

Preface

This volume includes eight papers that were prepared as part of a research project, "Housing and the Financial Crisis," by the National Bureau of Economic Research. The papers examine various aspects of the housing convulsion and its aftermath: describing what happened to prices and construction during and after the housing boom across and within US metropolitan areas; considering the role of credit, capital flows, and other factors as precipitating causes of the housing boom and bust; and evaluating the role of government-sponsored enterprises in the housing market. These papers were presented at a conference in Cambridge, Massachusetts, on November 17–18, 2011.

We are grateful to the Smith Richardson Foundation for its financial support of the project, which also encompassed a conference, "Behavioral Finance and Housing Bubbles," organized by Christopher Mayer and held on April 14, 2012, at the University of Chicago, and a conference, "Housing in the Aftermath of the Financial Crisis," organized by Joseph Gyourko and held in Cambridge, Massachusetts, on July 24–25, 2012. We would also like to thank Carl Beck, Helena Fitz-Patrick, Denis Healy, Lita Kimble, Brett Maranjian, and Alterra Milone for their efforts on behalf of this volume and its associated conferences, and James Poterba for providing the impetus for this endeavor.

Postmortem for a Housing Crash

Edward L. Glaeser and Todd Sinai

Introduction

The remarkable boom and bust of America's housing markets during the first decade of the twenty-first century now joins the stock market gyrations of the 1920s and the dot com bubble of the late 1990s in the pantheon of great asset market swings. The twenty-city Case-Shiller repeat sales housing price index rose 70 percent in real terms between April 2001 and April 2006, the peak of the market. By November 2011, the index had declined by 40 percent from the peak, leaving housing prices approximately where they were at the start of 2000.

This great housing market crash did as much damage to the received wisdom about housing markets and housing policy as it did to the portfolios of households and financial institutions. Traditional economic models, with their assumptions of hyper-rational consumers with sensible assessments of future price movements, seem difficult to reconcile with price swings in markets like Las Vegas, where real housing prices rose by 71 percent in the thirty-six months before April 2006, only to fall by 65 percent in subsequent years. The unincorporated area outside Las Vegas has abundant land and little land market regulation, so how could buyers really believe that prices could stay so far above the costs of producing homes?

Edward L. Glaeser is the Fred and Eleanor Glimp Professor of Economics at Harvard University and a research associate and director of the Urban Economics Working Group at the National Bureau of Economic Research. Todd Sinai is associate professor of real estate and business economics and public policy at the Wharton School at the University of Pennsylvania and a research associate of the National Bureau of Economic Research.

For acknowledgments, sources of research support, and disclosure of the authors' material financial relationships, if any, please see http://www.nber.org/chapters/c12618.ack.

The great housing convulsion destroyed the view that housing prices would always remain close to construction costs in unregulated markets (Glaeser, Gyourko, and Saiz 2008) and that price movements could be completely explained by changes in interest rates (Poterba 1984). Perhaps, most obviously, the crash banished the old myth that housing prices could only go up. Millions of underwater homeowners make it abundantly clear that houses are no different from any other asset in their ability to climb and crash.

Just as the crash changed our understanding of housing markets, it changed views about housing policy. While there were certainly economists who questioned the wisdom of pro-borrowing policies like the Home Mortgage Interest Deduction and the implicit subsidies enjoyed by Fannie Mae (the Federal National Mortgage Association) and Freddie Mac (the Federal Home Loan Mortgage Corporation), these policies were widely popular among politicians and voters of both parties. Subsidized mortgages were perceived not only as a tool to encourage the alleged social benefits of home ownership, but also as a path toward financial stability for ordinary Americans. Fannie Mae and Freddie Mac were supposed to be self-sufficient entities that created little risk for taxpayers.

The costs to taxpayers of bailing out these entities has been estimated at near $200 billion, and millions of foreclosures call into question the wisdom of using subsidized borrowing to encourage asset accumulation. But there remains considerable uncertainty about what housing policy should do now, when housing markets remain weak, and in the future. A more libertarian view argues for less public intervention in housing markets. An alternative viewpoint argues for more action, at least as long as prices and construction remain low, to bolster housing markets, and hopefully thus the larger economy.

This essay is an introduction to a volume meant to make sense of the housing convulsion and its aftermath. We organized this essay, and to a lesser extent the chapters in the volume, around three broad questions. First, we focus on description. What actually happened to prices and construction during and after the housing boom? America is not one housing market, and the boom hardly hit every market equally. Even among the Case-Shiller metropolitan areas, which represent an unrepresentatively volatile set of America's cities, there were places that experienced little price movement during the boom. Between April 2000 and April 2006, real prices in the Dallas area increased by less than 2 percent.

Three of the chapters in the volume address the core facts of the boom and bust. The first one, by Todd Sinai, presents a far-ranging look at price movements at the metropolitan area level, and presents six stylized facts about housing prices movements throughout the United States. The second chapter, by Andrew Haughwout, Richard W. Peach, John Sporn, and Joseph Tracy, focuses on the supply side of the market. They document key facts about building and land prices during the boom, document the changing industrial structure of the building industry, and investigate the role that the supply side of the market played in determining the nature of the boom and bust.

The third chapter, by David Genesove and Lu Han, examines both prices and permitting behavior, but focuses within, rather than across, metropolitan areas. Their work illustrates that even within a single metropolitan area, some neighborhoods experienced significantly more appreciation than others. They document that the boom seems to have particularly increased prices in areas with relatively short commute times, and that the gradients of prices with respect to commuting time seems to have flattened during the bust. These facts can be interpreted as supporting the view that the boom was associated with temporarily high valuations of genuine neighborhood assets, like proximity to jobs.

The second section of this introduction focuses on the causes of the boom, and inevitably changes in credit conditions play a dominant role in the search for causes. There are, of course, alternate explanations for the boom, and we discuss some of them in this introduction. Case and Shiller have persistently argued for the importance of unrealistic expectations about future house price appreciation and, in hindsight, the assumptions of many buyers during the boom appear to have been wildly mistaken. But there are at least three reasons why irrational expectations–based explanations have garnered less attention from housing economists than credit market–based explanations.

First, it is hard to think of erroneous expectations as being an exogenous variable, appearing out of nowhere and fueling housing price growth. If we think of price growth assessments as reflecting some deeper cause, then that pushes toward understanding the deeper causes rather than the mediating force of expectations. Second, there is no clear explanation of why irrational exuberance would show up so demonstrably in some markets, like Phoenix, and not in others, like Dallas. Finally, economics has a long and valuable tradition of attempting to exhaust rational explanations for market phenomena rather than embracing human error. The focus on the rational provides discipline for economic theorizing, even if it misses important components of human behavior.

Most non-credit-related "rational" explanations of the housing boom are relatively easy to disprove. For example, traditional theories would suggest that rising incomes could increase demand for housing and explain a price increase, but incomes were not rising nearly fast enough during the 2000 to 2006 period to explain the boom. Supply limitations may explain some of the variation in prices across America's metropolitan areas, but it is hard to imagine that supply conditions were changing quickly enough during the few years of the current millennium to explain a massive housing price increase.

Conversely, real interest rates were falling during much of the 2000 to 2006 period, and conventional models suggested that this decline might even be enough to explain a large portion of rising housing prices in many metropolitan housing markets (Mayer, Himmelberg, and Sinai 2005). In addition, there seems to have been a proliferation of easy credit during this time period, epitomized by the rise in subprime lending, that may have increased the number of people who had access to the credit needed to buy housing. As such, it is at least possible that easy credit explains a significant amount of the housing boom.

Supporters of the credit market theory note that the boom coincided with a period of time when risk spreads were extremely low by historical standards. In 2006, many lenders appear to have believed that both home buyers and the Greek government had almost no chance of defaulting. It is less clear whether this coincidence reflects a causal chain that runs from credit availability to high housing prices, or whether it reflects an overall climate of extreme optimism that simultaneously impacted home buyers, mortgage lenders and the buyers of Greek debt. Chapter 4, by Keys, Piskorski, Seru, and Vig, details the evolution of mortgage financing during the boom. They document the tremendous increase in subprime and "Alt-A" lending, and present evidence suggesting that increased securitization decreased lending standards. They document that securitization becomes more common for borrowers with FICO scores above 620, and that defaults rise, rather than fall, for borrowers with FICO scores that put them above this quantity.

The chapter by Donghoon Lee, Christopher Mayer, and Joseph Tracy (chapter 5) focuses on the rise of second liens during the boom. These second liens often made it possible for borrowers to get mortgages with essentially no money down. During the bust, these second liens create a conflict of interest between mortgage servicers who own second liens and owners of first liens. The servicers presumably have an interest to encourage payment on the second lien, even if the borrower is not servicing the first lien.

Chapter 6, by Favilukis, Kohn, Ludwigson, and Van Nieuwerburgh, then elegantly exposits the view that easy credit caused the run-up in housing prices. In their model, easy credit comes from a savings glut outside the United States. They parameterize a model and show that given their assumptions, the decrease in lending standards could have caused the price run-up. They also present some evidence linking price growth and bank loan officers' reports of their willingness to supply credit.

Chapter 7 by Glaeser, Gottlieb, and Gyourko offers an alternative take on the credit market hypothesis. They argue that there are several reasons why a conventional user cost model of housing will overstate the predicted link between credit conditions and housing prices, including elastic supply and mean reversion of interest rates. They then argue that the more modest link, predicted by a perhaps more realistic model, is supported by the long-run data and that this modest link implies that easier credit cannot explain more than a fraction of the boom in housing price and that tighter credit can similarly explain little of the bust.

The final section of this chapter and the final chapter in this volume focuses on the future of housing policy. In this introduction we discuss briefly a broader range of public policy considerations around housing, including the Federal Housing Administration, and the Home Mortgage Interest Deduction. Chapter 8, by Dwight Jaffee and John Quigley, specifically focuses on the Government-Sponsored Enterprises (or GSEs), Fannie Mae and Freddie Mac. Jaffee and Quigley describe the history of the GSEs and their repeated crises. Their analysis suggests that the GSEs received an implicit government subsidy, and much of the benefit of that subsidy went to GSE shareholders. Moreover, even if the GSEs are not themselves responsible for the boom and bust, they seem to have done relatively little to steady the market.

The chapter then discusses broader options for the future of the GSEs and in particular the possibility of shrinking their role enormously. The authors' evidence calls into question the view that the GSEs are absolutely vital for the functioning of housing markets. It is certainly quite possible that the cost of these enterprises, at least in their current form, significantly exceeds their benefits.

The great housing convulsion is a major event for housing research—an event so significantly large that it could even herald a paradigm shift within the field. The essays in this volume attempt to collect what we know about the nature and causes of the boom. Our hope is that this provides a starting point for future major advances in housing research.

The Anatomy of the Boom and Bust

The nationwide contours of the housing market boom and subsequent bust are well known. The Case-Shiller price index may not be nationally representative, but it does capture the basic shape of events nationwide. After six long years of nominal price stagnation and real price declines from 1991 to 1997, prices began to rise again. During all but one of the first five years of the most recent decade, the twenty-city price index increased by 10 percent or more; the exception year was 2001 when, despite deep economic troubles, nominal prices still managed to increase by over 7 percent.

The Case-Shiller increase somewhat overstates the national boom because it overrepresents America's more volatile housing markets. Except for late 2004 and 2005, nominal annual price growth in the Federal Housing Finance Agency's index, which represents a far wider range of metropolitan areas, does not top 10 percent. Yet while that index typically shows annual growth rates of 6 to 7 percent, it still shows the same basic pattern of a rapid increase in price growth around the end of 2007, followed by a sustained period of robust price increases that lasts until 2006, and steady price declines since that date.

This national pattern provides one depiction of the past decade, but it is an incomplete story. The first three chapters in this volume enrich the national picture first by providing subnational data (chapter 1), data on housing supply (chapter 2), and intra-metropolitan information (chapter 3). The variation within the United States is important, not just in detailing the larger picture, but providing data with which we can test various explanations of the boom and bust.

Figure I.1 shows the relationship between changes in the Federal Housing Finance Agency (FHFA) Price index between 2001 and 2006, divided by the 2001 index level, and changes in the price index between 2006 and 2011, also dividing by the 2001 index level. We adjust for changes in the nationwide consumer price index. We deflate by the 2001 index level for both periods so that the changes are in comparable units.

The figure illustrates that the growth in prices, from trough to peak, was highly variable. Some cities, like Las Vegas, experienced extraordinary swings, while others, like Houston, were far more stable. Chapter 1 also emphasizes that the distribution of price growth has a very fat tail. The average market experienced real price growth of about 55 percent, but 57 percent of markets experienced price growth, trough-to-peak, below that amount. When Sinai weights by the number of housing units in the market in 1990, the price distribution becomes even more skewed, as some of the largest markets experienced particularly robust growth, which is one reason why the Case-Shiller price index, which is skewed toward larger markets, finds larger average growth than the FHFA index.

The ephemeral nature of the boom is also illustrated by the robust correlation between the sizes of the boom and bust. The slope of the line in the figure is –0.95, so that if an area saw its prices rise by 50 percent between 2001 and 2006, that area's house prices were, on average, up only 2.5 percent over the entire decade. Such mean reversion is not uncommon in housing and other asset markets (Cutler, Poterba, and Summers 1991), but typically it is far milder than the figure suggests. Glaeser et al. (2011), for example, estimate a –0.32 coefficient for five-year changes on lagged figure year changes over a longer time period, which is about one-third of the coefficient shown in the picture.[1] The extraordinary magnitude of mean reversion in the 2001 to 2011 period suggests that the last boom was unrelated to enduring economic fundamentals.

That heterogeneity is itself an important fact about the boom, in part because it relates to different theories about the boom's cause. If this enormous heterogeneity is to be compatible with a common national shock to housing demand, caused perhaps by a common national shock to credit conditions, then there must be extremely large differences in housing supply, as suggested by Glaeser, Gyourko, and Saiz (2008). Alternatively, this heterogeneity might mean that a common national factor, like easier credit,

---

1. These results are not exactly comparable since they also control for year and area fixed effects, but even without those the estimated mean reversion levels are far smaller.

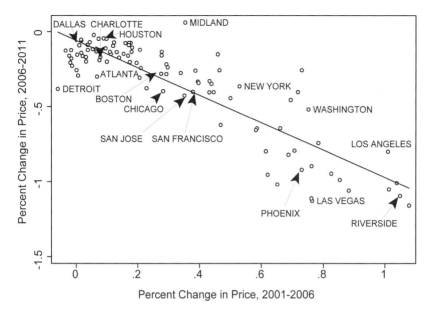

Fig. I.1   Percent house price growth (2001–2006) versus percent house price declines (2006–2011) by housing market
Note: House price growth calculated from the Federal Housing Finance Agency's House Price Index.

had different impact in different areas depending on local factors, such as the number of borrowers that were previously unable to access credit, as in Mian and Sufi (2009). A final explanation is that the booms were fueled by location-specific factors, perhaps including unrealistic expectations about local long-run trends that were not driven by any common national shock.

One clue offered by the heterogeneous price changes is that the places that boomed in the 2000s also boomed during the previous run-up in housing prices during the late 1980s. While the magnitude of the more recent price rise is far larger, there is a strong correlation between boom markets across the two episodes. This fact is compatible with the view that housing supply elasticity, which is presumably relatively constant over time, helps explain the cross-area heterogeneity. It is only compatible with the hypothesis that emphasizes a common national shock interacting with different local conditions, if indeed it was essentially the same national shock that operates during both periods, such as easier credit. If the boom was the result of lots of little local shocks, then there would have to be some reason why those shocks were so similar in the 2000s and the 1980s.

The cross-area heterogeneity is also helpful in testing the hypothesis that changes in underlying fundamentals can explain the boom. The Sinai essay addresses fundamentals both by controlling for rents and by controlling for underlying economic variables such as local income levels. Neither of these variables can explain much of the variation in prices over the boom, which pushes us toward theories that reflect the cost of capital or expectations about housing price appreciation—both of which should impact the price-to-rent ratio—and away from theories that emphasize changes in the fundamental demand for housing in particular areas.

A final interesting geographic fact is that the price growth was disproportionately present in coastal metropolitan areas. While there were some inland areas, such as Las Vegas, that experienced extreme price movements, overall, the interior of the country was far more stable. The coastal areas typically have more restrictions on housing supply, and more robust local economies that have shown remarkable resilience over many decades. The geographic clustering also reminds us that at least geographically proximate markets do seem to be somewhat linked, as documented by Sinai and Souleles (2005).

The Genesove and Han chapter focuses within metropolitan areas. During the latest boom, there was more price growth in the center of metropolitan areas, although that was not the case during the 1980s (Glaeser and Gottlieb 2012). The Genesove and Han chapter documents that the prices declined more sharply with commuting time during the boom than after it, which also suggests that prices rose more sharply close to employment centers.

Genesove and Han suggest a supply-side story for explaining this effect. Areas that are further away from employment centers effectively have more land in which to deliver housing. That extra supply can mute the price impact of demand increases. An alternative view suggests that price growth during the boom was associated with overly optimistic assessments of the value of urban assets, including access to core employment sectors. If these assets were temporarily overvalued during the boom, then we should expect to see more of a price decline in these areas during the bust.

While the examples of Phoenix and Las Vegas during the boom showed that extreme price growth was still possible in areas with apparently elastic supply, supply is still important both in shaping price growth and in determining the long-term real consequences of the boom. After all, the supply elasticity determines the extent to which a temporary price boom translates into real investment in housing and commercial real estate throughout the country. Understanding the magnitude of oversupply during the boom is also important if we are to estimate how long it will take for the American construction industry to resume more normal building levels.

Chapter 2 begins by putting the housing boom of the last decade into a broader historical perspective. Measured by housing starts per capita, the construction boom never reached the heights hit in the 1960s, 1970s, and 1980s. However, while those booms had a relatively short duration, and were followed by short, sharp downturns, the more recent building boom

Fig. I.2   Number of new housing units and number of new households, 1968–2011
Notes: Numbers in thousands. "New Households" is an average of the current year, the previous year, and the next year.

lasted for almost fifteen years. The construction bust after that boom has been more extreme than during the earlier upturns, perhaps because this boom lasted for so many years. As a share of gross domestic product, the recent building boom was fully as big as in earlier years, which reflects higher building costs and the larger structures that have become more prevalent. Moreover, the recent boom was almost all driven by increases in single-family, not multifamily, construction.

The amount of building needs to be related to the rate of household formation. Figure I.2 shows the long-run paths of household formation and changes in the number of new housing units in the United States. During the earlier booms, increases in building were matched with increases in the numbers of new households. During the more recent boom, construction occurred without any similar increase in number of households.

Haughwout et al. emphasize the changing demographic trends within America to explain the shifts. In earlier decades, the number of younger Americans was growing rapidly, as the baby boomers moved into adulthood. In recent years, the growth in younger age cohorts has been modest, but there were increases in the numbers of older Americans. Indeed, this demographic shift led Mankiw and Weil (1989) twenty years ago to predict a great housing bust. The fact that the building boom occurred despite the aging of America is fairly remarkable.

Haughwout et al. also illustrate the mismatch between construction and population growth at the state level. Throughout the 1990s, there is a fairly tight connection between overall state population growth and the number of housing starts. Between 2000 and 2005, however, housing starts seemed to be much higher than would be warranted due to population growth in many states, such as Arizona and Nevada. In other areas, such as California, population growth and housing starts remain closely connected.

This surfeit of building meant that there was a great deal of excess housing, even during the height of the boom, and a significant increase in nonseasonal vacancy rates. The vacancy rates were particularly high in the South. Typically, rising prices are associated with supply shortfalls, but during the boom the supply response was so enormous that housing was actually abundant. It remains puzzling that this glut did not do more to limit housing price growth.

The Haughwout et al. chapter also examines changes within the industrial organization of the building community. During the boom, building was increasingly dominated by larger builders and those builders increasingly built up large inventories of land. The consolidation of the building industry is striking. In 1990, the ten largest builders accounted for less than 10 percent of US construction, but by 2005, they were responsible for over 22 percent of American building. The authors emphasize the large number of company acquisitions over this period, and that larger builders typically rely less on bank financing, which means that they may face less scrutiny toward their construction projects.

Their large land inventories meant that the builders had also become big land speculators. Well-financed, presumably well-informed building companies were accumulating vast amounts of land. This presumably suggests that beliefs about increasing land values were quite widespread—it was not just ordinary homeowners who were gambling on real estate markets during this time period—and it meant that many builders found themselves in dire financial straits after the boom, leading to further distress within that industry.

The Causes of the Boom and Bust: Easy Credit and Other Explanations

It is easier to describe the events of the 2001 to 2011 decade than it is to explain them. The price boom was so much more extreme than during previous periods that it is hard to find exogenous forces that could possibly have explained such a serious price fluctuation. Classical explanations of price fluctuations emphasize changes in fundamentals, such as sizable shocks to housing demand created by rising income levels, or shocks to housing supply, such as increased limitations on construction. Yet it is hard to find such fundamental shifts. Certainly, the American economy was not experiencing a particularly unusual boom over these years.

Supply constraints do not appear to have been particularly tight in many boom areas, such as Las Vegas and Phoenix. While there were certainly stories suggesting that land was becoming less available in the Las Vegas region (Nathanson and Zwick 2011), the massive numbers of new homes built in the area makes it hard to believe that restrictions on supply were becoming all that onerous. Relatively flat rents also belie the view that changes in the demand and supply of housing drove the housing price boom.

An alternative view emphasizes the role of credit markets in driving the change. Chapter 4 by Keys, Piskorski, Seru, and Vig describes the evolution of mortgage financing during the boom. During the early years of this millennium, mortgage originations increased dramatically, but the initial wave was overwhelmingly originated by GSEs. The GSE mortgage originations appear to have increased fivefold, from roughly $500 billion to $2.5 trillion during their peak in 2002. That peak largely represented mortgage financing during an era of historically low interest rates.

Starting in 2002, there was a substantial increase in Alt-A and subprime mortgages originated through 2005 and 2006. While the GSEs remained the largest mortgage originator during this time period, the combined class of Alt-A and subprime mortgages exceeded GSE originations by 2005. After 2006, these riskier classes of mortgages declined dramatically.

As subprime and Alt-A mortgages became more prevalent, they were also increasingly securitized. The securitization rate for this class of mortgages was below 50 percent in 2001 and increased to over 90 percent by 2007. This time-series fact seems to support Keys, Piskorski, Seru, and Vig's contention that an increasing ability to securitize mortgages helped enable the vast flow of Alt-A and subprime credit to mortgage borrowers.

Over this period of increased securitization, some—but not all—characteristics of nonagency debt also evolved. There was little change in FICO scores over the boom, and the gap between prime and subprime lenders in this important measure of riskiness remained relatively constant. However, second liens became more important in the nonagency market, and average cumulative loan-to-value ratios eventually reached over 95 percent, meaning that borrowers were putting very little money down. Among the same group of borrowers, an increasing share of loans was made without complete documentation, further supporting the view that credit became more available in this group.

Keys, Piskorski, Seru, and Vig then document the apparent increase in the ease of securitizing risky mortgages. The time between origination and securitization fell from sixteen months to six between 2000 and 2006, suggesting that ability to pass along even risky mortgages had steadily increased. At the same time, the number of tranches in the typical subprime mortgage pool was increasing. Increasing numbers of tranches were often associated with a greater transformation of initially quite risky mortgages into pools of mortgages that appeared much safer because they contained the safest tranches of the mortgage pool. Of course, after the mortgage bust, many of those apparently safer tranches proved to remain quite risky.

Some of the most compelling evidence for the importance of securitization in producing lax credit is the evidence for a discontinuity in the treatment of borrowers around the 620 FICO score. In many cases, the FICO score of 620 has proved to be a rule of thumb that determines whether a mortgage can be securitized. Keys, Piskorski, Seru, and Vig show in their loans data that there is a vast discrete jump in the amount of prevalence of securitized low documentation mortgages at the 620 FICO score point, which seems to confirm the view that this was a real cutoff. The time to securitize also declines discretely at the 620 point.

If securitization leads to a reduction in the level of lender scrutiny, then we might expect to see a jump in the level of scrutiny for mortgages with borrowers under the 620 FICO point because, below that level, lenders expect to carry the risks of the mortgage themselves. Keys, Piskorski, Seru, and Vig do find that there are substantially higher delinquency rates just above the 620 FICO score cutoff. While it is in principle possible that this discontinuity reflects rules of thumb other than securitization per se, it is at least quite reasonable to think that securitization was one of the reasons why delinquency rates increase at the 620 point.

Keys, Piskorski, Seru, and Vig also examine the rash of foreclosures since the crash. Many authors have argued that there are too many foreclosures, and too few loan modifications, even relative to the interests of lenders. The significant losses involved in foreclosure would seem to create strong incentives to modify loans, although it is possible that it is just too difficult to identify borrowers for whom modification would actually deter default. Widespread modifications have the problem of reducing lender revenues for many mortgages that would have stayed current without any modification. An alternative hypothesis is that securitization makes renegotiation more difficult by creating diverse ownership and agents who are likely to just follow the letter of the contract.

Keys, Piskorski, Seru, and Vig show that independent servicers tend to foreclose more quickly. They also find that banks are less likely to foreclose on mortgages that they hold themselves. These facts seems to link securitization with the large numbers of foreclosures, which suggests an added reason to be wary of the securitization process.

In chapter 5 Lee, Mayer, and Tracy look at one particular aspect of the credit boom—the rise in second liens. There are two prevalent forms of second liens: home equity lines of credit (or HELOCs) and closed-end second liens (CES). The HELOCs are typically given to more creditworthy borrowers and are often used to supplement standard forms of borrowing, such as credit card debt. Closed-end seconds are more often given to riskier borrowers, and these are more often used to actually fund the purchase of the home, allowing the borrower to put relatively little of their own money down.

Both forms of second liens increased dramatically over the boom. The HELOCs remained the larger form of second lien, but CES increased dramatically in its share of overall second lien balances. Closed-end seconds were particularly common after nonprime first loans, and they were particularly common in areas that experienced extreme price fluctuations during the boom. They seem to have been a significant part of the credit explosion that accompanied the boom.

Delinquency rates for CES liens are quite high and close to the delinquency rates for subprime mortgages. Delinquency rates for HELOCs are substantially lower, and more comparable to the delinquency rates on auto loans. The delinquency rates for both types of second liens that were originated at the peak of the boom (2004 to 2006) are much higher than second liens originated during earlier years, which at least suggests that lending standards had been substantially relaxed for these forms of credit as well.

One of the great puzzles about second lien delinquency is that in principle, they should be more likely to be delinquent than first mortgages, which are technically senior debt. Yet in many cases, borrowers keep their second mortgages current while defaulting on their first mortgages. Lee, Mayer, and Tracy document this fact and present three interesting explanations for why this might be occurring, including the government-created incentives to default on primary mortgages and personal liability for second liens.

The Favilukis, Kohn, Ludwigson, and Van Nieuwerburgh chapter goes a step further back and attempts to understand the explosion of credit that was contemporaneous with the bubble. They argue that there was an increase in the supply of credit coming from outside the United States. They document the tremendous flow of credit into the United States during the boom years, and the relatively low interest rates during the time period.

They then perform panel regressions where they link loan officers' perceptions of the ease of supplying credit with price increases. While it is possible that rising house prices led loan officers to increase the supply of credit rather than the reverse, these regression results support the idea that there is a link between credit availability and the price growth during the boom.

In chapter 7 Glaeser, Gottlieb, and Gyourko present a somewhat contrarian view of credit and the boom. While they do not dispute there was a substantial increase in the amount of lending during the boom, they argue that neither theory nor empirical work suggests that the level of price increases can be easily explained by the changes in credit. They suggest that standard rational models of home-buyer behavior suggest a relatively weak link between credit variables and home prices. One reason for this weak link is that buyers who purchase homes during easy credit periods should expect some mean reversion of interest rates and credit conditions, which should cause them to expect to sell during periods when credit is less available.

The authors provide some empirical work suggesting that the historic link between real interest rates and housing prices is in line with the predictions of a simple rational model and far too small to explain the boom. Finally, they also provide some evidence on aggregate changes in loan-to-value ratios and loan acceptance ratios. While there were significant changes in these variables in specific subsets of the borrower population across the whole US market, these measures of credit availability do not appear to have changed enough to explain the boom in prices.

Chapter 7 also reminds us that the bust happened despite a period of persistently low interest rates. However, it is possible that other changes in the credit market may have helped prod housing market declines. For example, subprime borrowers found it more difficult to borrow during the bust. Moreover, the decline coincided with the introduction of new credit instruments, such as synthetic collateralized debt obligations, that made it easier for some investors to short the housing market. Of course, that introduction is itself endogenous and may reflect the desire of some savvy investors to short a market that seemed to them to be headed for a fall.

These facts do not imply that widespread credit availability was not important to the boom. But the link between credit and housing price growth does not seem to be sufficient to be the sole explanation. Instead, it seems more likely that credit interacted with other conditions, like buyer overoptimism, during the 2000 to 2006 period, and helped create the cocktail that spurred growth.

Public Policy in the Wake of the Crash

Even if we do not fully understand the causes of the great housing convulsion, the convulsion itself seems to call out for rethinking Federal housing policy. The government-sponsored enterprises are the most pressing area for reform. They were nationalized in the wake of their collapse, and no one has argued that the status quo, where they remain wards of the state, is a reasonable permanent solution. The Jaffee and Quigley chapter, which ends this volume, provides an overview of the history of the GSEs and a discussion of policy options going forward.

Fannie Mae got its start in the Great Depression to provide liquidity for mortgage lenders. It first acquired private shareholders in 1954 and was privatized in 1968. In 1970, Freddie Mac was create to generate competition for Fannie Mae. Together, they insure trillions of dollars of mortgages, bearing the potential default risk. At their height, they collectively also held $1.5 trillion worth of retained mortgages, which creates added interest rate risk.

While federal officials repeatedly attempted to signal that the federal government was not liable for the GSE debt, the market never seemed to believe these signals. Fannie and Freddie were regularly able to borrow at interest rates that were remarkably close to those paid by the US Treasury and far below interest rates paid even by the most secure AAA company.

The natural conclusion is that the market was sure that these entities would be bailed out, and of course, subsequent events have proven those investors to be correct. The combination of private ownership, and the ability to borrow with an implicit Federal guarantee, seems almost certain to lead to too much risk-taking. Shareholders stood to profit enormously when times were good, and the government bore the risk during downturns. The eventual collapse of the companies seems almost inevitable.

Yet the path forward seems unclear. One option is complete privatization. Yet the entities were private before the crash. It is not clear that the government can commit itself not to bail out private entities in the future. A second approach is to provide public backstop insurance for a fee, which recognizes that the government will be on the hook in the case of a catastrophe. A third approach is to keep the entities in public hands, and to allow them to gradually be competed into irrelevance. One proposal is for them to gradually decrease the upper limit on conforming loans. A second proposal is to increase the origination fees, which will hopefully ensure that they compete poorly relative to the private sector.

All approaches carry risks. The government may charge too little for catastrophic insurance, which will mean that the subsidization of these entities continues. A purely public entity may end up charging excessively low origination fees for political reasons, which will also lead to taxpayer losses. A purely private alternative may also lead to subversion of the political process. The ultimate decision about the appropriate path forward depends as much on an assessment of political risk as any appraisal of the housing market.

The great housing convulsion also raises other policy questions. How much should the government be intervening to reduce foreclosures? Chapter 4 suggests that securitization may have led to too few loan modifications. If foreclosures create externalities, as suggested by Campbell, Giglio, and Pathak (2011), this may lead to further social losses. This creates some case for federal encouragement of loan modifications, but modification programs can also lead to social waste, especially if they end up encouraging delinquencies, as suggested by Lee, Mayer, and Tracy.

The great housing convulsion even calls into question the Federal policy of subsidizing home borrowing through the home mortgage interest deduction. If subsidized borrowing leads to excessive risk-taking by ordinary Americans, then this policy may lead to a foreclosure society rather than an ownership society. Reconsidering such massive long-standing housing policies seems like a critical topic for future research.

Conclusion

The chapters in this volume examine the nature of the housing boom and its causes. The boom was not uniform. It was far stronger in some regions than in others. The regions that experienced the biggest booms between 2001 and 2006 have also experienced the biggest busts since then. The boom was associated with a massive increase in construction, as well as price fluctuations. Indeed, the fact that abundant construction in markets like Phoenix, Miami, and Las Vegas seemed to do so little to moderate the price boom remains an enduring puzzle. The construction boom and bust reminds us of the ability of the housing market to drive shifts in the real economy.

Easy credit, enabled by securitization and a wave of foreign lending, remains the most plausible explanation of the boom, yet even this explanation leaves many holes. The price growth seems to have been too high, at least relative to historic precedent and standard rational models, to be explained by the flow of lending. It seems likely that easy credit was necessary for the boom, but it seems unlikely to be a sufficient cause. Other forces were also at work.

The policy path forward also remains murky. The GSEs do seem to be a critical area of policy interest, but it remains unclear whether they should be privatized or kept as public entities. Hopefully, whatever path is chosen will reflect a serious understanding of the risks that occur when a private profit-maximizing entity enjoys an implicit government guarantee. It is also reasonable to rethink other Federal interventions in the housing market, such as the home mortgage interest deduction, given that we have been given such compelling evidence that home prices can fall dramatically as well as rise.

But while policy questions remain open, the events of the past decade make one point clearly. Housing is a critical part of the American economy and its study cannot be seen as a minor topic. Until we better understand housing markets and their fluctuations, we seem doomed to repeat the mistakes of the past and we risk again experiencing a painful real estate roller coaster that carries financial markets along in its wake.

In Memoriam

Our friend and colleague John Quigley passed away in April 2012, after his contribution to this volume was written. John contributed greatly to the project represented by this book, as he did in so many ways throughout the field of housing economics. His presence will be greatly missed, but his intellectual legacy will remain vibrant.

References

Campbell, John, Stefano Giglio, and Parag Pathak. 2011. "Forced Sales and House Prices." *American Economic Review* 101 (5): 2108–31.

Cutler, David, James Poterba, and Lawrence Summers. 1991. "Speculative Dynamics." *Review of Economic Studies* 58 (3): 529–46.

Glaeser, Edward L., Joshua D. Gottlieb, and Kristina Tobio. 2012. "Housing Booms and City Centers." *American Economic Review* 102 (3): 127–33.

Glaeser, Edward L., Joseph Gyourko, Eduardo Morales, and Charles Nathanson. 2011. "Housing Dynamics." Working Paper, May 20.

Glaeser, Edward L., Joseph Gyourko, and Albert Saiz. 2008. "Housing Supply and Housing Bubbles." *Journal of Urban Economics* 64 (2): 198–217.

Himmelberg, Charles, Christopher Mayer, and Todd Sinai. 2005. "Assessing High House Prices: Bubbles, Fundamentals and Misperceptions." *Journal of Economic Perspectives* 19 (4): 67–92.

Mankiw, Gregory N., and David N. Weil. 1989. "The Baby Boom, the Baby Bust, and the Housing Market." *Regional Science and Urban Economics* 19 (2): 235–58.

Mian, Atif, and Amir Sufi. 2009. "The Consequences of Mortgage Credit Expansion: Evidence from the US Mortgage Default Crisis." *Quarterly Journal of Economics* 122 (4): 1449–96.

Nathanson, Charles, and Eric Zwick. 2011. "Arrested Development: A Theory of Supply-Side Speculation in the Housing Market." Working Paper.

Poterba, James. 1984. "Tax Subsidies to Owner-Occupied Housing: An Asset-Market Approach." *Quarterly Journal of Economics* 99 (4): 729–52.

Sinai, Todd, and Nicholas Souleles. 2005. "Owner Occupied Housing as a Hedge against Rent Risk." *Quarterly Journal of Economics* 120 (2): 763–89.

1

House Price Moments in Boom-Bust Cycles

Todd Sinai

The United States experienced a remarkable boom and bust in house prices in the 2000s. According to the Fiserv Case-Shiller ten-city index, house prices grew by 125 percent in real terms from their trough in 1996 to their peak in 2006 and subsequently fell by 38 percent over the next five years. The impacts of this house price cycle have been wide-ranging and severe.

Explaining the causes of this episode of house price growth and decline and its effects on the rest of the banking sector and the real economy is the subject of much current research, some of which is collected in this volume. Potential explanations of the boom and bust in house prices include changing interest rates, subprime lending, irrational exuberance on the part of home buyers, a shift to speculative investment in housing, contagion and fads, and international capital flows.[1]

Todd Sinai is associate professor of real estate and business economics and public policy at the Wharton School at the University of Pennsylvania and a research associate of the National Bureau of Economic Research.

This chapter was prepared for the NBER's "Housing and the Financial Crisis" conference on November 17 and 18, 2011. I am grateful to Karl Case, Ed Glaeser, Charles Himmelberg, the conference participants, and the two book reviewers for their helpful comments and to Gordon MacDonald for his excellent research assistance. The Research Sponsors' Program of the Zell-Lurie Real Estate Center at Wharton and the Smith-Richardson Foundation provided financial support. For acknowledgments, sources of research support, and disclosure of the author's material financial relationships, if any, please see http://www.nber.org/chapters/c12619.ack.

1. A complete set of references for the potential causes of the house price boom in the 2000s is beyond the scope of this article. However, an interested reader might find the following citations of use. For discussions of the explanatory potential of interest rates, see Glaeser, Gottlieb, and Gyourko (2010); Himmelberg, Mayer, and Sinai (2005); Mayer and Sinai (2009); and Campbell et al. (2009). For subprime lending, see Pavlov and Wachter (2009); Mian and Sufi (2009); Wheaton and Nechayev (2008); and Lai and Van Order (2010). Arguments in favor of irrational bubbles can be found in Case and Shiller (2003) and Shiller (2005, 2006). Barlevy and Fisher (2011); Bayer, Geissler, and Roberts (2011); and Robinson and Todd (2010) examine the issue

The goal of this chapter is to describe a set of patterns in house prices among housing markets in the United States and to compile a set of empirical facts that potential explanations of the housing boom and bust should seek to explain. While some of the empirical relationships detailed here have been discussed to varying degrees in prior research, this paper seeks to assemble a broad collection of empirical facts. A unified theory of housing booms and busts would presumably be able to explain the entire set of facts. Of course, it is possible that there is no single mechanism that generated all the economic fluctuations that were experienced, and that a combination of causes needs to be explored.

For this chapter, I consider only house price dynamics. Evaluating the many potential determinants of these housing market dynamics is generally outside the scope of this chapter. However, the role of demand fundamentals, such as rents, income, and employment, is lightly addressed. Other potentially important contributors to housing market dynamics are the purview of other authors in this volume, such as Haughwought et al.'s chapter on the supply side of housing markets; Glaeser, Gottlieb, and Gyourko's chapter on interest rates; and Keys et al.'s chapter on housing finance. In addition, I broadly define housing markets as metropolitan statistical areas (MSAs), intended to correspond to labor market areas that workers are willing to commute amongst. During the boom-bust, there were also important within-MSA house price dynamics. These dynamics are addressed by Genesove and Han in this volume as well as Ferreira and Gyourko (2011) and Bayer, Geissler, and Roberts (2011).[2]

I highlight six stylized facts. First, despite the sizable boom-bust pattern in house prices at the national level, individual housing markets in the United States experienced considerable heterogeneity in the amplitudes of their cycles. The seventy-fifth percentile MSA experienced 111 percent trough-to-peak growth in real house prices in the 1990s and 2000s (using Federal Housing Finance Agency [FHFA] data), whereas the twenty-fifth percentile MSA had only 32 percent trough-to-peak real house price growth.

Second, the boom-bust of the 2000s bears remarkable similarities—as well as some differences—to the boom-bust of the 1980s. We observe two types of MSAs in the data. One set experienced house price cycles in both the 1980s and the 2000s, whereas the other set experienced a boom-bust only in the 2000s. The MSA-level correlation in trough-to-peak real house price growth in the late 1980s and the early 2000s for all MSAs is quite high

---

of speculative investment demand contributing to house price booms. Burnside, Eichenbaum, and Rebelo (2011) consider contagion ("social dynamics") and fads. Favilukis, Ludvigson, and Van Nieuwerburgh (2011) show that foreign capital flows into the United States could, in general equilibrium, lead to increases in the price-to-rent ratio for owner-occupied houses that match the aggregate US time series.
    2. I also limit my attention to US housing markets. Burnside, Eichenbaum, and Rebelo (2011) document house price dynamics in eighteen Organization for Economic Cooperation and Development (OECD) countries.

at 0.45 and would be higher still if those MSAs that did not experience a 1980s cycle at all were excluded.

Third, housing markets also experienced differences in the timing of their cycles. Most MSAs in the 1990s saw their house prices bottom either between 1990 and 1993 or between 1996 and 1997, and house prices generally peaked in 2006 and 2007. In the 1980s, house prices peaked between 1986 and 1990. Potential explanations for housing booms, therefore, need to generate both differences in the amplitude and timing of price changes across MSAs.

Fourth, the largest booms and busts, and their timing, seem to be clustered geographically. The largest amplitude cycles in the boom/bust of the 1990s and 2000s occurred in coastal MSAs and in Florida. These geographic concentrations also had price peaks and troughs that started at similar times, but distinct from the rest of the country.

Fifth, other interesting patterns emerge when one considers annual house price growth, rather than house price changes from trough to peak and back again. In particular, the cross-sectional variance of annual house price changes increases in booms and decreases in busts.

Lastly, these five patterns remain even when house prices are purged of demand fundamentals such as rents, incomes, or employment. Although changes in fundamentals are correlated with changes in house prices, cycles in these fundamentals do not have the same amplitude as price cycles and the time pattern of the growth in fundamentals does not match the timing of the growth in house prices. In fact, controlling for demand fundamentals makes the remaining boom-bust patterns in house prices even starker.

Collectively, these facts limit the possible explanations of the housing boom and bust. The fact that changing demand fundamentals cannot match the boom/bust pattern of house prices indicates that the house price cycles were due to changes in the price of owning a home rather than changes in the underlying demand for a place to live. However, the factors that are commonly believed to determine asset prices—the cost of credit, changing growth expectations, or time-varying risk premia—often vary over time only at the national level and thus cannot account for the different magnitudes of the booms and busts across metropolitan areas. Some have postulated that a national factor, such as the availability of subprime mortgages, might interact with local characteristics, such as the elasticity of housing supply, to create different-sized booms across MSAs. However, those explanations do not address why the booms would start at different times in different MSAs. Another set of explanations postulate that idiosyncratic MSA-specific conditions, such as differential availability of subprime mortgages, an influx of speculators, or excessive optimism, led to booms in a subset of MSAs. However, the remarkable similarity between the location and size of the booms of the 1980s and 2000s implies that, for this to be explanation, those same conditions must have reoccurred in the same MSAs.

The remainder of this chapter proceeds as follows. I first describe the data used in the chapter and the algorithm for identifying peaks and troughs in each MSA's time series. In section 1.2, I describe the aggregate national patterns in house price dynamics. Section 1.3 makes the point that MSAs can vary considerably from the national average and documents heterogeneity in the amplitude of the housing boom/bust of the 1990s and 2000s. It also shows that house price booms were typically followed by house price busts. The similarities and differences between the housing boom of the 1980s and the boom of the 2000s is discussed in section 1.4. The next section documents the fact that MSA-level house prices hit their troughs and peaks in different years. Section 1.6 shows that MSAs with similar amplitudes and timing in their housing booms and busts are clustered near each other geographically. Section 1.7 moves from the trough-to-peak house price growth concept to consider annual growth in house prices and the distribution of that growth rate across MSAs. I briefly discuss housing demand fundamentals in section 1.8, finding that house price cycles remain even conditional on cycles in housing fundamentals. Finally, section 1.9 briefly concludes.

1.1   Data

The primary source of data is the FHFA's quarterly house price index from data on repeat sales of homes. By comparing repeat transactions on houses that sell multiple times, the index controls for the size or quality of the house to the extent that the house is not renovated. The most significant benefit of the data is that it is available over a very long time (it is reliable as early as 1980) and for a large number of MSAs. However, to be included in the index's sample, the houses need to actually transact—and multiple times at that—and have conforming mortgages securitized by Fannie Mae or Freddie Mac. This sample of houses may not be representative of the overall housing stock and may not reflect the full volatility of the underlying housing market. In addition, the FHFA indexes are normalized within each MSA and thus cannot be used for cross-MSA house price comparisons. The FHFA data contains 344 MSAs with data between 1990 and 2010 and 163 MSAs with data covering 1980 through 2010. I annualize the data by averaging the index over the four quarters in a calendar year and convert the price indexes from nominal to real terms by deflating using the Consumer Price Index (CPI) (all urban consumers).

The FHFA repeat sales index is augmented with rent data from Reis Inc. Reis surveys "class A" apartment buildings, which are typically among the nicest in a given market, and adjusts the rents for concessions, such as months of free rent, to calculate a measure of effective rent. This is the rent concept we use as a proxy for rental values of owner-occupied houses. Because the Reis and FHFA indexes measure two different quantities of housing—the housing stock comprised by the apartment buildings in the Reis data can be quite different than the housing stock in the single-family detached houses in the FHFA data—I will not try to interpret the differences in house price levels versus rents in a given MSA. Instead, in section 1.8, I will compare the growth in FHFA prices to the growth in Reis rents, which merely requires that the growth in rents for apartments tracks the growth in (unobserved) rental value of houses.

As an alternative to using apartment rents as a proxy for housing demand, one could use demand fundamentals. For that reason, I collect data on median per capita income by MSA and employment by MSA from the Bureau of Labor Statistics (BLS). Income is converted into real dollars using the CPI.

Much of the analysis in this chapter concerns the peaks and troughs of housing cycles. The algorithm to determine those troughs and peaks starts by determining the peak of house prices in the 2000s. For each MSA, that peak is defined by first finding all the local maxima—years where the average annual real house price exceeds that of the adjacent years—in the 1999 through 2010 period and then choosing the local maximum with the highest real house price. After that, the algorithm works backward in time: it finds the local minimum—a year where house prices are lower than in the adjacent years—in the period prior to the 2000s peak year that is closest in time to the 2000s peak year and calls it the 1990s trough. The next preceding local maximum is labeled the 1990s peak, and the local minimum that precedes it is called the 1980s trough. Some MSAs do not have cyclical enough house prices for there to be local maxima and minima for all possible peaks and troughs. In those cases, the algorithm defines only those peaks and troughs it can identify. In addition, the trough in house prices in the 2000s is defined as the lowest real house price subsequent to the 2000s peak. However, that so-called trough often occurs in 2010, the last year of the data, and thus may not reflect the actual bottom in house prices. The peak/trough algorithm is repeated for all the MSA-level economic variables in the data set—house prices, apartment rents, median incomes, and MSA employment—as well as the ratios of house prices to rents, incomes, and employment[3]

1.2   National Patterns

The history of national average house prices in the United States is by now well-known. According to data from the FHFA, real house prices rose more

3. Burnside, Eichenbaum, and Rebelo (2011) apply a related algorithm to house price data for eighteen countries. Two differences are that they smooth quarterly house price growth using a five-quarter moving average and they require the price change in a run-up to exceed a minimum bound before calling it a boom. Ferreira and Gyourko (2011) apply a more rigorous econometric procedure to identify house price troughs across US metropolitan areas and Census tracts from structural breaks in house price growth. Davidoff (2012) identifies house price peaks by choosing the date that minimizes the standard deviation in annual house price growth rates before and after the peak and estimates trough-to-peak house price growth by assuming fixed dates for the troughs.

than 55 percent between the mid-1990s and the end of 2006 and had declined by almost 17 percent by late 2010. A national boom-bust in house prices also was experienced in the 1980s, with real prices rising nearly 15 percent between the mid-1980s and late 1989 and subsequently falling by 8 percent. This data is plotted in figure 1.1. The dashed line, labeled "HPI" (house price index) corresponds to the FHFA national series, deflated by the CPI, and is normalized so that it equals one in 1990.[4]

Another index, Fiserv Case-Shiller, uses a similar repeat-sales methodology but, unlike the FHFA index, is not limited to housing transactions with conforming mortgages and does not exclude sales of foreclosed homes. The real Fiserv Case-Shiller index is plotted in figure 1.1, in the dotted line, for comparison with the FHFA index. The Fiserv Case-Shiller index demonstrates substantially more volatility than the national FHFA index, more than doubling between 1997 and 2007 and subsequently falling by about one-third. However, the Fiserv Case-Shiller index in this figure is a composite of just ten cities, and it turns out that the differences in volatility between the FHFA index and the Case-Shiller index is more a function of the composition of cities that make up the index than of the composition of housing transactions within a city.[5] To show this, we plot (with a dash-dot line) a composite real FHFA index for the same ten cities that are in the Fiserv Case-Shiller ten-city composite index. The two ten-city indexes are quite similar, with the Fiserv Case-Shiller index exhibiting slightly more volatility. This chapter uses the FHFA series because the data covers a longer time span—for many MSAs, it starts (reliably) in 1980 rather than Fiserv Case-Shiller's 1987—and because it covers more metropolitan areas. However, based on figure 1.1, the results should be similar if other house price indexes are used.

1.3   Heterogeneity in Amplitude

The national pattern of house price dynamics masks considerable heterogeneity within the United States. One way to see this cross-MSA variation is to consider the amplitude of the trough-to-peak and peak-to-trough cycles in house prices experienced across various housing markets. Appendix Table A reports these statistics for each MSA in the data. In the 1990s and 2000s, most MSAs did not experience nearly the price growth reflected in the national average. However, a number of MSAs experienced considerably more growth, skewing the distribution of house price growth. The dispersion in the cumulative real price growth from each MSA's trough to peak is graphed in figure 1.2. For instance, the solid line plots a kernel estimate of the distribution of

---

4. These sorts of aggregate house price dynamics were initially modeled in a stock-flow framework, such as DiPasquale and Wheaton (1994).

5. The Fiserv Case–Shiller index is also publicly available as a twenty-city composite index.

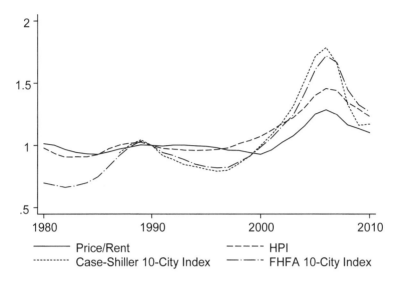

Fig. 1.1   National real house price indexes

Note: Indices are normalized to their 1990 price.

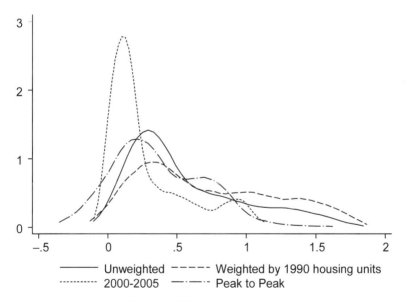

Fig. 1.2   Distribution of 1990s and 2000s trough-to-peak cumulative real house price growth

Source: Data comes from FHFA, deflated by the CPI.

Notes: Figure plots the distribution of MSA cumulative real house price growth between (a) the house price trough of (typically) the 1990s and the house price peak of (typically) the mid-2000s; (b) 2000 and 2005; (c) the house price peak of the late 1980s and early 1990s and the peak of the mid-2000s.

total real price growth for the entire set of MSAs available in the FHFA data, weighting each MSA equally. Most MSAs, 57 percent, experienced real house price growth below the national average growth of 55 percent. Indeed, the mode of the distribution is below 50 percent. However, the right tail of the price growth distribution is skewed, with a number of MSAs experiencing a doubling or more in their real house prices over the period.

The skewness across MSAs in trough-to-peak real house price growth is accentuated when the MSA observations are weighted by their 1990 population of households. This result can be seen in the dashed line in figure 1.2. The peak of the distribution is reduced, with the mass redistributed to the right. This change implies that the highest trough-to-peak house price growth in the 1990s and 2000s was experienced by larger cities, so weighting by the number of households reduces the emphasis at the low-growth portion of the distribution and shifts out the right tail of the distribution.

Most of the skewness in house price growth in the 1990s and 2000s arises from exceeding the prior house price peak of the 1980s and 1990s rather than from recovering to the prior high-price-level after the trough of the 1990s. Evidence can be found in the dashed-dotted line, which is a kernel density estimate of the real house price growth between the real house price peak in the 2000s and the prior peak in house prices, which typically occurred in the late 1980s. That distribution, which is unweighted, looks very similar to the unweighted distribution of trough-to-peak real house price growth, but shifted a bit to the left.

Finally, the heterogeneity in trough-to-peak growth is not due to differences in the length of the boom. Even over a fixed time span there is considerable heterogeneity and skewness in real house price growth. This fact can be seen in the dotted line, which corresponds to house price growth over the fixed 2000 through 2005 period, rather than over the trough-to-peak period window that can vary in length. Although the mass of low-growth MSAs is greater under this fixed-time period measure, there is still considerable skewness. This pattern indicates that house prices in some MSAs grew at a higher average rate, not just for a longer period. Another potential fixed-duration measure of growth would be to compute house price growth over the five years subsequent to each MSA's trough of the 1990s, rather than using 2000 as a base year for all MSAs. The distribution generated by that approach looks very similar to the 2000 to 2005 distribution plotted in figure 1.2.

That the skewness in the distribution of MSA house price growth during the 1990s and 2000s boom is not due to differences in the length of the boom is especially evident in figure 1.3, which plots the kernel density estimate of the geometric average trough-to-peak growth rate. Most of the MSAs averaged between 0 and 5 percent real house price growth during their run-ups. However, there is a sizable tail of MSAs with annualized house price growth rates ranging between 5 and 15 percent. That tail is larger when we weight

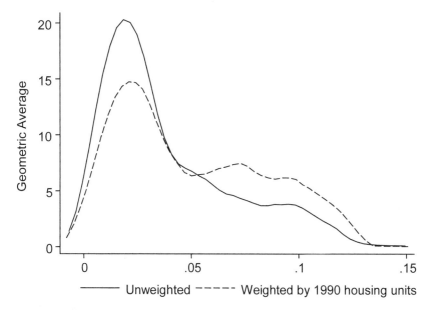

Fig. 1.3   Distribution of 1990s and 2000s trough-to-peak average real house price growth

Source: Data comes from FHFA, deflated by the CPI.

Notes: Figure plots the distribution of MSA *average* real house price growth between the house price trough of (typically) the 1990s and the house price peak of (typically) the mid-2000s.

by each MSA's population of housing units, depicted by the dashed line, indicating that larger cities experienced higher average house price growth rates during the most recent boom.

A similar degree of heterogeneity across MSAs can be observed in the house price declines from the peak of the 2000s through 2010, graphed in the solid line in figure 1.4. In this chart, a larger positive number corresponds to a greater decline in real house prices after the peak in the mid-2000s. Most MSAs experienced price declines, as measured by the FHFA data, of well less than the 17 percent national average. The modal decline in house prices is less than 10 percent. However, many MSAs experienced 30, 40, or even 50 percent price declines. While these MSAs are atypical, they nonetheless constitute a sizable tail. However, it is worth emphasizing that while the sample period ends in 2010, the housing collapse did not. The data do not yet allow us to compute a complete peak-to-trough measure.[6]

---

6. Just as there are a host of possible explanations for the run-up in house prices, there are many possible contributors to the bust. One potentially exacerbating factor is foreclosures, discussed in Campbell, Giglio, and Pathak (2011).

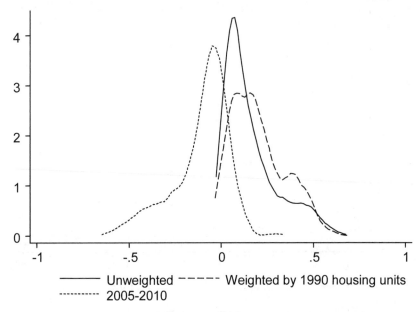

Fig. 1.4   Distribution of 2000s peak-to-trough cumulative real house price declines
Source: Data comes from FHFA, deflated by the CPI.
Notes: Figure plots the distribution of MSA cumulative real house price growth between (a) the house price peak of (typically) the mid-2000s and the subsequent house price trough, often 2010, and (b) 2005 and 2010.

Even within the truncated time period, the most populous MSAs, on average, experienced larger real house price declines after their peaks. This can be seen in the dashed line, which weights each MSA observation by its number of households. The density is shifted to the right.

The dotted line in figure 1.4 graphs the distribution of house price declines between 2005 and 2010 for comparison to the 2000 to 2005 distribution in figure 1.2. A positive number indicates that house prices fell between 2005 and 2010. Some MSAs had negative declines—which correspond to increases in house prices between 2005 and 2010—because house prices in most MSAs peaked between 2006 and 2008 and so 2005 to 2010 spans a period of price growth and subsequent decline. In many MSAs, the growth in prices between 2005 and the peak was greater than the decline from the peak to 2010, which yields a point to the left of zero. Still other MSAs had a larger house price collapse than run-up.

It is typically the case that those MSAs that experienced the greatest run-up in prices in the 1990s and 2000s also faced the largest subsequent house price declines, even recognizing that house prices still might continue to decline after 2010.[7] This pattern can be seen in figure 1.5, which plots for 249 of the MSAs in the FHFA data the decline in log real house prices after the peak of the 2000s on the vertical axis, and the growth in log real house prices from the 1990s trough to the 2000s peak on the horizontal axis. The dashed line is the fitted bivariate regression line where each MSA is weighted equally. The upward slope (0.641 with a standard error of 0.034) indicates that the magnitudes of the price run-ups and run-downs are correlated. The dotted line weights the MSAs by the population of housing units and yields a slightly lower slope (0.518 with a standard error of 0.031). This indicates that larger MSAs had busts that were less correlated with their preceding booms.

The MSAs that are furthest away from the origin in figure 1.5 experienced boom-bust cycles with the greatest amplitudes. These mainly include a number of MSAs in Florida, such as Naples with a 173 percent real price run-up, Miami (160 percent), and Fort Lauderdale (142 percent), and others in California, such as Salinas (165 percent), Santa Barbara (162 percent), Riverside/San Bernardino (158 percent), and Modesto (141 percent).

However, the decline in real house prices is not (yet) equal to the prior increase. The solid 45-degree line in figure 1.5 demarcates the decline in log house prices that would be necessary to undo all the price growth from the 1990s trough to the house price peak of the 2000s. Nearly all of the MSAs lie below this line, indicating that their real house prices at their lowest point after the peak of the 2000s were still above where they were in the prior trough of the 1990s. This is not surprising since, in most MSAs in 2010, the economic fundamentals that contribute to housing demand had not reverted to mid-1990s levels. Even so, some MSAs that have notably been suffering from a secular economic decline have real house prices in the late 2000s that were lower than what they were in the mid-1990s. These include many rust-belt MSAs, such as Detroit, Warren, and Flint, Michigan, Fort Wayne, Indiana, and parts of Ohio. Other MSAs whose real prices fell more than they rose in the latest boom include some "bubble" MSAs, such as Las Vegas, Nevada, and Merced, California.[8]

The heterogeneity across MSAs in the boom-bust cycle of house prices

---

7. Glaeser et al. (2011) highlight a similar phenomenon over the 1980 to 1990s time period, that US housing markets exhibit long-run mean reversion and short-run serial correlation in house price growth. They use a fixed time window rather than MSA-specific peaks and troughs, but the idea is the same. This evidence is extended in Glaeser, Gyourko, and Saiz (2008). They, too, use the same endpoint dates for all MSAs when defining booms: 1982 to 1989, 1989 to 1996, and 1996 to 2006. We also observe a correlation in house price booms and subsequent busts in the 1980s to 1990s period. It is not graphed, but the bivariate regression coefficient is reported in table 1.1.

8. Glaeser, Gyourko, and Saiz (2008) note that new house construction during booms could cause house prices to fall below their level in prior troughs because housing supply could increase more than demand fundamentals.

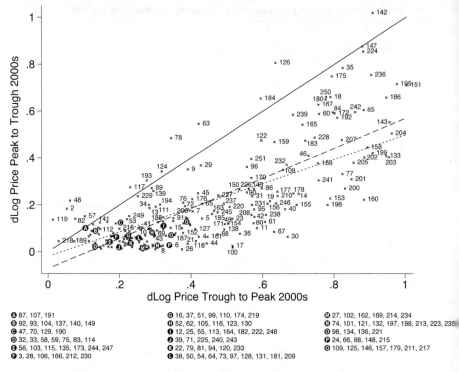

A 87, 107, 191
B 92, 93, 104, 137, 140, 149
C 47, 70, 129, 190
D 32, 33, 58, 59, 75, 83, 114
E 56, 103, 115, 135, 173, 244, 247
F 3, 28, 106, 166, 212, 230

G 16, 37, 51, 99, 110, 174, 219
H 52, 62, 105, 116, 123, 130
I 12, 25, 55, 113, 164, 182, 222, 248
J 39, 71, 225, 240, 243
K 22, 79, 81, 94, 120, 233
L 38, 50, 54, 64, 73, 97, 128, 131, 181, 209

M 27, 102, 162, 169, 214, 234
N 74, 101, 121, 132, 197, 198, 213, 223, 235
O 98, 134, 136, 221
P 24, 66, 88, 148, 215
Q 109, 125, 146, 157, 179, 211, 217

Fig. 1.5   Real house price growth and decline, 1990s–2000s, by MSA

Source: Data comes from FHFA, deflated by the CPI.

Notes: Figure plots the change in log MSA real house prices between the house price trough of (typically) the 1990s and the house price peak of (typically) the mid-2000s against the subsequent house price decline. The solid line demarcates the decline in log house prices that would exactly undo the prior growth in log prices. The straight lines are the fitted bivariate regression lines, the dashed one uses unweighted observations, and the dotted one uses observations weighted by 1990 housing units. Numbers in figs. 1.5, 1.6, 1.9, 1.10, 1.19, and 1.21 correspond to the following list:

1. Abilene, TX
2. Akron, OH
3. Albany, GA
4. Albany–Schenectady–Troy, NY
5. Albuquerque, NM
6. Alexandria, LA
7. Allentown–Bethlehem–Easton, PA–NJ
8. Amarillo, TX
9. Ann Arbor, MI
10. Appleton, WI
11. Asheville, NC
12. Athens–Clarke County, GA
13. Atlanta–Sandy Springs–Marietta, GA
14. Atlantic City–Hammonton, NJ
15. Auburn–Opelika, AL
16. Augusta–Richmond County, GA–SC
17. Austin–Round Rock–San Marcos, TX
18. Bakersfield–Delano, CA
19. Baltimore–Towson, MD
20. Baltimore–Towson, MD
21. Baton Rouge, LA
22. Beaumont–Port Arthur, TX
23. Bellingham, WA
24. Binghamton, NY
25. Birmingham–Hoover, AL

26. Bismarck, ND
27. Bloomington, IN
28. Bloomington–Normal, IL
29. Boise City–Nampa, ID
30. Boulder, CO
31. Bremerton–Silverdale, WA
32. Brownsville–Harlingen, TX
33. Buffalo–Niagara Falls, NY
34. Canton–Massillon, OH
35. Cape Coral–Fort Myers, FL
36. Casper, WY
37. Cedar Rapids, IA
38. Champaign–Urbana, IL
39. Charleston, WV
40. Charleston–North Charleston–Summerville, SC
41. Charlotte–Gastonia–Rock Hill, NC–SC
42. Charlottesville, VA
43. Chattanooga, TN–GA
44. Cheyenne, WY
45. Chicago–Joliet–Naperville, IL (MSAD)
46. Chico, CA
47. Cincinnati–Middletown, OH–KY–IN
48. Cleveland–Elyria–Mentor, OH
49. Colorado Springs, CO
50. Columbia, MO

51. Columbia, SC
52. Columbus, GA–AL
53. Columbus, OH
54. Corpus Christi, TX
55. Corvallis, OR
56. Dallas–Plano–Irving, TX (MSAD)
57. Dayton, OH
58. Decatur, AL
59. Decatur, IL
60. Deltona–Daytona Beach–Ormond Beach, FL
61. Denver–Aurora–Broomfield, CO
62. Des Moines–West Des Moines, IA
63. Detroit–Livonia–Dearborn, MI (MSAD)
64. Dothan, AL
65. Dover, DE
66. Dubuque, IA
67. Duluth, MN–WI
68. Eau Claire, WI
69. El Paso, TX
70. Elkhart–Goshen, IN
71. Erie, PA
72. Eugene–Springfield, OR
73. Evansville, IN–KY
74. Fargo, ND–MN
75. Fayetteville, NC

76. Fayetteville–Springdale–Rogers, AR–MO
77. Flagstaff, AZ–UT
78. Flint, MI
79. Florence, SC
80. Fort Collins–Loveland, CO
81. Fort Smith, AR–OK
82. Fort Wayne, IN
83. Fort Worth–Arlington, TX (MSAD)
84. Fresno, CA
85. Ft. Lauderdale–Pompano Bch.–Deerfield Bch., FL (MSAD)
86. Gainesville, FL
87. Gary, IN (MSAD)
88. Grand Forks, ND–MN
89. Grand Rapids–Wyoming, MI
90. Greeley, CO
91. Green Bay, WI
92. Greensboro–High Point, NC
93. Greenville, NC
94. Greenville–Mouldin–Easley, SC
95. Gulfport–Biloxi, MS
96. Hagerstown–Martinsburg, MD–WV
97. Harrisburg–Carlisle, PA
98. Hattiesburg, MS
99. Hickory–Lenoir–Morganton, NC
100. Houma–Bayou Cane–Thibodaux, LA
101. Houston–Sugar Land–Baytown, TX
102. Huntington–Ashland, WV–KY–OH
103. Huntsville, AL
104. Indianapolis–Carmel, IN
105. Iowa City, IA
106. Jackson, MS
107. Jackson, TN
108. Jacksonville, FL
109. Janesville, WI
110. Joplin, MO
111. Kalamazoo–Portage, MI
112. Kankakee–Bradley, IL
113. Kansas City, MO–KS
114. Kennewick–Pasco–Richland, WA
115. Killeen–Temple–Fort Hood, TX
116. Knoxville, TN
117. Kokomo, IN
118. La Crosse, WI–MN
119. Lafayette, IN
120. Lafayette, LA
121. Lake Charles, LA
122. Lakeland–Winter Haven, FL
123. Lancaster, PA
124. Lansing–East Lansing, MI
125. Las Cruces, NM
126. Las Vegas–Paradise, NV
127. Lawrence, KS
128. Lexington–Fayette, KY
129. Lima, OH
130. Lincoln, NE
131. Little Rock–North Little Rock–Conway, AR
132. Longview, TX
133. Los Angeles–Long Beach–Glendale, CA (MSAD)
134. Louisville–Jefferson County, KY–IN
135. Lubbock, TX
136. Lynchburg, VA
137. Macon, GA
138. Madison, WI
139. Mansfield, OH
140. McAllen–Edinburg–Mission, TX
141. Memphis, TN–MS–AR
142. Merced, CA
143. Miami–Miami Beach–Kendall, FL (MSAD)
144. Milwaukee–Waukesha–West Allis, WI
145. Minneapolis–St. Paul–Bloomington, MN–WI
146. Mobile, AL
147. Modesto, CA
148. Monroe, LA
149. Montgomery, AL
150. Myrtle Beach–North Myrtle Beach–Conway, SC
151. Naples–Marco Island, FL
152. Nashville–Davidson–Murfreesboro–Franklin, TN
153. Nassau–Suffolk, NY (MSAD)
154. New Orleans–Metairie–Kenner, LA
155. New York–White Plains–Wayne, NY–NJ (MSAD)
156. Newark–Union, NJ–PA (MSAD)
157. Niles–Benton Harbor, MI
158. Oakland–Fremont–Hayward, CA (MSAD)
159. Ocala, FL
160. Ocean City, NJ
161. Odessa, TX
162. Oklahoma City, OK
163. Olympia, WA
164. Omaha–Council Bluffs, NE–IA
165. Orlando–Kissimmee–Sanford, FL
166. Owensboro, KY
167. Palm Bay–Melbourne–Titusville, FL
168. Panama City–Lynn Haven–Panama City Beach, FL
169. Parkersburg–Marietta–Vienna, WV–OH
170. Pensacola–Ferry Pass–Brent, FL
171. Philadelphia, PA (MSAD)
172. Phoenix–Mesa–Glendale, AZ
173. Pittsburgh, PA
174. Pocatello, ID
175. Port St. Lucie, FL
176. Portland–Vancouver–Hillsboro, OR–WA
177. Poughkeepsie–Newburgh–Middletown, NY
178. Provo–Orem, UT
179. Pueblo, CO
180. Punta Gorda, FL
181. Raleigh–Cary, NC
182. Reading, PA
183. Redding, CA
184. Reno–Sparks, NV
185. Richmond, VA
186. Riverside–San Bernardino–Ontario, CA
187. Roanoke, VA
188. Rochester, MN
189. Rochester, NY
190. Rockford, IL
191. Rocky Mount, NC
192. Sacramento–Arden-Arcade–Roseville, CA
193. Saginaw–Saginaw Township North, MI
194. Salem, OR
195. Salinas, CA
196. Salt Lake City, UT
197. San Angelo, TX
198. San Antonio–New Braunfels, TX
199. San Diego–Carlsbad–San Marcos, CA
200. San Francisco–San Mateo–Redwood City, CA (MSAD)
201. San Jose–Sunnyvale–Santa Clara, CA
202. San Luis Obispo–Paso Robles, CA
203. Santa Ana–Anaheim–Irvine, CA (MSAD)
204. Santa Barbara–Santa Maria–Goleta, CA
205. Santa Cruz–Watsonville, CA
206. Santa Fe, NM
207. Santa Rosa–Petaluma, CA
208. Savannah, GA
209. Scranton–Wilkes-Barre, PA
210. Seattle–Bellevue–Everett, WA (MSAD)
211. Sheboygan, WI
212. Sherman–Denison, TX
213. Shreveport–Bossier City, LA
214. Sioux City, IA–NE–SD
215. Sioux Falls, SD
216. South Bend–Mishawaka, IN–MI
217. Spokane, WA
218. Springfield, IL
219. Springfield, MO
220. St. Cloud, MN
221. St. Joseph, MO–KS
222. St. Louis, MO–IL
223. State College, PA
224. Stockton, CA
225. Syracuse, NY
226. Tacoma, WA (MSAD)
227. Tallahassee, FL
228. Tampa–St. Petersburg–Clearwater, FL
229. Toledo, OH
230. Topeka, KS
231. Trenton–Ewing, NJ
232. Tucson, AZ
233. Tulsa, OK
234. Tyler, TX
235. Utica–Rome, NY
236. Vallejo–Fairfield, CA
237. Vineland–Millville–Bridgeton, NJ
238. Virginia Beach–Norfolk–Newport News, VA–NC
239. Visalia–Porterville, CA
240. Waco, TX
241. Washington–Arlington–Alexandria, DC–VA–MD–WV (MSAD)
242. West Palm Beach–Boca Raton–Boynton Beach, FL (MSAD)
243. Wichita Falls, TX
244. Wichita, KS
245. Wilmington, DE–MD–NJ (MSAD)
246. Wilmington, NC
247. Yakima, WA
248. York–Hanover, PA
249. Youngstown–Warren–Boardman, OH–PA
250. Yuba City, CA
251. Yuma, AZ

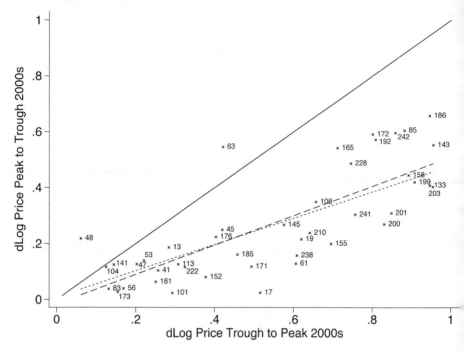

Fig. 1.6   Real house price growth and decline, 1990s–2000s, by Reis subset of MSAs

Note: See the notes to figure 1.5. This figure uses the subset of MSAs that also are in the Reis sample.

can be seen more clearly in figure 1.6, which reports the same trough-peak-trough price cycle as figure 1.5, but which restricts the sample of MSAs to those also covered by the Reis data. These forty-three MSAs are among the largest in the United States. The MSAs furthest from the origin—those with the largest price increases and decreases include most of California and South Florida, plus Phoenix, Arizona. Texas cities, such as Houston, Dallas, and Fort Worth had negligible price cycles and are close to the origin. Philadelphia, Baltimore, Seattle, New York, and Boston are in the middle. Only Cleveland and Detroit are above the 45-degree line, where their post-boom real house prices are below the level of their prior trough.

Those MSAs that are below the dashed and dotted fitted regression lines experienced a greater ratio of price increase to subsequent decrease than did the cities above the regression line. Some MSAs in close proximity experienced similar trough-to-peak price growth but dissimilar price declines. For example, as reported in appendix table 1A.1, both Los Angeles and San Bernardino/Riverside experienced 157 percent price growth between 1997 and 2006. However, prices in Los Angeles fell "just" 34 percent subsequently, compared to 48 percent in San Bernardino. In San Francisco, prices rose 129 percent from trough to peak and 124 percent in nearby Sacramento.

But real prices have fallen by 44 percent from the peak in Sacramento and only 24 percent in San Francisco. However, it is worth repeating that none of these cities have necessarily yet reached their new price trough and so judgments about price declines should be tempered.

This heterogeneity across MSAs has important implications for the possible explanations of the housing boom and subsequent bust. In particular, the many explanations that postulate a single common national factor, such as a national change in overall credit market conditions or widespread optimism about house price growth, cannot generate different price dynamics across housing markets. To account for the heterogeneity across MSAs, a change in a national factor, such as the cost of mortgage credit, would have to interact with an MSA-specific characteristic, such as the elasticity of supply, in order to generate housing cycles of different magnitudes across MSAs.[9]

Another possibility is that some precipitating factor for the boom and bust might simply have varied differentially across metropolitan areas over time. For example, if subprime credit availability increased in some MSAs, as in Mian and Sufi (2009), and subprime loans were capitalized into higher house prices (Pavlov and Wachter 2009), then some of the house price boom potentially could have been caused by local variation in credit supply. However, in order to be the sole explanation of the heterogeneity in the data, the growth in subprime credit would have to be largest in the MSAs with the most extreme booms, and subprime credit would have to be commensurately withdrawn during the bust. Indeed, there is evidence that the availability of subprime credit was a contributing factor to the boom. Mian and Sufi (2009) suggest that differences in credit availability could account for 40 percent of the price growth in the boom. Of course, even if differences across MSAs in the housing boom could be explained by idiosyncratic differences in subprime lending, or some other precipitating factor such as housing speculation (Bayer, Geissler, and Roberts 2011), it begs the question of why that factor would be more prevalent in particular MSAs. It could be the case that subprime lending or speculative investing happened to be located in particular MSAs for reasons that were based on exogenous characteristics. Or, perhaps, the growth in those activities was based on features of or expectations about the local housing market. In either case, lending or speculation may be a symptom rather than the true underlying cause. Burnside, Eichenbaum, and Rebelo (2011) propose a model of fads to explain this sort of housing market heterogeneity that appears to be unrelated to any observable underlying factor.

1.4   Similarity with the 1980s

The same MSA-level heterogeneity in house price growth rates that characterized the boom-bust cycle that peaked in the 2000s also was present

---

9. Examples of this approach include Himmelberg, Mayer, and Sinai (2005) for interest rates and Brunnermeier and Julliard (2008) for money illusion.

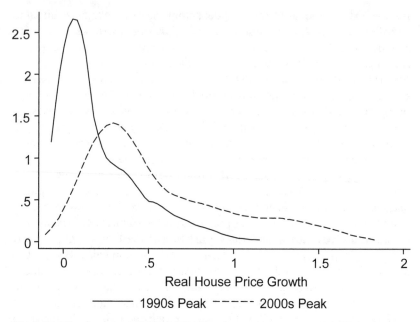

Fig. 1.7   Distribution of 1980s–1990s trough-to-peak cumulative real house price growth

Source: Data comes from FHFA, deflated by the CPI.

Note: Figure plots the distribution of MSA cumulative real house price growth between the house price trough of (typically) the 1980s and the house price peak of (typically) the late 1980s to early 1990s.

in the preceding house price cycle that peaked in the late 1980s. Figure 1.7 compares the unweighted distribution of real house price growth rates from the 1990s trough to the 2000s peak, as computed in figure 1.2, to the distribution of real house price growth rates from the 1980s trough to the peak of the late 1980s and early 1990s. Both boom-bust cycles demonstrated considerable dispersion across MSAs in trough-to-peak house price growth. A large fraction of the distribution of MSA house price growth during the 1990s boom, which is described by the solid line, is below 25 percent. However, the tail extends to growth of more than 100 percent. The dashed line, which corresponds to the boom that peaked in the 2000s, shows that the mass of the distribution of price growth in that run-up was shifted slightly more to the right than in the prior boom, up to about 50 percent increases in real house prices. The 2000 boom also had a thicker right tail, extending to more than 150 percent cumulative growth.

Both periods also exhibited dispersion in house price declines after their respective peaks. In figure 1.8, the kernel density of the decline in real house prices after the peak of the late 1980s (the solid line) is nearly the same as the density of real house price declines after the peak of the late 2000s (the

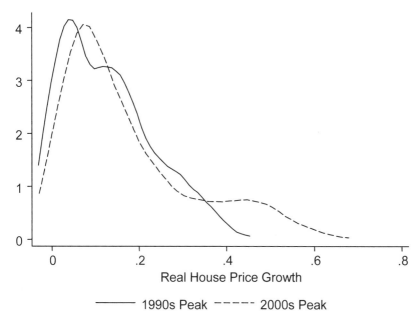

Fig. 1.8   Distribution of 1990s–2000s peak-to-trough cumulative real house price declines

Source: Data comes from FHFA, deflated by the CPI.

Note: Figure plots the distribution of MSA cumulative real house price declines between the house price peak of (typically) the late 1980s to early 1990s and the house price trough of (typically) the mid-1990s.

dashed line). The more recent housing bust reveals a somewhat larger house price collapse across most MSAs as the distribution of house price declines is shifted to the right. On top of that, the extent of the house price declines in the most recent bust is not yet fully known, whereas the 1990s bust is complete. That suggests that the most recent bust promises to be even more sizable than the house price collapse of the 1990s.

In addition, the MSAs that boomed in the 2000s largely were the same MSAs that boomed in the 1980s, with a few notable exceptions. This relationship can be seen in figure 1.9, which plots each MSA's trough-to-peak change in log real house prices during the cycle that peaked in the 2000s against trough-to-peak log house price changes during the 1980s cycle. Every MSA that had a 1980s cycle—even if it was small—is included in the sample, yielding 124 MSAs. On average, there is a positive relationship between house price growth in the two cycles, with higher trough-to-peak price growth in the 1980s predicting greater trough-to-peak price growth in the more recent cycle. This pattern can be seen in the dashed and dotted lines, which correspond to the unweighted and population-weighted bivariate regression lines, respectively. The MSAs that experienced considerable

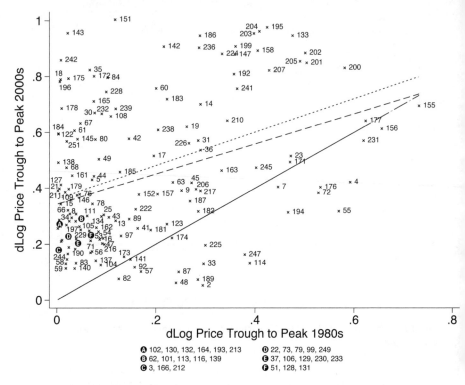

Fig. 1.9   Real house price growth, 1980s–1990s versus 1990s–2000s, by MSA

Source: Data comes from FHFA, deflated by the CPI.

Notes: Figure plots the cumulative change in MSA log real house prices between the house price trough of (typically) the 1990s and the house price peak of (typically) the mid-2000s against the trough-to-peak change in log house prices in the boom of the 1990s. The solid 45-degree line demarcates the log point increase in 2000s prices that would exactly equal the increase in 1980s prices. The straight lines are the fitted bivariate regression lines, the dashed one uses unweighted observations, and the dotted one uses observations weighted by 1990 housing units.

volatility in the 2000s, such as Boston, New York, and San Francisco, also had large house price run-ups in the 1980s, and thus can be found away from the origin on the right side of the chart. Other MSAs, such as Nashville, Austin, and Minneapolis, had relatively low amounts of house price growth in both cycles and are close to the origin. Nearly all cities, however, experienced more house price growth in the 2000s cycle than in the 1990s and thus are above the solid 45-degree line. Rather, those that experienced *above-average* high price growth in the 1980s typically also had above-average house price growth in the 2000s. An exception to this rule is the group of declining MSAs, such as Rochester, New York, Fort Wayne, Indiana, and Dayton, Ohio, which had little house price growth in both the 1980s and the 2000s.

There is one significant group of outliers to this general pattern. A cohort of MSAs experienced outsized house price growth in the 2000s but rela-

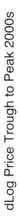
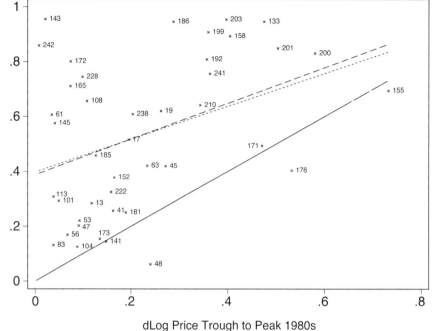

Fig. 1.10   Real house price growth, 1980s–1990s versus 1990s–2000s, by Reis subset of MSAs

Note: See the notes to figure 1.9. This figure uses the subset of MSAs that also are in the Reis sample.

tively little price growth in the 1980s. This set of MSAs is located in the upper left of the graph, close to the Y-axis and far from the X-axis. This group includes many MSAs that were poster children for the recent housing bubble—Miami and much of South Florida, Phoenix, Arizona, Las Vegas, Nevada, and Riverside/San Bernardino, California—as well as others that were less visible, such as Salt Lake City.

For legibility, figure 1.10 graphs the same information for the smaller sample of MSAs that also have data available from Reis. The outliers in the upper left quadrant, such as South Florida and Phoenix, are more evident in this figure. The California MSAs of San Bernardino, Orange County, San Diego, and Oakland also lie above the regression line but, unlike the Florida MSAs, they did exhibit a cycle in the 1980s, albeit a muted one.

The parallel between the 1980s and the 2000s presents a challenge for popular theories of the housing boom. Many of the commonly raised culprits for the most recent boom were simply not factors in the 1980s. For example, the subprime lending boom was an innovation of the 2000s. Thus, while Mian and Sufi (2009) attribute 40 percent of the 2002 to 2005 increase in house prices to the growth of subprime lending, it could not also have caused the house price cycle two decades earlier. It seems more likely that some recurring cause induced both housing booms than that two different factors separated by more than two decades caused matching housing booms across MSAs. The similarities between the 1980s and the 2000s also are hard for the Burnside, Eichenbaum, and Rebelo (2011) theory of fads to explain. It is hard to believe that fads randomly happened to recur, with similar degrees of intensity, in the same US housing markets. By contrast, the European data in Burnside, Eichenbaum, and Rebelo does not exhibit the same repeated housing cycles as the US data, making their theory more appropriate for that context.

Another challenge raised in this section is how to explain the aberrant MSAs. While most MSAs have regular housing booms and busts of varying magnitudes, others such as Phoenix, Las Vegas, the Inland Empire of California, and much of South Florida clearly experienced an unusual event in the boom of the 2000s. A key task for an explanation of the housing boom is to distinguish these MSAs that underwent an unusual event from the remainder. Did something different take place in the handful of MSAs that experienced house price swings only in the 2000s?

1.5   Heterogeneity in Timing

Popular discussion tends to refer to the start and end of the housing "bubble" as if there were a particular point in time in which price growth began in all MSAs and another date at which the bubble ended. In practice, those dates varied widely across MSAs. Figure 1.11 charts the distribution of trough and peak dates for the house price peak of the 1980s (in white), the trough of the 1990s (in black), and the peak of the 2000s (cross-hatched). (Appendix table 1A.1 reports these dates for each MSA in the data.) Each distribution spans a number of years. For most MSAs, the 1980s peak in real house prices occurred between 1986 and 1990. However, some MSAs peaked in the early 1980s and others peaked well into the 1990s. The early dates typically correspond to MSAs whose house prices peaked in the early 1980s, declined through the early-1990s, and then rose until the mid-2000s. For example, Denver's real house price peaked in 1983, reached a trough in 1991, and peaked again in 2005. The MSAs with the latest peaks typically did not experience a 1980s cycle at all. Rather, their house prices fell until the late 1980s, then rose steadily until the late 2000s. However, Portland, Oregon, for example, experienced a slight house price dip after the tech boom of the late 1990s, and so the algorithm characterized that period as a local house price maximum. Leaving aside the extreme outliers in the dates of the peak, considerable heterogeneity remains over the five years spanning 1986 through 1990.

The dates of the subsequent trough in house prices are bimodal. One concentration occurs in the early 1990s, between 1990 and 1993, with a large number of MSAs hitting their troughs in 1991. The other concentration

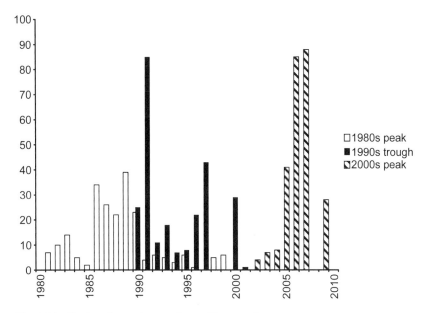

Fig. 1.11   Peak and trough years for real house prices

Note: Figure plots the histogram of peak and trough years for real house price cycles. See section 1.1 for details on the data construction.

takes place around 1996 and 1997. About thirty MSAs have troughs in 2000 or 2001. These MSAs typically experienced a small dip in house prices after a run-up in the late 1990s, before their house prices continued their climb through the late 2000s. The algorithm counts the small hiccup in house price growth as a local minimum and identifies it as a trough even if, like in Scranton, Pennsylvania, house prices reach a nadir again in the mid-1990s. Again, leaving aside the outliers, there is considerable dispersion across dates of the trough of house prices.[10]

By contrast, the peak of house prices in the 2000s was much more concentrated than either the previous trough or peak. The MSA-level house prices topped out primarily in 2006 and 2007, with about forty MSAs reaching their house price peaks in 2005. Despite this relatively high concentration, there is still considerable heterogeneity. House prices in twenty-six MSAs peaked before 2005 and a comparable number of MSAs had peaks in 2009.[11]

---

10. Independently, Ferreira and Gyourko (2011) have estimated the starting date of the boom of the 2000s at the MSA level using a quarterly MSA-level house price index of their own construction and a more rigorous econometric procedure. They also find considerable dispersion in starting dates.

11. Davidoff (2012) finds that most MSAs' house prices peak around Q2 of 2007 and, for those that do not, the difference between their house prices in Q2 of 2007 and house prices at their actual peaks is small.

This heterogeneity in timing presents another hurdle for theories that attribute the housing boom(s) and bust(s) to a common national factor. Even if that factor interacts with MSA-level characteristics to induce different amplitudes of the housing market boom across MSAs, the timing of the start, peak, and end of the house price cycle should be similar. For example, the decline in interest rates in the 2000s applied to all MSAs in the United States. Even if those MSAs varied in their elasticities of housing supply or expectations of future house price appreciation—both of which could induce a differential effect of interest rates on house prices—to the extent house prices increased when interest rates fell, it should have occurred simultaneously across MSAs.

1.6   Geographic Clustering

Although MSAs differ in the timing and amplitude of their house price cycles, MSAs with similar house price cycles tend to be located near each other. This pattern is especially evident in the trough-to-peak and peak-to-trough house price growth around the boom-bust of the 1990s and 2000s. Figure 1.12 maps the growth in real house prices between the 1990s trough and the 2000s peak, by MSA. Lighter-shaded MSAs had less trough-to-peak house price growth and darker-shaded MSAs experienced more. The darkest-shaded MSAs, those with 70 percent or more growth in house prices, were mainly located on the west coast of the United States, the Northeast Corridor (Washington DC, Philadelphia, New York, and Boston), and in the state of Florida. Most of the rest of the United States is shaded light grey, indicating relatively lower house price growth, with the exception of the areas around Denver, Salt Lake City, and Casper, Wyoming. (House prices in the latter city more than doubled between 1989 and 2007.) Even among the dark-shaded subset of MSAs, the coastal MSAs experienced more growth in prices than did the slightly more inland MSAs. For example, central Florida had less trough-to-peak real house price growth than did coastal Florida. In addition, major cities had greater house price growth during this period than did neighboring areas. For example, the Portland, Oregon, MSA had more price growth than the areas just to its south, and the Boston area experienced more house price growth than the areas to its west.

Since the MSAs that had house price booms also tended to have house price busts, it follows that the house price declines of the late 2000s are also spatially concentrated. This pattern can be seen in figure 1.13. The west coast of the United States, the northeast, and Florida experienced the largest concentrations of house price declines. However, the pattern within those areas is partially reversed from the prior house price run-up. The coastal MSAs and large cities experienced relatively less of a house price collapse by 2010 than did the more inland MSAs or the areas around the cities. However, house prices in those coastal MSAs still fell by more than in the MSAs in

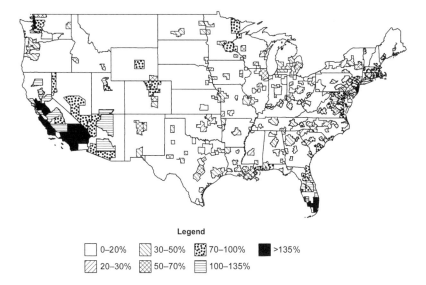

Legend

☐ 0–20% ◫ 30–50% ▦ 70–100% ■ >135%

▨ 20–30% ▧ 50–70% ▤ 100–135%

Fig. 1.12   Geography of trough-to-peak house price growth, 1990s to the 2000s

Source: Data comes from FHFA, deflated by the CPI.

Note: Figure maps the MSA cumulative real house price growth between the house price trough of (typically) the 1990s and the house price peak of (typically) the mid-2000s.

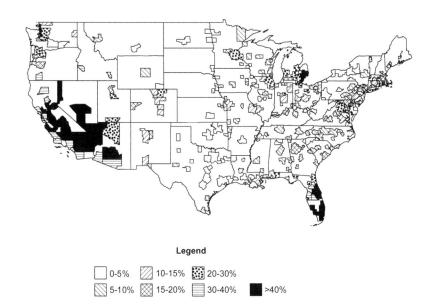

Legend

☐ 0-5% ▨ 10-15% ▦ 20-30% ■ >40%

◫ 5-10% ▧ 15-20% ▤ 30-40%

Fig. 1.13   Geography of peak-to-trough house price growth, 2000s

Source: Data comes from FHFA, deflated by the CPI.

Note: Figure maps the MSA cumulative real house price declines between the house price peak of (typically) the mid-2000s and the subsequent trough.

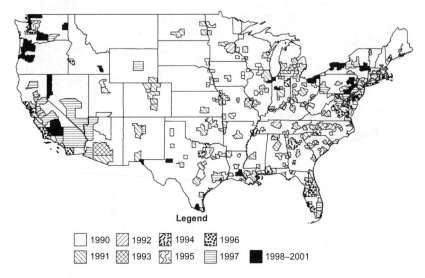

Legend

☐ 1990 ▨ 1992 ▨ 1994 ▨ 1996
▧ 1991 ▨ 1993 ▨ 1995 ☰ 1997 ■ 1998–2001

Fig. 1.14   Starting date of the 1990s and 2000s boom
Source: Data comes from FHFA, deflated by the CPI.
Note: Figure maps the date of the house price trough of (typically) the 1990s.

the middle of the country, reflecting the fact that they also experienced a greater house price rise.

Similar geographic clustering can also be seen in the starting date of the boom of the 2000s. This information is mapped in figure 1.14, with a darker shade for MSAs that had a later start date for the boom. The same areas that experienced the largest booms/busts appear to have started their cycles later.[12] The estimated coefficient in a bivariate regression of the trough-to-peak house price growth on the date of the trough is 0.019 (0.004 standard error) for 249 metropolitan areas. When the observations are weighted by the number of housing units, the estimated coefficient rises to 0.025 (0.005).

By contrast, in figure 1.15, the dates of the peak of the 2000s house price boom are much more uniformly distributed across the country. Indeed, there is no discernible statistical correlation between the magnitude of the preceding boom and the timing of the subsequent peak in the 2000s.

This geographic clustering might provide an opportunity to uncover the source of the housing boom. It is possible that neighboring MSAs have similar observable or unobservable characteristics that made them more susceptible to house price cycles. Or, perhaps housing booms propagate—by

12. Ferreira and Gyourko (2011) independently document similar MSA-level geographic clustering in the start of the boom. Their research emphasizes the initial jump in house prices at the start of the house price boom. Interestingly, they do not find geographic clustering at the MSA level in the magnitude of those initial price jumps.

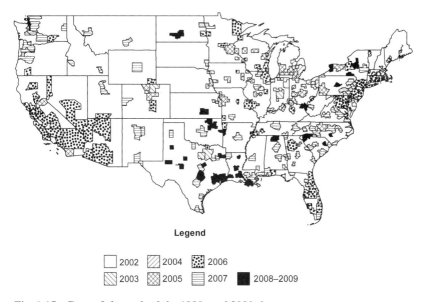

Legend

☐ 2002 ▨ 2004 ▦ 2006
▧ 2003 ▩ 2005 ▤ 2007 ■ 2008–2009

Fig. 1.15   Date of the peak of the 1990s and 2000s boom
Note: Figure maps the date of the house price peak of the mid-2000s. Data comes from FHFA, deflated by the CPI.

wealth transmission, or contagion of market information or sentiment—causing an MSA's housing market to follow its neighbor's.

1.7   Annual House Price Growth

Up to this point, this chapter has considered the distribution of trough-to-peak and peak-to-trough growth rates. However, the distribution of annual growth rates in MSA-level house price indexes also reveals some interesting patterns.

First, the cross-sectional distribution of one-year MSA-level house price growth rates widens considerably during housing booms and contracts during housing busts. That is, when house prices are highest, there is more dispersion across MSAs in the amount of house price growth. This pattern can be seen in figure 1.16, which plots the standard deviation of real house price growth over time. The standard deviation is computed across MSAs at a point in time. For example, the line in figure 1.16 starts in 1981. That year, the standard deviation across MSAs of their house price growth between 1980 and 1981 was just under 5 percent. During the next decade, as average house prices rose, the standard deviation of house prices also grew. By 1990, the peak of the boom, that standard deviation had grown to nearly 7 percent, indicating that the variation among MSAs in the amount of house price growth was greater at the top of the cycle. In the mid-1990s, as house

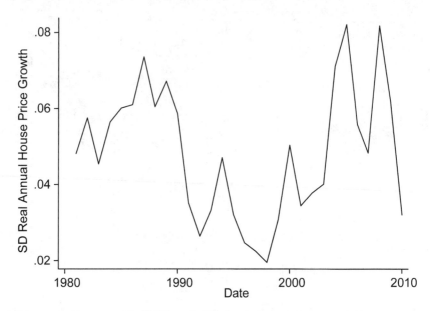

Fig. 1.16   The standard deviation of MSA-level annual real house price growth, 1981–2010

Source: Data comes from FHFA, deflated by the CPI.

Note: Figure graphs the standard deviation of annual real house price growth across MSAs in each year.

prices slumped, the cross-sectional variance also fell. But, in the boom of the 2000s, the standard deviation rose steadily with house prices to a peak of more than 8 percent.

While the standard deviation of house price growth rose in both the 1980s and the 2000s, there was one interesting difference between the two booms: In the 1980s boom, some MSAs experienced house price growth whereas others saw house prices decline. However, in the 2000s boom, almost all MSAs enjoyed house price increases. Figure 1.17 plots the distribution of annual house price growth by year. Within each year, there are 159 unweighted MSA-level observations on real house prices. The horizontal black line in the middle of each vertical black bar corresponds to the median MSA-level house price growth between the prior year and the current one. The median growth is positive between 1983 and 1989, reflecting the house price boom of that period. The cross-section dispersion increases toward the peak of the boom, in 1987, 1988, and 1989. As house prices fall through the late-1990s, the cross-sectional dispersion declines. However, during the entire 1983 to 1997 period, despite covering a significant aggregate house price boom and bust, the interquartile range (from the bottom to the top of the black bar) spanned zero. That is, some MSAs experienced real price declines in the

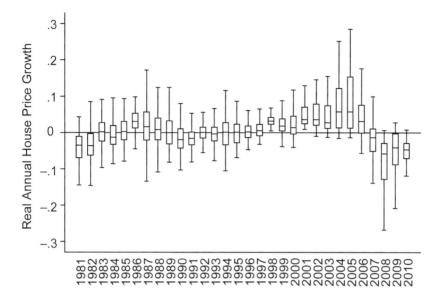

Fig. 1.17   The distribution of annual real house price growth, by year

Source: Data comes from FHFA, deflated by the CPI. Excludes outside values.

Notes: Figure plots the distribution of annual real house price growth across MSAs in each year. The black-outlined bar runs from the twenty-fifth to the seventy-fifth percentiles. The horizontal black line corresponds to the median.

same year that other MSAs experienced price growth. By 1998, that pattern was over, and during every year of the house price boom of the 2000s, with the exception of the post-Internet boom year of 2000, at least 75 percent of the MSAs (and often more) in each year experienced positive house price growth. In 2007, this was no longer true. Then, in every year between 2008 and 2010, more than 75 percent of MSAs faced house price declines.[13]

These patterns in annual growth rates highlight that something different was going on in the boom of the 2000s: house prices rose in all metropolitan areas, differing only by how much. But they also emphasize some important similarities across the housing booms. The increasing dispersion in annual house price growth indicates that some MSAs grew more rapidly than others, not that some just grew for a longer period of time. The cycle in dispersion also shows that there was not an equal shock to house price growth across MSAs; had there been, the entire distribution of house price growth would have shifted rather than expanding.

13. This pattern is consistent with Cotter, Gabriel, and Roll's (2011) finding of increased integration in MSA-level house prices in the 2000s.

1.8   House Price Cycles Remain after Controlling for Demand Fundamentals

Up to this point, this chapter has focused on house prices alone. But, as is widely recognized, there are two components that determine house prices. The first is the fundamental value of the housing service flow, rent. The rental value of housing is determined by factors that affect the demand for living in a particular location—income, household demographics such as marital status, and local amenities or wage levels—as well as the elasticity of housing supply. The second component is an asset pricing relationship that capitalizes a stream of future rental value into a current price.[14]

If the rental value of owner-occupied housing could be measured directly, housing cycles could be decomposed into cycles in the value of the housing service flow and cycles due to changes in asset pricing. Of course, owner-occupied houses are by definition not rented, and thus the econometrician does not observe the rental value of that set of houses. The prior literature takes three approaches to surmount that problem. One approach is to compare the rental value and prices for a set of matched rental and owner-occupied houses, as in Smith and Smith (2006). Another strategy is to assume that the growth rate in apartment rents, which are observed, is a good proxy for the growth rate in the unobserved rental value of owner-occupied housing, as in Himmelberg, Mayer, and Sinai (2005) or Campbell et al. (2009). A third tactic is to use demand shifters, such as household income, to estimate rental value within the context of an economic model, as in Glaeser, Gottlieb, and Gyourko's chapter in this volume.

In this section, I control for various measures of the underlying rental value of owner-occupied housing in each MSA to isolate the asset pricing component. Doing this makes the cyclical pattern of house prices, if anything, stronger.

One main reason for this outcome is that, while there are cycles in fundamentals, cycles in house prices are much larger. This can be seen clearly in figure 1.18, which plots the distribution of trough-to-peak growth in the 2000 boom for four MSA-level variables: Real house prices, real rent, real income, and employment.[15] House price growth, the solid line, has considerably more dispersion than any of the three measures of fundamentals.[16] A sizable fraction of MSAs experienced trough-to-peak real house price growth between 50 and 200 percent. However, very few MSAs experienced

---

14. See, for example, Meese and Wallace (1994) for an early exposition of this present value relationship for housing. The intuition is robust to an even more complete house pricing model, such as Ortalo-Magné and Prat (2010).

15. McCarthy and Peach (2004) show that the early stages of the house price boom of the 2000s may have been due to growth in demand fundamentals.

16. Haughwout et al. (2011) shows that house price growth is correlated with growth in the price of raw land.

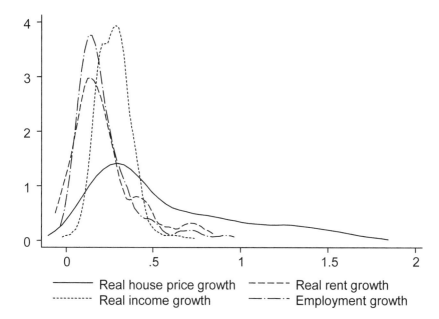

Fig. 1.18   Trough-to-peak growth in real house prices and housing demand fundamentals, 1990s–2000

Source: Data comes from FHFA, Reis, and BLS.

Note: Figure graphs the distribution of cumulative growth in real house prices, real rents, real MSA income, and MSA employment from each variable's trough in the 1990s to its peak in the 2000s.

more than 50 percent trough-to-peak growth in housing demand fundamentals, and none experienced more than 100 percent growth.[17]

Not only are the run-ups in fundamental values muted relative to house prices, the relationship between trough-to-peak growth and the subsequent peak-to-trough decline is attenuated. Figure 1.19 plots a cycle in real apartment rents. Each MSA's troughs and peaks in real rent are computed using the same algorithm that was applied to house prices. Then, figure 1.19 graphs the peak-to-trough change in log real apartment rents in the 2000s against the trough-to-peak log change in the 1990s and 2000s for the subset of forty-three MSAs for which we have rent data. Most MSAs experienced less than a 40 log point trough-to-peak growth in rent and less than a 20 point decline from their rent peak through 2010. However, a handful of MSAs—including the San Francisco Bay area, Denver, and New York—experienced much larger rent cycles. Most MSAs lie below the solid 45-degree line, indicating

17. Figure 1.18 uses different trough and peak dates for each variable, thus the trough-to-peak growth is calculated over a different sample window. However, it makes little difference in this figure if we instead compute trough-to-peak growth for each demand fundamental using the trough and peak dates for the real house price index.

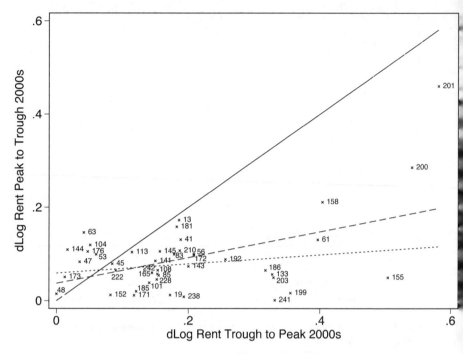

Fig. 1.19   Real rent growth and decline, 1990s–2000s, by Reis subset of MSAs

Source: Data comes from Reis, deflated by the CPI.

Notes: Figure plots the MSA cumulative change in real log rents between the rent trough of (typically) the 1990s and the rent peak of (typically) the mid-2000s against the subsequent rent decline. The solid 45-degree line demarcates the log point decline in rents that would exactly undo the prior growth in rents. The straight lines are the fitted bivariate regression lines, the dashed one uses unweighted observations, and the dotted one uses observations weighted by 1990 housing units.

that rents have not fallen as much as they rose during their booms. All the exceptions are rust-belt MSAs with very little rent growth, such as Detroit, Milwaukee, and Pittsburgh. The dashed line corresponds to the unweighted bivariate regression and shows that, on average, MSAs that enjoyed more rent growth during their booms also experienced greater percentage rent declines through 2010. (The estimated coefficient on the trough-to-peak change in log real rent is 0.276 with a standard error of 0.079.) However, when each MSA is weighted by its number of housing units, displayed in the dotted line, we do not obtain a statistically significant correlation. (The estimated coefficient is 0.098 with a standard error of 0.070.)

In fact, all bivariate relationships discussed in this chapter are stronger for house prices than for housing demand fundamentals. This fact can be seen in table 1.1. The top panel of table 1.1 uses the subsample of MSAs for which we have rent data from Reis. Each row corresponds to a different bivariate

Table 1.1   Bivariate regression results

	Real house prices (1)	Real rent (2)	Real income (3)	Employment (4)	P/R (5)	P/income (6)	P/emp. (7)
	Reis sample						
Regress peak-to-trough log changes in the 2000s on trough-to-peak log changes in the 1990s and 2000s (N = 43/43/./33/./.)[a]	0.471 (0.072)	0.098 (0.070)			0.783 (0.060)		
Regress peak-to-trough log changes in the 1990s on trough-to-peak log changes in the 1980s and 1990s (N = 42/41/30/27/33/43/38)	0.220 (0.110)	−0.153 (0.155)	−0.158 (0.065)	−0.084 (0.051)	0.608 (0.120)	0.306 (0.140)	−0.108 (0.180)
Regress trough-to-peak log changes in the 2000s on trough-to-peak log changes in the 1980s and 1990s (N = 42/41/30/30/33/43/38)	0.598 (0.185)	0.318 (0.307)	−0.303 (0.226)	0.195 (0.173)	0.381 (0.177)	0.866 (0.163)	0.660 (0.180)
	Full FHFA sample						
Regress peak-to-trough log changes in the 2000s on trough-to-peak log changes in the 1990s and 2000s (N = 249)	0.518 (0.031)						
Regress peak-to-trough log changes in the 1990s on trough-to-peak log changes in the 1980s and 1990s (N = 165/147/92/203/189)	0.233 (0.053)		−0.068 (0.032)	−0.090 (0.022)		0.378 (0.067)	−0.026 (0.088)
Regress trough-to-peak log changes in the 2000s on trough-to-peak log changes in the 1980s and 1990s (N = 165/137/81/203/189)	0.598 (0.094)		−0.117 (0.094)	0.167 (0.097)		0.968 (0.080)	0.772 (0.086)

[a]Income and employment data are available only through 2008, not enough time to assess peak-to-trough growth after the boom of the 2000s.

regression where the unit of observation is an MSA and each observation is weighted by the MSA's number of households. For a given variable, the first row regresses the peak-to-trough change in the log of that variable after the peak in the 2000s on the preceding trough-to-peak log change. The second row repeats the strategy for the boom/bust of the 1980s and 1990s. The third row regresses trough-to-peak log differences over the boom of the 2000s on trough-to-peak log differences over the preceding boom. The bottom panel repeats the regressions using the full FHFA sample of MSAs.

Each column of table 1.1 corresponds to a different variable of interest, and the estimated slope coefficient from the bivariate regression is reported in the cell. Cells are empty when there is not enough data for an estimate. For example, there is no rent variable in the FHFA data set, so columns (2) and (5) of the bottom panel are empty. Likewise, columns (2), (3), (6), and (7) of the top row of each panel are empty because the income and employment data do not extend far enough to allow an estimate of how much they changed after the peak of the 2000s.

In the first row and column of table 1.1, peak-to-trough real house price declines subsequent to the peak of the 2000s were 4.7 log points larger for every additional 10 log point increase in house price growth. (The estimated coefficient is 0.471 with a standard error of 0.072.) The analogous coefficient from the previous boom is just half that magnitude, at 0.220 (0.110). But house price growth is highly correlated between the two booms. The estimated coefficient of 0.598 shows that an MSA with 10 log points more trough-to-peak house price growth in the 1980s and 1990s on average experienced nearly 6 log points more house price growth in the 2000s boom. The bottom panel, which uses the full sample, finds similar estimated coefficients.

The second column repeats the same analyses with MSA-level real rent, the third column with real income, and the fourth column with MSA employment. In none of these columns are the estimated coefficients as large as the corresponding ones for real house prices. In addition, in most cases in the top panel they are not statistically distinguishable from zero.

Another way to see the contribution of swings in asset prices net of fundamentals to housing booms and busts is to normalize by a measure of fundamentals. Figure 1.20 plots the trough-to-peak distribution of growth between the trough of the 1990s and the peak of the 2000s in the price-to-rent, price-to-income, and price-to-employment ratios. The price-to-rent multiple should reflect the influence of factors that potentially affect housing asset pricing, such as interest rates, credit availability, expected future growth in the value of the housing service flow, adjustments for the relative riskiness of owning versus renting, and any mispricing in the housing market, while conditioning out differences across MSAs in current supply/demand fundamentals. The price-to-income and price-to-employment ratios are alternative measures that normalize by demand shifters in case rent growth for apartments does not parallel the growth in the implicit rental value of

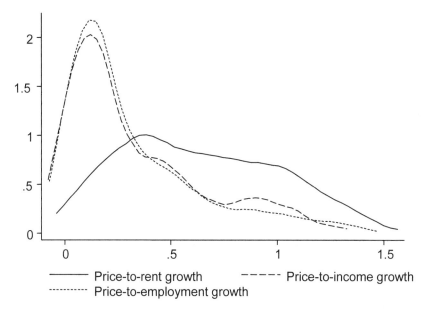

Fig. 1.20   Trough-to-peak growth in price-to-fundamentals ratios, 1990s–2000
Source: Data comes from FHFA, Reis, and BLS.
Note: Figure graphs the distribution of cumulative growth in the price-to-rent, price-to-income, and price-to-employment ratios from each variable's trough in the 1990s to its peak in the 2000s.

owner-occupied houses. Growth in the price-to-rent ratio exhibits nearly as much dispersion over the boom as growth in prices alone, ranging from zero to 150 percent. Growth in the price-to-income and price-to-employment ratios are more concentrated below 50 percent, but this is due to differences in the composition of MSAs that make up the full sample and the MSAs for which we have rent data. The Reis MSAs simply had more house price growth during this boom. When we plot all three series using the same subset of MSAs that are in the Reis sample, all three distributions look quite similar. The price-to-income and price-to-employment growth distributions parallel the shape of the price-to-rent distribution, but are shifted to the left by about 10 percentage points of growth.

Even though there is not much evidence of cycles in underlying demand fundamentals in this simple analysis, after controlling for the influence of fundamentals the boom-bust relationships documented in this chapter get stronger. Figure 1.21 plots the peak-to-trough decline after the 2000s peak in the log price-to-rent ratio against the trough-to-peak growth. There is a strong positive relationship—those MSAs that experienced the largest run-ups in their price-to-rent ratios also experienced the largest subsequent declines—and it is a tighter cyclical relationship than in the analogous chart

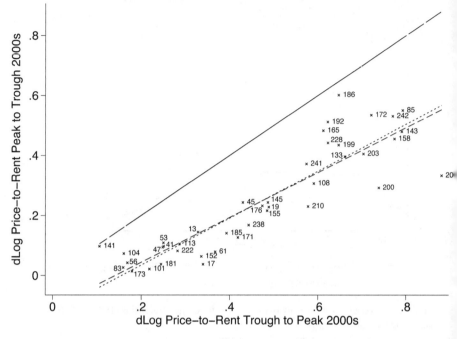

Fig. 1.21   Price-to-rent ratio growth and decline, 1990s–2000s, by Reis subset of MSAs

Source: Data comes from Reis and FHFA.

Notes: Figure plots the MSA cumulative change in the log price-to-rent ratio between the R/P trough of (typically) the 1990s and the R/P peak of (typically) the mid-2000s against the subsequent R/P decline. The solid line demarcates the log point decline in R/P that would exactly undo the prior growth in R/P. The straight lines are the fitted bivariate regression lines, the dashed one uses unweighted observations, and the dotted one uses observations weighted by 1990 housing units.

for house prices alone (figure 1.6, which uses the same sample of MSAs). The MSAs lie closer to the regression line—the adjusted *R*-squared that corresponds to the weighted bivariate regression line is 0.81 in figure 1.20 and just 0.53 in figure 1.6. In addition, the regression line is closer to the 45-degree line that signifies the point where the price-to-rent ratio has reverted to its prior trough levels.

The last three columns of table 1.1 report the estimated coefficients for the set of bivariate regressions on the price-to-rent, price-to-income, and price-to-employment ratios. There is a stronger boom-bust pattern in price-to-rent ratios than in house prices alone in the booms of the 2000s and the 1980s and 1990s (the first two rows). However, the link between the run-up of the 1980s and the run-up in the 1990s and 2000s was stronger in house prices than in price-to-rent ratios. This pattern does not persist with our other two measures of fundamentals. For price/income, the boom-bust relationship is

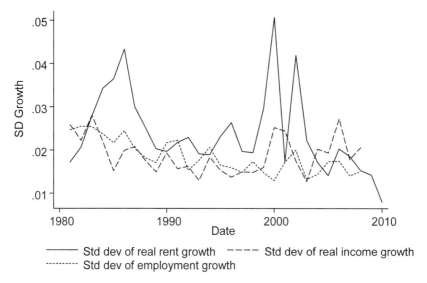

Fig. 1.22   The standard deviation of MSA-level annual growth in demand fundamentals

Source: Data comes from Reis and BLS, deflated by the CPI.

Note: Figure graphs the standard deviations of annual real rent, real income, and employment growth across MSAs in each year.

tighter during the 1980s and 1990s cycle and the 1980s booms are more correlated with the 1990s and 2000s booms. By contrast, price-to-employment does not exhibit much of any boom/bust cycle in the 1980s, but MSAs with high growth in price-to-employment in the 1990s and 2000s were also likely to experience high growth in the same ratio in the 1980s boom.

Turning back to annual growth rates, the growth in housing demand fundamentals does not show the same increases in cross-sectional dispersion during booms as we saw in house prices. Figure 1.22 plots the standard deviation (across MSAs) in each year's growth in rents, income, and employment, between 1981 and 2010 for rent and between 1981 and 2008 for income and employment. The cross-sectional dispersion in income and employment growth—the dashed and dotted lines, respectively—is relatively constant over the sample period. The standard deviation in rent growth, by contrast, is higher in the mid- to late 1980s and in the early 2000s, ahead of the house price peaks in the two booms in our sample period.

The variation in rent growth over the cycles is small relative to the variation in house prices and thus the standard deviation in house prices shown in figure 1.16 must be largely due to changes in the asset pricing of houses across MSAs. In fact, because the increase in variation in rents leads the increase in variation in house prices, purging rent growth from house price growth reveals an even starker pattern of greater dispersion in the changes

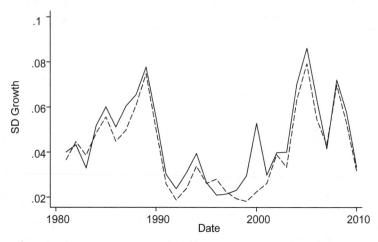

Fig. 1.23   **Standard deviations of conditional and unconditional annual house price growth**

Source: Data comes from Reis and FHFA, deflated by the CPI.

Note: Figure graphs the standard deviations of real house prices and the residuals from an MSA-level regression of real house price growth on real rent growth.

in asset pricing of houses during booms. To demonstrate this, we regressed real house price growth on real rent growth and graphed the standard deviation of the residual by year in the dashed line in figure 1.23.[18] The solid line repeats the standard deviation of real house price growth from figure 1.16. The standard deviation of annual house price growth net of rent growth increases in house price booms, rises steadily to the house price peaks, and is low in the troughs. It is evident from figure 1.23 that the volatility of house price growth outside of housing booms was due to growth in rents or cor-related housing demand fundamentals, whereas the volatility of house price growth inside of housing booms can be attributed to asset pricing factors.

It is worth noting that these patterns cannot be due merely to some MSAs experiencing house price growth in booms and others not. Since the standard deviation increases through the booms, figure 1.23 implies that house price growth must accelerate throughout the boom. Figures 1.24 and 1.25 provide evidence that the entire distribution of house price growth expands in booms. Figure 1.24 plots the distribution of real rent growth by year. The largest dispersion can be found in the mid-1980s and the late 1990s. In the 1983 through 1986 and the 1995 through 2000 periods, the top 75 percent

18. We obtain similar results if we plot the standard deviation of growth in the price-to-rent ratio rather than the residual from the price versus rent regression. The estimated coefficient on rent growth in the bivariate regression of real house price growth on real rent growth is 0.750 with a standard error of 0.054.

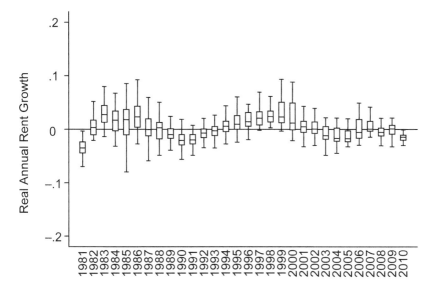

Fig. 1.24   **The distribution of annual real rent growth, by year**

Source: Data comes from Reis, deflated by the CPI. Excludes outside values.

Notes: Figure plots the distribution of annual rent growth across MSAs in each year. The black-outlined bar runs from the twenty-fifth to the seventy-fifth percentiles. The horizontal black line corresponds to the median.

of MSAs nearly always had positive rent growth. But in the height of the booms of the late 1980s and the mid-2000s, more than 75 percent of MSAs experienced real rent declines. Figure 1.25 plots the distribution of the residuals from the regression of real house price growth on real rent growth. Here, the dispersion was the largest during the booms of the late 1980s and mid-2000s. However, during the peak of the 1980s boom, house price growth conditional on rent growth was much more equally likely to be negative as positive. By contrast, in the run-up to the peak of the 2000s, almost all MSAs in every year between 2001 and 2005 experienced positive house price growth even conditional on rent growth. And, in the subsequent bust, between 2008 and 2010, almost all MSAs experienced declines in the house price growth residual.

The fact that the stylized facts established in this chapter are even more pronounced once demand fundamentals are accounted for suggests that the significant contributor to housing cycles comes from factors that affect the asset pricing of houses. If house price growth and declines were due to a changing desire for having a place to live, or an increase in the amount of housing demanded by households, it would be reflected in rents or incomes. Instead, the cycles must be due to waxing and waning of the taste for *owning* a house. Potential explanations that are compatible with changing taste for home ownership include credit market factors, such as changes in interest

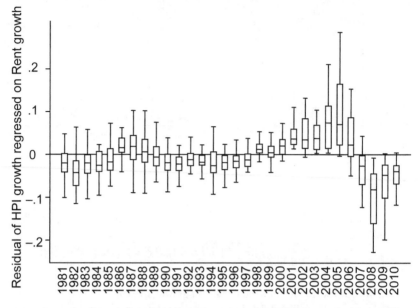

Fig. 1.25   The distribution of conditional annual real house price growth, by year

Source: Data comes from REIS and FHFA, deflated by the CPI. Excludes outside values.
Notes: Figure graphs the distributions of the residuals from an MSA-level regression of real
house price growth on real rent growth. The black-outlined bar runs from the twenty-fifth to
the seventy-fifth percentiles. The horizontal black line corresponds to the median.

rates, or changing expectations, such as optimism about house price growth.
However, given the empirical patterns documented earlier in this chapter,
some of these possibilities are unlikely.

1.9   Conclusion

This chapter has documented several empirical patterns in real house
prices in the United States over the last three decades. During that span,
many housing markets experienced two boom-bust periods in house prices.
However, that pattern was far from universal. A large fraction of housing
markets had no booms or busts, or just one. Even among cyclical housing
markets, the amplitude of house price increases or decreases varied greatly,
and the start dates and end dates of each boom were widely dispersed. In
addition, during the house price boom-bust of the 1990s and 2000s, nearly
all MSAs experienced house price growth during the boom and nearly all
MSAs faced house price declines in the bust. In the prior housing cycle,
many MSAs faced real house price declines even during the boom and many
MSAs experienced real house price growth during the bust.

Despite these differences across metropolitan areas and between the two housing cycles, there were also considerable similarities along these same dimensions. Housing markets that enjoyed the largest house price booms also faced the largest subsequent price declines. Those MSAs that had the largest boom/bust cycle in the 1980s also typically had the largest cycles in the most recent housing episode, though much of Florida and Phoenix, Arizona are exceptions to that pattern. Neighboring MSAs experienced similar timing and magnitudes of their cycles in the 1990s and 2000s, but not so much in the 1980s.

In addition to these facts about trough-to-peak and peak-to-trough growth rates, annual house price changes became more widely dispersed near the peak of the national house price cycle in both the 1980s and 2000s cycles.

Finally, these patterns persist even when demand fundamentals such as rents, median incomes, or MSA-level employment are netted out of prices. Indeed, controlling for growth in apartment rents makes the boom-bust cycle in house price growth even clearer.

This chapter has been agnostic about the possible causes of house price cycles. However, the accumulation of empirical facts limits the set of feasible explanations. Common national factors cannot easily generate differences in the amplitude of house price cycles across MSAs unless they interact with MSA-specific characteristics and, even then, are hard to reconcile with the variation across MSAs in the start or end date of booms and busts. Potential explanations that depend solely on differences across MSAs in the amount of new housing construction are at odds with the fact that cycles in price-to-rent ratios exhibit the same MSA-level heterogeneity as prices. Even if new construction attenuates house price growth in a given MSA, that new housing supply should also reduce the clearing rent, leaving price-to-rent ratios high.[19] Other models that emphasize how differences in initial conditions can yield variation in booms and busts across MSAs need to also explain how the cycles in house prices or price-to-rent ratios can repeat over decades within MSAs and why MSAs with similar cycles are located in geographically concentrated clusters.[20] While much progress has been made on understanding the phenomena of house price booms and busts, it is clear that much work remains to be done.

19. Glaeser, Gyourko, and Saiz's (2008) model sidesteps this issue by incorporating adaptive expectations, so differences across MSAs in the elasticity of supply lead to differences in short-run growth expectations. Those expectations should be capitalized into the price-to-rent ratio, though their model does not make that explicit.

20. This category of explanations includes "fads," such as Burnside, Eichenbaum, and Rebelo (2011), and subprime mortgages, such as Mian and Sufi (2009), since subprime mortgages were not prevalent in the 1980s. By contrast, Ferreira and Gyourko (2011) speculate that contagion could spread local housing booms to other areas.

Appendix

Table 1A.1   Real house price trough and peak dates and cumulative growth rates, by MSA

MSA	1980s trough	1990s peak	1990s trough	2000s peak	1980s trough to 1990s peak (%)	1990s peak to 1990s trough (%)	1990s trough to 2000s peak (%)	2000s peak to 2010 (%)
Abilene, TX	1984	1999	1990	2009	34	1	30	2
Akron, OH	1992	1993	2000	2005	0	1	5	17
Albany, GA	1982	1989	1994	2007	81	25	20	8
Albany-Schenectady-Troy, NY	1982	1986	2000	2007	7	15	52	6
Albuquerque, NM			1991	2007			54	13
Alexandria, LA	1983	1989	1991	2009	56	24	41	3
Allentown-Bethlehem-Easton, PA-NJ	1982	1984	2000	2007	3	31	50	16
Amarillo, TX	1985	1989	1990	2007	29	3	36	2
Ann Arbor, MI		1986	1993	2005		5	48	30
Appleton, WI		1987	1991	2005		3	29	10
Asheville, NC		1986	1991	2007		3	79	10
Athens-Clarke County, GA	1982	1987	1993	2007	13	8	38	9
Atlanta-Sandy Springs-Marietta, GA	1984	1989	1994	2006	34	12	33	17
Atlantic City-Hammonton, NJ	1989	1990	1996	2006	1	22	101	22
Auburn-Opelika, AL	1983	1987	1991	2007	9	3	41	10
Augusta-Richmond County, GA-SC	1981	1985	1997	2007	22	13	24	6
Austin-Round Rock-San Marcos, TX	1985	1986	1990	2009	1	38	67	2
Bakersfield-Delano, CA	1982	1989	2000	2006	30	24	120	48
Baltimore-Towson, MD	1981	1982	1997	2006	0	11	86	19
Baton Rouge, LA	1982	1983	1991	2007	1	34	48	3
Beaumont-Port Arthur, TX	1987	1995	1990	2009	60	30	24	3
Bellingham, WA			2000	2007		2	67	13
Billings, MT		1987	1997	2007			37	3
Binghamton, NY	1982	1987	1991	2009	10	35	36	2
Birmingham-Hoover, AL						7		9

City								
Bismarck, ND		1987	1991		2009	13	45	1
Bloomington, IN		1989	1990		2006	3	27	2
Bloomington-Normal, IL		1987	1991		2004	8	21	6
Boise City-Nampa, ID		1981	1996		2007	7	53	31
Boulder, CO	1981	1982	1990	8	2005	15	95	6
Bremerton-Silverdale, WA	1988	1994	1997	33	2007	2	77	21
Brownsville-Harlingen, TX			1991		2007		13	3
Buffalo-Niagara Falls, NY	1983		2000	35	2009	15	14	1
Canton-Massillon, OH	1985		1990	3	2003	0	33	18
Cape Coral-Fort Myers, FL	1985		1996	7	2006	11	128	54
Casper, WY	1989		1997	34	2007	0	71	7
Cedar Rapids, IA	1985		1990	4	2005	1	24	6
Champaign-Urbana, IL		1989	1993		2006	10	26	6
Charleston, WV		1987	1990		2007		19	2
Charleston-North Charleston-Summerville, SC	1983		1995		2007	17	94	17
Charlotte-Gastonia-Rock Hill, NC-SC	1985		1993	18	2007	7	29	10
Charlottesville, VA	1984		1996	16	2007	5	78	14
Chattanooga, TN-GA	1982		1991	11	2007	9	34	6
Cheyenne, WY		1983	1991	8	2006	22	56	3
Chicago-Joliet-Naperville, IL (MSAD)	1982		1991	31	2006	1	52	22
Chico, CA		1981	1997		2006	13	107	34
Cincinnati-Middletown, OH-KY-IN	1985		1991	10	2005	2	22	12
Cleveland-Elyria-Mentor, OH	1985		2000	27	2004	0	6	20
College Station-Bryan, TX		1986						
Colorado Springs, CO	1981		1991	9	2006	20	65	11
Columbia, MO	1986		1993		2006		29	6
Columbia, SC	1984		1995	7	2007	7	24	5
Columbus, GA-AL		1988	1991		2007	12	32	9
Columbus, OH	1985		1991	10	2005	2	25	13
Corpus Christi, TX	1981		1982	9	2007	35	28	6
Corvallis, OR	1988		2000	77	2003	4	37	10
Dallas-Plano-Irving, TX (MSAD)	1982		1995	7	2005	32	18	4
Davenport-Moline-Rock Island, IA-IL		1988	1991					4
Dayton, OH	1982		1991	19	2005	2	11	14

(continued)

Table 1A.1   continued

MSA	1980s trough	1990s peak	1990s trough	2000s peak	1980s trough to 1990s peak (%)	1990s peak to 1990s trough (%)	1990s trough to 2000s peak (%)	2000s peak to 2010 (%)
Decatur, AL	1991	1993	1996	2009	2	4	14	2
Decatur, IL	1988	1989	1991	2005	2	2	12	4
Deltona-Daytona Beach-Ormond Beach, FL	1981	1987	1997	2006	22	13	113	44
Denver-Aurora-Broomfield, CO	1981	1983	1991	2005	4	25	83	12
Des Moines-West Des Moines, IA	1982	1983	1991	2005	4	7	33	9
Detroit-Livonia-Dearborn, MI (MSAD)	1984	1990	1991	2004	26	0	52	42
Dothan, AL			1991	2007			25	7
Dover, DE		1990	2000	2007		10	54	19
Dubuque, IA	1987	1989	1990	2006	2	2	38	3
Duluth, MN-WI	1987	1989	1990	2006	5	0	88	8
Eau Claire, WI	1987	1988	1991	2005	2	5	61	7
El Paso, TX		1983	2000	2007		28	35	7
Elkhart-Goshen, IN		1986	1991	2005		10	21	11
Erie, PA	1985	1989	1990	2005	7	1	19	4
Eugene-Springfield, OR	1986	1999	2000	2007	70	2	47	18
Evansville, IN-KY	1985	1986	1991	2004	2	14	26	8
Fargo, ND-MN			1991	2006			31	3
Fayetteville, NC			1991	2009			14	1
Fayetteville-Springdale-Rogers, AR-MO	1981	1982	1991	2006	5	12	46	19
Flagstaff, AZ-UT		1987	1990	2006		7	128	28
Flint, MI	1984	1992	1993	2005	7	0	41	38
Florence, SC	1987	1988	1991	2009	1	3	23	4
Fort Collins-Loveland, CO	1982	1983	1991	2005	8	15	78	11
Fort Smith, AR-OK			1991	2009			22	4
Fort Wayne, IN	1984	1987	1994	2002	13	11	8	13
Fort Worth-Arlington, TX (MSAD)	1982	1986	1996	2003	4	30	14	4
Fresno, CA	1988	1992	1997	2006	11	16	121	45

		1981	1997	2006		15	142	45
Ft. Lauderdale-Pompano Bch.-Deerfield Bch., FL (MSAD)								
Gainesville, FL		1986	1993	2007		14	82	24
Gary, IN (MSAD)	1987	1998	2000	2007	28	2	11	9
Grand Forks, ND-MN		1991	1991	2007			40	3
Grand Junction, CO				2007				15
Grand Rapids-Wyoming, MI	1984	1989	1993	2005	16	3	34	24
Greeley, CO		1986	1991	2003		19	74	22
Green Bay, WI		1986	1991	2005		5	42	13
Greensboro-High Point, NC	1983	1988	1993	2005	17	9	12	7
Greenville, NC		1987	1993	2007		10	15	7
Greenville-Mauldin-Easley, SC		1981	1991	2009		8	24	4
Gulfport-Biloxi, MS		1988	1991	2007		16	78	17
Hagerstown-Martinsburg, MD-WV		1990	1996	2006		6	74	30
Harrisburg-Carlisle, PA	1984	1989	1991	2007	14	2	26	6
Hattiesburg, MS			1992	2007			43	8
Hickory-Lenoir-Morganton, NC	1987	1989	1991	2007	3	1	25	5
Houma-Bayou Cane-Thibodaux, LA			1990	2009			68	2
Houston-Sugar Land-Baytown, TX	1981	1982	1997	2009	5	40	34	2
Huntington-Ashland, WV-KY-OH	1989	1990	1991	2009	0	4	29	1
Huntsville, AL		1987	1997	2009		15	18	2
Indianapolis-Carmel, IN	1985	1988	1991	2003	9	2	13	11
Iowa City, IA	1988	1989	1990	2005	5	1	30	5
Jackson, MI				2005				29
Jackson, MS	1982	1986	1991	2007	4	20	20	6
Jackson, TN			1992	2006			10	9
Jacksonville, FL	1981	1986	1995	2006	11	15	93	29
Janesville, WI	1988	1989	1990	2006	2	0	47	14
Joplin, MO			1992	2006			24	7
Kalamazoo-Portage, MI	1985	1988	1991	2005	6	1	35	17
Kankakee-Bradley, IL		1998	2000	2007		2	16	9
Kansas City, MO-KS	1984	1987	1993	2005	4	14	36	12
Kennewick-Pasco-Richland, WA	1988	1994	1997	2006	48	11	14	1
Killeen-Temple-Fort Hood, TX			1991	2007			18	3

(continued)

Table 1A.1 continued

MSA	1980s trough	1990s peak	1990s trough	2000s peak	1980s trough to 1990s peak (%)	1990s peak to 1990s trough (%)	1990s trough to 2000s peak (%)	2000s peak to 2010 (%)
Knoxville, TN	1985	1987	1991	2007	5	6	35	7
Kokomo, IN			1991	2002			26	24
La Crosse, WI-MN		1986	1991	2006		11	51	4
Lafayette, IN		1999	2000	2002		1	1	13
Lafayette, LA		1982	2000	2009		36	25	3
Lake Charles, LA			1992	2009			34	3
Lake County-Kenosha County, IL-WI (MSAD)				2006				21
Lakeland-Winter Haven, FL	1985	1986	1996	2006	0	14	81	38
Lancaster, PA	1984	1990	2000	2007	25	8	31	7
Lansing-East Lansing, MI		1981	1993	2005		14	37	29
Las Cruces, NM		1986	1991	2007		14	42	12
Las Vegas-Paradise, NV		1982	1997	2006		19	89	55
Lawrence, KS	1988	1989	1991	2005	1	6	51	9
Lexington-Fayette, KY	1982	1983	1993	2006	7	13	28	5
Lima, OH	1985	1988	1993	2005	4	4	22	12
Lincoln, NE	1985	1986	1991	2005	1	6	30	10
Little Rock-North Little Rock-Conway, AR	1982	1986	1991	2007	7	19	25	4
Longview, TX	1985	1986	1992	2009	1	20	32	1
Los Angeles-Long Beach-Glendale, CA (MSAD)	1984	1990	1997	2006	61	34	158	34
Louisville-Jefferson County, KY-IN	1984	1989	1991	2005	9	2	35	7
Lubbock, TX		1981	1991	2009		28	16	1
Lynchburg, VA		1988	1991	2007		2	40	6
Macon, GA	1984	1987	1992	2007	8	10	15	10
Madison, WI	1981	1982	1990	2006	0	4	64	9
Mansfield, OH	1987	1988	1991	2004	3	4	34	23
McAllen-Edinburg-Mission, TX	1990	1994	2000	2007	4	6	12	6
Medford, OR				2006				35

City								
Memphis, TN-MS-AR	1984	1987	1994	2006	16	12	16	12
Merced, CA	1985	1991	1997	2006	24	20	148	64
Miami-Miami Beach-Kendall, FL (MSAD)	1981	1982	1991	2007	2	13	160	42
Milwaukee-Waukesha-West Allis, WI				2006			13	13
Minneapolis-St. Paul-Bloomington, MN-WI	1985	1987	1992	2005	4	7	78	23
Missoula, MT				2007				8
Mobile, AL	1985	1986	1991	2007	4	17	45	10
Modesto, CA	1984	1990	1997	2006	43	27	141	58
Monroe, LA			1991	2009			35	1
Montgomery, AL			1991	2007			13	9
Myrtle Beach-North Myrtle Beach-Conway, SC			1994	2007			71	23
Naples-Marco Island, FL	1985	1990	1996	2006	12	8	173	51
Nashville-Davidson—Murfreesboro—Franklin, TN	1982	1987	1992	2007	18	15	46	8
Nassau-Suffolk, NY (MSAD)		1988	1996	2006		28	120	20
New Orleans-Metairie-Kenner, LA			1991	2007			65	11
New York-White Plains-Wayne, NY-NJ (MSAD)	1982	1988	1997	2006	108	28	100	18
Newark-Union, NJ-PA (MSAD)	1982	1988	1997	2006	93	28	85	19
Niles-Benton Harbor, MI	1985	1990	1991	2007	23	1	46	11
Oakland-Fremont-Hayward, CA (MSAD)	1984	1990	1996	2006	50	24	144	36
Ocala, FL			1996	2006			88	37
Ocean City, NJ		1989	1997	2006		18	142	20
Odessa, TX	1991	1992	2001	2009	3	8	56	6
Oklahoma City, OK	1981	1983	1991	2007	8	42	30	2
Olympia, WA	1988	1995	1996	2007	39	1	59	16
Omaha-Council Bluffs, NE-IA	1982	1983	1991	2005	0	13	33	9
Orlando-Kissimmee-Sanford, FL	1981	1986	1996	2006	8	15	104	42
Owensboro, KY	1988	1989	1992	2002	0	8	19	6
Palm Bay-Melbourne-Titusville, FL		1981	1997	2006	0	25	113	47
Panama City-Lynn Haven-Panama City Beach, FL			1991	2006			113	31
Parkersburg-Marietta-Vienna, WV-OH			1991	2006			26	3
Pensacola-Ferry Pass-Brent, FL		1986	1991	2006		16	76	27
Peoria, IL				2007				3
Philadelphia, PA (MSAD)	1982	1989	1997	2006	60	19	64	11

(continued)

Table 1A.1   continued

MSA	1980s trough	1990s peak	1990s trough	2000s peak	1980s trough to 1990s peak (%)	1990s peak to 1990s trough (%)	1990s trough to 2000s peak (%)	2000s peak to 2010 (%)
Phoenix-Mesa-Glendale, AZ	1982	1986	1993	2006	8	23	123	45
Pittsburgh, PA	1982	1993	1997	2005	14	2	17	3
Pocatello, ID	1989	1998	2000	2007	26	4	25	7
Port St. Lucie, FL	1983	1984	1997	2006	2	18	121	53
Portland-Vancouver-Hillsboro, OR-WA	1988	1999	2000	2007	70	1	50	20
Poughkeepsie-Newburgh-Middletown, NY	1983	1988	1997	2006	86	32	90	23
Provo-Orem, UT	1985	1986	1990	2007	1	12	98	22
Pueblo, CO	1982	1983	1991	2006	2	15	49	11
Punta Gorda, FL	1982	1989	1997	2006		17	117	48
Racine, WI				2006				16
Raleigh-Cary, NC	1982	1986	1992	2007	21	12	28	6
Reading, PA	1982	1989	2000	2007	33	18	37	10
Redding, CA	1987	1991	1997	2006	25	15	105	38
Reno-Sparks, NV	1982	1983	2000	2006	0	5	81	48
Richmond, VA	1982	1989	1996	2007	14	8	58	15
Riverside-San Bernardino-Ontario, CA	1984	1990	1997	2006	33	33	157	48
Roanoke, VA	1982	1988	1991	2007	31	3	42	7
Rochester, MN		1985	1995	2005		8	38	14
Rochester, NY	1982	1988	2000	2005	33	22	8	4
Rockford, IL	1985	1987	1990	2007	2	0	18	12
Rocky Mount, NC		1986	1993	2003		11	11	10
Sacramento-Arden-Arcade-Roseville, CA	1984	1991	1997	2005	43	26	124	44
Saginaw-Saginaw Township North, MI	1983	1984	1991	2004	1	1	32	26
Salem, OR	1987	1999	2000	2007	59	1	37	18
Salinas, CA	1982	1990	1997	2006	53	17	165	51
Salt Lake City, UT	1985	1986	1990	2007	1	17	118	18
San Angelo, TX	1991	1993	1997	2009	2	3	31	3

City								
San Antonio-New Braunfels, TX		1984	1991	2007		36	32	4
San Diego-Carlsbad-San Marcos, CA	1983	1990	1996	2005	43	25	148	34
San Francisco-San Mateo-Redwood City, CA	1982	1989	1996	2006	79	24	129	24
San Jose-Sunnyvale-Santa Clara, CA	1983	1989	1995	2006	66	23	134	27
San Luis Obispo-Paso Robles, CA	1981	1990	1996	2006	65	30	142	33
Santa Ana-Anaheim-Irvine, CA (MSAD)	1985	1989	1997	2006	49	31	160	33
Santa Barbara-Santa Maria-Goleta, CA	1983	1990	1996	2006	50	25	162	40
Santa Cruz-Watsonville, CA	1984	1990	1996	2006	63	20	135	32
Santa Fe, NM	1988	1995	1997	2007	32	4	49	16
Santa Rosa-Petaluma, CA	1984	1990	1996	2006	53	19	127	38
Savannah, GA		1986	1991	2007		13	77	15
Scranton-Wilkes-Barre, PA		1993	2000	2007		6	26	5
Seattle-Bellevue-Everett, WA (MSAD)	1985	1990	1995	2007	41	3	90	21
Sheboygan, WI	1989	1990	1991	2006	0	0	49	11
Sherman-Denison, TX	1991	1992	1994	2006	0	1	20	6
Shreveport-Bossier City, LA	1985	1986	1991	2007	1	29	31	2
Sioux City, IA-NE-SD		1990	1990	2003			29	4
Sioux Falls, SD		1990	1990	2007			36	3
South Bend-Mishawaka, IN-MI	1984	1988	1991	2005	10	5	22	9
Spokane, WA	1988	1995	2000	2007	34	6	48	13
Springfield, IL		1987	1990	2005		2	3	4
Springfield, MO		1986	1991	2007		14	24	8
St. Cloud, MN			1991	2006			66	17
St. Joseph, MO-KS		1987	1991	2005		2	39	7
St. Louis, MO-IL	1982	1987	1993	2006	17	12	38	11
State College, PA			1990	2009			32	1
Stockton, CA	1984	1990	1997	2006	40	26	141	57
Syracuse, NY	1982	1988	1997	2006	35	25	22	3
Tacoma, WA (MSAD)	1988	1995	1996	2007	31	1	75	23
Tallahassee, FL		1983	1994	2007		13	61	21
Tampa-St. Petersburg-Clearwater, FL	1981	1986	1995	2006	10	15	111	39
Toledo, OH	1985	1989	1991	2004	5	3	29	21
Topeka, KS	1982	1984	1993	2005	2	17	21	6

(continued)

MSA	1980s trough	1990s peak	1990s trough	2000s peak	1980s trough to 1990s peak (%)	1990s peak to 1990s trough (%)	1990s trough to 2000s peak (%)	2000s peak to 2010 (%)
Trenton-Ewing, NJ	1982	1988	1997	2006	86	31	77	18
Tucson, AZ	1982	1986	1991	2006	9	13	95	31
Tulsa, OK	1981	1983	1992	2009	5	35	23	1
Tyler, TX			1991	2007			25	3
Utica-Rome, NY		1989	1997	2009		25	33	2
Vallejo-Fairfield, CA	1984	1990	1997	2006	33	24	147	53
Vineland-Millville-Bridgeton, NJ		1989	2000	2007		16	63	19
Virginia Beach-Norfolk-Newport News, VA-NC	1982	1988	1997	2007	23	13	84	15
Visalia-Porterville, CA	1988	1992	2000	2006	13	16	98	44
Waco, TX			1991	2009			22	2
Washington-Arlington-Alexandria, DC-VA-MD-WV (MSAD)	1982	1989	1997	2006	44	20	113	26
Waterloo-Cedar Falls, IA				2006				3
Wausau, WI				2005				8
West Palm Beach-Boca Raton-Boynton Beach, FL (MSAD)	1982	1983	1997	2006	1	17	136	45
Wichita Falls, TX			1991	2007			19	4
Wichita, KS	1985	1986	1991	2009	2	19	16	2
Wilmington, DE-MD-NJ (MSAD)	1981	1989	1997	2006	49	16	61	15
Wilmington, NC		1987	1991	2007		4	89	19
Yakima, WA	1989	1998	2000	2007	46	3	18	5
York-Hanover, PA		1989	2000	2007		7	38	12
Youngstown-Warren-Boardman, OH-PA	1987	1989	1990	2004	3	3	26	14
Yuba City, CA		1991	1997	2006		19	117	48
Yuma, AZ	1994	1995	1997	2006	2	2	76	33

References

Barlevy, Gadi, and Jonas Fisher. 2011. "Mortgage Choices and Housing Speculation." Federal Reserve Bank of Chicago Working Paper 2010–12, June 15.

Bayer, Patrick, Christopher Geissler, and James Roberts. 2011. "Speculators and Middlemen: The Role of Flippers in the Housing Market." NBER Working Paper no. 16784. Cambridge, MA: National Bureau of Economic Research.

Brunnermeier, Markus, and Christian Julliard. 2008. "Money Illusion and Housing Frenzies." *Review of Financial Studies* 21 (1): 135–80.

Burnside, Craig, Martin Eichenbaum, and Sergio Rebelo. 2011. "Understanding Booms and Busts in Housing Markets." NBER Working Paper no. 16734. Cambridge, MA: National Bureau of Economic Research.

Campbell, John, Stefano Giglio, and Parag Pathak. 2011. "Forced Sales and House Prices." *American Economic Review* 101 (5): 2108–31.

Campbell, Sean, Morris Davis, Joshua Gallin, and Robert Martin. 2009. "What Moves Housing Markets: A Variance Decomposition of the Rent-Price Ratio." *Journal of Urban Economics* 66:90–102.

Case, Karl E., and Robert J. Shiller. 2003. "Is There a Bubble in the Housing Market?" *Brookings Papers on Economic Activity* 2:299–342. Washington, DC: Brookings Institution.

Cotter, John, Stuart Gabriel, and Richard Roll. 2011. "Integration and Contagion in US Housing Markets." Working Paper, October 12. Available at SSRN: http://ssrn.com/abstract=1945975.

Davidoff, Tom. 2012. "Supply Elasticity and the Housing Cycle of the 2000s" *Real Estate Economics,* forthcoming.

DiPasquale, Denise, and William Wheaton. 1994. "Housing Market Dynamics and the Future of House Prices." *Journal of Urban Economics* 35 (1): 1–27.

Favilukis, Jack, Sydney Ludvigson, and Stijn Van Nieuwerburgh. 2011. "Macroeconomic Implications of Housing Wealth, Housing Finance, and Limited Risk Sharing in Equilibrium." New York University-Stern Working Paper, January.

Ferreira, Fernando, and Joseph Gyourko. 2011. "Anatomy of the Beginning of the Housing Boom: US Neighborhoods and Metropolitan Areas, 1993–2009." NBER Working Paper no. 17374. Cambridge, MA: National Bureau of Economic Research.

Glaeser, Edward, Joshua Gottlieb, and Joseph Gyourko. 2010. "Can Cheap Credit Explain the Housing Boom?" NBER Working Paper no. 16230. Cambridge, MA: National Bureau of Economic Research

Glaeser, Edward, Joseph Gyourko, Eduardo Morales, and Charles Nathanson. 2011. "Housing Dynamics." 2011 Meeting Papers, no. 307. Society for Economic Dynamics.

Glaeser, Edward, Joseph Gyourko, and Albert Saiz. 2008. "Housing Supply and Housing Bubbles." *Journal of Urban Economics* 64:198–217.

Haughwout, Andrew, Richard Peach, John Sporn, and Joseph Tracy. 2011. "The Supply Side of the Housing Boom and Bust of the 2000s." FRBNY Working Paper, November 6. Federal Reserve Bank of New York.

Himmelberg, Charles, Chris Mayer, and Todd Sinai. 2005. "Assessing High House Prices: Bubbles, Fundamentals, and Misperceptions." *Journal of Economic Perspectives* 19 (4): 67–92.

Lai, Rose, and Robert Van Order. 2010. "Momentum and House Price Growth in the United States: Anatomy of a Bubble." *Real Estate Economics* 38 (4): 753–73.

Mayer, Christopher, and Todd Sinai. 2009. "US House Price Dynamics and Behavioral Finance." In *Policy Making Insights from Behavioral Economics,* edited by

Christopher L. Foote, Lorenz Goette, and Stephan Meier, 261–95. Boston: Federal Reserve Bank of Boston.

McCarthy, Jonathan, and Richard Peach. 2004. "Are Home Prices the Next 'Bubble'?" *FRBNY Economic Policy Review* December:1–17.

Meese, Richard, and Nancy Wallace. 1994. "Testing the Present Value Relation for Housing Prices: Should I Leave My House in San Francisco?" *Journal of Urban Economics* 35:245–66.

Mian, Atif, and Amir Sufi. 2009. "The Consequences of Mortgage Expansion: Evidence from the US Mortgage Default Crisis." *Quarterly Journal of Economics* 124 (4): 1449–96.

Ortalo-Magné, Francois, and Andrea Prat. 2010. "Spatial Asset Pricing: A First Step." CEPR Discussion Paper no. 7842. London: Center for Economic Policy Research.

Pavlov, Andrey, and Susan Wachter. 2009. "Subprime Lending and Real Estate Prices." *Real Estate Economics* 39:1–17.

Robinson, Breck, and Richard Todd. 2010. "The Role of Non-Owner-Occupied Homes in the Current Housing and Foreclosure Cycle." Federal Reserve Bank of Richmond Working Paper no. 10-11, May.

Shiller, Robert. 2005. *Irrational Exuberance,* 2nd ed. Princeton, NJ: Princeton University Press.

———. 2006. "Long-Term Perspectives on the Current Boom in Home Prices." *The Economists' Voice* 3 (4): 4.

Smith, Gary, and Margaret Hwang Smith. 2006. "Bubble, Bubble, Where's the Housing Bubble?" *Brookings Papers on Economic Activity* 1:1–63. Washington, DC: Brookings Institution.

Wheaton, William, and Gleb Nechayev. 2008. "The 1998–2005 Housing 'Bubble' and the Current 'Correction': What's Different This Time?" *Journal of Real Estate Research* 30 (1): 1–26.

2

The Supply Side of the Housing Boom and Bust of the 2000s

Andrew Haughwout, Richard W. Peach, John Sporn, and Joseph Tracy

2.1 Four Questions about Housing Supply over the 2000s Cycle

The boom and subsequent bust of housing construction and prices over the 2000s is widely regarded as a principal contributor to the financial panic of 2007 and the ensuing "Great Recession." As of this writing, it appears that single-family housing starts are finally beginning a gradual recovery roughly seven years after their previous peak in 2005:Q3. Nonetheless, the overall level of housing starts and sales remain at depressed levels as the economy slowly resolves the legacy of excess supply and sharply lower prices. Based on the CoreLogic national index, home prices have fallen 30 percent from their peak in early 2006, returning to levels that prevailed in mid-2003. Roughly one in four homeowners with a mortgage has combined mortgage loan balances that exceed the value of the property. Over 2.6 million foreclosures have been completed since 2008 with 1.9 million

Andrew Haughwout is a vice president in the Research and Statistics Group at the Federal Reserve Bank of New York. Richard W. Peach is a senior vice president in the Macroeconomic and Monetary Studies Function of the Federal Reserve Bank of New York. John Sporn is an assistant economist in the Research and Statistics Group at the Federal Reserve Bank of New York. Joseph Tracy is an executive vice president and senior advisor to the president at the Federal Reserve Bank of New York.

These views are those of the authors and do not necessarily reflect the views of the Federal Reserve Bank of New York or the Federal Reserve System. The authors would like to thank David Crowe, Stephen Melman, and Elliot Eisenberg of the National Association of Home Builders (NAHB) for providing various data and suggestions. We would also like to thank Dan Oppenheim from Credit Suisse, Nishu Sood from Deutsche Bank, and Joshua Pollard from Goldman Sachs for sharing their knowledge of the home-building sector. Sarah Stein provided expert assistance with the CoStar land sales data. For acknowledgments, sources of research support, and disclosure of the authors' material financial relationships, if any, please see http://www.nber.org/chapters/c12620.ack.

foreclosures in process.[1] Another 1.3 million loans are currently ninety or more days delinquent and very likely to move into the foreclosure process.

Much has been written about the demand side of this pronounced housing cycle, in particular the innovations in mortgage finance and loosening of underwriting standards that greatly expanded the pool of potential home buyers. In this chapter, we take a closer look at developments on the supply side of the housing market, and bring prior theories and previous analysis of housing supply face-to-face with data from the 2000s cycle. We focus our discussion on four key issues.

First, how much excess housing production occurred during the boom phase of the cycle and how far along is the correction? While it is now clear that too much housing was built in the United States in the boom phase, identifying how much and where overbuilding occurred remain important issues. We also explore the issue of whether supply elasticity played a role in that geographic dispersion. Our results suggest that 3 to 3.5 million excess housing units were produced during the boom. Excess housing production was a national phenomenon, but excess supply is positively related to housing supply elasticities.

Second, we look at trends in the characteristics of new single-family homes built prior to, during, and after the construction boom to assess what effect, if any, the boom may have had on those trends. The number of excess units put in place during the boom is only a partial measure of its distortive effect on resource allocation; to be complete we must also understand the quality of those units. The effect of booms on asset quality is ambiguous in theory, so evidence from the housing market, where the quality of new construction compared to the existing stock is relatively easy to measure, is valuable. We find that throughout the boom, the quality of new units—both observable and unobservable—appears to have remained high.

Our third question is how the home-building industry changed as prices boomed during the 2000s. We present new evidence regarding the restructuring of the industry that took place from the mid-1990s to the mid-2000s and ask whether this restructuring may have contributed in some way to the overbuilding that took place. We find that a significant amount of consolidation occurred in the industry over this period, as large builders got larger and increasingly relied on the equity markets to finance their projects. These large builders appear to have been major contributors to oversupply as they had projects in the pipeline even after prices began to fall, and in spite of the fact that capital markets signaled this risk well before banks began to tighten lending standards.

Finally, we address the important question of whether these large developers reaped excess profits from the boom, or whether excess demand simply

---

1. See OCC and OTS Mortgage Metric Reports. Comptroller of the Currency, Administrator of National Banks, and Office of Thrift Supervision, US Department of the Treasury.

drove up land values in specific markets, enriching landowners. We present new evidence on transaction volumes and prices for vacant land during the boom and bust, and combine them with our estimates of excess returns in the building industry. In addition, we examine whether large builders earned on average excess returns over this period of consolidation. In addition, we explore whether any excess returns were higher during the height of the housing boom. These data allow us to conclude that both builders and landowners shared in the excess profits generated by the boom.

2.2   Literature Review

Among our four questions, the first—documenting excess supply and its sources—has received the most attention in previous literature. There is considerable interest in evaluating the efficiency of various asset markets, including housing. Case and Shiller (1989) report evidence of serial correlation in quality-adjusted housing returns. If housing markets were fully efficient, then future housing returns could not be predicted based on current information. There are frictions on both the demand side and the supply side of the housing market that might lead to imperfect arbitrage. On the demand side, housing is heterogeneous in a number of dimensions and there are significant transaction costs associated with buying and selling property. On the supply side, there are time frictions involved in the supply of new housing that limit how quickly builders can respond to any mispricing. There may also be costs of adjustment in housing supply that cause builders to spread any supply response out over time (Topel and Rosen 1988). These results imply that builders could get caught with excess supply in the pipeline if prices turn quickly and unexpectedly.

Rosenthal (1999) tests for inefficiencies on the supply side, taking into account that builders cannot instantaneously supply new housing to the market. He uses data on single family detached housing sales in Vancouver, BC, from 1979 to 1989 to estimate a quality-adjusted price of housing using hedonic regressions. An error correction model is estimated to determine how quickly deviations in quality-adjusted prices from building costs are dissipated. The results for a standard building indicate that 96 percent of a short-run price shock disappears within two quarters. When estimates of these price shocks are added to a construction equation, they are not significant. This is consistent with additional evidence that during this period builders required two to three quarters to complete a construction project. Consequently, the observed price shocks were on average too short-lived for builders to earn excess profits by adjusting their construction activity in response to the shocks. Rosenthal concludes that any inefficiencies must originate in the land markets.

Glaeser, Gyourko, and Saiz (2008) explore the role of housing supply elasticity in how possible housing bubbles would manifest themselves in different markets. Their model predictions are that any irrational demand during a bubble will result in higher prices and a more prolonged duration of the bubble in markets where housing is less elastically supplied. In contrast, in markets with relatively elastic supply, bubbles should result in more new residential investment and consequently less of a price response. This muted price response also makes it likely that the bubble will be shorter in duration. They test these predictions using the proxy for housing supply elasticity developed in Saiz (2010).[2] Their estimates confirm that prices react relatively more than quantities in housing markets with inelastic supply, and that as a consequence periods of significantly high prices relative to replacement costs on average last longer. However, they note that several of the markets that experienced the largest booms in the recent cycle have high measured supply elasticities. These markets also demonstrated little variability of prices relative to replacement costs prior to the recent cycle. While having an elastic housing supply limits the likelihood of a serious housing bubble in a local market, it clearly does not prevent one from happening.

While an elastic supply of housing can limit the price rise associated with a temporary period of irrational exuberance in demand, given the durability of housing the larger supply response during the boom means that prices may fall below their preboom levels once demand again reflects fundamental factors.[3] Housing supply is nearly completely inelastic at the current stock of housing for prices below replacement costs (Glaeser and Gyourko 2008). This implies that if housing demand reverts back to its preboom level when the bubble bursts, then prices will overshoot to the down side in elastically supplied markets.

This is illustrated in figure 2.1, which contrasts two local housing markets—one with a completely inelastic short-run housing supply curve, $S(I)$, and one with an elastic short-run supply curve, $S(E)$. The replacement cost of housing is given by C and initially both markets start out with prices equal to replacement cost at point A. A housing bubble develops, which shifts out housing demand in both markets from D_0 to D_1. There is no supply response in the inelastic market so prices ration this irrational exuberance by increasing to $P_1(I)$ as indicated at point C. In contrast, in the elastic supply market both prices and new housing supply react to the outward shift in demand. As a consequence, prices adjust by less than in the inelastic market, rising only to $P_1(E)$ as indicated at point B. When the bubble bursts, assume that demand reverts back to D_0. Prices in the inelastic market decline back to their prebubble level of P_0. However, due to the new housing supply added to the

2. This proxy is the percent of land within a 50 kilometer radius area that has a slope of less than 15 degrees.

3. The tendency for house prices to "overshoot" on the down side will be magnified if lending standards are significantly tightened during the bust phase of the housing cycle and to the extent that the bursting of the housing bubble weakens fundamental housing demand due to higher rates of unemployment.

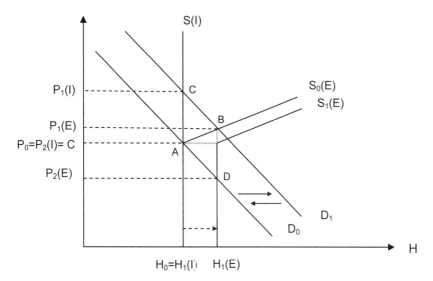

Fig. 2.1   House price dynamics in inelastic and elastic supply markets

elastic market and the durable nature of housing, prices in the elastic market overshoot on the downward side to $P_2(E) < P_0$.[4] As fundamental demand begins to expand in the elastic supply market, prices will adjust upward, but there will initially be no new building activity. Once prices have recovered to the replacement cost, new supply will again be added to the market. Over-building, to the extent that it occurs, has important consequences for local housing markets.

There is also an emerging literature on rational models of overbuilding. DeCoster and Strange (2010) argue that rational overbuilding may occur in markets with uncertainty due to herding behavior by builders. They explore statistical and reputational models of herding behavior (see Banerjee 1992 and Welch 1992). In statistical herding, a builder may choose to ignore a bad signal about future demand prospects in the market if this builder can infer that other builders have received more positive signals. This tendency to ignore bad signals is more pronounced if the market is characterized by lead-ing builders who are perceived as having high-quality information regard-ing market conditions and who may act as "first movers" in the market. In a market characterized by a few large builders and many small builders, statistical herding is most likely to be exhibited by the small builders who are attempting to free ride on the information gathered and acted upon by the large builders. Changes in market structure in the building industry can

4. If lending standards are tightened following the bust relative to the preboom period, then the demand for housing will be contracted even further, magnifying the downward overshoot in prices. Also, if the burst of the housing bubble results in a recession that increases unemploy-ment then this will further put downward pressure on home prices.

impact the likelihood of overbuilding due to statistical herding. As a market becomes more concentrated, there is a trade-off between the increased likelihood that the smaller builders will discount their signals and follow the market leaders and the possible greater reliability of the signals received by the market leaders. Reputational herding may take place if banks have imperfect information on the quality of developers. The likelihood that a bank will cut off funding to a particular builder may be lower if that builder mimics the actions taken by another builder. This type of herding adds noise to the signal that the bank uses to attempt to discriminate between the builders.

2.3   How Much Overbuilding Occurred during the Boom?

A question of interest is how much excess supply was created during the boom in housing construction. To begin to answer that question, figure 2.2 presents a half-century time series of housing starts per 1,000 people, broken out by single-family and multifamily units. From the mid-1960s to the late 1980s, housing production expressed in these terms was quite volatile around a downward trend. Then, from the early 1990s until 2005, a strong upward trend was evident, particularly for single-family units. Following the peak in 2005, total housing starts fell a cumulative 75 percent by 2009. A very gradual increase occurred in 2010 and 2011, particularly for multifamily units, but the 2011 level of starts per 1,000 people was still 72 percent below the 2005 level.

At first glance, the level of housing starts per 1,000 people at the peak in 2005 does not appear to be particularly high, especially when compared

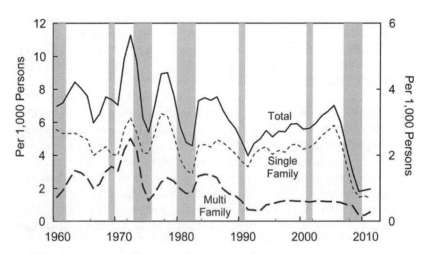

Fig. 2.2   Single and multifamily housing starts over total population
Source: Census Bureau.
Note: Shading reflects NBER recessions.

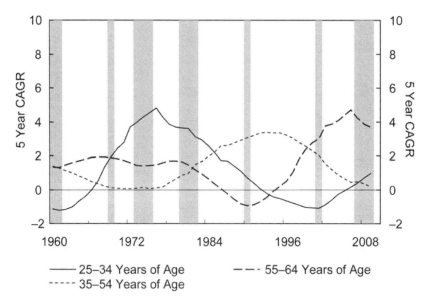

Fig. 2.3   Population growth by age cohort
Source: Census Bureau.
Note: Shading reflects NBER recessions.

to what occurred in the 1960s and 1970s. However, the underlying demographic conditions of the country were fundamentally different in these two periods. These underlying demographic dynamics can have important long-term impacts on the level of demand for housing (Mankiw and Weil 1989). As shown in figure 2.3, up until the mid-1970s, the number of people in the twenty-five to thirty-four year age group (the post World War II baby boom) was growing very rapidly. People at this stage of the life cycle tend to establish independent households for the first time such that the headship rate for this age group is quite a bit higher than for people under twenty-five years of age (figure 2.4). In the second half of the 1970s, the number of people in the thirty-five to fifty-four age group, whose headship rate makes another distinct jump upward, began to increase rapidly. These age-specific population growth rates, along with some increase in age-specific headship rates, resulted in a rising aggregate headship rate (figure 2.5). This meant that the demographically driven number of households was rising quite a bit faster than the underlying population.

In contrast, from the mid-1990s through the mid-2000s the number of people in the twenty-five to thirty-four year age group was actually declining, while the growth rate of those thirty-five to fifty-four years of age was slowing sharply. At the same time, the number of people aged fifty-five to sixty-four was rising rapidly. In addition, headship rates for individual age

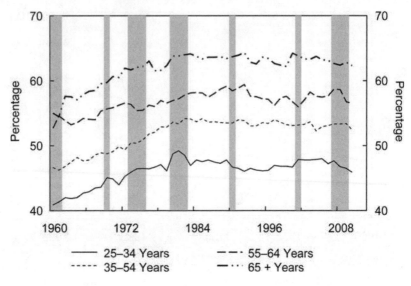

Fig. 2.4   Headship rates by age cohort
Source: Census Bureau.
Note: Shading reflects NBER recessions.

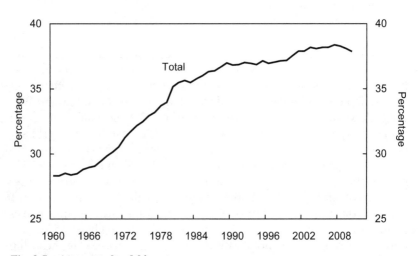

Fig. 2.5   Aggregate headship rate
Source: Census Bureau.
Note: Shading reflects NBER recessions.

cohorts generally peaked in the 1980s and have since been relatively stable to slightly declining. These factors combined to keep the overall US headship rate essentially flat since the mid-1980s. As a result, the underlying trend growth of the number of households was limited to the growth of the population, which was slowing rapidly from the mid-1990s onward. Thus,

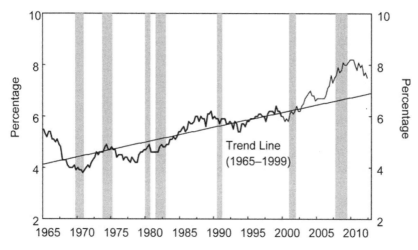

Fig. 2.6   Vacancies as a percent of total housing units (excluding seasonal vacancies)
Source: US Bureau of the Census, Housing Vacancy Survey, and authors' calculations.
Note: Shading reflects NBER recessions.

referring back to figure 2.2, from a demographic perspective, housing starts per 1,000 people should have continued to trend gradually lower from the mid-1990s onward. The order of magnitude of the resulting overbuilding relative to underlying demographic trends can be estimated in different ways with different data sources. But as we shall see, the resulting estimates are roughly similar.

One approach is based on the Census Bureau's Housing Vacancy Survey. This survey provides quarterly estimates of the stock of housing and its occupancy status. Figure 2.6 presents an aggregate vacancy rate for the US housing stock based on that data. To construct this vacancy rate, the numerator is the number of units vacant for rent, vacant for sale, and units in the category "held off the market for other reasons." The number of units in this latter category has historically been quite modest and usually reflected units in the probate process. However, the number of units in this category has risen rapidly over the recent past, apparently reflecting units that have been taken back by lenders (held in their real estate owned [REO] inventory) but not yet offered for sale or rent. The denominator is the numerator plus all occupied units intended for year-round use. A trend line fitted through the time series for the period from 1965 through 1999 suggests that there has been a slight secular uptrend in this vacancy rate. Since the early 2000s the actual value has consistently been above the trend line, with the actual value peaking in 2010:Q2 and moving slightly lower since then.

Figure 2.7, which is derived from this same housing vacancy data program, presents an estimate of the number of "excess" housing units, meaning vacant units above a rough estimate of normal or equilibrium vacancies.

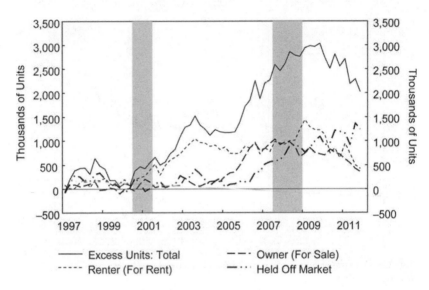

Fig. 2.7   **Excess supply of housing**
Source: US Bureau of the Census, Housing Vacancy Survey, and authors' calculations.
Note: Shading reflects NBER recessions.

In this particular case, separate estimates of equilibrium vacancy rates are derived for single- and multifamily units for sale, single- and multifamily units for rent, and single- and multifamily units held off the market for other reasons. Excess units are defined as units in each of these six categories above the number of units implied by the equilibrium vacancy rates. The estimate of the number of excess units peaked at around 3 million in mid-2010, which provides a rough estimate of the amount of "overbuilding" of housing that occurred during the boom. Since then the number of excess units has been gradually declining, reaching around 2 1/4 million by mid-2012. The number of excess units for sale and for rent has declined fairly sharply while the number of units held off the market has continued to rise.

An alternative measure of the amount of overbuilding that occurred is the difference between the cumulative sum of the number of housing units started relative to the amount of new housing units needed to meet the trend rate of growth of the number of households. Figure 2.8 provides such an estimate. Based on the rate of growth of the population and its age structure, we estimate that the trend rate of growth of households over the period since the mid-1990s is about 1.17 million per year. Due to losses from the existing stock due to fires, floods, and obsolescence, we estimate that about 1.4 million housing starts per year are needed to provide housing for the 1.17 million new households. Starting from 1995, we cumulate the number of housing starts minus 1.4 million (the solid line curve) and the change in the number of households minus 1.17 million (the dotted line curve). The

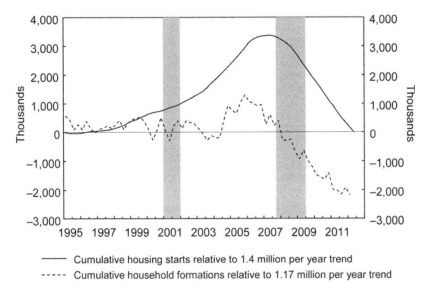

Fig. 2.8   **Cumulative housing production and household formations relative to trend**
Source: US Bureau of the Census and authors' calculations.
Note: Shading reflects NBER recessions.

difference between the two curves is an estimate of overproduction. Strictly from the standpoint of production, the maximum overbuilding was achieved in 2007:Q2 at about 3.4 million units. However, likely due to the strength of the economy and labor markets, household formations were running above trend at that point, so relative to the actual number of households the peak excess production occurred in 2009:Q1 at around 3.5 million units. In terms of both timing and number, this result is similar to that based on the vacancy data.

Figure 2.8 also provides some insight into why this most recent housing downturn has been so protracted. Since mid-2007, a period of five years, housing starts have been below the 1.4 million trend, such that as of mid-2012 the excess production that began in the mid- to late 1990s has been worked off. However, due to the weakness of the economy, the rate of household formations has fallen well below trend. Thus, while from a pure production standpoint we no longer have an excess supply, vacancy rates remain above their longer run equilibrium values. Figure 2.9 provides additional insight into the issue of household formations. Not only are they running well below the demographic trend, the growth that is occurring is more than accounted for by renter households while owner households continue to decline. While still at relatively low levels, over the past year there has been a considerably larger percentage increase of multifamily housing starts than of single-family starts.

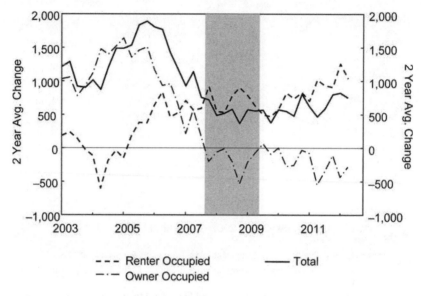

Fig. 2.9   Household formations by type
Source: US Bureau of the Census and authors' calculations.
Note: Shading reflects NBER recessions.

Table 2.1 provides some regional detail on the measure of excess housing units based on the Housing Vacancy Survey, which provides annual data for the four major census regions that corresponds to the national data that is provided on a quarterly basis. Using the same methodology as employed in the construction of figure 2.7, table 2.1 presents the regional distribution of total excess housing units in 2009 and 2011 and compares it with the regional distribution of total housing units. In 2009 the largest share of excess units was in the South, followed by the Midwest, where in both cases the share of excess units exceeded the corresponding share of the housing stock. In contrast, in the Northeast the share of excess units was roughly half its share of the total housing stock. By 2011 the picture had changed. The West's share of excess units declined significantly, the South's share declined modestly, while the shares of the Northeast and Midwest increased by about 4 and 5.5 percentage points, respectively. Of course, these changes reflect both trends in housing production and demographic trends such as relative population growth rates.

To focus specifically on the issue of excess production and where it occurred, figure 2.10 presents a scatter plot of combinations of population growth and housing starts per 1,000 people for each of the individual states. Each of the black dots in the chart represents population growth (expressed at a compound annual rate) over the period from 1990 to 2000 and the average level of housing starts per 1,000 people over the same time period for each of the fifty states. Note the fairly tight positive relationship

Table 2.1   **Shares of excess housing vacancies by region**

	2009		2011	
	Share of stock	Share of excess units	Share of stock	Share of excess units
Northeast	18.0	9.4	17.9	13.3
Midwest	22.4	26.1	22.3	31.5
South	37.9	43.9	38.0	42.0
West	21.7	20.6	21.7	13.2
Total	100.0	100.0	100.0	100.0

Source: Authors' calculations based on Housing Vacancy Survey data.

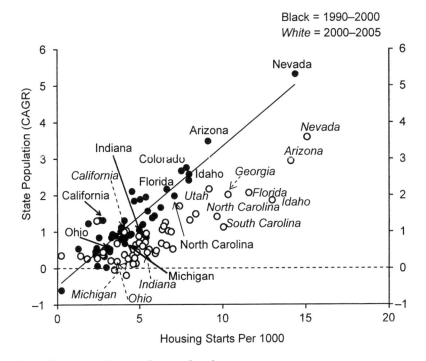

Fig. 2.10   Population growth versus housing starts

indicated by the close clustering of the black dots relative to the regression line. Focusing on this period, the supply side of the housing market showed a tremendous ability to scale production rates to a wide variation in local population growth rates. There is no evidence that housing supply lagged population growth by any significant degree even in the fastest growing states such as Arizona and Nevada.[5]

5. If there were significant costs of adjustment to housing supply, this might show up as the black dots associated with the fast-growing markets tending to be to the left of the regression line.

The white dots in figure 2.10 represent the combinations of population growth rates and housing starts per 1,000 people for each state over the period from 2000 to 2005. Note that virtually all states moved to the right relative to the earlier decade, meaning an increase in housing starts for a given population growth rate. That is, the housing boom from a supply perspective was to a degree a national phenomenon. The magnitude of shift, however, tended to be larger for those states that experienced above-average population growth in the 1990s. This can be seen for three of the four "sand states."[6] The population growth rate in Florida was fairly constant relative to the 1990s, while the rate of housing supply per capita nearly doubled. Arizona experienced a slight slowing in its population growth rate, but like Florida its rate of housing supply per capita increased significantly, growing by roughly a third. Unlike the other sand states, Nevada experienced a significant slowdown in its rate of population growth. However, the rate of housing supply in Nevada in 2000 to 2005 did not respond to this slowdown, resulting in Nevada's white dot being significantly to the right of the regression line.[7] Three other states that stand out in figure 2.10 in terms of a high rate of housing construction relative to population growth are Georgia, North Carolina, and South Carolina. The fact that housing supply increased relatively the most in these three states as well as the sand states may reflect that home builders were producing a product geared toward people at the later stages of their careers who might have been looking for a second home or a retirement home.[8]

Figure 2.11 addresses the issue of how these increases in housing production during the 2000 to 2005 period are related to available measures of the elasticity of supply of new housing. On the horizontal axis of the chart we measure for each state the percentage distance of the 2000 to 2005 housing starts per 1,000 people from the value predicted by the regression line of the 1990 to 2000 period given the 2000 to 2005 rate of population growth. On the vertical axis we plot elasticities of supply as estimated by Saiz (2010), where all of the elasticities for the MSAs in a state were averaged to provide a state estimate.[9] Also shown is a least squares regression line fitted through the scatter diagram. While there is a great deal of dispersion around that line, the upward slope is statistically significant (t-statistic of 3.74). Similarly, figure 2.12 presents the relationship between that same estimate of supply elasticity and the cumulative percent change of house prices over the period

6. The "sand states" refer to Arizona, California, Florida, and Nevada.
7. California is the only sand state that did not have a population growth rate in the 1990s that exceeded the national average. California's rate of housing supply in the 1990s was not significantly higher than what would be predicted from the regression relationship. During the boom, California's rate of housing supply did increase, but this increase only moved it to the regression line and not to the right of the regression line.
8. It should be noted, however, that housing starts are not necessarily the same as net additions to the stock of housing due to destruction and demolition of existing units.
9. Note that North Dakota was dropped from this diagram as it represented an extreme value for percentage difference from the regression line.

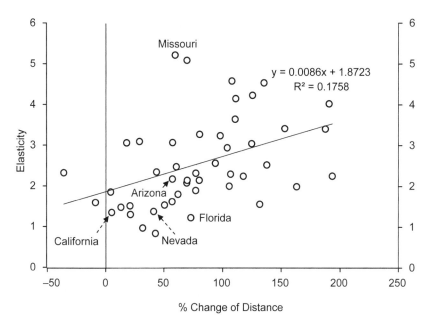

Fig. 2.11   Elasticity versus percent distance, 1990–2000 trend
Note: North Dakota excluded as outlier.

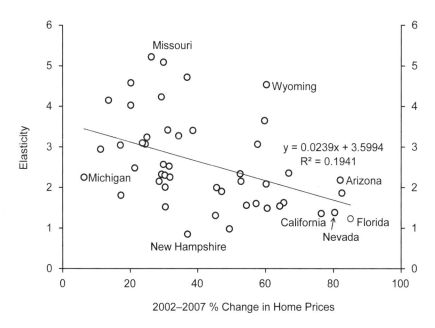

Fig. 2.12   Elasticity versus change in home prices

from 2002 to 2007. In this case the negative slope of the regression line is statically significant (t-statistic of -3.33).

2.4   Trends in Size, Amenities, and Quality

New homes produced for sale have been getting larger, with more bedrooms, bathrooms, and garages, for quite some time. Figure 2.13 presents the median size of new homes sold, measured in square feet, for the period from 1978 through 2011.[10] A trend line was fitted through the series for the period from 1978 through 1998, with that trend then extended from 1999 to 2011. While the median square footage in 2005 is 3.3 percent above that trend, that represents just 1.2 standard deviations of the residual of the estimated trend line, suggesting that the 2005 value is not significantly above what would be suggested by the established trend. Figure 2.14 presents the median size of the lot that the structure was built upon, also measured in square feet. Again, a trend line was fitted through the data for the period from 1976 to 1998 and then extended over the period from 1999 to 2011. Clearly, average lot size declined during the building boom years. The median lot size in 2004 was 8.3 percent below the estimated trend. Combined, the two trends indicate that during the boom years of the 2000s builders were economizing on the amount of land devoted to each unit, likely reflecting the fact that land prices were rising relatively rapidly. However, due to the wide variation in the median lot size over the period from 1976 to 1998, that 8.3 percent represents just 1.2 standard deviations of the residual of the estimated trend line. Note that the decline in median lot size from the mid-1990s through the mid-2000s was due in part to a modest increase of the share of units that were attached as opposed to detached. But the median lot size of attached units declined in a similar fashion.

Of course, changes in physical characteristics such as square footage and number of bathrooms do not capture changes in quality, such as the materials used and the level of skill and care employed in construction. It is certainly conceivable that as demand for new homes intensified, the quality of new homes, defined in this manner, slipped somewhat. To shed some light on this issue, we used American Housing Survey (AHS) data to estimate the percentage premium that home buyers place on new homes versus existing homes. All else equal, a new home is likely to command a premium as it is likely to require lower maintenance expenditures over an expected holding period. By estimating that premium for AHS surveys before and during the construction boom, we can observe how that premium changed over time.

The estimation procedure was as follows. From each AHS data set from 1985 through 2007 we create a sample of owner-occupied single-family homes purchased over the two-year period since the preceding AHS. The

---

10. These data are from the "Characteristics of New Homes Sold," which is part of the Census Bureau's statistical program called "New Residential Sales."

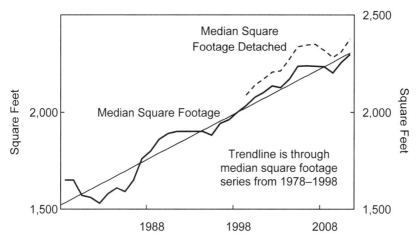

Fig. 2.13   Median square footage of new homes sold
Source: Census Bureau.
Note: Shading reflects NBER recessions.

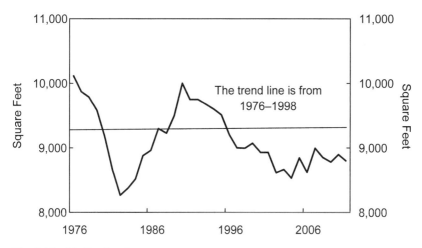

Fig. 2.14   Median lot size
Source: Census Bureau.

sample sizes range from a high of around 1,200 in 1995, of which roughly 20 percent were new homes, to a low of around 500 in 2007, of which 10 percent were new homes. We then estimate a hedonic regression of the log of the self-reported value of that home on a series of physical characteristics such as unit square footage, size of the lot, number of bedrooms, number of bathrooms, and so forth. We used as a guide for this regression the procedure used by the US Bureau of the Census in the construction of its constant-quality new home price series. We add to that procedure a dummy variable

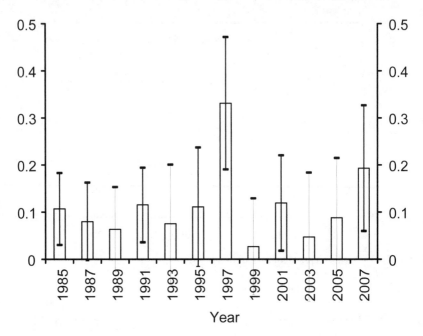

Fig. 2.15   The percent premium for a new home
Source: AHS.

for the purchase of a new home (defined as being built in the last two years) rather than an existing home. In addition, all regression include Standard Metropolitan Statistical Area (SMSA) fixed effects to control for any composition shifts in where new homes were being constructed over time.

Figure 2.15 presents the estimated new home premium for AHS years from 1985 through 2007. The black dashes above and below each estimate represent 90 percent confidence intervals. In seven of the twelve cases, that confidence internal includes zero. Given the volatility of the estimated premium and the rather wide confidence bands around the estimates, it does not appear that there was a systematic change in the premium during the period from the early 2000s through 2005 relative to what is was prior to and after that period.

2.5   Trends in the Home Building Industry

The home building industry has traditionally been characterized as having relatively low barriers to entry such that there are a large number of firms producing a relatively few number of units per year. Indeed, 79 percent of the builder members of the National Association of Home Builders started ten or fewer homes in 2010. However, a characteristic of the housing boom from the early 1990s through the mid-2000s is the pronounced growth of market share of a relatively few number of firms, the bulk of which were

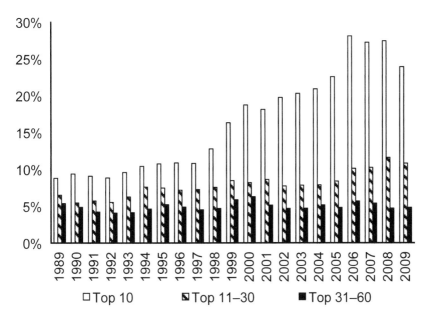

Fig. 2.16   Share of new home sales by size of home builder
Source: Builder Magazine, Census Bureau.

publicly owned and, to a large extent, financed directly through capital markets rather than financial intermediaries such as banks. This consolidation within the building industry has been discussed by others (see Ambrose 2009, 2010 and Frey 2003). Following, we update some of this prior analysis. In addition, we explore whether any excess returns were higher during the height of the housing boom. Finally, we look at whether the capital markets provided more timely signals than the banking industry for builders to start to reduce their activity levels.

Figure 2.16 provides a time series of the share of new home sales accounted for by the top ten to top sixty builders by size. In 1990 the top sixty builders accounted for 20 percent of new home sales (as defined by the Census Bureau), while the top ten builders accounted for 9.4 percent. Over the next fifteen years there was steady consolidation in the industry, such that by 2005 the top sixty accounted for 36 percent and the top ten for 22.6 percent. For this increase in share of the top ten builders to occur, it means that these firms captured roughly one-third of the increase in sales that occurred over that period. The top sixty largest firms accounted for nearly half of the increase. It is also interesting to note that the ten largest firms experienced additional large increases in market share over the period from 2006 through 2008. However, this increase occurred when overall sales and prices were declining, and reflected the fact that the large builders had accumulated a large inventory of homes in their production pipelines.

This rapid growth by the largest builders reflected a mix of internal or

Table 2.2   Total closings and percentage change from mergers and acquisitions

Company	1993	2004	Change 1993–2004	Percent through acquisition/merger
D. R. Horton	1,668	44,005	42,337	45.1
Pulte Homes	9,798	38,612	28,814	38.7
Lennar Corp.	4,634	36,204	31,570	55.7
Centex Corp.	11,685	32,896	21,211	15.6
KB Homes	5,982	26,937	20,955	63.2
Beazer Homes USA	2,496	16,437	15,921	72.9
The Ryland Group	8,319	15,101	6,782	19.9
Hovnanian Enterprises	3,671	14,586	10,915	105.8
M.D.C. Holding	3,344	13,876	10,532	20.5
NVR	4,248	12,749	8,501	7.0
Total	55,845	251,383	195,538	46.1

Source: Builder Magazine, Mergers Online, and NAHB Economics. See http://mydigimag.rrd .com/publication/?i=37093&p=61.

"organic" growth as well as growth through acquisitions. Table 2.2 shows the growth in closings by the top ten builders over the period from 1993 to 2004, and the decomposition by organic versus acquisition. For the group as a whole, 46 percent of their growth in closings over the eleven-year period leading up to the peak was due to acquisitions. As one might expect, there were multiple motivations for these acquisitions. But in conversations with leading analysts of this industry, the prime motivation appears to have been to obtain land and local expertise in promising markets.

There are several dimensions on which large and small builders differ. Small builders are to a large extent reliant on bank financing. Their ability to launch new construction projects and to continue building spec homes depends on the willingness of those banks to extend financing. The scrutiny of the builder's activities by the lender can be surprisingly intense. In contrast, large builders are much less reliant on banks, obtaining the bulk of their financing through issuance of debt and equity directly in capital markets. Thus, the ability of these large builders to expand their balance sheet is determined by the willingness of markets to advance more funds.

A second distinction is that large builders are vertically integrated from land acquisition and development, construction, marketing, and mortgage financing. This organization helps these builders exploit scale economies involved in large development projects and to have a broader source of revenues and potential profits. It is also possible that by being involved in each segment of the production and distribution chain, large builders had an informational advantage in the markets they operated in.

To shed light on these points, table 2.3 presents the balance sheet of Toll Brothers, a well-known publicly traded home builder, as of April of 2005, right around the peak of new home construction. At that time assets totaled

$5.4 billion, of which 80 percent was the firm's inventory of lots, homes under construction, and completed homes. Liabilities totaled $3.1 billion, of which notes issued in the capital markets represented 43 percent. Bank financing, consisting of loans payable (the used portion of a credit line extended by a consortium of banks) and the mortgage subsidiaries warehouse line of credit, represented just 17 percent of total liabilities. The debt to equity ratio of the firm was 1.35.

Table 2.4 shows the building lot inventory data for the top ten builders from 2002 to 2008. The lot inventory is broken down into lots that were owned by the builders, lots where the builders held options to purchase, and lots that were part of joint ventures. The last column converts the total

Table 2.3   Large home builder balance sheet

Toll Brothers Inc. and Subsidiaries as of April 30, 2005		
Assets	($ in thousands)	% of total assets
Cash and cash equivalents	566,668	11
Inventory	4,299,587	80
Property, construction and office equipment, net	63,649	1
Receivables, prepaid expenses and other assets	152,009	3
Mortgage loans held for sale	78,663	1
Customer deposits held in escrow	76,681	1
Investment in and advances to unconsolidated entities	114,196	2
Total assets	5,351,453	100
Liabilities		% of total liabilities
Loans payable	358,922	12
Senior notes	845,914	28
Senior subordinated notes	450,000	15
Mortgage company warehouse loan	69,108	2
Customer deposits	389,265	13
Accounts payable	202,918	7
Accrued expenses	611,340	20
Income taxes payable	147,964	5
Total liabilities	3,075,431	100
Equity		
Common stock	776	
Additional paid in capital	251,646	
Retained earnings	2,051,056	
Unearned compensation	(834)	
Treasury stock	(26,622)	
Total Equity	2,276,022	

Table 2.4   Lot inventory for top-ten builders

Year	Inventory				Percent change	Percent of total change			Year's supply
	Total	Owned	Optioned	JV		Owned	Optioned	JV	
2008	655,734	459,014	170,491	26,229	(33)	(43)	(44)	(13)	4.0
2007	976,896	595,907	312,607	68,383	(35)	(26)	(67)	(7)	4.6
2006	1,497,799	733,922	659,032	104,846	(24)	(4)	(93)	(3)	5.1
2005	1,981,488	752,965	1,109,633	118,889	19	38	25	37	6.8
2004	1,659,661	630,671	1,028,990	0	13	38	62	0	6.6
2003	1,473,000	559,740	913,260	0	59	26	74	0	5.4
2002	928,719	417,924	510,795	0					4.8

Source: Builder Magazine and NAHB.
Notes: JV indicates "joint-venture." Parentheses indicates negative changes.

inventory into a year's supply at the prevailing sales rate. The first thing to note is that the inventory of lots grew quite rapidly over the period from 2002 to 2005, suggesting that these builders remained quite optimistic about future sales prospects even as the market was approaching its peak. Indeed, in terms of years' supply the builders were substantially lengthening their investment in land, from 5.4 years in 2003 to 6.8 in 2005.

As we know now, single-family housing starts peaked in 2005:Q3 and home prices peaked roughly one year later. It appears that the top ten builders responded aggressively to this turn of events. From 2005 to 2006, the largest builders reduced their lot inventory by 24 percent. Almost all of this reduction, 97 percent, was through the lots that they held options on. Options continued to be the dominant adjustment mechanism as well in 2007, with 67 percent of the shrinkage accounted for by optioned lots. It is not until 2008 that the adjustment process is roughly balanced between percentage reductions in owned and optioned lots. Note, however, that lots are only one portion of a builder's inventory. While we do not have data on homes either under construction or completed for these large builders, the macro data indicate that it took quite a bit longer to reduce inventories in those categories.

Another feature of the increase in housing production from the mid-1990s through the mid-2000s was that an increasing share of single-family units was "built for sale" (figure 2.17). Built for sale, sometimes referred to as a "spec" or speculative start, refers to situations where the land and structure are sold in one transaction. An example is when a home builder develops a section of land, putting in roads and utilities, and then begins selling indi-

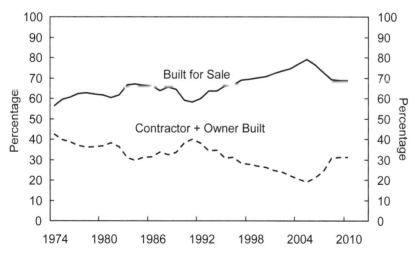

Fig. 2.17   Share of new single-family homes completed built for sale
Source: Census Bureau.

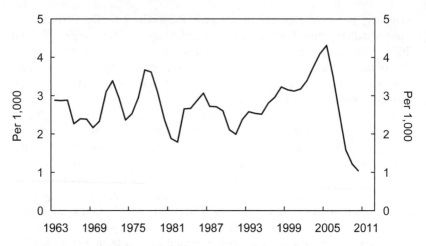

Fig. 2.18   New single-family homes sold per 1,000 people
Source: Census Bureau.

vidual lots with houses—either already completed, under construction, or not yet started. In contrast, contractor- or owner-built units are cases in which an individual or firm already owns the land and either hires a general contractor or acts as their own general contractor.[11] Monthly data on sales of new single-family homes refers only to sales of "spec" units, and the sale can occur at various stages—completed, under construction, or even not started. Due to the shift toward construction of single-family units, and the shift toward speculative units within the single-family market, sales of new single-family homes per 1,000 people in 2005 reached the highest of the entire period for which there is data (dating back to 1963) (figure 2.18).

The shift toward more speculative building also meant that even though new housing starts declined abruptly and remain quite low to this day, the home building industry ended up with a large inventory of units in their production pipeline that took quite some time to unwind. Figure 2.19 presents the inventory of new single-family homes for sale broken down into the categories of not started, under construction, and completed. As house prices peaked in many markets in early 2006, builders began to reduce their units not started and under construction. The pace of contraction was faster in units under construction, which may reflect the continuing option value of keeping improved lots on hand in case markets stabilized. Completed units did not reach their peak until late 2007, nearly a year and a half after the slowdown was under way in units under construction. The inventory of

11. It is also the case that an increasing share of multifamily starts were built for sale, likely as condominiums, as opposed for the rental market.

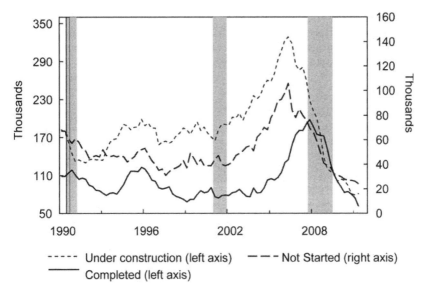

Fig. 2.19   New single-family homes for sale by stage of completion
Source: US Bureau of the Census.
Note: Shading reflects NBER recessions.

completed units for sale has only recently returned to levels that prevailed prior to the boom. A question that we will return to is whether builders were too slow to respond to changing demand conditions in their respective markets, contributing to an excess of housing inventory.

This review of the macro data and the data on individual firms in the home builder industry suggests that one of the reasons the housing downturn has been so severe and so prolonged is the industry, particularly the largest firms, built up such substantial inventories of lots and homes at various stages of production. As the largest firms tend to obtain financing from capital markets rather than banks, an interesting question is whether the capital markets were providing any early indications that this inventory represented a significant downside risk to their earning should demand turn out to be weaker than expected. In figure 2.20 we compare a fixed weighted index of the equity prices for six large home builders and the Federal Reserve's Senior Loan Officer Opinion Survey (SLOOS) data on lending standards for mortgage loans.[12] For the SLOOS, values above (below) zero indicate that standards

---

12. In order to create the fixed weight equity index, we collected Bloomberg's market capitalization and equity time series for a subset of home builders. Specifically, we selected home builders that had a large market presence before the housing bust and are still in operation today. The home builders in our equity index are: Toll Brothers Inc., Pulte Group Inc., Lennar Corp., DR Horton Inc., Hovnanian Enterprises Inc., and Beazer Homes USA Inc. Keeping

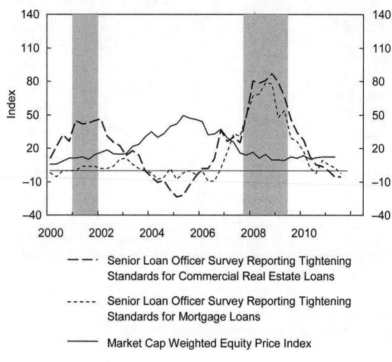

Fig. 2.20   Equity price index and various measures of the SLOOS

Source: WRDS, Bloomberg, and authors' calculations.

Note: Shading reflects NBER recessions. The weight used in the equity price index is the market capitalization at the peak of the housing starts series for each security in the index.

on net are reported to be tighter (looser) since the prior survey. We can see that bank lending standards were being loosened from 2004 to mid-2006. The SLOOS indicates that lending standards began to tighten in the fourth quarter of 2006. In contrast, the home builder equity price index peaks in August 2005, more than a year earlier than the onset of tightening by banks. By the end of the third quarter of 2006, the home builder equity price index had declined by 45 percent. Figure 2.21 summarizes analyst equity recommendations for the major builders. Again, we see a sharp drop-off in "buy" recommendations in the third quarter of 2005 matched by a pickup in "sell" recommendations. Finally, figure 2.22 shows a market capitalization weighted average of short interest in the major builders. This series picks up in the second quarter of 2006. While the SLOOS data is not a perfect measure of when banks would have been tightening their lending to small

---

the market capitalization fixed at Q1:2006, the quarter in which housing starts peaked, we then created a market capitalization weighted average of the quarterly equity prices of each home builder. The resulting series was then indexed to equal 100 for the first quarter of 2006.

Fig. 2.21 Equally weighted analyst equity recommendations
Source: WRDS.

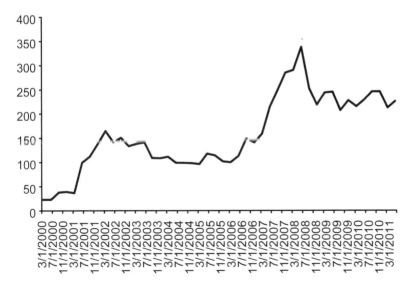

Fig. 2.22 Market capitalization weighted home builder short interest
Source: Bloomberg and authors' calculations.
Notes: Index = 100 at the peak of housing starts Q1:2006. Market capitalizations are contemporaneous to the short interest data.

builders, these comparisons suggests that the capital markets did provide the large builders with a substantially earlier signal to pull back than the small builders likely received from their banks.[13]

2.6   Land Markets during the Boom and Bust

Builders' use of vacant lot inventories, whether owned outright or optioned, suggests an important role for vacant land as a potential driver of builder costs, and ultimately house prices. In addition to the cost and access to capital just discussed, the cost of building a new home consists of construction labor and material costs, along with the cost of developable land. Davis and Heathcote (2007) and Davis and Palumbo (2008) estimate the value of residential land nationally and in metropolitan areas, respectively, using a combination of the cost of construction and the value of housing in place. Davis and his coauthors conclude that the value of land rose sharply in the United States during the housing boom, particularly in metro areas that experienced the largest house price booms.

Given the prominent role that land inventories played on builders' balance sheets during the 2000s housing cycle, we supplement the Davis analysis with information from vacant land transactions for select metropolitan areas. Vacant land may exhibit different dynamics from land with a housing unit already in place, since the latter reflects the value of the particular structure present, as we argued earlier and as shown in figure 2.1. In addition, our data allow a parcel-level analysis of the evolving prices and quantities as well as the features of vacant land that was selling in the metro areas for which we have data.

Our land sales data come from the COMPS data set produced by the CoStar Group. Residential land sales—as opposed to other real estate transactions—are distinguished by the buyer's intention, as reported to CoStar, to use the *land* for construction of residential units, rather than to build other types of projects or to use structures currently present. Figures 2.23 and 2.24 display the residential land price indexes and log number of acres sold in eight Metropolitan Statistical Areas (MSAs) with inelastic and elastic housing supplies, respectively, as estimated by Saiz (2010). For comparison purposes, CoreLogic's overall House Price Indexes (HPIs) for each MSA are reported as well.[14] Several features of the land sales data are noteworthy.

First is the amount of acreage transacted over time and space. In the figures, the bars show the four-quarter moving average of the natural log of acres sold.[15] Perhaps unsurprisingly, the great majority of land sold for resi-

13. It is interesting to note, however, that smaller builders apparently were not caught with such large inventories of homes under construction or already completed.

14. In the case of South Florida, we use the Miami MSA HPI.

15. We use natural logs because a few markets completely dominate the acreage calculations; plotting acreage itself with consistent axes yields figures that are hard to see in comparison with Atlanta and especially Phoenix.

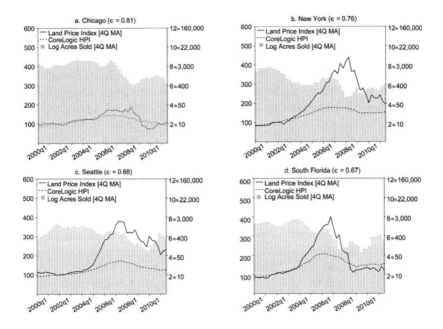

Fig. 2.23   Land prices in select markets with relatively inelastic supply

Sources: CoreLogic, CoStar, authors' calculations. Elasticity estimates from Saiz (2010).

Note: Acreage, right scale; land and house price indexes, left. South Florida comprises the Miami, Fort Lauderdale, and West Palm Beach MSAs.

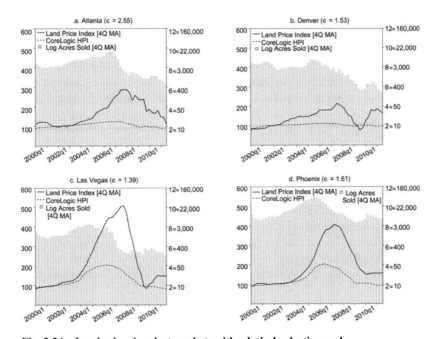

Fig. 2.24   Land prices in select markets with relatively elastic supply

Sources: CoreLogic, CoStar, authors' calculations. Elasticity estimates from Saiz (2010).

Note: Acreage, right scale; land and house price indexes, left.

dential development came from the more elastically-supplied MSAs (figure 2.24). In those cities, particularly Atlanta and Phoenix, quarterly sales of 10,000 to 20,000 acres of land for residential development were common throughout the boom. During 2005, CoStar reported average quarterly land transactions in Phoenix alone that exceeded 50,000 acres. In inelastically supplied cities like Chicago, peak land sales were closer to 3,000 acres a quarter. Land sales volumes in all cities track house prices relatively closely and began to fall quickly after the HPI peaks.

Also shown in figures 2.23 and 2.24 are land price indexes. In order to abstract from changes in the mix of properties being sold over time, we create a quarterly price index that controls for such traits as location, presence of a structure, level of preparation for building, and characteristics of the transaction. The index we employ here is interpretable as the price paid in a standard arms-length transaction for an unimproved square foot of centrally-located residential land relative to some benchmark period (2001:Q4) for that city.[16]

Land prices exhibit some interesting dynamics in these cities. First, as expected given relatively steady increases in building costs during the boom, raw land price increases frequently outstripped house price increases. In constrained markets like New York, Seattle, and South Florida, vacant land prices tripled or quadrupled during the boom, as theory would predict. However, perhaps as evidence of housing prices that were straying from fundamentals, even elastic markets experienced rapid price appreciation during the housing boom. In Denver, for example, raw land prices doubled between late 2001 and the end of 2006; in Las Vegas they quintupled.

Land prices in elastic and inelastic markets are more distinguished by their tendencies during the bust, from 2007 to 2010, as anticipated by our discussion of figure 2.1. In cities with elastic housing supplies (figure 2.24) nominal prices reversed course soon, although not immediately, after the housing market peak, and had generally reverted to their 2001 levels by the end of 2010. In cities with inelastic supply, residential land prices fell after the house price peak, but now seem to have firmed (again, in nominal terms) at levels 50 to 100 percent above their 2001 levels. South Florida, a victim of extreme overbuilding in spite of inelastic supply, is an exception. There, raw land prices are currently about where they were in 2001.

The price dynamics shown in figures 2.23 and 2.24 control for property location, but, like most other information on housing prices, are calculated at the MSA level, making it difficult to determine the price dynamics at different points in the metropolitan landscape. Our data, however, allow a

---

16. Haughwout, Orr, and Bedoll (2008) describe the development of the land price index for one of the sample cities, New York; other cities' indexes are constructed similarly. To control for the influence of outliers, the indexes are constructed from a trimmed sample, excluding the 1 percent of transactions with the highest and lowest actual prices per square foot. Indexes are smoothed using a four-quarter moving average.

Table 2.5   Residential land price dynamics across the metropolitan landscape

	Boom, 2000–2006			Bust, 2007–2010		
City	Inner 25%	Middle 50%	Outer 25%	Inner 25%	Middle 50%	Outer 25%
Atlanta	6.4%	13.4%	17.0%	–14.1%	–2.3%	–10.8%
Chicago	7.9	8.6	11.6	0.1	4.3	–21.9
Denver	5.2	14.6	19.8	2.4	–4.8	4.0
LA Basin	21.5	18.4	19.5	–10.8	–17.2	–8.2
Las Vegas	26.2	31.3	28.5	–29.5	–28.7	–19.2
New York	22.9	24.9	22.2	–14.6	–13.7	–10.4
Orlando	17.7	21.8	11.2	–26.9	–8.2	26.0
Philadelphia	18.4	7.0	15.7	5.2	2.2	2.8
Phoenix	19.1	22.6	50.5	–11.7	–19.1	–27.3
Portland	17.7	9.9	16.9	–10.0	–5.0	–20.2
Seattle	12.4	18.6	13.2	–10.5	–7.5	–1.7
South Florida	20.5	25.9	29.3	–25.5	–16.2	–31.6
Tampa	26.4	26.4	24.3	–14.4	8.2	15.3
Tucson	15.6	16.7	20.6	–2.4	–4.0	–0.7
Washington	20.0	1.6	16.3	–13.9	19.4	19.4
Unwtd. mean across cities	17.2	17.4	21.1	–11.8	–6.2	–5.6
Unwtd. std. dev. across cities	6.6	8.3	9.8	10.3	12.0	17.2

Source: CoStar Group; authors' calculations.
Note: Figures in the table are compound average annual growth rates for the specified periods.

finer look at the geography of the land boom and bust, and table 2.5 reports these results for fifteen large cities. In each city, a measure of the center is created—typically the tallest building—and land transactions are grouped according to whether they are among the 25 percent (of plots sold) in closest proximity to the center, the 25 percent farthest from the center, or the middle 50 percent.

The mean figures, reported at the bottom of the table, reflect some general tendencies across the cities: during the boom (2000 to 2006) prices rose in all parts of the average metropolitan area; in the bust they fell in all parts. Generally speaking, the boom was the strongest on the fringe, and the bust was weakest there as well. Thus the housing cycle of the 2000s was associated with a flattening of the price gradient in these metros.

But the overall data mask substantial heterogeneity, as the large standard deviations indicate. In some cities—Atlanta, Denver, Phoenix, South Florida—the boom was noticeably concentrated on the fringe. In others, particularly supply-constrained cities like New York, Los Angeles, and Seattle, land prices in the center more or less kept pace with price changes on the fringe, leaving the gradient either unchanged or, in some cases, steeper.

2.7   Who Got the Profits—Builders or Landowners?

As noted earlier, the large builders likely benefited from scale economies in terms of lower material costs, cheaper funding, and greater production efficiencies. An important question is whether the combination of consolidation among the largest builders and a housing boom led to large builders earning excess returns. To explore this question, we created a monthly equity returns series for publicly traded builders. In each month, we calculate the market capitalization-weighted average equity return by month. Our data runs from January 1990 to May 2012. We then disaggregate this equity return series into a series for the top-ten builders based on market capitalization in each month, and a series of the non-top ten builders.[17] We estimate simple market models by regressing the builder monthly equity return on a market return. We use the Russell 2000 Index as our market return.

The market model results are presented in table 2.6. Specifications (1) and (2) report results for the overall builder equity returns, while specifications (3) and (4) focus on the non-top–ten builders, and specifications (5) and (6) focus on the top-ten builders. Two things stand out from specification (1). First, the building industry as a whole does not display any higher or lower cyclicality than does the overall market. The estimated beta for the industry is equal to one. Second, for the more than twenty years covered by the data, the building industry earned an average annual excess return of 20 percent.[18] Specification (2) checks to see if the excess returns to the building industry changed during the height of the housing boom. The data indicate that outside of the period from January 2000 to June 2005 the building industry earned on average an annualized excess return of 13 percent.[19] However, during the housing boom the average annualized excess return increased significantly to 48 percent.

Both the large average excess returns overall and the significant increase in these excess returns during the housing boom raise the question of to what extent these excess returns were going to all publicly traded builders or only the largest of the firms. To explore this we turn to our disaggregated return series. Specifications (3) and (4) report results for the non-top–ten builders. The data indicate that outside of the period of the housing boom, the non-top–ten builders did not earn on average any excess returns. However, during the housing boom, they earned average excess returns of 43 percent. In addition, while the overall building industry has a market beta of one, the non-top–ten builders have a market beta of 1.4, which is statistically higher than one. In contrast, looking at specifications (5) and (6), which focus just

17. Over the period the top-ten builders accounted for between 80 to 95 percent of the total market capitalization of all publicly-traded builders.
18. The annualized compound excess return is given by $(1.01573)^{12} - 1$.
19. June 2005 was the peak of the home builders' sentiment series collected by the National Association of Home Builders.

Table 2.6   **Market model estimates for building industry stock returns**

	All public builders		Non–top-ten builders		Top-ten builders	
	(1)	(2)	(3)	(4)	(5)	(6)
Alpha	1.573**	0.996**	0.747	−0.004	1.625**	1.066**
	(0.382)	(0.434)	(0.639)	(0.730)	(0.392)	(0.446)
Alpha interaction (1/00–6/05)		2.346**		3.058**		2.278**
		(0.871)		(1.467)		(0.895)
Beta	1.001**	1.004**	1.399**	1.404**	0.979**	0.982**
	(0.066)	(0.066)	(0.111)	(0.111)	(0.068)	(0.067)

Notes: Market model regresses the monthly capitalization weighted stock market returns for publicly traded builders (r_{bt}) on the monthly returns for the Russell 2000 Index (r_{mt}). The estimation period is from January 1990 to May 2012. A unit change is 1 percent. Coefficient estimates are given with standard errors in parentheses. Top-ten builders are based on market capitalization in each month. Market model reported in specifications (1), (3), and (5) is given by: $r_{bt} = \alpha + \beta r_{mt} + \varepsilon_t$, where ε_t is the excess return in month t. The expanded market model reported in specifications (2), (4), and (6) is given by: $r_{bt} = \alpha + \alpha_I I_{1/00–6/05} + \beta r_{mt} + \varepsilon_t$, where $I_{1/00–6/05}$ is an indicator variable that takes a value of one over the period from January 2000 to June 2005.
**Significant at the 5 percent level.

on the returns for the top-ten builders, the data indicate that they earned on average excess returns of 14 percent outside of the housing boom period, and that these average excess returns increased to 48 percent during the boom—only slightly higher than for the non-top–ten builders.

2.8   Conclusion

Our description of the supply side of the housing boom and bust cycle of the 2000s reveals many changes in the structure and costs of the home-building industry. Many of these developments might have been expected to provide some cushion against the possibility that the housing market would stray far above fundamental valuations for an extended period. The increased concentration of the industry in the decade leading up to the boom meant that large shares of the market were held by large firms with substantial market information. In addition, these firms' reliance on deep public capital markets, rather than special arrangements with individual financial intermediaries, brought with it close investor and analyst scrutiny of the marketplace and firms' positions and strategies. Smaller builders could easily observe the actions taken by the large builders operating in their markets and to free ride on the market information available to the larger builders. Furthermore, the use of land options by large builders allowed them, if market conditions changed, to exit projects before purchasing land and embarking on difficult-to-reverse building projects. The concentration of new building activity in fast-growing, supply elastic markets in areas like

Phoenix and Las Vegas meant that new housing should have helped to limit and then to offset price increases that were originally driven by demand shifts.

Were a housing expert to be told only of these developments, without knowing what actually transpired in the housing market during the 2000s, he might well have taken some comfort that conditions were in place to discourage a market that strayed far from fundamentals. Yet while many factors may have been expected to constrain price increases and make the supply side of the market more responsive to market conditions, as a whole they were insufficient to forestall both a bubble in prices and a significant oversupply of units. It is impossible to determine how much worse things might have been absent these supply-side developments, but it seems clear in retrospect that on their own, favorable supply-side conditions cannot be exclusively relied upon to restrain the effects of major, but temporary, demand shocks.

Appendix
Sources and Definitions of Data

The US Census Bureau is the primary source of data on both the stock of existing housing and the production of new housing. The information presented in this chapter is derived from several different Census housing data programs. The following summarizes those sources and some key definitions. The following website provides background information on the housing construction and sales data program: http://www.census.gov/construction /nrs/about_the_surveys/.

Housing Units Authorized (Building Permits)

Monthly data on building permits for single- and multifamily housing units are released as part of the "New Residential Construction" release. The building permits data are derived from the "Building Permits Survey" (BPC), which is a representative sample of permit-issuing authorities.

New Privately Owned Housing Units Started (Housing Starts)

Monthly data on single- and multifamily housing starts, units under construction, and units completed are also released as part of the "New Residential Construction" release. A housing unit is considered to be started "when excavation begins for the footings or foundation of a building." A housing unit is considered to be completed "when all finished flooring has been installed." These data are generated by the "Survey of Construction" (SOC), which begins with a sample of individual building permits. On a monthly basis, census field representatives contact the individual or firm to whom the permit was issued to determine dates of starts and completions as well as physical characteristics of the units. If the unit is for sale, the eventual sales date and price are obtained, while if the unit is for rent the eventual date of occupancy (absorption) and rent are obtained.

New Residential Sales (New Home Sales)

Monthly data on new single-family homes sold, for sale, and median and average sales prices are released in the "New Residential Sales" release, the information for which is also derived from the SOC. In this data set, new single-family homes sold or for sale are defined as units "built for sale," sometimes referred to as a "spec" or speculative sale, in which the land and structure are sold in one transaction. In contrast, contractor- or owner-built units are cases in which an individual or firm already owns the land and either hires a general contractor or acts as their own general contractor. Thus, new single-family homes sold are a subset of single-family housing starts and permits. A new single-family home is defined as sold "with the signing of a sales contract or the acceptance of a deposit." New single-family home sold and for sale can be in one of three categories: completed, under construction, or not started.

Included within the New Residential Sales data program is annual data on the characteristics of new homes sold. This information is also used to construct a quarterly Price Index for New One-Family Homes Sold Including Value of Lot, which is a constant quality price index based on hedonic methods.

Housing Vacancies and Home Ownership

Quarterly data on the housing stock of the United States and its occupancy status are derived from the Housing Vacancy Survey (HVS). Housing units are occupied, by owners or renters, or are vacant. There are several categories of vacancies including for rent, for sale, rented or sold but not yet occupied, and other. Within the other category are units held for occasional use, units temporarily occupied by persons whose usual residence is elsewhere, and other, which includes units held for settlement of an estate. Finally, there is a category of "vacant but for seasonal rather than year-round use."

References

Ambrose, Brent W. 2009. "Housing After the Fall: Reassessing the Future of the American Dream." Working Paper. Pennsylvania State University, Institute for Real Estate Studies, February.

————. 2010. "The Homebuilding Industry: How Did we Get Here?" *Institute for Real Estate Studies* 2 (Spring): 2–6.

Banerjee, Abhijit V. 1992. "A Simple Model of Herd Behavior." *Quarterly Journal of Economics* 107 (August): 797–817.

Case, Karl E., and Robert J. Shiller. 1989. "The Efficiency of the Market for Single-Family Homes." *American Economic Review* 79 (March): 125–37.

Davis, Morris A., and Jonathan Heathcote. 2007. "The Price and Quantity of Residential Land in the United States." *Journal of Monetary Economics* 54 (November): 2595–620.

Davis, Morris A., and Michael G. Palumbo. 2008. "The Price of Residential Land in Large US Cities." *Journal of Urban Economics* 63 (January): 352–84.

DeCoster, Gregory P., and William C. Strange. 2010. "Developers, Herding, and Overbuilding." Working Paper. Bowdoin College, Department of Economics, May.

Frey, Elaine F. 2003. "Building Industry Consolidation." *Housing Economics* August:7–12.

Glaeser, Edward, and Joseph Gyourko. 2008. "Arbitrage in Housing." In *Housing and the Built Environment: Access, Finance, Policy,* edited by Edward Glaeser and John Quigley, 113–48. Cambridge: Lincoln Land Institute of Land Policy.

Glaeser, Edward L., Joseph Gyourko, and Albert Saiz. 2008. "Housing Supply and Housing Bubbles." *Journal of Urban Economics* 64 (September): 198–217.

Haughwout, Andrew, James Orr, and David Bedoll. 2008. "The Price of Land in the New York Metropolitan Area." *Current Issues in Economics and Finance, Second District Highlights* 14 (3): April/May.

Mankiw, N. Gregory, and David N. Weil. 1989. "The Baby Boom, the Baby Bust, and the Housing Market." *Regional Science and Urban Economics* 19 (May): 235–58.

Rosenthal, Stuart S. 1999. "Residential Buildings and the Cost of Construction: New Evidence on the Efficiency of the Housing Market." *The Review of Economics and Statistics* 81 (March): 288–302.

Saiz, Albert. 2010. "The Geographic Determinants of Housing Supply." *Quarterly Journal of Economics* 125 (August): 1253–96.

Topel, Robert, and Sherwin Rosen. 1988. "Housing Investment in the United States." *Journal of Political Economy* 96 (4): 718–40.

Welch, Ivo. 1992. "Sequential Sales, Learning, and Cascades." *Journal of Finance* 47 (June): 695–732.

A Spatial Look at Housing Boom and Bust Cycles

David Genesove and Lu Han

3.1 Introduction

This chapter adopts a spatial perspective on supply conditions in housing markets, both within and across urban areas. We investigate empirically how the behavior of prices over the boom-bust cycle of housing markets differs according to the location within the urban area and across urban areas according to the area's size. We take commuting minutes as the appropriate measure of distance from the urban center.

Within markets, we distinguish between households with a longer and shorter commuting time to work. On the presumption that building is easier the further out one gets from the urban center, we expect that a given common increase in demand throughout an urban area will lead to a relatively smaller price response and relative greater quantity response the further away from the center one gets. To test for this, we ask whether households with a shorter commuting trip report relatively higher values for their homes in years when prices are high.

Using the 2005 to 2010 microdata of the American Community Survey (ACS), we find that to be essentially true: controlling for Metropolitan Statistical Area (MSA) cross-year effects, we find that house values decline faster with commuting time in the years 2005 to 2008 than in the bust years of 2009 and 2010. The flatter price gradient of the last two years is consistent

David Genesove is associate professor of economics at Hebrew University of Jerusalem. Lu Han is the Petro-Canada Junior Professor of Business Economics at the Rotman School of Management, University of Toronto.

We thank our discussants, Denise DiPasquale and Stuart Rosenthal, and other participants at the NBER "Housing Market and the Financial Crisis" conference for helpful comments. For acknowledgments, sources of research support, and disclosure of the authors' material financial relationships, if any, please see http://www.nber.org/chapters/c12621.ack.

with a common demand bust, with spatial variation in supply conditions. This result holds when we consider various subsamples: recent home movers, household heads that work in the central city, and those that commute by car. The result continues to hold when we control for household predicted income, whose effect on house value we also permit to vary by year so as to capture the differential effect of the post-2008 recession across income groups. It is also robust to time varying housing attributes effects.

We then consider the spatial patterns of the growth in rents over the period. We find that rents also decline faster with commuting time in the boom years, although the change in the rate of decline is about half that of prices. That would be suggestive of there being a bubble component along with a "legitimate" increase then dissipation of current demand, except that the difference between the two rates of decline is insignificant.[1]

We also examine whether the change in the number of permits over the cycle differs between central and noncentral city counties within MSAs. The difference in the relationships is extremely noisy and we are unable to find any significant difference.

Across markets, we distinguish between cities with longer and shorter average commuting time. The geometry of expanding areas yields a simple property for the supply elasticity: because the area of a circle, or any slice of it, increases with the square of its radius, while the circumference increases linearly, the additional housing built in response to a given price increase is a smaller percentage of the overall stock, the larger is the city. Thus larger cities should have a less elastic supply curve, so that in response to a common demand shock across cities, prices should rise proportionately more and construction less in the larger cities. We argue that the measure of a city should be its mean commuting time.

To check this cross-market hypothesis, we regress the first difference in the yearly FHFA (Federal Housing Finance Administration, formerly OFHEO) MSA-level price indices on year dummies and the interaction of those dummies with (demeaned) average Census 2000 commuting time in the MSA, over the 1975 to 2009 period, using a sample of 258 MSAs. We find a strongly significant positive correlation between the overall housing price change and the slope of the relationship between housing price changes and average commuting time. In other words, when price growth rises on average nationally, it rises relatively more in cities with higher average commuting time. When overall price growth (i.e., in the mean average commuting MSA) increases by 1 percent, price growth in an MSA with a 1 standard deviation greater average commute (2.8 minutes) is predicted to grow one-tenth of a percent more.

---

1. Like Glaeser, Gyourko, and Saiz (2008), although we use the language of bubbles, nothing we present here can be considered a strict test of the presence of a bubble. Based on the analysis of prices in this chapter alone, a demand story could be told. However, the rapid increase and fall of home prices in the United States around the 2006 peak, with no accompanying movement in general economic conditions until 2008, is certainly suggestive of the presence of a bubble.

We also investigate how the relationship between permits and price growth depends on the average commuting time. We find that log MSA level permits are increasing in price growth, but that the extent of the increase is decreasing in average commuting time: given a 1 percent greater price growth, a 1 standard deviation greater average commute decreases the predicted increase in log permits by 0.3 log points. That effect is more than doubled if we distinguish between periods of nominal price increases and decreases. Together, the quantity and price responses are consistent with MSAs responding differentially to a common demand shock, with supply elasticity declining in the size of the urban area.

We begin with the within-market analysis in section 3.2. We first present our argument in detail, then present the data, the estimation procedure, and then the results. In section 3.3, we follow the same sequence of topics for the cross-market analysis. We relate our analysis and our findings to the existing literature in section 3.4. We conclude in section 3.5.

3.2   Within-Market Spatial Variation in House Price, Rents, and Building Permits

At any given distance from the center of an urban area, we see a mixture of developed and undeveloped land, due to differential expectations across landowners, historical accidents, local zoning variation, topographical variation, and a multitude of other factors. Overall, however, since the price of housing falls with distance from the center, there is likely to be a greater and greater share of undeveloped land the further out one gets. That, in turn, implies a greater possibility of a significant supply response the more distant one is from the center. That this is so empirically is the obvious inference from Burchfeld et al. (2006), who show that building on previously undeveloped parcels of land in and around urban areas is far more common the less developed is the area surrounding that parcel.[2] Furthermore, where housing prices are lower, building will be less dense, and so there will be a greater opportunity to substitute higher density with lower density. Positive demand shocks that are common across an urban area are therefore likely to be translated mostly into price increases in the city center, with little quantity increase, and translated into more development and little price change near the edge.

There are forces that may act in the opposite direction. Redevelopment closer in to the urban center might be at higher density than previously (the

2. The maps in that paper show new land development occurring overwhelmingly along the edges of the previously developed area. Their figure VI shows an inverted U relationship between the probability of development of a previously undeveloped parcel as a function of the percentage of the surrounding square kilometer that is previously undeveloped. It is the rising part of the relationship that is most relevant for urban areas, as that is where they are located, on average (table X in the same paper).

Burchfeld et al. [2006] data only reveal whether there is any development, not its density). Land use regulations may differ within an urban area, and might be systematically more stringent in the suburbs, especially if higher income people live there and they have a greater willingness to pay for a low density environment; indeed, Glaeser and Ward (2009) have shown that in the greater Boston area, historically less dense areas adopt tougher regulations. Historical development patterns may also mean that inner city structures are more depreciated and so more likely to be replaced; Brueckner and Rosenthal (2009) provide evidence for this. Overall, however, it does appear that supply opportunities are greater further away from the core: Brueckner and Rosenthal (2009) also show that new building is a greater proportion of the existing stock the further out one gets from the urban center.[3] In any case, whether the supply response through undeveloped land is sufficiently important to outweigh these other factors is ultimately an empirical question.

Note also that the argument for a greater quantity response and smaller price increase at greater distances from the center cannot be supported by a model of homogenous households. In that case, the required indifference of occupants among all locations implies that preferences alone determine relative prices. Rather, there must be some element of heterogeneity and consequent clustering that permits local supply conditions to matter for relative prices.

Finally, we note that commuting time is the appropriate measure of distance from the urban core if most of the disutility from residing at a distance from the central business district arises from the time resources devoted to going to and from work (White 1988). Housing prices will then decline with distance from the core at a rate given by the decline in commuting *time* from the core, and the share of undeveloped land and supply possibilities should vary accordingly.

3.2.1   Data

The main data source used for the within-market analysis is the public use microdata samples of the ACS for 2005 through 2010. Each year's sample includes roughly 1.3 million owner-occupied and rental housing units. We do not use earlier years' data because in those years geographical identifiers below the state level were not available and the geographical coverage was also much smaller. The variables we take from the survey are subjects' reports on the home value if the unit is owned or annual rent if it is rented, commuting time to work and commuting modes, physical home attributes, utility costs associated with their residence, taxes paid (for owner-occupied

3. Using the ACS data described later to investigate the same relationships uncovered by Brueckner and Rosenthal (2009), but in terms of commuting minutes rather than miles, we have found that building age is decreasing in commuting time, up to a 100 minute commute, and that post-2000 dwellings as a percentage of all dwellings is increasing the commute up to 30 minutes and then more or less constant thereafter.

homes), and the PUMA (Public Use Microdata Area) and state identifiers for both the respondent's place of residence and place of work.[4]

We take the MSA to define the urban area. Although the ACS does not include an MSA identifier, in almost all cases a PUMA can be matched to a unique MSA. We drop observations whose residents reside in a PUMA that does not belong to an MSA. Those with a residence in one of the ten PUMAs that overlap more than one MSA are dropped.[5] In part of our analysis, we distinguish between PUMAs that contain a central city of the MSA and those that do not. Not all PUMAs have a central city status identifier, however.

For part of our analysis, we restrict the sample to homeowners who report having moved to the given housing unit in the last twelve months. These are about 6.5 percent of all households. The logic of concentrating on such households is that their valuations may be closer to the market value, given that they have just recently purchased their home. However, twelve months is not necessarily "recent" in such a volatile environment.

Our regressor of interest is commuting time, which measures the time it takes to commute from the house to work, as reported by the head of the household. This almost always equals an alternative measure calculated as the difference between the time the respondent reports leaving the home and the time he or she gets to work. Two factors, however, are likely to make reported commuting time a noisy measure of the housing unit's distance in commuting time to the core.

First, households differ in how they commute, and some modes are more pleasant than others. Consequently, prices will drop more quickly with commuting time along a ray along which commuting to the center requires several buses rather than a comfortable subway ride. We handle this in part by including dummy variables for the type used. For a more thorough treatment, we redo our analysis on the subsample for which the household head drives (nearly 90 percent of the total sample).

Second, the household may commute in the direction of the core, but not all the way, or may not commute in the direction of the core, but rather cross-commute; that is, around the circle and not into it. Indeed, Anas and Rhee (2007) show that most commuting is not to the central core. The resulting noise is likely to bias the coefficient on commuting time downwards in magnitude by the reliability ratio; consequently, the difference in measured coefficients across years will also be a downward biased estimate of the true

---

4. We drop vacant, occupied but neither owned nor rented, mobile home, trailer, boat, RV, and van units, homes without complete kitchen facilities or telephones, Puerto Rico, and units with zero or more than nine bedrooms, or zero rooms. We also drop observations that do not report commuting time (about 2.5 percent of the data) and owner-occupied households that do not report taxes (a little over 1 percent of the data).

5. On average, there are about six PUMAs per MSA. Some large MSAs, such as Log Angeles-Long Beach, contain more than sixty PUMAs.

Table 3.1   Summary statistics of commuting time to work (in minutes)

	Mean	S.D.	25th	Median	75th	N
			Owner-occupant sample			
All	30.89	23.83	15	25	40	1,817,977
Recent movers	31.39	23.92	15	25	40	119,031
Drivers	29.82	22.31	15	25	40	1,717,938
			Renter sample			
All	28.15	23.00	15	20	35	695,557
Recent movers	26.75	22.07	15	20	30	251,420
Drivers	25.60	20.28	15	20	30	559,617

Source: ACS (2005–2010)
Note: S.D. = standard deviation.

difference. To mitigate such bias, we include a dummy variable for whether the household commutes to the PUMA that contains the central core. More importantly, we redo our analysis for the subsample of households whose head commutes to that PUMA.

Note that although we speak as if there is a single center in the MSA, the presence of multiple centers in a given MSA would not in and of itself affect the quality of the commuting variable as a proxy for supply conditions. With multiple centers, prices will decline at the same rate, in commuting time, from the closest center (in a world of homogenous workers and jobs). The commuting time of households who work in the closest center to their residence will still indicate commuting time distance and so supply conditions. It is the commuting time of workers who work outside of the centers, or at a center other than the one closest to their residence, that leads to the noise in the variable.

The top panel of table 3.1 presents the summary statistics on commuting time for homeowners. The average commuting time is at 30.89 minutes, just a touch over half an hour. The median is 25 minutes. There is a large variation in commuting time across households, as seen in the standard deviation of 24 minutes, and by the 25 minute difference between the twenty-fifth and seventy-fifth percentiles. However, commuting time does not vary much across the samples: the average for the recent mover sample is only half a minute more, and for the driver sample, a minute less, and the twenty-fifth, fiftieth, and seventy-fifth percentiles remain constant across the samples.

Table 3.2's two top panels present summary statistics for the log house value sample by year, with the top panel corresponding to the overall home-owner sample, and the second panel to the recent mover sample. The first column shows the annual difference in the yearly, MSA-wide average log value, averaged across the MSAs in our sample. The second column shows the same as a weighted (by the number of observations in the second year in each MSA) mean across MSAs; thus it is essentially the mean annual differ-

Table 3.2   **Summary statistics of house price/rent growth (in %)**

	Mean (1)	Weighted mean (2)	Cross-MSA S.D. (3)
All owner-occupants (N = 1,817,283)			
2005–2006	8.85	9.09	6.12
2006–2007	4.56	4.15	4.64
2007–2008	–2.43	–3.21	7.55
2008–2009	–5.30	–7.01	9.32
2009–2010	–2.80	–3.94	6.31
Recent mover owner-occupants (N = 119,023)			
2005–2006	8.39	9.03	14.07
2006–2007	2.98	2.56	15.17
2007–2008	–5.97	–6.04	17.29
2008–2009	–6.68	–9.98	22.94
2009–2010	–6.02	–6.99	19.09
All renters (N = 695,557)			
2005–2006	3.54	3.48	9.07
2006–2007	3.39	4.29	5.03
2007–2008	3.76	3.60	4.88
2008–2009	3.18	3.04	5.20
2009–2010	0.74	0.49	5.43

Source: ACS (2005–2010).

Notes: Column (1) presents the simple mean of the cross-MSA mean of house price growth; column (2) presents the weighted mean, where weights equal the number of observations within each MSA for a given year; column (3) presents the cross-MSA standard deviation around the simple mean.

ence in the average log value in the entire sample. The all owner-occupants panel shows values increasing dramatically between 2005 and 2006 at about 9 percent, increasing further at half that rate over the next year to a peak in 2007, then declining over the next three years by a cumulative 9.5 percent or 14 percent. Half of the decline takes place between 2008 and 2009 alone. The third column shows that there is substantial variation in growth rates across MSAs.

The pattern for recent movers (about 6.5 percent of owner-occupants) is qualitatively similar, with values growing over the first two years and declining over the next three. Quantitatively, however, it differs substantially: the 2006 to 2007 increase is much weaker, and the subsequent declines much greater—the latter by about 3 percent in each year. Here, too, 2008 and 2009 registers the greatest decline, but it stands out less. The standard deviation across MSAs is two or three times as great as that for the overall sample.

What explains the difference between the two panels? It is not differences in geographical composition across MSAs between the overall and the recent mover samples, as columns (1) and (3) show the simple mean and standard deviation across MSAs.

One possible explanation is that in a downturn, recent movers are a self-selected sample of individuals that adjust to the fall in prices. The sample of recent movers is likely to have a disproportionate share of individuals who are insusceptible to factors that hinder selling when prices fall. Their immunity may be due to a lack of loss aversion, or being new buyers (entirely, or to the specific MSA market) who are not "tied" to the recent high prices either as a reference point or through portfolio composition, their having purchased their previous home with little debt. The loss averse may be as unwilling to admit to the loss in value when reporting it as they are unwilling to realize it financially; equity lock-in should not affect a respondent's assessment of market conditions, but will affect his own reservation price for the property, and that may be what he reports. This would explain why the reported values for the high growth period of 2005 to 2006 are so similar in the two panels, while in the subsequent years, in which there is a slowdown and then a decline in prices, the growth rates are smaller for the recent mover panel.

An alternative explanation is that recent movers are more aware of market conditions than nonmovers. They thus report values that are more up to date and more market-specific than those reported by nonmovers, whose information lags that of market conditions. Nonmovers may also not carefully distinguish between news that reports on their market and on the national market, and so may smooth values across MSAs as well. According to this explanation, nonmovers underestimate the slowdown in the market between 2006 and 2007, do not recognize the extent of the decline over the next three years, and miss the extent of differences in growth rates across the areas.

If we are to use self-reported home values to explore the movement of prices, then we need some evidence that values track prices. Others have explored this issue before (e.g., DiPasquale and Somerville 1995; Kiel and Zabel 1999; and Bucks and Pence 2008), but given the dramatic movements in our sample, and in light of previous evidence that sellers are reluctant to recognize losses, we find it appropriate to reexamine the issue with our sample. We are unable to check the relationship at the sub-MSA level, which is the focus of this part of the chapter, as we lack any such indices, but we can at least do so at the MSA level. We begin with a comparison of the figures in table 3.2 to the annual growth rates of the two leading sets of repeat sale price indices, that of the FHFA and Fiserv Case-Shiller, which we show in table 3.3. All columns show the annual difference in the yearly average of the log of the quarterly or monthly (as appropriate) indices. Averaging over the year is appropriate since the ACS is conducted uniformly over the calendar year. The log transformation recovers the coefficient on the difference between the transaction year dummy and the previous year of sale dummy in the repeat sales regressions on which both sets of indices are based, thus making them comparable to our average of log house values.

Column (1) shows the annual growth rates of the purchase-only, national

Table 3.3   **Comparison mean house price growth (in %)**

	FHFA all purchase (1)	FHFA all transactions (2)	Unweighted FHFA all-transactions (restricted to ACS sample) (3)	Weighted FHFA all-transactions (restricted to ACS sample) (4)	Fiserv Case-Shiller National (5)	Fiserv Case-Shiller 10-City Composite (6)	Fiserv Case-Shiller 20-City Composite (7)	Unweighted ACS house price growth (restricted to Fiserv Case-Shiller sample) (8)	Weighted ACS house price growth (restricted to Fiserv Case-Shiller sample) (9)
2005–2006	5.89	7.49	7.02	7.51	5.07	7.11	7.30	10.05	9.77
2006–2007	0.22	1.56	1.74	1.45	-4.67	-4.53	-3.92	2.51	2.36
2007–2008	-7.67	-2.25	-3.89	-5.16	-17.20	-18.30	-17.16	-6.50	-5.85
2008–2009	-5.29	-3.56	-4.33	-5.61	-12.16	-13.86	-14.26	-13.47	-12.20
2009–2010	-3.00	-2.33	-3.60	-3.82	0.20	2.08	1.23	-7.36	-7.02

level FHFA index, and column (2) that for all transactions (i.e., including refinancing). In column (3) we have taken the average growth rate of the FHFA MSA indices for MSAs that appear in our sample; in column (4) they are weighted by the incidence of the MSA in our sample. Columns (5), (6), and (7) show the Fiserv Case-Shiller National ten City and twenty City Composite indices. Finally, in Columns (8) and (9) we reestimate the mean and weighted mean from the first two columns in the top panel of table 3.2, using observations with a residence PUMA in one of the twenty Fiserv Case-Shiller cities.

There are a number of observations to be made here. First, the Fiserv Case-Shiller indices show a decline already in 2006 and 2007, while the FHFA indices show a small increase or a leveling off (recall that our data show a moderate increase). In the next two years, the Fiserv Case-Shiller indices show huge declines; the FHFA indices also show declines but they are about 10 percentage points smaller than those of Fiserv Case-Shiller. Over the last pair of years, the FHFA indices continue to decline at a moderate rate, while the Fiserv Case-Shiller indices level off or increase somewhat. All this is well known. What is new is that households report values whose average growth rates are much more like the FHFA than Fiserv Case-Shiller figures. The higher declines in the post-bust period, and the smaller increase in 2006 and 2007 for the all-purchase index compared to the all-transaction index, are also reminiscent of the difference between the recent movers and the overall sample. However, by restricting the ACS sample to the twenty Fiserv Case-Shiller cities (Columns [8] and [9]), we can generate that index's dramatic decline for 2008 and 2009,[6] although the fit for the other years is not as good.

In table 3.4, we present regressions of the average log house value reported in the ACS for a given MSA and year on the log FHFA transaction index for that MSA and year, and MSA fixed effects. The regressions are weighted by the number of ACS observations in that MSA and year. There are four pairs of regressions, where the second of any pair also includes the lagged index. The four pairs cover the samples we will look: all owners, recent movers, owners who work in PUMAs whose central city status is defined, and owners who commute to a central city PUMA. In the ideal case, we would have a coefficient of one on the current index in the bivariate regression. Except for the recent mover sample, we do in fact obtain coefficients very close to one: 0.96 for the overall sample, and 1.01 for the last two samples. The coefficient of 1.21 for the recent movers sample indicates that those reports substantially "overreact" to the FHFA index. However, recall that the FHFA MSA index includes refinancing transactions, and it is not inconceivable that the assessments that underlie them smooth out purchase prices.

6. That the Fiserv Case-Shiller national index is so similar to its city composites throws some doubt on the representativeness of the underlying sample, the county composition of which is not known. This is especially so since the FHFA has shown that its index can mimic the twenty city Fiserv Case-Shiller composite in part by restricting the sample to those twenty cities.

Table 3.4   **Mean house value regressions on FHFA price index**

	Overall home owner		Recent mover		PUMAs w/ cent. city def.		Work in central city	
	(1)	(2)	(3)	(4)	(5)	(6)	(7)	(8)
lnHPI(t)	.96	.75	1.21	1.18	1.01	.72	1.01	.79
	(.02)	(.03)	(.05)	(.06)	(.04)	(.06)	(.03)	(.04)
lnHPI($t-1$)		.33		.03		.38		.32
		(.02)		(.05)		(.03)		(.04)
RMSE	.040	.028	.079	.079	.049	.041	.082	.077
No. of obs.	1,200	1,200	1,200	1,200	1,199	1,199	1,199	1,199

Note: RMSE = root mean square error.

In all four cases, the lagged price index has a positive and significant coefficient when it is included. For other than the recent mover sample, its share of the sum of the coefficients ranges between .29 to .35; for the recent movers sample, however, it is only .025 of the sum. This reinforces our earlier conclusion that recent movers' valuation are more in line with contemporary prices (or assessments) than that of other households. The sample that looks best when considering the bivariate regression is that of households who work in a central city PUMA, for which the estimated coefficient is insignificantly different from one; but, again, the lagged index gets a large weight when it is included.

Finally, our annual building permit issuance data come from the Census Bureau, which publishes the data for about 18,000 permit-issuing places from 1990 to 2009. We aggregate these place-level data to create the county-level data for the within-market analysis.

3.2.2   Estimation

To compare the within-market house price variation over the years in our sample, we estimate the following relationship:

$$(1) \quad lnP_{jit} = \sum_{t=2005}^{2010}(I_t \times COM_j)\gamma_{1t} + \sum_{t=2005}^{2010}(I_t \times COM_j^2)\gamma_{2t} + X_{jit}\beta + u_{it} + \varepsilon_{jit}.$$

Variable P_{jit} is self-reported home value for household j in MSA i in year t. The vector X_{jit} is a set of housing attributes, including dummies for three sizes of acreage, dummies for the number of bedrooms, whether the house is detached, the number of rooms and building age, and the log expenditures on electricity, natural gas, and water, as well as dummies for ten commuting methods. We also include a full set of MSA × year fixed effects (u_{it}), as is appropriate for a within-market analysis. These fixed effects control for the overall level of prices in the MSA for that year, so, equivalently, we are regressing the deviation of log value from the mean log value for that MSA and year. This, of course, differences out any MSA-level differences in local amenities, housing density, urban structure, geographical/regulation barriers, and so forth.

The variable of interest in this regression is COM_j, which indicates the self-reported commuting time. We interact this variable and its quadratic with the year dummies. Our goal is to compare the decline in values of two physically identical homes at different proximities to the urban center, from the boom to the bust in the cycle of the second half of the 2000s.

We focus on the change in the price gradient and not on its level since we are unable to control for *all* differences in physical housing attributes and local amenities. This is likely to impart a positive bias to the effect of distance on the level of values. The monocentric model and its variants predict that per-household housing quantity or quality increases in distance from the center, in response to the decreasing price of a standardized unit. Thus the measured effect of commuting time effect on home values will equal the sum of the effect on the value for some standard unit plus the effect on housing quality/quantity. However, for a given house, if the quality/quantity is relatively constant over time compared to large changes in the per standard unit value, the differences in the measured price gradient over time should come close to measuring the true changes in the price gradient. More formally, let $p_t(x)$ be the log price at distance x in year t, and $h_t(x)$ is log housing quantity/quality at distance x in year t, and specify those relationships as $p_t(x) = \alpha_t + x\gamma_t + u$ and as $h_t(x) = \alpha_t^* + x\gamma_t^* + \eta$. We run the regression

$$(2) \qquad v_{it} = (\alpha_t + \alpha_t^*) + x_{it}(\gamma_t + \gamma_t^*) + (u_{it} + \eta_{it}),$$

where $v(x)$ is the log of home value at distance x, that is, $v(x) = p(x) + h(x)$. Basic results from the monocentric city model predict that $\gamma_t < 0$, $\gamma_t^* > 0$; the sign of $\gamma_t + \gamma_t^*$ depends on the utility function. We assume that γ^* is constant over the five years of our sample. Given that assumption, the differences in the measured $\gamma_t + \gamma_t^*$ across years, which we estimate by the difference in the coefficients on the interaction of commuting time and year dummies, capture differences in γ over time. Thus our approach is analogous to difference-in-difference estimation.

Although the long durability of housing—coupled with the ACS's random sampling—makes a constant γ^* a reasonable assumption on which to base the empirical analysis, two factors are a cause of concern. The first is renovation and new construction at a standard, or size, different than the existing housing. If these differ systematically across locations with differing commuting times, our results will be biased. A second concern is sampling noise, especially in the smaller subsamples we use, and especially given that we need to control for MSA year effects. To mitigate the bias, and improve precision, we include the physical home attributes in our regressions. To test for robustness, we also interact them with year dummies.[7]

---

7. We also considered including log property taxes. In MSAs with market-based assessments, taxes are likely to do an excellent job of capturing variation in value across properties in a mar-

An underlying assumption behind our identification strategy is that the year-to-year growth in house prices is mostly driven by demand shocks, regardless of whether they reflect changes in economic fundamentals or a bubble, and not changes in supply. This assumption, although strong, is consistent with the approach taken in a number of papers, including Glaeser, Gyourko, and Saiz (2008), as well as the general presumption that the evolution of prices in this period constituted a bubble that then burst. Also, although supply-side stories have been offered for the increase in prices in the first part of the 2000s, we are not aware of any that have been offered for the bust.

Finally, although the motivating argument has assumed a common demand shock across the urban area, with a bubble and its bursting the leading explanation of the general pattern of prices over the period of our sample, the post-2007 economic downturn is likely to have affected poorer areas more harshly. Since high income groups live further out, any change in the price gradient over that time period may conceivably be reflecting variation in the deterioration of the labor market, and thus in the demand for housing, across income levels. To account for this, we include predicted income (based on the household's age and occupation group) interacted with the year time dummies. We use predicted and not actual income to avoid including a feedback income effect, whereby a decrease in an individual's housing wealth leads it to work harder.

3.2.3   Results

Baseline Results

Table 3.5 presents the regression described in equation (1). Column (1) presents our baseline regression, using the full sample of owner-occupants. For clarity of presentation, we group pairs of years together in the interaction terms. For example, COM*0506 is the product of a dummy variable equal to one if the year is either 2005 or 2006, zero otherwise, and the commuting time (measured in units of 10 minutes). The results predict that in 2005 and 2006, a home with a commuting time of the median 25 will have a value that is $100 \times [-.028 \times 2.5 + .0012 \times (2.5)^2] = -6.4$ percent that of a similar home with a zero minute commute. As noted in the previous section,

---

ket at a given time, thus soaking up much of the regression error and making the estimates more precise; variations in the tax rate will be captured by the MSA-year fixed effect. Unfortunately, taxes may do too good a job if they also capture variation across time within a market. This will occur if assessments are updated frequently, and are in line with market developments at the sub-MSA level. In the extreme case, if assessed values track changes in the value of individual properties (or more exactly, on average with commuting time), the estimated coefficients on commuting time will not reflect changes in the price gradient, once taxes are included. Taxes will then be masking the very change we are looking for. Had we taxes for a given year, say 2005, this problem would not arise, but the reported taxes are for the year of the survey. If we do include taxes, the estimated rotation of the price gradient falls, but with minimal gain in precision, so that there is no added precision that might compensate for the bias.

Table 3.5   House value regressions (all owner-occupants and recent movers)

	(1)	(2)	(3)	(4)
COM*0506	−0.027	−0.036	−0.030	−0.033
	(0.002)	(0.0019)	(0.004)	(0.003)
COM*0708	−0.029	−0.038	−0.030	−0.035
	(0.002)	(0.002)	(0.005)	(0.004)
COM*0910	−0.012	−0.026	−0.015	−0.021
	(0.003)	(0.003)	(0.005)	(0.005)
COM^2*0506	0.0012	0.0017	0.0014	0.0015
	(1.31e−04)	(1.18e−04)	(2.09e−04)	(2.00e−04)
COM^2*0708	0.0013	0.0017	0.0014	0.0016
	(1.29e−04)	(1.15e−04)	(2.63e−04)	(2.57e−04)
COM^2*0910	4.34e−04	0.0011	6.81e−04	9.15e−04
	(1.72e−04)	(1.53e−04)	(3.49e−04)	(3.39e−04)
Vector of predicted Income*year dummies	No	Yes	No	Yes
Price difference at median 2009–2010	−0.028	−0.058	−0.034	−0.047
	(0.007)	(0.006)	(0.012)	(0.011)
Price Difference at Median 2005–2006	−0.059	−0.079	−0.065	−0.072
	(0.004)	(0.004)	(0.008)	(0.007)
Difference between 2009–2010 and 2005–2006	0.031	0.021	0.031	0.025
	(0.005)	(0.005)	(0.010)	(0.010)
F–stat.		74.56		28.19
(p-value)		(0.000)		(0.000)
Sample	Full	Full	Recent	Recent
Observations	1,513,018	1,513,018	104,116	104,116

Source: The home owner sample from the ACS (2005–2010).

Notes: The dependent variable is the log of house value. All regressions include MSA × year fixed effect and house characteristics. Standard errors in parentheses are clustered at the MSA level. Commutin time is measured in a unit of 10 minutes. *F*-stat. reports the statistics for the joint test that coefficient interaction of predicted income with year dummy equal to zero.

that estimate is likely to be biased. But we are interested in its difference over time. The results predict that in 2009 and 2010, a home with the median commuting time of 25 minutes will have a value that is $100 \times [−.012 \times 2.5 + .0004 \times (2.5)^2] = −2.8$ percent that of a similar home with a zero minute commute. We take the difference between the 2009 and 2010 difference in values at the median and zero commuting minutes and the 2005 and 2006 difference as our measure of the rotation of the price gradient. As we see in the bottom panel of the table, it is 3.1 percent (rounding is responsible for the discrepancy with our calculation in the text) with a standard error of a mere 0.5 percent.

In column (2) we add predicted income and its interaction with the year pair dummies. Including these variables reduces the estimated rotations by a third, to .021, but it remains significant, with a *t*-statistic of about 4. Closer inspection reveals that the fall comes from including predicted income and not the interaction with the year pairs (although the interactions are jointly highly significant).

In columns (3) and (4), we restrict the sample to recent movers. As noted earlier, we presume that their assessments will be closer to the market value. In column (3), we obtain very similar results to those in our baseline regression of column (1). The estimates are noisier, but far less than what one would expect from the substantially smaller sample: the standard error on the rotation of the price gradient is only doubled to 1.0 percent. The estimate itself is 3.1 percent, the same that we got for the whole sample. As before, including predicted income and its interaction with the year pairs reduces the estimated rotation, but now only to 2.5 percent, and the difference is such that it would not fail a Hausman test.

Whether or not we restrict the sample to recent movers, all four specifications show that the coefficients on the linear component on commuting time are negative and significant in all years, while the coefficient on the quadratic components are positive. The marginal effect is negative up to at least 105 minutes. Although, as noted earlier, this result is not necessary for our identification strategy, it is nonetheless heartening to see that the estimates are consistent with the underlying assumption that the data are well-represented by a monocentric city model, with much of the variation in housing quantity accounted for.

These regressions constrain the coefficients on the physical home attributes to be constant over time. One possible objection is that the hedonic prices of these attributes might differ across years, and it is these changing prices, along with the correlation of attributes with commuting time, that explains our results. To see if this is so, table 3.6 allows for year-varying coefficients on the lot size and number of bedroom dummies. As one can clearly see, doing so barely changes our core estimates. The largest change is in the rotation of the recent mover sample, which drops from 3.1 percent in table 3.5 to 2.8 percent here. Neither does adding interactions of additional physical home attributes have any noticeable effect on the estimates (regressions not shown).

In order to reduce the noise in the commuting time variable due to cross-commuters and those who commute in the direction of the central city, but only part way, we next restrict the sample to households whose heads work in the central city. This subsample has only 85,200 observations, or about 4.7 percent of the owner-occupants. The subsample is so much smaller because it throws out not only those who do not commute to the central city but also those households whose head works in a PUMA whose central city status is not defined by the Census Bureau.

Table 3.7 presents the results. To establish a comparable baseline, we first consider the sample of observations belonging to a PUMA whose central city status is defined. This is about one-third of the sample. Our baseline regression run on this subsample is presented in column (1). The estimated

Table 3.6   House value regressions (all owner-occupants and recent movers)

	(1)	(2)	(3)	(4)
COM*0506	−0.027	−0.036	−0.029	−0.033
	(0.002)	(0.0019)	(0.004)	(0.003)
COM*0708	−0.029	−0.038	−0.030	−0.035
	(0.002)	(0.002)	(0.005)	(0.004)
COM*0910	−0.013	−0.026	−0.017	−0.022
	(0.003)	(0.003)	(0.005)	(0.005)
COM^2*0506	0.0012	0.0017	0.0014	0.0015
	(1.33e−04)	(1.19e−04)	(2.11e−04)	(2.02e−04
COM^2*0708	0.0013	0.0017	0.0014	0.0016
	(1.29e−04)	(1.15e−04)	(2.62e−04)	(2.56e−04
COM^2*0910	4.65e−04	0.0011	7.56e−04	9.52e−04
	(1.69e−04)	(1.51e−04)	(3.40e−04)	(3.34e−04
Vector of predicted Income*year dummies	No	Yes	No	Yes
Price difference at median 2009–2010	−0.029	−0.058	−0.037	−0.049
	(0.007)	(0.006)	(0.011)	(0.011)
Price Difference at median 2005–2006	−0.059	−0.078	−0.065	−0.072
	(0.005)	(0.004)	(0.008)	(0.007)
Difference between 2009–2010 and 2005–2006	0.030	0.020	0.028	0.023
	(0.004)	(0.004)	(0.010)	(0.010)
F-stat.		68.41		24.53
(p-value)		(0.000)		(0.000)
Sample	Full	Full	Recent	Recent
Observations	1,513,018	1,513,018	104,116	104,116

Source: Home owner sample from the ACS (2005–2010).

Notes: The dependent variable is the log of house value. All regressions include MSA × year fixed effect and house characteristics, and allow the year-varying coefficients on the lot size and the number of bed rooms. Standard errors in parentheses are clustered at the MSA level. Commuting time is measured in unit of 10 minutes. F-stat. reports the statistics for the joint test that coefficients interaction of predicted income with year dummy equal to zero.

rotation effect is 3.8 points, as compared to the 3.1 percent from the corresponding column from table 3.6. Restricting the sample to central city commuters (column [3]) increases the magnitude of all six coefficients on the linear and quadratic commuting times, consistent with the restriction reducing the errors in variable problem. The estimated rotation of the price gradient is roughly doubled, to a significant 7.1 percent, with a t-statistic of 5.4. Adding predicted income and its interactions (column [4]) has little effect.

Table 3.8 repeats the same exercise as in table 3.7, except that here we do not pair up years, but show separate effects for each year. This table shows the evolution of the price gradient over time in finer detail. The gradient remains very nearly constant over the first four years of the sample. This is so despite the fact that those four years include periods of growth and decline. Then, in 2009, once the markets are in the depths of the decline, the gradient becomes substantially flatter. The coefficient on the linear term is cut at

Table 3.7   **House value regressions (MSAs with defined central city PUMAs)**

	(1)	(2)	(3)	(4)
COM*0506	–0.021	–0.029	–0.041	–0.044
	(0.003)	(0.003)	(0.007)	(0.007)
COM*0708	–0.021	–0.029	–0.047	–0.049
	(0.003)	(0.003)	(0.008)	(0.007)
COM*0910	–0.004	–0.016	–0.009	–0.017
	(0.004)	(0.004)	(0.008)	(0.008)
COM^2*0506	0.0010	0.0014	0.002	0.002
	(1.90e–04)	(1.84e–04)	(5.53e–04)	(5.08e–04)
COM^2*0708	0.0010	0.0014	0.002	0.002
	(1.86e–04)	(1.75e–04)	(4.77e–04)	(4.28e–04)
COM^2*0910	2.42e–04	8.09e–04	7.35e–04	4.84e–04
	(2.52e–04)	(2.29e–04)	(5.33e–04)	(5.18e–04)
Vector of predicted Income*year dummies	No	Yes	No	Yes
Price difference at median 2009–2010	–0.009	–0.017	–0.021	–0.039
	(0.008)	(0.007)	(0.017)	(0.017)
Price difference at median 2005–2006	–0.047	–0.029	–0.092	–0.097
	(0.007)	(0.005)	(0.017)	(0.016)
Difference between 2009–2010 and 2005–2006	0.038	0.012	0.071	0.058
	(0.008)	(0.005)	(0.013)	(0.013)
F-stat.		46.79		27.42
(p-value)		(0.000)		(0.000)
Sample	Full	Full	Work in central cities	Work in central cities
Observations	452,051	452,051	71,397	71,397

Source: Home owner sample from the ACS (2005–2010).

Notes: Columns (1) and (2) are restricted to observations in MSAs with a central city PUMA. Columns (3) and (4) are restricted to the sample that contains households working in central cities only. The dependent variable is the log of house value. All regressions include MSA × year fixed effects and house characteristics. Standard errors in parentheses are clustered at the MSA level. Commuting time is measured in a unit of 10 minutes. *F*-stat. reports the statistics for the joint test that coefficients interaction of predicted income with year dummy equal to zero.

least in half, and substantially more in the central city commuters' sample, while the coefficient on the quadratic term drops substantially as well. The year 2010's gradient looks similar. It is very clear that there is a substantial break in the gradient "series" and that it takes place between 2008 and 2009.

Robustness Checks

An additional concern is that commuting time may not adequately represent the disutility from commuting, which may depend on the means of transportation. We have included dummies for different commuting methods, but that obviously will not control for variations in the marginal disutility. To address this concern more fully, we have run all the previous regressions with the further restriction that the household head commutes

Table 3.8   **House value regressions: Separate year interaction effects**

	(1)	(2)	(3)	(4)
COM*05	−0.023	−0.030	−0.040	−0.043
	(0.005)	(0.005)	(0.011)	(0.011)
COM*06	−0.020	−0.029	−0.044	−0.045
	(0.003)	(0.003)	(0.009)	(0.009)
COM*07	−0.022	−0.029	−0.045	−0.047
	(0.004)	(0.004)	(0.008)	(0.008)
COM*08	−0.020	−0.028	−0.049	−0.051
	(0.004)	(0.004)	(0.011)	(0.011)
COM*09	−0.006	−0.017	−0.005	−0.011
	(0.004)	(0.004)	(0.008)	(0.008)
COM*10	−5.59e−05	−0.015	−0.015	−0.026
	(0.005)	(0.004)	(0.010)	(0.011)
COM^2*05	0.0011	0.0015	0.002	0.0018
	(0.0003)	(0.0003)	(0.0007)	(0.0007)
COM^2*06	0.0010	0.0014	0.002	0.0021
	(0.0002)	(0.0002)	(0.0007)	(0.0006)
COM^2*07	0.0012	0.0015	0.002	0.0020
	(0.0002)	(0.0002)	(0.0005)	(0.0005)
COM^2*08	0.0009	0.0013	0.002	0.0020
	(0.0002)	(0.0002)	(0.0006)	(0.0006)
COM^2*09	0.0005	0.0009	−0.0002	4.73e−05
	(0.0003)	(0.0003)	(0.0006)	(0.0005)
COM^2*10	−0.0002	0.0006	0.0007	0.0010
	(0.0003)	(0.0003)	(0.0007)	(0.0008)
Vector of predicted Income*year dummies	No	Yes	No	Yes
Price difference at median 2009–2010	−0.007	−0.034	−0.023	−0.042
	(0.007)	(0.006)	(0.013)	(0.014)
Price Difference at Median 2005–2006	−0.047	−0.064	−0.093	−0.098
	(0.009)	(0.006)	(0.015)	(0.015)
Difference between 2009–2010 and 2005–2006	0.040	0.030	0.069	0.055
	(0.009)	(0.009)	(0.020)	(0.021)
F-stat.		17.99		7.15
(p-value)		(0.000)		(0.000)
Sample	Full	Full	Work in central cities	Work in central cities
Observations	452,051	452,051	71,397	71,397

Source: Home owner sample from the ACS (2005–2010).

Notes: Columns (1) and (2) are restricted to observations in MSAs with a central city PUMA. Columns (3) and (4) are restricted to the sample that contains households working in central cities only. The dependent variable is the log of house value. All regressions include MSA × year fixed effects and house characteristics. Standard errors in parentheses are clustered at the MSA level. Commuting time is measured in a unit of 10 minutes. F-stat. reports the statistics for the joint test that coefficients interaction of predicted income with year dummy equal to zero.

to work by driving. None of our results change in any substantive way, which is to be expected given that nearly 90 percent of all owner-occupants commute by car to work.

In comparing across years, the analysis has thus far implicitly used the nationwide average movement in prices or values as indicators of the state of overall market conditions. However, there are differences across cities in the extent and timing of the price appreciation and depreciation over our period of analysis. We thus check to see whether using the MSA level FHFA house price indices instead of year dummies generates the same results. To do so, we replace the interaction of commuting minutes and year dummies with the interaction of commuting minutes and the growth in the MSA price index.

Table 3.9 shows the resulting regression for the sample of households whose head works in the central city. The first column controls for MSA cross-year fixed effects and physical house attributes, as usual. The coefficient of $-.041$ in column (1) implies that when prices grow at a 1 percent lower rate, the absolute slope of the price gradient decreases by .04 percent per commuting minute. Thus prices at a 25-minute commute fall one-tenth of a percent more than prices at the center for every 1 percent decline in overall price.

At a 16 percent decline, which corresponds to the decline between 2006 and 2010, according to both the valuations reported in the ACS and the FHFA All Purchase Index, the estimated rotation is thus 1.6 percent. That is exactly one-half of our baseline estimate, and less than a quarter of that

Table 3.9   **House value regressions on FHFA price indices (work in central city sample)**

	(1)	(2)	(3)	(4)
COM	−0.016	−0.015	−0.013	−0.016
	(0.002)	(0.002)	(0.000)	(0.002)
COM*(ΔlnHPI)	−0.041	−0.044		
	(0.023)	(0.019)		
COM*(ΔlnHPI)*I{ΔlnHPI > 0}			−0.075	−0.021
			(0.031)	(0.025)
COM*(ΔlnHPI)*I{ΔlnHPI < 0}			−0.007	−0.069
			(0.035)	(0.028)
lnHPI		1.094		1.097
		(0.054)		(0.056)
Lagged lnHPI		−0.062		−0.054
		(0.089)		(0.089)
MSA × year fixed effects	Yes	No	Yes	No
MSA fixed effects		Yes		Yes

Source: ACS (2005–2010).

Notes: The dependent variable is the log house value. "HPI" is the MSA FHFA house price indices. Standard errors in parentheses are clustered at the MSA level. Commuting time is measured in units of 10 minutes. The number of observations is 85,143.

from the work in central subsample. Using the Fiserv Case-Shiller decline of 31 percent brings the estimate in line with that of the baseline estimates, but not quite one-half that of the work-in-central-city sample.

In column (2) we replace the MSA cross-year fixed effects with the price index and its lag and MSA fixed effects. The estimates on the commuting terms remain essentially unchanged. In the next two columns we allow the gradient to shift with a differential magnitude according to whether growth is positive or negative, by replacing the interaction of commuting time and MSA price growth with the following two variables: COM × ΔlnHPI × $I\{\Delta ln$HPI $> 0\}$ and COM × ΔlnHPI × $I\{\Delta ln$HPI $\leq 0\}$. Both the durability of housing and our earlier result that the price gradient shifted when prices fell over the latter part of the 2005 to 2010 period but not when they rose suggest that allowing for such an asymmetry might be important. We obtain ambiguous results: when MSA cross-year effects are included (column [3]), we find that the price gradient shifts most when prices are rising; when the price index is included instead, we find the opposite.

Within-Market Spatial Variation in Rents

We now turn to consider the rents of rented dwellings. Unlike house prices, for which expectations over future conditions matter, rents are determined solely by current demand and current supply. The comparative behavior of rents to prices over a boom and bust cycle can thus give us some sense of whether the price movement was the result of a positive shock to current demand for housing services that then dissipated, or a bubble. (Of course, an increase in expected future demand that is then undone is indistinguishable from a bubble.) If it is a temporary shock to current demand, then the rent gradient should become flatter in the bust, just as for prices. If it is a bubble, than the spatial pattern of rents should remain constant over time. That is, unless the boom has persisted long enough for a substantial overhang to have developed, in which case rents should fall more where supply is more elastic. Thus, for a bubble, the rent gradient should either remain constant over time, or become steeper in the bust.[8]

We first turn back briefly to table 3.2, where the bottom panel presents the annual average growth in rents. Here, rents behave very differently than self-reported values and price indices. In contrast to the boom and bust cycle displayed by the latter, rents increase steadily year after year, at about 3.5 percent a year, until 2010, when they essentially stagnate at the 2009 level. This is clearly at odds with any explanation of the boom and bust of prices over the 2000s based on changing current demand for housing services.

Table 3.10 presents results from regressing log rents on the same set of

---

8. Obviously, any overhang will affect prices as well; however, since prices will incorporate the gradual disappearance of the overhang with the normal growth in demand, the effect on prices should be substantially less.

Table 3.10   Rent regressions (work in central city sample)

	(1)	(2)	(3)	(4)	(5)	(6)
COM*0506	-0.026	-0.029	-0.035	-0.036	-0.002	-0.006
	(0.009)	(0.008)	(0.010)	(0.010)	(0.012)	(0.012)
COM*0708	-0.014	-0.017	-0.02	-0.024	-0.008	-0.003
	(0.008)	(0.007)	(0.008)	(0.007)	(0.011)	(0.010)
COM*0910	-0.004	-0.013	-0.017	-0.024	0.014	0.004
	(0.009)	(0.008)	(0.009)	(0.008)	(0.014)	(0.001)
COM²*0506	6.95e-04	0.0016	0.0020	0.002	-6.96e-04	-3.48e-04
	(4.66e-04)	(5.85e-04)	(6.64e-04)	(6.56e-04)	(9.04e-04)	(9.46e-04)
COM²*0708	3.17e-04	8.38e-04	9.30e-04	0.001	-2.25e-04	9.57e-05
	(4.66e-04)	(4.21e-04)	(5.17e-04)	(4.77e-04)	(6.33e-04)	(5.84e-04)
COM²*0910	3.17e-05	8.27e-04	0.001	0.001	-8.64e-04	-1.88e-04
	(6.94e-04)	(6.03e-04)	(5.77e-04)	(5.77e-04)	(0.0011)	(9.72e-04)
Predicted income with year interactions	No	Yes	No	Yes	No	Yes
Price difference at median 2009–2010	-0.008	-0.027	-0.036	-0.051	0.030	0.009
	(0.019)	(0.016)	(0.019)	(0.017)	(0.029)	(0.023)
Price difference at median 2005–2006	-0.056	-0.061	-0.076	-0.076	-0.021	-0.017
	(0.018)	(0.017)	(0.022)	(0.021)	(0.023)	(0.024)
Difference between 2009–2010 and 2005–2006	0.048	0.034	0.040	0.025	0.051	0.026
	(0.019)	(0.018)	(0.025)	(0.026)	(0.025)	(0.024)
F-stat.		5.17		0.66		6.04
(p-value)		(0.007)		(0.52)		(0.003)
Sample	All rentals	All rentals	Rented apartments	Rented apartments	Rented houses	Rented houses
Observations	25,182	25,182	14,975	14,975	10,207	10,207

regressors as in tables 3.5, 3.6, and 3.7: year dummies, their interaction with commuting time and with the square of commuting time, and attributes of the unit. The sample is restricted to households whose heads commute to the central city. The first two columns show the results on the sample of all renters, with the interactions of predicted income and year dummies controlled for in column (2) but not so in column (1). We first note that the rent gradients are downward sloping over the vast majority of the support of commuting time. In the early years, commuting time decreases rents until 105 minutes, similarly to what we saw for values; in 2009 and 2010, however, it turns up at 51 minutes (the ninety-fourth percentile), although the quadratic term is insignificant. The estimation rotation is 3.9 percent, and is significant. Thus we can reject the pure bubble hypothesis, under which rents would have fallen equally along the commuting time dimension, or fallen less at the center due to overhang. A weaker test is to check whether rents rotate up with the housing bust less than prices themselves. The point estimate for the rotation is about half that of the 7.1 percent we obtained in table 3.7 for the parallel sample of owner-occupants who commute to the central city, but the difference between the two is insignificant.

The next four columns distinguish between rented apartments (columns [3] and [4]) and rented houses (columns [5] and [6]). The distinction might be an important one, since nominal rigidity in rents is much more prevalent in single-family dwellings than in apartments, likely because apartments are much more likely to be owned by corporations, partnerships, and large investors (Genesove 2003). Thus we might expect that the gradient for houses would be relatively constant over time. Nonetheless, we find a positive rotation of the rent gradient in both categories, with that for houses much bigger and significant only.

Thus, surprisingly, although the aggregate behavior of reported rents is very different from that of both reported values and price indices, the variation in the temporal behavior of rents across commuting time is qualitatively similar to that of prices. Taken by itself, the similarity in the spatial behavior is consistent with a dramatic temporary increase in current demand in the bust period that gets undone between 2008 and 2009. It is not consistent with either a bubble that gets pricked, or an increase in future expected demand that then goes away; in such cases, the rent gradient would have stayed constant or because of the overhang, become steeper.

Within-Market Spatial Variation in Building Permits

Although the focus of this chapter is on prices, since our analysis does presume that building in the city center is more difficult than building outside it, we now turn to ask whether building in the urban center is indeed less responsive to price increases. We aggregate up county-level permit data to the set of central city counties and noncentral city counties, in each MSA, for those counties for which permit data are available. We consider only those

Table 3.11   **Summary statistics of permits**

	(1)	(2)	(3) = (1) – (2)	(4)	(5)
			Central-noncentral difference	First difference of central-Noncentral difference	
	Log permits				
	Central	Noncentral		Mean	S.D.
2005	6.36	7.60	1.23	—	—
2006	6.22	7.43	1.21	–0.02	0.30
2007	5.93	7.17	1.24	0.03	0.32
2008	5.48	6.71	1.23	–0.01	0.30
2009	5.17	6.43	1.26	0.03	0.38

Notes: The building permits are obtained at the county level from the Census (1990–2009) and aggregated up to the set of central and noncentral counties in each of the 141 MSAs that have both central and noncentral counties.

141 MSAs for which we are able to obtain permit data for both central and noncentral city counties. In columns (1) and (2) of table 3.11 we present the log of the number of permits in the central city counties and the noncentral city counties, respectively, averaged across the MSA by year, from 2005 to 2009, with the difference given in column (3). Because the coverage of counties is not complete (although the sample is balanced), and the number of permits is not normalized by the existing housing stock, we cannot infer the relative degree of building in these two sets of areas. Column (4) shows the first difference in these figures, however, and thus shows us how the extent of building moves differentially over the cycle. Column (5) shows the standard deviation of these changes across MSAs. With 141 MSAs, the standard error on the mean first differences in column (4) are thus about 0.03. There is clearly no evidence that the relative number of permits within the urban areas varies over the period.

In table 3.12, we ask whether the number of permits increases less with price growth in central city counties than in noncentral city counties, as would be implied by a smaller supply elasticity closer in to the urban center when demand shocks dominate supply shocks. That it is price growth that should be expected to be correlated with permits and not the price levels follows naturally from the fact that permits essentially indicate the change in supply. Mayer and Somerville (2000) show that this logic follows from the standard monocentric city model, specifically Capozza and Helsley (1989). To account for replacement investment, we nonetheless allow for a price level effect by adding the current price level as well and not simply the difference. Underlying this investigation is of course an assumption that supply shifts are substantially less variable than demand shifts.

Column (1) shows the regression of the within-MSA log difference in permits between central and noncentral city counties on the MSA-level price

Table 3.12   Permit regressions

	(1)	(2)	(3)	(4)	(5)	(6)
lnHPI	0.27		−0.16		0.20	
	(0.30)		(0.15)		(0.20)	
Δ lnHPI	1.32	1.29	0.28	0.22	0.18	0.25
	(1.15)	(1.11)	(0.48)	(0.49)	(0.51)	(0.51)
Trend					−0.013	−0.010
					(0.004)	(0.003)
Sample period	2005–2009	2005–2009	1990–2009	1990–2009	1990–2009	1990–200
Number of obs.	585	585	2,222	2,222	2,222	2,222

Notes: The MSA fixed effects are included in each regression. Standard errors are in parentheses.

index and its first difference, over the 2005 to 2010 period. Neither variable is close to being significant. In column (2) we drop the price level, but this does not improve the precision on the first difference. Columns (3) and (4) repeat the estimation over the entire period for which we have data, from 1990 to 2010, and columns (5) and (6) add a trend term. In none of the regressions is there a statistically significant relationship.

3.3   Cross-Market Spatial Variation in House Price and Building Permits

So far, our analysis has focused on the spatial variation in house price growth among housing units within the same market, where the variation is collapsed to the time to commute dimension. It is natural to extend the use of commuting time as a proxy for supply conditions to the cross-market level. In this section, we first derive a theoretical relationship between average commuting time and housing supply elasticity across markets. It is based on the geometry of expanding areas. We then empirically test this relationship by examining how house prices and building permits vary across markets with different average commuting time, and how these effects vary with the stages of the housing market cycle.

The intuition for the theoretical result is shown in figure 3.1. If all the additional housing built in response to a price change is built on the margins of a circular city, the increased stock will equal the circumference of the circle. As the total housing stock in the city is the area of the circle, the percentage change in the housing stock for a given absolute price change should be decreasing in the city radius. In considering the supply elasticity, we need to consider a given percentage increase in price, of course, and prices are higher in bigger cities. But it is only the location rents component of prices that increases with city size, and in Capozza and Helsley's (1989) dynamic version of the monocentric city model, which we base our analysis on, it increases linearly. The presence of the remaining components of price, agricultural rents, and construction costs, ensure then that supply elasticity

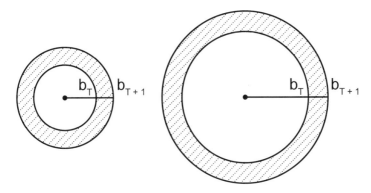

Fig. 3.1   **Graphical illustration of supply elasticity with respect to city size**

is inversely proportional to the city radius. As the following analysis also shows that the proper measurement of the radius is maximum commuting time, not distance per se, we show that supply elasticity is inversely related to commuting time.

In developing our argument, we follow Mayer and Somerville (2000) and Green, Malpezzi, and Mayo (2005) in deriving an elasticity of supply based on Capozza and Helsley (1989). We view our presentation as somewhat more transparent, however. Consider, then, a set of cities that have developed in line with that model. The cities are of different sizes, perhaps because they were established at different points in the past, or perhaps because they have different transportation infrastructures that yield different commuting costs.

Now consider a shock to demand that takes the form of an enhanced willingness to pay in the city. The greater price will induce an increase in the housing stock. In line with Capozza and Helsley (1989), all new development takes place at the city edge. (In practice, redevelopment in the city core is certainly possible. However, as discussed in section 3.2, the empirical literature generally shows that supply opportunities are much greater at the edge.)[9] Assume that households are willing to pay α percent above the current fundamental price at the city edge. That means an absolute price increase at the city edge of $\Delta P = \alpha P_E$, where P_E is the current price at the edge. Capozza and Helsley (1989) show that

$$P_E = A + C + Tf(g, r)z_E,$$

where A is the discounted value of land use in its undeveloped state (agricultural rent) and C is the conversion cost, which we should see here as the construction cost of the housing structure. The last term represents the

9. To control for the possibility that some cities develop more in the core than others, our empirical specifications include MSA fixed effects and the interactions between year dummies and supply constraint proxies, such as the Wharton Residential Land Use Regulation Index and the undevelopable land share.

discounted value of location rents, with T the time cost of commuting a unit distance, z_E the distance from the center to the edge, g population growth, r the interest rate, and f a function that is increasing in g and decreasing in r.

Define the absolute rate at which prices decline with distance from the city center as k. Then the city edge grows out an additional $\Delta z = k^{-1}\Delta P$ from the center. The additional area that is developed is $2\pi z_E\Delta z = 2\pi k^{-1}\alpha\{[A + C]z_E + Tf(g,r)z_E^2\}$. (See figure 3.1. Like the aforementioned papers, we assume a constant lot size.) Since the area of a circular city is z_E^2, we obtain that the percentage increase in the housing stock is $2k^{-1}\alpha\{[A + C]/z_E + Tf(g,r)\}$. Since $k = T/r$ (a dwelling at one unit of distance closer to the center is worth the discounted value of the time cost of commuting a unit distance more), the supply elasticity of housing is

$$
(3) \qquad \eta = 2r\left\{\frac{[A+C]}{(Tz_E)} + f(g,r)\right\}.^{10}
$$

As is often done, we will assume that the opportunity cost of the land plus the construction cost, $A + C$, do not vary substantially across cities. The housing supply elasticity is thus decreasing in the maximum commuting time (Tz_E), increasing in future population growth g, and increasing in the sum of the opportunity cost of land and construction costs $(A + C)$.

Our focus is on commuting time. Importantly, the previous argument shows us that the proper measure of a city's size as a factor of supply elasticity is commuting minutes and not kilometers. The term that appears in the supply elasticity is the maximum commuting time, but given the greater sensitivity of the maximum to measurement error, we substitute the average commuting time, which is two-thirds of the maximum under this model.[11]

If demand shocks are a national phenomenon (as Cotter, Gabriel, and Roll [2011] show to be increasingly the case) that add a willingness to pay to inverse demand of a constant percentage over current prices, then the foregoing implies that prices should rise relatively more in larger cities. In smaller cities, they will be undone by massive building along the edge, which will keep prices from increasing too much.

3.3.1   Data

To test these implications, we look at the differential movement of MSA-level house prices across time according to the average commuting time of

---

10. Green, Malpezzi, and Mayo (2005) derive the semi-elasticity of housing supply from the Capozza-Helsley model as $2(r - g)/(Tz_E)$. Multiplying this by P_E yields our result. Assuming $g = 0$, our expression also reduces to that implicit in Saiz (2010). His central claim is that the supply elasticity is decreasing the undevelopable share of the city. Given the population, this is so: to fit in the same number of households in a semicircle as in a circle, the former must extend further out from the origin, and so by precisely the argument given here, must have a smaller supply elasticity.

11. With a fixed lot size, the mean is proportional to the maximum: since the number of dwellings at distance z from the center is $2\pi z$, mean commuting time is $2\pi T\int_0^{z_E} z^2 dz/2\pi\int_0^{z_E} z dz = 2/3 Tz_E$.

the MSA. We measure house prices with MSA-level FHFA all transaction (i.e, purchase plus refinancing) indices. This covers a somewhat different set of MSAs than the ACS data. We also consider a much longer window: 1976 to 2009. The sample of 257 MSAs is heavily unbalanced due to different starting times, which are distributed between 1975 and 1993. While the price series is at a quarterly frequency, we use the averaged annual data, since our focus is on patterns over a cycle, not on higher frequency, seasonal effects. As before, we obtain the housing permit data from the US Bureau of the Census. We aggregate across places to create metropolitan-area-level aggregate permits. Annual permits data are available for 1990 to 2009. In some regressions, we also control for measures of growth to control for g. We also at times condition on the interaction with year dummies of other proxies for determinants of housing supply, notably the updated Wharton Residential Land Use Regulatory Index (WRLURI) (Gyourko, Saiz, and Summers 2008) and Saiz's undevelopable land share (Saiz 2010).

To measure commuting time in each location, we use the average number of minutes needed for a one-way trip to work among workers sixteen years and over from the 2000 Census. The mean average commuting time is 22 minutes, with a standard deviation of 2.66 minutes. The MSAs with the longest average commuting time are New York, NY (37.4 minutes); Newburgh, NY-PA (34.6); Bremerton, WA (34.4); Monmouth Ocean, NJ (33.8); and Washington, DC (33.5). Those with the shortest are Grand Forks, ND-MN (16.0 minutes); Dubuque, IA (16.7); Waterloo-Cedar Falls, IA (17.1); Great Falls, MT (17.2); and Bismarck, ND (17.4). Figure 3.2 reports the histogram of average commuting time. Note that our measure of average commuting time does not vary over time; there should therefore be little concern of an endogeneity bias in which positive demand shocks both increase prices and increase congestion and thus commuting time.

3.3.2   Cross-MSA Variation in House Prices

The brief argument we laid out implies that when demand increases, price will increase more in markets with longer average commuting time. The argument has nothing to say about demand decreases (nor has the underlying Capozza and Helsley [1989] model), but fortunately, most of the period of our sample is one of price increases. Coupled with the assumptions that (a) demand shocks are much more variable than supply shocks, and (b) demand shocks are heavily correlated across MSAs (Cotter, Gabriel, and Roll 2011), the claim implies that when overall prices increase, prices will increase more in high average commuting MSAs.

Our procedure has two stages. In the first stage, we estimate the following regression model:

$$y_{it} = \sum_{t=1975}^{2009} I_t \alpha_t + \sum_{t=1975}^{2009} (I_t \times COM_j)\beta_t + \sum_{t=1975}^{2009} (I_t \times X_j)\gamma_t + u_i + \varepsilon_{it}.$$

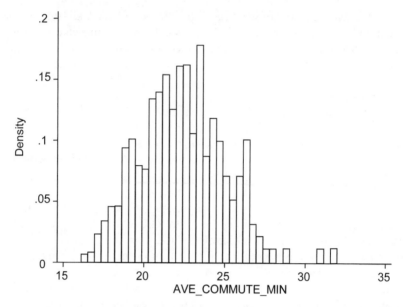

Fig. 3.2   Histogram of average commuting time (mean = 22.39 min., sd = 2.66 min.)

The dependent variable is the first difference in the log of the house price index in MSA i at year t.[12] Variable I_t is a dummy for year t, COM_i indicates the demeaned, average commuting time in MSA i from the year 2000 Census, and X_j indicates other possible determinants of the supply elasticity. Finally, MSA fixed effects are included. These effects control for, among other things, trends in market-specific geographical feature and regulatory constraints, and unchanging amenities.

With demeaning and MSA fixed effects, the parameter α_t reflects the overall housing price growth in year t. The parameter β_t reflects, in a given year t, how the price growth varies across markets with different average commuting time. Figure 3.3 shows the time series of the estimated parameters, that of the raw estimates on the left and that of the residuals from regressions of each on controls to be included in regressions below on the right.

In the second stage, we explore the relationship between β_t and α_t. If longer average commuting time indeed proxies for more inelastic housing supply, then we should expect that when overall house prices increase, house prices will increase more in the MSAs with longer commuting time than in others; that is, that β_t and α_t should be positively correlated over time. We

---

12. The index is equal to $100\exp(\psi_t)$, where ψ_t is the estimated coefficient on the year t variable that takes values $\{1, -1, 0\}$ according to whether t is the year of sale, previous sale, or neither, in the regression with log price as the dependent variable. Thus taking the log of the index yields ψ_t, the measured price growth, plus a constant.

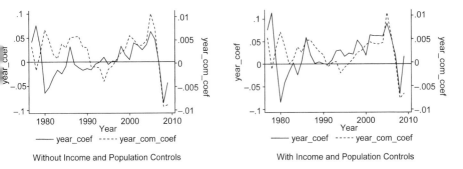

Fig. 3.3   Cross-MSA house price analysis

Note: Estimated α_t and β_t, from the Regression of First Difference of log Price Index on Year Dummies and Interaction of Year Dummies with Average Commuting Time.

wish to examine this relationship through the regression $E[\beta_t|\alpha_t] = a_0 + a_1\alpha_t$.[13] The argument we outlined earlier implies that a_1 should be positive.

Of course, we do not observe β_t and α_t, but only their estimates $\hat{\beta}_t$ and $\hat{\alpha}_t$. We thus face a measurement error problem, which implies that the ordinary least square (OLS) estimate of a_1 will be biased: it converges to the sum of the attenuation of the true value (due solely to the measurement error in $\hat{\alpha}_t$) and an additional bias of the sign of the covariance between the estimation errors of the two coefficients. However, since we can estimate the distribution of those errors, using the standard asymptotic results on the distribution of OLS estimates, we can form the following consistent method of moments à la Fuller (1987) and Buonaccorsi (2010):

$$\alpha_1^{MOM} = \frac{\{S_{\alpha\beta} - Q_{\alpha\beta}\}}{\{S_{\alpha\alpha} - Q_{\alpha\alpha}\}},$$

where $S_{\alpha\beta}$ is the sample covariance of $\hat{\beta}_t$ and $\hat{\alpha}_t$, $S_{\alpha\alpha}$ is the sample variance of $\hat{\alpha}_t$, $Q_{\alpha\beta} \equiv (1 + 1999 - 1976)^{-1} \sum_{t=1976}^{1999} \sigma_{\alpha\beta t}^2$, $Q_{\alpha\alpha} \equiv (1 + 1999 - 1976)^{-1} \sum_{t=1976}^{1999} \sigma_{\alpha\alpha t}^2$, $\sigma_{\alpha\alpha t}$ is the estimated standard error on $\hat{\alpha}_t$, and $\sigma_{\alpha\beta t}^2$ is the estimated covariance of $\hat{\alpha}_t - \alpha_t$ and $\hat{\beta}_t - \beta_t$. Where there are no other regressors other than the year dummies and their interaction with commuting time, $\sigma_{\alpha\beta t}^2$ equals minus the regression error variance time the product of the mean of the commuting variable divided by the variance of the same, where the mean and variance are taken over the set of MSAs in the sample for that year. Since we use the deviation of average commuting minutes from its mean, $Q_{\alpha\beta}$ is very nearly zero (it is not exactly zero as the sample is not balanced). Thus in our case

13. We mean this as not only a projection, and attribute no casual interpretation to it. We estimate a regression coefficient since correcting it for errors in variables is more straightforward than correcting a correlation estimate.

the method of moments estimator corrects the OLS estimator essentially for attenuation bias (the error in α).[14]

Table 3.13 reports the estimates from the second-stage regressions. Since the first stage uses the growth rate in the nominal housing price index, α_t includes the inflation rate, and so we first adjust $\hat{\alpha}_t$ by subtracting off the inflation rate. In the baseline specifications of column (1), which shows the "naïve" (OLS) coefficient, and column (2), which shows the method of moments estimator, we see that the coefficients on (the adjusted) $\hat{\alpha}_t$ are positive and statistically significant at the 1 percent level, consistent with our hypothesis. The coefficient of 0.047 implies that in a year in which house prices increase on average by 1 percent, the price in an MSA whose average commuting time is 2 standard-deviations longer than the sample mean (that is, 28 minutes instead of 22.4 minutes) will increase by about 26 percent $(0.047 * (28 - 22.4) \times 100$ percent) more than the average. The method of moments estimator is nearly exactly the same as the naïve estimator, since here the attenuation bias is small, as the year effects are precisely estimated relative to the large changes in overall housing prices over time.

The remaining columns in table 3.13 show that the positive and significant relationship between $\hat{\beta}_t$ and $\hat{\alpha}_t$ is robust to a number of specification changes. First, in column (3), we include the year variable in the second-stage regression to control for the time trend; the trend is insignificant, and the estimated commuting time effect is unaffected. Second, we address the concern that the first-stage regression for the baseline specification does not adequately control for other conditions that affect the elasticity of supply. In the next three columns, we consider the Wharton land regulation index and Saiz's undevelopable land share, by adding their interaction with the year dummies to the set of regressors. Column (5) shows the method of moments estimator, for which the estimated regression coefficient of $\hat{\beta}_t$ on $\hat{\alpha}_t$ is more than one-half that of previously, although it remains significant. Once again, adding a trend has no effect on the OLS estimate. Another determinant of supply elasticity is growth, as equation (3) shows. In columns (7) through (9) we add the interactions of population growth and average income growth to the set of regressors. The method of moments estimator is again reduced relative to the baseline, although less so, and it remains positive and significant. In the last set of columns, we add in both sets of alternative supply constraints. The results are like those in columns (4) through (6), where only the land regulation index and the undevelopable share are included.

Thus we can conclude that when prices rise overall, they rise more in high average commuting cities—a result predicted by the simple geometry of expanding areas, in the context of highly correlated and similarly sized MSA-level demand shocks. This result holds even when controlling for

---

14. This is not the case when we include other regressors. However, in practice, most of the bias comes from the attenuation component.

Table 3.13   Second-stage of the cross-MSA price variation analysis

	(1)	(2)	(3)	(4)	(5)	(6)	(7)	(8)	(9)	(10)	(11)	(12)
$\hat{\beta}_t$												
$\hat{\alpha}_t$	0.047	0.050	0.050	0.012	0.020	0.014	0.025	0.035	0.030	0.003	0.012	0.007
	(0.020)	(0.004)	(0.020)	(0.014)	(0.003)	(0.014)	(0.015)	(0.003)	(0.015)	(0.010)	(0.002)	(0.009)
Time trend	No	No	−0.0001	No	No	−0.00004	No	No	−0.00009	No	No	−0.00009
			(0.0001)			(0.00005)			(0.00006)			(0.00004)
Population and income controls	No	No	No	No	No	No	Yes	Yes	Yes	Yes	Yes	Yes
Other supply constraints	No	No	No	Yes	Yes	Yes	No	No	No	Yes	Yes	Yes
Estimation method	OLS	MOM	OLS	OLS	MOM	OLS	OLS	MOM	OLS	OLS	MOM	OLS

Notes: The independent variable is $\hat{\alpha}_t$, the estimated coefficient on I_t, the dummy variable for year t, adjusted for inflation. The dependent variable is $\hat{\beta}_t$, the estimate of the coefficient on the interaction of the (demeaned) average commuting time with I_t. Data sources for first stage: (1) MSA-level FHFA Office of Federal Housing Enterprise Oversight (OFHEO) house price indices (1976–2009), time averaged over the year. (2) Average commuting time from the 2000 Census data. The first-stage regression regresses lnHPI or ΔlnHPI on year MSA fixed effects, dummies, and the interactions of average commuting time and year dummies. "Population and income controls" refers to the interaction of population growth and average income growth with year dummies. "Other supply constraints" refers to the interaction of the WRLURI and Saiz's undevelopable land share with year dummies. MOM = method of moments.

regulatory and topological supply proxies that have previously been used in the literature.

3.3.3   Cross-MSA Variation in Building Permits

We now ask whether building activity increases more with prices in markets with low average commuting time, as we argued earlier. To test this, we estimate the following regression:

$$ln\text{PERMIT}_{it} = \alpha_0 ln\text{HPI}_{it} + \alpha_1 \Delta ln\text{HPI}_{it} + \beta\Delta ln\text{HPI}_{it} \times \text{COM}_i + \gamma' X_{it} + e_i + \varepsilon_{it},$$

where i indexes the metropolitan areas, t represents the years from 1990 to 2009, COM_i indicates the average commuting time in MSA i, $ln\text{HPI}_{it}$ indicates the inflation-adjusted log of the FHFA house price index in MSA i in year t, $\Delta ln\text{HPI}_{it}$ is its first difference, X_{it} is income and population and their growth rates, and e_i is an MSA fixed effect.

The coefficient α_1 indicates how construction activities are associated on average with price changes, while β captures how that association varies with average commuting time. Since, according to the argument we developed earlier, the elasticity of supply is decreasing in average commuting time, we expect β to be negative. As before, we expect permits to be most strongly correlated with the price changes rather than its level (Mayer and Somerville 2000), but we also include the price level to account for depreciation.

We present the estimates in table 3.14 using single-family permits (the estimates for total permits are very similar). Column (1) shows the regression without income and population. It shows a highly significant positive association between the price change and the level of permits, with every 1 percent increase in price growth associated with about a 4 percent increase in permits. As predicted by our theoretical argument, that relationship is

Table 3.14	Permit regressions				
	(1)	(2)	(3)	(4)	(5)
	Single-family permits				
ΔlnHPI	0.02	0.12	0.13	0.41	0.06
	(0.12)	(0.13)	(0.13)	(0.14)	(0.17)
Δ lnHPI	4.23	4.21	4.09	1.87	5.89
	(0.19)	(0.19)	(0.18)	(0.33)	(0.55)
lnHPI*COM	−0.095	−0.071	−0.074	−0.146	−0.25
	(0.046)	(.043)	(0.044)	(0.077)	(0.12)
Other controls		Income, population	Income, population Δ Income Δ Pop	Income, population	Income, population
Observations	2,559	2,559	2,559	1,173	846

Note: The building permits are obtained at the MSA level from the Census (1990–2009). All regressions include MSA fixed effects.

decreasing in the average commuting time in the MSA: a 1 standard deviation (2.8 minute) greater average commute decreases the predicted increase in single-family home permits given a 1 percent greater price growth rate from 4.16 percent to $(4.16 - 2.8 \times 0.095) \times 100$ percent = 3.89 percent. The price level is irrelevant. The magnitude of the coefficient on the interaction term falls somewhat, from $-.095$ to $-.071$, when income and population are added (column [2]), but is not further affected when their growth rates are also added (column [3]), and remains significant.

Because housing is a durable good, the argument that we laid out is most appropriate for positive demand shocks. Yet the relationship apparently holds for both positive and negative shocks. Column (4) restricts the sample to observations in which the (real) price index change is positive, which is two-thirds of the sample. The coefficient on the interaction term doubles in magnitude, to -0.15, and remains significant. Column (5) considers the remaining third of the sample, those with a fall in the price index. The estimated coefficient is, at -0.26, even larger in magnitude, and significant.[15]

3.4   Related Literature

Our work is related to several strands of the housing literature. First, it relates to the literature on MSA-level supply elasticity, which has received increasing attention over the last few years, after having been overshadowed by a much more voluminous literature on demand (e.g., Rosenthal 1999). Recent work has related housing supply elasticity to a number of factors, such as land use regulation (Linneman et al. 1990; Gyourko, Saiz, and Summers 2008) and the share of buildable land (Glaeser, Gyourko, and Saiz 2008; Saiz 2010). In our empirical cross-market analysis, we control for regulation and topography, but highlight the implications of a new supply elasticity proxy—commuting time, which essentially stems from differences in the urban form.

Second, prior research on spatial variation in house price movements has mostly focused on across-market differences. Examples include Glaeser, Gyourko, and Saiz (2008), Van Nieuwerburgh and Weill (2010), and Saiz (2010). As shown in this chapter and elsewhere (e.g., Guerrieri, Hartley, and Hurst 2010), there is significant and systematic within-city variation in house price growth. Thus, both the within-market and cross-market analysis are essential to understanding house price movements. Our work adds to this literature by looking at a single indicator of supply conditions whose variation within- and cross-markets determines the extent of the response of both price and quantity to demand in both contexts.

---

15. We drop the income and population growth terms in the split sample regressions as they are insignificant. The results are robust to including them or dropping the income and population levels.

Despite its importance, the literature on within-market house price movements is relatively thin. Case and Mayer (1995) and Case and Marynchenko (2002) examine house price movements during the 1980s and early 1990s across zip codes within Boston, Chicago, and Los Angeles. More recently, Landvoigt, Piazzesi, and Schneider (2012) use an assignment model to explain the greater appreciation of low-quality homes in San Diego. Guerrieri, Hartley, and Hurst (2010) explore house price changes across neighborhoods within Chicago, and find that poor areas adjacent to rich areas appreciate more quickly than other areas. Molloy and Shan (2010) use data on a large number of zip codes and municipalities from 1981 to 2008, and find that a 10 percent increase in gas prices leads to a 10 percent decrease in construction in locations with a long average commuting time relative to other locations, but to no significant change in house prices.

While both of these last two papers control for commuting time in the price analysis, the within-market analysis in this chapter differs from their analysis both in its focus and in its implementation. While their papers concentrate on the variation in demand-side determinants (neighborhood gentrification opportunities and the budget share of gas prices), ours is concerned with differing supply elasticities. In the implementation, our work differs in allowing the effect of commuting time to differ across years and MSAs, and, indeed, that is our focus.

As noted earlier, Green, Malpezzi, and Mayo (2005) also derive the supply elasticity from the Capozza and Helsley (1989) model. They estimate a supply elasticity for each MSA by the OLS estimate of an MSA-specific regression of permits per population on average prices, and then regress that estimate on a number of variables, including log population, a per unit distance commuting time (i.e., T), and a land use regulation proxy. Their sample is much smaller than ours, comprising only forty-five MSAs.

3.5 Conclusion

Recent work by Glaeser, Gyourko, and Saiz (2008) has shown, both theoretically and empirically, that house prices increase more during housing booms in places where housing supply is less elastic. In this chapter, we follow their insight and explore the role of a new supply proxy—commuting time—in explaining the within-market and cross-market variation in how house price varies with stages of the market cycle.

In the within-market analysis, we use self-reported home values from the 2005 to 2010 ACS samples to examine the changing relationship between housing price growth and commuting time. Consistent with the notion that building is easier to build at the city edge, we find that the price gradient became flatter in the bust, implying prices fell more in the center than at the city's edge. We do not, however, find any changing relationship over the short part of the boom (2005 to 2006/2007). These results are very similar to the findings on land prices in Haughwout et al.'s chapter 2 in this volume, although their distance metric—physical distance from the city's tallest building, grouped and normalized by the distribution of land transactions in each city—is different from ours, and they consider only fifteen large cities. Their table 2.4 shows no difference in the boom years increase in land prices between the middle half and the inner quarter, but a much greater fall for the inner quarter in the bust years.[16]

We also find that rents behave qualitatively in the same manner as values. Indeed, we are unable to reject the hypothesis that the price and rent gradients rotate to the exact same degree in the bust. However, the point estimates indicate that the rotation of the rent gradient is more muted than that of prices, which is what we expect from the bursting of an asset bubble, with some overhang effect on rents.

We also consider housing price growth across markets. We argue that the supply elasticity should be smaller in cities with larger average commuting time. Consistent with that, we find that when prices increase overall, prices rise more in MSAs with greater average commuting time, even when controlling for regulatory and topological supply constraint proxies previously used in the literature. We have also checked whether the cross effects of commuting time, and the supply constraints, can explain the finding in Sinai's chapter 1 in this volume that the cross-sectional dispersion in housing price growth is greater in booms, but we have found no significant relation between the variance and the mean of predicted price growth across years.

As a complementary analysis to that of prices, we also investigate how permits behave over the cycle. Within markets, we find no evidence that the log difference in permits issued in the central and noncentral counties of MSAs differ over that or other cycles. Across markets, however, we find that a given increase in prices is associated with a smaller increase in permits, the greater is average commuting time.

Since Rosenthal's (1999) lament on the limited work on the supply side of housing, a number of studies have identified regulation and topographical conditions as determinants of supply elasticity. Relying on both economic-spatial reasoning and empirical evidence broadly consistent with it, this chapter has shown commuting time, at both the cross-market and within-market level, to be an important determinant of supply elasticity as well.

References

Anas, A., and H. Rhee. 2007. "When Are Urban Growth Boundaries Not Second-Best Policies to Congestion Tolls?" *Journal of Urban Economics* 61:263–86.

16. The comparison of the middle half to the inner quarter is most akin to our gradient rotation, which compares predicted values at the median and zero commuting minutes. They are able to observe the boom from 2000 on.

Brueckner, J., and S. Rosenthal. 2009. "Gentrification and Neighborhood Housing Cycles: Will America's Future Downtowns Be Rich?" *The Review of Economics and Statistics* 91 (4): 724–43.

Bucks, B., and K. Pence. 2008. "Do Borrowers Know Their Mortgage Terms?" *Journal of Urban Economics* 64 (2): 218–33.

Buonaccorsi. 2010. *Measurement Error: Models, Methods, and Applications.* Boca Raton, FL: Chapman and Hall/CRC.

Burchfield, M., H. G. Overman, D. Puga, and M. A. Turner. 2006. "Causes of Sprawl: A Portrait from Space." *Quarterly Journal of Economics* 121 (2): 587–633.

Capozza, D., and R. Helsley. 1989. "The Fundamentals of Land Prices and Urban Growth." *Journal of Urban Economics* 26 (3): 295–306.

Case, K., and M. Marynchenko. 2002. "Home Appreciation in Low- and Moderate-Income Markets." In *Low Income Homeownership: Examining the Unexamined Goal,* edited by Nicolas Retsinas and Eric Belsky. Cambridge, MA, and Washington, DC: Joint Center for Housing Studies at Harvard University and Brookings Institution Press.

Case, K., and C. Mayer. 1995. "The Housing Cycle in Eastern Massachusetts: Variation among Cities and Towns." *New England Economic Review* March/April: 24–40.

Cotter, J., S. Gabriel, and R. Roll. 2011. "Integration and Contagion in US Housing Markets." October 18. Available at Social Science Research Network: http://ssrn .com/abstract=1945975.

DiPasquale, D., and C. T. Somerville. 1995. "Do House Price Indices Based on Transacting Units Represent the Entire Stock? Evidence from the American Housing Survey." *Journal of Housing Economics* 4 (3): 195–229.

Fuller, W. 1987. *Measurement Error Models.* Hoboken, NJ: John Wiley and Sons.

Genesove, D. 2003. "Nominal Rigidity in Apartment Rents." *Review of Economics and Statistics* 85 (4): 844–53.

Glaeser, E., J. Gyourko, and A. Saiz. 2008. "Housing Supply and House Bubbles." *Journal of Urban Economics* 64 (2): 198–217.

Glaeser, E., and B. Ward. 2009. "The Causes and Consequences of Land Use Regulation: Evidence from Greater Boston." *Journal of Urban Economics* 65 (3): 265–78.

Green, R., S. Malpezzi, and S. Mayo. 2005. "Metropolitan-Specific Estimates of the Price Elasticity of Supply of Housing and Their Sources." *American Economic Review P&P* 95 (2): 334–39.

Guerrieri, V., D. Hartley, and E. Hurst. 2010. "Endogenous Gentrification and Housing Price Dynamics." NBER Working Paper no. 16237. Cambridge, MA: National Bureau of Economic Research.

Gyourko, J., A. Saiz, and A. Summers. 2008. "A New Measure of the Local Regulatory Environment for Housing Markets: The Wharton Residential Land Use Regulatory Index." *Urban Studies* 45:693.

Kiel, K., and J. Zabel. 1999. "The Accuracy of Owner-Provided House Values: The 1978–1991 American Housing Survey." *Real Estate Economics* 27 (2): 263–98.

Landvoigt, T., M. Piazzesi, and M. Schneider. 2012. "The Housing Market(s) of San Diego." NBER Working Paper no. 17723. Cambridge, MA: National Bureau of Economic Research.

Linneman, P., A. Summers, N. Brooks, and H. Buist. 1990. "The State of Local Growth Management." Harton Real Estate Working Paper no. 81. University of Pennsylvania.

Mayer, C., and T. Somerville. 2000. "Residential Construction: Using the Urban Growth Model to Estimate Housing Supply." *Journal of Urban Economics* 48 (1): 85–109.

Molloy, R., and H. Shan. 2010. "The Effects of Gasoline Prices on Household Location." Federal Reserve Board Finance and Economics Discussion Series Working Paper no. 2010-36.

Rosenthal, S. 1999. "Housing Supply: The Other Half of the Market." *Journal of Real Estate Finance and Economics* 18 (1): 5–8.

Saiz, A. 2010. "The Geographic Determinants of Housing Supply." *Quarterly Journal of Economics* 125 (3): 1253–96.

Van Nieuwerburgh, S., and P. Weill. 2010. "Why Has House Price Dispersion Gone up?" *Review of Economic Studies* 77 (4): 1567–606.

White, M. J. 1988. "Urban Commuting Journeys Are Not 'Wasteful.'" *Journal of Political Economy* 96 (5): 1097–110.

4

Mortgage Financing in the Housing Boom and Bust

Benjamin J. Keys, Tomasz Piskorski, Amit Seru, and Vikrant Vig

4.1 Introduction

The recent domestic financial crisis has become a global phenomenon. With "crisis-like" events unfolding on a regular basis around the world, it is easy to forget that the financial crisis started with the US subprime mortgage market. This is the same part of the market that not so long ago was heralded as a financial innovation that would help propel millions of additional households toward achieving the American Dream. For the first half of the 2000s, it appeared that the American Dream was coming true for more and more households, as the housing market boomed and the home ownership rate hit an all-time high of 69 percent in 2004.

Over the boom period, however, the traditional methods of mortgage finance were undergoing a series of dramatic changes. While mortgages had

Benjamin J. Keys is assistant professor in the Harris School of Public Policy at the University of Chicago. Tomasz Piskorski is the Edward S. Gordon Associate Professor of Real Estate and Finance at Columbia Business School. Amit Seru is associate professor of finance and Neubauer Faculty Fellow at the Booth School of Business, University of Chicago, and a faculty research fellow of the National Bureau of Economic Research. Vikrant Vig is associate professor of finance at London Business School.

This chapter was prepared for the NBER's "Housing and the Financial Crisis" conference on November 17 and 18, 2011. We thank Edward Glaeser, Joseph Gyourko, Chris Mayer, Brian Melzer, Todd Sinai, Shane Sherlund, anonymous external reviewers, and participants at NBER preconference meetings for useful suggestions. We are grateful to Equifax, BlackBox Logic, 1010Data, and Zillow for their data, research support, and infrastructure that were invaluable for the analysis in this chapter. Daniel Hubbard, Laura Vincent, and James Witkin provided excellent research assistance. Piskorski acknowledges the funding from the Paul Milstein Center for Real Estate at Columbia Business School and the National Science Foundation. Seru acknowledges the funding from the Institute of Global Markets at the Booth School of Business at the University of Chicago. For acknowledgments, sources of research support, and disclosure of the authors' material financial relationships, if any, please see http://www.nber.org/chapters/c12624.ack.

been fixed- or adjustable-rate in the past, nontraditional products, such as hybrid adjustable-rate mortgages (ARMs) and negative amortization contracts, appeared on the scene. Previously rare mortgage products, such as low documentation loans, became commonplace. Borrowers now faced challenging decisions about what type of mortgage was right for them. These new products were financed largely through the expansion of private label securitization, which developed its own set of guidelines, norms, and partici-pants beyond the scope of Fannie Mae and Freddie Mac (the government-sponsored enterprises, or GSEs). The share of subprime mortgages in total originations increased from 6 percent in 2002 to 20 percent in 2006. As of 2006, the value of US subprime loans was estimated at $1.5 trillion, or 15 percent of the $10 trillion residential mortgage market.[1] And yet, just as quickly as these changes occurred, the mortgage market has reverted back to "conservative" underwriting standards, products, and financing in the current post-crisis environment.

In this overview, we trace the rapid evolution of mortgage financing from boom to bust and explore two crucial questions surrounding the market's rise and fall. First, why did the lending boom occur in the size and form that it did? Second, why has the foreclosure crisis been so cataclysmic, but also so heterogeneous across geography and loan types? We organize this chapter around these central questions.

First, in section 4.2, we present a broad set of descriptive statistics and facts regarding the rise and fall of the subprime mortgage market. The sub-prime market emerged in the late 1990s in a landscape dominated by the GSEs and traditional mortgage terms. We examine why financial innovation occurred in the time and form that it did. Next, we describe how innovation took two separate but complementary paths, through disintermediation and through mortgage contracts. The innovations of private label securitiza-tion had a meaningful impact on borrowers, lenders, and investors. These new channels of funding led to a rise in access to nontraditional mortgage products, which had significantly different features than those commonly found in the prime market. We discuss the trends in the availability of these products and the view of the market from its peak in 2006.

We then describe the subsequent housing bust, with an emphasis on the seismic impact that the housing crisis has had on mortgage finance. During the crisis, nontraditional mortgage products performed significantly worse than traditional mortgage contracts. We detail how this led to a collapse of the private label securitization market, and with it the disappearance of nontraditional mortgage products. The GSEs were put into conservator-ship by the federal government, but regained their market share back to over 90 percent of the market (in conjunction with the FHA). The thirty-

---

1. See Agarwal and Ho (2007).

year fixed rate mortgage dominated the post-crisis market, and still does today.

In section 4.3, we address the question of why there was a lending boom of this sort. We provide theoretical connections between the optimal financing choices of borrowers and lenders for the emergence of specific products, as well the development of the private label securitization channel for mortgage finance. These theories (e.g., Piskorski and Tchistyi 2010, 2011) also predict a connection between the concentration of these loans and borrowers' characteristics as well as regional house price movements, which are confirmed in the data.

This changed nature of lending had a broad impact on financial intermediation. In particular, we discuss the private securitization process and contrast it with the process used by the GSEs to create mortgage-backed securities. We argue further that, while these nontraditional products were made to inherently riskier borrowers, this is only part of the reason why these mortgages ended up with higher rates of default. We discuss empirical evidence that suggests that their high rates of default reflect not only the greater riskiness of these products and consumers on observable dimensions, but also the ex-ante impact of intermediation on lenders' screening incentives.

The motivation for this section derives from theories of financial intermediation that discuss the role of incentives to help solve moral hazard problems. In particular, balance sheet illiquidity provides a strong economic incentive for lenders to screen and monitor borrowers adequately (Diamond and Rajan 2001). We argue that ease of securitization—driven by the expansion of private label securitization—increased the liquidity of mortgage loans. This liquidity manifests itself on several empirically measurable dimensions such as securitization volume, securitization rates, and the time it takes to securitize a loan. Since securitization increases the liquidity of mortgage loans, a natural question of whether it blunts lenders' incentives to screen arises.

Indeed, the empirical evidence shows that greater loan liquidity did affect lenders' incentives to carefully screen borrowers. We discuss the results of a series of papers by Keys et al. (2009, 2010a, 2010b) and Keys, Seru, and Vig (2012) that provide empirical support for this view. We provide evidence on the heterogeneity of these effects by demonstrating that these effects were present (or easier to detect) among borrowers who took loans with more "soft information." Moreover, by contrasting this result with evidence from the GSE market and the full documentation non-GSE market, we argue that additional mechanisms—either through increased documentation requirements, better monitoring through representations and warranties, or reputational concerns—improved screening incentives of lenders when faced with differential ease of securitization.

More broadly, we discuss several other papers that demonstrate the altered structure of financial intermediation (e.g., Mian and Sufi 2009; Rajan, Seru, and Vig 2010; Loutskina and Strahan 2011). In particular, there was a shift in how much mortgage contracts relied on FICO and LTV (loan to value)—consistent with investors in the mortgage-backed securities (MBS) making decisions based solely on hard information variables. Moreover, we discuss evidence that identifies agency conflicts in the supply chain of credit. Here we emphasize the composition of originators contributing to the pool. We also discuss several papers that document changes to financial intermedia-tion as well as emphasize similar agency conflicts arising, particularly among privately securitized loans (e.g., Ashcraft and Schuermann 2008; Purnanan-dam 2011; Jiang, Nelson, and Vytlacil 2010; Nadauld and Sherlund 2009; and Demiroglu and James 2012).

We also ask if the regulatory structure in place was effective in curbing some of these conflicts. Our analysis shows that loans originated in securi-tization chains that were more heavily regulated performed *worse* than their less regulated counterparts—suggesting that regulation was largely ineffec-tual, findings that are consistent with those revealed in several congressional reports in the aftermath of the crisis.[2] Finally, we conclude this section of the chapter by discussing some of the broad themes that emerge from the empirical work, which have implications for designing private securitization markets going forward.

In section 4.4, we discuss the "prolonged" foreclosure crisis that has prompted a number of policy responses by the government. The crisis, in which house prices fell by 35 percent on average, led to a massive wave of foreclosures. Distressed borrowers who potentially could have renegotiated out of their delinquent (and often underwater) mortgages were rarely able to do so. Why was renegotiation so difficult? We outline two main factors for this difficulty. Both of these factors were aggravated with the general decline of the economy, which led to job losses and repayment problems for many households.

First, we discuss the ways in which aspects of financial intermediation made it more difficult to renegotiate. By its very nature, securitization induces separation of ownership (investors) and control (servicers/banks) of the agents responsible for conducting the renegotiations. The consequent coordination frictions between investors made it difficult to allow banks to conduct renegotiations, even if it may have improved their collective out-comes. We discuss overwhelming evidence in the literature that shows the importance of this factor in limiting renegotiation.

Second, we discuss another challenge to cost-effective mortgage renego-tiation: In practice, it may be difficult for the lenders and servicers to easily identify home owners who would default without help. Although millions of

---

2. The case of the Office of Thrift Supervision's (OTS's) turf war against the FDIC over the regulation of Washington Mutual is a well-known instance (see Agarwal, Lucca, et al. 2012).

home owners are "underwater" and therefore at risk of default, the majority of these home owners are still making timely mortgage payments and may continue doing so without receiving a mortgage modification.[3] It could be quite costly to extend benefits to all of these underwater home owners. One possible approach to this problem is to extend benefits only to home owners who are delinquent.[4] This approach, however, could induce home owners to default in order to obtain modification benefits even though they would not have defaulted otherwise. The extent of such "strategic" behavior crucially depends on the costs of delinquency and on the ability and willingness of households to behave strategically. We identify the extent of such strategic defaulters and argue that their intensity went up over time. We also discuss several factors (such as house prices, leverage) that are correlated with borrowers deciding to default while making payments on their other accounts. In addition, we also discuss recent research by Mayer et al. (2011) that provides empirical evidence that renegotiation programs *themselves* could also induce additional borrowers toward strategic behavior. Together, these findings suggest potential reasons why it may have been difficult for lenders to identify "eligible" borrowers to renegotiate with in a cost effective manner.

We conclude section 4.4 by discussing the nature of various federal programs that were implemented to curtail the foreclosure crisis. We discuss the objectives behind these programs and discuss recent research by Agarwal, Amromin, et al. (2012) that empirically evaluates the effects of the 2009 Home Affordable Modification Program (HAMP)—one of the largest policy interventions concerning residential mortgage debt that provided intermediaries (servicers) with sizable financial incentives to renegotiate mortgages. Their research suggests that the ability of government to quickly induce changes in the behavior of large intermediaries through financial incentives is quite limited, underscoring significant barriers to the effectiveness of such polices.

We end the chapter by providing a broad perspective on the future of mortgage finance and lessons learned from the last tumultuous decade. Our main takeaway is that the way in which mortgages were financed, above and beyond the characteristics of the individual loan or borrower, had an impact on both the likelihood that the loan was originated and the likelihood that the loan would be renegotiated. However, to be clear, securitization is an important innovation and should be a central part of the mortgage market going forward. The challenge now is to design the securitization chain so as to align incentives between borrowers, lenders, issuers, and investors.

3. See, for example, March 2011 Written Testimony of David H. Stevens, Assistant Secretary of Housing–Federal Housing Administration Commissioner, US Department of Housing and Urban Development.

4. For example, a number of modification programs have made benefits available only to home owners who failed to make at least two monthly mortgage payments (such homeowners are at least "sixty days delinquent"). See Citigroup (2009).

4.2   The Housing Boom and Bust

4.2.1   Growth in Private Label Securitization and the Changed Nature of Lending

The modern subprime market developed around the fringes of the prime market, with initial efforts in the mid-1990s to provide loans to borrowers who were credit-constrained, (temporarily) cash-flow constrained, or less creditworthy than the prime "conforming" standards. These loans generally required less money down than prime loans, and thus carried higher interest rates to offset additional risk.

Figure 4.1 shows the volume of subprime originations over time, as compared to the GSEs, Jumbo, and Alt-A loans (the figure includes both purchase and refinance loans). Loans with these types of subprime term structures were relatively new, so little was known about how borrowers

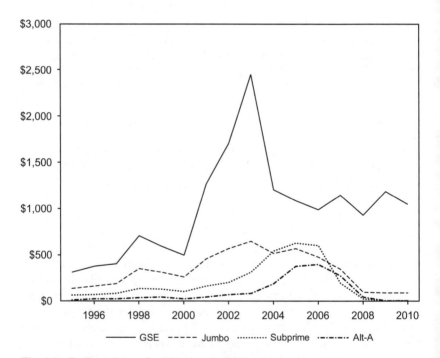

Fig. 4.1   Dollar volume of originations in GSE and private market

Source: www.insidemortgagefinance.com.

Notes: This figure presents the volume of originations (in billions of dollars), both purchase and refinance mortgages, by segment of the mortgage market from 1995 to 2010. The spike in GSE originations in 2002 and 2003 reflects the refinance boom during that period. Subprime originations increased from near zero in the late 1990s to over $500 billion during the peak years of the boom (2004 to 2006).

would repay. Loans began to default at a faster than anticipated rate in the late 1990s, in conjunction with the dot-com bubble and the turmoil in world markets, and the market briefly scaled back its operations. However, house prices continued to increase and interest rates dropped in the early 2000s, and the subprime market revived rapidly. As house prices rose, potentially distressed borrowers were able to either sell their home or refinance into a new mortgage, obscuring any weaknesses with the structure or sale of these new nontraditional mortgage products (Belsky and Richardson 2010). Not until house prices began to fall did the weaknesses of these products become fully apparent (Demyanyk and Van Hemert 2009). Overall, during 2001 to 2006 the dollar volume of subprime originations ballooned from $65 billion in 1995 to over $500 billion by 2006 (www.insidemortgagefinance.com). By 2006, the subprime market was 20 percent of the overall market (by origination volume), up from 6 percent in 2001.

Figure 4.2 shows that not only were there more loans originated but also that more of them were securitized to the private market: subprime/Alt-A

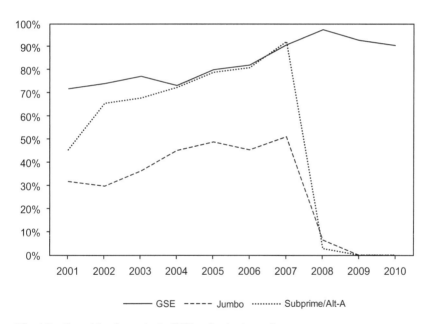

Fig. 4.2   Securitization rates in GSE and private market

Source: www.insidemortgagefinance.com.

Notes: This figure presents securitization rates of conforming loans sold to the GSEs, Jumbo loans, and subprime/Alt-A loans. The GSE loans were more likely to be securitized over the housing boom, but Jumbo and subprime/Alt-A both increased their rates of securitization far more dramatically. Securitization rates of subprime/Alt-A loans rose from less than 50 percent in 2001 to over 80 percent in 2006. The graph shows the collapse of the nonprime market in 2008, as loans originated outside of the purview of the GSEs are generally no longer securitized.

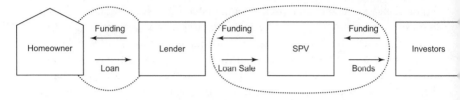

Fig. 4.3   Securitization process in the private market

Notes: This figure provides a simplistic view of the securitization process of subprime residential backed-mortgage securities. After a potential home owner approaches a lender for a mortgage, the lender screens the borrower based on information variables such as credit scores and other indicators of potential financial health of the borrower. Once a loan contract has been accepted, the loans are pooled together in a deal by an issuer. The deal is then tranched and rated before being sold to investors. After sale, the payments and day-to-day management of the deal are handled by the trustee of the SPV. The deals usually have several credit enhancements, which potentially allow the deal to achieve a high rating.

securitization rates went up from less than 50 percent in 2001 to over 80 percent by 2006 (also see Chomsisengphet and Pennington-Cross 2006).

What does private securitization entail? Figure 4.3 provides a stylized description of this process. After a potential borrower approaches a lender for a mortgage, the lender screens the borrower based on information such as credit scores and other indicators of potential financial health of the borrower. Once a loan contract has been accepted, the loans are pooled together in a deal by an issuer. The deal is then tranched and rated before being sold to investors. After sale, the trustee of the SPV (Special Purpose Vehicle) handles the payments and day-to-day management of the deal. The deals usually have several credit enhancements that potentially allow portions of the deal to achieve a high rating. The most popular of these is overcollateralization, where a collateral cushion "over" what was pledged to investors was kept in the deal.

It is worth noting that this process differed from the well-established GSE securitization process. First, the sale in private securitization does not ensure investors from default risk. Second, and more importantly, lenders who sell loans to the GSEs must follow strict guidelines. Their large size allows the GSEs to coordinate and implement standardized practices across various agents in the supply chain of credit. We will reiterate these differences both when we discuss some of our results on the relationship between securitization and screening (section 4.3.2), between securitization and loan renegotiation (section 4.4), and also in our discussion of lessons drawn from the evidence presented in this overview (section 4.5). We now describe the evolution of each of the agents in the supply chain of credit—borrowers, lenders, and investors—over the boom period in turn.

Borrowers

The best way to show how borrowers financed by the subprime market changed during the boom period is to plot average loan characteristics over time. First, we present the time series of average credit scores across three groups of nonprime borrowers. We focus our attention on the category of "subprime" borrowers, defined here based on the B&C classification of securitized loan pools in the Loan Performance (LP) database. For comparison, we provide information on credit scores on parts of nonprime mortgage segments that followed underwriting standards closer to the GSEs (Alt-A and Jumbo loans). As is evident from figure 4.4, part A, relative to Alt-A and Jumbo loan borrowers, subprime borrowers had significantly lower credit scores (Mayer, Pence, and Sherlund 2009). However, average FICO scores were largely constant in these three subsections of the nonprime market over time. One could also make comparisons with the average credit scores of GSE borrowers over the same time period and reach similar conclusions.

Second, borrowers were able to increase their leverage and decrease their monthly payments by using these new products. As shown in part B of figure 4.4, while the leverage on the first-lien on the homes grew early on, it stabilized around 87 percent. However, there was also a massive increase in the debt taken on second liens (see also Mian and Sufi 2010). The combined LTV (CLTV, which measures the debt from both the first and second liens) increased from 85 percent to 95 percent between 2001 and 2006 (averaged for loans that report CLTV), a finding that is similar to figures reported in Sherlund (2008). This result has been interpreted in the literature as willingness by lenders to provide easier credit—partly due to high house price growth expectations—to borrowers who were willing to buy larger houses and investors who were willing to buy multiple houses.

Third, there was also a dramatic change in the nature of credit on another margin. Lenders were also increasingly willing to reduce the documentation requirements for loans. "Low documentation" mortgages, where less information was collected and verified on potential borrowers' income and assets, had once been extremely rare and usually reserved for high-income, high-wealth entrepreneurs who had difficulty documenting their resources. As investors came to accept FICO and LTV as sufficient statistics for loan default (Rajan, Seru, and Vig 2010), more borrowers provided less documentation. Part C of figure 4.4 shows the dramatic rise in the proportion of loans with incomplete documentation. Prior to 2000, fewer than 20 percent of new subprime loans were originated with low or no documentation; by 2006, this figure approached a full 50 percent of new subprime originations.

Lenders

Changes to the process of financial intermediation came about concurrently with changes in the composition of mortgage lenders. In contrast to lenders that followed the model of originating the loans as per GSE guidelines and selling to GSEs, lenders in this segment catered primarily to the private market. The largest subprime lenders financed their mortgages through a line of credit, and generally did not intend to retain loans on their books. The subprime lending market was concentrated, with the top

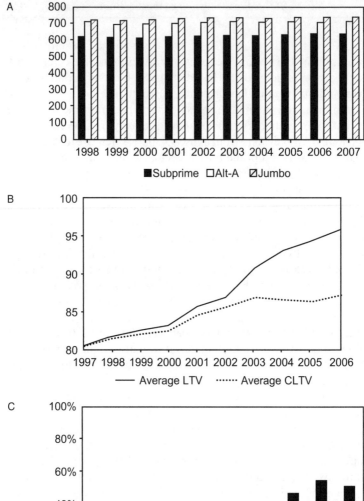

Fig. 4.4 Evolution of FICO, LTV/CLTV, and percent low documentation loans in private market

Source: LP database.

Notes: This figure shows the changes to basic borrower and loan quality during the housing boom. Part A shows the average FICO score of borrowers for three types of loans. Although subprime borrowers had lower scores on average than Alt-A or Jumbo borrowers, there was very little change in either the level or difference over the course of the boom. In contrast, part B shows the dramatic increase in CLTV ratios over the boom. While average LTV rose in the late 1990s and early 2000s, CLTV rose sharply beginning in 2003. Part C presents the percent of loans made without complete documentation in the private market. The fraction of low documentation loans peaked at over 50 percent of the private market in 2006.

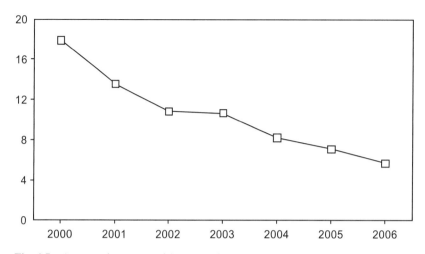

Fig. 4.5   Average time to securitize a loan in private market

Notes: This figure reports the mean time (in months) between origination and securitization for loans sold in the private market. The sample of loans is securitized subprime deals in LoanPerformance database. The figure shows a progressive reduction in how "quickly" a loan could be sold to investors over time starting in 2000. On average, a loan that could be sold only in a year in 2002 was sold within five months during the peak of the subprime boom.

twenty-five lenders originating over 80 percent of all loans (in dollar terms) in the peak years, up from 60 percent in 2001 (www.insidemortgagefinance .com). These lenders tended to be specialists and sold relatively few loans to the GSEs (e.g., New Century, Ameriquest).

The change in the nature of financial intermediation can be observed in two ways. First, banks kept progressively fewer loans on their balance sheets over the housing boom. This can be seen from figure 4.2 regarding the trend in securitization rates over this period. Second, there was also a change in the speed with which these loans could be sold to the private markets. Figure 4.5 shows that on average it took over sixteen months to sell loans in 2000. However, this number saw a 300 percent reduction by 2006, to only five months' average time to sale. As we will argue in section 5.3.2, these changes had a dramatic effect on the nature of financial intermediation in this market.

Investors

While it is hard to provide any substantial data on whether there was a change in the nature of investors in mortgage-backed securities, we do provide one piece of evidence that is suggestive. In figure 4.6, we plot the average number of tranches into which cash flows of each pool in a given vintage year were divided. We collect information on the number of tranches across all subprime pools in a given year from Bloomberg. As can be observed from figure 4.6, the average number of tranches increased by roughly 150 percent from 2001 to 2006—increasing from about eight tranches to about twenty-five

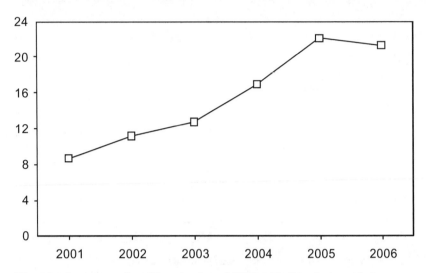

Fig. 4.6   Average number of tranches in an MBS pool in the private market

Notes: This figure reports the mean number of tranches across all the securitized subprime deals in the LoanPerformance database. We also cross-check that these tranches are similar to those reported in Bloomberg. In case of discrepancy, we do drop the deal. We did not get reliable information for 2000. As can be observed, there is a dramatic increase in number of tranches backed by the mortgage collateral progressively from 2001 to 2006.

per pool. This evidence suggests that there was a change in the clienteles that purchased the bonds backed by subprime collateral from 2001 to 2006.

This evidence is also consistent with the popular narrative that there was a change in the nature of credit supply driven by the global savings glut (as described, for instance, by Buiter 2008) as well as several regulated investors (like pension funds and insurance companies). In part, it has been argued that these investors were attracted to an asset that was rated AAA by the ratings agencies but also provided a better return than the low prevailing Treasury rates. We do not know of any research that provides direct and systematic evidence on the changes to the composition of investors in mortgage-backed securities during this period.

4.2.2   The Growing Importance of Less Traditional Mortgages

The increase in private label securitization and growth in prominence of less creditworthy, riskier borrowers was accompanied by significant innovations in mortgage design. While the traditional thirty-year fixed-rate mortgage remained a popular instrument, especially among more creditworthy borrowers, other less-traditional instruments gained market share beginning in the early 2000s. While nontraditional mortgages have been used in the past to some degree, during the boom of the 2000s these products were predominately offered to less creditworthy borrowers, allowing them easier access to credit. Most of these new loans were financed though the private label securitization channel. As we discuss in section 4.2.3, these nontraditional mortgages performed significantly worse than traditional mortgage contracts during the housing crisis.

Nontraditional mortgages can be classified in two main product categories. The first category of loans are short-term hybrid ARMs such as 2/28 and 3/27 loans, which carry a lower introductory "teaser" rate for the first two (or three) years, after which the rate typically resets to a higher, fully indexed level, for the remaining twenty-eight (or twenty-seven) years of the loan term. The second category consists of loans with a nontraditional amortization structure such as option ARMs or interest only loans. Unlike traditional fixed-rate mortgages (FRMs) or adjustable-rate mortgages (ARMs), option ARMs let borrowers pay only the interest portion of the debt or even less than that, while the loan balance can grow above the amount initially borrowed up to a certain limit, resulting in negative amortization. Under an interest-only loan, the borrower pays only the interest rate on the principal balance, with the principal balance unchanged, for a set term (usually five or ten years). At the end of the interest-only term, the principal balance is amortized for the remaining term. Finally, unlike traditional loans given to prime borrowers, many of these nontraditional mortgages carried costly prepayment penalties.

Short-term hybrid loans were the most popular category among subprime loans. Figure 4.7 shows the concentration of short-term hybrid adjustable

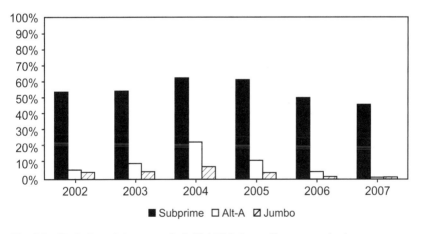

Fig. 4.7   Evolution of short-term hybrid ARMs by credit category in the private market

Source: LP database.

Notes: This figure shows the fraction of loans with short-term hybrid ARMs (2/28 or 3/27) by credit category in the nonprime market during the housing boom. These types of loans were particularly popular among subprime borrowers. Short-term hybrids made up more than half of all subprime originations during the boom years. This product was rarely used among Jumbo loans, and peaked in 2004 with 20 percent of the Alt-A market, but was generally not used as frequently as in the subprime market.

rate mortgages with a teaser rate period of up two years among subprime, Alt-A,[5] and most creditworthy (Jumbo) nonagency securitized loans. As we observe from figure 4.7, short-term hybrid adjustable-rate mortgages were most prevalent among subprime borrowers and overall accounted for more than half of these loans. Including the longer-term hybrid mortgages such as 3/27 ARMs, hybrid loans constitute more than 70 percent of all privately securitized subprime loans. Also we observe that these loans came into significant use among more creditworthy Alt-A borrowers in the 2003 to 2005 period, accounting for as much as 20 percent of all Alt-A loans originated in 2004. Few of these loans were given to most creditworthy Jumbo borrowers. By 2007, these loans became less popular and were limited almost exclusively to subprime borrowers. We also note that as the origination of subprime loans dramatically increased during the housing boom in the 2000s, so did the share of short-term hybrid loans among all loans originated during this period.

Loans with nontraditional amortization structures such as option ARMs or interest-only loans also experienced rapid growth during the housing boom in the 2000s. From 2003 through 2005, the originations of these loans grew from less than 10 percent of residential mortgage originations to about 30 percent.[6] Option adjustable-rate mortgages experienced particularly dramatic growth. They accounted for as little as 0.5 percent of all mortgages written in 2003, but their share soared to more than 12 percent of all originations in 2006 (LoanPerformance).

Figure 4.8 shows the concentration of loans with negative amortization among subprime, Alt-A, and Jumbo nonagency securitized loans. While the short-term hybrid loans were mostly a subprime product, negative-amortization loans were by far the most common among Alt-A borrowers. Barely any subprime borrowers took out negative-amortization loans, and no more than 10 percent of jumbo borrowers received these mortgages. Negative-amortization loans went from being relatively uncommon products in 2002 to capturing almost 40 percent of the Alt-A market in 2007, mostly due to a dramatic increase in 2004.

Similarly, figure 4.9 shows the concentration of loans with interest-only repayment structures among subprime, Alt-A, and Jumbo nonagency securitized loans. Interest-only loans were generally concentrated among most creditworthy borrowers, though not exclusively. For much of the sample period, more than half of new Jumbo loans followed an interest-only payment schedule, as did around 40 percent of Alt-A loans. By 2007, interest-only mortgages were almost as common among Alt-A borrowers as among more creditworthy borrowers.

---

5. The Alt-A category consists of loans that, for various reasons, are considered by lenders to be more risky than prime mortgages and less risky than subprime mortgages.
6. See Government Accountability Office (2006).

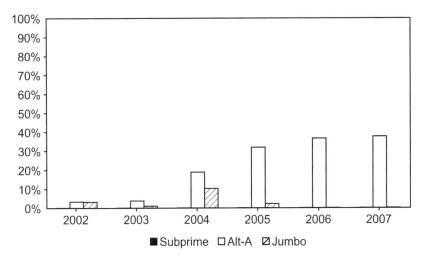

Fig. 4.8   Evolution of negative amortization loans by credit category in the private market

Source: LP database.

Notes: This figure shows the popularity of negative amortization loans in the private market. These loans were largely an Alt-A phenomenon and grew in popularity at the tail end of the housing boom, especially in high house price appreciation markets.

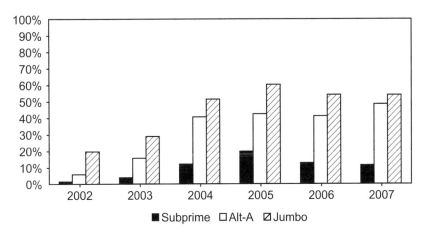

Fig. 4.9   Evolution of interest-only loans by credit category in the private market

Notes: This figure presents the use of interest-only loans in the nonprime mortgage market during the housing boom. Interest-only loans were extremely common in both the Alt-A and Jumbo segments but much less so in the subprime market. In 2005, over 50 percent of all Jumbo loans had an interest-only structure, while 40 percent of Alt-A loans had this structure.

Finally, we note that this growth in usage of nontraditional mortgages was accompanied by a significant increase in the usage of prepayment penalties. These clauses have been almost exclusively concentrated among less creditworthy borrowers (subprime and Alt-A). For example, among the 2/28 ARM loans originated in the 2003 to 2006 period more than 74 percent of these loans carry prepayment penalties. On the other hand, among Jumbo borrowers (who have stronger credit profiles) these clauses are virtually non-existent, with less than 3 percent of these loans having such clauses (www.loanperformance.com).

4.2.3   The Housing Bust and the Fall of Subprime Lending

House prices peaked in early 2006, and thereafter turned sharply downward. As figure 4.10 shows, by the end of 2008, national average house prices had fallen more than 30 percent from their peak, according to the Case-Shiller index. This precipitous decline exposed borrowers who had bought nontraditional products, put little money down, and anticipated to easily refinance before payments increased. These borrowers were quickly underwater on their mortgages and began to go into serious delinquency and enter the foreclosure process.

Figure 4.10 also shows the cumulative inventory of loans in foreclosure by product type. We observe that the percentage of loans in foreclosure has increased since 2008 for all product types, and the riskiest mortgages have been hit the hardest. For the universe of US residential mortgages, the cumulative foreclosure rate is 4.1 percent, yet nearly 15 percent of subprime loans and 19 percent of option ARMs are now in foreclosure. Conversely, the cumulative foreclosure rate for agency prime loans, traditionally seen as the

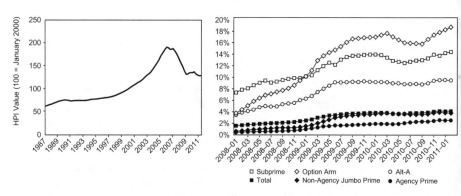

Fig. 4.10   National house price index and total cumulative foreclosure starts by product type

Source: LPS.

Notes: This figure shows the national house price index using S&P/Case–Shiller data for the period 1987 to 2011 in the left panel. The right panel presents cumulative foreclosure starts by different product category types starting 2008.

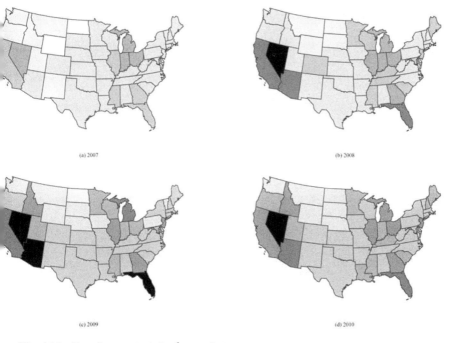

Fig. 4.11 Foreclosure starts by year and state

Source: Mortgage Bankers Association data on quarterly foreclosures across states.

Notes: The foreclosure start percentage values range from 0.97 to 13.85, white being the lowest and black the highest. North Dakota consistently has the lowest rate of foreclosure starts for each year, including the minimum of 0.97 in 2007. The maximum foreclosure start percentage of 13.85 is seen in Nevada in 2009, which has the highest rate of foreclosure starts in all years except 2007, in which Michigan holds the highest foreclosure start rate of 4.56.

safest group of mortgages, is a relatively modest 3.5 percent (although still substantially elevated relative to its historical average). We see that option ARMs were initially less likely to be in foreclosure than subprime loans, but this trend dramatically reversed over the past three years. This is likely due to the exhaustion of negative amortization limits of option ARMs that temporarily allowed for heavily reduced interest payments.

Figure 4.11 shows foreclosure starts by state for 2007 to 2010. The percentage values of outstanding loans starting the foreclosure process range from 0.97 to 13.85, with white being the lowest, and increasing in density to black as the highest. North Dakota consistently has the lowest rate of foreclosure starts for each year, including the minimum of 0.97 in 2007. The maximum foreclosure start percentage of 13.85 is seen in Nevada in 2009, which has the highest rate of foreclosure starts in all years except 2007, when Michigan took the top spot with a foreclosure start rate of 4.56. Figure 4.12 shows the inventory of loans in foreclosure by state in the same period (measured in Q2 of each year). The foreclosure inventory values range from

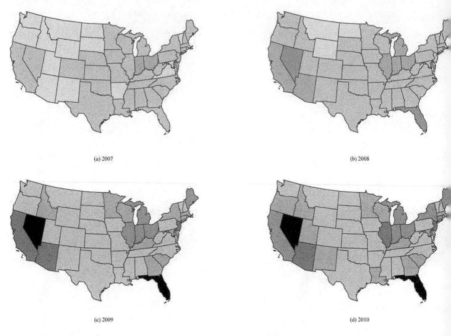

(a) 2007

(b) 2008

(c) 2009

(d) 2010

Fig. 4.12   Foreclosure inventory by year and state

Source: Mortgage Bankers Association data on quarterly foreclosures across states.

Notes: The foreclosure inventory percentage values range from 0.47 to 14.04, light gray being the lowest and black the highest. The lowest inventory percentage of 0.47 is in Oregon in Q2:2007, with North Dakota consistently having the lowest foreclosure inventory percentage for each Q2:2008, Q2:2009, and Q2:2010. The maximum foreclosure inventory percentage of 14.04 is seen in Florida in Q2:2010. Florida also has the highest foreclosure inventory percentage in Q2:2008 and Q2:2009, while Ohio holds the Q2:2007 maximum for foreclosure inventory percentage at 3.6.

0.47 to 14.04 percent, with white being the lowest, and increasing in density to black as the highest. The lowest foreclosure inventory percentage of 0.47 is in Oregon in 2007, with North Dakota consistently having the lowest foreclosure inventory percentage for each of the other years. The maximum foreclosure inventory percentage of 14.04 is seen in Florida in 2010. Florida also has the highest percentage in 2008 and 2009, while Ohio holds the 2007 maximum at 3.6 percent.

It is clear from figure 4.12 that the inventory of homes in foreclosure increased during the period between 2007 and 2010. In 2007, the inventory was largely concentrated in the Midwest, particularly in Indiana and Ohio, states that had been hit hard by unemployment due to the decline of the manufacturing sector. However, as time passed, the foreclosure inventory in these states remained relatively constant, while the heaviest foreclosure load moved into the states characterized by a dramatic housing bubble, such as Nevada, Florida, California, and Arizona. Generally, the same states that show high inventory growth also have high growth in foreclosure starts (figure 4.11), suggesting that inventory growth had more to do with an increase in the number of loans entering foreclosure than a bottleneck in the system preventing foreclosures from being processed and sold. With more recent data, we would potentially be able to see the effects of the "robo-signing" litigation and foreclosure moratoria on growth in foreclosure inventories.

Figures 4.11 and 4.12 also indicate that there is significant geographic dispersion in foreclosure rates. We observe high foreclosure rates in states such as Arizona, California, and Florida. On the other hand, foreclosure rates are low in states such as Colorado and Kansas. This geographical dispersion in foreclosure starts is closely related to the geographical dispersion in the extent of housing boom and bust. States with high house price appreciation and subsequent price collapse have experienced much higher rates of foreclosures compared to the states where changes in house prices were less pronounced. For example, as figure 4.13 indicates, Miami experienced a very significant boom and bust in house prices in 2000s, while Denver saw much more moderate house price changes in the same period. Correspondingly, as we observe from figures 4.11 and 4.12, foreclosures are high in Florida and low in Colorado.

As a wave of delinquencies and foreclosures swept through the states with the largest house price bubbles, MBS and collateralized debt obligations (CDO) markets suffered severe losses. Many of these delinquencies wiped

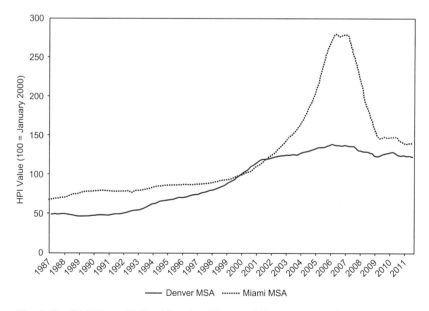

Fig. 4.13   S&P/Case–Shiller Miami and Denver MSA house price indices
Source: S&P/Case–Shiller data.

out subordinated tranches and even tranches that were designated triple-A by the rating agencies lost significant value. As investors developed an understanding of the risk of existing loan pools and the difficulty in pricing these pools in the midst of a declining market, the private market for mortgage-backed securities suffered a massive contraction. Whereas over $1 trillion was privately securitized in 2005 (subprime + Alt-A + Jumbo), there were essentially no private securitization deals in 2008 (see figures 4.1 and 4.2).

Private label securitization was no longer a viable distribution channel for mortgages, and this financial innovation was effectively discontinued for the time being. Banks either ceased to originate the types of loans that were previously distributed to the nonagency secondary market, or else originated the loan with the intent to hold them on their balance sheets (or to be sold if/when the private market returns).

In September 2008, the federal government took both Fannie Mae and Freddie Mac into conservatorship, effectively nationalizing over $5 trillion in MBS and guarantees. The GSEs were allowed to continue to guarantee MBS and also to purchase securities to keep their portfolio roughly constant in size. Fannie and Freddie sharply tightened underwriting standards and broadly instituted "declining market" policies to avoid making loans in markets with falling house prices. The new conforming standard became lower LTV ratios, higher FICO scores, and full documentation and verification of income and assets. Recent congressional efforts have been made to reduce the conforming loan limit as well.

With the private market shut down and Fannie and Freddie constrained by conservatorship, the Federal Housing Administration (FHA) stepped in to fill the financing void. The FHA was largely on the sidelines during the housing boom of the early 2000s, in part due to federal limits on the size of their loans that did not keep pace with the conforming limit. The Economic Stimulus Act of 2008 raised limits on the size of FHA-guaranteed loans, and the agency has continued to offer high LTV loans (97 percent) to high-quality, full documentation borrowers. In 2009 and 2010, the FHA backed 24 percent of all originations, which were subsequently securitized through Government National Mortgage Association (GNMA) pools.

By tightening underwriting standards, the second dimension of financial innovation—nontraditional mortgage products—also went into dormancy. Nearly all loans originated after the crisis have been thirty-year fixed-rate mortgages, with only 8 percent of new originations as ARMs in 2009 and 2010, and essentially no originations of nontraditional products such as interest-only or low documentation loans that proliferated during the boom years.

The crisis may have temporarily halted financial innovation in the mortgage market, or even reversed its course, but these innovations continue to have a direct impact on borrowers. First, borrowers with nontraditional products have been much more likely to go into default and subsequent foreclosure. Furthermore, in section 4.4, we describe the role of the securitization chain on the foreclosure process and the frictions introduced when a borrower's delinquent mortgage is owned by a dispersed group of investors. But before we investigate the housing bust, we will explore why subprime products emerged in the first place.

4.3   Subprime Products' Emergence and Impact

High default rates among and big losses to lenders and investors in the declining housing market have focused academics' and policymakers' interests on nontraditional mortgage products. One can broadly think of two ways of justifying the emergence of these new products, mostly financed by the private label securitization market. According to the efficiency view, the emergence of these products represented a financial innovation that relaxed households' borrowing constraints in a way that benefited both borrowers and lenders (at least from ex ante perspective, given their possibly overly optimistic expectations regarding the evolution of key variables such as house prices). The alternative view is that these products were designed or misused so that some market participants (e.g., lenders, underwriters) could benefit at the expense of others (e.g., borrowers, MBS investors). We now discuss these views in turn and discuss some empirical evidence that lends support to both of these views.

4.3.1   An Efficiency View of Mortgage Product Development

According to the efficiency explanation, either markets had limited efficiency before the development of these products or the underlying economic environment changed sufficiently to justify such development. Consequently, nontraditional mortgages have facilitated an extension of credit to riskier borrowers benefiting both borrowers and lenders (at least from the ex ante perspective).

There are several theoretical papers supporting this view. Piskorski and Tchistyi (2011) provide a formal analysis of optimal mortgage design in a dynamic setting with stochastic growth in house price and income, costly foreclosure, and a risky borrower who requires incentives to repay his debt. They show that in such a setting the features of optimal lending from the perspective of borrowers and lenders are parallel to some key aspects of subprime mortgages.[7] In particular, during an economic boom when house prices (and borrowers' incomes) are expected to grow it is optimal to extend credit to less creditworthy borrowers, provide them with lower initial payments set to increase over time, and increase borrowers' access to credit as their houses appreciate. This maximizes the benefits of house price appre-

---

7. See also Makarov and Plantin (2011), who study loans with teaser rates in equilibrium with myopic borrowers.

ciation for the borrower and lender.[8] Their model also predicts that a housing slump would result in the tightening of borrowers' access to credit, a foreclosure wave among the least creditworthy, and increased mortgage modification efforts.

In a related analysis, Piskorski and Tchistyi (2010) study optimal mortgage design in a dynamic setting with costly foreclosure, stochastic market interest rate, and a borrower with risky income who requires incentives to repay his debt. They show that the features of the optimal mortgage in such a setting are consistent with an adjustable-rate mortgage with negative amortization (such as an option ARM). The negative amortization provides flexibility for the borrower to cover possible low income realizations, which in turn lowers chances of default inefficiencies. The adjustable interest rate also allows for more efficient management of default risk. Gains from using the optimal contract relative to simpler mortgages are the biggest for those who face more income variability, buy expensive houses given their income level, or make little or no down payment.

The analysis of Piskorski and Tchistyi (2011) implies that mortgages with deferred payments, such as 2/28 and 3/27 ARMs or negative amortization loans, should be more prevalent in locations with higher expected house price and income growth. Also such loans should be concentrated among less creditworthy (subprime or Alt-A) borrowers; that is, those with lower credit scores and lower or more variable incomes (or higher debt-to-income ratios). The analysis of Piskorski and Tchistyi (2010) also implies a high concentration of mortgages with negative amortization among riskier borrowers who at the same time are sufficiently sophisticated to manage such products.

The data appear to be broadly consistent with the key predictions of Piskorski and Tchistyi (2010, 2011). First, figure 4.7 indicates that mortgages with short-term teaser rates are mostly concentrated among risky subprime borrowers. Figure 4.8 indicates that loans with negative amortization features are highly concentrated among riskier borrowers (Alt-A), who at the same time are likely more financially sophisticated than subprime borrowers.[9]

Second, table 4.1 shows the results of regressions when the dependent variable takes the value 1 if a loan is a short-term hybrid ARM (initial rate period between eighteen months and forty-two months), a negative-

---

8. Early default by the borrower in the boom is costly to the lender, as it does not allow the borrower to use future house appreciation for loan repayment. At the same time, the lender, in order to break even, has to make money on the loan in good times (i.e., periods with prolonged house price growth), as he is likely to lose money in bad times (e.g., during housing crisis). Hence, the interest rate is scheduled to increase over time during the boom. On the other hand, the borrower can afford to pay higher interest rates in the future and is less likely to default in good times, since he can borrow more as the home appreciates in value.

9. See also Cocco (2011), who provides empirical evidence, using the UK household data, that borrowers who took out interest-only mortgages were more likely to have higher future income.

Table 4.1   **Short-term hybrid and deferred-amortization regressions**

	Pr(short-term hybrid ARM = 1) (1)	Pr(IO/neg – am = 1) (2)
LTV	0.001***	–0.003***
	(60.14)	(–389.79)
FICO	–0.003***	0.009***
	(–2158.73)	(519.05)
HPI growth	0.191***	0.260***
	(71.44)	(84.65)
Dummy (low documentation)	0.037***	0.064***
	(177.2)	(266.03)
Other controls	Yes	Yes

Notes: This table reports a pair of regressions where the dependent variable in the first regression (1) is an indicator that takes the value 1 if the loan is a short-term hybrid ARM; the dependent variable in the second regression (2) is an indicator that takes the value 1 if the loan is interest-only or negative-amortization. House price growth is a variable that measures the extent of local house price growth during two years prior to mortgage origination. The values in parentheses are the *t*-statistics.
***Significant at the 1 percent level.
**Significant at the 5 percent level.
*Significant at the 10 percent level.

amortization loan, or an interest-only loan; it takes the value 0 otherwise. Not surprisingly, there is a strong negative coefficient on the origination FICO score. These instruments were mostly concentrated among buyers with lower credit quality. Similarly, low-documentation loans were more likely to be in one of these categories. The relationship with loan-to-value ratio is negative overall, but less clear; this is because Alt-A borrowers (who were more likely to get interest-only or negative-amortization loans) tend not to have high LTV ratios, while subprime borrowers (who were more likely to get short-term hybrid ARMs but not to get deferred-amortization loans) usually do have high LTVs. Lastly, borrowers in "housing bubble" states (California, Nevada, Arizona, and Florida) were significantly more likely to receive these loans than borrowers in the rest of the country. Again, in these very simple regressions, the broad correlations in the data seem consistent with the economic arguments outlined above.

Finally, we note that the very high concentration of prepayment penalties among subprime borrowers compared to their low usage among more creditworthy, prime borrowers has been viewed as one of the key pieces of evidence that lending to risky borrowers was inefficient or predatory.[10]

10. For example, a 2003 report from the Center for Responsible Lending by Goldstein and Son states that: "While some subprime lenders claim that borrowers actually choose prepayment penalties in order to lower the costs of their loan, borrower choice cannot explain the 80% penetration rate of prepayment penalties in subprime loans in comparison to the 2% penetration rate in the competitive, more transparent, conventional market. The wide disparity

However, Mayer, Piskorski, and Tchistyi (2010) show that when considering improvements in a borrower's creditworthiness (such as positive wealth shocks) as one of the reasons for refinancing mortgages, prepayment penalties serve an important role by helping to ensure that mortgage pools are not becoming disproportionately composed of the riskiest borrowers over time. Enforcement of longer-term lending contracts through prepayment penalties allows lenders to charge lower mortgage rates, which reduce the risk of costly default, and to extend credit to the least creditworthy borrowers. This increases welfare, with the riskiest borrowers benefiting the most.[11] Consequently, a high concentration of prepayment penalties among the riskiest borrowers can be an outcome of an efficient equilibrium in a mortgage market. Mayer, Piskorski, and Tchistyi (2011) also provide empirical evidence consistent with this view.

To summarize, recent theoretical research suggests that nontraditional mortgage products and their high concentration among riskier borrowers may represent a financial innovation benefiting both borrowers and lenders (at least from an ex ante perspective). This research also implies that we should observe high default rates on these new products during the housing crisis.[12]

It is important to note, however, a few key limitations of the aforementioned efficiency results. First, the borrower and lender need to be able to form correct expectations regarding the evolution of key variables (including house prices and income). However, we note that even if this condition is not satisfied, we could think of the aforementioned results as explaining the structure of mortgage contracts given the beliefs of borrowers and lenders. Second, the features of mortgage lending that are optimal at the individual level may have negative consequences at the aggregate level, since the borrower and the lender do not take into account the potential negative externalities that their contract might impose on others. In that sense, mortgage contracts that are ex ante beneficial for borrowers and lenders may overall decrease welfare (due, for example, to the negative externalities of foreclosures). Finally, in deriving optimal contracts, the aforementioned studies assume that the borrower does not face a self-control problem. Borrowers

---

between the prime and subprime market penetration rates shows that subprime consumers do not "choose" prepayment penalties in any meaningful sense. Rational subprime borrowers with market power should prefer them no more often, and probably less often, than conventional borrowers so that they can refinance into a conventional loan at a significantly lower rate as soon as credit improves" (6).

11. This result is related to Dunn and Spatt (1985), who study the role of due-on-sale clauses and prepayment penalties in a two-period setting in which the borrowers receive ex post stochastic shocks to the incremental utility received from selling the house (from mobility). They show that such clauses may enhance welfare by improving risk-sharing opportunities of borrowers.

12. See Corbae and Quintin (2011) and Campbell and Cocco (2011) for quantitative analysis of defaults on mortgages with deferred payment schedules.

lacking self-control might abuse access to credit (such as a negative amortization feature), leading to inefficiently high default rates.[13]

If we assume that mortgage product innovation was beneficial to borrowers and lenders (at least from the ex ante perspective), a natural question arises as to why this development had not occurred earlier. There are number of potential explanations. First, since the mid-1990s, mortgage lenders significantly increased their ability to gather and process information. Information technology reduced the costs incurred in the mortgage origination process, and assisted lenders in learning about the credit quality of borrowers and the value of collateral.

Second, during the 2000s, long-term interest rates sustained significant declines that coincided with a vast inflow of capital from abroad into US bond markets (e.g., from China). This led to a significant decline of lenders' cost of capital. Finally, the development of the private label securitization market may have provided better risk-sharing opportunities to investors, thus further reducing the cost of capital. Lower mortgage origination costs coupled with lower cost of capital could have resulted in the extension of credit to less creditworthy borrowers. As nontraditional mortgages can benefit exactly these borrowers, this extension of credit could have triggered widespread development and usage of these products by riskier borrowers.

All these developments occurred in conjunction with each other, and hence through general equilibrium effects that could affect and feed on each other. We note that coinciding with these developments in the mortgage market had been a marked increase in the demand for housing, including second homes, which contributed to fast growth in house prices.[14] This exuberant environment, in conjunction with anticipated house price appreciation, could provide an additional rationale for the usage of nontraditional mortgages.

Alternative Views on Mortgage Product Development

An alternative view on mortgage product development postulates that these products were designed or misused so that some market participants (e.g., lenders, underwriters) could benefit at the expense of others (e.g., borrowers, MBS investors). For example, mortgages with teaser rates or negative amortization can allow lenders and mortgage underwriters to defer realization of losses. Hence, these products could facilitate manipulation of the market perception of the risks of these products. In other words, such mortgage contracts may have made the securitization of riskier collateral

13. See Barlevy and Fisher (2010), who present a model and empirical evidence that suggests that speculating borrowers in areas that saw more house price growth increased their demand for deferred amortization loans.

14. See, among others, Khan (2008) and Favilukis, Ludvigson, and Van Nieuwerburgh (2010) for recent general equilibrium studies of house price determination.

easier or more profitable to lenders and underwriters at the expense of less sophisticated MBS investors. For example, the recent research by Ben-David (2011) suggests that risky subprime lending was associated with artificially inflated transaction prices that allowed sellers of these loans to overstate their quality and earn higher fees. Inflated transactions were common in low-income neighborhoods and were associated with high default rates in the crisis. Moreover, mortgages with a deferred payment schedule, whose returns can be more sensitive to real estate prices than standard contracts, could allow managers of highly levered financial institutions to take on excessive risk (asset substitution).[15]

Alternatively, these nontraditional mortgage products could have allowed lenders to profit at the expense of less sophisticated borrowers. For example, borrowers may not have been fully aware of mortgage resets or existence of the prepayment penalty at the time of signing a contract. Recent research by Bucks and Pence (2008) shows that many borrowers are uninformed about the terms of their mortgage, and this is particularly true for those who have an ARM structure. A more complex nature of these products could have facilitated obfuscation of the true payment structure of these loans. Although direct evidence on lenders extracting rents from mortgage borrowers is difficult to obtain and quantify, in the payday-lending environment, recent work by Melzer (2011) has found that access to payday lenders actually exacerbates debt and bill repayment. This suggests that lenders are potentially able to extract excessive rents from some households.[16]

A full empirical investigation of these alternative hypotheses is challenging, as they often have similar implications as the efficiency view discussed in section 4.2.3. For example, if these products were used to deter recognition of losses and lower the market perception of their risk, we would expect a high concentration of deferred payment/amortization mortgages among less creditworthy borrowers. But according to the efficiency view, we should also see a high concentration of such products among less creditworthy borrowers. However, as we discuss in the next section, there is some evidence that these new forms of lending, coupled with growth in private label securitization, may have adversely affected the incentives of some market participants.

4.3.2   Did the Changed Nature of Financing Affect Financial Intermediation?

Did the dramatic changes in the nature of lending impact the behavior of agents engaged in intermediation? General theories of financial intermediation argue that banks help channel resources from savers to users of capital. However, to be able to do so, they must be provided adequate incentives—in

---

15. See Landier, Sraer, and Thesmar (2010) for discussion of this argument.

16. For a theoretical model of poorly informed borrowers and predatory lending, see Bond, Musto, and Yilmaz (2005).

part through the illiquidity of long-term investments on their balance sheet. However, securitization changes the lending framework from "originate and hold" to "originate and distribute," and increases the distance between a home owner and the ultimate bearer of the mortgage's risk. A loan sale to an investor results in information loss: some characteristics of the borrower that are potentially observable by the originating lender are not transmitted to the final investor. Since the price paid by investors depends only on verifiable information transmitted by the lender, this process could introduce a moral hazard problem: the lender originates loans that rate highly based on the characteristics that affect its compensation, even if the unreported information implies a lower quality.[17] It is possible, of course, that regulatory oversight, reputational considerations, or sufficient balance sheet risk may prevent moral hazard on the part of lenders. Understanding the effects of existing securitization practices on screening is thus an empirical question.

How would one detect changes in lenders' origination incentives? In general, the quality of a mortgage loan is a function of both hard and soft information that the lender can obtain about the borrower (see Stein 2002). Hard information, such as a borrower's FICO credit score, is easy to verify; conversely, soft information, such as the borrower's future job prospects, is costly to verify. In the absence of securitization, a lender should internalize the benefits and costs of acquiring both kinds of information and adequately invest in both tasks. With securitization, hard information is reported to investors; soft information, which is difficult to verify and transmit, remains unreported. Investors therefore rely only on hard information to judge the quality of loans. This may eliminate the lender's incentive to collect and evaluate soft information. Consequently, conditional on observable borrower and loan characteristics, borrowers that receive loans may become worse along the soft information dimension as the ease of securitization increases. Therefore, by comparing the default rates, conditional on hard information (observables), one can infer the changes in lenders' screening effort on the margin of soft information.

We now discuss evidence that suggests that subprime securitization did in fact impact lenders' screening incentives. Most of the work discussed here surveys our own work but we will also discuss other evidence in the literature that supports these arguments.

Evidence from Keys, Mukherjee, Seru, and Vig

In Keys et al. (2010a, henceforth KMSV), the authors asked whether increased access to secondary mortgage markets affected whether lenders were willing to originate loans and the quality of those loans. Making a

---

17. The same tension exists in the multitasking framework of Holmstrom and Milgrom (1991): an agent compensated for specific tasks ignores other tasks that also affect the payoffs of the principal.

causal claim requires isolating differences in channels that impact lender behavior and loan outcomes that depend on securitization but are independent of contract and borrower characteristics. The authors used a rule of thumb in the subprime market that generated an exogenous increase in ease of securitization of loans around a particular credit score. This allowed them to identify whether an increase in the ease of securitization had any impact on lenders' screening effort.

Keys et al. identified a rule of thumb in the nonagency investor market related to credit scores, based originally on Fannie and Freddie guidelines. A FICO score above 620 was considered "strong," whereas scores below 620 were perceived as lower quality and deserving of increased scrutiny. Although these GSE guidelines did not apply to the nonagency securities market, whether loans had FICO scores above or below 620 became a commonly used summary statistic in securities prospectuses. Keys et al. argued that adherence to this cut-off by investors (e.g., investment banks, hedge funds), generated an increase in demand for securitized loans just above the credit cut-off relative to loans below this cut-off. This "ease of securitization" can be measured on several dimensions, such as the number of loans securitized, the securitization rate (conditional on origination), or the time it takes a lender to sell a loan.

There are a number of additional ways to measure ease of securitization and establish that there was a systematic difference around FICO = 620 for low documentation loans, the most information-sensitive type of loan being originated. Figure 4.14, part A, presents the distribution of low documentation securitized subprime loans by individual FICO score around the FICO of 620 threshold. The figure shows that there were nearly twice as many loans securitized just above 620 than just below it. An alternative way of evaluating this changed ease of securitization is by examining the conditional securitization rate; that is, conditional on a lender originating a loan, the probability that it is sold. In part B of figure 4.14, KMSV show that low documentation loans originated with FICO scores just above 620 are significantly and discontinuously more likely to be sold than those below 620. Finally, another measure of how "liquid" a loan is the speed with which the loan is sold. If a loan is sold quickly, that frees up lenders' capital requirements and also reduces their "warehousing" risk. Part C shows that low documentation loans just above 620 were sold to the private market over one month faster than loans below the 620 threshold. Thus from the lenders' perspective, if two identical borrowers applied for a low documentation loan, but one had a credit score of 619 and the other a score of 621, the lender knew the ease of selling was higher above FICO = 620.

The next figure, figure 4.15, shows that this differential "ease of securitization" had a direct impact on lenders' screening decisions. Because investors purchase securitized loans based only on hard information, the cost of collecting soft information is internalized by lenders to a lesser extent when

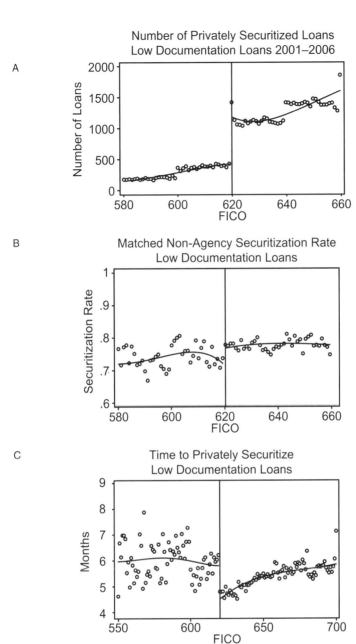

Fig. 4.14 Ease of securitization of private low documentation loans (2001–2006)

Notes: Part A presents the distribution of low documentation securitized subprime loans in the LPS database originated between 2001 and 2006. Part B shows the securitization rate of low documentation loans in the LPS database originated between 2001 and 2006. Propensity Score reweighting is used to attribute unsold loans to the agency or nonagency market. Part C depicts the average time it takes for loans in the LPS database originated between 2001 and 2006 to be securitized to the private nonagency market. The longer it takes for a loan to be securitized, the costlier it may be for the bank, due to either the opportunity cost of capital or risk of loan delinquency.

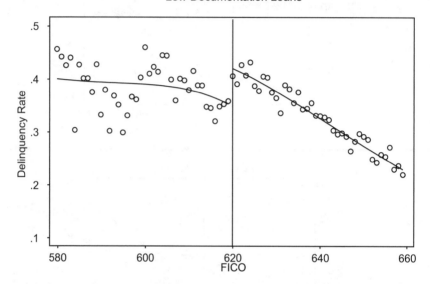

Fig. 4.15   Delinquency rate of private low documentation loans (2001–2006)

Notes: This figure shows the 60+ day delinquency rate for low documentation loans sold to the private market in the LPS database originated between 2001 and 2006. Propensity score re-weighting is used to assign unsold loans to the agency or nonagency market based on observable loan characteristics.

screening borrowers at 620+ than at 620–. Therefore, by comparing loan portfolios on either side of the credit score threshold, one can assess whether differential access to securitization led to changes in lenders' decisions to offer these loans to consumers with nearly identical risk profiles. Low documentation subprime loans just above 620 were significantly more likely to default than those loans just below 620. Thus differences in the performance of these loans (differential screening) can be attributed to differential access to the secondary mortgage market.

Keys, Seru, and Vig (2012) also show that lenders had private information about these loans that was not provided to investors and differed systematically around FICO = 620. In particular, using data from an anonymous large subprime lender (who went bankrupt during the subprime bust), they find that in this lender's pool of originated loans, there are more self-employed borrowers just above 620 than just below 620. These borrowers have more variable income and were likely greater credit risks than borrowers steadily employed by firms. However, despite the fact that this information was maintained in the lender's database, and potentially used in their internal underwriting process, this information was not transmitted to investors purchasing these loans. Exploring the time-series relationship, they further find that variation in access to the secondary market is strongly related to variation in screening the low documentation subprime market. In short, there are no samples or environments where differences in default around the cut-off were not related to differences in the ease of securitization.[18]

This evidence can be interpreted as suggesting that providing more documentation (in the case of full documentation loans sold to the non-GSEs), or additional mechanisms to monitor and constrain lenders (in the case of the GSEs, underwriting software, reps and warranties, and reputation risks all fall into this category) may have limited the amount of soft information available for lenders to differentially screen on. However, it is also worth noting that although the Keys et al. (2012) methodology does not uncover differential loan performance in some markets, this does not necessarily mean that lenders were not influenced by the ease of access in other markets.

Broader Patterns in the Market and Other Evidence

While work in KMSV focused on establishing the causal link between securitization and screening, there are several patterns in the broader market that suggest this link was not restricted locally around FICO of 620. To evaluate broader effects, it is useful to note what the increased securitization of subprime loans implies for lender behavior. Securitization increases the distance between lenders and investors, making it difficult to contract on every possible variable (see Stein 2002). In particular, only hard, easily verifiable information is reported to investors and the soft information, which is difficult to verify and transmit, remains unreported. Therefore, due to the greater distance between originators and investors, the interest rate on new loans may depend increasingly on hard information reported to the investor. Also, due to the loss of soft information, the interest rate on a loan may become an increasingly poor predictor of loan performance.[19]

18. In Keys et al. (2010a), the possibility that the 620 rule of thumb was in fact unrelated to securitization, but instead reflected lenders choosing an optimal screening cut-off, was considered, tested, and rejected. In that paper, the authors used changes in antipredatory lending laws in New Jersey and Georgia as a natural experiment to vary access to secondary markets. During periods when lenders were constrained from easily accessing nonagency securitization markets, the differences around the 620 threshold in both loan sales and loan performance disappeared. However, the differences reappeared once the laws were weakened and the originate-to-distribute model was up and running again in these states. Support of the optimal lender rule of thumb has been provided by Bubb and Kaufman (2009, 2011), who claim to find differences in default rates without any differences in the ease of securitization in the non-Jumbo market. Keys, Seru, and Vig (2012) show that Bubb and Kaufman's results are due to their combining loans from different secondary markets into one analysis. When analyzed separately, even using Bubb and Kaufman's data set and definitions, the same patterns emerge: differences in loan performance and differences in the ease of securitization around FICO of 620 for low documentation loans sold to nonagency investors. There are no differences in loan performance at the threshold for any other types of loans.

19. With securitization, there is an information loss, since the lender offers the same interest rate to both good and bad types of borrowers at the same interest rate (see Rajan, Seru, and Vig 2010). As a result, in a high securitization regime, the interest rate becomes a noisier predictor of default for the loan pool.

Rajan, Seru, and Vig (2010) provide evidence for both these predictions. In particular, using a large database on securitized subprime loans across different US lenders, they find that over time the interest rate on new loans relies increasingly on a small set of variables. Specifically, the R^2 of a regression of interest rates on borrower FICO credit scores and loan-to-value (LTV) ratios increases from 9 percent for loans issued in the period 1997 to 2000 to 46 percent for 2006 loans. Further confirmation comes from the dispersion of interest rates; conditioning on the FICO score, the standard deviation of interest rates on new loans shrinks over time. Second, Rajan et al. show that with increased securitization the interest rate becomes a worse predictor of default likelihood on a loan. In particular, the pseudo-R^2 of this logit regression declines with securitization, suggesting that the interest rate loses some of its ability to predict loan defaults. In related work, Loutskina and Strahan (2011) find that as lenders sought a national presence, they lost any geographic informational advantages they previously had acquired, and no longer performed "informed" underwriting based on local (soft) knowledge of markets.

There are several other papers that also suggest a link between changed nature of supply of credit due to subprime securitization and the quality of loans that were originated. First, Mian and Sufi (2009) investigate causes of the expansion in subprime mortgage credit and find evidence consistent with an increase in lending supply and defaults that are correlated with securitization activity. Using zip code-level data, they find that places that had greater securitization rates were places in which subprime credit increased most dramatically. In a similar spirit, Purnanandam (2011) uses the exogenous shut down of the private label securitization market to evaluate the quality of loans that were originated by lenders who intended to securitize them, and compare these to loans that were not intended to be securitized. His evidence suggests that banks active in pursuing an originate-to-distribute model of lending did not expend as many resources in screening their borrowers.

Next, Jiang, Nelson, and Vytlacil (2010) use data from one of the top subprime lenders in the United States and a similar identification strategy as KMSV to find that increases in securitization reduced the lender's origination standards. In addition, the paper shows that observing ex post default patterns on unsold loans and comparing them with default patterns of sold loans to make inferences on the ex ante connection between securitization and screening are misplaced. The reason is that most subprime lenders originated all loans with intent to sell and loans that were ex post unsold were of lower quality; for instance, they suffered an early payment default.[20]

Finally, Nadauld and Sherlund (2009) use the timing of a reduction in Securities and Exchange Commission (SEC)-mandated capital requirements

---

20. A similar point was also made in KMSV (2010b).

to identify the impact of intermediation on increases in subprime credit. They find that when capital requirements were reduced, more mortgage credit was supplied to neighborhoods with high house price appreciation and to subprime borrowers. The results corroborate the view that increased access to the secondary mortgage market weakened lenders' screening incentives.

Were These Patterns Related to Agency Conflicts in the Supply Chain?

While most of the work just discussed evaluates whether there was a change in loan quality when the nature of financing changed, it does not assess what parts of the securitization chain were affected. As discussed earlier, there are several agents involved in the supply chain of credit, from brokers and lenders who originate the loan, to issuers and underwriters who package the loans before they are sold to investors. As discussed in detail in Ashcraft and Schuermann (2008), there are potentially multiple agency conflicts between various participants in the supply chain of credit that can affect the quality of loans originated. While this narrative is convincing, it is a narrative that is generally difficult to test empirically.

The reason that Ashcraft and Schuermann (2008) and earlier work were not able to empirically evaluate the changes in behavior of these agents in response to changes in ease of securitization is that it requires detailed data that was not easily available. We now present some suggestive evidence based on new data that is consistent with agent incentives playing an important role in loan performance. We also discuss several new papers in the literature that have also used similar data sources and provide evidence that confirms the presence of agency conflicts in the supply chain.

To conduct our analysis, we need information beyond what is provided in the databases we listed earlier. In particular, we need to collect information on the composition of originators contributing to a mortgage pool as well as information on other agents in the supply chain of credit such as issuers and underwriters of the pool. This information is available in the prospectus document of a deal. However, reading all deal prospectuses is a time-consuming task. We therefore randomly sample mortgage-backed securities (MBS) deals over the period 2004 to 2007 and cover roughly 1,200 mortgage pools spread across these years. We restrict attention to these years since the availability of prospectuses of mortgage pools in the earlier periods is limited.

Using the information available in these deals we construct a variable that we employ in our analysis. In particular, we use information on the originators who contribute loans to a deal. Most prospectuses list information on originators as well as their contribution to the pool. This allows us to construct a variable that reflects whether a pool has relatively higher number of "small originators" contributing to it. We use this measure to test whether the performance of loans in a pool is reduced if it is more difficult to monitor the incentives of agents originating the risk. More specifically, we construct an indicator variable ("minor contributors") that takes a value of 1 if the pool consists of more than one lender that is not a major contributor. We then evaluate the performance of the same vintages of loans that are securitized by pools with or without these minor contributors.

Panel A of table 4.2 presents the results of this regression. The dependent variable here is the proportion of loans (dollar-weighted) in a given

Table 4.2   Delinquency in privately securitized mortgage pools and characteristics of agents in the supply chain

A. Different characteristics of agents in supply chain of credit				
	%60+ (1)	%90+ (2)	%60+ (3)	%90+ (4)
Subordination level	0.001*** (11.03)	0.002*** (8.01)	0.001*** (11.03)	0.002*** (8.19)
Dummy (minor originators)			0.003** (2.42)	0.008*** (3.58)
Observations	832	832	832	832
R^2	0.24	0.18	0.25	0.19
Other controls	Yes	Yes	Yes	Yes
Vintage fixed effects	Yes	Yes	Yes	Yes

B. Originators with different regulatory oversight		
	%60+ (1)	%90+ (2)
Subordination level	0.001*** (11.03)	0.002*** (8.19)
Dummy (originators largely nonbank)	–0.002** (2.30)	–0.004** (1.97)
Observations	832	832
R^2	0.25	0.19
Other controls	Yes	Yes
Vintage fixed effects	Yes	Yes

Notes: This table reports regressions that relate the quality of the pool with various pool-level characteristics and characteristics of agents originating the loans. The dependent variable in each regression is the dollar volume of loans that are sixty-day delinquent or ninety-day delinquent within twenty-four months of origination. The regressions include controls for average pool FICO, interest rate, LTV, the proportion of loans that are low documentation, and the proportion of loans that are ARM. In addition, we also include origination vintage time effects.

***Significant at the 1 percent level.
**Significant at the 5 percent level.
*Significant at the 10 percent level.

mortgage pool that became late on their payments by sixty or ninety days within twenty-four months of originating the loan (percent 60+ or percent 90+). In the first two columns, we examine if the baseline results of the pools for which we have complete information (830 out of 1,200) seem sensible. In particular, we include the subordination level of the pool—the percent of lower tranches that are affected before the top tranches of the pool are affected—an indication of risk. As is expected, we find that subordination levels are positively related to the subsequent quality of the pool—that is, there is a higher cushion for deals that have a higher proportion of risky loans. In these regressions we include other pool-level variables that measure the quality of the collateral (e.g., average pool FICO, LTV, interest rates, percent low documentation loans, percent ARM loans).

In the next set of columns ([3] and [4]), we regress the variable we discussed before and find indeed that pools with more minor lenders contributing loans performed worse. Even though these are admittedly naïve regressions that may not account for other important factors affecting delinquencies, these results are suggestive of agency problems affecting the quality of originations from the securitization chain.

The evidence we provided in this section is consistent with several other studies. First, the findings are broadly in line with KMSV (2009), where the authors used the FICO = 620 as a source of differential ease of securitization and evaluated which factors alleviated or aggravated differential screening by lenders. In particular, they also find that more stringent broker laws across states—with several states requiring brokers who originate mortgages to post "surety" bonds—are associated with higher quality originations. These findings are also broadly consistent with Jiang, Nelson, and Vytlacil (2009), who find that broker-originated loans for a large subprime lender performed significantly worse than those originated by the bank's own loan officers. Notably, their specification and data allow them to account for several hard information variables that the bank collects but may not pass to investors or data-vendors (beyond those as employed in our analysis). Nevertheless, the finding that loans originated by brokers are of worse quality remains.

Finally, more generally, these results are also consistent with Demiroglu and James (2012), who show that the quality of loans originated in pools that have the same institution undertaking the tasks of originating, sponsoring the deal, as well as servicing the loans tended to be of significantly better quality. This was true both when the authors looked at delinquencies as well as foreclosures of a large number of deals—with effects most pronounced for deals originated during the housing boom.

What about Regulation?

Did regulation have any bite in alleviating the reduction in lending standards? The subprime mortgage market consists of lenders who perform similar tasks—origination and distribution—but are differentially regulated. Deposit-taking institutions (banks/thrifts and their subsidiaries) undergo rigorous examinations from their regulators: the Office of the Comptroller of the Currency, Office of Thrift Supervision, Federal Deposit Insurance Corporation, and the Federal Reserve Board (see Agarwal, Luca, et al. 2012). Non-deposit-taking institutions, on the other hand, are supervised relatively lightly. To evaluate if more oversight led to better underwriting we compare the quality of loans originated by banks and compare them to those originated by nondepository institutions.

To conduct our tests, we classify lenders in our sample into banks, thrifts, subsidiaries of banks/thrifts, and independent lenders. Each loan in the database is linked to an originating lender. However, it is difficult to directly discern all unique lenders in the database since the names are sometimes spelled differently and in many cases are abbreviated. We manually identified the unique lenders from the available names when possible. In order to ensure that we are able to cover a majority of loans in our sample, we also obtained a list of top fifty lenders (by origination volume) for each year from 2001 to 2006, previously published by the publication *Inside B&C Mortgage*. Across years, this yields a list of 105 lenders. Using the list we are able to identify some abbreviated lender names, which otherwise we might not have been able to classify. Subsequently, we use Form 10-K proxy statements and lender websites (whenever available) to classify the lenders into two categories—*banks*, which comprise all lenders that are banks, thrifts, or subsidiaries of banks and thrifts, and *independents*. An example of a bank in our sample would be Bank of America, while Ameriquest is an example of an independent lender.

In panel B of table 4.2, we examine the performance of the same vintages of loans that are securitized by banks relative to those securitized by independents. In particular, we regress the proportion of loans (dollar-weighted) in a given mortgage pool that became late on their payments by sixty or ninety days within twenty-four months of originating the loan (percent 60+ or percent 90+). The results in columns (1) and (2) suggest that pools where loans are primarily originated by independent lenders tend to perform better as compared to those where banks primarily originated the loans. While we realize that this is a limited comparison—the characteristics of borrowers, contractual terms, and other institutional features may differ in ways not accounted for by our simple specification and controls—we are provided comfort by the observation that KMSV reached the same conclusion with a superior identification strategy.

These results are consistent with the institutional reasons discussed in Van den Heuvel (2008) where most of the focus of the regulation across institutions was on "balance-sheet" items rather than "off-balance" sheet activities such as subprime mortgage loans that were primarily intended to be securitized and were, therefore, considered as "off-balance" sheet.

Implications

The main implication that can be drawn from this line of research is that skin in the game and mechanisms for monitoring and enforcement play an important role in the performance of mortgages, and hence mortgage bonds. In particular, complete documentation of income and assets, as well as the reputation/exclusionary threat by the GSEs to constrain lender behavior, appear to have led to better outcomes than in the private low documentation subprime market. In the absence of these checks on lender strategic behavior, it appears that lenders differentially screened borrowers, and that mechanisms such as retaining a junior portion of the security may provide significant incentives for lenders to conduct more careful screening.

In addition, the results related to state-level variation in broker laws again support the view that agency problems are mitigated in instances where agents involved in the supply chain of credit had more "stakes" involved. These findings are also confirmed when loans were pooled across different lenders—potentially making it harder for the issuer to monitor the quality of the loan pool. Furthermore, the finding that loan pools where the issuer and the underwriter were the same institution had better performance also supports the idea that the participants in the credit chain have differing incentives, and that when aligned can be used to reduce the agency problems and resulting lower quality of the pool.

Our results also have another important implication. They suggest that there is substantial heterogeneity in how the agency conflicts manifest themselves across different types of products. In particular, we find a great deal of heterogeneity across market segments in the ability of lenders to behave strategically. This finding does not necessarily support the view that the Dodd–Frank mandate of 5 percent risk retention is the optimal amount of risk retention in the mortgage market. In some segments of the market, 5 percent may not be enough to strengthen incentives, while in others, retaining a 5 percent portion of the loan pool may be prohibitively costly to fund private label securitizations. Although our results provide broad support for skin in the game, we would need a more complete model of pool performance and information frictions to quantify the optimal level of risk retention for a given type of underlying mortgage asset.

4.4   The Foreclosure Crisis and the Challenges of Renegotiation

Since 2007, as the housing crisis unfolded, the number of foreclosures reached unprecedented levels. What was behind the high number of defaults and foreclosures? First, almost by definition, the most important factor was a decline in the level of house prices that put many home owners under-water—that is, those borrowers had a negative amount of equity in their homes. This decline was accompanied by an increase in unemployment and a broad economic recession that put additional stress on borrowers' willingness and ability to pay their loans.[21]

In addition, in such an environment one would expect high foreclosure rates on nonagency securitized mortgages since, as discussed before, these loans tended to have higher loan-to-value ratios and were made to riskier borrowers (and more sensitive to systemic risk). Indeed, nonagency securitized mortgages accounted for more than half of the foreclosure starts during the first two years of the crisis, despite their much smaller market share (see Piskorski, Seru, and Vig 2010). However, there was also concern among academics and policymakers that the high foreclosure rate on securitized mortgages might also partly reflect misaligned incentives in origination of these products and its adverse impact on screening and underwriting standards (see section 4.3.2). Furthermore, there was also a concern that several other factors could have impeded effective renegotiation of these mortgages, thereby aggravating the foreclosure crisis. We now discuss some of these reasons in turn.

4.4.1   Challenges to Effective Renegotiation of Residential Mortgages

Securitization

There are compelling arguments that in times of significant adverse macro shocks, debt forgiveness and loan renegotiation can create value for both borrowers and lenders (Bolton and Rosenthal 2002; Piskorski and Tchistyi 2011). However, as of early 2009, the general perception was that there were far too few mortgage modifications performed by lenders and servicers, and that even those that were performed were not effectively helping borrowers avoid losing their homes. This was particularly troubling given the significant deadweight costs of foreclosure due to lack of incentives for borrowers to maintain their homes (see Melzer 2012), as well as negative externalities of foreclosure (see, e.g., Campbell, Giglio, and Pathak 2011).

As most of the early foreclosures occurred among nonagency securitized loans, a debate ensued regarding whether dispersed ownership and potential agency frictions brought about by the securitization of residential mortgages inhibited renegotiation of loans at risk of foreclosure. In the case of a securitized loan, the servicer acts as an agent of the investors and makes the crucial decision of how to handle a delinquent loan: choosing to pursue either a

---

21. According to the option-theoretic literature, borrowers default on their mortgage when the value of the house falls below the current value of the mortgage (see, among others, Kau, Keenan, and Kim [1994] and Deng, Quigley, and Van Order [2000]) This may imply that the optimal default trigger is such that the borrower has negative equity measured as ratio of the loan balance to the current market value of the house. This theory assumes that the borrower has full access to credit markets for unsecured credit such that default is unaffected by liquidity considerations and income fluctuations. We note, however, that in a setting in which the borrower values the home more than its "market" value and/or faces default costs, the default can be triggered by liquidity shocks.

foreclosure or a modification of the mortgage. A number of commentators and academics have argued that servicers' financial incentives, legal constraints and uncertainty in servicers' contracts, and coordination problems among multiple investors may have inhibited renegotiation of securitized loans, thereby aggravating the foreclosure crisis.[22]

Existing research has been consistent with this view. Piskorski, Seru, and Vig (2010) examine whether securitization impacts loan servicers' renegotiation decisions, focusing on their choice to foreclose a delinquent loan. Conditional on a loan becoming seriously delinquent, they find a significantly lower foreclosure rate associated with bank-held loans when compared to similar securitized loans. Across various specifications with numerous controls and origination vintages, they find that the foreclosure rate of delinquent bank-held loans is 3 to 7 percent lower in absolute terms (13 to 32 percent in relative terms).

They further confirm these results in a quasi-experiment that exploits plausibly exogenous variation in securitization status of a delinquent loan. In particular, the quasi-experiment involved using repurchase clauses (either due to early pay defaults or due to violations of reps and warranties) that legally obligate originators to purchase back any securitized loans that become delinquent, typically within ninety days of the loan being securitized. Piskorski, Seru, and Vig (2010) use this feature to construct two groups: securitized loans that become delinquent just before ninety days and were taken back by the originator and serviced as if the loan was bank-held (treatment group); securitized loans that become delinquent just after ninety days and continued to be serviced as securitized loans (control group). Since both types of loans are securitized to start with, the repurchase feature allows them to circumvent any ex ante selection on unobservable concerns by providing plausibly exogenous variation in the securitization status of a delinquent loan. By comparing the foreclosure rates of distressed loans in the treatment and control groups, they are able to show that securitization induced foreclosure bias in the decisions of lenders and servicers.

While the foreclosure results of Piskorski and colleagues are consistent with securitization impacting renegotiation, the authors did not have "direct" data on the renegotiation decisions of lenders.[23] However, this data was collected by the Office of the Comptroller of the Currency. Trends in the OCC data confirm that results Piskorski, Seru, and Vig (2010) are driven by differences in lenders' renegotiation decisions—renegotiation rates were higher for bank-held loans, and these renegotiations were both more

---

22. See, among others, Gelpern and Levitin (2009); Mayer, Morrison, and Piskorski (2009); Posner and Zingales (2009); White (2009a, 2009b).
23. These results also are consistent with Gan and Mayer (2006) and Ambrose, Sanders, and Yavas (2011). These papers find that servicers change their behavior toward renegotiations depending on whether they own a first-loss position for the loans they service.

aggressive (e.g., had a higher principal reduction) and more effective (had a lower redefault rate conditional on receiving a modification).

While the OCC data is suggestive, it is not conclusive. The data provides trends and averages without adequately accounting for different loan and borrower. This deficiency was overcome in Agarwal et al. (2011a, 2011b), who use data on direct renegotiations. Exploiting within-servicer variation in these data, they find that bank-held loans are more likely to be modified than comparable securitized mortgages (4.2 to 5.8 percent in absolute terms). Moreover, they establish that these differences in renegotiation rates explain the lower foreclosure rate of bank-held loans relative to comparable securitized mortgages. They also show that modifications of bank-held loans are more efficient. These findings have subsequently been also confirmed independently in a recent paper by Zhang (2011). The paper also discusses why using "indirect imputation" methods to infer renegotiations had led to biased inferences by some studies such as Adelino, Gerardi, and Willen (2010) (also see the discussion in Piskorski, Seru, and Vig 2010).

Finally, Agarwal, Zhang, et al. (2011), use an alternative strategy to reveal another manner in which securitization induces impediments to renegotiation. In particular, they document that when there is a difference in the ownership of liens on the house (second and first liens are sold to different sets of investors), the likelihood of liquidation is higher by 3.6 percent points in six months (60 percent in relative terms). They also find that the efficiency of renegotiation on a given loan (in terms of redefault rates) is lower for loans that suffer more from this problem.

Overall, this literature supports the view that frictions introduced by securitization created significant challenges to effective renegotiation of residential loans. While most of the studies just described focus on establishing that securitization introduced impediments in renegotiation during the early phase of the crisis period, there is no evidence on how these effects were spread heterogeneously across parts of the United States. We provide some evidence to this end by focusing on one particular aspect—the impact of foreclosure laws. In the United States, many states protect borrowers by imposing restrictions on the foreclosure process. This may make it difficult for servicers to foreclose in states where these laws make it harder to foreclose (i.e., in creditor unfriendly states). We investigate if these laws interacted with the impediments that securitization imposed on the renegotiation process.

While we lack data on direct renegotiations, we use foreclosure rates on distressed loans as a proxy. As previous research confirms, this is a reasonable variable if one is interested in capturing renegotiations on distressed loans. We follow Pence (2006) and classify states into those where foreclosure laws are creditor friendly (called "tough" states) and for states where these laws are creditor unfriendly (called "weak" states).

Table 4.3 reports the estimates from a regression evaluating the impact of securitization on foreclosure rates of distressed loans in the two different

Table 4.3   Foreclosures on distressed loans by securitization status across states with differing foreclosure rights

	2005:Q1	2005:Q2	2005:Q3	2005:Q4	2006:Q1	2006:Q2	2006:Q3	2006:Q4
A. Weak liquidation states								
Dependent variable: Foreclosure on distressed loans (%)	16.8	15.6	14.3	15.9	17.2	13.5	11.2	7.3
Bank-held dummy	-0.044***	-0.036***	-0.033***	-0.049***	-0.023**	-0.035***	-0.032***	-0.011***
	(5.64)	(4.73)	(6.37)	(5.48)	(2.40)	(6.28)	(7.90)	(5.25)
MSA fixed effects	Yes	Yes	Yes	Yes	Yes	Yes	Yes	Yes
Other controls	Yes	Yes	Yes	Yes	Yes	Yes	Yes	Yes
N	13,217	17,249	16,679	15,746	16,087	16,290	14,273	11,872
B. Strong liquidation states								
Dependent variable: Foreclosure on distressed loans (%)	28.7	28.3	27.5	29.5	31.8	27.9	25.5	22.3
Bank-held dummy	-0.048***	-0.057***	-0.056***	-0.080***	-0.087***	-0.080***	-0.092***	-0.069***
	(5.98)	(7.87)	(6.26)	(8.93)	(8.47)	(10.81)	(9.74)	(12.82)
MSA fixed effects	Yes	Yes	Yes	Yes	Yes	Yes	Yes	Yes
Other controls	Yes	Yes	Yes	Yes	Yes	Yes	Yes	Yes
N	22,122	29,013	29,953	29,125	26,662	25,703	22,694	18,035

Notes: This table reports the marginal effects of a logit regression relating foreclosure on distressed loans and securitization status of a loan across states with differing liquidation laws. We follow Pence (2006) in classifying these states as weak (judicial) and tough (nonjudicial) foreclosure states. A loan is classified as distressed if it becomes sixty-day delinquent. In all the regressions we include MSA fixed effects and nonlinear controls of FICO, LTV, interest rates, and loan amounts. We also control for whether a loan is insured, whether it is an FRM (fixed-rate mortgage) or ARM, the term of the loan, and the age of the loan at its delinquency. The sample is from LPS database and is based on loans originated between 2005 to 2006. The payment status on these loans is tracked until the first quarter of 2008.

MSA = metropolitan statistical area.

***Significant at the 1 percent level.

**Significant at the 5 percent level.

*Significant at the 10 percent level.

sets of states. On average, delinquent loans in states with tough liquidation laws are about twice as likely to default as delinquent loans in states with weak liquidation laws (28 percent to 14.2 percent). This is consistent with the patterns reported in Mian, Sufi, and Trebbi (2011), who find higher fore-closure rates in tougher states as well. More importantly for our purpose, we find that, conditional on being seriously delinquent, the difference in the foreclosure rates between securitized and portfolio loans is much higher for those loans that are originated in states with creditor-friendly laws; that is, states that allow for quick foreclosure and house repossession.

Although we account for a number of observable characteristics, it is possible that these differences are driven by some unobservable factors. However, we note that these correlations are consistent with basic economic arguments that support the view that creditor friendly rights are benefi-cial to both lenders and borrowers, at least from the ex ante perspective (by facilitating the provision of credit). Our evidence suggests that strong creditor rights can also have some negative consequences by exacerbating the renegotiation frictions imposed by securitization. It is possible that the magnitude of the current crisis was not fully anticipated by investors and borrowers and so they did not provision for this contingency. Consequently, less creditor friendly laws potentially provided additional time to borrow-ers, investors, and government to intervene in order to change the nature of mortgage servicing.

What about Other Factors?

While the securitization of mortgages did impact renegotiation rates, it is clearly not the only factor impeding renegotiations; the renegotiation rate on delinquent bank-held loans is not 100 percent. What other factors were crucial in impeding renegotiations? We now discuss some of the salient fac-tors that have emerged in the literature and also provide some evidence that supports their importance.

Identifying "Eligible Borrowers"

An important challenge in designing cost-effective mortgage modification programs is how to develop eligibility criteria that efficiently identify home owners who are likely to default unless they receive help. In practice, it is difficult to identify these at-risk homeowners. Although millions of home owners are "underwater" and therefore at risk of default, the majority of these home owners are still making timely mortgage payments and may continue doing so without receiving a mortgage modification.[24] It could be quite costly to extend benefits to all of these underwater home owners. One possible solution to this problem is to extend benefits only to home

24. See, for example, Stevens (2011).

owners who are delinquent.[25] This approach, however, could induce home owners to default in order to obtain modification benefits even though they would not have defaulted otherwise. The extent of such "strategic" behavior crucially depends on whether costs of delinquency are sufficiently high to deter it for most home owners. In addition, moral considerations or bounded rationality may decrease a borrower's ability or willingness to behave strategically (see, e.g., Guiso, Sapienza, and Zingales 2009; Bhutta, Dokko, and Shan 2010).

But what is the extent of strategic borrowers in the economy and how could they be identified? We now provide some evidence that tries to identify such "strategic defaulters" using additional borrower payment data from credit bureaus. The analysis suggests that the rate of strategic defaults did increase dramatically as house prices decreased.

In classifying borrowers as "strategic" or not, we took all the loans in the BlackBox database. We then matched borrowers who took these loans to credit bureau data from Equifax and obtained the entire payment history of these borrowers across different credit products. We define a borrower as "strategically" defaulting if the borrower stops paying a delinquent mortgage loan (i.e., a borrower who became sixty-day delinquent for the first time and remained seriously delinquent), while concurrently paying on all non-HELOC (home equity line of credit) revolving debt in the next six months.[26]

Figure 4.16 shows the fraction of borrowers who become sixty-day delinquent for the first time, classified as "strategic defaulters." As we can observe, strategic default was rare prior to the crisis. Less than 2 percent of borrowers fall in this category among the mortgages that went delinquent in mid-2005. This is not surprising, as house prices were still increasing. In contrast, by mid-2010 close to 20 percent of borrowers can be classified as strategic defaulters.[27]

Figure 4.17 shows the fraction of "strategic defaulters" by origination vintage. Again, the fraction of strategic defaulters is low for early origination vintages, as these borrowers experienced significant house price appreciation. However, this fraction increases over time, as was shown earlier.

25. For example, a number of modification programs have made benefits available only to home owners who failed to make at least two monthly mortgage payments. See Citigroup (2009).

26. Note that we are not ascribing a moral judgment on this behavior, as it may be optimal for a household to repay certain debts while ignoring others. Households face a dynamic debt service problem and maintaining some access to unsecured credit—paying off credit card bills first, for instance, while missing four straight mortgage payments, may be an optimal choice given the delays in the foreclosure process. While some call this behavior "ruthless," one could just as easily also call it "optimizing" behavior.

27. We also note that in mid-2005 close to 20 percent of newly delinquent borrowers could exit their delinquency by paying off their loans (e.g., selling the house or refinancing the mortgage). This fraction drops to virtually 0 percent by 2009. This is hardly surprising, as by this year the private refinancing market collapsed and house prices suffered significant decline.

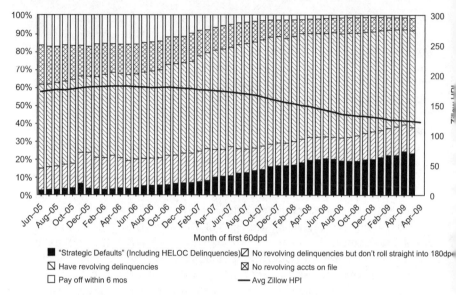

Fig. 4.16   Strategic defaults over time

Notes: This figure presents the borrowers defined to be "strategically defaulting" over time. A borrower is defined as doing so if the mortgage loan progressively goes from its 60 dpd for the first time to 180 dpd, while concurrently making payments on all non-HELOC revolving debt. In this chart, "Pay off within 6 mos" takes precedence over other categories, so, for example, if a loan pays off and also has no revolving accounts on file, it will be classified as paid off.

Moreover, the shorter the loan age, the bigger is the fraction of strategic defaulters, reaching more than 10 percent for loans originated in 2006 and 2007. In figure 4.18 we also plot the fraction of strategic defaulters as a function of house price change in their location. The areas with the largest house price declines have the largest share of strategic defaulters. In the areas where house prices experienced more than a 40 percent decline in prices from the peak, strategic defaulters account for about 20 percent of all mortgage defaults.

To investigate this further, in unreported tests we estimate a regression where the dependent variable is whether or not the delinquency is classified as a strategic default (as defined before). The loans used in the regressions are all loans originated between 2003 and 2007 that roll sixty days past due (dpd) for the first time with nonmissing control variable information. We find that the probability of a default being strategic increases with origination year. We also augment this specification and also include the usual loan level controls such as interest rate, origination FICO and LTV, documentation type, and loan type. We further find that having a 100-point increase in origination FICO increases the likelihood of a default being strategic by 4.38 percent. That borrowers with higher creditworthiness are more likely to engage in strategic defaults is consistent with survey evidence in Guiso,

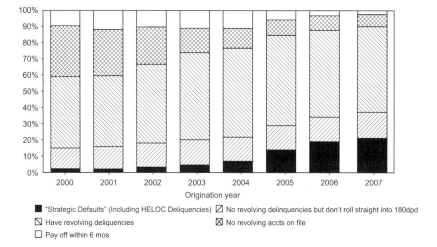

Fig. 4.17 Strategic defaults by origination vintage

Notes: This figure presents the borrowers defined to be "strategically defaulting" over time for various vintages. A borrower is defined as doing so if the mortgage loan progressively goes from its 60 dpd for the first time to 180 dpd, while concurrently making payments on all non-HELOC revolving debt. In this chart, "Pay off within 6 mos" takes precedence over other categories, so, for example, if a loan pays off and also has no revolving accounts on file, it will be classified as paid off.

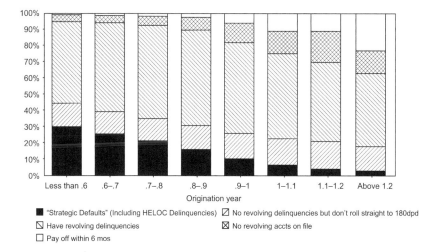

Fig. 4.18 Strategic defaults by change in HPI

Notes: This figure presents the borrowers defined to be "strategically defaulting" over time across regions with differential HPI changes over the period 2001 to 2009. A borrower is defined as doing so if the mortgage loan progressively goes from its 60 dpd for the first time to 180 dpd, while concurrently making payments on all non-HELOC revolving debt. In this chart, "Pay off within 6 mos" takes precedence over other categories, so, for example, if a loan pays off and also has no revolving accounts on file, it will be classified as paid off.

Sapienza, and Zingales (2011). Likewise more levered loans (those with higher LTV) are more likely to display strategic default. We also add in a variable that identifies the house price change from origination, equal to current OFHEO (Office of Federal Housing Enterprise Oversight) HPI/ origination HPI (housing price index). The results reveal that if the HPI of a property decreases compared to the origination HPI, then the likelihood of the default being strategic becomes greater. For example, a 20 percent decrease in the house prices since loan origination increases the likelihood of strategic default by almost 5 percent (more than a 50 percent increase in relative terms).

Overall, these are sizable magnitudes of borrowers who are current on revolving debt but remained seriously delinquent on their mortgage in the six straight months. We also note that our definition of "strategic default" is very stringent. If we were to take other definitions—for example, the fraction of borrowers who become seriously delinquent at some point of time on their mortgage while being subsequently current on their revolving debt—the proportion of such borrowers is *much higher.* Figure 4.16 indicates this clearly. It shows that among borrowers who became seriously delinquent for the first time in April 2009, almost 40 percent were current on their revolving accounts during the next six months.

The previous evidence suggests that a sizable fraction of "underwater" borrowers who defaulted on their loans appear to be not financially constrained and so had discretion of whether or not to default on their mortgages.[28] We now highlight a related issue that is faced by lenders designing a renegotiation program—the impact of the program in inducing strategic behavior by an additional set of borrowers. In particular, mortgage modification programs targeted at delinquent borrowers may encourage some borrowers who would otherwise stay current on their mortgage to default in order to obtain the benefits of a modification.

This tension underlying any modification initiative is illustrated in recent research by Mayer et al. (2011). The paper provides direct evidence on whether home owners respond strategically to news of mortgage modification programs. The authors exploit plausibly exogenous variation in modification policy induced by lawsuits against Countrywide Financial Corporation, which agreed in October 2008 to offer modifications to seriously delinquent borrowers with subprime mortgages throughout the country. Using a difference-in-difference framework, they find that Countrywide's relative delinquency rate increased more than 10 percent per month immediately after the program's announcement. The borrowers whose estimated default rates increased the most in response to the program were those who appear to have been the least likely to default otherwise, including those

---

28. Note that we have been able to identify "strategic defaulters" by merging several data sets—many of which were not available for lenders during the crisis period. Moreover, it is not clear that using up-to-date payment information across products to identify such "behavior" is legal from a lender's perspective.

with substantial liquidity available through credit cards and relatively low combined loan-to-value ratios. Their results suggest that strategic behavior should be an important consideration in designing mortgage modification programs (see also Agarwal, Amromin, et al. 2012).

Overall, the evidence in this section suggests that identifying "eligible" borrowers is a significant challenge for lenders interested in renegotiating with borrowers. There are some borrowers who—given the substantial negative equity in their homes—strategically defaulted on their mortgage payments. In addition, the design of a renegotiation program itself could induce other borrowers to strategically default. The magnitudes of both of these factors seem large enough to have potentially deterred lenders from renegotiating at a higher rate than has been observed.[29]

Political Influence

Furthermore, we discuss if there is evidence that banks' servicing decisions were also influenced by political pressure. In particular, it is plausible that banks may postpone foreclosures on their own delinquent loans in response to political pressure. Agarwal, Dinc, et al. (2011) provide evidence that is consistent with this conjecture. They show that the start of foreclosure on a delinquent loan is delayed if the loan is located in a congressional district whose representative is a member of the Financial Services Committee in the US House of Representatives.

We show below that these political effects may not have been only limited to bank-held loans by conducting a different variant of tests used in Agarwal, Dinc, et al. (2011). In table 4.4 we conduct our analysis on securitized loans to assess if the time it takes to foreclose on a loan varies depending on whether the servicer is likely to be affected more by political and regulatory pressure. We use the time it takes to foreclose a loan (in months) as the dependent variable and measure it as the time it takes from the incidence of a loan becoming sixty days delinquent until the completion of foreclosure process. The analysis uses data on nonagency securitized mortgages that were foreclosed in the 2004–2010 period (from the BlackBox database) and uses standard controls as well as origination year fixed effects, as well as fixed effects for the year when the foreclosure process began. Importantly, we use servicer information at the loan level to classify them as "independent" if the entity does not have substantial holdings of their own loans and are not directly involved in loan origination process (e.g., Ocwen or Litton). The excluded category consists of the loans handled by big bank servicers (e.g., Citi or Bank of America).

Column (1) of table 4.4 shows that, all else equal, independent servicers

---

29. The problem of cost-effective design of mortgage modification programs is complicated further by the observation that some of the "strategic defaulters" may be the best candidates for mortgage modification due to their financial ability to service debt. In other words, a group of borrowers with potentially promising modification targets can also display a larger scope for strategic behavior in response to a mortgage modification program.

Table 4.4   Number of months from last sixty dpd to end of foreclosure

Dependent variable	(1)	(2)	(3)
Average number of months to foreclosure	16.94	19.66	14.16
	All	2004–2007	2008–2010
Independent servicer	−0.766***	−0.569***	−0.857***
	(52.44)	(23.83)	(49.83)
Other controls	Yes	Yes	Yes
Origination year fixed effects	Yes	Yes	Yes
Foreclosure began year fixed effects	Yes	Yes	Yes
N of loans	1,598,700	808,351	790,349
R^2	0.192	0.103	0.120

Notes: The dependent variable is the number of months from a loan going 60 dpd for the last time to the loan leaving the sample as a finished foreclosure. The main explanatory variable is whether the servicer of a loan is an independent servicer (= 1) or a big bank (= 0). In these regressions we include nonlinear controls of FICO, LTV, interest rates, and loan amounts. We also include a dummy for whether the loan was ARM or FRM. Finally, we also use origination year fixed effects as well as fixed effects for the year the foreclosure process began. The data comes from BlackBox database.

***Significant at the 1 percent level.
**Significant at the 5 percent level.
*Significant at the 10 percent level.

foreclose loans faster than big banks by about twenty-three days (0.76 of month), a relative reduction of 4.4 percent in foreclosure time. Columns (2) and (3) split the sample based on whether loans entered delinquency in the 2004–2007 period or in the 2008–2010 period, respectively. These results suggest that the gap in foreclosure time between big banks and independent servicers grew over time. We interpret these results as suggesting that big banks—possibly due to stronger political or regulatory pressures—were more lenient in processing foreclosures. Overall, these correlations suggest that political pressure may have played a role in delaying foreclosures, especially during the later end of the crisis.

Role of Servicer-Specific Factors

Finally, the renegotiation process may have been stymied (or perceived to be stymied) by several other factors. For instance, limited organizational capability or capacity constraints faced by some lenders and servicers during the crisis may have prevented these institutions from developing and implementing cost-effective mortgage modification programs. A recent paper by Agarwal, Amromin, et al. (2012) suggests that the sluggish pace of the loss mitigation process of mortgages following the crisis can be attributed (in part) to the inaction of servicers, likely due to their limited organizational capabilities. Moreover, the general downturn in the economy—leading to significant job loss—also contributed to the deepening of the foreclosure crisis.

Since foreclosures tend to result in significant deadweight losses for borrowers and lenders and impose negative externalities for neighborhoods, many federal, state, and local initiatives have been undertaken to combat the foreclosure crisis. We now discuss the most significant initiative undertaken by the federal government to address the factors that were perceived to be hindering renegotiations.

Government Intervention to Stem the Foreclosure Crisis

There were several reasons why the federal government intervened in the foreclosure crisis. First, as discussed before, foreclosures may exert significant negative externalities that make it socially optimal for government intervention to accelerate the rate of mortgage modifications relative to what lenders and servicers would do privately. Second, as we also discussed, servicers' financial incentives, legal constraints and uncertainty in servicers' contracts, and coordination problems among dispersed investors may have inhibited renegotiation of securitized loans. These coordination problems could be fixed if the government served as a coordinating entity. Third, some lenders and servicers may have become liquidity constrained during the crisis. Consequently, these institutions may not have had sufficient resources required to develop and implement mortgage modification programs. Providing them with subsidies for modification efforts could alleviate their financial constraints, allowing them to modify more loans. Finally, a government-initiated loan modification program could provide a framework to standardize modification efforts, resulting in possible economies of scale and a reduction in borrowers' idiosyncratic incentives to strategically default.

These arguments were central to the Obama administration implementing the Home Affordable Modification Program (HAMP) program, with the hope of bolstering the rate of modifications of residential loans. The HAMP program outline was presented on March 4, 2009. Its two main features consist of, first, a cost-sharing arrangement with mortgage holders and investors designed to help reduce monthly payments on first-lien mortgages, and second, sizable financial incentives to servicers for modifying mortgages under the program.[30] The Treasury has also committed to use HAMP funds

---

30. The HAMP committed to onetime incentive payments to servicers of $1,000 for each completed renegotiation under the program. Servicers were also eligible for up to $1,000 in annual, ongoing pay-for-success incentive payments that would accrue if mortgage payments were made on time for three years after the renegotiation. These incentive payments are sizable relative to the regular annual fees for servicing, which amount to about 20 to 50 basis points of the outstanding loan balance ($400 to $1,000 per year for a $200,000 outstanding loan balance mortgage).

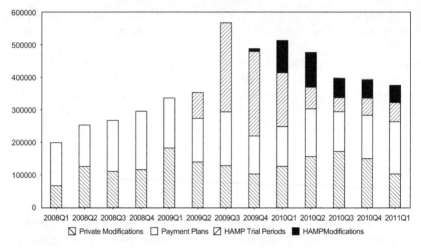

Fig. 4.19   Residential mortgage renegotiations in the United States (2008:Q1 to 2011:Q1)

Source: OCC and OTS Mortgage Metrics Reports, Q1:2009 to Q1:2011.

Notes: This figure presents the number and composition of mortgage renegotiations for residential mortgages over the period 2008:Q1 to 2011:Q1.

to provide both onetime and ongoing "pay-for-success" incentives to borrowers for making payments on modified loans.

When the program was introduced, new borrowers were to be accepted under the program until December 31, 2012. Program payments were to be made for up to five years after the date of entry into a Home Affordable Modification. According to the Government Accounting Office (2010), the budget allocated to HAMP overall was $50 billion of Troubled Asset Relief Program (TARP) funds, directed to encourage the modification of mortgages that financial institutions own and hold in their portfolios and mortgages held in private label securitization trusts. In addition, Fannie Mae and Freddie Mac provided an additional $25 billion to encourage servicers and borrowers to modify loans owned or guaranteed by the GSEs. The expectation of policymakers—given the number of severely indebted households—was that about three to four million home owners would receive assistance with their mortgages during forty-five months of the program.[31]

Figure 4.19 shows residential mortgage renegotiations performed in the OCC data covering more than 60 percent of the mortgage market. We note that just prior to the announcement of the HAMP program, almost 200,000 loans were modified in the first quarter of 2009. In addition, more than

31. This estimate was based on the number of home owners who were likely to be at risk of default (over 10 million homes), to have unaffordable loans (more than 8 million homes), to apply for a loan modification (5.5 million homes), and to pass the net present value (NPV) test (about 4 million homes). See Government Accountability Office (2009).

100,000 loans were renegotiated using repayment plans. We do observe some modest increase in the number of modified loans after the HAMP passage. However, most of it comes in the form of HAMP trial modifications, which may be subsequently converted into a permanent modification only if the modification is successful during the trial period (i.e., borrowers make payments per the changed contract that was offered on a trial basis, which typically takes about six months). This figure suggests that a majority of trial modifications were not converted into permanent modifications.

A detailed empirical analysis of the effects of HAMP using OCC data is provided by Agarwal, Amromin, et al. (2012). Using a difference-in-difference strategy that exploits variation in program eligibility criteria across comparable borrowers, they estimate that the program resulted in only modest increase in modifications. Overall, they find that the impact of the program will be substantially limited since they estimate that renegotiations induced by HAMP will reach just one-third of its targeted 3 to 4 million indebted households. This shortfall is in large part due to low renegotiation intensity of a few large servicers that responded at half the rate than others. They show that the muted response of these servicers cannot be accounted for by differences in contract, borrower, or regional characteristics of mortgages across servicers. Instead, their low renegotiation activity—which is also observed before the program—reflects servicer-specific factors that appear to be related to their preexisting organizational capabilities. Overall, their findings reveal that the ability of government to quickly induce changes in behavior of large intermediaries through financial incentives is quite limited, underscoring significant barriers to the effectiveness of such polices.

Current Status of the Foreclosure Crisis

More than 5 million US home owners lost their homes to foreclosure between 2007 and 2010.[32] More worrisome, an additional 11 million homeowners—nearly one out of every four with a mortgage—are at risk of foreclosure because their homes are worth less than what they owe to mortgage lenders.[33] As of fall 2011, foreclosure rates are still high by historical standards, with many more expected. The lack of success of either private or government programs suggests that many of the barriers to efficient foreclosure resolution are even more formidable than previously anticipated. The economic downturn has been both more severe and more persistent than many expected, and house prices have not yet bottomed out in many metropolitan areas. Furthermore, underwater home owners and those with limited income have been unable to meet LTV and DTI guidelines set out by federal modification and refinance programs.

The broader lesson from the foreclosure crisis and the glut of vacant hous-

32. See Chen (2010).
33. See CoreLogic (2012).

ing is that during the boom, residential investment likely reached such levels that resources were ex post inefficiently allocated toward home construction. In many markets, house price growth may have distorted the overall efficiency of productive activity in the economy. It may take some time for the economy to reallocate resources to other productive sectors from housing; among other challenges, it may also require significant retraining of the labor force. This reallocation process is also hampered due to the uncertainty surrounding the future of the GSEs. The current set of lenders are only originating loans eligible for sale to GSEs—the only game in town—while other private participants are reluctant to reenter the mortgage market in which they may have to potentially compete with even larger and stronger GSEs than what they had faced in the early 2000s.

4.5   Conclusion

In our discussion of the evolution of the mortgage finance, we have described several factors related to innovation and securitization that led us into the current crisis and factors that allowed the crisis to prolong. We feel that many of these factors have direct implications on issues relevant to policymakers as they embark on redesigning mortgage markets going forward. We now list broad themes that have emerged and the lessons we can draw on each of these based on our analysis.

4.5.1   Implication 1: Skin in the Game Matters, but Not All Securitizations Are Created Equal

The first implication that emerges clearly from our analysis is that skin in the game matters for improving the performance of the mortgage pool. Securitization—the act of creating distance between originators of risk and those that bear the risk—requires several actors, each with potentially different interests, in the supply chain of credit. Several pieces of evidence presented here suggest that these conflicting interests can lower the quality of the mortgage pool. We have also emphasized the importance of mechanisms that potentially counteract the weakened incentives of various agents in the supply chain when they respond to greater "ease of securitization."

Going forward, the future design of private securitization will likely implement this lesson by better aligning the interests of lenders, underwriters, and servicers with those of investors. To achieve this goal, it may be beneficial to enforce some mandatory retention of a fraction of lower tranche by originators/underwriters to better align their interests with those of investors. Such retention is consistent with predictions of contracting literature and a component of the Dodd-Frank financial reform act. For example, in a recent theoretical work Hartman-Glaser, Piskorski, and Tchistyi (2012) derive the optimal mortgage-backed security contract in a dynamic setting, in which a mortgage underwriter with limited liability can engage in costly hidden effort to screen borrowers and can sell loans to investors. They show that (a) the timing of payments to the underwriter is the key incentive mechanism, (b) the maturity of the optimal contract can be shorter than the maturity of the underlying mortgages, (c) and that bundling mortgages is efficient, as it allows investors to learn about underwriter effort more quickly due to an information enhancement effect. Interestingly, they demonstrate that requiring the underwriter to retain the "first loss piece" can closely approximate the optimal contract. We note, however, that the practical design of such mechanisms is challenging: the appropriate retention will usually vary as a function of collateral, and there is also a legitimate question of how such retention clauses will be enforced in practice.

To shed more light on the importance of risk retention mechanisms, we briefly compare the provision of incentives in the nonagency residential mortgage-backed security market with other asset-backed security markets and argue that all "securitization" is not created the same—that is, there are differences in the nature of financial intermediation across products, and these differences could lead to dramatic differences in their performance.

We begin by describing the differences between credit card and auto loan securitizations and the securitization of nonagency residential mortgages in terms of originators' incentives to screen. In contrast to nonagency mortgages, auto and credit card securitizers ask issuers explicitly to retain first loss pieces on their asset-backed securities transactions. For example, an issuer like Ford Motor makes loans to car buyers through its Ford Motor Credit finance unit, and retains junior loan pieces before underwriters securitize senior loans to be sold as securities. Similarly, in the case of credit card securitization, card issuers only securitize receivables; they do not securitize the accounts themselves. Consequently, the issuer controls the account and retains the "excess spread"—the revenue in surplus of what is needed to pay the asset-backed securities. This provides the issuer with additional "skin in the game."

Similarly, securitization by the GSEs differs from subprime loan securitization on several important dimensions. First, since the buyers of loans are concentrated, it is easier to coordinate and implement standard lending and servicing guidelines across lenders. In addition, because the lender-investor relationship is repeated more frequently than in the subprime market, it is also easier to reward or punish lenders and servicers by tracking the performance of collateral originated by different entities. In other words, reputation-based implicit contracts are easier to sustain in this market. Interestingly, the credit card and auto loan securities market, as well as the market for GSE-backed securities, did not experience a collapse similar to that of the private label securitization market.[34] This may suggest that stron-

---

34. A similar point is made by Benmelech, Dlugosz, and Ivashina (2012) in the context of securitizations in the corporate loan collateralized loan obligations (CLOs). They show that

ger mechanisms for aligning incentives between various parties involved could have played an important role in sustaining their functioning during the crisis.[35]

4.5.2   Implication 2: Focus on What Products Should Be or Should Not Be Securitized

Our work highlights that issues of moral hazard are important only if the collateral being originated has potentially significant unobservable information associated with it. If hard information variables sufficiently capture the credit quality of the collateral, problems of moral hazard may not be a big issue. In fact, this has been found to be true even within the nonagency part of the securitized markets. As has been shown in Keys et al. (2009, 2010a, 2010b) and Keys, Seru, and Vig (2012), the issue of screening on unobservables is important only if the hard information variables are not likely to be sufficient statistics for a borrower's credit quality. For example, a high FICO borrower is unlikely to have a great deal of unobservable information that, if the lender had carefully collected the information, would fundamentally alter the borrower's predicted default rate. Credit card securitized pools tend to have higher FICO than subprime mortgage securitized pools, suggesting that screening on unobservables might be less of a concern in credit card markets in general. Similarly, loans sold to GSEs have hard information that is likely to be closer to a sufficient statistic of borrowers' credit quality. As a result, screening on unobservables may not be as severe to begin with as it is in the subprime market.

This insight has parallels in the work on financial intermediation. A large body of work shows that banks differ in technologies based on their size, which leads to differing comparative advantage on the products they originate. Small banks lend primarily to "soft information" intensive borrowers because the distance between the loan officers who originate the loan and the decision makers (loan officers) is shorter. Larger banks lend instead to borrowers with hard information, since there is potential information loss

---

mechanisms in place (including originator reputation) play a significant role in curbing adverse selection.

35. Another securitization structure—conduits—worked well during the crisis (Acharya, Schnabl, and Suarez 2011). We argue that this is the case because the issuers had enough "skin in the game." The conduit structure allows firms such as auto and credit card companies, which have loans on their balance sheets but are unable to access the unsecured commercial paper (CP) market at favorable rates to finance their assets in the asset-backed commercial paper (ABCP) market. Notably, the average age of an ABCP program's assets is significantly longer than the maturity of its commercial paper, and maturing paper is continually being repaid with the proceeds of new issues ("rolling"). This mismatch of assets and liabilities introduces liquidity risk into the ABCP product: should a conduit become unable to roll existing liabilities, the administrator must find another way to pay investors. To address these risks, most ABCP programs include explicit "liquidity backstops," or standing facilities that can be drawn upon in the event that the conduit is unable to rollover maturing paper, and which cover the conduit's obligations. The facility, either a loan or an asset purchase agreement, is generally provided by a commercial bank. Thus, the bank providing the liquidity facility has incentives to monitor the lenders originating the collateral that backs the pool due to threat of a run (as in Diamond and Rajan 2001).

between loan officers who originate the loan and decision makers (higher-level bank officials). This research suggests that large banks would face adverse selection on unobservables if soft information intensive borrowers were able to get loans from large banks.

Our findings are consistent with this evidence. Securitization creates a distance between the originator and the final bearer of risk, and therefore can be thought of as movement from a small bank to a large bank. Consequently, we find that loans where soft information is important are precisely the ones where informational problems occur—with investors holding loans that are worse on unobservables.

4.5.3   Implication 3: A Redesign of the Securitization Chain Should Not Ignore Other Agency Conflicts

The current crisis has also emphasized that the potential agency conflicts between underwriters and investors do not arise only during the mortgage origination process and its subsequent sale. Of great importance are also potential conflicts arising during the process of servicing these assets (Piskorski, Seru, and Vig 2010). Any new securitization design needs to anticipate these conflicts and allow investors better control of how their investments are managed. An important insight of our work is that an ideal securitization market would be more robust with better provisions for the possibility of mortgage workouts in a crisis. This could be achieved by building more state-contingencies into servicing contracts. For example, mortgages at risk of foreclosure could be transferred to special servicers according to similar rules as used in the commercial MBS market. Alternatively, some adjustments of mortgage terms due to changes in regional economic conditions may be directly built up into the mortgage contracts (see Shiller 2008; Piskorski and Tchistyi 2011). Moreover, the evidence provided by Mayer et al. (2011) suggests that more work should be done to design efficient mortgage modification programs that take into account borrowers' strategic responses to such policies.

4.5.4   Implication 4: Regulation That Proclaims That "One Size Fits All" Ignores the Evidence

Our results do not necessarily support the view that the Dodd–Frank mandate of 5 percent risk retention is the optimal amount of risk retention in the mortgage market. We find a great deal of heterogeneity across market segments in the ability of lenders to behave strategically; in some segments of the market, 5 percent may not be enough to strengthen incentives, while in others, retaining a 5 percent portion of the loan pool may be prohibitively costly to fund private label securitizations. Although our results provide broad support for skin in the game, we would need a complex structural model of pool performance and information frictions to estimate the optimal level of risk retention for a given type of underlying mortgage assets.

4.5.5   Important Caveats

While our line of research uncovers some potential costs of securitization, it is not questioning the potential benefits of this financial innovation. Securitization leads to better risk-sharing and can result in potentially financing value-creating investments that would otherwise be difficult to finance. There is large evidence in the literature on the benefits accruing to financially constrained banks, which, due to securitization, were able to fund new projects and sustain the adverse effects of monetary shocks on their balance sheets.

Were many of the effects we found ex ante priced by investors? While this is an important question, there are two obstacles in answering this question. First, data on the prices of various tranches in the MBS market is difficult to obtain. Most data vendors who provide the data make available prices that are "model" generated, rather than ones actually paid by investors. Second, it is hard to know what "correct" pricing means without a comprehensive structural model that maps various factors into a pricing function. Several papers show that the riskiness of the pool (as measured by ex post quality) and some ex ante pricing variable (like subordination rate) are positively correlated. Indeed, that is the same result we find (e.g., table 4.2, column [1]). However, without having a clear model to infer what the price should have been—given the riskiness of the pool—it is difficult to make assertions about optimal or correct pricing. As far as we are aware, no such model exists, but developing one is a fruitful area of future research.

It is important to note that while we refrain from making any welfare claims, there could have been distortions introduced in the real economy due to the effects we document, even if investors rationally priced the effect of securitization on screening. In particular, it is possible that regulators and rating agencies may have perceived some securitized assets to be less risky than they actually were if they relied on preboom data to evaluate the quality of securitized loans. As a result, banks' capital requirements may not have adjusted sufficiently for the risk of some securitized assets. Understanding the behavior of regulators and rating agencies in the period before and during the crisis remains another promising area of research.

Overall, our work seeks to emphasize that there are potential costs to the securitization process in practice, and that these costs must be recognized when designing the financial infrastructure for mortgage lending in the future.

Data Appendix

We use several sources of mortgage data to conduct our analysis. The first source of data is from LoanPerformance, who maintain a loan-level database that provides a detailed perspective on the nonagency securities market. The data includes, as of December 2006, more than 7,000 active home equity and nonprime loan pools that include more than 7 million active loans, with over $1.6 trillion in outstanding balances. LoanPerformance estimates that, as of 2006, the data covers over 90 percent of the universe of securitized nonprime loans. The data set includes all standard loan application variables such as the loan amount, loan-to-value (LTV) ratio, FICO credit score, and interest rate. The major limitation of the data set is that it does not have information on unsold loans.

Our next source of data comes from the Lender Processing Services (LPS) database (formerly "McDash"), which combines characteristics of the loan and borrower at the time of origination with monthly payment information. The LPS data contain loan-level information on unsold loans, loans securitized by government-sponsored enterprise (GSEs), and loans securitized through private investors. In addition, similar to the LoanPerformance data set, LPS also includes all standard loan application variables such as the loan amount, LTV ratio, FICO credit score, and interest rate. The downside of the data is that its coverage of subprime loans is significantly limited, especially for loans originated prior to 2005.

Each of these data sets contains information about the property being financed by the borrower and the purpose of the loan. Specifically, we have information on the type of mortgage loan (fixed rate, adjustable rate, balloon, or hybrid) and the zip code where the dwelling is located. Typically, loans are classified as either for purchase or refinance, though in this chapter we focus exclusively on loans for home purchases. We restrict our sample to cover owner-occupied single-family residences, townhouses, or condominiums (single-unit loans account for more than 90 percent of the loans in our sample). We also drop nonconventional properties, such as those that are Federal Housing Administration (FHA)- or Veterans Administration (VA)-insured or pledged properties, and also exclude buy down mortgages. Only those loans with valid FICO scores are used in our sample.

In general, we assess borrower creditworthiness along two dimensions. First, we use borrower credit scores, known as "FICO" scores, as a measure of credit risk. These scores provide a ranking of potential borrowers by the probability of having some negative credit event in the next two years, with nearly all scores between 500 and 800 (see Avery et al. 1996). Second, we use the level of documentation of income and assets collected by the lender as a proxy of borrower quality. Documentation in the market (and reported in the database) is categorized as full, limited, or no documentation. Borrowers with full documentation verify both income and assets. Borrowers with limited documentation usually provide no information about their income but do provide some about their assets. "No-documentation" borrowers provide no information about income or assets, which is a very rare degree of screening lenience on the part of lenders. In our analysis, we combine limited and no-documentation borrowers and call them low-documentation borrowers.

Next, in some of our analysis we use information from a database of lenders' required disclosure to the federal government under the Home Mortgage Disclosure Act (HMDA). The HMDA data set, hosted at the Federal Reserve Bank of New York, covers the period from 1990 to 2008, though newer data have been collected, as lenders are still required to report this information. In several of our analyses we will use information from other sources (e.g., prospectuses of MBS). We discuss these sources closer to where we conduct the analysis.

Finally, in some of our analysis we use data that links two databases: (a) loan-level mortgage data on nonagency securitized mortgages collected by BlackBox Logic, and (b) borrower-level credit report information collected by Equifax. BlackBox data, which has similar coverage as the LP database, account for about 90 percent of all privately securitized mortgages. The BlackBox data, which are obtained from mortgage servicers and securitization trustees, include static information taken at the time of origination, such as mortgage date and amount, FICO credit score, servicer name, interest rate, term, and interest rate type. The BlackBox data also include dynamic data on monthly payments, mortgage balances, and delinquency status. Equifax is a credit reporting agency that provides monthly data on borrowers' current credit scores, payments and balances on mortgage and installment debt, and balances and credit utilization for revolving debt (such as credit cards and HELOCs). These databases were merged by 1010Data, a provider of data warehousing and processing, using a proprietary match algorithm.

We note that there is no consensus on definition of a "subprime" mortgage. The term subprime usually refers to a loan (mortgage, auto, etc.) that is viewed as riskier than a regular (prime) loan in the eyes of a lender. It is riskier because the expected probability of default for these loans is higher. There are several definitions of subprime available in the industry. A subprime loan can be (a) originated to a borrower with a low credit score and/or history of delinquency or bankruptcy, and/or poor employment history; (b) originated by lenders specializing in high-cost loans who sell few loans to the GSEs; (c) part of a subprime security (called B&C or Alt-A securities in Wall Street parlance); and/or (d) a mortgage (e.g., a 2/28 or 3/27 "hybrid" mortgage) generally not available in the market where the GSEs operate.

References

Acharya, Viral, Philipp Schnabl, and Gustavo Suarez. 2012. "Securitization without Risk Transfer." *Journal of Financial Economics.* Available online as of October 12, 2012: http://dx.doi.org/10.1016/j.jfineco.2012.09.004.

Adelino, Manuel, Kristopher Gerardi, and Paul S. Willen. 2010. "Why Don't Lenders Renegotiate More Home Mortgages? Redefaults, Self-Cures and Securitization." Federal Reserve Bank of Atlanta Working Paper.

Agarwal, Sumit, Gene Amromin, Itzhak Ben-David, Souphala Chomsisengphet, and Douglas D. Evanoff. 2011a. "Market-Based Loss Mitigation Practices for

Troubled Mortgages Following the Financial Crisis." Federal Reserve Bank of Chicago Working Paper no. 2011-03.

———. 2011b. "The Role of Securitization in Mortgage Renegotiation." *Journal of Financial Economics.* http://dx.doi.org/10.1016/j.jfineco.2011.07.005.

Agarwal, Sumit, Gene Amromin, Itzhak Ben-David, Souphala Chomsisengphet, Tomasz Piskorski, and Amit Seru. 2012. "Policy Intervention in Debt Renegotiation: Evidence from Home Affordable Modification Program." Working Paper. Available at SSRN: http://ssrn.com/abstract=2138314.

Agarwal, Sumit, Gene Amromin, Itzhak Ben-David, Souphala Chomsisengphet, and Yan Zhang. 2011. "Second Liens and the Holdup Problem in First Mortgage Renegotiation." Working Paper. Available at SSRN: http://ssrn.com/abstract=2022501.

Agarwal, Sumit, Gene Amromin, Itzhak Ben-David, and Serdar Dinc. 2011. "The Politics of Foreclosure." National University of Singapore, Working Paper.

Agarwal, Sumit, and Calvin T. Ho. 2007. "Comparing the Prime and Subprime Mortgage Markets." *Chicago Fed Letter,* Number 241.

Agarwal, Sumit, David Lucca, Amit Seru, and Francesco Trebbi. 2012. "Inconsistent Regulators: Evidence from Banking." NBER Working Paper no. 17736. Cambridge, MA: National Bureau of Economic Research.

Ambrose, Brent, Anthony Sanders, and Abdullah Yavas. 2011. "Special Servicers and Adverse Selection in Informed Intermediation: Theory and Evidence." Pennsylvania State University, Working Paper.

Ashcraft, Adam, and Til Schuermann. 2008. "Understanding the Securitization of Subprime Mortgage Credit." Federal Reserve Bank of New York Staff Report no. 318.

Avery, Robert, Raphael Bostic, Paul Calem, and Glenn Canner. 1996. "Credit Risk, Credit Scoring and the Performance of Home Mortgages." *Federal Reserve Bulletin* 82:621–48.

Barlevy, Gadi, and Jonas Fisher. 2010. "Mortgage Choices and Housing Speculation." Federal Reserve Bank of Chicago Working Paper.

Belsky, Eric S., and Nela Richardson. 2010. "Understanding the Boom and Bust in Nonprime Mortgage Lending." Harvard Joint Center for Housing Studies Working Paper.

Ben-David, Itzhak. 2011. "Financial Constraints and Inflated Home Prices during the Real Estate Boom." *American Economic Journal: Applied Economics* 3 (3): 55–78.

Benmelech, Efraim, Jennifer Dlugosz, and Victoria Ivashina. 2012. "Securitization without Adverse Selection: The Case of CLOs." *Journal of Financial Economics* 106 (1): 91–113.

Bhutta, Neil, Jane Dokko, and Hui Shan. 2010. "The Depth of Negative Equity and Mortgage Default Decisions." FEDS Working Paper 2010-35.

Bolton, Patrick, and Howard Rosenthal. 2002. "Political Intervention in Debt Contracts." *Journal of Political Economy* 110 (5): 1103–34.

Bond, Philip, David K. Musto, and Bilge Yilmaz. 2005. "Predatory Lending in a Rational World." Federal Reserve Bank of Philadelphia Working Paper no. 06-2.

Bubb, Ryan, and Alex Kaufman. 2009. "Securitization and Moral Hazard: Evidence from Credit Score Cutoff Rules." Federal Reserve Bank of Boston Working Paper no. 0905.

———. 2011. "Further Investigations into the Origin of Credit Score Cutoff Rules." NYU School of Law Working Paper.

Bucks, Brian K., and Karen M. Pence. 2008. "Do Borrowers Know Their Mortgage Terms?" *Journal of Urban Economics* 64 (2): 218–33.

Buiter, Willem H. 2008. "Lessons from the North Atlantic Financial Crisis." Paper presented at "The Role of Money Markets" Conference, Columbia Business School and the Federal Reserve Bank of New York. May 29–30.

Campbell, John Y., and Joao F. Cocco. 2011. "A Model of Mortgage Default."
    NBER Working Paper no. 17516. Cambridge, MA: National Bureau of Economic
    Research.
Campbell, John Y., Stefano Giglio, and Parag Pathak. 2011. "Forced Sales and
    House Prices." *American Economic Review* 101(5): 2108–31.
Chen, Celia. 2010. "Foreclosures Cloud the Housing Outlook." Moody's Analytics
    Regional Financial Review. November.
Chomsisengphet, Souphala, and Anthony Pennington-Cross. 2006. "The Evolution
    of the Subprime Mortgage Market." *St. Louis Federal Reserve Review,* January-
    February 88 (1): 31–56.
Citigroup Global Markets. 2009. "A Brief (and Complete) History of Loan Modi-
    fications." Working Paper.
Cocco, Joao F. 2011. "Understanding the Trade-offs of Alternative Mortgage Prod-
    ucts." Working Paper. Available at SSRN: http://ssrn.com/abstract=1572603.
Corbae, Dean, and Erwan Quintin. 2011. "Mortgage Innovation and the Foreclosure
    Boom." University of Texas–Austin, Working Paper.
CoreLogic. 2012. "CoreLogic Reports Negative Equity Increase in Q4 2011." http://
    corelogic.com/about-us/news/asset_upload_file909_14436.pdf.
Demiroglu, Cem, and Christopher M. James. 2012. "How Important Is Having Skin
    in the Game? Originator-Sponsor Affiliation and Losses on Mortgage-Backed
    Securities." *Review of Financial Studies* 25 (11): 3217–58.
Demyanyk, Yuliya, and Otto Van Hemert. 2009. "Understanding the Subprime
    Mortgage Crisis." *Review of Financial Studies.* doi:10.1093/rfs/hhp033.
Deng, Yongheng, John Quigley, and Robert Van Order. 2000. "Mortgage Termina-
    tions, Heterogeneity, and the Exercise of Mortgage Options." *Econometrica*
    68:275–307.
Diamond, Douglas W., and Raghuram Rajan. 2001. "Liquidity Risk, Liquidity
    Creation, and Financial Fragility: A Theory of Banking." *Journal of Political
    Economy* 109 (2): 287–327.
Dunn, Kenneth B., and Chester S. Spatt. 1985. "An Analysis of Mortgage Contract-
    ing: Prepayment Penalties and the Due-on-Sale Clause." *Journal of Finance*
    40:293–308.
Favilukis, Jack, Sydney Ludvigson, and Stijn Van Nieuwerburgh. 2010. "The Macro-
    economic Effects of Housing Wealth, Housing Finance, and Limited Risk-Sharing
    in General Equilibrium." NBER Working Paper no. 15988. Cambridge, MA:
    National Bureau of Economic Research.
Gan, Yingjin, and Christopher Mayer. 2006. "Agency Conflicts, Asset Substitution,
    and Securitization." NBER Working Paper no. 12359. Cambridge, MA: National
    Bureau of Economic Research.
Gelpern, Anna, and Adam J. Levitin. 2009. "Rewriting Frankenstein Contracts: The
    Workout Prohibition in Residential Mortgage-Backed Securities." *Southern Cali-
    fornia Law Review* 82:1077–152.
Goldstein, Debbie, and Stacy Strohauer Son. 2003. "Why Prepayment Penalties Are
    Abusive in Subprime Home Loans." Center for Responsible Lending Policy Paper
    no. 4.
Government Accountability Office. 2006. *Alternative Mortgage Products: Impact on
    Defaults Remains Unclear, but Disclosure of Risks to Borrowers Could Be Improved.*
    GAO-06-1021, September.
———. 2009. *Treasury Actions Needed to Make the Home Affordable Modification
    Program More Transparent and Accountable.* GAO-09-837, July 23.
———. 2010. *Home Affordable Modification Program Continues to Face Implemen-
    tation Challenges.* GAO-10-556T, March 25.
Guiso, Luigi, Paola Sapienza, and Luigi Zingales. 2009. "Moral and Social Con-

straints to Strategic Default on Mortgages." NBER Working Paper no. 15145. Cambridge, MA: National Bureau of Economic Research.

Hartman-Glaser, Barney, Tomasz Piskorski, and Alexei Tchistyi. 2012. "Optimal Securitization with Moral Hazard." *Journal of Financial Economics* 104 (1): 186–202.

Holmstrom, Bengt, and Paul Milgrom. 1991. "Multitask Principal-Agent Analyses: Incentive Contracts, Asset Ownership, and Job Design." *Journal of Law, Economics, & Organization* 7:24–52.

Jiang, Wei, Ashlyn Aiko Nelson, and Edward Vytlacil. 2009. "Liar's Loan? Effects of Origination Channel and Information Falsification on Mortgage Delinquency." Indiana University Bloomington, School of Public and Environmental Affairs Research Paper no. 2009-06-02.

———. 2010. "Securitization and Loan Performance: A Contrast of Ex Ante and Ex Post Relations in the Mortgage Market." Working Paper. Available at SSRN: http://ssrn.com/abstract=1571300.

Kau, James B., Donald C. Keenan, and Taewon Kim. 1994. "Default Probabilities for Mortgages." *Journal of Urban Economics* 35:278–96.

Keys, Benjamin J., Tanmoy Mukherjee, Amit Seru, and Vikrant Vig. 2009. "Financial Regulation and Securitization: Evidence from Subprime Loans." *Journal of Monetary Economics* 56 (5): 700–20.

———. 2010a. "Did Securitization Lead to Lax Screening? Evidence from Subprime Loans." *Quarterly Journal of Economics* 125:307–62.

———. 2010b. "620 FICO, Take II: Securitization and Screening in the Subprime Mortgage Market." University of Chicago, Working Paper.

Keys, Benjamin J., Amit Seru, and Vikrant Vig. 2012. "Lender Screening and Role of Securitization: Evidence from Prime and Subprime Mortgage Markets." *Review of Financial Studies* 25 (7): 2071–108.

Khan, James A., 2008. "Housing Prices, Productivity Growth and Learning." Working Paper. Federal Reserve Bank of New York.

Landier, Augustin, David Sraer, and David Thesmar. 2010. "Going for Broke: New Century Financial Corporation, 2004–2006." IDEI Working Papers 649. Toulouse: Institut d'Économie Industrielle (IDEI).

Loutskina, Elena, and Philip E. Strahan. 2011. "Informed and Uninformed Investment in Housing: The Downside of Diversification." *Review of Financial Studies* 24 (5): 1447–80.

Makarov, Igor, and Guillaume Plantin. 2011. "Equilibrium Subprime Lending." *Journal of Finance,* forthcoming.

Mayer, Christopher, Edward Morrison, and Tomasz Piskorski. 2009. "A New Proposal for Loan Modifications." *Yale Journal on Regulation* 26:417–29.

Mayer, Christopher, Edward Morrison, Tomasz Piskorski, and Arpit Gupta. 2011. "Mortgage Modification and Strategic Behavior: Evidence from a Legal Settlement with Countrywide." NBER Working Paper no. 17065. Cambridge, MA: National Bureau of Economic Research.

Mayer, Christopher, Karen Pence, and Shane Sherlund. 2009. "The Rise in Mortgage Defaults." *Journal of Economic Perspectives* 23:27–50.

Mayer, Christopher, Tomasz Piskorski, and Alexei Tchistyi. 2010. "The Inefficiency of Refinancing: Why Prepayment Penalties Are Good for Risky Borrowers." *Journal of Financial Economics.* Available online October 13, 2012. http://dx.doi.org/10.1016/jfineco.2012.10.003.

Melzer, Brian. 2012. "Debt Overhang: Reduced Investment by Homeowners with Negative Equity." Kellogg School of Management, Working Paper.

———. 2011. "The Real Costs of Credit Access: Evidence from the Payday Lending Market." *Quarterly Journal of Economics* 126 (1): 517–55.

Mian, Atif, and Amir Sufi. 2009. "The Consequences of Mortgage Credit Expansion: Evidence from the US Mortgage Default Crisis." *Quarterly Journal of Economics* 124:1449–96.
———. 2011. "House Prices, Home Equity-Based Borrowing, and the US Household Leverage Crisis." *American Economic Review* 101 (5): 2132–56.
Mian, Atif, Amir Sufi, and Francesco Trebbi. 2011. "Foreclosures, House Prices, and the Real Economy." NBER Working Paper no. 16685. Cambridge, MA: National Bureau of Economic Research.
Nadauld, Taylor D., and Shane M. Sherlund. 2009. "The Role of the Securitization Process in the Expansion of Subprime Credit." Finance and Economics Discussion Series (FEDS) Working Paper no. 2009-28. Board of Governors of the Federal Reserve System.
Pence, Karen M. 2006. "'Foreclosing on Opportunity: State Laws and Mortgage Credit.'" *Review of Economics and Statistics* 88:177–82.
Piskorski, Tomasz, Amit Seru, and Vikrant Vig. 2010. "Securitization and Distressed Loan Renegotiation: Evidence from the Subprime Mortgage Crisis." *Journal of Financial Economics* 97:369–97.
Piskorski, Tomasz, and Alexei Tchistyi. 2010. "Optimal Mortgage Design." *Review of Financial Studies* 23:3098–140.
———. 2011. "Stochastic House Appreciation and Optimal Mortgage Lending." *Review of Financial Studies* 24:1407–46.
Posner, Eric A., and Luigi Zingales. 2009. "A Loan Modification Approach to the Housing Crisis." *American Law and Economics Review* 2009:1–33.
Purnanandam, Amiyatosh. 2011. "Originate-to-Distribute Model and the Subprime Mortgage Crisis." *Review of Financial Studies* 24 (6): 1881–915.
Rajan, Uday, Amit Seru, and Vikrant Vig. 2010. "The Failure of Models that Predict Failure: Distance, Incentives and Defaults." Chicago GSB Research Paper no. 08-19.
Sherlund, Shane M. 2008. "The Past, Present, and Future of Subprime Mortgages." FEDS Working Paper no. 2008-63. Board of Governors of the Federal Reserve System.
Shiller, Robert J. 2008. *The Subprime Solution: How Today's Global Financial Crisis Happened, and What to Do About It.* Princeton, NJ: Princeton University Press.
Stein, Jeremy C. 2002. "Information Production and Capital Allocation: Decentralized vs. Hierarchical Firms." *Journal of Finance* 57:1891–921.
Stevens, David H. 2011. "Legislative Proposals to End Taxpayer Funding for Ineffective Foreclosure Mitigation Programs." Written Testimony of David H. Stevens, Assistant Secretary of Housing, Federal Housing Administration. Hearing before the House Financial Services Committee's Subcommittee on Insurance, Housing, and Community Opportunity. March 2.
Van den Heuvel, Skander J. 2008. "The Welfare Cost of Bank Capital Requirements." *Journal of Monetary Economics* 55 (2): 298–320.
White, Alan M. 2009a. "Deleveraging the American Homeowner: The Failure of 2008 Voluntary Mortgage Contract Modifications." *Connecticut Law Review* 41:1107–31.
———. 2009b. "Rewriting Contracts, Wholesale: Data on Voluntary Mortgage Modifications from 2007 and 2008 Remittance Reports." *Fordham Urban Law Journal* 36:509–35.
Zhang, Yan. 2011. "Does Loan Renegotiation Differ by Securitization Status? An Empirical Study." Working Paper. Available at SSRN: http://ssrn.com/abstract =1773103.

5

A New Look at Second Liens

Donghoon Lee, Christopher Mayer, and Joseph Tracy

Second liens represent an important segment of the credit markets in the United States, but are often controversial and poorly understood. According to data from Equifax Credit Trends (August, 2011), consumers owe about $11.3 trillion to various lenders. Of that total, first mortgages represent about $8.16 trillion and second liens are another $800 billion.[1] The remaining $2.36 trillion includes auto and student loans and credit cards.

The run-up in second liens has often been blamed as a major contributor to the housing crisis, both because second liens facilitated a large increase in debt-financed consumption (Greenspan and Kennedy 2008) and also because second liens allowed potentially poorly qualified buyers to purchase homes with little cash as a down payment. Our data show that second

Donghoon Lee is a senior economist at the Federal Reserve Bank of New York. Christopher Mayer is the Paul Milstein Professor of Real Estate and professor of finance and economics at Columbia Business School, a visiting scholar at the Federal Reserve Bank of New York, and a research associate of the National Bureau of Economic Research. Joseph Tracy is an executive vice president and senior advisor to the president at the Federal Reserve Bank of New York.

The opinions, analysis, and conclusions of this chapter are those of the authors and do not indicate concurrence by the Board of Governors of the Federal Reserve System, the Federal Reserve Bank of New York, or their staffs. The authors wish to thank Daniel Hubbard and James Witkin for excellent research assistance, Ethan Buyon for comments, and Dataquick and Equifax for providing critical data for this chapter. The Milstein Center for Real Estate and the Richman Center for Business, Law, and Public Policy at Columbia Business School provided critical funding for this project. For acknowledgments, sources of research support, and disclosure of the authors' material financial relationships, if any, please see http://www .nber.org/chapters/c12623.ack.

1. Of the outstanding second liens, the bulk ($595 billion) are home equity lines of credit, which are revolving credit lines. In total, HELOCs are about the same size as all other types of revolving credit (credit cards) and thus represent an important part of consumer credit. Closed-end second liens are much smaller, representing about $158 billion, less than 10 percent of all other nonrevolving debt.

lien originations were always below $50 billion per quarter prior to 2001, but more than tripled to over $160 billion quarterly by 2005 and 2006. Total balances of second lien borrowings grew from under $200 billion to $1.1 trillion over the same time period. While much attention has been paid to piggyback second liens that helped borrowers purchase homes with small down payments, the bulk of the borrowing involved home equity lines of credit (HELOCs) (and closed-end second liens, or CES) that were taken out well after the borrower purchased the home. Such debt represented a tax-preferred way for many borrowers to use gains in home values to support increased consumption, help reduce other forms of debt, or to make improvements in their home.[2]

Today, since second liens rank as junior mortgage debt, they pose a potential risk to the banking system, as most second lien loans reside on lenders' balance sheets. Total outstanding second liens represent more than one-half of all bank capital ($1.4 trillion according to the Federal Financial Institutions Examination Council [FFIEC] Peer Group Average Report). However, lenders argue that second liens are more comparable to other types of consumer debt, rather than mortgages, and were originated according to the same or stricter standards that they offered other types of consumer debt. A key question, therefore, in evaluating the capitalization of many banks is how second liens perform relative to first liens and other consumer credit.

An additional issue with second liens involves potential conflicts of interest for servicers who manage first and second liens. Investors complain that servicers of second liens act in ways that prioritize payments to second liens over first liens.[3] According to these concerns, the largest banks that hold many second liens on their balance sheets also act as servicers on the associated securitized first liens. These lenders face potentially conflicting incentives between their fiduciary responsibilities as servicers and their interests to protect their second liens by either aggressively modifying first liens (at great cost to mortgage bond owners) or encouraging borrowers to miss first lien payments while remaining current on their second liens.

In a related vein, many analysts argue that second liens represent a serious public policy challenge, based on a view that second lien holders often get in the way of high loan-to-value (LTV) refinancing programs such as the Home Affordable Refinance Program (HARP) by refusing to agree to "resubordinate" to a newly issued first lien. Also, second liens are much more likely to be underwater than first liens, increasing the likelihood of a costly foreclosure. Martin Feldstein (2011) has proposed a program where

---

2. The tax deductibility of second liens depends on the use of proceeds. Generally speaking, interest on the first $100,000 of home equity borrowing is tax deductible regardless of the use of proceeds as long as the owner does not exceed $1 million of total outstanding mortgages. Beyond $100,000, interest on the borrowing might be tax deductible depending on whether the borrower uses the proceeds for improving the home.

3. See Frey (2011).

the government would subsidize 50 percent of the cost of writing-down negative equity to 110 percent LTV, which might impact an appreciable portion of second liens that are the most junior position relative to the first lien. Levitan (2009) has suggested that bankruptcy judges should have the right to "cram down" debt, forcing lenders to accept losses on the underwater portion of the first and second lien. Mayer, Morrison, and Piskorski (2009) propose a small "Second Lien Incentive Fee" to pay second lien holders to voluntarily surrender their claim rather than holding up the modification process. Mortgage-holders often take an even stronger view, arguing that giving any rights to second lien holders violates basic prioritization of claims. They suggest that second liens should be forced to accept a total write-off before first liens write off any principal or substantially reduce interest rates for borrowers.

On the other hand, banks argue that many (but not all) second liens, especially revolving home equity lines of credit (HELOCs),[4] were given primarily to the best quality borrowers and were underwritten to a great extent based on the credit quality of the borrower, not just the home value. Such mortgages are the equivalent to high-quality credit card loans, where if the borrower does not pay the lender has a claim on the borrower and not just on the home. They suggest that no one would propose that a credit card be written down—when a borrower is underwater but remains current on the mortgage, even though credit cards are also unsecured debt and thus might have lower priority, why should HELOCs be treated differently? While HELOCs and credit cards both impact the borrower's indebtedness and place demands on the borrower's cash flow, only HELOCs impact the borrower's equity position in the house. The equivalence of HELOCs and credit card debt depends on a critical question: Does the borrower's equity position have an independent impact on the probability of default on the HELOC, holding the borrower's total amount of debt constant?[5]

The law often supports the legal interpretation of second liens as personal recourse debt with equivalent priority to credit cards or student loans. In states where borrowers face personal recourse if they default on a first mortgage, second liens also have personal recourse against the borrower and his or her other assets. Even in states where first liens have no personal recourse,

---

4. A HELOC is a mortgage in which the lender agrees to give a borrower a line of credit up to some maximum amount, where the lender has a secured claim on the home in addition to a claim against the borrower.

5. For example, a second lien or a credit card balance with the equivalent minimum monthly payment would both raise the borrower's back-end debt-to-income (DTI) ratio by the same amount. However, the second lien would also raise the borrower's LTV, whereas the credit card balance would not. The question of the equivalence of second liens and credit card balances can be restated as: Holding the borrower's back-end DTI constant, does the borrower's LTV impact the likelihood that the borrower will default? In addition, a borrower's credit card balances are not required to be paid off if the borrower moves, whereas any second lien balances must be paid off if the house is sold.

borrowers still typically face personal liability for the second lien if they took out the second lien debt at any time after purchasing the home. That is, in nonrecourse states a second lien that is taken out at a later date would be recourse while a piggyback second lien (i.e., a second lien taken out at the same time as the first lien when the borrower purchases a home) would not have personal recourse to the borrower.

Government policies have attempted, without much success, to address problems with outstanding second liens. The HAMP (Home Affordable Mortgage Program) offers to pay second lien holders a nominal amount to cover costs of modifying or writing off second liens, but has resulted in only 76,218 such modifications as of April 2012, with fewer than 17,000 of them involving write-offs.[6]

While there has been relatively little empirical work that addresses these questions, three recent papers examine the prevalence and performance of second liens and provide the starting point for our analysis. Goodman et al. (2010) document that second liens were an important source of credit during the boom, with about one-half of all privately securitized mortgages having a second lien, and that second liens appear to perform better than privately securitized first liens. Andersson et al. (2011) examine data on mortgage payments and credit files (Office of the Comptroller of the Currency [OCC] Credit Bureau Data) for borrowers with nonprime, privately securitized mortgages combined with credit files from 2001 to 2009. The authors find that consumers have adjusted the relative order in which they pay their debts, moving from an environment where a default on credit card is much more likely to occur before a mortgage default to an environment where consumers are equally likely to initially miss mortgage or credit card payments. The authors attribute this finding to changes in the cost of servicing each type of debt, reduced or negative home equity, and the increased penetration of nonstandard mortgage products. The changing pecking order suggests that borrowers may be acting strategically by defaulting on their first lien in an attempt to obtain a modification, even while remaining current on their other debts.[7]

Jagtiani and Lang (2011) merge together data on mortgage performance (from Lender Processing Services–McDash) with credit report files (from Federal Reserve Bank of New York Consumer Credit Panel) to examine the relative order of payments for first and second liens. The paper finds that a large portion of delinquent borrowers on first liens keep their second liens current. Such behavior is more prevalent for HELOCs, where they argue that the ability to maintain a credit line is quite valuable, but is also quite common for closed-end second liens (CES), where the borrower takes out a mortgage for a fixed sum of money at one time.

6. Treasury Department, March 2012, "Making Home Affordable" Report.
7. This strategic behavior could be avoided if mortgage modifications were based on measures of payment stress such as the borrower's updated debt-to-income ratio, regardless of the payment status of the borrower.

This chapter considers a number of important issues with regard to second liens. We investigate these issues using information from Equifax credit reports and Dataquick deeds records. First, we look to understand the growth of second liens, including the credit quality of the borrowers. Next we examine where second liens were originated and how they might have contributed to (over) leverage during the boom. Finally, we consider how second liens perform relative to first liens. In particular, we examine why some borrowers choose to pay their second lien even as they are delinquent on their first lien.

In the following, we summarize our findings. In doing so, it is important to recognize that this chapter presents an attempt to summarize the data so that policymakers and analysts can better understand the second lien market and to spur additional analysis among economists. While results are sometimes suggestive of certain interpretations, we cannot in this analysis distinguish between supply and demand for credit. Thus, it is impossible to know whether some of these patterns reflect demand for second liens by various types of purchasers or constraints on the type of mortgages that lenders might approve.

1. Even though HELOCs and CES are both classified as second liens, they are quite different. The CES account for between 30 to 40 percent of the total second lien balances between 1999 and 2011 and have similar characteristics to nonprime first mortgages; they were often originated to borrowers with low credit scores and were more likely to be originated simultaneously with a first lien (so-called piggyback mortgage) and/or with nonprime first mortgages. The CES mortgage issuance peaked between 2005 and 2007, a time when deteriorating credit standards and peaking house prices led to very high subsequent default rates. By contrast, HELOCs are more closely related to conforming/prime first mortgages; HELOCs were originated to people with high credit scores, were often originated to borrowers with no first lien or a prime first mortgage, and were often originated well after the first lien had been taken out. The HELOC originations peaked in 2004, before the peak in home prices. Thus home-equity extraction, while important during the boom, seems to have taken place predominantly among relatively high-quality borrowers.

2. At the height of the housing market in 2006, as many as 40 to 45 percent of home purchases involved a piggyback second lien in coastal markets and bubble locations (Phoenix, Las Vegas, Miami). Slightly fewer piggybacks were used in more stable markets in the Midwest and South, and piggybacks were much less prevalent in declining markets like Cleveland and St. Louis. Second liens were strongly associated with the use of low down payments to purchase homes. While 10 to 20 percent of home purchases with a single mortgage involved a down payment of 5 percent or less (origination LTV $\geq$ 95 percent), about two-thirds of all purchases with a piggyback second lien

had a low down payment (origination combined loan-to-value, or CLTV $\geq$ 95 percent). Thus, piggyback second liens appear to have contributed to home purchases at times and in locations where home values likely exceeded fundamental values, potentially helping to fuel the housing bubble. Contrary to some claims about the use of second liens for speculation, second liens were somewhat more prevalent among owner-occupants than investors.

3. The CES performed similarly to nonprime mortgages, especially for CES originated between 2005 and 2007 and piggyback CES. The HELOCs performed much closer to prime first liens. More than 25 percent of the piggyback CES become 90+ days delinquent as of 2010 and 2011, but only 8 percent of HELOCs had similar serious delinquencies during the same period. The timing of origination and the credit quality of borrowers appear to explain most of these differences. In the last few quarters, however, HELOC delinquencies have been flat while delinquencies were falling for most other types of consumer credit.

4. We find a high correlation between the delinquency of first mortgages and their associated second liens. Borrowers are more likely to initially become delinquent on their first mortgages, but if the first mortgage delinquency persists, most second liens eventually default as well. For example, when a first mortgage reaches the 90 to 120 days delinquent stage, only about 21 percent of CES remain current four quarters later (31 percent for HELOCs). By contrast, about 70 percent of auto loans and 40 percent of all credit cards remain current four quarters after a serious mortgage delinquency.

5.1 Data

We utilize a variety of new data sets to examine aggregate trends in second lien usage, as well as individual use of second liens and subsequent repayment patterns. We start with Equifax Credit Trends 4.0 to examine overall credit usage. These data report information for all consumers whose credit records are reported to Equifax. Data are available from 2005 to the present.

Next we turn to the Federal Reserve Bank of New York Consumer Credit Panel (CCP), which comprises an anonymous and nationally representative 5 percent random sample of US individuals with credit files and all of their household members. In all, the data set includes credit information for more than 15 percent of the population, or approximately 37 million individuals in each quarter. The panel allows us to track individual borrowers and their loan accounts including first mortgages, second liens, credit cards, auto loans, and student loans over time. The CCP panel is based on Equifax consumer credit reports. Lee and van der Klaauw (2010) provide further details on the CCP data.

Due to the large size of the CCP data, we use a 0.1 percent sample of the population in our analysis. This includes about 240,000 individuals with credit reports in a given quarter. While joint accounts appear twice on the credit report—for example, one for the husband and a second for the wife—we combine these joint records into a single record where appropriate to remove any duplicates. Our sample for this chapter runs from 1999:Q1 to 2012:Q1, thus covering a more stable period before the subprime run-up, the housing boom, and the subsequent bust.

We face a number of data issues, which are described later. The credit files do not always clearly identify whether a loan is a first mortgage or a CES. We classify the loans with narrative codes of Freddie, Fannie, Federal Housing Administration (FHA), and Veterans Affairs (VA) as first mortgages, and loans with narrative codes of home equity loan, home improvement loan, and second mortgage as second liens. We believe that at least 80 percent of Freddie and Fannie loans and 100 percent of FHA and VA loans have correct narrative codes.[8] The HELOCs are easily identified since they are recorded as a revolving account type. There are some installment loans with no narrative codes indicating the type of loan. Among these unclassified installment loans, we currently drop from the sample those with an origination amount of less than $40,000 from the sample (our results are robust to keeping these loans and classifying them as CES). We treat mortgages with an origination balance of at least $40,000 that do not have a narrative code indicating that they are Freddie, Fannie, FHA, or VA loans as nonprime first liens. Care must be used in interpreting results for this class of loans. Nonprime first liens by construction in our data are a residual category, including not only subprime and Alt-A mortgages (the traditional category of nonprime), but also Jumbo-prime mortgages, some government-sponsored enterprise (GSE) prime mortgages that are not properly narrated, and some private label conforming loans. We have no way to externally validate differences among the various types of mortgages at this time.

The origination date is defined for our analysis by the quarter the loan appears on the credit report for the first time. However, there can be some delays between when a loan is actually originated and when it is reported to Equifax, so this classification may have some error in timing. The results are quite similar if we use the reported quarter of origination instead.

To examine the importance of second liens in financing of individual property purchases and, in particular, the extent to which second liens contributed to high leverage, we turn to Dataquick deeds records. Dataquick reports deeds records for the vast majority of home purchase and mortgage transactions. For this analysis, we examine purchase transactions only (no refinancings) and describe the financing of that purchase, including whether the transaction had a second mortgage (we combined HELOCs and CES for

---

8. Some loans initially contain the narrative code "Real Estate Mortgage," and only later in the life of the loan the narrative code is expanded to say, for example, "Freddie." In these cases, we classify them retroactively as if we observed the expanded narrative code from the outset.

this analysis), and whether the transaction involved an investor (defined as an owner whose property tax bill is sent to a different location than the purchase address).[9] We include data from 2001 to 2011, although many figures we report are cut off after 2007 due to the very small number of transactions involving a second lien after that time period. Our sample covers the forty largest metropolitan areas in the United States outside of Texas, where sale prices are not reported in the public records. We use data from a subset of metropolitan areas as described in the following section.

5.2   Origination and Growth of Second Liens

5.2.1   Aggregate Second Lien Lending Patterns

To examine the overall growth of the second lien market, we start with evidence from the CCP data. Figure 5.1 plots the number and dollar volume of second liens outstanding quarterly from 1999:Q1 to 2012:Q1. With over 20 million borrowers and more than $800 billion of outstanding credit, second liens represent a large and important source of credit for US consumers. At its peak at the end of 2007, second liens represented over $1.0 trillion of credit. Greenspan and Kennedy (2008) pointed to second liens as a key vehicle that allowed home owners to extract equity from their homes.

Figure 5.2 shows quarterly originations of second liens (figures 5.4 and 5.5 plot originations for CES and HELOCs separately). Although overall dollar volume peaked at the end of 2005, the aggregate data masks variation across the two types of credit. The HELOC originations peaked in 2005:Q4, and fell about 30 percent over the next two years, while CES originations continued rising, peaking in 2006:Q3 and remaining near their peak throughout 2007. Originations of new second liens fell off rapidly in 2008 and have since remained at about 15 to 20 percent of their level during the boom years. Second liens represented a strongly procyclical form of credit.

Next we consider the credit quality of borrowers who took out second liens and compare them to other mortgage borrowers. Figure 5.3 shows the share of various types of mortgages with an origination credit score above 700, an indication of loans given to high-quality borrowers. As with all types of mortgages, the share of high-quality borrowers declined from 2004 to 2007, although the CES and HELOC share declined less. Since most second liens were held on balance sheet, these results are consistent with balance sheet lenders pursing slightly higher quality borrowers than securitized lenders. Consistent with results from the Federal Reserve's Senior Loan Officer

---

9. Chinco and Mayer (2012) also define investor purchases based on the address of the property tax bill. In that paper, the authors show that the presence of outside investors helps cause price run-ups, contributing to bubbles in many housing markets.

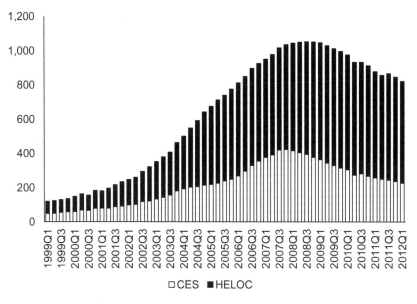

Fig. 5.1 Second lien balance ($B)

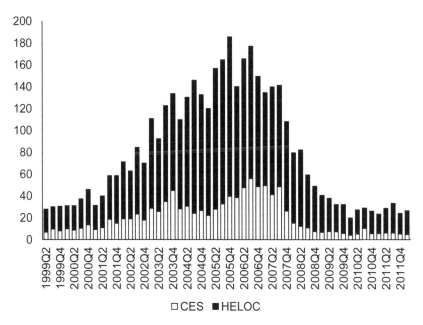

Fig. 5.2 Second lien originations ($B)

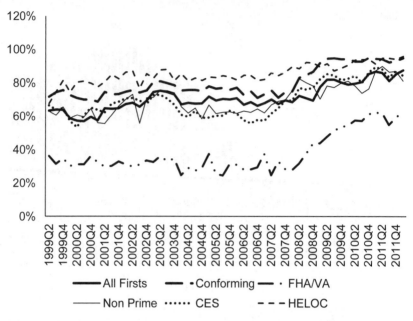

Fig. 5.3   Share of balances with Equifax risk score > 700 at origination

Survey[10], figure 5.3 shows that residential mortgage credit standards had risen to the highest levels in our sample period by late 2010.

Comparing second liens to first liens, it appears that CES credit quality moved with nonprime first liens, while HELOCs were more closely linked with the credit quality of prime mortgages. Around 60 percent of CES in the boom went to borrowers with a risk score over 700, similar to the overall share of such borrowers for first liens, and slightly higher than the share of high-quality borrowers in nonprime originations. The HELOCs remained focused on the highest quality borrowers. About 75 to 85 percent of HELOCs in the boom went to borrowers with FICO scores over 700, a greater share of such borrowers than even prime mortgages.

The linkage of CES with lower quality borrowers and HELOCs with higher quality borrowers is further supported when we compare the types of first liens for CES and HELOC borrowers. Figures 5.4 and 5.5 show the share of CES and HELOCs going to borrowers with various types of first liens as an alternative measure of credit quality. The largest share of CES mortgages went to borrowers with relatively low-quality nonprime mortgages. The large growth of CES mortgages in 2006 to 2007 primarily went to borrowers with nonprime first liens that would eventually default at very high rates. By comparison, HELOCs were more likely to go to borrowers

10. http://www.federalreserve.gov/boarddocs/SnloanSurvey/

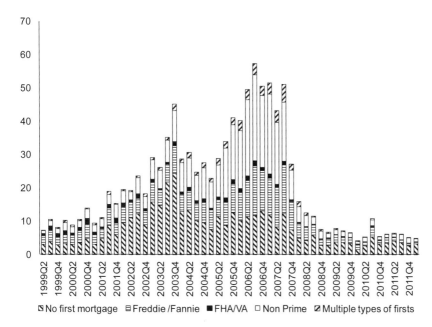

Fig. 5.4   CES originations, by type of first lien ($B)

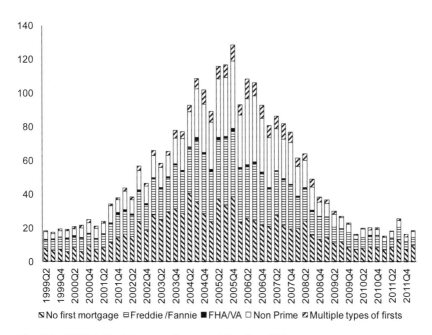

Fig. 5.5   HELOC originations, by type of first lien ($B)

with higher quality conforming mortgages or to borrowers without a first lien. The HELOC originations declined over 2006 to 2007, with a much smaller increase as compared to CES going to borrowers with nonprime first liens.

Finally, we consider the role of second liens in financing the purchase of a home versus their origination at a later date, possibly to extract home equity as in Greenspan and Kennedy (2008). Figures 5.6 to 5.9 track originations of second liens based on the type of first lien and how close in time the second lien was originated relative to the date the first lien was taken out. We allow for a small reporting lag in second lien origination, so liens taken out within two months are coded as simultaneous ("piggyback") second liens, while loans originated three to five months after origination are coded as being lagged one quarter, and so forth.

The data suggest that higher quality borrowers tended to take out second liens well after origination, whereas lower quality borrowers used second liens to help finance the purchase of the home. Following a prime first lien, most CES originations were taken out well after the origination date of the first lien. However, most CES originations for nonprime first liens were taken out as piggyback loans. Relatively few HELOCs were taken out as piggyback mortgages. Even HELOCs associated with nonprime first liens were usually taken out well after the date that the nonprime first mortgage was originated.

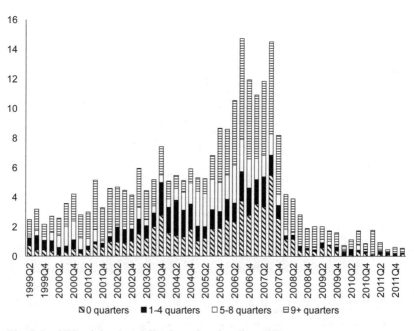

Fig. 5.6   CES originations following prime first liens ($B)

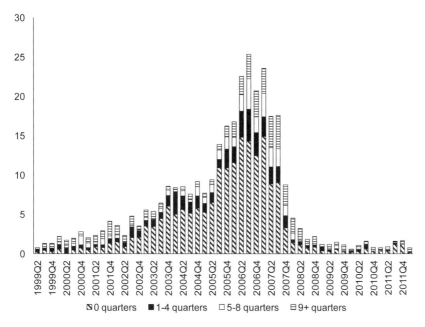

Fig. 5.7   CES originations following nonprime first liens ($B)

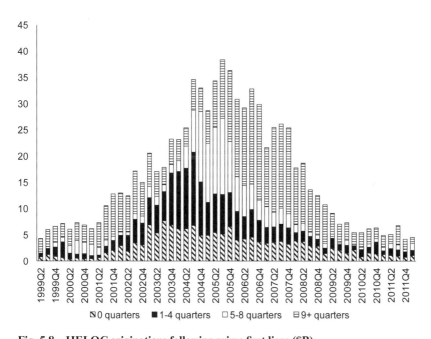

Fig. 5.8   HELOC originations following prime first liens ($B)

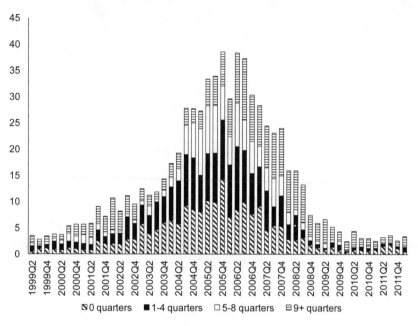

Fig. 5.9   HELOC originations following nonprime first liens ($B)

Thus, the data show that second lien originations grew rapidly during the boom period, but were composed of two very different products. The CES represented a minority of all second liens, but these loans were riskier on all dimensions, including peaking later in the cycle, being originated to lower credit quality borrowers, including borrowers with riskier first liens, and being more likely to be taken out as a piggyback loan.

5.2.2   Use of Second Liens to Enhance Leverage for Home Purchases

Next we turn to deeds records data from Dataquick to examine the amount of leverage for home purchases that utilized second liens. Our results show that second liens allowed borrowers to make very small down payments and were broadly used across the country. Also, owner-occupants were more likely to use second liens than investors. Viewing piggyback seconds as an alternative to private mortgage insurance for a low down payment mortgage, then the relative pricing differences could create an advantage of using a piggyback second that would increase in the expected duration of the mortgage. If investors planned to resell the property quicker than owner-occupants, then they would receive less value from this arbitrage.

We divide our sample into four groups of metropolitan areas, in a similar manner to Hubbard and Mayer (2009). These authors argue that mispricing was most pronounced in bubble markets like Las Vegas, Miami, and

Phoenix, whereas coastal markets followed a more typical pattern of house price appreciation from previous cycles. They show that other Midwest and Southern markets exhibited much less volatility over the cycle.

1. *Coastal cyclical markets*: Boston, New York, Washington, DC, Los Angeles, San Francisco, and San Diego
2. *Midwest/South stable markets*: Charlotte, Atlanta, Chicago, Denver, and Minneapolis
3. *Midwest declining markets*: Detroit, Cleveland, and St. Louis
4. *Bubble markets:* Las Vegas, Phoenix, Tampa, and Miami

Figure 5.10 plots the share of home purchases financed by piggyback second liens in each group of markets. Second liens grew with the increase in home prices in all markets, with the largest share of purchases being financed by second liens in bubble and coastal cyclical markets, followed by a slightly smaller share of purchases in Midwest/South stable markets, where home prices grew much less rapidly. The highest and most persistent use of second liens was in coastal cyclical markets, where homes appeared least affordable to many buyers. By contrast, Midwest declining markets exhibited a much lower share of piggyback second lien originations. Affordability in these markets was also better than in most other parts of the country. The use of piggyback second liens did not appear more concentrated in bubble markets

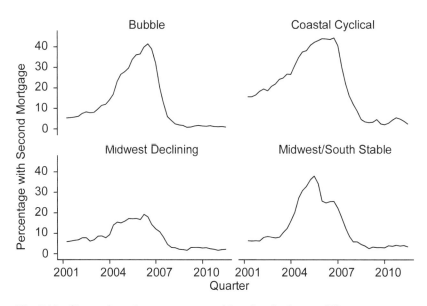

Fig. 5.10 **Share of purchases mortgages with a piggyback second lien**
Note: Graphs by market type.

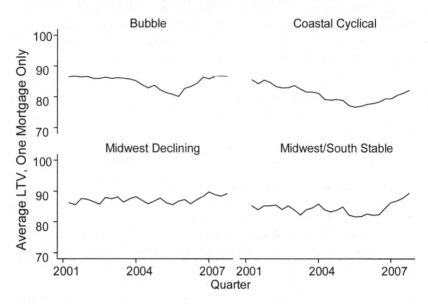

Fig. 5.11   Average LTV, purchase mortgages without a second lien
Note: Graphs by market type.

than many other metropolitan areas. In all locations, purchases with piggy-back mortgages fell off rapidly in 2008 and have not recovered.

We also examine the link between leverage and second lien use. Figures 5.11 to 5.14 show the impact of second liens on loan-to-value ratios (LTVs) for purchase mortgages. Our measure of loan-to-value includes both the first and second lien, which we refer to as the cumulative LTV (or CLTV). The data show very high CLTVs even for purchases financed by a single mortgage, averaging over 80 percent in almost all time periods.[11] Through much of the boom, purchases in coastal cyclical and Midwest/South stable markets had slightly lower CLTVs than purchases in bubble and Midwest declining markets. Nonetheless, the use of piggyback second liens was clearly tied to the lowest down payment purchases. Borrowers with a second lien had an average CLTV during the boom of at least 95 percent. About two-thirds of all such purchasers had a CLTV of 95 percent or more.

Figures 5.15 and 5.16 separate purchases between investors and owner-occupants. In all markets, second liens were more likely to be taken out by owner-occupants relative to investors. Among owner-occupants, second liens were most prevalent in coastal cyclical and bubble markets, where prices increased the fastest during the boom, peaking at 50 to 55 percent of

11. The high LTVs in the recent time period are surprising given the secondary market dominance of GSE mortgages. However, the FHA finances about one-half of all recent purchase mortgages and FHA mortgages can have as little as a 3 percent down payment.

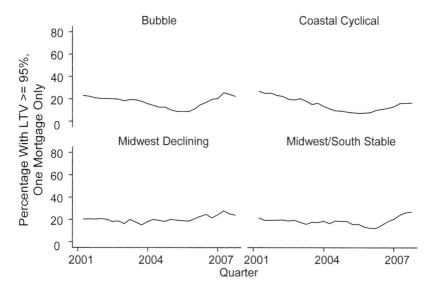

Fig. 5.12   Share of purchases with one mortgage and with an LTV ≥ 95 percent
Note: Graphs by market type.

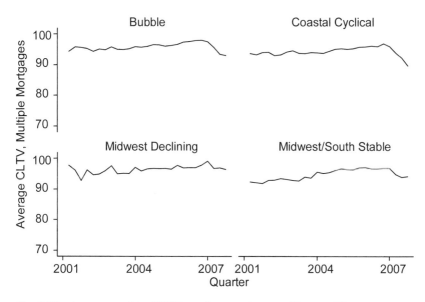

Fig. 5.13   Average combined LTV, purchase mortgages with second lien
Note: Graphs by market type.

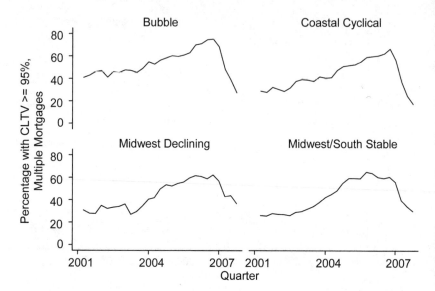

Fig. 5.14   Share of purchases with multiple mortgages with combined LTV ≥ 95 percent

Note: Graphs by market type.

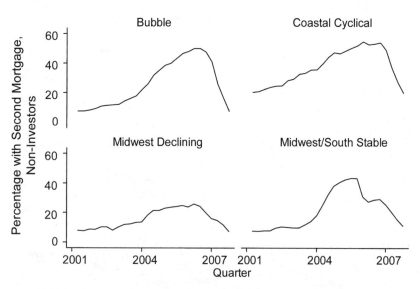

Fig. 5.15   Share of owner-occupied purchases with multiple mortgages

Note: Graphs by market type.

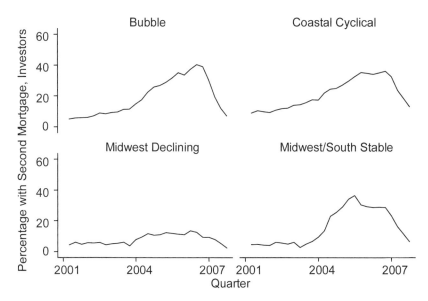

Fig. 5.16   Share of investor purchases with multiple mortgages
Note: Graphs by market type.

all purchases. Investors used second liens at a similar rate across all groups of markets with the exception of the declining markets, with usage peaking at 35 to 40 percent.

In summary, piggyback second liens grew rapidly in bubble, coastal cyclical, and Midwest/South stable markets during the housing boom. Mortgages with a piggyback second lien had very high origination CLTVs, with almost two-thirds of borrowers having a down payment of 5 percent or less, much higher CLTVs than for mortgages without a second lien. Owner-occupants more commonly used piggyback second liens than investors.

5.3   Performance of Second Liens and First Liens with an Affiliated Second Lien

Next we examine the performance of second liens relative to other types of consumer credit. Also, we provide evidence on the controversial claims that many borrowers appear to continue to pay their second lien while defaulting on their first lien.[12]

---

12. We do not formally model the default decision on first liens. For a summary of this literature, see Elul et al. (2011), for example.

5.3.1   Default Performance of Second Liens

We turn back to the CCP data to examine the performance of second liens relative to first liens and other types of credit, examining the percentage of borrowers that are ninety or more days delinquent on various forms of debt. Figure 5.17 compares the performance of CES and HELOCs to various types of first liens. The data show a sharp rise in second lien delinquencies that mirrors delinquencies of similar types of first liens, consistent with serious credit problems resulting from the weakening of underwriting standards discussed earlier, the sharp decline in home prices, and the high unemployment created by the Great Recession. The CES were delinquent at a similarly high rate as nonprime first liens, which are also the most common type of mortgages that the CES are attached to as a piggyback. Also, HELOCs defaulted at a similar rate to GSE-backed mortgages, which were originated to higher credit quality borrowers and defaulted at much lower rates than mortgages granted to riskier borrowers.[13]

However, in the last year, there has started to be a divergence between the performance of first and second liens that bears monitoring by analysts and regulators. Delinquency rates for second liens have not fallen as much as for most first mortgages, suggesting a possible change in performance of senior and junior debt. One possible explanation is that some HELOCs have an initial period (often five years) where the borrower pays interest only, but then the borrower must start paying off the principal, raising payments. Such an explanation deserves further attention, as it might preview poorer relative performance for HELOCs.

In figure 5.18, we compare delinquency rates for second liens to other types of consumer debt. It is worth noting the sharp rise in serious mortgage delinquencies, especially CES delinquencies, relative to serious delinquencies for auto loans or credit cards. Even while exhibiting a sharper rise over the last several years, recent delinquency rates on HELOCs are comparable to auto loans, which are considered a relatively safe form of consumer lending. However, in the last couple of quarters, HELOC delinquency rates have remained flat even as delinquency rates for auto loans and credit cards have been declining. The CES delinquency rates have declined relatively more than for HELOCs, possibly because the worst quality piggyback CES have now defaulted and the borrowers have lost their homes.

Finally, in figures 5.19 and 5.20 we turn to delinquency rates for piggyback second liens versus second liens taken out well after the home purchase while controlling for the year of origination. In all cases, piggyback second liens

13. Also of note is that after declining from the end of 2009 through mid-2010, 90+ delinquency rates for FHA mortgages have been rising for the past several quarters. See Gyourko (2011) and Caplin, Cororaton, and Tracy (2012) for more discussion of expected FHA credit losses.

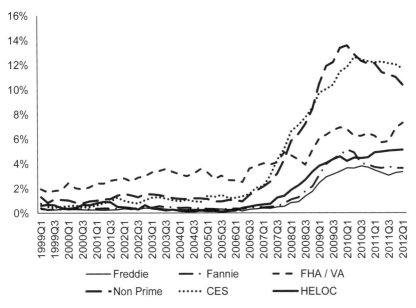

Fig. 5.17   **90+ delinquency rates for CES, HELOCs, FHA/VA, prime, and nonprime**

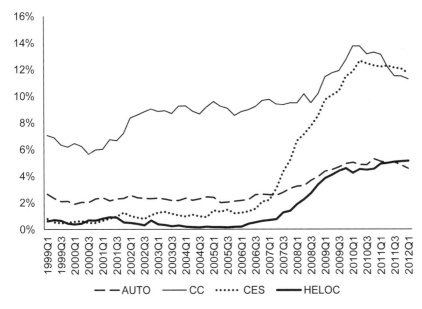

Fig. 5.18   **90+ delinquency rates for CES, HELOCs, credit cards, and auto loans**
Note: Balance weighted.

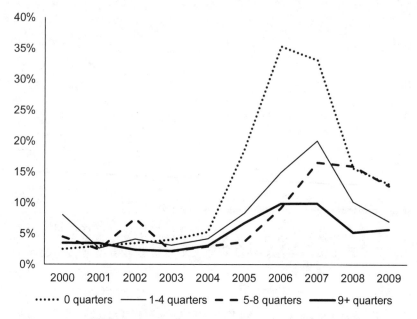

Fig. 5.19 90+ delinquency rates for CES originations, after the first lien origination, based on year of origination

Note: Delinquency defined by the last observation of the life of the loan.

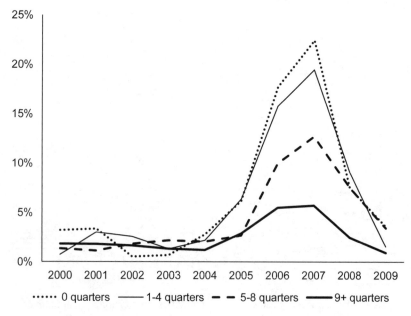

Fig. 5.20 90+ delinquency rates for HELOC originations, after the first lien origination, based on year of origination

perform much worse than second liens taken out subsequent to the purchase. In fact, generally across origination years, the longer the period of time between the origination of the first lien and the second lien, the lower the rate of subsequent delinquency. This effect is more pronounced for CES. Also, like first liens, the origination date has a large effect on performance, with the worst loans originated in 2006 and 2007 at the height of the housing boom and also at a time that lending standards had slipped the most.[14] However, second liens originated prior to 2005 became delinquent at very low rates.

5.3.2   Default Performance of Matched First and Second Liens

Next we turn to the default rate of matched first and second liens. Some commentators have observed that borrowers appear to default on first liens while the second lien remains current, with the strong implication that such behavior is a strong rejection of prioritization between senior and junior debt. Jagtiani and Lang (2011) present striking evidence in this regard, especially for HELOCs, showing that an appreciable portion of borrowers who are delinquent on their first lien remain current on their second lien. While some of our results are similar to Jagtiani and Lang, we interpret the evidence somewhat differently. The data show that the performance of linked first and second liens is more similar than different, especially when comparing the performance of second liens to other types of unsecured debt. For example, a much larger share of defaulted first lien borrowers remain current on their credit cards and auto loans a year later than on their second liens. We also find an increasing trend toward being delinquent of the first lien but not the second lien.

Figure 5.21 reports 90+ days delinquency rates for HELOCs and CES and the accompanying first mortgages when both are matched together. The top two lines represent serious delinquency rates for a CES that also has an attached first lien, and similarly for a first lien that has an attached CES. The performance of both the CES and the attached first lien are very similar today, although in earlier periods, especially in 2008 and 2009, the first lien appears to have defaulted at higher rates than CES. The difference in performance between first and second liens is more pronounced for HELOCs, where first liens default at a much higher rate than the accompanying HELOC. This result is consistent with the possibility that borrowers might continue to rely on a HELOC for credit even after facing problems on the first lien, as is suggested in Goodman et al. (2010) and Jagtiani and Lang (2011).

However, we do not believe that preserving access to HELOC credit is the most likely explanation for the lower default rates on HELOCs. For a borrower who is considering default, the safest way to preserve access to any

---

14. See Mayer, Pence, and Sherlund (2009) and Demyanyk and Van Hemert (2011) for evidence on the deteriorating credit quality of nonprime loans over this time period.

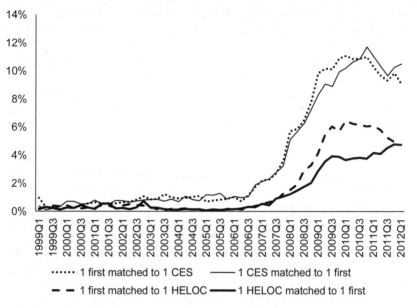

Fig. 5.21 First mortgage, CES, HELOC 90+ delinquency rate
Note: Conditional on matching a first and a second.

remaining HELOC credit after a default on the first lien is to draw on the remaining HELOC credit ahead of the default, either paying down other debt or depositing the funds for later use.[15] Consistent with this possibility, by the time a default occurs on the first lien, most borrowers have very little available credit left on their HELOCs; on average, only 10 percent of the outstanding credit line is available at the time of the first lien default. Also, it is not very hard to remain current on a HELOC. Usually, the required HELOC payment is typically quite small, comprising only the interest payment on the existing balance. In contrast, the first mortgage payment is much larger. Thus it is quite possible that the relatively high payment rate on HELOCs when the first mortgage is delinquent may be due to the low costs to keep the HELOC current, rather than to the borrower's active attempt to maintain the access to the HELOC credit line when such access is likely quite uncertain when facing a possible default.

To further explore the credit profile of borrowers who have defaulted on a first lien, table 5.1 reports the delinquency rate of various types of credit in the five quarters following the default. The top part of the table shows that, conditional on a first lien delinquency, about 80 percent of homeowners stop paying their CES within five quarters. While most HELOC borrowers also

15. This strategy would be more difficult for credit cards since they tend to have lower credit limits and they place restrictions on cash advances.

Table 5.1   **Percent of balances remaining current after first lien delinquency**

Credit type	1 Quarter	2 Quarters	3 Quarters	4 Quarters	5 Quarters
All states					
CES	27.5	28.3	26.5	24.5	20.9
HELOC	43.2	39.8	36.5	36.6	30.9
Recourse states (R)					
CES	30.6	30.8	29.4	25.4	23.2
Piggyback	23.3	24.2	23.6	22.5	15.8
Subsequent	38.0	37.6	34.1	31.7	27.1
Difference	14.7	13.5	10.5	9.2	11.3
HELOC	46.1	42.7	40.1	39.3	31.6
Piggyback	37.4	36.7	30.3	31.5	31.7
Subsequent	48.8	44.9	42.2	39.7	34.5
Difference	11.4	8.2	11.9	8.3	2.8
Nonrecourse states (NR)					
CES	22.8	24.4	21.7	23.0	16.4
Piggyback	16.5	17.4	18.2	23.6	18.3
Subsequent	29.2	33.3	27.4	25.2	14.3
Difference	12.7	15.9	9.2	1.7	−4.1
HELOC	40.0	36.8	31.9	33.1	29.6
Piggyback	32.4	28.8	21.0	18.1	17.6
Subsequent	43.6	37.9	36.4	37.6	38.5
Difference	11.2	9.1	15.4	19.6	20.9
CES: diff.(NR)-in-diff.(R)	−2.0	2.5	−1.3	−7.5	−15.4
HELOC: diff.(NR)-in-diff.(R)	−0.2	0.9	3.5	11.3	18.1

Note: Nonrecourse states include AK, AZ, IA, MN, MI, ND, OR, WA, WI, CA (purchase), and NC (purchase).

stop paying soon after a first lien delinquency, about 30 percent of HELOCs remain current even a year and a quarter later. This calculation removes first liens that cure after a 60+ delinquency. In our sample about 40 percent of first lien delinquencies cure within two quarters, consistent with the strong growth of mortgage modifications.

We also examine the impact of personal recourse on delinquency rates on second liens. Previous research by Ghent and Kudlyak (2011) suggests that borrowers on first liens default at a 30 percent higher rate in states that have no personal recourse relative to states where the borrower potentially faces personal liability for losses on the defaulted mortgage beyond the value of the foreclosed home.[16] Similar issues exist with second liens because of the differential personal liability associated with piggyback versus subsequent second liens in recourse states. In recourse states, the borrower always

16. See Ghent and Kudlyak (2011, table 1) for a listing of recourse and nonrecourse states.

maintains personal liability on both the first and second lien to the extent that there is an unpaid balance on the second lien in a default. In other words, in recourse states, the extent of personal liability on a second lien is always the same as for the first lien. However, for nonrecourse states, the existence of personal liability depends on when the second lien was taken out. For second liens taken out at the time of purchase to help finance the home, the borrower also maintains nonrecourse status on the second lien. However, the borrower is personally liable for any subsequent second liens taken out after the purchase is completed.

The differential legal treatment of piggyback and subsequent second liens in nonrecourse states presents an opportunity to perform a simple differences-in-differences comparison: (a) How do piggyback versus subsequent second liens perform after the default on the first lien? (b) Does the difference in performance between the piggyback and subsequent second lien vary depending on whether the borrower is in a recourse or nonrecourse state? This analysis allows us to control for differences in the types of borrowers in recourse versus nonrecourse states as well as differences between piggyback and subsequent second lien borrowers.

The first result in table 5.1 is that second liens taken out subsequent to the first lien are more likely than piggyback seconds to remain current following a delinquency on the first lien. This difference is more persistent over time for a HELOC as compared to a CES. These findings are indicated by comparing piggyback and subsequent seconds in recourse states. To see if second liens that are recourse loans are even more likely to remain current, we compare the differences between subsequent and piggyback seconds across recourse and nonrecourse states. If recourse is important, then we would expect this difference-in-difference to be positive. The data indicates that recourse does not appear to induce borrowers with CES loans or HELOC loans to be more likely to remain current subsequent to a delinquency on their first lien.[17]

Table 5.2 shows the performance of credit card and auto debt following a delinquency on a first mortgage. Borrowers appear to make many of these debt payments a year or more after defaulting on their first lien. Borrowers who default on their first mortgage remain current on their auto loan 70 percent of the time for a year or more after a first mortgage delinquency. These findings are consistent with the findings of Andersson et al. (2011) that home owners have a hierarchy of debt payments where the mortgage payment is no longer the most critical payment.

For many consumers in trouble, the car loan is the most critical payment to make, given that a default on a car loan can result in a quick repossession. Without a car, most households would have a hard time getting to work

---

17. Over the first three quarters after the first lien delinquency, the difference-in-differences values are quite small for both HELOC and CES. While the values diverge a little bit from zero in the fourth and fifth quarters post-delinquency, the number of observations diminishes and we do not put a lot of weight on the small reported differences.

Table 5.2   **Percent of balances remaining current after first lien delinquency**

Credit type	1 Quarter	2 Quarters	3 Quarters	4 Quarters	5 Quarters
CES	27.5	28.3	26.5	24.5	20.9
HELOC	43.2	39.8	36.5	36.6	30.9
Auto loan	79.2	78.0	78.5	70.0	70.7
Credit card	46.8	41.8	43.8	40.2	38.9

Notes: Sample includes all first liens that remain delinquent over the indicated period. About 40 percent of delinquent first liens "cure" within 4 quarters of first becoming delinquent.

Table 5.3   **Change over time in payments on second liens when first lien is seriously delinquent**

% current if first lien is 60+ delinquent	CES	HELOC
2008:Q2	16.2	29.2
2010:Q2	22.0	42.2
2011:Q2	25.7	37.8

or looking for a job. The results for credit cards are more mixed. About 40 percent of those who default on their first lien continue to pay their credit card. Credit cards can be a source of additional credit to an unemployed household and similar to HELOCs, the minimum payment to keep the credit card account current is relatively small. For example, Cohen-Cole and Morse (2010) find that the availability of credit is as important as house prices in predicting delinquency on a mortgage. In the event of a personal bankruptcy, credit card and HELOC debt would often be treated similarly. Unpaid HELOC debt (and most second lien debt) would typically be converted to unsecured debt in a bankruptcy if the total of all secured real estate debt (first liens plus all subsequent liens) exceeds the value of the home.

Finally, we examine changes in second lien performance over time when the first lien has defaulted. Table 5.3 shows that the performance of second liens once the first lien has become delinquent has improved since 2008. The improvement may be due to increased numbers of first lien borrowers seeking mortgage modifications while remaining current on their second lien.

We consider three possible explanations for why some borrowers remain current on their second liens even a year beyond a continuing serious delinquency on their first lien.

Behavioral cash management: When facing a loss of income, some borrowers may follow a strategy of paying as many bills as possible each month. Given that the first lien mortgage has the largest monthly payment, these households will initially go delinquent on their first lien mortgage. These households plan to become current in the future when their income has been restored. As we noted earlier, the one exception to the payment order by payment size strategy appears to be auto loans.

Strategic default: Borrowers may strategically default on their first lien, since most mortgage modification programs were targeted to seriously delinquent first liens. While some borrowers might have had resources to pay the first lien and strategically defaulted to obtain a modification,[18] others might have only been able to cover a portion of their mortgage payments and so chose the second lien to increase their chances of getting help. Modification flags were only added to our consumer credit panel data only starting in 2011:Q1. This initial modification information only indicates that a mortgage was modified, not when it was modified. For modifications that occur subsequent to 2011:Q1, we can ascertain the timing of the modification. This data limitation makes it difficult for us to investigate the merits of the strategic default hypothesis.

Personal liability: As noted earlier, most borrowers who default on a second lien, with the exception of those who have a piggyback CES in a nonrecourse state, still face personal liability on their debt, the same way they would if they defaulted on a credit card or student loan. Our simple difference-in-difference evidence does not find support for this hypothesis.

5.4   Conclusion

We use data from credit report and deeds records to better understand the role of second liens in contributing to the housing boom and subsequent foreclosure crisis. Overall, second liens appear to have allowed borrowers to take on additional leverage, although it is not possible to say whether borrowers might have turned to higher LTV first liens if attractively priced second liens were not available. However, part of the reason that second liens were attractively priced is that many second liens were originated to higher quality borrowers than the average first lien borrowers. Within the category of second liens, HELOCs appear to be the best credit quality, with relatively few piggyback originations, higher quality borrowers at origination, and a smaller percent originated near the peak of the housing boom. Closed-end second lien characteristics were worse on all these dimensions. While home equity extraction appears to be large factor behind increased borrowings, especially for HELOCs, such borrowings went to relatively high-quality borrowers who likely would have had access to some additional credit even without using a HELOC.

Second liens were quite prevalent at the top of the housing market, with as many as 45 percent of home purchases involving a piggyback second lien

---

18. See Mayer et al. (2011). In this paper, the authors show that the offer of a mortgage modification program can increase default rates on a first lien by about 20 percent, with the biggest increase among borrowers who apparently have the financial resources to pay.

in coastal markets and bubble locations, but a somewhat smaller prevalence of piggyback second liens in more stable or declining markets in the Midwest and South. Second liens were strongly associated with the use of low down payments to purchase homes. Owner-occupants used second liens to help finance a higher percentage of purchases than investors. These data are consistent with the hypothesis that piggyback second liens allowed some borrowers to purchase homes with especially low down payments who might otherwise have not been able to afford a home. That said, it is not possible to demonstrate a causal link between second liens borrowings and the housing bubble and subsequent collapse.

The default rate on a second lien is generally similar to that of the first lien on the same home, although about 20 to 30 percent of borrowers will pay the second lien for more than a year while remaining seriously delinquent on their first mortgage. By comparison, about 40 percent of credit card borrowers and 70 percent of auto loan borrowers will continue making payments one year after defaulting on their first mortgage. This behavior is caused by a combination of several reasons, including strategic default on the first lien to obtain a modification, behavioral explanations that depend in part on borrowers directing available funds to the accounts with the smallest minimum payments, and the fact that defaults on second liens very rarely result in the loss of a home.

Finally, we show that the relatively low delinquency rates for HELOCs have remained flat in recent quarters even as delinquency rates are falling for most other types of credit. Given that the bulk of outstanding second liens are HELOCs, such performance could signal that problems are not over for some lenders with large portfolios of HELOCs on their balance sheet.

References

Andersson, Fredrik, Souphala Chomsisengphet, Dennis Glennon, and Feng Li. 2011. "The Changing Pecking Order of Consumer Defaults." SSRN Working Paper no. 1939507. Social Science Research Network.

Caplin, Andrew, Anna Cororaton, and Joseph Tracy. 2012. "Is the FHA Creating Sustainable Homeownership?" NBER Working Paper no. 18190. Cambridge, MA: National Bureau of Economic Research.

Chinco, Alex, and Christopher Mayer. 2012. "Distant Speculators and Asset Bubbles in the Housing Market." Working Paper, Columbia Business School. April.

Cohen-Cole, Ethan, and Jonathan Morse. 2010. "Your House or Your Credit Card, Which Would You Choose? Personal Delinquency Tradeoffs and Precautionary Liquidity Motives." SSRN Working Paper no. 1939507.

Demyanyk, Yulia, and Otto Van Hemert. 2011. "Understanding the Subprime Mortgage Crisis." *Review of Financial Studies* 24 (6): 1848–80.

Elul, Ronel, Nicholas Souleles, Souphala Chomsisengphet, Dennis Glennon, and

Robert Hunt. 2011. "What 'Triggers' Mortgage Default." *The American Economic Review Papers and Proceedings* 100 (2): 490–94.

Feldstein, Martin. 2011. "How to Stop the Drop in Home Values." *New York Times,* October 13.

Frey, William. 2011. *Way Too Big to Fail: How Government and Private Industry Can Build a Fail-Safe Mortgage System,* edited by Isaac M. Gradman. Greenwich: Greenwich Financial Press.

Ghent, Andra, and Marianna Kudlyak. 2011. "Recourse and Residential Default: Evidence from US States." *The Review of Financial Studies* 24 (9): 3139–86.

Goodman, Laurie S., Roger Ashworth, Brian Landy, and Ke Yin. 2010. "Second Liens: How Important?" *The Journal of Fixed Income* 20 (2): 19–30.

Greenspan, Alan, and James Kennedy. 2008. "Sources and Uses of Equity Extracted from Homes." *Oxford Review of Economic Policy* 24 (1): 120–44.

Gyourko, Joseph. 2011. "Is FHA the Next Housing Bailout?" A Report Prepared for the American Enterprise Institute.

Hubbard, R. Glenn, and Christopher J. Mayer. 2009. "The Mortgage Market Meltdown and House Prices." *The B.E. Journal of Economic Analysis & Policy* 9 (3) Symposium: Article 8.

Jagtiani, Julapa, and William Lang. 2011. "Strategic Defaults on First and Second Lien Mortgages during the Financial Crisis." *The Journal of Fixed Income* 20 (4): 7–23.

Lee, Donghoon, and Wilbert Van der Klaauw. 2010. "An Introduction to the FRBNY Consumer Credit Panel." Federal Reserve Bank of New York Staff Report no. 479.

Levitan, Adam. 2009. "Resolving the Foreclosure Crisis: Modification of Mortgages in Bankruptcy." *Wisconsin Law Review* 565–655.

Mayer, Christopher, Edward Morrison, and Tomasz Piskorski. 2009. "Essay: A New Proposal for Loan Modifications." *Yale Journal on Regulation* 26 (2): 417–29.

Mayer, Christopher, Edward Morrison, Tomasz Piskorski, and Arpit Gupta. 2011. "Mortgage Modification and Strategic Default: Evidence from a Legal Settlement with Countrywide." NBER Working Paper no. 17065. Cambridge, MA: National Bureau of Economic Research.

Mayer, Christopher, Karen Pence, and Shane Sherlund. 2009. "The Rise in Mortgage Defaults." *Journal of Economic Perspectives* 23 (1): 23–50.

International Capital Flows
and House Prices
Theory and Evidence

Jack Favilukis, David Kohn, Sydney C. Ludvigson,
and Stijn Van Nieuwerburgh

6.1 Introduction

The last fifteen years have been marked by a dramatic boom-bust cycle in real estate prices, a pattern unprecedented both in amplitude and in scope that affected many countries around the globe and most regions within the United States (figure 6.1). Over the same period, there were economically large fluctuations in international capital flows. Countries that exhibited the largest house price increases also often exhibited large and increasing net inflows of foreign capital that bankrolled sharply higher trade deficits. Economists have debated the role of international capital flows in explaining these movements in house prices and asset market volatility more generally. A common hypothesis is that house price increases are positively related to a rise in the country's net foreign inflows, either because they directly cause house price increases (perhaps by lowering real interest rates), or because other factors simultaneously drive up both house prices and capital inflows.

Jack Favilukis is a lecturer of finance at the London School of Economics. David Kohn is a PhD student in economics at New York University. Sydney C. Ludvigson is professor of economics at New York University and a research associate of the National Bureau of Economic Research. Stijn Van Nieuwerburgh is professor of finance and director of the Center for Real Estate Finance Research at Stern School of Business at New York University and a research associate of the National Bureau of Economic Research.

Prepared for the National Bureau of Economic Research "Housing and the Financial Crisis" conference, November 17–18, 2011, Cambridge, Massachusetts. We are grateful to seminar participants at the NBER "Housing and the Financial Crisis" conference November 2011 and the HULM conference April 2012, and to John Driscoll, Victoria Ivashina, Steven Laufer, and Nikolai Roussanov for helpful comments, and to Atif Mian and Amir Sufi for data. For acknowledgments, sources of research support, and disclosure of the authors' material financial relationships, if any, please see http://www.nber.org/chapters/c12626.ack.

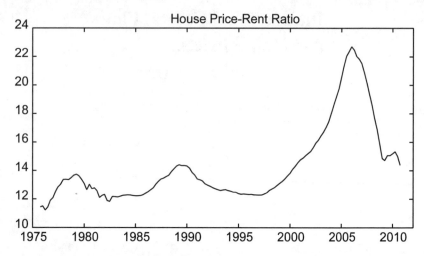

Fig. 6.1   Price-rent ratio in the United States

Notes: The figure plots an aggregate price-rent ratio index for the United States from 1975:Q4 to 2010:Q4. Rent is rent for primary residence, constructed from the Shelter component of the Consumer Price Index for all urban consumers, SA, last month of each quarter. Data available from the Bureau of Economic Analysis of the US Department of Commerce. Price is the Core Logic National House Price Index (SA, Jan. 2000 = 100). The price-rent ratio has been normalized to equal the level, in 1975:Q4, of the quarterly price-rent ratio constructed from the flow of funds housing wealth and National Income and Products data on housing consumption.

In this chapter, we study both theory and evidence that bears on this hypothesis, focusing on the unprecedented boom-bust cycle in housing markets that took place over the last fifteen years.

We argue that changes in international capital flows played, at most, a small role driving house price movements in this episode and that, instead, the key causal factor was a *financial market liberalization* and its subsequent reversal that took place in many countries largely independent of international capital flows. Financial market liberalization (FML hereafter) refers to a set of regulatory and market changes and subsequent decisions by financial intermediaries that made it easier and less costly for households to obtain mortgages, borrow against home equity, and adjust their consumption.

By contrast, we argue that net capital flows into the United States over both the boom and the bust period in housing have followed a largely independent path, driven to great extent by foreign governments' regulatory, reserve currency, and economic policy motives. Consider the value of foreign holdings of US assets minus US holdings of foreign assets, referred to hereafter as *net foreign asset holdings* in the United States, or alternatively, as the US *net liability position*. A positive change in net foreign asset holdings indicates a capital inflow, or more borrowing from abroad.[1] As we show in the following, from 1994 to 2010, only the change in net foreign holdings of US *securities* (equities, corporate, US Agency and Treasury bills and bonds) shows any discernible upward trend. Moreover, among securities, the upward trend has been driven entirely by an increase in net foreign holdings of US assets considered to be safe stores-of-value, specifically US Treasury and Agency debt (referred to hereafter simply as US "safe" assets). Yet inflows into these securities, rather than declining during the housing bust, have on average continued to increase. Importantly, foreign demand for US safe assets is dominated by Foreign Official Institutions, namely government entities that have specific regulatory and reserve currency motives for holding US Treasuries and other US-backed assets, and that face both legal and political restrictions on the type of assets that can be held (Kohn 2002). Such entities take extremely inelastic positions, implying that when these holders receive funds to invest, they buy US Treasuries regardless of the price (Alfaro, Kalemli-Ozcan, and Volosovych 2011; Krishnamurthy and Vissing-Jorgensen 2007).

We interpret these recent events through the lens of the theoretical models in Favilukis, Ludvigson, and Van Nieuwerburgh (2010), henceforth FLVNa, and Favilukis, Ludvigson, and Van Nieuwerburgh (2011), henceforth FLVNb. These papers study the economic consequences of both the US FML (and its reversal) and, at the same time, empirically calibrated fluctuations in net capital inflows into the US riskless bond market. The model environment is a two-sector general equilibrium framework with housing and nonhousing production where heterogeneous households face uninsurable idiosyncratic and aggregate risks. Given the assets available in the model economy and collateralized financing restrictions, individuals can only imperfectly insure against both types of risk. We argue that these frameworks can account for the observed boom-bust pattern in house prices simultaneously with the continuing trend toward greater net capital inflows into US securities over both the boom and the bust.[2] Fluctuations in the model's price-rent ratio are driven by changing risk premia, which vary endogenously in response to cyclical shocks, the FML and its subsequent

---

1. What we have defined as net foreign asset holdings, or the US net liability position, is equal to the negative of the US *net international investment position* in the US Bureau of Economic Analysis balance of payments system. A country's resource constraint limits its expenditures on (government and private) consumption and investment goods, fees, and services, to its domestic output *plus* the change in the market value of its net liabilities (*minus* the change in the net international investment position). Thus a country's ability to spend in excess of domestic income in a given period depends positively on the change in its net foreign liabilities.

2. There was considerable volatility in the changes of net foreign asset holdings in the United States during the financial crisis in 2008 and 2009. Nevertheless, we show in the following that the changes in holdings were still higher at the end of the sample in 2010 than they were at the peak of the housing boom in 2006.

reversal, and capital inflows. In FLVNa, house prices rise in the boom period because of a relaxation of credit constraints and decline in housing-related transactions costs, both of which reduce risk premia. Conversely, the reversal of the FML raises housing risk premia and causes the housing bust.

In contrast to the FML, an inflow of foreign money into domestic bond markets plays a small role in driving home prices in the models of FLVNa and FLVNb, despite its large depressing influence on interest rates. The reason is that a capital inflow into the safe bond market—by itself—*raises* risk premia on housing and equity, as domestic savers are forced out of the safe bond market and into risky securities. (We emphasize the words "by itself" here because this increase in risk premia is more than offset by the simultaneous *decline* in risk premia during the boom caused by the FML, as discussed later.) At the same time, the capital inflow stimulates residential investment and an expected increase in the housing stock. So while low interest rates in isolation tend to raise home prices, these general equilibrium consequences tend to reduce them, thereby limiting the scope for a capital inflow to increase home prices significantly. It follows that the sharp rise in price-rent ratios during the boom period must be attributed to an overall decline in risk premia and *not* to a fall in interest rates. Many alternative theories that can account for the positive correlation between house prices and capital inflows in the boom period are not able to explain the bust period, in which house prices collapsed but inflows into countries like the United States continued.

By FML we mean an outward shift in the broad availability of credit, at any given initial level of credit demand and borrower quality. This includes, as in the US housing boom, an increase in maximal loan-to-value (LTV) ratios (e.g., the fraction of loans with combined—first and second—mortgage LTV ratios above 80 percent or 90 percent, an increase in the prevalence of new mortgage contracts (option-adjustable-rate mortgages [ARMs], interest-only and negative amortization loans, loans to households with low FICO scores), a reduction in documentation requirements (asset and income verification), a rapid increase in the use of private label securitization, and a reduction in fees (as well as in time and effort) associated with refinancing a mortgage or obtaining a home equity line of credit. The widespread relaxation of credit standards is well-documented (see the following discussion). Consistent with this evidence, microeconomic evidence in Mian and Sufi (2009) shows that mortgage credit expansion and house price growth in the boom were concentrated in areas with a large fraction of subprime mortgages and securitization of these mortgages, and *not* in areas with improved or improving economic prospects. Thus, this component of credit availability to households—accompanied by government deregulation of financial institutions and widespread changes in the way housing assets were financed and traded—appears to have fluctuated, to great extent, independently of current and future economic conditions.

But credit availability can also change endogenously in response to fluctuations in the aggregate economy and to revisions in expectations about future economic conditions, including house price growth. This information is reflected immediately in collateral values that constrain borrowing capacity. As in classic financial accelerator models (e.g., Bernanke and Gertler 1989; Kiyotaki and Moore 1997), *endogenous* shifts in borrowing capacity imply that economic shocks have a much larger effect on asset prices than they would in frictionless environments without collateralized financing restrictions. Both exogenous and endogenous components of time-varying credit availability to households are operative in the model of FLVNa.

While endogenous fluctuations in credit availability are clearly important in theory, it is unclear how quantitatively important they have been empirically, especially in the recent housing boom-bust episode. Some researchers have argued that credit availability is primarily driven by the political economy, and in particular by political constituencies that influence bank regulation related to credit availability (e.g., Mian, Sufi, and Trebbi 2010; Rice and Strahan 2010; Boz and Mendoza 2010; Rajan and Ramcharan 2011b). Such a component to credit availability could in fact be independent of economic fundamentals, expectations of future fundamentals, and credit demand.

Using observations on credit standards, capital flows, and interest rates for the United States and for a panel of eleven countries, we present evidence on how these variables are related to real house price movements in recent data. Our main measure of credit standards is compiled from quarterly bank surveys of senior loan officers, carried out by national central banks as part of their regulatory oversight. We consider this a summary indicator of fluctuations in the variables associated with an FML, as described earlier. The surveys specifically address changes in a bank's *supply* of credit, as distinct from changes in its perceived demand for credit. We find for the United States that this measure of credit supply, by itself, explains 53 percent of the quarterly variation in house price growth over the period 1992 to 2010, while it explains 66 percent over the period since 2000. By contrast, controlling for credit supply, various measures of capital flows, real interest rates, and aggregate activity (collectively) add less than 5 percent to the fraction of variation explained for these same movements in home values. Credit supply retains its strong marginal explanatory power for house price movements over the period 2002 to 2010 in a panel of international data, while capital flows have no explanatory power. Moreover, credit standards continues to be the most important variable related to future home price fluctuations even when it has been rendered statistically orthogonal to banks' perceptions of credit demand, and even when controlling for expected future economic growth and expected future real interest rates. Taken together, these findings suggest that a stark shift in bank lending practices—conspicuous in the FML and its reversal—was at the root of the housing crisis.

The rest of this chapter is organized as follows. The next section discusses theoretical literature that has addressed the link between house prices, capital flows, and/or credit supply. To provide a theoretical frame of reference, here we also describe in detail the predictions of FLVNa for house price movements. Section 6.3 turns to the data, presenting stylized facts on international capital flows, interest rates, and credit standards. Section 6.4 presents an empirical analysis of the linkage between capital flows and house price fluctuations, controlling for measures of credit supply, economic activity, and real interest rates. Section 6.5 concludes. The appendix provides details on the data we use and on our estimation methodology.

6.2   Theories

A number of studies have addressed the link between house prices and capital flows, focusing on the recent boom period in housing. For brevity, we will refer to the period of rapid home price appreciation from 2000 to 2006 as the *boom* period in the United States, and the period 2007 to present as the *bust*.

The *global savings glut* hypothesis (Bernanke 2005; Mendoza, Quadrini, and Rios-Rull 2007; Bernanke 2008; Caballero, Farhi, and Gourinchas 2008; Caballero and Krishnamurthy 2009) contends that a number of possible events (the Asian financial crisis in the late 1990s being one frequently cited) led to an increase in savings in developing countries, notably China and emerging Asia, which sought safe, high-quality financial assets that their own economies could not provide. Because of the depth, breadth, and safety of US Treasury and Agency markets, those savings predominantly found their way to the United States. To the extent that saving in developed nations remained roughly unchanged by these events, the increase in savings in developing nations would cause an increase in worldwide savings, hence the global savings glut. Some have directly linked these capital flow patterns to higher US home prices, arguing that low interest rates (driven in part by the capital inflow) were a key determinant of higher house prices during the boom (e.g., Bernanke 2005; Himmelberg, Mayer, and Sinai 2005; Bernanke 2008; Taylor 2009; Adam, Marcet, and Kuang 2011). In a similar spirit, Caballero and Krishnamurthy (2009) identify the start of the housing boom with the Asian financial crisis, which fueled the demand for US risk-free assets. In their model, Asian savers turn to US assets, resulting in a net capital inflow for the United States. Global interest rates then fall in their model because the US economy is presumed to grow more slowly than the rest of the world.

Laibson and Mollerstrom (2010) have criticized the global savings glut hypothesis by noting that an increase in worldwide savings should have led to an investment boom in countries that were large importers of capital, notably the United States. Instead, the United States experienced a consumption boom that accompanied the housing boom, suggesting that saving worldwide was not unusually high. Laibson and Mollerstrom (2010) present an alternative interpretation of the correlation between home values and capital flows during the boom based on asset bubbles. Assuming a bubble in the housing market, they argue that the rise in housing wealth generated by the bubble led to higher consumption, which in turn led to greater borrowing from abroad and a substantial net capital inflow to the United States. A similar idea is presented in Ferrero (2011), but without the bubble. Ferrero studies a two-sector representative-agent model of international trade in which lower collateral requirements facilitate access to external funding and drive up house prices.

Others have argued that preference shocks and a desire for smooth (across goods) consumption can generate a correlation between house prices and capital inflows. Gete (2010) shows that consumption smoothing across tradable (nonhousing) goods and nontradable (housing) goods can lead to a positive correlation between house prices and current account deficits. With an exogenous increase in the home country's preference for housing, productive inputs in the home country are reallocated toward housing production, so that housing consumption can rise. But with a preference for smooth consumption across goods, the tradable nonhousing good (presumed identical across countries) will then be imported from abroad, leading to capital inflows to the home country.

The abovementioned theories fall into two broad categories: those that rely on higher domestic demand to drive both house prices and capital inflows in the same direction (Gete 2010; Laibson and Mollerstrom 2010; Ferrero 2011), and those that rely on capital inflow–driven low interest rates to drive up house prices (Bernanke 2005; Himmelberg, Mayer, and Sinai 2005; Bernanke 2008; Taylor 2009; Caballero and Krishnamurthy 2009; Adam, Marcet, and Kuang 2011). While these papers were motivated by observations on housing and capital flows during the housing *boom,* they also have implications for the housing bust. The former imply that the housing bust should be associated with a reversal of domestic demand, leading to a capital outflow. The latter imply that the housing bust should be associated with a rise in real interest rates, driven by a capital outflow.

As we show in the following, recent data pose a number of challenges to these theories. First, while it is true that real interest rates were low throughout the boom period, they have remained low and have even fallen further in the bust period. Second, while capital certainly flowed into countries such as the United States during the boom period, there is no evidence of a clear reversal in this trend during the bust period.[3] These observations suggest

---

3. Some empirical studies document a positive correlation between house prices and capital inflows to the United States, but these studies typically have data samples that terminate at the end of the boom or shortly thereafter (e.g., Aizenman and Jinjarak 2009; Kole and Martin 2009).

that the economic and political forces responsible for driving capital flows and house prices over the entire period were, to a large extent, distinct. Later we present empirical evidence that neither capital inflows nor real interest rates bear a strong relation to house prices in a sample that includes both the boom and the bust.

We interpret these recent events through the lens of the theoretical models in FLVNa and FLVNb, focusing specifically on the model in FLVNa in which an FML and its reversal are studied. Rather than reproducing the mathematical description of the model here, we simply describe it verbally and refer the reader to the original papers for details. Our focus here is on empirical evidence relating home prices to various indicators as a means of distinguishing among theories. Next we describe the model in FLVNa, and explain how it differs from the abovementioned theories.

6.2.1   The Housing Boom-Bust: A Theory of Time-Varying Risk Premia

The FLVNa paper studies a two-sector general equilibrium model of housing and nonhousing production where heterogenous households face limited risk-sharing opportunities as a result of incomplete financial markets. A house in the model is a residential durable asset that provides utility to the household, is illiquid (expensive to trade), and can be used as collateral in debt obligations. The model economy is populated by a large number of overlapping generations of households who receive utility from both housing and nonhousing consumption and who face a stochastic life cycle earnings profile. We introduce market incompleteness by modeling heterogeneous agents who face idiosyncratic and aggregate risks against which they cannot perfectly insure, and by imposing collateralized borrowing constraints on households.

Within the context of this model, FLVNa focus on the macroeconomic consequences of three systemic changes in housing finance, with an emphasis on how these factors affect risk premia in housing markets, and how risk premia in turn affect home prices. First, FLVNa investigate the impact of changes in housing collateral requirements.[4] Second, they investigate the impact of changes in housing transactions costs. Taken together, these two factors represent the theoretical counterpart to the real-world FML discussed before. Third, FLVNa investigate the impact of an influx of foreign capital into the domestic bond market. They argue that all three factors fluctuate over time and changed markedly during and preceding the period

4. Ferrero (2011) also assumes a relaxation of credit constraints to explain the housing boom. A key distinction between his model and FLVNa, however, is that Ferrero studies a two-country representative agent model, so an increase in borrowing by the domestic agent is only possible with an increase in lending from the rest of the world, hence a higher current account deficit. By contrast, in FLVNa, borrowing and lending can happen within the domestic economy between heterogeneous agents, so housing finance need not be tied to foreign savings. Thus, a reversal of the FML in a setting like that of Ferrero's would necessitate a capital outflow, whereas in FLVNa it does not.

of rapid home price appreciation from 2000 to 2006, and the subsequent bust. In particular, the boom period was marked by a widespread relaxation of collateralized borrowing constraints and declining housing transactions costs (including costs associated with mortgage borrowing, home equity extraction, and refinance). The period was also marked by a sustained depression of long-term interest rates that coincided with a vast inflow of capital into US safe bond markets. In the aftermath of the credit crisis that began in 2007, the erosion in credit standards and transactions costs has been sharply reversed.[5] We provide evidence on this following.

The main impetus for rising price-rent ratios in the model in the boom period is the simultaneous occurrence of positive economic shocks and a financial market liberalization, phenomena that generate an endogenous decline in risk premia on housing and equity assets. As risk premia fall, the aggregate house price index relative to aggregate rent rises. An FML reduces risk premia for two reasons, both of which are related to the ability of heterogeneous households to insure against aggregate and idiosyncratic risks. First, lower collateral requirements directly increase access to credit, which acts as a buffer against unexpected income declines. Second, lower transactions costs reduce the expense of obtaining the collateral required to increase borrowing capacity and provide insurance. These factors lead to an increase in risk-sharing, or a decrease in the cross-sectional variance of marginal utility. The housing bust is caused by a reversal of the FML and of the positive economic shocks and an endogenous decrease in borrowing capacity as collateral values fall. These factors lead to an accompanying rise in housing risk premia, driving the house price-rent ratio lower. Almost all of the theories discussed previously are silent on the role of housing risk premia in driving house price fluctuations.[6]

It is important to note that the rise in price-rent ratios caused by a financial market liberalization in FLVNa must be attributed to a decline in risk premia and not to a fall in interest rates. Indeed, the very changes in housing finance that accompany a financial market liberalization drive the endogenous interest rate up, rather than down. It follows that, if price-rent ratios rise after a financial market liberalization, it must be because the decline in risk premia more than offsets the rise in equilibrium interest rates that is attributable to the FML. This aspect of an FML underscores the importance of accounting properly for the role of foreign capital over the housing cycle. Without an infusion of foreign capital, any period of looser collateral requirements and lower housing transactions costs (such as that which characterized the housing boom) would be accompanied by an *increase* in equilibrium interest rates, as households endogenously respond to the improved

5. Streitfeld (2009) argues that, since the credit crisis, borrowing restrictions and credit constraints have become even more stringent than historical norms in the preboom period.
6. An exception is Caballero and Krishnamurthy (2009), but they do not study housing nor the FML and its reversal.

risk-sharing opportunities afforded by a financial market liberalization by reducing precautionary saving.

To model capital inflows, FLVNa introduce foreign demand for the domestic riskless bond into the market-clearing condition. This foreign capital inflow is modeled as driven by governmental holders who inelastically place all of their funds in domestic riskless bonds. Foreign governmental holders have a perfectly inelastic demand for safe securities and place all of their funds in those securities, regardless of their price relative to other assets. Later we discuss data on US international capital flows that supports this specification of the net capital flows in the United States over the last fifteen years.

The model in FLVNa implies that a rise in foreign purchases of domestic bonds, equal in magnitude to those observed in the data from 2000 to 2010, leads to a quantitatively large decline in the equilibrium real interest rate. Were this decline not accompanied by other, general equilibrium effects, it would lead to a significant housing boom in the model. But the general equilibrium effects imply that a capital inflow is unlikely to have a large effect on house prices *even if* it has a large effect on interest rates. One reason for this involves the central role of time-varying housing risk premia. In models where risk premia are held fixed, a decline in the interest rate of this magnitude would be sufficient—by itself—to explain the rise in price-rent ratios observed from 2000 to 2006 under reasonable calibrations. But with time-varying housing risk premia, the result can be quite different. Foreign purchases of US bonds crowd domestic savers out of the safe bond market, exposing them to greater systematic risk in equity and housing markets. In response, risk premia on housing and equity assets rise, substantially offsetting the effect of lower interest rates and limiting the impact of foreign capital inflows on home prices.

There is a second offsetting general equilibrium effect. Foreign capital inflows also stimulate residential investment, raising the expected stock of future housing and lowering the expected future rental growth rate. Like risk premia, these expectations are reflected immediately in house prices (pushing down the national house price-rent ratio), further limiting the impact of foreign capital inflows on home prices. The net effect of all of these factors is that a large capital inflow into safe securities has, at most, a small positive effect on house prices.

It is useful to clarify the two opposing forces simultaneously acting on housing risk premia in the model of FLVNa. During the housing boom, there is both an FML and a capital inflow. As explained, the FML *lowers* risk premia, while foreign purchases of domestic safe assets *raise* risk premia. Under the calibration of the model, the decline in risk premia resulting from the FML during the boom period is far greater than the rise in risk premia resulting from the capital inflow. On the whole, therefore, risk premia on housing assets fall, and this is the most important contributing factor to the increase in price-rent ratios during the boom. During the bust, modeled as a reversal of the FML but not the capital inflows, risk premia unambiguously rise even as interest rates remain low. The rise in risk premia drives the decline in house-price rent ratios.

These features of the model represent significant differences from other theories of capital flows and house prices. They permit the model to explain not just the housing boom, but also the housing bust, in which house price-rent ratios fell dramatically, even though interest rates remained low and there has been no clear reversal in the trend toward capital inflows into the US bond market. Moreover, they underscore the importance of distinguishing between interest rate changes (which are endogenous) and credit supply. In the absence of a capital inflow, an expansion of credit supply in the form of lower collateral requirements and lower transactions costs should lead, in equilibrium, to higher interest rates, rather than lower, as households respond to the improved risk-sharing/insurance opportunities by reducing precautionary saving. Instead we observed low real interest rates, generated in the model of FLVNa by foreign capital inflows, but the inflows themselves are not the key factor behind the housing boom-bust.

To illustrate the independent role of house prices and capital inflows in the model, figure 6.2 plots the transition dynamics for both the aggregate price-rent ratio and for foreign holdings of domestic assets over the period 2000 to 2010 from the model of FLVNa. The figure shows the dynamic behavior of the price-rent ratio in response to a series of shocks designed to mimic both the state of the economy and housing market conditions over the period 2000 to 2010. The economy begins in year 2000 at the stochastic steady state of a world with "normal" collateral requirements (i.e., fraction of home value that must be held as collateral) and housing transactions costs calibrated to roughly match the data prior to the housing boom of 2000 to 2006. In 2001, the economy undergoes an unanticipated shift to a new steady state, in which there is an FML with lower collateral requirements and lower transactions costs, calibrated to match the changes in these variables during the boom period, as well as an unanticipated increase in foreign holdings of US bonds from 0 to 16 percent of GDP. This 16 percent increase is calibrated to match the actual increase in net foreign holdings of US securities over the period 2000 to 2010. Along the transition path, foreign holdings of bonds are increased linearly from 0 to 16 percent of GDP from 2000 to 2010. The adjustment to the new stochastic steady state is then traced out over the seven-year period from 2001 to 2006, as the state variables evolve. Finally, starting in 2007 and continuing through 2010, the economy is presumed to undergo a surprise reversal of the financial market liberalization but not the foreign capital inflow.

Figure 6.2 shows that the house-price rent ratio rises by 39 percent over the period 2000 to 2006 and then falls by 17 percent over the period 2006 to 2010. By contrast, foreign holdings of domestic riskless bonds, denoted B_t^F,

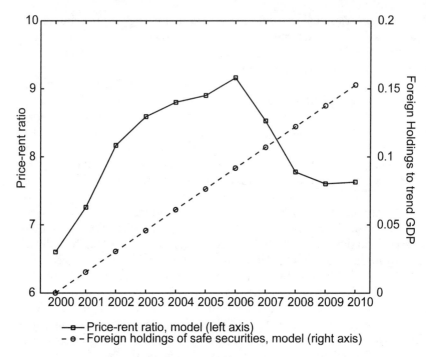

Fig. 6.2   Price-rent ratio and foreign holdings in FLVNa

Source: Favilukis, Ludvigson, and Van Nieuwerburgh (2010).

Notes: The figure plots the transition dynamics of the aggregate price-rent ratio and foreign holdings of the safe asset in the model of Favilukis, Ludvigson, and Van Nieuwerburgh (2010), for the period 2000 to 2010. The dynamics are driven by a sequence of aggregate economic shocks designed to mimic the business cycle over this period, a financial market liberalization in 2000, and a reversal of this liberalization in 2007, as well as the foreign flows depicted in the figure.

rise at a constant rate throughout the boom-bust period. Although foreign holdings rise mechanically over time and are crudely calibrated to match the long-term (trend) increase in holdings over the entire ten-year period (rather than matching the year-by-year fluctuations), the figure nevertheless shows that capital flows are not a key determinant of the boom-bust pattern in the price-rent ratio in this model, despite the large decline in interest rates generated by these inflows. In the data, the increase in the price-rent ratio (series shown in figure 6.1) over the period 2000:Q4 to 2006:Q4 is 49.9 percent (calculated in the same way as in the model), while over the bust (2006:Q4 to 2010:Q4) it declined 34.0 percent. The model captures 78 percent of the run-up in this measure and 49 percent of the decline.

The relationship between capital inflows and risk premia in FLVNa and FLVNb is worthy of emphasis. In equilibrium, higher capital inflows into the safe bond market *raise* risk premia on housing and equity, rather than lower them. This runs contrary to the argument, made by some, that the free flow of capital across borders should be associated with a reduction in risk premia (e.g., Geithner 2007). Here, foreign purchases of the safe asset make both equity and housing assets *more risky.* Both the risk premium and Sharpe ratio for equity and housing rise when there is a capital inflow, for two reasons. First, the increase in foreign money forces domestic residents as a whole to take a leveraged position in the risky assets. This by itself increases the volatility of asset and housing returns, translating into higher risk premia. Second, domestic savers are crowded out of the bond market by foreign governmental holders who are willing to hold the safe asset at any price. As a result, they become more exposed to systematic risk in the equity and housing markets. This means that the equity and housing Sharpe ratios must rise, as domestic savers shift the composition of their financial wealth toward risky securities. In addition, the volatility of the stochastic discount factor rises and there is a decrease in risk-sharing, as measured by the cross-sectional variance of marginal utility growth.

Of course, the effect of a capital inflow on house prices depends not only on the housing risk premium, but also on the risk-free interest rate. Although a capital inflow drives the housing risk premium up, in the model of FLVNa it drives the risk-free rate down by more, so a capital inflow still leads to a modest increase in the price-rent ratio.[7] In this model, an inflow of foreign capital calibrated to match the increase in foreign ownership of US Treasuries and US agency debt over the period 2000 to 2010 has a large downward impact on the equilibrium interest rate, which falls from 3.45 percent to 0.39 percent. The magnitude of this decline is close to the reduction in real rates observed in US bond market data over the period 2000 to 2006.

With this discussion as theoretical background, we now turn to an analysis of the data on capital flows, interest rates, and credit standards over the boom-bust period.

6.3   Trends in Capital Flows, Interest Rates, Credit Supply

While the notion of a global savings glut is controversial, recent data clearly suggest a reallocation of savings away from the developed world, and toward the developing world, the so-called *global imbalances* phenomenon. Unlike any prior period, global financial integration allowed for the channeling of one country's excess savings toward another country's real estate boom. Such financing occurred directly, for example, by German banks' purchases of US subprime securities, but also indirectly through the US Treasury and Agency bond markets. As the world's sole supplier of a global

---

7. Changes in expected future aggregate rent growth also can effect the price-rent ratio. The numbers here refer to a comparison of stochastic steady states, however, in which the expected rental growth rate is the same in both steady states (equal to the deterministic growth rate of the economy).

reserve currency, the US experienced a surge in foreign ownership of US Treasuries and Agency bonds. Agency bonds refers to the debt of the two government-sponsored enterprises (GSEs) Freddie Mac and Fannie Mae, as well as to the mortgage-backed securities that they issue and guarantee. Due to their ambivalent private-public structure and their history as agencies of the federal government, private market investors (including foreign investors) have always assumed that the debt of Freddie Mac and Fannie Mae was implicitly backed by the US Treasury. That implicit backing became an explicit backing in September 2008 when Freddie Mac and Fannie Mae were taken into government conservatorship. See Acharya, Richardson, et al. (2011) for details on the GSEs.

In this section, we discuss in detail data showing the trends in capital flows, US real interest rates, and the relaxation and subsequent tightening of housing credit constraints and credit standards.

6.3.1   International Capital Flows

The Treasury International Capital (TIC) reporting system is the official source of US securities flows data. It reports monthly data (with a six-week lag) on foreigners' purchases and sales of all types of financial *securities* (equities, corporate, Agency, and Treasury bonds). We refer to these monthly transactions data as the *TIC flows data.* The TIC system also produces periodic benchmark surveys of the market value of foreigners' net *holdings,* or net asset *positions,* in US securities. Unlike the flows data, these data take into account the net capital gains on gross foreign assets and liabilities. We refer to these as the *TIC holdings data.* The holdings data are collected in detailed surveys conducted in December of 1978, 1984, 1989, and 1994, in March 2000, and annually in June from 2002 to 2010. The survey data on holdings is thought to be of higher quality than the flows data because it more accurately accounts for valuation effects (Warnock and Warnock 2009).[8]

The Bureau of Economic Analysis (BEA) in the US Department of Commerce also provides annual estimates of the value of accumulated stocks (holdings) of US-owned assets abroad and of foreign-owned assets in the United States. We will refer to these as the *BEA holdings data.* These include estimates of holdings of securities, based on the TIC data, as well as estimates of holdings of other assets such as foreign direct investment (FDI), US official reserves, and other US government reserves. We refer to the sum of these other assets plus financial securities as *total assets.* In recent data, the main difference between the BEA estimate of net foreign holdings of total assets and its estimate of net foreign holdings of total securities is

---

8. As explained in Warnock and Warnock (2009), reporting to the surveys is mandatory, with penalties for noncompliance, and the data are subjected to extensive analysis and editing. Data on foreign holdings of US securities are available at http://www.treasury.gov/resource-center /data-chart-center/tic/Pages/index.aspx.

attributable to FDI, where, since 2006, the value of US FDI abroad has exceeded the value of foreign FDI in the United States.[9]

The BEA defines the US *net international investment position* (NIIP) as the value of US-owned assets abroad minus foreign-owned assets in the United States. The overall change in the NIIP incorporates capital gains and losses on the prior stock of holdings of assets. Thus, the total change in US gross foreign assets equals net purchases by US residents plus any capital gains on the prior stock of gross foreign assets, while the total change in US foreign liabilities equals net sales of assets to foreign residents plus any capital gains accrued to foreigners on their US assets. The change in the NIIP is the difference between the two. Capital gains are the most important component of valuation changes on the NIIP.

The BEA also collects quarterly and annual estimates of *transactions* with foreigners, including trade in goods and services, receipts and payments of income, transfers, and transactions in financial assets. We refer to these as the *BEA transactions data.* The transactions data measure the current account (CA). Since the CA transactions data only measure purchases and sales of assets, they do not adjust for valuation effects that must be taken into account in constructing the international investment *positions* (holdings) of the United States, as just discussed.[10]

When thinking about the recent boom-bust period in residential real estate, a question arises as to which measure of capital flows to study. Obstfeld (2011) documents an increase in the sheer volume of financial trade across borders, and argues that it could be positively correlated with financial instability. Moreover, he shows that the amplitude of pure valuation changes in the NIIP has grown in tandem with the volumes of gross flows. Because the CA ignores such valuation changes, our preferred measure would therefore be a measure of total changes in net foreign *holdings* of assets rather than changes in net *transactions.* Unfortunately, data on net foreign asset holdings are only readily available in the United States, and then only annually. (For the empirical work following, we construct our own quarterly estimate of these holdings for securities.) Outside the United States, only the transactions-based CA data are available. Thus, when we use international data we use the CA as a measure of capital flows, bearing in mind the limitations of these data for measuring changes in actual asset holdings.

Since net foreign asset holdings data are available for the United States, when working with US data we focus most on net foreign holdings as a measure of capital flows (although for completeness we also present empirical results using the CA as a measure of capital flows). Within net foreign

---

9. These data are available at http://www.bea.gov/international/index.htm.

10. See the adjustments for valuations effects at http://www.bea.gov/international/xls/intinv10_t3.xls.

holdings, we focus on changes in holdings of financial *securities,* rather than changes in holdings of total *assets.* We argue that the former are far more relevant for residential real estate than the latter. Recall that the most important difference between the two, espeçfially in recent data, is attributable to flows in FDI. But it is unclear how relevant FDI is for the housing market. For example, during much of the housing boom, the value of net foreign holdings on FDI fell, implying a net capital *outflow* on those types of assets. This fact is hardly consistent with the notion that capital *inflows* to the United States helped finance the housing boom.

What flowed *in* during the housing boom was foreign capital directed at US Treasury and Agency securities. There are several reasons we expect these assets—unlike FDI—to be directly related to the US housing market. First, foreign purchases of Agency securities allowed the government-sponsored enterprises (GSEs) Fannie Mae and Freddie Mac to broaden their market for mortgage-backed securities (MBS) to international investors, funding the mortgage investments themselves. Thus, an inflow of capital into US Agencies can in turn free up US banks to fund additional mortgages. Second, because mortgage rates are often tied to Treasury rates, large foreign Treasury purchases could in principle directly affect house prices through their effect on interest rates. In addition, low Treasury rates could lead US banks in search of yield to undertake more risky mortgage investments (see Maddaloni and Peydro [2011] for evidence that banks increase the riskiness of investments in low interest rate environments). In summary, because the FDI streams are largely divorced from the US housing market, the most appropriate measure of capital flows for our purpose is not net foreign holdings of total assets but instead total securities.

Figure 6.3 shows the movement in various measures of international capital flows into the United States, relative to trend GDP, in annual data from 1976 to 2010. Plotted are the *change* in net foreign holdings of total assets, total securities, and in what we will call US "safe" securities (defined as Treasuries and Agencies). We refer to a capital inflow as a positive change in holdings, and vice versa for a capital outflow. Also plotted is the current account deficit. Figure 6.3 shows that there is considerable volatility in these measures during the housing boom and the subsequent financial crisis, with particularly sharp increases in the change in net foreign holdings of US assets from 2007 to 2008. This corresponds to an upward spike in the change in the US net foreign liability position in 2008 (change in net foreign holdings of total assets in the figure). This series declines from 2008 to 2009 and increases again from 2009 to 2010. Comparing the endpoints of these series in 2010 to their values in 2006, we see that—by any measure of assets—inflows (or the change in holdings) were higher at the end of the sample in 2010 than they were at the peak of the housing boom at the beginning of 2006 (end of 2005).

To get a better sense of the trends in these series, figure 6.4 plots the same measures of international capital flows, but computed as four-year moving

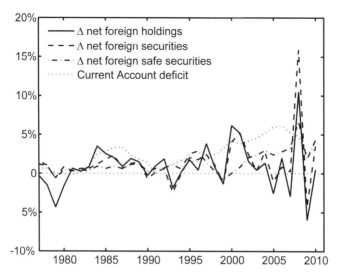

Fig. 6.3 Measures of US capital flows

Source: US Department of Commerce, Bureau of Economic Analysis.

Notes: Net foreign holdings of total assets is foreign-owned assets in the United States minus US-owned assets abroad. Net foreign holdings of total securities is defined as foreign-owned US government securities plus US Treasury securities plus US securities other than Treasury securities minus US-owned foreign securities. Net foreign holdings of safe securities is defined as US government securities plus Treasury securities. (We do not subtract off US holdings of foreign government securities, since these carry at least exchange-rate risk.) The current account deficit is imports of goods and services and income payments less exports of goods and services and income receipts less net unilateral current transfers. All series are expressed relative to trend GDP (obtained from a Hodrick–Prescott trend). The sample is annual, 1976 to 2010.

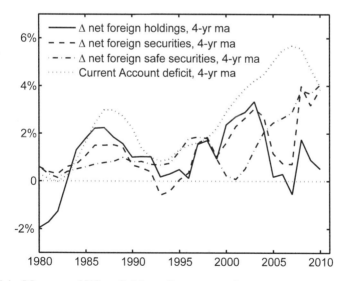

Fig. 6.4 Measures of US capital flows, four-year moving average

Source: US Department of Commerce, Bureau of Economic Analysis.

Notes: See figure 6.3. The sample is annual, 1980 to 2010.

averages. The figure shows that changes in net foreign holdings of total assets show little trend movement over the entire boom-bust period 2000 to 2010, but if anything they trended *up* during the *bust* period from 2006 to 2010, while they trended *down* in the *boom* from 2002 to 2006. A similar pattern holds for net foreign holdings of total securities, except that here, inflows are much more sharply positive during the housing bust period. So where are the inflows during the housing boom? In US safe securities.

The only assets for which we observe a significant increase in capital inflows during the boom period are those we defined earlier as US safe securities, comprised of Treasury and Agency debt. We have argued earlier that these assets are likely to be the most relevant for housing markets, and indeed the change in net foreign holdings of these securities was positive and increasing throughout the boom period, from 2001 through the beginning of 2006, which we take as the peak of the housing boom. At the same time, however, inflows into these securities, like the other categories of assets, continued to rise during the bust period, implying that the US borrowing from abroad in these securities increased further from the beginning of 2006 to end 2010, rather than declined.

The only measure in figure 6.4 that suggests a decline in the rate at which the United States is borrowing from abroad is the current account deficit, pointing to a significant incongruence with the holdings data. (We discuss this further later.) Despite the volatility in the holdings data, the bust period still exhibited relatively high average inflows of foreign capital into all forms of US securities, mirroring capital gains on US Liabilities relative to US assets abroad, as well as a net flight into US safe securities, in 2008. The CA deficit (or, equivalently, the capital account) omits these significant valuation changes during the financial crisis. We view this as a serious shortcoming of the CA as a measure of international capital flows, since such valuation adjustments surely have wealth effects that in general equilibrium would influence the extent to which US households can consume at rates that exceed domestic income. At the end of the sample in 2010, figure 6.4 shows that there is a decline in the (moving average trend) inflows to total assets from the end of 2008 to the end of 2010. But this decline is barely discernible in total securities and is not at all present in US safe securities. The discrepancy is again net flows into FDI, which we have already argued are largely divorced from the housing market.

How can we reconcile the large decline in the current account deficit from the end of 2005 to the end of 2010, with the observation that the change in net foreign holdings of total US assets rose over this period (figure 6.3)? Comparing 2010 to 2005 (year end), the current account deficit fell by $274,876 million, while the year-end change in net foreign holdings of total US assets (relative to trend GDP) rose by $395,440 million. The discrepancy is attributable to valuation effects, which the current account ignores. Indeed, 126 percent of the discrepancy over this period is attributable to valuation effects (–26 percent is attributable to a statistical discrepancy and other small adjustments between the current and capital account flows). Thus, the decline in the current account deficit from 2005 to 2010 suggests a decline in the rate at which US liabilities are increasing, when in fact this rate has increased, primarily because the change in capital gains foreign residents enjoyed on US assets from 2005 to 2010 far exceeded the change in capital gains accruing to US residents on their assets abroad. But these valuation adjustments came primarily from assets other than what we have defined as US safe assets. (This is perhaps not surprising since these assets are far less volatile than is risky capital.) A breakdown suggests that only 15.6 percent of these valuation adjustments (specifically of the change in these adjustments from 2005 to 2010) came from adjustments on US safe assets. A much larger 39.7 percent came from financial securities other than safe securities, and the majority (44.7 percent) came from valuation adjustments on assets other than financial securities (including both safe and nonsafe financial securities).

We can also compute the fraction of the *cumulative* change in net foreign holdings of safe assets from the end of 2005 to the end of 2010 that is attributable to valuation changes versus transactions. Over this period, transactions account for 92.6 percent, while valuation changes account for just 7.3 percent. This shows that, even accumulating over the entire bust period, there continues to be a strong inflow of capital into US safe securities that is not attributable merely to valuation changes.

To summarize, during the housing boom, only US capital inflows on *securities* (equities, corporate, US Agency and Treasury bills and bonds) show any discernible upward trend. Among securities, the upward trend has been driven almost entirely by an increase in net foreign holdings of US safe assets, specifically US Treasury and Agency debt. Yet net inflows on these securities, rather than declining during the housing bust, have continued to increase.

We now provide more detail on the flows to US safe securities. To get a better sense of the quantitative importance of these flows to US safe assets, the solid line of figure 6.5, measured against the left axis, plots the combined foreign holdings in billions of US dollars of short-term and long-term US Treasuries and Agencies. The dashed line, measured against the right axis, shows long-term (not short-term) foreign holdings of Treasuries and Agencies relative to the amount of long-term marketable debt outstanding. Figure 6.6 plots total foreign holdings of US Treasuries and Agencies relative to the size of the US economy, measured as trend GDP.

The figure shows that foreign holdings of US Treasuries were modest until the mid-1990s. In December 1994, foreign holdings of long-term Treasuries were $464 billion, which amounted to 19.4 percent of marketable Treasuries outstanding and to 6.4 percent of US trend GDP. Foreign holdings of long-term Agencies were $121 billion, which amounted to 5.4 percent of

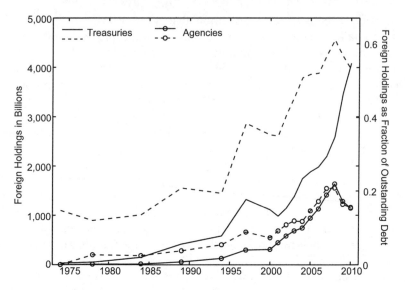

Fig. 6.5   Foreign holdings of US safe assets

Source: US Treasury International Capital System's annual survey of foreign portfolio holdings of US securities.

Notes: The figure plots foreign holdings of US Treasuries and US Agencies (circles). US Agencies denotes both the corporate bonds issued by the government-sponsored enterprises and the mortgage-backed securities guaranteed by them. The solid lines denote the amount of long-term and short-term holdings, in billions of US dollars, as measured against the left axis. The dashed lines denote the long-term foreign holdings relative to the total amount of outstanding long-term (marketable) debt. The foreign holdings data are available for December 1974, 1978, 1984, 1989, 1994, 1997, March 2000, and annually from June 2001 until June 2010.

outstanding Agencies and 1.5 percent of trend GDP. Over the course of the Asian financial crisis, these holdings doubled. By March 2000, toward the end of the crisis, foreign holdings of long-term Treasuries and Agencies were $884 billion and $261 billion, respectively, corresponding to 35.3 percent and 7.3 percent of the amounts outstanding. Total foreign holdings of Treasuries and Agencies increased from 9.8 percent to 14.8 percent of trend GDP. Caballero, Farhi, and Gourinchas (2008) argue that the Asian financial crisis represented a negative shock to the supply of (investable/pledgeable) assets in East Asia, and led their investors to increase their investments in US bonds, one of the scarce risk-free assets available worldwide.

During the housing boom from 2000 to 2006, the increase in foreign holdings of safe assets continued at an even more rapid pace. Total foreign holdings of Treasuries and Agencies more than doubled, from $1,418 billion in March 2000 to $3,112 billion in June 2006. Foreign holdings of long-term Treasuries went from 35.3 percent to 52.0 percent of the total amount of Treasuries outstanding, while holdings of long-term Agencies went from 7.3 percent to 17.2 percent. Most of the rise in foreign holdings of Treasuries took place by 2004, while most of the rise in Agencies took place from 2004

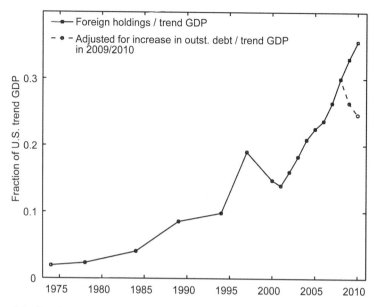

Fig. 6.6   Foreign holdings relative to GDP

Source: US Treasury International Capital System's annual survey of foreign portfolio holdings of US securities.

Notes: The solid line denotes foreign holdings of US Treasuries and Agencies relative to US trend GDP (squares). Trend GDP is computed with a Hodrick–Prescott filter (Hodrick and Prescott 1997). The dashed line (circles) asks what the foreign holdings relative to trend GDP would have been if the foreign holdings relative to the amount of debt outstanding declined the amount they did but the amount of debt outstanding relative to trend GDP was held at 2008 values for the years 2009 and 2010. The foreign holdings data are available for December 1974, 1978, 1984, 1989, 1994, 1997, March 2000, and annually from June 2001 until June 2010.

to 2006. Total foreign holdings of Treasuries and Agencies increased from 14.8 percent to 23.7 percent of trend GDP. The boom in US house prices, which started at the end of 1994 and accelerated after 2000, coincided with a massive inflow of foreign capital in safe US assets.

At the same time, however, capital inflows in the US safe assets continued to rise during the housing bust and financial crisis. Figure 6.5 shows that between June 2006 and June 2010, total foreign holdings of Treasuries and Agencies rose from \$3,112 billion to \$5,232 billion, or from 23.7 percent to 35.5 percent of trend GDP. The share of outstanding long-term Treasuries held by foreign investors also increased from 52.0 percent in 2006 to 61.1 percent in 2008 before falling back to 53.0 percent in 2010. The reduction in 2010 is attributable to a large increase in the total quantity of marketable Treasuries outstanding in 2009 and 2010 (which rose from 33.2 percent of trend GDP in 2008 to 54.9 percent in 2010), rather than to a reduction in nominal foreign holdings. The latter actually continued to increase rapidly from \$2,211 billion in 2008 to \$3,343 billion in 2010. The dashed line in figure 6.6 is a foreign holdings-to-trend GDP series that we have adjusted in 2009 and 2010 to reflect the large increase in the quantity of Treasury debt outstanding that occurred in 2009 and 2010. The adjusted series equals the level of foreign holdings as a fraction of trend GDP that *would have* occurred in 2009 and 2010 had Treasury debt outstanding as a fraction of trend GDP been fixed at its 2008 level. The dashed line shows that the increase in foreign holdings of US Treasuries in 2009 and 2010 is less than proportional to the increase in outstanding Treasuries over those years. In this relative sense, therefore, foreigners have become less willing to hold US Treasuries. According to the adjusted series there is a reduction in foreign holdings as a fraction of trend GDP, from 30.0 percent of trend GDP in 2008, to 24.6 percent in 2010, suggesting that a substantial "unwind" of foreign positions in US Treasuries may be under way, at least relative to the total amount of US debt being issued.

Although there has so far been no reduction in nominal foreign holdings of US Treasuries during the housing bust, the financial crisis did lead to a substantial reduction in nominal foreign holdings of US Agencies. While foreign holdings of Agencies still rose from 17.2 percent in 2006 to 20.8 percent of the amount outstanding in 2008, they fell back sharply to 15.6 percent of the amount outstanding in 2010, even as the amount outstanding remained flat.

Foreign Official Holdings

An important aspect of recent patterns in international capital flows is that foreign demand for US Treasury securities is dominated by Foreign Official Institutions. Krishnamurthy and Vissing-Jorgensen (2007) find that demand for US Treasury securities by governmental holders is extremely inelastic, implying that when these holders receive funds to invest they buy US Treasuries, regardless of their price. As explained in Kohn (2002), government entities have specific regulatory and reserve currency motives for holding US Treasuries and face both legal and political restrictions on the type of assets that can be held, forcing them into safe securities.

Data from the TIC system breaks out what share of foreign holdings of US Treasuries is attributable to Foreign Official Institutions, which are government entities, mostly central banks. Foreign Official Institutions own the vast majority of US Treasuries in recent data: in June 2010 Foreign Official Institutions held 75 percent of all foreign holdings of US Treasuries. That share has always been high and has risen from 58 percent in March 2000 to 75 percent in June 2010. Indeed, 75 percent represents a *lower bound* on the fraction of such securities held by Foreign Official Institutions, since some prominent foreign governments purchase US securities through offshore centers and third-country intermediaries, purchases that would not be attributed to Foreign Official entities by the TIC system—see Warnock and Warnock (2009). Foreign Official Institutions also accounted for 64 percent of the foreign holdings of Agencies in June 2010.

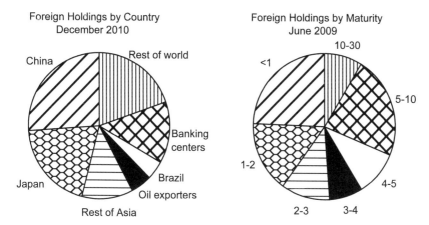

Fig. 6.7   **Foreign holdings by maturity and by country**

Source: US Treasury International Capital System's annual survey of foreign portfolio holdings of US securities.

Notes: The right panel shows the share of foreign holdings of US Treasuries and Agencies for different maturity ranges, expressed in years. The data are for June 2009 (table 14a of the 2009 TICS report). Fifty-one percent of the Agency holdings are reported to be of maturity twenty-five to thirty years. These are thirty-year mortgage-backed securities, which have a nominal maturity of thirty years but an effective maturity of about seven years because of prepayment. We reallocate these thirty-year Agency holdings across maturities so that they have a weighted average maturity (WAM) of seven years. The resulting series for the maturity of foreign holdings of US Agencies has a WAM of 6.4 years instead of the original 17.7 years. Total long-term foreign holdings have a WAM of 5.2 years. Once we add the short-term Treasury holdings, which are one year or less in maturity, the WAM drops to 4.6 years. The left panel shows the foreign holdings as of December 2010 by country groups. China excludes Hong Kong, which is part of "Rest of Asia." Banking centers consist of the United Kingdom, the Caribbean, Luxembourg, Belgium, and Ireland.

Asian central banks (China, Japan, Korea) have acquired massive US dollar reserves in the process of stabilizing their exchange rate. The share of foreign holdings is higher for long-term than for short-term securities. The left panel of figure 6.7 shows the foreign holdings as of December 2010 by country groups. China excludes Hong Kong, which is part of "Rest of Asia." Banking centers consist of the United Kingdom, the Caribbean, Luxembourg, Belgium, and Ireland. It is widely believed that China holds a nontrivial fraction of its safe dollar assets through financial intermediaries in the UK and in other banking centers (Warnock 2010). The graph then suggests that as much as two-thirds of safe US assets is held by Asian countries. China (narrowly defined) held nearly $1,500 billion in Treasuries and Agencies in June 2010; Japan held nearly $1,000 billion.

The right panel of figure 6.7 shows the share of foreign holdings of US Treasuries and Agencies for different maturity ranges, expressed in years. The data are for June 2009. As the caption explains, the maturity of the Agency holdings is adjusted to account for the prepayment option embedded in mortgage-backed securities. Total long-term and short-term foreign holdings have a weighted average maturity of 4.6 years. About a quarter of foreign holdings have a maturity of one year or less. Fully half of all holdings have a maturity below three years. This suggests that a substantial reduction in foreign holdings of US safe assets could occur over a relatively short period without an outright fire-sale of long-term bonds, if current holders simply stopped rolling over existing positions.

Longer-Term Trends in Net Foreign Holdings of Securities

We have emphasized the special relevance for the US housing boom-bust cycle of US securities considered to be safe stores-of-value (i.e., US Treasury and Agency debt). But is worth emphasizing that, even over a longer period of time, foreign holdings of these securities behave similarly to total net foreign holdings of all securities. The reason is that foreign holdings of US securities other than Treasuries and Agencies are roughly equal in magnitude to US holdings of securities abroad. Figure 6.8 makes this point visually; net foreign holdings of all securities other than US Treasury and Agency debt as a fraction of US Trend GDP have hovered close to zero since 1994, even as net foreign holdings of safe securities have soared. This shows that all of the long-term upward trend in net foreign holdings of US securities since 1994 has been the result of an upward trend in net foreign

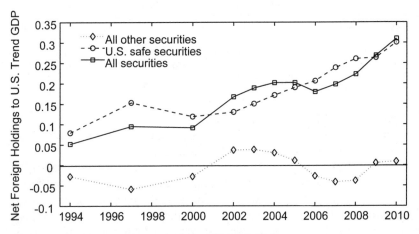

Fig. 6.8   Net foreign holdings relative to US trend GDP

Source: US Treasury International Capital System's annual survey of foreign portfolio holdings of US securities.

Notes: The solid line (squares) denotes total net foreign holdings of long-term securities (the net foreign liability position of the United States) relative to US trend GDP. Net foreign holdings are defined as foreign holdings of US securities minus US holdings of foreign securities. We define as net foreign holdings of safe securities to be foreign holdings of US Treasuries and Agencies. (We do not subtract off US holdings of foreign government securities, since these carry at least exchange-rate risk.) The dashed line (circles) denotes the thus constructed net foreign holdings in safe securities, while the dotted line (diamonds) denotes the net foreign holdings in all other securities. The data are available for December 1994, December 1997, March 2000, and annually from June 2002 until June 2010.

holdings of US *safe* securities; net foreign holdings of other securities are almost exactly zero in June of 2010. Thus the long-term downward trend in the US net international investment position is well described by the foreign holdings of US safe assets. Of the safe assets foreigners hold, 70 percent (on average) over the period 1994 to 2010 are held in US Treasuries. The large US current account deficits in the boom period are, to a large extent, the mirror image of the increase in foreign holdings of US safe assets.[11] This is true in the aggregate net flows to the United States, but also for China. China's cumulative current account surplus between 2003 and 2007 largely matches up with its acquisitions of US Treasuries and Agencies (Bernanke 2011).

Risky Mortgage Holdings

Although net flows into securities other than Treasuries and Agencies have hovered around zero, there were substantial *gross* flows across borders into private-label products such as mortgage-backed securities (MBS), collateralized debt obligations (CDO), and credit default swaps (CDS) with nonprime residential or commercial real estate as the underlying or as the reference entity. Because an average of 80 percent of such private-label MBS principal received a AAA rating from the credit ratings agencies and earned yields above those of Treasuries (see US Treasury Department 2011), large foreign (as well as domestic) institutional investors were able and willing to hold these assets on their books. The TICS data indicate that foreigners held $594 billion of nonagency mortgage-backed securities in June 2007. By June 2009, these holdings more than halved to $266 billion, after which they stabilized at $257 billion in June 2010. Less than 10 percent of these are held by foreign official institutions (US Treasury Department 2011).

Bernanke (2011) shows interesting cross-country differences in the composition of countries' US investment portfolio. China and emerging Asia held three-quarters of their US investments in the form of Treasuries and Agencies in 2007. Their share of all AAA-rated securities was 77.5 percent, while the AAA-rated share of all US securities outstanding was only 36 percent. European (as well as domestic) investors held only about one-third of their US portfolio in the form of AAA-rated assets. Not only did Europeans invest in non-AAA corporate debt, they accumulated $500 billion in US asset-backed (largely mortgage-backed) securities between 2003 and 2007.

In addition to their different risk profiles over the housing cycle, Europe and Asia differ by their current account positions. While the Asian economies ran a large current account surplus, financing the purchases of US assets with large trade surpluses, Europe had a balanced current account over this period. It financed the purchases of risky US assets by issuing external liabilities, mostly equity, sovereign debt, and asset-backed commercial paper

---

11. Though, as discussed earlier, an important discrepancy between the current account data, based on transactions, and the net foreign assets holdings data, is that the former do not fully adjust for valuation effects that are captured in the international holdings data.

(ABCP). A prototypical example of European holdings were AAA-rated tranches of subprime MBS held by large banks through lightly-regulated off-balance sheet vehicles, and financed with ABCP (Acharya, Schnabl, and Suarez 2012).

6.3.2   US Interest Rates

We have seen that the long-term upward trend in net foreign holdings of US securities since 1994 has been the result of an upward trend in net foreign holdings of US safe securities. The rise in net holdings by foreigners over time has coincided with a downward trend in real interest rates, as illustrated in figure 6.9. The real annual interest rate on the ten-year Treasury bond fell from 3.78 percent at the start of 2000 to 1.97 percent by the end of 2005, while the ten-year Treasury Inflation Protected (TIPS) rate fell from 4.32 percent to 2.12 percent over this period. Real rates fell further to all-time lows during the housing bust. The real ten-year Treasury bond rate declined from 2.22 percent to –0.42 percent from 2006:Q1 to 2011:Q3, while the TIPS rate declined from 2.20 percent to 0.08 percent.

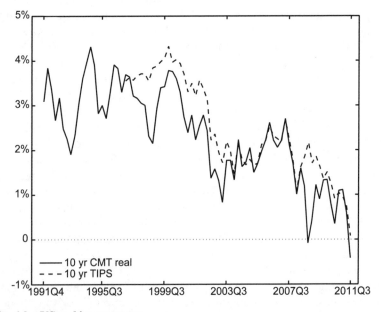

Fig. 6.9   US real interest rates

Sources: US Treasury, Survey of Professional Forecasters. From 2003 to 2011, US Treasury; from 1997 to 2002, data are obtained from J. Huston McCulloch, http://www.econ.ohio-state .edu/jhm/ts/ts.html. The complete sample runs from 1991:Q4 to 2011:Q3.

Notes: "10yr TIPS" is the yield on Treasury inflation protected securities (TIPS) adjusted to constant maturities, corresponding to the third month of each quarter. "10yr CMT real" is the ten-year constant maturity Treasury bond rate minus expectations of the average annual rate of CPI inflation over the next ten years from the Survey of Professional Forecasters, in percent per annum.

Empirically, Bernanke, Reinhart, and Sack (2004) find evidence for lower Treasury yields around periods of Japanese purchases of US Treasuries in the 2000 to 2004 period, while Warnock and Warnock (2009) estimate that twelve-month flows equal to 1 percent of GDP are associated with a 19 basis point reduction in long rates. They also find US mortgage rates to be affected. The effects are large. Had the twelve months ending in May 2005 seen zero foreign official purchases of US Treasury and agency bonds, their results suggest that, ceteris paribus, US long rates would have been about 80 basis points higher.

6.3.3   Financial Market Liberalization

While there is little doubt that inflows of foreign capital into US Treasury and Agency markets are associated with lower long-term real interest rates, there is no direct evidence that they have played an important role in raising house prices during the boom. We argued earlier that there are good theoretical reasons to doubt the hypothesis that lower interest rates had a quantitatively large effect on house prices during the boom. Empirically, Glaeser, Gottlieb, and Gyourko (2010) concur and find that even when the house price impact of lower interest rates should be stronger (at a low initial rate), they account for, at most, one-fifth of the observed change in housing prices. We present additional evidence on this in the following.

What, then, accounts for the dramatic rise in US house prices during the boom if not low interest rates? A key missing element in this scenario is the shift in credit standards and housing transactions costs, summarized earlier as an FML and its reversal. The widespread relaxation of credit standards is well-documented (see Nichols, Pennington-Cross, and Yezer 2005; Favilukis, Ludvigson, and Van Nieuwerburgh 2010; and Ferrero 2011 for more details). Moreover, a growing body of empirical evidence directly links measures that identify changes in credit *supply* (as opposed to changes in demand) to movements in asset prices.

Loan-to-Value Ratios

Many different aspects of mortgage lending over the 2000 to 2010 period are consistent with a relaxation of credit standards. It may seem that an obvious way to measure relaxation of credit standards is to study loan-to-value ratios. Several studies have observed that average or median loan-to-value ratios did not increase much over time; see, for example, the contribution by Glaeser, Gottlieb, and Gyourko in this volume (chapter 7). There are at least three problems with using average LTV ratios as an indicator of tightness of credit constraints. First, average loan-to-value ratio measures usually mix in mortgages for house purchases with those for refinancing. The latter category of mortgages have much lower LTV ratios because the borrowers often have accumulated substantial amounts of home equity already. These refinancing are quantitatively important because, during the housing boom, mortgage interest rates came down persistently, leading to a massive refinancing boom. The share of refis in originations was 63 percent in 2002, 72 percent in 2003, and around 50 percent in 2004 to 2006 (data from www .insidemortgagefinance.com).

Second, the average loan-to-value ratio are typically based only on the first lien on the house. But often, new borrowers would take out an 80 per-cent LTV first lien and then a second (and possibly third) lien (closed-end second or home equity line of credit). By the end of 2006 households rou-tinely were able to buy homes with 100 percent or higher financing using a piggyback second mortgage or home equity loan. The fraction of house-holds with second liens rose dramatically during the boom. For subprime loans, that fraction rose from 3 percent in 2002 to 30 percent; for Alt-A loans it rose from 3 percent to 44 percent.[12] In addition, second or third liens were often the way in which existing home owners tapped into their home equity, often several quarters after they took out the original mortgage. This equity extraction through second liens is in addition to extraction via cash-out refinancing, another innovation of the boom that became increas-ingly prevalent. The contribution in this volume by Lee, Mayer, and Tracy (chapter 5) shows that second lien balances grew from about $200 billion at the start of 2002 to over $1 trillion by the end of 2007. It also shows that the prevalence of second mortgages rose in every US region from below 10 percent at the start of the boom (bit higher in coastal cyclical markets) to around 40 percent in 2006 (except for the Midwest declining region, which peaks at a 20 percent share).

What this evidence suggests is that we should look at combined LTVs (CLTVs), combining all liens on a property, at the time of purchase. And to gauge how credit constraints affected the marginal household, we should look at the right tail of that CLTV distribution. Lee, Mayer, and Tracy (chap-ter 5, this volume) show that the average LTV at purchase for properties *with one lien* stayed rather constant over the boom—if anything, it declined a bit. Likewise, the share of purchases with one mortgage with an LTV greater or equal to 95 percent also stays constant. By contrast, the share of purchases *with multiple mortgages* with a CLTV greater or equal to 95 percent rises dra-matically in every region. The nationwide increase is from about a 25 percent

---

12. An indirect indicator of the prevalence of the use of second mortgages is the fraction of first liens with LTV exactly equal to 80 percent. This fraction rose substantially between 2002 and 2006, as shown by Krainer, LeRoy, and Munpyung (2009). They also show that the fraction of FRMs with LTV greater than 80 percent decreased from 22 percent to 6 percent over this period. Their hypothesis is that mortgage lending underwent a shift from a practice of achieving greater home-buyer leverage by simply increasing the LTV on the first lien (common prior to the housing boom), to a practice of achieving such greater leverage by combining an exactly 80 percent LTV first lien with a second lien taken out simultaneously (common during the housing boom). In short, during the housing boom high LTV ratios were achieved by taking out piggyback second mortgages rather than by loading all leverage onto the first lien, as was previous practice. Consistent with this hypothesis, Krainer, LeRoy, and Munpyung (2009) find that the default rate on first lien mortgages with exactly 80 percent LTV ratios was higher than that on first lien mortgages that had either 79 percent or 81 percent LTV ratios.

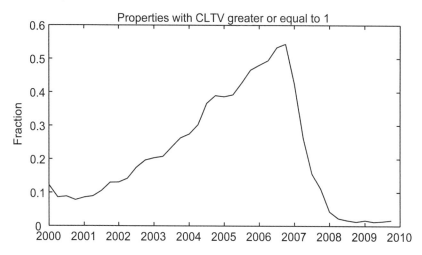

Fig. 6.10   **Fraction of properties in LA County with cumulative LTV ratios greater or equal than 100 percent**
Source: Laufer (2011).
Note: The figure plots the cummulative loan-to-value ratio at the time of purchase for homes in Los Angeles County.

share to about a 60 percent share. At the peak, about two-thirds of purchase mortgages with a second lien had a CLTV of 95 percent or more. Keys et al., chapter 4 in this volume, show that the average CLTV on subprime loans increases from 80 percent in 1997 to 96 percent in 2006.

A recent study using detailed data on mortgages in Los Angeles county shows the dramatic easing of credit constraints over the boom period and subsequent reversal in another way. Figure 6.10 from Laufer (2011) shows the share of properties in LA county with CLTVs at purchase above 100 percent for all loans except nonconventional loans (Federal Housing Administration [FHA] and Veterans Affairs [VA] loans). That share rises from 8 percent in 2001 to 54 percent in the fourth quarter of 2006, before collapsing. The sharp drop in this series beginning in 2007 and reaching zero by 2008 reflects a significant reduction in the maximum LTV ratio permitted by mortgage originators, since home values (in the denominator) were simultaneously falling.

Finally, there is a widespread belief that house price appraisals, done at the time of mortgage origination, were upward biased during the boom. This would downward bias LTV and CLTV ratios. As a result, what may look like flat or modestly increasing (average) CLTVs may in fact be increasing CLTVs once measured relative to the true value of the property.

Other Aspects of Credit Availability

The behavior of CLTV ratios in the boom and bust does not do full justice to several aspects of the increased availability of mortgage credit. New mortgage products became available to borrowers that were previously unable to obtain mortgage credit. The share of subprime mortgage originations (to borrowers with low FICO credit scores) went from less than 10 percent of originations in 2002 to 40 percent of originations by 2006, growing from $120 billion in originations in 2001 to $600 billion in 2006 (www.insidemort gagefinance.com). Likewise, the fraction of mortgages made to households with debt-to-income ratios above 40 percent rose from 33 percent to 50 percent over the same period (Haughwout et al. 2011). The Alt-A market, which grew from $60 billion in originations in 2002 to $400 billion in 2006, predominantly served households with low or no documentation (asset and income verification). The fraction of Alt-A loans with full documentation declined from 41 percent in 2002 to 19 percent in 2006. Complex mortgages, defined by Amromin et al. (2011) as mortgages with low initial payments, grew from about 2 percent of originations in 2002 to 30 percent of total originations in 2006. Complex mortgages are non-fully amortizing loans, including the interest-only mortgages studied by Barlevy and Fisher (2011), option ARMs (pick-a-payment mortgages), negative amortization loans, loans with teaser rates, and loans with balloon payments. Complex mortgages often went to households with higher than average incomes, living in higher than average expensive housing markets. In addition to making house purchases available to some households that would otherwise not have been able to own a home, complex mortgages may also have allowed other households to buy a larger house than what they otherwise would have been able to afford.

Finally, private label securitization played an important role in providing the funding for all these new mortgages. Keys et al. (chapter 4, this volume) show that the fraction of subprime loans that was securitized increased from about 50 percent in 2001 to 90 percent in 2007, before collapsing to 0 in 2008. The fraction of conforming loans that were securitized also increased from 70 percent to 90 percent during the boom, and has stabilized at that level.

Exogenous Changes in Credit Supply

Moreover, a growing body of empirical evidence directly links measures that identify changes in credit supply (as opposed to changes in demand) to movements in asset prices.

Adelino, Schoar, and Severino (2012) exploit exogenous variation in the government-controlled conforming loan limit (CLL) as an instrument for changing credit supply. The CLL determines the maximum size of a mortgage that can be purchased or securitized by Fannie Mae or Freddie Mac. Because these loans were widely understood to have the implicit (and since 2008, explicit) backing of the US government, borrowers in the market for loans that fall below the CLL have easier access to credit at less costly terms. Changes in the CLL are set annually and depend on the previous year's limit plus the change in the median national house price. These movements are clearly exogenous to individual mortgage transactions, local housing markcts, and the local economy. Using data on single-family house purchases in ten metropolitan statistical areas between 1998 and 2006, Adelino, Schoar, and Severino show that houses that became newly eligible for a conforming loan just after an increase in the CLL saw significant price increases relative to similar houses that were already below the limit before the CLL increase.

Rajan and Ramcharan (2011a) exploit interstate banking restrictions to study the effect of credit supply on land prices in the early twentieth century United States. Regulations at the time stipulated that banks could not lend across state borders. They argue that the number of banks in this era proxied for credit supply, with more banks indicating higher supply. They show that the number of banks in a county positively predicts land prices independently of fundamentals likely to move credit demand for land (commodity prices). They also find that the number of banks in neighboring in-state counties affects land prices more than the number of banks in equidistant counties out of state. Since banks were prohibited from lending across state borders, it is difficult to form a coherent story for this latter fact that does not involve credit supply.

In a similar spirit, Favara and Imbs (2011) identify movements of credit supply in more recent data (since 1994) by studying bank branching restrictions. Even though interstate banking (i.e., cross-state ownership of banks) was made legal after the passage of the Interstate Banking and Branching Efficiency Act of 1994, US states retained the right to erect barriers to interstate branching. They study branching deregulations since 1994 and show that they significantly affect the supply of mortgage credit. With deregulation, the number and volume of originated mortgage loans rise, while denial rates fall, echoing evidence in Mian and Sufi (2009). This deregulation has no effect on a placebo sample, formed of independent mortgage companies that should not be affected by the regulatory changes. Deregulation leads to greater supply of mortgage credit, which they find leads to significantly higher house prices.

Our main measure of credit availability is based on quarterly bank lending surveys for countries in the Euro Area and the United States. For the United States, we use the Senior Loan Officer Opinion Survey on Bank Lending Practices (SLOOS), collected by the Federal Reserve. An important aspect of this survey is that it asks banks to explicitly distinguish between changes in the *supply* of credit as distinct from the *demand* for credit, on bank loans to businesses and households over the past three months. Thus in principle, answers to the appropriate questions are able to identify a movement in supply separately from a movement in demand. We focus on questions related to *mortgage* credit supply to *households*. The detailed information is considered highly reliable because the surveys are carried out by central banks, which are also bank regulators with access to a large amount of information about a bank's operations, including those reflected in loan applications and balance sheet data.

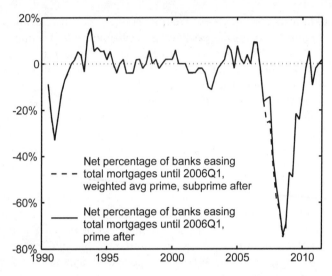

Fig. 6.11   Net percentage of US banks reporting easier credit standards

Source: US Survey of Senior Loan Officers, 1990:Q2 to 2011:Q2.

Notes: The figure reports the percentage of banks that reported easing of credit standards on mortgages, less the percentage that reported tightening of standards. A positive number indicates that more banks reported easing than tightening. A negative number indicates the opposite (more banks tightening than easing). Until 2006, surveys did not distinguish between prime and subprime mortgages. Beginning in 2007:Q1, the figure shows the net percentage easing for two series: prime mortgages only, and a weighted average of prime and subprime mortgages, where weights are computed based on the shares of prime and subprime in total mortgages, as described in the appendix.

Data for other countries are from bank lending surveys conducted by national central banks, and the European Central Bank (ECB). The survey questions are modeled after the US Survey of Senior Loan Officers. (See the appendix for data sources.) We use these data in the following empirical analysis.

For the US SLOOS survey, banks indicate easing, tightening, or no change in lending standards compared to the previous three months. We use the net percentage of banks that have eased their lending standards on mortgage loans as a measure of credit supply. This is the difference between the percentage of banks reporting easing and the percentage of banks reporting tightening, thus a positive figure indicates a net easing of lending standards, considering all bank respondents.

Figure 6.11 reports the net percentage of banks easing over time. We denote this variable CS_t. According to this measure, there was a significant easing of standards from 2002 to 2006, and a very sharp tightening afterwards. Notice that this measure does not weight banks by their relative importance in the mortgage market, nor does it weight the responses by the degree of tightening. Thus, it is not an indicator of the strength of credit easing or tightening, only of its breadth. Moreover, until 2007, the survey did not distinguish between prime and subprime mortgages. The figure shows clearly a broad tightening of credit standards beginning at the end of 2006. A cursory investigation of the figure suggests that the easing of standards in the boom was more modest. One must be careful in interpreting this series, however. There is a long string of observations starting in 1998 and continuing through 2006 that shows a net easing of credit standards. Recall that the survey asks banks about how their standards have changed *relative to the pervious three months*. Thus a series of observations indicating easier credit conditions relative to previous quarters by a few important banks in the mortgage space, once cumulated, could indicate a significant relaxation of underwriting standards.

We can relate *CS* to the growth in mortgages outstanding. Before doing so, figure 6.12 shows the *share* of mortgages outstanding by holder, over time. The line labeled "GSE portfolio and pools" are Agency and GSE-backed

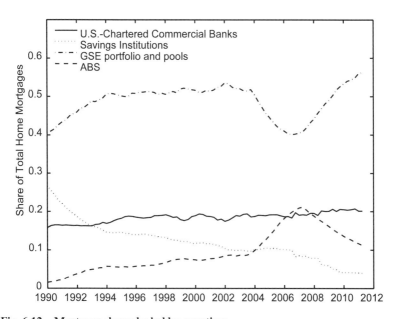

Fig. 6.12   Mortgage shares by holder over time

Source: Federal Reserve, flow of funds, table L.218. Sample 1990:Q1 to 2011:Q2.

Notes: "ABS" is home mortgages by issuers of asset-backed securities that are special purpose vehicles (SPVs), entities established by contractual arrangement to hold assets and to issue debt obligations backed by the assets. "US Chartered Commercial Banks" refers to mortgages held by US-chartered commercial banks. "Savings Institutions" refers to state-chartered savings banks, federal savings banks, cooperative banks, and savings and loan associations. "GSE portfolio and pools" refers to mortgages held as MBS assets in the portfolio of government-sponsored enterprises plus mortgages held in Agency- and GSE-backed mortgage pools not on GSE balance sheets prior to 2010:Q1.

mortgage pools, comprised only by conforming mortgage loans.[13] The line labeled "ABS" refers to issuers of asset-backed securities. Issuers of asset-backed securities are special purpose vehicles (SPVs) of the non-GSE banking system, entities established by contractual arrangement to hold assets and to issue debt obligations backed by the assets but moved off the balance sheet of the parent company. Note that the mortgages held in ABS were comprised entirely of *nonconforming* loans, since the conforming loans were all held in the GSE portfolio and pools. The figure shows a significant change in the composition of loans from 2002 to 2007: a sharp rise in the share of ABS, which mirrors a sharp fall in the share of GSE loans. This indicates a shift in the composition of mortgage lending, away from conforming debt and toward nonconforming debt, a trend that was subsequently reversed after 2007.

Table 6.1 shows that the short-term trends in *CS* are related to these very changes in the *composition* of lending over the boom-bust period. We investigate the relation between the four-quarter moving average value of the SLOOS net percentage indicator *CS* shown in figure 6.11, and year-over-year growth in mortgage credit outstanding, by holder. The table reports results from a regression of the latter on the former. The first column shows the relation over the full sample 1991:Q1 to 2010:Q4. This column shows that *CS* is positively related to growth in ABS and negatively related to growth in mortgages held in GSE pools. The last row shows the results from a regression of the *ratio* of ABS to GSE pools. Variable *CS* is positively related to growth in this ratio. Thus the percentage of banks reporting an easing of credit standards is associated with a shift in the composition of loans, toward nonconforming loans and away from conforming loans. The subsequent columns show that this result is unique to the boom-bust period 2000 to 2010. In both the boom (2000 to 2006) and bust (2007 to 2010), *CS* is positively related to the ratio ABS/GSE, but it is negatively related to this ratio in the years prior to this boom-bust cycle (1991:Q1 to 1999:Q4).

In the empirical work following, we will focus on the quarterly loan survey data on mortgage credit standards as a measure of credit supply. In thinking about these data, it is instructive to consider how they may relate to the notion of credit availability in FLVNa. In that model, an FML involves both a reduction in transactions costs associated with buying and selling the housing asset, and a change in collateralized borrowing constraints. Consider the borrowing constraint component, which takes the form:

$$(1) \qquad -B_{t+1}^i \leq (1 - \varpi) P_t H_{t+1}^i, \qquad \forall a, t$$

13. Prior to 2010:Q1, only a small fraction of GSE mortgage pools were held in portfolio at Fannie Mae and Freddie Mac; most were held off-balance sheet in special purpose vehicles (SPVs). Beginning in 2010:Q1, almost all Fannie Mae and Freddie Mac mortgage pools were consolidated on Fannie Mae's and Freddie Mac's balance sheets as a result of new accounting standards issued by the Financial Accounting Standards Board (FASB), statements 166 and 167, pertaining to Securitizations and Special Purpose Entities. We have consolidated the two into a single series, labeled "GSE portfolio and pools."

where B^i_{t+1} is the amount of bonds household i owns at the beginning of period $t+1$, P_t denotes the relative price of housing in units of the nonhousing consumption good (P_t is the time t price of a unit of housing of fixed quality and quantity), and H^i_{t+1} is the housing stock owned by household i at the beginning of period $t+1$. A negative value for B^i indicates a borrowing position. This equation represents the collateral constraint in the model, where $0 \le \varpi \le 1$. It says that households may borrow no more than a fraction $(1 - \varpi)$ of the value of housing, implying that they must post collateral equal to a fraction ϖ of the value of the house. This constraint can be thought of as a down-payment constraint for new home purchases, but it also encompasses collateral requirements for home equity borrowing against

Table 6.1   **Regression of mortgage growth by holder on credit standards**

Mortgage holder	1991:Q1–2010:Q4	2000:Q1–2006:Q1	2000:Q1–2010:Q4	1991:Q1–1999:Q4
All	0.024	0.000	0.033	–0.006
	(3.73)***	(0.00)	(4.86)***	(–1.41)
	[0.24]	[–0.04]	[0.40]	[0.00]
ABS	0.097	0.356	0.125	–0.259
	(3.91)***	(2.00)	(4.65)***	(–4.69)***
	[0.20]	[0.24]	[0.44]	[0.38]
Banks	0.019	–0.022	0.025	0.014
	(3.82)***	(–0.26)	(4.25)***	(0.92)
	[0.10]	[–0.03]	[0.17]	[0.01]
Savings	0.088	0.160	0.101	0.070
	(3.50)***	(1.95)	(3.72)***	(2.22)**
	[0.39]	[0.29]	[0.45]	[0.19]
GSE	–0.013	–0.146	–0.014	–0.036
	(–2.37)**	(–3.30)***	(–2.26)**	(–3.60)***
	[0.11]	[0.53]	[0.15]	[0.25]
ABS/GSE	0.110	0.50	0.140	–0.217
	(4.76)***	(2.41)**	(4.78)***	(–4.68)***
	[0.26]	[0.34]	[0.48]	[0.37]

Notes: Regressions of year-to-year growth (from $t - 4$ to t) of variable on column (1) on a four-quarter moving average of $CS = (CS_t + CS_{t-1} + CS_{t-2} + CS_{t-3})/4$ and a constant. Variable CS_t has been standardized; a positive value for this variable means that banks reported eased credit conditions relative to the previous quarter. The row labeled "All" refers to regressions of total home mortgages outstanding on the moving average of CS_t. "ABS" refers to home mortgages growth owned by issuers of asset-backed securities. "Banks" refers to growth in mortgages held by US-chartered commercial banks. "Savings" refers to growth in mortgages held by savings institutions. "GSE" refers to growth in mortgages held as MBS assets in the portfolio of government-sponsored enterprises plus mortgages held in Agency- and GSE-backed mortgage pools not in GSE balance sheets prior to 2010:Q1. "ABS/GSE" refers to the growth in the ratio of ABS to GSE. Data are from Federal Reserve, flow of funds table L.218.

***Significant at the 1 percent level.
**Significant at the 5 percent level.

existing homes. The constraint gives the maximum combined LTV ratio for first and second mortgages and home equity withdrawal.

The paper by FLVNa asks how a plausibly calibrated change in its value (along with a calibrated change in housing transactions costs) changes the equilibrium outcome. Thus, one way credit supply can change is via a change in the fraction $(1 - \varpi)$ of the home's value that must be held as collateral. But, as just discussed, borrowing capacity will fluctuate endogenously with the collateral value $P_t\, H^i_{t+1}$ even if that fraction remains unchanged. This represents an endogenous change in borrowing capacity, driven by economic shocks and accompanied by revisions in expectations about future economic conditions. These factors get immediately reflected in house prices, which affects borrowing capacity and the tightness of the constraints. We argue that *either* of these represent a change in credit supply in the sense that they are related to a borrower's access to funds via his or her credit constraint. Moreover, the two could be correlated (expectations of a decline in economic activity could lead to an increase in ϖ), as they are in the transition dynamics studied by FLVNa and displayed in figure 6.2.[14]

6.4   International Evidence on House Price Fluctuations

We have seen in the abovementioned that the United States experienced large capital inflows and commensurate current account deficits at the same time that it experienced strong growth in house prices. The same is true for countries such as Iceland, Ireland, and Spain. In fact, during the boom, there is a positive cross-country correlation of current account deficits with house price growth on the one hand (Ferrero 2011; Laibson and Moller-strom 2010; Gete 2010) and with value added and the labor share of the construction industry on the other hand (Gete 2010). Using data that ends before the bust, Aizenman and Jinjarak (2009) provide a precise estimate of the relationship between house prices and external imbalances: a 1 standard deviation increase in lagged current account deficits is associated with a 10 percent appreciation of real estate prices.

Panel A of table 6.2 replicates the flavor of these results for the boom period and extends the sample to a larger set of countries. It reports real house price growth (deflated by the Consumer Price Index [CPI]), cumulative current account deficits, and cumulative residential investment over the period 2000:Q1 to 2006:Q4, with the last two variables measured relative to GDP in 2006:Q4. Countries such as Germany, Switzerland, China, and

14. The transition dynamics are an exploration of movements between stochastic states with different values for ϖ (as well as the housing transactions costs). An important aspect of the transition is that the exogenous changes in borrowing capacity are correlated with endogenous changes in borrowing capacity, because the exogenous and unexpected decline in ϖ is calibrated to coincide with an economic boom, which bolsters collateral values and endogenously relaxes borrowing constraints.

Table 6.2   **Cross-country house price statistics**

	Panel A 2000:Q1–2006:Q4			Panel B 2006:Q4–2010:Q4		
	Real HP gr. (% change)	CA def. (cum.)/ GDP2006 (%)	Res. inv. (cum.)/ GDP2006 (%)	Real HP gr. (% change)	CA def. (cum.)/ GDP2006 (%)	Res. inv. (cum.)/ GDP2006 (%)
Australia	55	24	35	17	23	27
Austria	1	–8	29	20	–17	19
Belgium	18	–17	32	10	–1	26
Canada	46	–10	35	10	6	30
China	–1	–22	38	–6	–50	63
Czech Republic	20	19	18	4	14	16
Denmark	64	–16	32	–20	–15	22
Estonia	387	47	19	–47	26	21
Euro Area	32	0.04		–3	2.4	
Finland	37	–35	39	8	–15	28
France	85	–3	36	1	7	22
Germany	–16	–17	38	–3	–29	23
Greece	50	39	42	–22	62	23
Hungary	40	39	25	–27	15	14
Iceland	64	57	28	–28	62	21
Ireland	60	8	57	–40	15	26
Israel	–16	–6	27	34	–14	22
Italy	35	7	29	–2	12	21
Korea	25	–12	29	–4	–9	20
Luxembourg	71	–51	13	–3	–38	14
Netherlands	28	–31	37	–7	–27	26
New Zealand	73	30	35	–10	29	23
Norway	46	–73	21	9	–68	16
Poland	–2	18	16	33	29	11
Portugal	–6	51	42	2	51	18
Russia	157	–39	8	10	–30	12
Slovenia	46	8	11	1	18	10
Spain	87	28	45	–16	35	30
Sweden	61	–35	17	15	–36	15
Switzerland	12	–75	28	13	–40	15
United Kingdom	78	13	21	–6	9	14
United States	64	30	32	–36	17	13
Corr. CA def.	0.23	1.00	0.22	–0.38	1.00	–0.14
Corr. HP gr.	1.00	0.23	–0.25	1.00	–0.38	–0.09

Notes: House prices are deflated by CPI. The data are from different national sources (see appendix), mostly quarterly, except for Germany (annual), Luxembourg (annual, and until 2009), Italy (semiannual), and Japan (semiannual). The CPI is collected by EIU from national sources. For Slovenia, series begins in 2003:Q1; for Russia in 2001:Q1. The CA deficit data are from IMF, and SAFE for China. The CA balances are accumulated and deflated by 2006 GDP (collected by EIU), all in current US dollars. For Belgium, CA data 2000:Q1 to 2001:Q4 are from NBB, via OECD. Residential investment is from Eurostat and national sources. Residential investment is accumulated and deflated by 2006 GDP, all in current national currency. For France, Hungary, Poland, Switzerland, and Russia, residential investment data are available only through 2009.

Austria accumulated large current account surpluses and exhibited slow house price growth and modest residential investment, while countries such as the United States, Spain, the United Kingdom, Portugal, Greece, Estonia, New Zealand, and Australia attracted lots of external capital, exhibited large rises in house prices, and experienced significant residential investment booms. In the boom period, there is a positive cross-country correlation between average house price changes and average current account deficits equal to 23 percent. There is also a negative cross-country correlation between residential investment and house price growth: countries with more residential investment experienced lower house price growth, consistent with the idea that residential investment drives up the expected housing stock and drives down the expected future growth rate on the dividend to housing (rent).

It is tempting to conclude that the excess savings of the first group of countries found its way to the real estate industry in the second group of countries and fueled the housing boom there. However, as argued earlier, general equilibrium considerations suggest that large inflows into safe assets need not lead to large house price booms because the effect of lower interest rates is offset by a rise in risk premia and an expected increase in the housing stock from higher residential investment. This may help explain why the current account patterns from the boom period persisted in many countries during the housing bust, while house prices and residential investment patterns obviously did not. Panel B of table 6.2 shows that the cross-country correlation between house price changes and current account dynamics reverses in the bust sample from 2006:Q4 to 2010:Q4. The cross-country correlation between the current account deficit and house price growth is now −38 percent. By itself, this negative correlation is certainly not consistent with the notion that capital inflows cause higher house price growth. Nor is it consistent with the hypothesis that capital inflows lead to a relaxation of credit standards, which in turn causes higher house price growth. To further explore these issues, we now turn to a statistical analysis of the relation between house price changes (or changes in price-rent ratios), measures of capital flows, credit standards, and interest rates.

6.4.1   Regression Analysis

In this section we undertake a basic empirical analysis of correlations among house prices and other variables.

A few words about the data are in order. First, with regard to an international panel of data, we are limited to far fewer time-series observations given the availability of bank lending survey data for non-US countries. These data extend only from 2002:Q4 to 2010:Q4. For this reason we also look separately at regressions for the United States alone, where data reaches back much further, starting in 1990:Q4.

Second, as explained in the appendix, the data on bank lending standards differs somewhat by country. When we analyze the United States alone, we use the *net percentage easing* indicator plotted earlier as a measure of credit standards. For the other countries, the surveys are generally modeled after the US SLOOS survey, but the way the survey results are aggregated can differ. For nine of the eleven countries for which there exist data on credit standards (Austria, Belgium, Euro Area, France, Korea, Portugal, Spain, United States, Ireland) we have available, or can construct, a *diffusion index* of credit standards or a *scale transformation* thereof (some countries report a *mean value* indicator—see the appendix—which is a scale transformation of the diffusion index) with the information reported by the central banks. This diffusion index, however, is not a scale transformation of the *net percentage* indicator discussed earlier, and there are two countries (Canada and the Netherlands) that report only the net percentage indicator. For the panel regressions that we report on here, we simply use all these data together in one regression, even though the credit standards measure for two countries (Canada and the Netherlands) are not a scale transformation of the other countries' measures. Results, available on request, show that the findings are virtually unchanged if we exclude these two countries. Finally, we standardize these bank lending survey measures, country by country, by subtracting the mean and dividing by the standard deviation, for the period 2002:Q4 to 2010:Q4. This ensures that (at least for the nine countries for which we have a diffusion index or mean value indicator) the credit supply measure for each country is in the same units. The appendix provides more details on the credit supply data by country.

Third, we use a measure of the change in net foreign holdings of US securities as our main measure of international capital flows into the United States. (Although for completeness, we also report results using the CA [current account] deficit.) Annual net foreign holdings estimates are compiled by the BEA in their international investment data, year-end positions, thereby providing annual observations. All the rest of our data are quarterly, however. Instead of limiting ourselves to annual observations, we form an estimate of the *quarter*-end net foreign liability position of the United States in total securities, by employing a methodology to interpolate between the year-end positions, taking into account the quarterly *transactions* data in these same securities. The procedure ensures that our estimate of the holdings at the end of the fourth quarter of a given year is equal to the recorded value from the annual holdings data. The details of this procedure are described in the appendix. We simply note here that it provides a quarterly measure of the change in net foreign holdings of US assets. We use this measure in the regressions that follow.

We now present results from a regression analysis using these and other data. We emphasize that, in presenting these next results, we do not make claims about causality. Later we will provide some additional discussion and evidence on the question of causality.

Table 6.3 Quarterly panel regressions (2002:Q4–2010:Q4), eleven countries

		Real House price growth on			
Regression	Cons.	CAdef/GDP	CS	(CAdef/GDP)$x CS$	R^2
1	0.005	–0.055			0.01
	(1.52)	(–0.73)			
2	0.004		0.005		0.06
	(1.69)		(3.24)***		
3	0.005	–0.018	0.005		0.07
	(1.62)	(–0.29)	(3.26)***		
4	0.005	–0.009		0.083	0.05
	(1.58)	(–0.14)		(5.34)***	
5	0.005		0.004	0.060	0.09
	(1.96)		(3.20)***	(6.61)***	

Notes: Panel data estimation with fixed effects. CAdef/GDP is current account deficit divided by the country's GDP. Variable CS is net percentage of banks reporting easing of credit; a positive value indicates more banks eased than tightened credit conditions with respect to previous quarter. The column labeled "Cons" gives the coefficient on the regression constant. Credit conditions have been standardized country by country. Driscoll–Kraay corrected t-statistics in parentheses (lags = 3). Eleven countries included are Austria, Belgium, Canada, Euro Area, France, Ireland, Korea, Netherlands, Portugal, Spain, and the United States. There are 363 observations in total.
***Significant at the 1 percent level.

We begin with evidence from the panel of eleven countries mentioned earlier. For these countries, we have quarterly observations from 2002:Q4 to 2010:Q4 on real house price growth, the current account deficit, and credit standards. The variable CS in these regressions is a diffusion index measure that, when increased, indicates an *easing* of credit standards. A detailed description of all of these data, including data sources, is given in the appendix. Table 6.3 reports the results of a panel fixed-effects regression of real house price growth on the current account, CS, and interactions of these variables. The variable CAdef/GDP is the current account *deficit,* divided by the country's GDP.

Table 6.3 shows that CAdef/GDP bears a *negative* relation to contemporaneous real house price growth (though it is not statistically significant), suggesting that, if anything, capital inflows are associated with a decline in house prices, rather than a boom.[15] By contrast, the credit standards measure CS is statistically significant and positive, implying that an increase in CS (an easing of credit standards) leads to an increase in real house price growth (row 2). Row 3 shows that CS remains the only significant determinant of house price growth when both variables are included, while rows

15. We use the Driscoll and Kraay (1998) consistent covariance-matrix estimates to produce heteroskedasticity consistent standard errors that are robust to general forms of autocorrelation and cross-sectional (spatial) correlation between the residuals.

4 and 5 document some interaction effects: countries and time periods in which there was an increase in credit supply experienced a larger increase in house price growth if they also ran current account deficits. But, controlling for this, CAdef/GDP has a statistically insignificant marginal effect on house price growth (row 4), while CS by itself has a strongly significant marginal effect (row 5). The R^2 statistics range from 6 to 9 percent whenever CS_t is included in the regression, either by itself or interactively with CAdef/GDP. These results provide little support for the hypothesis that capital inflows played an important role in driving the changes in house prices internationally over the recent boom-bust period.

To interpret the magnitudes of the coefficients on CS, recall that this variable is standardized, so a one-unit increase in this measure implies a 1 standard deviation increase around its mean. The coefficient is 0.005, which implies that a 1-standard deviation increase in CS leads to a 50 basis point rise in quarterly real house price growth, roughly a 2 percent rise at an annual rate. This increase represents about one-quarter of a 1 standard deviation change in quarterly US real house price growth (2.0 percent).

To investigate a longer time frame, we now turn to an analysis of US time series data. Table 6.4 presents results from regressions using the same variables as in table 6.3, but this time only for the United States. The US data are quarterly and span the period 1990:Q2 to 2010:Q4. Row 1 shows that CAdef/GDP has no effect, by itself, on real house price growth. This variable explains 2 percent of the quarterly variation in real US house price growth. By contrast, CS is strongly statistically significant, and by itself explains

Table 6.4   **Quarterly regressions for United States (1990:Q2–2010:Q4)**

Regression	Cons.	Real house price growth on CAdef/GDP	CS	Adj. R^2
1	−0.006	0.207		0.02
	(−1.35)	(0.92)		
2	0.001		0.016	0.53
	(0.27)		(9.94)***	
3	−0.011	0.365	0.017	0.62
	(−2.68)***	(2.54)**	(10.32)***	

Notes: See table 6.3. The column labeled "Cons." reports coefficients on the constant in the regression. CAdef is current account deficit, GDP is gross domestic product, both from the US Department of Commerce, BEA. Variable CS is a measure of credit standards from the SLOOS survey that gives the net percentage of banks that reported easier credit conditions. A positive value for this variable therefore indicates an easing of credit conditions, while a negative value indicates a tightening. We standardize the credit standards variable by dividing by the standard deviation and subtracting its mean based on data for the full sample. Newey and West (1987) corrected *t*-statistics in parentheses.

***Significant at the 1 percent level.

**Significant at the 5 percent level.

53 percent of the quarterly variation in house price growth. When we include both CAdef/GDP and CS in the regression, the current account now has a statistically significant and positive effect, and this adds to the regression model's ability to explain the data: the adjusted R^2 rises by 9 percentage points to 62 percent. But this happens because, over this sample, the CS and CAdef/GDP are again *negatively* correlated rather than positively correlated (capital inflows are associated with a tightening of credit rather than an easing). Since credit supply is so strongly positively related to house price growth, removing its effects by including it in the regression along with CAdef/GDP allows the regression to distinguish a modest positive role for the current account.

To interpret the magnitude of the coefficients on CS reported in table 6.4, recall that we standardize this variable so a one-unit increase is equal to a 1 standard deviation increase. The coefficient estimate in row 2 implies that a 1 standard deviation increase in CS leads to a 0.016 unit (160 basis point) rise in quarterly US house price growth, roughly a 6.6 percent increase at an annual rate. This increase represents about three-quarters of a 1 standard deviation change in quarterly US real house price growth (2.15 percent).

For comparison, table 6.5 shows output from the same regressions but restricted to the subsample that only includes the recent boom-bust period: 2000:Q1 to 2010:Q4. The results with respect to the relation between CAdef/GDP and house price growth are little changed: in this subsample the variable explains none of the variation in the growth of residential real estate prices in a univariate regression. But credit standards explains a much larger fraction of the variation in house price growth in this sample: CS now explains 66 percent of the quarterly variation in house price growth (row 2). The coefficient is also larger, equal to 0.019 in row 2. A 1 standard deviation increase in CS in this subsample leads to a 190 basis point rise in quarterly real house price growth, roughly a 7.6 percent increase at an annual rate. This quantitatively large effect represents 88 percent of a 1 standard deviation change in quarterly US real house price growth. Moreover, unlike the results for the full sample, even when included in the regression along

Table 6.5   Quarterly regressions for United States (2000:Q1–2010:Q4)

| Regression | Real house price growth on | | | |
	Cons.	CAdef/GDP	CS	Adj. R^2
1	–0.018	0.435		0.01
	(–0.96)	(1.02)		
2	0.007		0.019	0.66
	(1.76)		(11.43)***	
3	–0.003	0.214	0.019	0.66
	(–0.17)	(0.57)	(11.90)***	

Note: See table 6.4.
***Significant at the 1 percent level.

Table 6.6   **Quarterly regressions for United States (1990:Q2–2010:Q4)**

Regression	Cons.	ΔNFL$_t$	CS	Adj. R^2
	Real house price growth on			
1	0.003	–0.142		0.06
	(0.76)	(–1.46)		
2	0.001		0.016	0.53
	(0.27)		(9.94)***	
3	0.000	0.036	0.016	0.53
	(0.06)	(0.89)	(8.75)***	

Notes: See table 6.4. Variable ΔNFL$_t$ is change in total net foreign US liabilities in total securities (where quarter-end positions have been estimated as described in the chapter), divided by trend GDP. The trend is measured using a Hodrick and Prescott (1997) filter.
***Significant at the 1 percent level.

with CS, CAdef/GDP is statistically unrelated to house price growth in all of the regression specifications over this subperiod. To summarize, to the modest extent that the current account bears any relation to US house price growth, it does so only in samples *prior to* the recent housing boom-bust. There is no relation between these variables in the recent boom-bust cycle.

Returning to the full sample, table 6.6 shows the same regressions when we replace CAdef/GDP with our quarterly measure of the change in the net foreign holdings of total securities (the change in the US net foreign liability position in securities), divided by trend GDP. We denote this variable ΔNFL_t. The results indicate that this variable has no effect on US house price growth, whether it is included in the regression by itself or jointly with CS_t. The modest effect we found from current account deficits on house price growth in the long US sample disappears once we replace the current account deficit by a better measure of capital inflows.

So far we have investigated only contemporaneous correlations between house prices, capital flows, and credit standards. Table 6.7 shows results from *forecasting* regressions of real house price growth, $\Delta\ln(P)$ in period $t + H$, on variables known at time t. (Analogous results for the price-rent ratio rather than price growth are nearly identical and are available upon request.) We report results from long-horizon forecasts of house price growth on CS_t by itself (row 1); on CS_t, ΔNFL_t, and the real ten-year T-bond rate, r_t^{10} (row 2); and on CS_t, ΔNFL_t, r_t^{10}, and the growth in real GDP, ΔGDP_t (row 3). The first column of results reports results from the $H = 0$ ahead forecasts (contemporaneous correlations), and the following four columns report results from the one-, two-, three-, and four-quarter ahead forecasts of these house price measures.

Table 6.7 shows that credit standards are strongly statistically significantly related to the change in the log of real house prices at all future horizons. Indeed, this variable explains 47 percent of the one-, two-, and three-quarter ahead variation, and 41 percent of the four-quarter ahead variation. By

Table 6.7   Regressions of $\Delta \ln(P_{t+H})$ on CS, covariates (1991:Q4–2010:Q4)

			US data			
			Forecast horizon H			
Row	Regressors	Contemp.	1	2	3	4
1	CS_t	0.015	0.015	0.028	0.041	0.050
		(9.63)***	(7.00)***	(5.46)***	(4.76)***	(4.09)***
		[0.52]	[0.47]	[0.47]	[0.47]	[0.41]
2	CS_t	0.018	0.016	0.032	0.054	0.071
		(6.29)***	(4.11)***	(3.87)***	(4.71)***	(4.57)***
	ΔNFL_t	0.036	–0.026	0.018	0.218	0.435
		(0.79)	(–0.40)	(0.12)	(1.04)	(1.62)
	r^{10}_t	–0.004	–0.003	–0.009	–0.019	–0.027
		(–1.10)	(–0.72)	(–1.24)	(–2.33)**	(–2.31)**
		[0.53]	[0.48]	[0.49]	[0.53]	[0.50]
3	CS_t	0.017	0.016	0.033	0.054	0.070
		(6.19)***	(4.30)***	(4.25)***	(5.00)***	(4.67)***
	ΔNFL_t	0.058	–0.024	0.012	0.216	0.456
		(1.10)	(–0.36)	(0.07)	(0.87)	(1.37)
	r^{10}_t	–0.005	–0.003	–0.008	–0.019	–0.028
		(–1.23)	(–0.63)	(–0.99)	(–2.00)**	(–2.20)**
	ΔGDP_t	0.568	0.036	–0.153	–0.032	0.449
		(1.60)	(0.09)	(–0.19)	(–0.03)	(0.27)
		[0.54]	[0.47]	[0.48]	[0.53]	[0.49]

Notes: Variable P is Core Logic National House Price Index. The column labeled "Contemp." reports coefficients from a regression of contemporaneous house price growth on variables; that is, $ln(P_t)$ – $ln(P_{t-1})$ on CS_t. For all other columns, results are reported for forecasting regressions; for example $\Delta ln(P_{t+H}) = ln(P_{t+H}) - ln(P_t)$ on CS_t. Variable CS is net percentage of banks reporting easing of credit; a positive value indicates more banks eased than tightened credit conditions with respect to previous quarter. Credit conditions have been standardized. Variable ΔNFL is change in total net foreign holdings of securities, adjusted as described in the chapter, divided by trend GDP. Variable r^{10} is real ten-year bond yield: ten-year constant maturity rate in last month of quarter minus ten-year ahead inflation forecast median response, from Survey of Professional Forecasters. Variable ΔGDP is real GDP growth. Newey-West corrected t-statistics appear in parentheses. Adjusted R^2 in brackets.
***Significant at the 1 percent level.
**Significant at the 5 percent level.

contrast, the other explanatory variables add very little to the explanatory power of the house price forecasting regression. Moreover, the change in US net foreign liabilities, ΔNFL_t, has a *negative* effect on house price growth, one quarter ahead. The real interest rate does have a statistically significant negative effect on house price growth in the three- and four-quarter ahead regressions. The coefficient on the net foreign liabilities indicator ΔNFL_t is statistically insignificant at every forecast horizon.

The evidence just presented indicates that house price growth is correlated with lags of CS_t. Case and Shiller (1989) have pointed out that house price growth is correlated with its own lags. Since CS_t is strongly contemporaneously correlated with house price growth, and since house price growth is

Table 6.8   **Quarterly long-horizon regressions**

		Panel A			
		$\ln(P_{t+H}) - \ln(P_t)$ on Forecast horizon H			
Row	Regressors	1	2	3	4
1	$\Delta \log(HP_t)$	0.86 (9.29)*** [0.70]	1.58 (6.41)*** [0.65]	2.35 (5.85)*** [0.69]	2.95 (4.98)*** [0.63]

		Panel B			
		$\ln(P_{t+H}) - \ln(P_t)$ on Forecast horizon H			
1	e_{CS}	0.76 (5.01)*** [0.23]	1.33 (4.08)*** [0.19]	2.07 (4.59)*** [0.22]	2.71 (4.42)*** [0.22]

Notes: See table 6.7. Results for US data 1991:Q4 to 2010:Q4. Variable lnP_{t+H} is log of real house price index, measured by the Core Logic index and deflated by the CPI; e_{CS} is the residual from a regression of $\Delta\log(HP_t)$ on CS_t; CS is credit supply. Positive credit supply means banks eased credit conditions with respect to previous quarter.
***Significant at the 1 percent level.

correlated with its own lags, it stands to reason that there may be significant information overlap in lagged values of CS_t and in lagged house prices for future house prices. Indeed this is what we find, as table 6.8 shows, suggesting that part of the reason house price growth is correlated with its own lags is that house price growth is correlated with lags of credit standards, and credit standards matter for house prices. Panel A of table 6.8 shows that the one-quarter lagged value of house price growth explains 70 percent of house price growth next period. But panel B of table 6.8 shows that a residual from a regression of house price growth on contemporaneous credit standards CS_t only explains 23 percent of next period's house price growth. For the four-quarter horizon, the residual only explains 22 percent while the raw series explains 63 percent. This evidence suggests that the effects of credit standards on house prices explain most (but not all) of the serial correlation in quarterly house price growth.

To summarize, the evidence just discussed suggests that bank loan officers' accounts of their willingness to supply more mortgage credit are strongly statistically related to house price movements, both contemporaneously and in the future, and both in the United States and in international data. By contrast, data on capital flows, real interest rates, and GDP growth at best add modestly to explanatory power of these statistical models, and most of the time they are found to add nothing. We now turn to a discussion of whether these movements in credit supply are exogenous to other factors.

6.4.2   Are Movements in Credit Supply Exogenous?

While the previous evidence strongly suggests that bank credit standards and credit availability matter for home values, with increases in credit supply associated with higher home prices, there is nothing in the evidence to suggest that such movements in credit standards are exogenous to the state of the economy or to expectations about future economic conditions, including the direction of future home prices. Nor is there any theoretical reason to expect them to be. As in classic financial accelerator models, endogenous shifts in collateralized borrowing capacity imply that economic shocks have a much larger effect on asset prices than they would in frictionless environments without collateralized financing restrictions. Bank loan surveys on credit standards could in principle elicit information on either or both forms of a borrower's access to funds, and we have no way of knowing from the survey questions how much of any given change in standards is represented by one or the other. In our view, *either* of these represents a movement in credit availability, and both could be important for home prices.

Still, don't endogenous movements in credit supply raise a question of causality? If credit standards move in response to changing economic conditions, which in turn alter expectations of future home price movements, then how do we rule out the possibility that (current and future) home prices affect credit availability rather than the other way around? The answer, we argue, is that we do not rule this out nor should we seek to, since the direction of causality is not central for the question of whether credit availability plays a role in driving asset price fluctuations. A natural benchmark is a complete markets environment, where borrowing constraints and transactions costs play no role in the equilibrium allocations. Indeed, it is hard to understand why credit standards would be correlated at all with asset values in such an environment. With incomplete markets, credit availability can have a large dynamic impact on asset prices even if fluctuations in that availability are completely endogenous. From this perspective, as long as we have a clean measure of credit supply, as distinct from credit demand, any correlation of credit supply with asset prices is evidence that credit supply matters for asset prices.

These considerations lead to two questions. The SLOOS survey explicitly asks banks to distinguish movements in credit supply from movements in credit demand, but there may be some residual correlation between the two. First, are movements in credit supply still associated with home price movements once we eliminate the correlation between credit supply and credit demand? Second, does the credit supply measure that we study have an exogenous component that still affects house prices once we control for expectations about future economic conditions and once we take out possible linkages between international capital flows and credit supply?

Table 6.9 presents evidence pertaining to these questions. To do so, we first

Table 6.9   Regressions of $\Delta \ln(P_{t+H})$ on CS, covariates (1991:Q4–2010:Q4)

			US Data			
			Forecast horizon H			
Row	Regressors	Contemp.	1	2	3	4
	CS_t	0.015	0.015	0.028	0.041	0.050
		(9.63)***	(7.00)***	(5.46)***	(4.76)***	(4.09)***
		[0.52]	[0.47]	[0.47]	[0.47]	[0.41]
	$\varepsilon_{CD,t}$	0.015	0.015	0.027	0.038	0.047
		(7.20)***	(5.50)***	(4.39)***	(3.94)***	(3.54)***
		[0.48]	[0.43]	[0.41]	[0.40]	[0.35]
	$\varepsilon_{CD,t}$	0.018	0.015	0.031	0.052	0.068
		(5.28)***	(3.50)***	(3.22)***	(3.67)***	(3.58)***
	ΔNFL_t	0.023	−0.038	−0.012	0.164	0.368
		(0.51)	(−0.55)	(−0.08)	(0.71)	(1.23)
	r^{10}_t	−0.004	−0.003	−0.009	−0.020	−0.028
		(−1.13)	(−0.76)	(−1.22)	(−2.10)**	(−2.08)**
		[0.50]	[0.44]	[0.43]	[0.46]	[0.43]
	$\varepsilon_{CD,t}$	0.013	0.012	0.028	0.051	0.070
		(2.95)***	(2.11)**	(2.30)**	(3.01)***	(3.10)***
	ΔNFL_t	0.017	−0.044	−0.019	0.162	0.372
		(0.38)	(−0.61)	(−0.12)	(0.70)	(1.24)
	r^{10}_t	−0.002	−0.002	−0.007	−0.019	−0.028
		(−0.51)	(−0.36)	(−0.95)	(−1.99)	(−2.11)**
	$\Delta GDP_{t\to t+4}$	0.011	0.008	0.008	0.002	−0.003
		(2.32)**	(1.33)	(0.69)	(0.15)	(−0.15)
		[0.55]	[0.46]	[0.43]	[0.45]	[0.42]
	$\varepsilon_{NFL,t}$	0.014	0.014	0.029	0.046	0.060
		(6.04)***	(6.22)***	(6.11)***	(7.85)***	(8.15)***
		[0.39]	[0.41]	[0.48]	[0.58]	[0.57]
	$\varepsilon_{GFL,t}$	0.015	0.014	0.026	0.038	0.048
		(4.98)***	(3.90)***	(3.25)***	(3.05)***	(2.89)***
		[0.47]	[0.41]	[0.39]	[0.39]	[0.36]

Notes: See table 6.7. Variable lnP_{t+H} is log of real house price index, measured by the Core Logic index and deflated by the CPI; $e_{CD,t}$ is the residual from regressing CS (net percentage of banks' reporting easing of mortgage credit) on a constant and the variable CD (net percentage of banks reporting higher demand for mortgage credit). Variable $e_{NFL,t}$ is the residual from regressing CS on a constant, the variable ΔNFL, and 3 lags of ΔNFL; $e_{GFL,t}$ is the residual from regressing CS on a constant, the variable ΔGFL, and 3 lags of ΔGFL. The residuals have been standardized. Variable ΔNFL is change in total net foreign holdings of securities, adjusted as described in the chapter, divided by trend GDP. Variable ΔGFL is change in total gross foreign holdings of securities, adjusted in the same manner as NFL, divided by trend GDP; r^{10} is real ten-year bond yield: ten-year constant maturity rate in last month of quarter minus ten-year ahead inflation forecast, median response, from Survey of Professional Forecasters. Variable $\Delta GDP_{t\to t+4}$ is median forecasted real GDP growth between periods t and $t+4$, from the Survey of Professional Forecasters. Row 1 is repeated from table 6.7 for ease of comparison. Newey–West corrected t-statistic in parentheses (lags = 4). Adjusted R^2 in brackets. Seventy-seven quarterly observations.

***Significant at the 1 percent level.

**Significant at the 5 percent level.

regress the raw credit supply series CS_t on the SLOOS survey's measure of credit demand (the net percentage of banks reporting higher credit demand), and take the *residual* of this regression $\varepsilon_{CD,t}$, as a measure of credit supply. (After obtaining this residual we standardize it so as to give it the same units the raw measure used previously had.) We also replace current GDP growth from the previous regressions with the *expected* GDP growth rate for the year ahead, $\Delta GDP_{t \to t+4}$, as measured by the Survey of Professional Forecasters (SPF) median forecast. In these regressions, we continue to use our measure of capital inflows, ΔNFL_t, and the real ten-year T-bond rate, r_t^{10}, as additional explanatory variables. Notice that r_t^{10} is itself a forward-looking variable since it equals the nominal ten-year T-bond rate minus the *expected* ten-year inflation rate (also from the SPF, median forecast). Thus, once we include these forecasts of future economic activity and r_t^{10} as additional predictor variables, any remaining role for our residual credit supply measure $\varepsilon_{CD,t}$ in explaining house price movements must be independent of expectations of future real activity or inflation.

Table 6.9 shows that the residual credit supply measure $\varepsilon_{CD,t}$ by itself explains about the same amount of variation in house price growth as does the raw series CS_t (given in row 1), and this is true no matter what other variables we include as additional regressors. The table also shows that expected future GDP growth $\Delta GDP_{t \to t+4}$ has significant explanatory power for house price growth contemporaneously but does not help predict *future* house price growth, consistent with the notion that such expectations are reflected immediately in asset prices and collateral values. Even so, the residual supply measure $\varepsilon_{CD,t}$ maintains its marginal explanatory power for contemporaneous movements in $\Delta \ln(P)$. When it comes to forecasting *future* house price changes, only the residual credit supply measure $\varepsilon_{CD,t}$ displays any clear predictive power: expectations of future GDP growth, real interest rates, and the change in US net foreign liabilities all have a statistically negligible effect of $\Delta \ln(P_t)$. The change in US net foreign liabilities, ΔNFL_t, again has a negative (but statistically insignificant) effect on house price growth, one and two quarters ahead. The forecasting regressions for horizons ranging from one to four quarters ahead using all four predictor variables explain about the same amount of variation in future house price growth as does the residual credit supply measure alone, indicating that none of them are strongly related to future house price growth once we control for credit supply.

A related question on the exogeneity of credit supply movements concerns the relationship between international capital flows and credit supply. Could international capital flows have been a causal factor contributing to the changing supply of credit, thereby indirectly contributing to the housing boom and bust through their influence on credit supply? The remaining rows of table 6.9 provide evidence on this question. To address this question, we again construct residual credit supply measures by regressing the raw credit supply CS_t series on the contemporaneous values and three quarterly lags of two different measures of international capital flows: ΔNFL_t, and an analogous measure of the change in *gross* flows, ΔGFL_t, constructed in the same way as ΔNFL_t except that we do not net out US holdings of foreign assets from the foreign holdings data. We then take the residuals from these regressions, denoted $\varepsilon_{NFL,t}$ and $\varepsilon_{GFL,t}$ respectively, as measures of changes in credit supply that are unrelated to current and past changes in international capital flows.

Rows 5 and 6 present the results from regressions of house price growth on $\varepsilon_{NFL,t}$ and $\varepsilon_{GFL,t}$. Comparing row 1 with rows 5 and 6, we see that these residual credit supply measures explain almost the same amount of variation in house price growth as does the raw series CS_t, indicating that the bulk of the credit supply variation that is related to house price movements is in fact orthogonal to movements in capital flows. Moreover, the first-stage regression results (not reported) indicate that current and lagged credit flows have a *negative* effect on credit supply CS_t, contradicting the hypothesis that credit flows into the United States contributed to an easing of credit supply during the housing boom, and vice versa during the housing bust. In short, there is no evidence from these data to support the hypothesis that international capital flows were causally related to the changes in credit supply that were responsible for the housing boom and bust.

To summarize, when we control for expectations about future economic conditions and when we purge the credit standards measure of any residual demand or capital flow effects, we still find that credit supply has an economically large effect on house price movements. Indeed, these exogenous movements in credit supply appear to be the main driver of the credit supply-house price link we find. We close this section by noting that the model in FLVNa produces qualitatively similar results when performing such regressions on simulated data. To conserve space, these results are not reported but are available upon request.

6.5 Conclusion

In this chapter we have studied the empirical relationship between house price changes and international capital flows, focusing in particular on the extraordinary boom-bust period in the housing market from 2000 to 2010. We have argued that foreign capital flows into safe US securities—US Treasury and Agency bonds—played an important role in understanding the low interest rates in the last decade and quantitatively account for all of the upward trend in the US net foreign liability position over this period. Many countries that saw large housing booms and busts attracted foreign capital, as witnessed by their large current account deficits. Much of this capital seems to have found its way into residential investment and mortgage credit extension.

Despite these stylized facts, we have argued here that the same capital inflows that lowered interest rates and supported the mortgage boom over this period had only a small impact on house prices. Although the housing boom was characterized by sharp increases in the rate at which capital flowed into the United States, the bust and its aftermath occurred with no clear reversal in the trend toward healthy capital inflows into US assets considered to be safe stores-of-value and integral to housing finance. While US borrowing from abroad may ultimately decline, home values have not waited to do so, having already given up almost all of their gains during the boom years. This simple observation is reflected in our statistical analysis of the relationship between home prices, capital flows, credit standards, and interest rates, not only in the United States, but also internationally: capital flows have little if any explanatory power for residential real estate fluctuations in samples that include both the boom and the bust. We have also argued on theoretical grounds that capital inflows—even those that significantly decrease domestic interest rates—need not have large effects on domestic real estate prices if they simultaneously push up the housing risk premium and the expected stock of future housing.

A quantitatively meaningful account of the massive boom and bust in house prices must therefore rely on (at least one) alternative element. We argue here that the missing element is the financial market liberalization in the mortgage space (and its subsequent reversal), which made it easier and cheaper during the boom period for homeowners to purchase a house or to borrow against existing home equity. The relaxation of credit constraints, by itself, is a powerful force for higher house prices in general equilibrium theory. Easier access to mortgage credit increases households' ability to withstand income shocks, and it reduces the risk premium households require to invest in risky assets like houses. In addition, lower transaction costs associated with new or refinanced home mortgages and home equity lines of credit raise the liquidity of houses, and therefore their price.

We have presented evidence that these mechanisms appear to have operated in the United States, but also in countries other than the United States. Using observations on credit standards, capital flows, interest rates, and house prices, we find that, of these variables, only the bank lending survey measure of credit standards explains either current or future home price fluctuations, with credit supply explaining 53 percent of the quarterly variation in US house price growth over the period 1992 to 2010, and 66 percent over the boom-bust period from 2000 to 2010. By contrast, the other variables combined add less than 5 percent to the fraction of quarterly variation in house price changes explained, once we control for credit standards.

Our chapter is silent on the origins of the financial market liberalization in credit standards and its subsequent reversal, but it is worthwhile to conclude by briefly considering some possibilities. A first possibility is that mortgage lenders were confronted with exogenous changes in technology that affected mortgage finance. The boom period was characterized by a plethora of such changes, including the birth of private label securitization, collateralized debt obligations, credit default swaps, and automated underwriting coupled with new credit scoring techniques employed in that underwriting (Poon 2009). These specific innovations have been directly linked to the surge in mortgage credit and house price growth by Mian and Sufi (2009) and Keys et al. (chapter 4, this volume). Second, during the period leading up to and including the housing boom, numerous legislative actions were undertaken that had the effect of giving banks far more leeway to relax lending standards than they had previously. In this regard, Mian, Sufi, and Trebbi (2010) mention 700 such housing-related legislative initiatives that Congress voted on between 1993 and 2008, while Boz and Mendoza (2010) highlight the 1999 Gramm-Leach-Bliley and the 2000 Commodity Futures Modernization Acts. Third, in the period leading up to and including the housing boom, regulatory oversight of investment banks and mortgage lenders weakened substantially (Acharya and Richardson 2011). For example, the regulatory treatment of AA-or-better rated private label residential mortgage-backed securities was lowered in 2002 to the same lesser regulatory capital level as that which applied since 1988 to MBS issued by the Agencies. Overall, regulatory capital requirements were in practice further relaxed as banks ostensibly removed MBS assets from their balance sheets by selling them to SPVs with far less restrictive capital requirements than those assets would have faced had they remained on the bank balance sheets. The removal of these assets from bank balance sheets was illusory, however, since banks extended credit and liquidity guarantees to the SPVs, effectively undoing the risk-transfer (but not the lowered capital requirement) and forcing them to reclaim the MBS on their balance sheets when those assets began to lose value (Acharya, Schnabl, and Suarez 2012). These changes took place in an environment where private sector mortgage lenders where engaged in a "race to the bottom" in credit standards with the government-sponsored enterprises, which experienced similar regulatory changes and increasing investor awareness of the implicit government guarantees that were afforded these enterprises (Acharya, Richardson, et al. 2011). Faced with such changes in their regulatory environment, we hypothesize that prior to the boom, mortgage lenders formed expectations of higher future house price growth, leading to more and riskier mortgages in equilibrium, as in the optimal contracting framework of Piskorski and Tchistyi (2010). The bust was characterized by a tightening of regulatory oversight (Acharya, Cooley, et al. 2011), which appears to have contributed to the reduction in credit availability that occurred at the end of the housing boom. The exact mechanisms through which credit standards were dramatically relaxed and reversed remains an important topic for future research.

There are several other interesting questions for future research. First, it is often hypothesized that international capital flows themselves contributed to a relaxation of lending standards during the housing boom. As we show here, however, this explanation is not consistent, especially in the United States, with the housing bust period, in which credit standards dramatically tightened but capital inflows to US safe securities remained high on average and real interest rates low. Neither net capital flows nor gross capital flows into the United States have any explanatory power for current or future bank lending standards in our sample. More research is needed on this question. Second, why is capital flowing from relatively productive economies, like China, Germany, Japan, Switzerland, and so forth, to relatively unproductive economies like Spain, the United States, Greece, and Italy? Moreover, why is capital flowing into safe assets like US Treasuries? We have argued here that purchases of US safe assets appear to be driven by reserve currency motives and political constraints by governmental holders in the source countries (see Alfaro, Kalemli-Ozcan, and Volosovych 2011), but more research is needed on this issue as well. Finally, for the most part we focused on the relationship between *net* capital flows and house prices. Other researchers (notably Obstfeld 2011), have argued that *gross* flows in international financial assets may lead to financial market instability. Future work should investigate the link between gross flows and prices of all kinds of assets, including real estate, equity, and bond markets.

Appendix

This appendix provides details on all the data used in this study, including data sources. The last section also includes some additional details about the estimation procedures used.

House Price Data

Data on house prices are deflated by a consumer price index (CPI). The data are from different national sources, mostly quarterly, except for Germany (annual), Luxembourg (annual, and until 2009), Italy (semiannual), and Japan (semiannual). The CPI is collected by Economist Intelligence Unit (EIU) and from national sources. For Slovenia the series begins in 2003:Q1; for Russia in 2001:Q1.

United States

For regressions involving the house prices in the United States, we use the Core Logic National House Price Index (SA, Jan. 2000 = 100). This is a repeat-sales price index that is based on the universe of mortgages (conforming and nonconforming).[16] House prices are deflated using consumer price index (All urban consumers, US city average, All items) from the Bureau of Labor and Statistics (http://www.bls.gov/cpi/). The monthly data are averaged over the quarter and rebased at 2005 = 100, so real house prices are in 2005 US dollars. Regressions of growth rates use log changes, $\log(HP_t)$ − $\log(HP_{t-1})$ for contemporaneous changes, and $\log(HP_{t+H})$ − $\log(HP_t)$ for H horizon changes.

For regressions using the aggregate price-rent ratio, we construct an index by combining a measure of rent, for primary residences, constructed from the Shelter component of the Consumer Price Index for all urban consumers, SA, last month of each quarter, with the Core Logic measure of house prices. Data for rent are available from the Bureau of Economic Analysis of the US Department of Commerce. The price-rent ratio has been normalized to equal the value in 1975:Q4 of the quarterly price-rent ratio constructed from the flow of funds housing wealth and National Income and Products data on housing consumption.

International Data

House prices are deflated using consumer price indices for each country, from national sources. For the Euro Area we deflate with the Harmonized Index of Consumer Prices for the Euro Area 17, all items. Data sources for residential real estate are given in table 6A.1.

Current Account Data

Current Account is measured as the current account *deficit*. Data are available from the International Monetary Fund (IMF) for all countries except China. For China, data are from State Administration of Foreign Exchange, SAFE. The CA balances are accumulated and deflated by 2006 GDP (collected by Economist Intelligence Unit, EIU), in current US dollars. For Belgium, CA data 2000:Q1 to 2001:Q4 are from the National Bank of Belgium, provided by the Organization of Economic Cooperation and Development (OECD).

United States: (CAdef/GDP)$_t$ is current account *deficit* over nominal GDP, at current market prices. Balance of current account is from the Bureau of Economic Analysis, US International Transactions Accounts Data, in millions of dollars, not seasonally adjusted. The GDP data is from the Bureau of Economic Analysis, National Economic Accounts, in billions

16. Other indexes are available only for conforming mortgages. For example, the Federal Housing Finance Administration (FHFA) measure is based only on conforming mortgages and therefore misses price changes associated with nonconforming mortgages. Like the Core Logic measure, the Case–Shiller measure is also based on the universe of mortgages, but it has substantially smaller geographic coverage than the Core Logic measure.

Table 6A.1   **Data sources for house prices**

Australia	Australian Bureau of Statistics. Exist. dwellings (8 CITIES), PER DWEL., Q-ALL NSA. (1)
Austria	Oesterreichische National Bank. All dwellings (VIENNA), PER SQ.M., Q-ALL NSA. (1)
Belgium	EXISTING DWELLINGS, PER DWEL., Q-ALL NSA. (1)
Canada	Teranet-National Bank of Canada. Comp. 6 Cities (monthly, averaged to quarterly using sales pair count).
China	National Bureau of Statistics of China. Land prices, Resid. and Commercial, Q-ALL NSA. (1)
Czech Republic	Czech Statistical Office. House prices.
Denmark	Statistics Denmark. ALL SINGLE-FAMILY HOUSE, PER DWEL, Q-ALL NSA.
Estonia	Statistical Office of Estonia. Av. price per sq.m., 2-rooms and kitchen, Tallinn (1). 2009 onwards, 55–70m2.
Euro Area	European Central Bank. Euro area 17 (fixed composition); New and existing dwellings; Not S.A.
Finland	Statistics Finland. EXISTING HOUSES, PER SQ.M, Q-ALL NSA. (1)
France	National Institute of Statistics and Economic Studies. Existing Dwellings, Q-ALL NSA. (1)
Germany	Deutsche Bundesbank, based on data provided by BulwienGesa AG. Existing Dwellings, Y-ALL NSA. (1)
Greece	Bank of Greece. ALL DWELL. (URBAN GREECE EX. ATHENS), PER SQ.M, NSA. (1)
Hungary	FHB Bank. FHB House Price Index (actual buying and selling transaction data of residential real estate).
Iceland	Icelandic Property Registry. ALL DWELLINGS (GR. REYKJAVK), PER SQ.M, M-ALL NSA. (1)
Ireland	Economic and Social Research Institute (ESRI). ALL DWELLINGS, PER DWELLING., Q-ALL NSA. (1)
Israel	Central Bureau of Statistics. Prices of Dwellings (Until September 2010–Owner Occupied Dwellings).
Italy	Bank of Italy. ALL DWELLINGS, PER SQUARE M., H-ALL NSA. (1)
Korea	Kookmin Bank in Korea. ALL DWELLINGS, M-ALL NSA. (1)
Luxembourg	Central Bank of Luxembourg. ALL DWELLINGS, Y-ALL NSA. (1)
Netherlands	Statistics Netherlands. Existing own homes. Dwellings: all. Price index purchase prices.
New Zealand	Reserve Bank of New Zealand. All dwellings, Q-ALL NSA. QVL. (1)
Norway	Statistics Norway. All dwellings, Q-AVG, NSA. (1)
Poland	Central Statistics Office. Price of a square meter of usable floor space of a residential building.
Portugal	Inteligência de Imobiliário. All dwellings, PER SQUARE METER, M-ALL NSA. (1)
Russia	Federal State Statistics Service. EXISTING DWELLINGS, PER SQUARE M, Q-ALL NSA. (1)
Slovenia	Statistical Office of the Republic of Slovenia. Existing Dwellings, Q-ALL NSA. (1)
Spain	Bank of Spain. All dwellings, PER SQUARE M., Q-ALL NSA. (1)
Sweden	Statistics Sweden. ALL OWNER-OCCUPIED DWELLINGS, PER DWEL., Q-ALL NSA. (1)
Switzerland	Swiss National Bank. ALL 1-FAMILY HOUSES, PER DWELLING, Q-ALL NSA. (1)

Table 6A.1	continued
United Kingdom	Office for National Statistics. All dwellings (ONS), PER DWEL., M, Q-ALL NSA. (1)
United States	Federal Housing Finance Agency. Family Houses, Q-ALL NSA (all transactions, FHFA). (1)

Notes: Series (1) can be found at the Bank of International Settlements website, http://www.bis.org statistics/pp.htm.

of current dollars, seasonally adjusted at annual rates; we transform it to quarterly rates dividing by four.

International data: $(CA\text{def}/GDP)_t$ is current account *deficit* over nominal GDP, at current market prices. Data from International Monetary Fund, in millions of US dollars, and GDP data are collected by the Economist Intelligence Unit on nominal GDP (USD), quarterly.

Residential Investment

Residential Investment data are from Eurostat and national sources, as indicated in table 6A.2. Residential investment is accumulated and deflated by 2006 GDP, all in current national currency. For France, Hungary, Poland, Switzerland, and Russia, data is available only until 2009.

Data on Credit Standards

United States

The variable CS_t is a net percentage index that indicates the percentage of banks relaxing credit standards for mortgage loans (both *considerably* and *somewhat*), with respect to the previous quarter, minus the percentage of banks tightening credit standards (both *considerably* and *somewhat*). This indicator is taken from the Senior Loan Officer Opinion Survey on Bank Lending Practices for the United States, published by the Federal Reserve. They report the net percentage of banks *tightening* standards. The negative of this is the net percentage of banks easing standards, which we use in our empirical work. This is a quarterly survey of approximately sixty large domestic banks and twenty-four US branches and agencies of foreign banks. Questions cover changes in the standards and terms of the banks' lending and the state of business and household demand for loans. These data are available since May 1990, when the survey then began including approximately twenty questions designed to measure changes in credit standards and terms on bank loans and perceived changes in the demand for bank credit. See http://www.federalreserve.gov/boarddocs/snloansurvey/.

Table 6A.2   **Data sources for residential investment**

Australia	Australian Bureau of Statistics. Private Gross fixed capital formation, Dwellings, Total, $ millions
Austria	Eurostat.
Belgium	National Bank of Belgium. Gross fixed capital formation, dwellings, current prices, millions of euros.
Canada	Statistics Canada. Capital formation in residential structures, current prices, national currency, NSA.
China	National Bureau of Statistics China (NBSC). Total Inv. Residential Buildings in the whole country, million yuan.
Czech Republic	Eurostat.
Denmark	Eurostat.
Estonia	Eurostat.
Euro Area	No data.
Finland	Eurostat.
France	Eurostat.
Germany	Eurostat.
Greece	Eurostat.
Hungary	Eurostat.
Iceland	Eurostat.
Ireland	Central Statistics Office Ireland. Gross Dom. Physical Cap. Formation at current prices. Fixed capital, Dwellings.
Israel	Central Bureau of Statistics. Gross Domestic Capital Formation. Residential Buildings, current prices.
Italy	Eurostat.
Japan	Cabinet Office, Gov. of Japan, Billions of Yen, nominal Private residential investment, not SA.
Korea	Bank of Korea, Gross fixed capital formation in residential buildings, current prices, Bil. Won.
Luxembourg	Eurostat.
Netherlands	Eurostat.
New Zealand	Statistics New Zealand. Gross Fixed Capital Formation, Residential buildings, current prices, $ millions.
Norway	Norway Statistics. Gross fixed capital formation, Dwellings (households). Current prices (mill. NOK)
Poland	Eurostat.
Portugal	Eurostat.
Russia	Federal State Statistics Service. Investment in fixed capital, in residential houses, current prices, billions rubles.
Slovenia	Eurostat.
Spain	Eurostat.
Sweden	Eurostat.
Switzerland	Eurostat.
United Kingdom	Eurostat.
United States	US Bureau of Economic Analysis. Fixed Investment, Residential, Billions of dollars.

Notes: Most of the series are from national sources via Eurostat. Gross fixed capital formation, in construction work: housing, millions of national currency, current prices.

We focus on the question that asks about residential mortgage loans at each bank. From 1990:Q2 (beginning of the survey) to 2006:Q4, the question is about residential mortgage loans in general:

> Over the past three months, how have your bank's credit standards for approving applications from individuals for mortgage loans to purchase homes changed?

The recommendations for answering this question state

> If your bank's credit standards have not changed over the relevant period, please report them as unchanged even if the standards are either restrictive or accommodative relative to longer-term norms. If your bank's credit standards have tightened or eased over the relevant period, please so report them regardless of how they stand relative to longer-term norms. Also, please report changes in enforcement of existing standards as changes in standards. (See http://www.federalreserve.gov/boarddocs/snloansurvey/ for more details.)

From 2007:Q1 onwards, the question is asked for each of three categories of residential mortgage loans: prime residential mortgages, nontraditional residential mortgages, and subprime residential mortgages. The answer to this question can be one of the following: tightened considerably, tightened somewhat, remained basically unchanged, eased somewhat, eased considerably. Responses are grouped in "Large Banks" and "Other Banks." The index, however, is calculated using information of "all respondents." Given that the question is referenced to the past three months, we date the index with respect to the quarter when changes to lending standards occurred (as opposed to when the responses are collected, i.e., net percentage reported in July 2011 is the net percentage for 2011:Q2). In the report beginning in 2007:Q1, a distinction is made between prime and subprime mortgages in the survey. In the regressions using US credit supply, CS is a weighted average of prime and subprime mortgages: (net percentage easing on prime)*weight plus (net percentage easing on subprime)*(1 − weight), where weight is 0.75 for 2007 and 0.95 for 2008. After that weight equals 1, because no bank reported that they originated subprime mortgages. The earlier weights are based on the paper http://www.jchs.harvard.edu/publications/finance/UBB10-1.pdf, page 85, figures 1 through 3. These numbers are approximately the average share of banks that originated subprime residential mortgages, according to the survey (23 percent for 2007 and 8 percent for 2008). Results are not sensitive to using one or the other set of numbers.

We standardize the net percentage indicator by subtracting the mean and dividing by the standard deviation.

International Data

Variable CS_t stands for credit standards for housing loans. Data are from bank lending surveys conducted by national central banks and the European Central Bank. The survey questions are modeled after the US Survey of Senior Loan Officers. Central Banks report the information in different ways. Some Central Banks report net percentages, some report diffusion indices, and some report mean values. *Net percentage* is the percentage of banks loosening (or tightening) credit standards with respect to the previous quarter minus the percentage of banks tightening them (or relaxing). *Diffusion index* is the percentage of banks loosening (or tightening) credit standards "considerably" with respect to the previous quarter multiplied by 1 plus the percentage of banks loosening (or tightening) credit standards "somewhat" multiplied by 0.5 minus the percentage of banks tightening (or relaxing) "somewhat" times 0.5, minus the percentage of banks tightening (or relaxing) "considerably" times 1. *Mean values:* each answer receives a value from 1 to 5 (where for 5, the bank reported that relaxed the credit standards "considerably," 3 did not change them, and 1 is a "considerable" tightening), and the mean value for each quarter is reported.

Mean values are a scale transformation of the diffusion index, but the net percentage indicator is not. There are nine countries for which we can construct either the diffusion index (Austria, Belgium, Euro Area, France, Korea, Portugal, Spain, United States) or a mean value (Ireland) with the information reported by the central banks. We have a larger set of eleven countries for which we have only information on the net percentage (Canada and the Netherlands). We standardize these indices, country by country, by subtracting the mean and dividing by the standard deviation, for the period 2002:Q4 to 2010:Q4.

A positive value for CS_t reflects easing credit conditions with respect to the previous quarter, and units are in terms of standard deviations.

Micro data for each country are not publicly available, but each of the abovementioned countries publishes an indicator (net percentage, mean index, diffusion index) that reflects the change in credit conditions in the country. The data sources are summarized in table 6A.3. For Austria, Belgium, Euro Area, France, Ireland, Netherlands, Portugal, and Spain, the survey is based on the Bank Lending Survey conducted by the ECB. See http://www.ecb.int/stats/money/surveys/lend/html/index.en.html. The European Central Bank's website states:

> The survey addresses issues such as credit standards for approving loans as well as credit terms and conditions applied to enterprises and households. It also asks for an assessment of the conditions affecting credit demand. The survey is addressed to senior loan officers of a representative sample of euro area banks and will be conducted four times a year. The sample group participating in the survey comprises around 90 banks from

all euro area countries and takes into account the characteristics of their respective national banking structures.

We focus on question 8 from the ECB survey, Item 8.1, Loans for house purchase:

Over the past three months, how have your bank's credit standards as applied to the approval of loans to households changed?

Respondents can reply with one of the following answers: tighten considerably, tighten somewhat, basically unchanged, ease somewhat, or ease considerably.

For Korea and Canada, the raw questions in the survey differ somewhat. The survey for Korea is from the Korean Survey of Lending Attitudes, which asks about households' "housing lending." The diffusion index is the sum of the responses of significant increase plus responses of moderate increase minus responses of a significant decrease minus responses of moderate decrease times 0.5, divided by 100. For Canada, the Balance of Opinion survey delivers only a net percentage indicator based only on overall lending conditions (inclusive of residential mortgages but also of other forms of credit). The net percentage indicator we use is minus a weighted percentage of surveyed financial institutions reporting tightened credit conditions plus the weighted percentage reporting eased credit conditions.

Finally, when we analyze the international data in panel regressions, for the United States, we construct a diffusion index (rather than use the net percentage indicator) from the data reported by the Senior Loan Officer Opinion Survey on Bank Lending Practices for the United States, published by the Federal Reserve. Data for 2007 onwards is a weighted average of prime and subprime mortgages, with the following weights for prime mortgages: 2007, 0.75; 2008, 0.95; 2009 and 2010, 0.

Data sources for each country are given in table 6A.3.

Estimation Details

This section presents several details pertaining to our empirical estimation.

Estimating Quarterly Net Foreign Holdings of US Assets

This section describes how we estimate quarterly net foreign holdings of US assets by combining annual positions data. Annual net foreign holdings estimates are compiled by the BEA in their international investment data, year-end positions, thereby providing annual observations.[17] To form

---

17. The BEA year-end holdings data begin in 1976. This is in contrast to the TIC data on asset holdings, which is reported annually only starting in 2002. Thus, the BEA constructs its

Table 6A.3   Data sources for credit standards

Austria	Oesterreichische Nationalbank. Bank Lending Survey.
Belgium	Nationale Bank van Belgie. Bank Lending Survey.
Canada	Bank of Canada. Senior Loan Officer Survey. Lending conditions: Balance of Opinion.
Euro Area	European Central Bank. Bank Lending Survey.
France	Banque de France. Bank Lending Survey.
Ireland	Central Bank of Ireland. Bank Lending Survey. Mean.
Korea	Bank of Korea, Financial System Review. Survey Bank Lending Practices. Lending attitude.
Netherlands	De Nederlandsche Bank. Bank Lending Survey.
Portugal	Banco de Portugal. Bank Lending Survey.
Spain	Banco de Espana. Bank Lending Survey.
United States	Federal Reserve. Senior Loan Officer Opinion Survey.

Notes: For countries other than Korea and Canada, surveys follow the BLS survey conducted by the European Central Bank. In that survey, the questions attained for our purpose are Q8.1 and Q13.1, about mortgage credit. We construct diffusion indices based on this question for use in the panel regressions. For Korea, we use the "Lending Attitude" diffusion index for households' housing, and for Canada we use the "Overall Balance of Opinion" diffusion index.

quarter-end net foreign liability position of the United States in total securities, we employ a methodology to interpolate between the year-end positions, taking into account the quarterly *transactions* data in these same securities.[18]

Let nh_{Q4} be the value of net foreign holdings of total securities observed at the end of quarter Q4 of a given year, where net foreign holdings are defined as foreign holdings of US securities minus US holdings of foreign securities. These data are available from the BEA year-end positions table. Let $\widehat{nh}_q$ be an estimate that we will form of the value of these net foreign holdings at the end of quarter q in that same year. Let nt_q be net transactions in those securities during that quarter, where net transactions are net foreign purchases (gross foreign purchases less gross foreign sales) of US-owned securities minus US net purchases (gross US purchases less gross US sales) of foreign-owned securities. These data are available from the BEA international transactions table. To obtain estimates of quarterly holdings for the three quarters within a year, we accumulate according to

$$\widehat{nh}_q = \widehat{nh}_{q-1} + nt_q + \mathrm{adj}_q$$

where

own estimate of year-end positions prior to 2002 using as raw inputs the TIC flows data and the periodic TIC benchmark surveys of holdings. The BEA year-end data are located at http://www.bea.gov/international/xls/intinv10_t2.xls

18. The data on international transactions in financial securities are in the balance of payments data set, found at http://www.bea.gov/international/xls/table1.xls.

$$\text{adj}_q = \text{gap}_{Q4} * w_{q,Q4}$$

$$w_{q,Q4} \equiv \frac{\left|nt_q\right|}{\sum_{k=0}^{3}\left|nt_{Q4-k}\right|}$$

$$\text{gap}_{Q4} \equiv (nh_{Q4} - nh_{Q4-4}) - \sum_{k=0}^{3} nt_{Q4-k}.$$

The above recursion ensures that our estimate of the holdings at the end of Q4 of a given year, $\widehat{nh}_{Q4}$, is equal to the recorded value from the annual holdings data, nh_{Q4}. For all other quarters within a year, the above recursion forms an estimate of holdings at the end of the quarter, which is equal to the estimated net holdings from last quarter, plus the net transactions in that quarter, plus an adjustment. The adjustment is equal to the *gap* between the change in measured holdings from the year in which the quarter resides and the previous year and the cumulation of all the quarterly transactions over the year, times a weight, where the weight is given by that quarter's value of net transactions relative to the value over the entire year. Thus, quarters for which net transactions were higher in absolute value receive a greater weight in the adjustment. Notice that, in the absence of any valuation adjustments, the cumulation of all the quarterly transactions over the year would equal the total change in net foreign holdings or year-end positions. The observed change in year-end positions takes into account the valuation changes, and gap_{Q4} is the difference between the observed change in year-end positions and the cumulation of the quarterly transactions. Thus, roughly speaking, the adjustment adj_q captures the pure valuation effects that are not reflected in the cumulation of transactions but are reflected in the total change in net foreign holdings. The weights $w_{q,Q4}$ give quarters with a larger value of transactions more weight in the adjustment.

US Regressions

For the contemporaneous quarterly regressions we report Newey–West corrected standard errors (and t-statistics) using 4 lags. For the long horizon quarterly regressions we use lags equal to max{Horizon − 1,4}, to take into consideration the use of overlapping data.

Panel Regressions

We use a balanced panel from 2002:Q4 to 2010:Q4 for ten countries plus the Euro Area: Austria, Belgium, Canada, Euro Area, France, Ireland, Korea, the Netherlands, Portugal, Spain, United States. The choice of sample period is determined by the availability of a balanced panel for data on credit standards (European Central Bank conducts the Bank Lending Survey since 2002:Q4), and quarterly house prices (for Italy and Germany we only have annual data on house prices, for Hungary only semiannual data on credit conditions, and for Poland we only have data on credit conditions since 2003:Q4). We also use a subsample of nine countries where we drop Canada and the Netherlands (see previous information on credit standards). The Euro Area consists of seventeen countries: Austria, Belgium, Cyprus, Estonia, Finland, France, Germany, Greece, Ireland, Italy, Luxembourg, Malta, the Netherlands, Portugal, Slovakia, Slovenia, and Spain. We construct log changes $\log(HP_t) - \log(HP_{t-1})$ for contemporaneous changes, and $\log(HP_{t+H}) - \log(HP_t)$ for H horizon changes.

For the contemporaneous quarterly regressions, we report the robust standard errors (and t-statistics) using the Driscoll-Kraay statistic, with lags = 3 (default). For the quarterly long horizon regressions, we use instead number of lags equal to max{Horizon − 1,3} to take into account the use of overlapping data. For more on the Driscoll–Kraay statistic, see Hoechle (2007) and Driscoll and Kraay (1998).

References

Acharya, V. V., T. Cooley, M. Richardson, and I. Walter. 2011. *Regulating Wall Street: The Dodd–Frank Act and the New Architecture of Global Finance.* Wiley Finance Series. Hoboken, NJ: John Wiley and Sons.

Acharya, V. V., and M. Richardson. 2011. *Restoring Financial Stability: How to Repair a Failed System.* Wiley Finance Series. Hoboken, NJ: John Wiley and Sons.

Acharya, V. V., M. Richardson, S. Van Nieuwerburgh, and L. J. White. 2011. *Guaranteed to Fail: Freddie, Fannie, and the Debacle of US Mortgage Finance.* Princeton, NJ: Princeton University Press.

Acharya, V. V., P. Schnabl, and G. Suarez. 2012. "Securitization without Risk Transfer." Forthcoming, *Journal of Financial Economics.*

Adam, K., A. Marcet, and P. Kuang. 2011. "House Price Booms and the Current Account." NBER Working Paper no. 17224. Cambridge, MA: National Bureau of Economic Research.

Adelino, M., A. Schoar, and F. Severino. 2012. "Credit Supply and House Prices: Evidence from Mortgage Market Segmentation." NBER Working Paper no. 17832. Cambridge, MA: National Bureau of Economic Research.

Aizenman, J., and Y. Jinjarak. 2009. "Current Account Patterns and National Real Estate Markets." *Journal of Urban Economics* 66 (2): 75–89.

Alfaro, L., S. Kalemli-Ozcan, and V. Volosovych. 2011. "Sovereigns, Upstream Capital Flows, and Global Imbalances." Unpublished Paper, Harvard Business School.

Amromin, G., J. Huang, C. Sialm, and E. Zhong. 2011. "Complex Mortgages." NBER Working Paper no. 17315. Cambridge, MA: National Bureau of Economic Research.

Barlevy, G., and J. D. Fisher. 2011. "Mortgage Choices and Housing Speculation." Federal Reserve Bank of Chicago, Working Paper no. 2010-12.

Bernanke, B. S. 2005. "Remarks by Governor Ben S. Bernanke at the Sandridge Lecture." Virginia Association of Economics. Richmond, Virginia, March 10.

———. 2008. "Remarks by Chairman Ben S. Bernanke at the International Monetary Conference." Barcelona, Spain (via satellite), June 3.

————. 2011. "International Capital Flows and the Returns to Safe Assets in the United States 2003–2007." *Banque de France Financial Stability Review* 15:13–26.

Bernanke, B. S., and M. Gertler. 1989. "Agency Costs, Net Worth and Business Cycle Flutuations." *American Economic Review* 79:14–31.

Bernanke, B. S., V. R. Reinhart, and B. P. Sack. 2004. "Monetary Policy Alternatives at the Zero Bound: An Empirical Assessment." *Brookings Papers on Economic Activity* (2):1–100. Washington, DC: Brookings Institution.

Boz, E., and E. Mendoza. 2010. "Financial Innovation, the Discovery of Risk, and the US Credit Crisis." CEPR Discussion Paper no. 7967. Center for Economic Policy Research.

Caballero, R. J., E. Fahri, and P.-O. Gourinchas. 2008. "An Equilibrium Model of 'Global Imbalances' and Low Interest Rates." *American Economic Review* 98 (1): 358–93.

Caballero, R. J., and A. Krishnamurthy. 2009. "Global Imbalances and Financial Fragility." *American Economic Review Papers and Proceedings* 99:584–88.

Case, K. E., and R. J. Shiller. 1989. "The Efficiency of the Market for Single-Family Homes." *American Economic Review* 79 (1): 125–37.

Driscoll, J. C., and A. C. Kraay. 1998. "Consistent Covariance Matrix Estimation with Spatially Dependent Panel Data." *The Review of Economics and Statistics* 80 (4): 549–60.

Favara, G., and J. Imbs. 2011. "Credit Supply and the Price of Housing." 2011 Meeting Paper no. 1342. Society for Economic Dynamics.

Favilukis, J., S. C. Ludvigson, and S. Van Nieuwerburgh. 2010. "The Macroeconomic Effects of Housing Wealth, Housing Finance and Limited Risk-Sharing in General Equilibrium." NBER Working Paper no. 15988. Cambridge, MA: National Bureau of Economic Research.

————. 2011. "Foreign Ownership of US Safe Assets: Good or Bad?" Unpublished Paper, New York University.

Ferrero, A. 2011. "House Prices Booms and Current Account Deficits." Unpublished Paper, Federal Reserve Bank of New York.

Geithner, T. 2007. "Remarks by New York Federal Reserve President Timothy Geithner at the Council on Foreign Relations." C. Peter McColough Roundtable Series on International Economics. New York, January 11.

Gete, P. 2010. "Housing Markets and Current Account Dynamics." Available at SSRN: http://ssrn.com/abstract=1558512. Social Science Research Network.

Haughwout, A., J. Tracy, R. Peach, and E. Okah. 2011. "Mortgages Defaults and the Credit Crunch." Federal Reserve Bank of New York Unpublished Paper.

Himmelberg, C., C. Mayer, and T. Sinai. 2005. "Assessing High House Prices: Bubbles, Fundamentals and Misperceptions." *Journal of Economic Perspectives* 19 (4): 67–92.

Hodrick, R., and E. C. Prescott. 1997. "Post-War US Business Cycles: A Descriptive Empirical Investigation." *Journal of Money, Credit, and Banking* 29:1–16.

Hoechle, Daniel. 2007. "Robust Standard Errors for Panel Regressions with Cross-Sectional Dependence." Available at http://fmwww.bc.edu/repec/bocode/x/xtscc_paper.pdf.

Kiyotaki, N., and J. Moore. 1997. "Credit Cycles." *Journal of Political Economy* 105 (2): 211–48.

Kohn, D. L. 2002. "Panel: Implications of Declining Treasury Debt. What Should the Federal Reserve Do as Treasury Debt Is Repaid?" *Journal of Money, Credit, and Banking* 34 (3): 941–45.

Kole, L. S., and R. F. Martin. 2009. "The Relationship between House Prices and the Current Account." Working Paper, Board of Governors of the Federal Reserve System.

Krainer, J., S. F. LeRoy, and O. Munpyung. 2009. "Mortgage Default and Mortgage Valuation." Working Paper Series 2009–20. San Francisco: Federal Reserve Bank of San Francisco.

Krishnamurthy, A., and A. Vissing-Jorgensen. 2007. "The Demand for Treasury Debt." NBER Working Paper no. 12881. Cambridge, MA: National Bureau of Economic Research.

Laibson, D., and J. Mollerstrom. 2010. "Capital Flows, Consumption Booms and Asset Bubbles: A Behavioural Alternative to the Savings Glut Hypothesis." *Economic Journal* 120:354–74.

Laufer, S. 2011. "Equity Extraction and Mortgage Default." Working Paper, New York University.

Maddaloni, A., and J.-L. Peydro. 2011. "Bank Risk-Taking, Securitization, Supervision, and Low Interest Rates: Evidence from the Euro-Area and the US Lending Standards." *Review of Financial Studies* 24 (6): 2121–65.

Mendoza, E. G., V. Quadrini, and J.-V. Rios-Rull. 2007. "Financial Integration, Financial Deepness and Global Imbalances." NBER Working Paper no. 12909. Cambridge, MA: National Bureau of Economic Research.

Mian, A., and A. Sufi. 2009. "The Consequences of Mortgage Expansion: Evidence from the US Mortgage Default Crisis." *Quarterly Journal of Economics* 124 (4): 1449–96.

Mian, A., A. Sufi, and F. Trebbi. 2010. "The Political Economy of the US Mortgage Default Crisis." *American Economic Review* 100:67–98.

Newey, W. K., and K. D. West. 1987. "A Simple, Positive Semi-Definite, Heteroskedasticity and Autocorrelation Consistent Covariance Matrix." *Econometrica* 55:703–38.

Nichols, J., A. Pennington-Cross, and A. Yezer. 2005. "Borrower Self-Selection, Underwriting Costs, and Subprime Mortgage Credit Supply." *Journal of Real Estate Finance and Economics* 30:197–219.

Obstfeld, M. 2011. "Financial Flows, Financial Crises, and Global Imbalances." Keynote address to the 15th International Conference on Macroeconomic Analysis and International Finance. University of Crete, Greece, May 26–28.

Piskorski, T., and A. Tchistyi. 2010. "Optimal Mortgage Design." *Review of Financial Studies* 23:3098–140.

Poon, M. A. 2009. "From New Deal Institutions to Capital Markets: Commercial Consumer Risk Scores and the Making of Subprime Mortgage Finance." *Accounting, Organizations and Society* 35 (5): 654–74.

Rajan, R., and R. Ramcharan. 2011a. "The Anatomy of a Credit Crisis: The Boom and Bust in Farm Land Prices in the United States in the 1920s." In *PIEP: Research Group on Political Institutions and Economic Policy.* Cambridge, MA: Weatherhead Center for International Affairs, Institute for Quantitative Social Sciences. Available at http://conferences.wcfia.harvard.edu/piep/publications/anatomy-credit-crisis-boom-and-bust-farm-land-prices-united-states-1920s.

———. 2011b. "Constituencies and Legislation: The Fight over the McFadden Act of 1927." NBER Working Paper no. 17266. Cambridge, MA: National Bureau of Economic Research.

Rice, T., and P. E. Strahan. 2010. "Does Credit Competition Affect Small-Firm Finance?" *The Journal of Finance* 65 (3): 861–89.

Streitfeld, D. 2009. "Tight Mortgage Rules Exclude Even Good Risks." *New York Times,* Saturday, July 11.

Taylor, J. B. 2009. *Getting off Track: How Government Actions and Interventions Caused, Prolonged, and Worsened the Financial Crisis.* Stanford: Hoover Institution Press.

US Treasury Department. 2011. *Report on Foreign Portfolio Holdings of US Securities, as of June 30, 2010.* Department of Treasury, Federal Reserve Bank of New York, Board of Governors of the Federal Reserve System.

Warnock, F. 2010. "Two Myths About the U.S. Dollar." *Center for Geoeconomic Studies Capital Flows Quarterly.* Council on Foreign Relations Press, September.

Warnock, F. E., and V. C. Warnock. 2009 "International Capital Flows and US Interest Rates." *Journal of International Money and Finance* 28:903–19.

Can Cheap Credit Explain
the Housing Boom?

Edward L. Glaeser, Joshua D. Gottlieb,
and Joseph Gyourko

7.1   Introduction

From the beginning of 2001 to its cyclical peak in April of 2006, the Standard and Poor's/Case–Shiller Twenty City Composite Index rose by nearly 60 percent in real terms and then fell by just over one-third before reaching a plateau in May of 2009. The volatility of the Federal Housing Finance Agency (FHFA) repeat-sales price index was less extreme but still severe. That index rose by just over 50 percent in real terms between 1996 and 2006 and then fell by 19 percent in real terms between the end of 2006 and the end of 2009. The real value of this index fell by another 11 percent as of the fourth quarter of 2011.[1] As many financial institutions had invested

Edward L. Glaeser is the Fred and Eleanor Glimp Professor of Economics at Harvard University and a research associate and director of the Urban Economics Working Group at the National Bureau of Economic Research. Joshua D. Gottlieb is assistant professor of economics at the University of British Columbia. Joseph Gyourko is the Martin Bucksbaum Professor of Real Estate and chairperson of the Real Estate Department at the Wharton School, University of Pennsylvania, and a research associate of the National Bureau of Economic Research.

We are grateful to our discussants, Gadi Barlevy and Morris Davis; to an anonymous reviewer; to Thomas Barrios, Owen Lamont, Carolin Pflueger, Jeremy Stein, Paul Willen, Justin Wolfers, and seminar participants at Harvard University, the University of Pennsylvania, the NBER conference on "Housing Markets and the Financial Crisis," the 2010 AREUEA Mid-Year Meetings, and the 2010 Conference on Urban and Regional Economics for valuable comments; and to Fernando Ferreira, Karen Pence, and Amit Seru for providing data. Jiashou Feng and Charlie Nathanson provided excellent research assistance. Glaeser and Gottlieb thank the Taubman Center for State and Local Government for financial support. Gottlieb also thanks the Harvard Real Estate Academic Initiative and the Institute for Humane Studies. Gyourko thanks the Research Sponsors Program of the Zell/Lurie Real Estate Center at Wharton. For acknowledgments, sources of research support, and disclosure of the authors' material financial relationships, if any, please see http://www.nber.org/chapters/c12622.ack.

1. The monthly index values for the Standard & Poor's/Case–Shiller Index are available at http://www.standardandpoors.com/indices/sp-case-shiller-home-price-indices/en

in or financed housing-related assets, the price decline helped precipitate enormous financial turmoil.

Much academic and policy work has focused on the role of interest rates and other credit market conditions in this great boom-bust cycle. One common explanation for the boom is that easily available credit, perhaps caused by a "global savings glut," led to low real interest rates that substantially boosted housing demand and prices (e.g., Himmelberg, Mayer, and Sinai 2005; Mayer and Sinai 2009; Taylor 2009). Others have suggested that easy credit market terms, including low down payments and high mortgage approval rates, allowed many people to act at once and helped generate large, coordinated swings in housing markets (Khandani, Lo, and Merton 2009). Favilukis, Ludvigson, and Van Nieuwerburgh (2010) have argued that the relaxation of credit constraints combined with a decline in housing transactions costs can account for much of the recent boom. These easy credit terms may themselves have been a reflection of agency problems associated with mortgage securitization (Keys et al. 2009, 2010; Mian and Sufi 2009, 2010; Mian, Sufi, and Trebbi 2008).

If correct, these theories provide economists with the comfortable sense that we understand one of the great asset market gyrations of our time; they would also have potentially important implications for monetary and regulatory policy. However, economists are far from reaching a consensus about the causes of the great housing market fluctuation. Shiller (2005, 2006) long has argued that mass psychology is more important than any of the mechanisms suggested by the research cited earlier. Skeptics of an especially strong role for interest rates include Glaeser and Gyourko (2008) and Greenspan (2010). Bubb and Kaufman (2009) provide a counterpoint to the argument that agency conflicts within mortgage securitization programs contributed to the issuance of significantly riskier loans.

This uncertainty leads us to reevaluate the link between housing markets and credit market conditions, to determine if there are compelling conceptual or empirical reasons to believe that changes in credit conditions can explain the past decade's housing market experience. For credit markets to be able to explain the large recent price movements, there must have been a substantial change in credit market conditions during the periods when housing prices were booming and busting, and credit markets must influence house prices.

Certainly, the real long rate dropped substantially during the housing boom, and the implied impact of interest rates on house prices is quite large according to the static version of Poterba's (1984) asset market approach to house valuation. Between 1996 and 2006, the real ten-year Treasury yield

---

/us/?indexId=spusa-cashpidff--p-us----. We use the seasonally-adjusted monthly figures as of May 2012 for the twenty-city index and the relevant monthly All Urban Workers Consumer Price Index (CPI-U) from the Bureau of Labor Statistics to compute real changes. The FHFA series is downloadable at http://www.fhfa.gov/Default.aspx?Page=87, and we used index numbers as of 2012(1).

fell by 120 basis points, and declined by an even larger 190 basis points from 2000 to 2005, when housing prices boomed the most. Recent research implies a semielasticity of housing prices with respect to real rates of over 20 (Himmelberg, Mayer, and Sinai 2005, hereafter HMS), meaning that a 100 basis point change in real rates should be associated with roughly a 20 percent increase in price.[2] The combination of a nearly 200 basis point decline in real interest rates and semielasticity of 20 suggests that the change in real rates could account for the bulk of the 50 percent-plus boom in prices experienced in the aggregate US data.

But there are two reasons to question this conclusion. First, a more comprehensive user cost model, which we present in section 7.2 of this chapter, predicts much lower price impacts than suggested by those using Poterba's (1984) framework (e.g., HMS 2005). Second, the actual empirical relationship between house prices and interest rates is much weaker than that implied by the standard pricing model used in housing market analysis.

The model analyzed in section 7.2 illustrates various reasons why the impact of interest rates in particular may be much less strong than has been traditionally suggested by the asset market approach to house prices. First, the link between house prices and interest rates can be reduced substantially by weakening the connection between private discount rates and market interest rates. The standard asset market approach presumes that private discount rates and market rates always move together. This relationship means that lower current rates raise the present value of future appreciation, and hence increase current willingness to pay. The sizable impact of current discount rates on the value of future gains leads standard models to predict a large impact of interest rates on prices, especially in high price growth environments. But if private discount rates do not move with market rates, because buyers are credit constrained, then this channel is eliminated, and the connection between interest rates and prices is substantially muted.

The nature of housing supply provides another reason why interest rate effects need not be large, at least in some markets. If supply is highly elastic in the relatively short run, then house prices should be pinned down by fundamental production costs, as suggested by Glaeser, Gyourko, and Saiz (2008). In that case, any demand shifter, whether interest rate-related or not, simply engenders sufficient new production to keep prices from rising above the level where developers can cover all production costs and earn a normal entrepreneurial profit.

While it certainly is possible that buyers are not as forward-looking as our extensions of the Poterba model presume, the essence of any asset market approach to house valuation is that buyers form expectations about future price changes. More generally, we are quite open to the possibility

---

2. The semielasticity is defined as the derivative of the logarithm of housing prices with respect to the real interest rate.

that buyers are far less rational than these models suggest, but there is no consensus yet on the right alternative to rational expectations. Certainly, it is a mistake to think that standard economic reasoning necessarily predicts an extremely strong relationship between interest rates and housing prices.

In Glaeser, Gottlieb, and Gyourko (2010), we also show that when interest rates are volatile and mean revert, expected mobility and the ability to refinance can also reduce the predicted interest rate elasticity of house prices by three-quarters. If buyers in low-interest rate environments anticipate having to sell their homes in periods with higher rates, the link between current rates and house prices is weakened. Another mechanism muting the impact of higher rates is that buyers may anticipate the ability to access lower rates in the future via refinancing. As long as buyers also anticipate that current rates will not remain low (or high) in perpetuity, the interest rate elasticity of house prices will be lower.

As we document in section 7.3, the data largely are consistent with the modest implied semielasticity of house prices with respect to interest rates implied by our expanded model. For example, the simple bivariate relationship between log house prices and the real long rate, as measured by the ten-year Treasury rate corrected for inflation expectations, implies that a 100 basis point fall in rates is associated with barely a 7 percent increase in house prices, as measured by the FHFA index between 1980 and 2008. Larger price effects are found by restricting the sample to years after 1984, but they do not survive inclusion of a simple national time trend. As theory suggests, we find that real rates have their strongest impact when rates are low and in markets where housing supply is relatively inelastic. Our results support HMS's (2005) insight that price impacts should be stronger at lower initial rates of interest, but even when rates change from a low base, a 100 basis point fall in real rates is associated with only an 8 percent rise in real house prices, independent of trend.

While there are good reasons to question the empirical authority of less than thirty years of time series data, these results are quite in line with the predictions of our model. Thus, both theory and data suggest that lower real rates cannot account for more than one-fifth of the boom in house prices.

We then use our estimated coefficients to assess the portion of the price increase that can be explained by interest rate changes over different time periods: (a) the full boom period of 1996 to 2006; (b) the period of largest change in rates; and (c) the initial housing bust of 2006 to 2008. Assuming that the semielasticity of prices with respect to the interest rate is 6.8, the 120 basis point drop in the real long rate between 1996 and 2006 predicts a price increase of about 8 percent, which is less than one-fifth of the actual increase in prices over this period. If we cherry-pick the time period and focus on the years from 2000 to 2005 during which real rates changed most, we find that declining rates can explain almost 45 percent of the 29 percent real price increase that actually occurred during that period. But, this truly is cherry picking, as real rates also fell during the bust since 2006, and obviously cannot account for the fall in prices in that period.

These results should not, however, be interpreted as suggesting that monetary policy was either wise or appropriate. Housing is only part of the economy, and monetary policy should be evaluated in a broader context. Even within the housing sector, it is possible that a sharp rise in the Federal Funds rate could have substantially limited price increases by interacting with buyers' expectations during the boom. But this speculation only highlights the need for more research on the broader issue of buyers' expectations.

In sections 7.4 and 7.5, we investigate two other changes in mortgage credit markets: mortgage approval rates and down payment requirements. One difficulty with assigning much credit, or blame, for the boom to these factors is that the measured values of both variables seem to have remained remarkably constant over the housing cycle. For example, Home Mortgage Disclosure Act (HMDA) data show that approval rates were 78 percent in 2000 and in 2005. The median loan-to-value (LTV) ratio among buyers in our data was no higher in 2005 than in 1999. And, our data indicate that there is nothing new about having at least 10 percent of purchasers buying with little or no equity.[3]

That said, there is good reason to be skeptical about interpreting either data series as signaling little or no change in effective credit conditions. For example, if the quality of loan applicants declined substantially during the boom, then relatively constant approval rates or loan-to-value ratios could, in fact, reflect much easier credit conditions. The number of applications did trend up sharply during the boom, and characteristics of that pool also changed (e.g., the number of single applicants as opposed to two-person applications spiked, minority applicants increased more than white applicants, etc.). We try to infer an underlying approval rate series from the available data in several ways. First, we just assume an upward trend in the number of ill-qualified people applying for mortgages. Second, we assume that a fixed fraction of the growth in the number of accepted mortgage applications reflects growth in approval rates. Both of these approaches suggest that the true underlying approval rate could have increased substantially over the boom.

To estimate the impact that rising approval rates or changing loan-to-value ratios should have had on price, we then need to multiply the growth in approval rates by a coefficient linking approval rates and prices. Our model predicts only modest impacts for each. Down payments should matter when private discount rates and market rates are not identical. After all, if you can borrow and lend at the same rate, you are indifferent between

---

3. The loan-to-value data are from DataQuick, a private data vendor to the real estate industry, and are discussed more fully later in the chapter.

paying all cash or leveraging your home purchase. Even if borrowers are credit constrained and private discount rates are very high (i.e., well above 10 percent), the implied semielasticity of lowering down payments never exceeds two, according to our model. Hence, even very large changes of 10 percentage points in loan-to-value ratios would lead to no more than a 20 percent change in house prices.

The most natural interpretation of a higher approval rate is that it boosts the demand for housing. Thus, if lenders change from approving 50 percent of would-be buyers to approving 60 percent of would-be buyers, that essentially reflects a 20 percent increase in the market demand for housing. Given standard housing supply elasticities of two and demand elasticity estimates of less than one, this would be associated with less than a 7 percent increase in prices. The model's predictions of modest marginal effects on prices are largely confirmed in the data. However, important endogeneity concerns make robust analysis of these variables difficult. Empirically, we do not have strong instruments to deal with the likelihood that bank behavior regarding lending conditions not only could influence the housing market, but could be influenced by it.

Using our theory-inspired elasticity of prices with respect to approval rates, and our implied approval rate series, we estimate that even a large increase in approval rates should have predicted a price increase of no more than 14 percent, which is one-quarter of the increase that America experienced. We can, however, explain the post-2006 decline.

Still, the combination of standard econometric concerns about the robustness of estimated marginal effects on prices with worries about the measurement of these two credit market variables themselves means that no firm conclusions can be reached about the role of these particular aspects of the credit market. We find no evidence that these factors did account for the boom and bust in house prices, but that is very different from convincingly concluding they did not play a more prominent role. More research with different and better data will be needed to pin down their effects empirically.

Similar conclusions hold for loan-to-value ratios. Since they did not increase by much on average over the boom, they could not explain it, even if we had estimated large marginal effects on house prices. Unlike interest rates and like approval rates, loan-to-value ratios move in the right direction to help account for the 2006 to 2008 bust.

In sum, we doubt that any single or simple story can explain the movement in house prices, especially over the past decade. While our analysis indicates that one plausible explanation of that boom, easy credit conditions—and low interest rates especially—cannot account for most of what happened to prices, we are not able to offer a compelling alternative hypothesis. We suspect that Case and Shiller (2003) are correct and the overoptimism illustrated by their surveys of recent home buyers was critical, but this just pushes the puzzle back a step. Why were buyers so overly optimistic about prices? Why did that optimism show up during the early and middle years of the last decade, and why did it show up in some markets but not others? Irrational expectations are surely not exogenous, so what explains them?

7.2   The Theoretical Link between Interest Rates and Housing Prices

In this section, we follow the path laid out by Poterba (1984) and reevaluate the theoretical predictions about the connection between interest rates, housing prices, and other credit market variables. The myriad challenges in empirically estimating the connection between these variables and prices increase the value of simple, robust theoretical predictions about these relationships. We have chosen a simple model, close in spirit to the benchmark user cost model, that treats interest rates and other credit market variables such as approval rates and loan-to-value ratios as exogenous variables that have the potential to influence housing prices and quantities.

We begin by analyzing interest rates, and follow the literature in this part. There is less guidance from the literature on how to approach loan-to-value ratios and approval rates. To model approval rates, we will assume that there is a fraction of the population each period that is kept out of the housing market because they cannot get credit. We assume that an increase in approval rates is a reduction in the share of people who cannot get loans, and that will operate essentially as a shift outward in the demand for housing. Changes in loan-to-value ratios may also operate by enabling formerly credit constrained people to buy homes, but we separate out the approval effect from the loan-to-value effect. In our model, higher loan-to-value ratio will raise housing demand because formerly credit constrained people are now able to take out larger loans.

In the first subsection, we assume that the housing stock is fixed, rents are constant, and prices are determined so that buyers will be financially indifferent between owning and renting. Within that framework, we provide a closed-form solution when interest rates are time invariant, and in Glaeser, Gottlieb, and Gyourko (2010) we show simulated results when interest rates follow a stochastic process. In the second subsection, we endogenize housing supply in the location in question. In that case, home buyers are not only indifferent between buying and renting, but also between living in the impacted community and a reservation locale.

7.2.1   Fixed Housing Supply and Fixed Interest Rates

We focus on the choice of a consumer moving to a particular area in year t, who is deciding whether to buy or rent a home. Equilibrium requires the marginal consumer to be indifferent between the two choices, and if consumers are homogeneous, then everyone will be indifferent between buying and renting.

In this subsection, we treat housing supply and rent as exogenous. We further assume that the home owners and renters are homogenous, risk-neutral, and face random mobility shocks. With probability δ each period, a shock will force the consumer to vacate his or her new home or rental property. This shock might be a taste shock (e.g., a divorce or a marriage) or an economic shock (e.g., a new job opportunity elsewhere).

If the consumer chooses to rent, she pays the rental rate R_{t+j} in each period $t + j \geq t$ as long as she remains in this unit. If she chooses to buy, she is required to make a down payment of θ times the price, which is denoted P_t. Home owners finance the rest of the mortgage, rolling over the debt each period at an interest rate r per period. Thus the nominal debt is kept constant at $(1 - \theta)P_t$ until they move out. We deflate the interest rate cost by $1 - \varphi$, where φ should be thought of as the relevant tax rate, to reflect the deductibility of mortgage payments (all costs should be thought of as being paid in after-tax dollars). Owners must also pay property taxes (also corrected for federal tax deductibility) and maintenance costs in period $t + j$ equal to $\tau(1 + g)^j P_t$, where g is the growth rate of maintenance expenditures.

Our first approach to valuing the home follows the usual method of treating the rental flow as exogenous, and derives a standard pricing formula. We assume that there are no cash constraints, and that renting and owning must have equal expected costs spread over the (uncertain) duration of the individual in the locale.

We consider the discounted flow of costs as of time t. That is, expenditures at time $t + j$ are discounted at an annual rate of ρ. We assume that rental and interest payments come at the end of each period. The expected outlays from renting over the duration of the lease are therefore:

(1)
$$\sum\nolimits_{j=1}^{\infty} \left(\frac{1-\delta}{1+\rho} \right)^j \frac{1}{1-\delta} R_{t+j-1}.$$

Assuming that rents grow at a constant rate g equal to the growth of maintenance costs, so that $R_{t+j} = (1 + g)^j R_t$, then the net present value of expected rental payments is $R_t / (\rho_t + \delta + \delta g - g)$.

In the case of buying with a down payment of θP_t, the expected costs of ownership are the expected value of:

(2)
$$\theta P_t + \sum\nolimits_{j=1}^{\infty} \left(\frac{1-\delta}{1+\rho} \right)^j \frac{1}{1-\delta} \left\{ \begin{array}{l} r(1-\varphi)(1-\theta)P_t + \tau(1+g)^{j-1} P_t \\ -\delta[P_{t+j} - (1-\theta)P_t] \end{array} \right\}.$$

The first term, θP_t, represents the required down payment. To this is added the sum of future expected interest rate payments (equal to $r(1 - \varphi)(1 - \theta)P_t$ in each period) and future maintenance and property tax payments (equal to $\tau(1 + g)^{j-1} P_t$ in each period). Finally, we subtract capital appreciation (equal to $P_{t+j} - (1 - \theta)P_t$ when the sale finally occurs).

The net present value of housing costs to an owner is thus:

$$(2') \qquad P_t \left(\frac{\theta\rho + (1-\theta)(1-\varphi)r - g + \tau + g(1-\theta)(1-\delta)^{\frac{\rho-(1-\varphi)r}{\rho+\delta}}}{\rho + \delta + g\delta - g} \right).$$

If the net present values of renting and owning costs are equal, then the rent-to-price ratio will satisfy:

$$(2'') \qquad \frac{R_t}{P_t} = \theta\rho + (1-\theta)(1-\varphi)r - g + \tau + g(1-\theta)(1-\delta)\frac{\rho-(1-\varphi)r}{\rho+\delta}.$$

This purely static formula is analogous to the one used by Poterba (1984) and HMS (2005). This formula does not allow us to consider elastic housing supply, but it does allow us to explore another critical issue: the connection between the private discount rate and market interest rates.

The asset market approach to housing prices typically assumes that future costs are discounted at the market rate of interest net of taxes. This is natural if individuals are investing funds at this market rate. In that case, an investment of one dollar at time t yields a return of $[1 + (1 - \varphi)r]^j$ at time $t + j$, and the rent-to-price formula simplifies to $R_t/P_t = (1 - \varphi)r - g + \tau$. This formula can also be understood in real terms. If the inflation rate is denoted π, the real growth of the rental rate (and housing prices) is denoted $\hat{g}$ and the real interest rate is denoted $\hat{r}$, then $R_t/P_t = (1 - \varphi)\hat{r} - \hat{g} - \varphi\pi + \tau$ As Poterba (1984) taught us, higher rates of inflation will increase the tax subsidy to housing and raise the level of prices relative to rents. These standard formulae also suggest that down payment requirements have no impact since the market and private rates of interest are identical.

But individuals need not discount the future at the market interest rate. Some home buyers, especially young ones, are likely to have little or no other assets and be credit-constrained in their spending on other goods (Mayer and Engelhardt 1996; Haurin, Wachter, and Hendershott 1995). If so, they may discount future gains at a rate that is both higher than the market rate and potentially varies independently of the market rate. Because investing in owner-occupied homes is challenging for the large institutional investors who probably set prices in liquid securities markets (e.g., government bonds), it seems plausible for the marginal investor to be one of these constrained households, and hence for the pricing kernel to vary between housing and securities markets.

To explore the implications of this segmentation, we let $\rho = \hat{\rho}(\hat{r}) + (1 - \varphi)\pi$, so that the real private discount rate, $\hat{\rho}(r)$, can respond to the market interest, $\hat{r}$, but need not move one-for-one. The rent-to-price ratio is then:

$$\frac{R_t}{P_t} = \hat{\rho}(\hat{r}) - \varphi\pi + (1 - \theta)(1 - \varphi)\hat{r} - \hat{g} + \tau$$
$$+ (\hat{g} + \pi)(1 - \theta)(1 - \delta)\frac{\hat{\rho}(\hat{r}) - (1-\phi)\hat{r}}{\hat{\rho}(\hat{r}) + (1-\phi)\pi + \delta}.$$

If rents (R_t), inflation (π), and the growth rate of rents and maintenance $(\hat{g})$ are held constant, the derivative of the log price with respect to the real market rate of interest $(\hat{r})$ is:

$$(3) \quad \frac{\partial Ln(P_t)}{\partial \hat{r}}$$

$$= -\frac{(1-\varphi)\left[1-\theta-\frac{(\hat{g}+\pi)(1-\theta)(1-\delta)}{\hat{\rho}(\hat{r})+(1-\varphi)\pi+\delta}\right]+\hat{\rho}'(\hat{r})\left[\theta+\frac{(\hat{g}+\pi)(1-\theta)(1-\delta)((1-\varphi)(\hat{r}+\pi)+\delta)}{(\hat{\rho}(\hat{r})+(1-\varphi)\pi+\delta)^2}\right]}{\theta\hat{\rho}(\hat{r})-\varphi\pi+(1-\theta)(1-\varphi)\hat{r}-\hat{g}+\tau+(\hat{g}+\pi)(1-\theta)(1-\delta)\frac{\hat{\rho}(\hat{r})-(1-\varphi)\hat{r}}{\hat{\rho}(\hat{r})+(1-\varphi)\pi+\delta}}.$$

This quantity is decreasing with $\hat{\rho}'(\hat{r})$, so a higher sensitivity of private discount rates to public interest rates makes those interest rates more powerful in determining prices.

Two natural benchmarks for this relationship are when $\hat{\rho}'(\hat{r}) = (1 - \varphi)$, which is the case assumed by the asset market approach (i.e., private home buyers discount at the market rate), and when $\hat{\rho}'(\hat{r}) = 0$, where discounting depends purely on private preferences and is independent of real market rates. We calibrate the semielasticity under these two assumptions, shown in table 7.1. We first assume that the market rate and the private discount rate are the same, so that $\hat{\rho}(\hat{r}) = (1 - \varphi)\hat{r}$; and then in column (2), we assume that these variables are decoupled. Within each column, we compute the semielasticity for a range of interest rates.

For our benchmark semielasticities, shown in column (1), we assume that $\hat{g} = 0.01$, which corresponds to an average real growth rate of housing prices of 1 percent. We let $\pi = 0.032$, which corresponds to the average inflation rate over the past quarter century. We let the real interest rate range from 3 percent ($\hat{r} = 0.03$), which corresponds to a nominal rate of 7.2 percent, to 7 percent ($\hat{r} = 0.07$). The marginal tax rate is 25 percent ($\varphi = 0.25$). We assume a 20 percent down payment requirement ($\theta = 0.2$). In line with previous work in this area, we calibrate noninterest costs of home ownership to be 3.5 percent per year ($\tau = 0.035$; Poterba and Sinai 2008). Individuals have a 6 percent chance of moving each year ($\delta = 0.06$), which is substantially lower than the typical US rate of changing residences (which is 15.5 percent) to reflect home owners' lower mobility.[4] Perhaps most importantly, this calculation assumes that $\hat{\rho}(\hat{r}) = (1 - \varphi)\hat{r} = 0.03$, so the private discount rate equals the marginal rate at the point where we are taking a derivative. This assumption, which we drop beginning in column (3), allows us to focus on the fact that the private rate may not move with the market rate, rather than the possibility that the private rate is substantially different from the market rate.[5]

---

4. Ferreira, Gyourko, and Tracy (2010) report a two-year mobility rate for home owners of 12 percent.
5. Technically, we assume that the private rate is epsilon larger than the market rate, so that market rate remains slightly below the private discount rate when the derivative is taken.

Table 7.1   **Interest rate semielasticities with inelastic housing supply**

	(1)	(2)	(3)	(4)	(5)	(6)
Discount rate linked?	Yes	Yes	No	No	No	No
Mobility (δ)	6%	6%	6%	6%	0%	6%
Down (θ)	20%	20%	20%	2%	20%	20%
Growth ($\hat{g}$)	1%	2%	1%	1%	1%	2%
Real interest rate						
$\hat{r} = 0.03$	–18.99	–25.42	–8.05	–10.70	–4.70	–8.62
$\hat{r} = 0.04$	–15.96	–20.27	–7.45	–9.66	–4.49	–7.93
$\hat{r} = 0.05$	–13.76	–16.85	–6.93	–8.81	–4.29	–7.35
$\hat{r} = 0.06$	–12.10	–14.42	–6.48	–8.10	–4.12	–6.85
$\hat{r} = 0.07$	–10.79	–12.61	–6.09	–7.49	–3.95	–6.41

Notes: This table reports calculated values of the semielasticity of house prices with respect to interest rates under various parameter assumptions. In the baseline scenario, shown in column (1), annual growth of rents and costs is $\hat{g} = 0.01$, annual inflation is $\pi = 0.032$, the marginal tax rate is $\varphi = 0.25$, the down payment is $\theta = 0.2$ of the purchase price, noninterest costs of homeownership are $\tau = 0.035$, and annual mobility is $\delta = 0.06$. When discount rates are linked to interest rates, $\hat{\rho}(\hat{r}) = (1 - \varphi)\hat{r}$, and $\hat{\rho}(\hat{r}) = 0.055$ otherwise. The semielasticity is evaluated at various initial real interest rates $\hat{r}$.

When the real interest rate is 0.03 (and hence the real private discount rate is 0.0225), the semielasticity is –19, as reported in column (1). This represents a very high degree of price responsiveness, comparable to that discussed by HMS (2005). The magnitude drops to 16 if the real interest rate is 0.04, which is reported in the next row of column (1). As the real rate rises to 0.07, the elasticity drops down to about 11, but these results suggest a large impact of interest rates on prices unless real rates themselves are quite high.

The second column of table 7.1 increases the real growth rate of fundamental values and ownership costs from $\hat{g} = 0.01$ to $\hat{g} = 0.02$. This increases interest rate responsiveness by changing the potential for capital gains should the family move.

To begin exploring the impact of changing assumptions about the discount rate, we can simplify equation (3) under the baseline parameterization. With these values, at a real interest rate of $\hat{r} = 0.03$, the semielasticity can be written as $-(\partial Log(P_t))/\partial \hat{r} = 8.3 + 10.2\hat{\rho}'(\hat{r})$. When $\hat{\rho}'(\hat{r}) = 1 - \varphi$, the case shown in column (1), the semielasticity is –16. When discount rates are delinked from interest rates, so $\hat{\rho}'(\hat{r}) = 0$, the semielasticity falls to –8.3. The connection between $\hat{\rho}$ and $\hat{r}$ nearly doubles the predicted relationship between prices and interest rates. Lower levels of $\hat{r}$ or higher levels of $\hat{g}$ will raise the predicted relationship, but the sensitivity to $\hat{\rho}'(\hat{r})$ remains. For instance, if $\hat{g} = 0.02$, then $-(\partial Log(P_t))/\partial \hat{r} = 9.3 + 14.7\hat{\rho}'(\hat{r})$, in which case the semielasticity ranges from 9.3 to 20.3.

Columns (3) through (6) of table 7.1 report results when interest rates and discount rates are no longer tied together. In this case, we assume that the discount rate is $\hat{\rho}(\hat{r}) = 0.055$. We chose this value so that $\hat{\rho} > (1 - \varphi)\hat{r}$ for all of our values of $\hat{r}$. It is easy for us to imagine that individuals are more impatient than the market, but considerably harder to believe that they are more patient, since this would presumably lead them to invest up to the point where their marginal rate of substitutions between periods equals the market interest rate.

As column (3) demonstrates, eliminating the discount rate–interest rate connection cuts the semielasticity from 19 to 8 when $\hat{r} = 0.03$ and from 8 to 6 when $\hat{r} = 0.07$. Not only does the level of the semielasticity fall dramatically, but so does its sensitivity to $\hat{r}$. The impact of down payment requirements under this new assumption can be seen by comparing column (3) to column (4). In column (4), we reduce the down payment from $\theta = 0.2$ to $\theta = 0.02$, and find significantly higher elasticities at the lower value. They now range from 7.5 when $\hat{r} = 0.07$ to 10.7 when $\hat{r} = 0.03$. Higher rates now affect the buyers' choice set, making them more sensitive to these costs.

The fifth column eliminates mobility ($\delta = 0$) and shows substantially lower interest rate elasticities of around 4.[6] This result obtains because mobility reduces the amount of time that borrowers expect to pay the interest rate, and thereby increases the effective discount rates. This can be seen most clearly in the price-rent formula given in equation (2″), where mobility δ is added to the discount rate ρ. The final column again increases the real growth rate from $\hat{g} = 0.01$ to $\hat{g} = 0.02$. As in the move from column (1) to column (2), this change increases interest rate sensitivity, but the effect here is smaller.

There are two reasons why the connection between market and private discount rates can matter so much. First, when private discount rates and market interest rates move together as in the standard asset market approach, higher market rates make future appreciation less valuable to a buyer, dampening housing demand. Similarly, lower rates increase the value of future price growth, raising demand and increasing the sensitivity of house prices to interest rates. However, if private discount rates do not move with market rates, then future price gains no longer become more valuable as market rates fall, and less valuable as rates rise. The second reason for the difference comes from the opportunity cost of the down payment. In the asset market approach, higher interest rates increase the opportunity cost of the down payment, but with a private discount rate, that is no longer the case.

While the link between discount rates and interest rates has a powerful impact on semielasticities, one further force that we do not investigate here is the introduction of stochastic interest rates. In Glaeser, Gottlieb, and Gyourko (2010), we show that when interest rates are volatile and mean revert, the current rate becomes dramatically less important for buyers than

---

6. In Glaeser, Gottlieb, and Gyourko (2010) we show that the effect of mobility is reversed when interest rates are mean-reverting. In that case, mobility reduces interest rate responsiveness because home owners anticipate having to sell when interest rates have returned back toward an average level.

it is in the present model. This occurs for two reasons. Most directly, buyers who can refinance their mortgages need not pay the current interest rate indefinitely. Since the current rate no longer determines the cost of all future interest payments, it has less of an impact on buyers' demand. Even more significantly, volatile interest rates imply volatile house prices. If buyers in low interest rate environments anticipate having to sell their homes subsequently, and rates may have changed, they rationally expect to receive capital gains or losses from this sale. This expected reversion of prices further mutes the impact of current rates on buyers' willingness to purchase housing. The impact of interest rate volatility on the semielasticity with respect to current rates increases with home owners' mobility and with the ease of mortgage refinancing.

While this model aims to increase the realism of the user cost analysis, there are other channels by which credit costs could have driven price growth. We have modeled credit constraints as a disconnect between private and market discount rates, but looser borrowing constraints might foster a credit-driven demand from absentee investors. In addition, families' expectations of future price growth could change in the face of laxer credit conditions. Changing credit availability could also affect an area's composition, leading to multiplier effects through other buyers' purchase or default decisions. Finally, the static model we employ here does not permit us to examine the effects of interest rate changes on the numerous risk premia embodied in mortgages, or conversely of these premia on rates (Campbell and Cocco 2011). The time-varying rates we examine in Glaeser, Gottlieb, and Gyourko (2010) can be viewed as one reduced-form approach to modeling this risk.

We next enrich the model by incorporating explicit changes in down payment requirements and mortgage denials.

7.2.2   The Impact of Down Payment Requirements on Prices

Cheap credit could potentially influence housing prices through high loan-to-value ratios, easy approval rates, and a whole range of phenomenon often associated with, but not limited to, subprime lending (Coleman, LaCour-Little, and Vandell 2008). We now turn to the effect of down payment requirements and approval rates.

In our core model, there is a fixed supply of housing and essentially an infinite supply of homogenous buyers, which implies that there is no way to generate sensible predictions about approval rates. Under these model assumptions, rejecting 10 or 50 percent of prospective buyers will make no difference to price. Hence, we will consider the impact of approval rates only in the next section when we allow heterogeneity of buyers, which generates a downward sloping demand for housing, and an elastic housing supply.

The basic model can, however, generate implications about the impact of changes in down payment effects. In the case of a constant interest rate, differentiating the log of house price with respect to θ, the down payment level, yields:

$$(4) \quad \frac{\partial Ln(P_t)}{\partial \theta}$$

$$= -\frac{(\hat{\rho}(\hat{r})-(1-\varphi)\hat{r})\left(1-\frac{(\hat{g}+\pi)(1-\delta)}{\hat{\rho}(\hat{r})+(1-\varphi)\pi+\delta}\right)}{\theta\hat{\rho}(\hat{r})-\varphi\pi+(1-\theta)(1-\varphi)\hat{r}-\hat{g}+\tau+(\hat{g}+\pi)(1-\theta)(1-\delta)\frac{\hat{\rho}(\hat{r})-(1-\varphi)\hat{r}}{\hat{\rho}(\hat{r})+(1-\varphi)\pi+\delta}}.$$

This equals zero when individuals discount at the market rate; that is, $\hat{\rho}(\hat{r}) = (1 - \varphi)\hat{r}$. In other words, in the classic asset market approach to housing prices, down payment levels should not matter since home buyers discount at the market rate and are indifferent between paying cash and borrowing. An easier ability to borrow will not matter if people are not credit constrained.

Down payment levels do, however, start to matter if $\hat{\rho}(\hat{r}) > (1 - \varphi)\hat{r}$, meaning that the buyer would like to borrow more at the market rate.[7] In a sense, the connection between down payment requirements and prices therefore becomes something of a test of whether individuals are credit constrained.

For example, table 7.2 shows the implied semielasticity if $\hat{g} = 0.01$, $\pi = 0.032$, $\hat{r} = 0.04$, $\delta = 0.06$, $\varphi = 0.25$, and $\tau = 0.035$, and we vary the value of both θ and $\hat{\rho}$. If the private real discount rate is 0.09 or less (columns [1] and [2]), the implied elasticity is less than 0.77 even at very low down payments of 1 percent. If we choose very high real private discount rates of 0.15 or above (columns [3] and [4]), the implied semielasticity can climb to 2 if down payment requirements are very low. If the private discount rate is around 0.2, a 5 percentage point change in the down payment requirement could create a price increase of as much as 10 percent. Given standard economists' beliefs about discount rates, we would expect to find a semielasticity between 0.4 and 0.8. These effects do not change significantly when we allow for time-varying interest rates, and are not particularly sensitive to our other parameter values.

It is noteworthy that our model assumes that buyers are homogenous, so that the characteristics of the marginal buyers are unchanged when the down payment rate varies. If lower down payments allow less patient (or more overly optimistic) people to borrow, the impact on prices could be larger.

7.2.3   Endogenous Housing Supply

We now expand the model to incorporate worker heterogeneity and housing supply. In order for this expanded model to be tractable, we fix interest rates and eliminate mobility, so individuals live in their new homes permanently. We assume that there is a distribution of potential buyers, some of whom value the city more than others. In this case, we focus on overall housing demand instead of the own-rent arbitrage relationship. Ensuring

---

7. This requires that $\hat{\rho}(\hat{r}) + (\delta - \varphi)\pi + \delta > \hat{g}(1 - \delta)$, which we assume to hold.

Table 7.2   **Price responsiveness to down payment requirements for varying private discount rates and down payment requirements**

	$\hat{\rho} = 0.06$	$\hat{\rho} = 0.09$	$\hat{\rho} = 0.15$	$\hat{\rho} = 0.20$
$\theta = 0.2$	0.37	0.67	1.15	1.47
$\theta = 0.1$	0.38	0.72	1.3	1.73
$\theta = 0.05$	0.39	0.75	1.40	1.90
$\theta = 0.01$	0.40	0.77	1.48	2.05

Notes: This table reports various values of the semielasticity of house prices with respect to down payment requirements, calculated using equation (4) in the text.

that workers are on the margin between owning and renting would not pin down the number of people in the area, which is needed to determine the housing demand. Thus we focus on the decision of whether to buy in the community or not, and do not focus on the unit's capital structure. In this framework, the net discounted cost of buying a house equals $(\theta + ((1 - \theta)(1 - \varphi)r)/\rho + \tau/(\rho - g))P_t$, which reduces to $(1 + \tau/(\rho - g))P_t$ if $(1 - \varphi)r = \rho$.

Each year, potential buyer i receives a nominal dollar-denominated flow of utility from living in the house of $A_t(i) = (1 + g)^t A(i)$, where $A(i)$ is the person-specific taste for the area. $A(i)$ has a Pareto distribution with parameter $1/\gamma$, so there are $KA^{-1/\gamma}$ buyers at time t with valuations $A(i)$ that are greater than A. We also assume that only an independently distributed fraction α of buyers get approved for mortgages. As a result, if there are N_t buyers at time t, then there will be $(\alpha K)^\gamma N_t^{-\gamma}$ approved buyers with values of $A(i)$ greater than A. Since the marginal buyer at time t compares the discounted future value of housing flow utility to the present-value cost of buying, housing demand satisfies:

$$(5) \qquad \frac{(1+g)^t}{\rho - g}(\alpha K)^\gamma N_t^{-\gamma} = \left(\theta + \frac{(1-\theta)(1-\varphi)r}{\rho} + \frac{\tau}{\rho - g}\right)P_t.$$

We can think of this as demand for the housing in a particular city, holding the options available elsewhere fixed. Alternatively, the value $A(i)$ can reflect the heterogeneous benefits from owning a home, if the utility from renting is held constant, or in principle, it might even reflect the benefits of moving into a housing unit at all, relative to cohabitating with a parent or friend.

Our second key assumption is that I_t new homes are built each period and that the price of supplying new homes is $(1 + g)^t c I_t^\beta$ (for $I_t \geq 1$). At each point in time, the number of homes being sold must equal N_t, so the housing supply equation is: $(1 + g)^t c N_t^\beta = P_t$. The supply elasticity linking the number of homes supplied (I_t) to the price, $(\partial Log(I_t))/(\partial Log(P_t))$, which we denote ε_P^D, equals $1/\beta$. The demand elasticity linking the number of buyers to the price, $-(\partial Log(N_t))/(\partial Log(P_t))$, which we denote ε_P^D, will equal $1/\gamma$.

Together, housing supply and demand yield:

(6) $$N_t = \left(\frac{(\alpha K)^\gamma}{c(\theta\rho + (1-\theta)(1-\varphi)r - g\theta - g^{\frac{(1-\theta)(1-\varphi)r}{\rho}} + \tau)} \right), \text{ and}$$

(7) $$P_t = \frac{(1+g)^t (\alpha^\beta K^\beta c)^{\gamma/(\beta+\gamma)}}{\left(\theta\hat{\rho}(\hat{r}) + (1-\theta)(1-\varphi)\hat{r} - \varphi\pi - \hat{g} + \tau - (\hat{g}+\pi)(1-\theta)\frac{(1-\phi)\hat{r} - \hat{\rho}(\hat{r})}{\hat{\rho}(\hat{r}) + \pi(1-\varphi)} \right)^{\beta/(\beta+\gamma)}}.$$

These calculations somewhat alter the semielasticity of prices with respect to the interest rate, which now equals:

(8) $$\frac{\partial Ln(P_t)}{\partial \hat{r}}$$

$$= -\frac{\varepsilon_P^D}{\varepsilon_P^D + \varepsilon_P^S} \frac{\theta\hat{\rho}'(\hat{r}) + (1-\theta)(1-\varphi) - (\hat{g}+\pi)(1-\theta)(1-\varphi)\frac{\hat{\rho}(\hat{r})+\pi(1-\varphi))-\hat{\rho}'(\hat{r})(\hat{r}+\pi)}{(\hat{\rho}(\hat{r})+\pi(1-\varphi))^2}}{\theta\hat{\rho}(\hat{r}) + (1-\theta)(1-\varphi)\hat{r} - \varphi\pi - \hat{g} + \tau - (\hat{g}+\pi)(1-\theta)\frac{(1-\varphi)\hat{r}-\hat{\rho}(\hat{r})}{\hat{\rho}(\hat{r})+\pi(1-\varphi)}}.$$

If $\hat{g} = 0.01$, $\pi = 0.032$, $\hat{r} = 0.04$, $\theta = 0.2$, $\tau = 0.035$, $\varphi = 0.25$, and $\hat{\rho}(\hat{r}) = 0.03$, then this expression becomes $-\varepsilon_P^D/(\varepsilon_P^D + \varepsilon_P^S)(17.5\hat{\rho}'(\hat{r}) + 2.8)$, which ranges from $-2.8\varepsilon_P^D/(\varepsilon_P^D + \varepsilon_P^S)$ when $\hat{\rho}'(\hat{r}) = 0$ to $-16\varepsilon_P^D/(\varepsilon_P^D + \varepsilon_P^S)$ when $\hat{\rho}'(\hat{r}) = 1 - \varphi$. Personal discounting reduces interest rate sensitivity, but so does increasing supply elasticity. If ε_P^S goes to zero when housing supply is perfectly inelastic, then the semielasticity goes to $-17.5\hat{\rho}'(\hat{r}) - 2.8$, while the semielasticity goes to zero when housing supply is perfectly elastic.

What is a reasonable value of $\varepsilon_P^D/(\varepsilon_P^D + \varepsilon_P^S)$? Saiz (2008) reports supply elasticities ranging from as low as 0.6 to as high as 5 across different markets; Topel and Rosen (1988) found a national supply elasticity of 2, and we use that as our core estimate.

The value of ε_P^D is less clear since demand elasticities are typically estimated for the intensive margin (the amount of housing services each person consumes) rather than the extensive margin (the number of people in each city). The literature suggests the former elasticities are around 0.7 (Polinsky and Ellwood 1979). Saiz (2003) provides an alternative estimate. He found that a 9 percent increase in population, due to the plausibly exogenous Mariel boatlift, is associated with an 8 to 11 percent increase in rents in the short run.[8] This shock would seem to be equivalent to an increase in the baseline population in our model, perhaps an increase in K, with fixed supply, so his estimates seem to imply that γ is approximately one (we will use that value, but its imprecision for our purpose is acknowledged).[9]

If, for lack of a better alternative, we can take 1 as a measure of ε_P^D and 2 as our measure of ε_P^S, then moving from a model with inelastic housing supply to elastic housing supply causes the interest rate–price relationship to fall

8. Saiz (2007) finds similar effects looking at increases in immigration throughout the country.
9. Saiz's experiment looks at a shock to the entire rental population, not to the flow of new buyers. We think that this suggests that his estimate is likely to be higher relative to a shock to the flow created by an increase in the approval rate, but he is looking at renters who may be somewhat more flexible in their preferences.

Table 7.3   **Interest rate semielasticities with elastic housing supply**

	(1)	(2)	(3)	(4)	(5)	(6)
Supply elasticity (ε_P^S)	0.5	0.5	2	2	4	4
Discount rate linked?	Yes	No	Yes	No	Yes	No
Mobility (δ)	6%	6%	6%	6%	6%	6%
Down (θ)	20%	20%	20%	20%	20%	20%
Growth ($\hat{g}$)	1%	1%	1%	1%	1%	1%
Real interest rate						
$\hat{r} = 0.03$	−12.66	−3.13	−6.33	−1.57	−3.80	−0.94
$\hat{r} = 0.04$	−10.64	−2.99	−5.32	−1.50	−3.19	−0.90
$\hat{r} = 0.05$	−9.17	−2.86	−4.59	−1.43	−2.75	−0.86
$\hat{r} = 0.06$	−8.06	−2.74	−4.03	−1.37	−2.42	−0.82
$\hat{r} = 0.07$	−7.19	−2.64	−3.60	−1.32	−2.16	−0.79

Notes: This table reports calculated values of the semielasticity of house prices with respect to interest rates under various parameter assumptions. In the baseline scenario, shown in column (1), annual growth of rents and costs is $\hat{g} = 0.01$, annual inflation is $\pi = 0.032$, the marginal tax rate is $\varphi = 0.25$, the down payment is $\theta = 0.2$ of the purchase price, noninterest costs of homeownership are $\tau = 0.035$, and annual mobility is $\delta = 0.06$. When discount rates are linked to interest rates, $\hat{\rho}(\hat{r}) = (1 - \varphi)\hat{r}$, and $\hat{\rho}(\hat{r}) = 0.055$ otherwise. The semielasticity is evaluated at various initial real interest rates $\hat{r}$.

by two-thirds. Table 7.3 shows this effect for various values of the supply elasticity. Columns (1) and (2) show the interest rate semielasticity when ε_P^S = 0.5, columns (3) and (4) increase it to $\varepsilon_P^S = 2$, and columns (5) and (6) show results with $\varepsilon_P^S = 4$. Both when discount rates are linked to interest rates, as in the traditional model, and when they are separated, supply responses dramatically reduce the interest rate semielasticities. Supply elasticity thus provides us with yet another reason why the impact of interest rates on prices will be lower than in the canonical model.

7.2.4   The Price Impact of Approval Rates

This framework also enables us to consider more seriously the impact of higher approval rates, which in the model means a higher value of α. If lower down payment requirements operate by enabling credit constrained people to borrow more, then the elasticity of prices with respect to approval rates will equal $1/(\varepsilon_P^D + \varepsilon_P^S)$. The elasticity of units sold with respect to approval rates equals $\varepsilon_P^S/(\varepsilon_P^D + \varepsilon_P^S)$. If, for example, the approval rate across the entire population increased by 60 percent to 80 percent, the number of units sold would increase by 18 percent and prices would rise by 9 percent. The largest price effect would occur if ε_P^D equals zero, and in that case, the impact on prices of approving an extra 20 percent of the population for mortgages would be 15 percent. In that case, the quantity increase would be exactly one-third.

If cheap credit acted primarily by enabling more people to buy homes, then theory and past work on housing gives us some idea of the kind of effect that such a shock to demand would be expected to have. Even a very large increase in approval rates, of 20 percentage points, would be predicted—by standard housing models—to have a relatively modest impact on long-run price, as long as supply remained modestly elastic. We will return to this in the impact section later.

A key assumption needed for these results is that increasing the approval rates essentially just shifts out the demand curve. It is certainly conceivable that higher approval rates particularly impact buyers with disproportionately high or low levels of demand. For example, if the poor are particularly likely to be on the approval margin, and if the poor have relatively less willingness to pay for housing, then the impact of higher approval rates would be lower than the effects discussed here. If the poor had high private discount rates and, hence, a lower willingness to pay for a house, then this would also make approval rates matter less than a standard shift out in the demand curve. Conversely, if higher approval rates disproportionately impact buyers with high demand, then the effect of approval rates can indeed be higher. As such, this becomes an empirical matter, but we do believe that theory suggests an approval rate price impact that is close to $1/(3 \times \text{Approval Rate})$.

7.3   Empirical Analysis of Interest Rates and Housing Prices

We begin the empirical section by examining the macroeconomic connection between interest rates and housing prices. We supplement this by looking at the connection between interest rates and construction activity. We also examine whether interest rate shocks have a larger impact in areas where housing supply is less elastic or where exogenous variables such as January temperature have long predicted positive housing price trends.

7.3.1   National Time Series Data

Real house prices are measured using the Federal Housing Finance Agency (FHFA) price index, deflated using the full Consumer Price Index (CPI-U, for all urban workers). Like the S&P/Case–Shiller price indices, the FHFA series attempts to correct for the changing quality of houses being sold at any point in time by estimating price changes with repeat sales.[10] The FHFA series begins in 1975, but we use data beginning in 1980 because the vast majority of metropolitan areas are covered on a consistent basis from that year onward. We use the FHFA instead of the S&P/Case–Shiller series (which includes home sales financed using nonconventional loans), because the Case–Shiller data begin in 1987 and include only twenty metropolitan areas. Table 7.4 presents the summary statistics from this data, with table 7.5

10. The FHFA index supplements the repeat sales data with appraisal data, but there is also a purchase-only index (available for a shorter time window beginning in 1991 and a smaller number of areas). We have duplicated our results with that shorter time series and there is little change in the findings.

Table 7.4   Time-series summary statistics

Variable	Years	Minimum	25th percentile	Median	75th percentile	Maximum	Mean	Standard deviation
Log single-family permits	29	13.2	13.7	13.8	14.01	14.3	13.8	0.28
Log real FHFA house prices	29	5.29	5.37	5.39	5.53	5.79	5.46	0.15
Real 10-year rate	29	0.011	0.024	0.035	0.0398	0.075	0.035	0.016
First difference of real 10-year rate	29	−0.017	−0.0052	−0.00074	−0.0038	−0.036	−0.000038	0.011
Romer and Romer shock	29	−0.015	−0.0026	0.0031	0.00603	0.019	0.00196	0.0075

Table 7.5   **MSA summary statistics**

Variable	Observations	Minimum	25th percentile	Median	75th percentile	Maximum	Mean	Standard deviation
Log MSA house prices	5,646	4.36	4.75	4.81	4.92	5.73	4.86	0.19
Raw MSA approval rates	5,646	0.0015	0.042	0.058	0.092	0.49	0.069	0.037
Mean LTV	924	0.17	0.69	0.74	0.79	0.95	0.73	0.096
Mean January temperature	298	5.9	24.7	32.1	44.6	71.4	34.7	12.9
Branching restrictiveness	298	0	1	3	3	4	2.2	1.4
Foreclosure procedure length	298	53	101	142	207	342	158.8	78.3
Land-use regulation	298	−1.89	−0.75	−0.13	0.68	5.01	0.051	0.99
Saiz housing supply elasticity	103	0.57	0.92	1.31	2.01	5.16	1.55	0.85

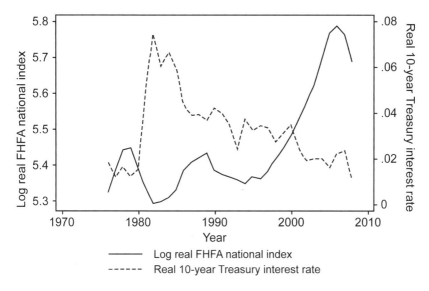

Fig. 7.1   Prices and interest rates
Sources: Federal Housing Finance Agency, Federal Reserve.

providing the analogous information on the other variables used in this section.

We use annual price data, even though higher frequency FHFA data is available, because the problems of intertemporal correlation of the error terms are reduced by using annual, rather than higher frequency data. Given the slow movement of housing prices, we believe that little is lost by focusing on year-to-year changes.

Real interest rates are constructed following the strategy outlined in HMS (2005). That is, we start with the ten-year Treasury bond rate and then correct for inflation with the Livingston Survey of inflation expectations. A long rate is used to approximate the duration of most mortgages. The Treasury rate rather than the actual mortgage rate is employed to reduce the feedback between events in the housing market and market rates. However, we have used alternative interest rates measures and found quite similar results.[11]

Figure 7.1 plots real interest rates and real housing prices over our full sample period from 1980 to 2008. The strong negative trend in real interest

11. For example, Shiller (2005, 2006) uses a different and simpler real rate that is created by subtracting the actual inflation rate from the nominal Treasury yield. His methodology results in somewhat weaker correlations of house prices with interest rates than we report later. Hence, our method (really HMS's [2005] method) certainly is not biasing the results downward. Experimentation with other interest measures (e.g., based on longer or shorter rates and fixed inflation expectations) do not change the results in an economically meaningful way. In addition, experimentation with different lag structures on rates found that the contemporaneous relationship between rates and prices is the strongest.

rates is clear, as real rates fall sharply from a peak of 7.5 percent in 1982 to 3.7 percent in 1989, before continuing downward at a more moderate pace. Ultimately, real ten-year rates hit a low of 1.6 percent in 2005 before rising slightly and then declining to 1.1 percent in 2008 as the Great Recession ensued. It is noteworthy that real house prices are flat over a significant part of this sample period, and the real FHFA index has virtually identical values in 1980 and 1997. Real house prices then appreciated by 49 percent from 1997 to the FHFA index peak in 2006, a period over which long real rates continued to fall.

Looking solely at this later time period, housing prices and interest rates seem to move in strongly opposite directions. This has lent support to some authors' claims of a strong connection between interest rates and housing prices (HMS 2005; Taylor 2009). However, over our nearly three decade sample period, the negative connection between interest rates and housing prices is much weaker. While real rates fell by 50 percent between 1982 and 1989, real house prices increased by only 15 percent. In some years, such as 1993, real rates dropped drastically and real house price growth was flat. Real house prices actually fell the following year, so this is not an issue of a lagged effect. Prior to the most recent housing boom, even extreme changes in real rates had only a modest impact on prices.

Table 7.6 more formally documents this relationship by reporting the results of a series of regressions of the log FHFA price index on real ten-year interest rates and other covariates. To correct for serial correlation and heteroskedasticity, we employ the standard Newey and West (1987) correction. The simplest bivariate regression of log real prices on real rates suggests that a 100 basis point fall in real rates is associated with a 0.0682 log point increase in house values (column [1]).[12] This coefficient is closely in line with the relatively low semielasticities reported for calculations with elastic housing supply or with discount rates separated from interest rates. This finding suggests that a 1-standard deviation fall in real interest rates (1.57 percentage points in our time period, as reported in table 7.4) is unlikely to increase housing prices by much more than 10 percent.

Of course, one should be suspicious that this univariate relationship is biased because of reverse causality (e.g., lower housing prices causing a reduction in real rates) or because other variables may be correlated, or even cause, movements in both variables. For example, higher levels of economic productivity might push interest rates up and increase the demand for housing. If we include a simple time trend to correct for any bias from omitted variables that are trending in one direction and that are correlated with both interest rates and prices, we find that a 100 basis point decline in long

12. The model suggests that inflation will also impact prices, and we have also estimated specifications including the inflation rate, which did little but increase our standard errors. Given that actual inflation includes housing-related variables, this endogeneity led us to prefer the specifications without inflation.

Table 7.6   Semielasticity of national house prices

Dependent variable	OLS log price (1)	OLS log price (2)	OLS log price (3)	OLS log price (4)	OLS price gr. (5)	OLS log price (6)	OLS log price (7)	OLS price gr. (8)
Real 10-year rate	-6.82*** (1.85)	-1.82 (1.16)	-10.5*** (2.58)	-1.16 (3.17)				
Change in real 10-year rate					-1.44** (0.53)			
Real 10-year rate, < 3.45%						-13.3*** (3.73)	-8.00*** (1.98)	
Real 10-year rate, > 3.45%						-3.05*** (0.85)	1.48 (1.56)	
Linear time trend		0.012*** (0.0036)		0.016 (0.0068)			0.012*** (0.0027)	
Romer and Romer shock								0.36 (1.37)
Constant	5.70*** (0.088)	5.47*** (0.055)	5.82*** (0.096)	5.42*** (0.14)	0.0081 (0.0090)	5.86*** (0.13)	5.63*** (0.052)	0.0075 (0.011)
Observations	29	29	24	24	29	29	29	29
R^2	0.50	0.72	0.57	0.71	0.16	0.61	0.81	0.0048
Years	1980–2008	1980–2008	1985–2008	1985–2008	1980–2008	1980–2008	1980–2008	1980–2008

Notes: The dependent variable is log average FHFA price index for elastic or inelastic cities, or one-year log price growth. Standard errors, in parentheses, are adjusted for heteroskedasticity and autocorrelation using the Newey–West method with 2 lags.

***Significant at the 1 percent level.

**Significant at the 5 percent level.

*Significant at the 10 percent level.

real rates now is associated with only a 1.82 percent increase in real house prices (table 7.6, column [2]). This effect is not significantly different from zero at standard confidence levels, but the standard error of the estimate is sufficiently tight to rule out anything more than a 4 percent impact on real prices from a 100 basis point decline in real rates, controlling for trend.[13]

These results are not materially affected even if the sample period is restricted to more recent years. That could be appropriate if one thought, for instance, that the early 1980s were sufficiently unusual, perhaps because of the volatility and possible mismeasurement of inflation expectations during those years.[14] Column (3) of table 7.6 reports the bivariate relationship between house prices and interest rates when the sample period is restricted to 1985 to 2008. The estimated impact of a 100 basis point fall in real rates increases to 0.105 log points. However, this effect also is very sensitive to inclusion of a simple time trend. Column (4) shows that the estimated coefficient drops to −1.16 when the trend in real prices is controlled for.

These regressions effectively have presumed that house prices are stationary. If house prices have a unit root, our previous estimates would be invalid. To address this possibility, in column (5) we regress changes in the logarithm of real housing prices on changes in the real interest rate. In this case, the estimated coefficient is −1.44, which is both small and fairly precisely estimated (standard error equal to 0.53). Hence, this specification also provides no support for a large impact of interest rates on house prices.

Poterba (1984), HMS (2005), and our model all suggest that changes in rates should have a larger impact on prices when rates themselves are lower. To test for this possibility, we estimate a piecewise linear spline function, with a break at the sample real interest rate median of 3.45 percent. Column (6)'s result shows that a 100 basis point decline in real interest rates is associated with a significantly higher 13.3 percent increase in real house prices when that change occurs within a low rate environment. However, this effect also is sensitive to including a time trend, as our seventh regression shows: detrended prices rise by only 8 percent when rates fall by 100 basis points from an already low level (i.e., from somewhere between 1.1 percent

13. Experimentation with other time varying controls such as real per capita GDP found that they generally lowered the estimated interest rate elasticity. Following Favilukis et al., chapter 6 in this volume, we also added measures of lending standards from Federal Reserve Bank's Senior Loan Officer Opinion Survey on Bank Lending Practices (SLOOS), which did not noticeably affect the interest rate estimates for the sample period for which the SLOOS data are available. Of course, there is the fear that these variables also are endogenous with respect to housing prices. Because adding these controls only reinforces the empirical point that the measured relationship between housing prices and interest rates is modest, we report only univariate and detrended results.

14. The median Livingston Survey inflation forecasts drop sharply from 9.9 percent to 5.8 percent between 1980 and 1984, which is the largest change (by far) over any five-year period in our sample.

and 3.45 percent).[15] Again, this estimate is well in line with our calculations when assuming elastic housing supply or separate interest rates and discount rates. The coefficient when rates are high is positive and indistinguishable from zero. An 8 percent price impact of a 100 basis point change in real rates certainly is not negligible, but as we shall see, it is far too small to explain much of the recent boom.

One problem throughout all of these estimates is that interest rates may themselves be endogenous to house prices. For example, heavy demand for housing itself could push interest rates up. A crash in housing prices, like that experienced after 2006, might cause the Federal Reserve to lower nominal rates. To address this issue, we tried to use the Romer and Romer (2004) measure of monetary policy shocks to instrument for interest rates. This variable captures the component of monetary policy decisions that cannot be explained by variables such as macroeconomic conditions and prior rates that are known before the Federal Reserve Board (FRB) meeting. Unfortunately, this measure is only weakly correlated with interest rates over the 1980 to 2008 time period (with an F-statistic of 1). As such, we do not use it as an instrument for rates, but simply include it as an alternative measure of credit availability. The final regression in column (8) of table 7.6 shows that this variable essentially is uncorrelated with housing prices. We interpret this result as supporting the view that that the weak connection between interest rates and housing prices observed in the data is unlikely to reflect reverse causality.

7.3.2   Interest Rates and House Prices in Areas with Elastic and Inelastic Supply

Table 7.7 reproduces key regressions from table 7.6 for different sets of cities in which housing is more or less elastically supplied. Following Glaeser, Gyourko, and Saiz (2008), we split the sample of metropolitan areas into three groups based on Saiz's (2008) measure of constraints on supply elasticity, which itself is based on area topography. Summary statistics for this measure, and other metropolitan statistical area (MSA)–specific data are presented in table 7.5. We compute a house price index for each tercile of supply elasticity, weighting MSAs by their population in 2000.

The results in the first three columns, which are for the markets with the most elastic supplies of housing, indicate only a very modest housing price–interest rate relationship, as predicted by the model. The bivariate relationship reported in column (1) implies that a 100 basis point decline in real rates is associated with only 1.29 percent higher house prices (and the

15. The results throughout this table are similar when we use the log interest rate in place of the level, with the magnitude of the coefficient increasing from −6.82 to −7.12 in column (1) and from −1.82 to −1.94 when including a trend in column (2). Standard errors also increase very slightly.

Table 7.7   Differential elasticities by Saiz's supply elasticity

Sample of metro areas Dependent variable	OLS elastic log price (1)	OLS elastic log price (2)	OLS elastic log price (3)	OLS inelastic log price (4)	OLS inelastic log price (5)	OLS inelastic log price (6)
Real 10-year rate	−1.29 (1.19)	−0.39 (1.66)		−10.7*** (2.59)	−2.40** (0.91)	
Real 10-year rate, < 3.45%			−7.71*** (1.39)			−7.65** (3.52)
Real 10-year rate, > 3.45%			3.52*** (1.11)			0.41 (2.39)
Linear time trend		0.0022 (0.0038)	0.0017 (0.0021)		0.021*** (0.0045)	0.020*** (0.0042)
Constant	4.89*** (0.050)	4.85*** (0.077)	5.04*** (0.047)	5.25*** (0.13)	4.87*** (0.046)	5.01*** (0.083)
Observations	29	29	29	29	29	29
R^2	0.075	0.10	0.60	0.52	0.78	0.80

Notes: The dependent variable is log average FHFA price index for elastically supplied or inelastically supplied metropolitan areas. Standard errors, in parentheses, are adjusted for heteroskedasticity and autocorrelation using the Newey–West method with 2 lags. Data are from 1980 to 2008.

***Significant at the 1 percent level.

**Significant at the 5 percent level.

*Significant at the 10 percent level.

effect is not significantly different from zero). In column (2), we control for a trend in price and find an even smaller estimated impact of interest rates on prices in elastic markets. In column (3), we find that there is a significant effect when the rate occurs amidst relatively low interest rate environments. When we include a trend, a 100 basis point fall in real rates at these low levels is associated with nearly an 8 percent increase in prices. In this specification, the coefficient for changes in high interest rate environments is inexplicably positive.

Columns (4) through (6) report analogous results for the most inelastic markets. As basic price theory suggests should be the case in such markets, house prices are more sensitive to interest rates, as the simple bivariate relationship reports. Column (4) shows that a 100 basis point decline in real rates is associated with 10.7 percent higher house prices in these markets, but in column (5) we find that this coefficient drops by 75 percent when we control for a trend. Column (6) shows that most of this impact arises from rate changes in low interest rate environments. Still, the coefficient of −7.65 is modest compared to the volatility of price changes realized in inelastically supplied markets. Real prices more than doubled during the 1996 to 2006 boom in some of the coastal markets that have the most inelastic supplies of housing, so even large declines in interest rates cannot account for much of their price growth.[16]

7.3.3   Summary and Conclusions

It is hard to be overly confident about results drawn from thirty years of national data, but the data gives little support to the view that there is a large robust relationship between interest rates and prices. The strength of the empirical correlation between house prices and interest rates is much more consistent with the weaker relationship implied by our model when additional features are introduced and private discount rates need not equal market ones. Interest rates have very little ability to predict house prices independent of trend. A 100 basis point change in real rates is associated with no more than an 8 percent change (in the opposite direction) in detrended house prices, and that is only when the rate change is from a relatively low level.

In addition, there is no evidence that interest rates have a dramatic effect on quantities in the housing market. In appendix C, we report the regression analogues to table 7.6, using construction, rather than housing prices, as the dependent variable. Those findings increase our confidence in the robustness of the price impacts. Construction statistics are thought to be better measured than house prices because a permit is required for each house. Hence, one well might be worried about measurement error being responsible for the weak estimated relationship between house prices and interest rates if

16. Results using the Wharton Residential Land Use Regulatory Index (WRLURI) reported in Gyourko, Saiz, and Summers (2008) yielded qualitatively and quantitatively similar results.

Table 7.8   Predicted interest rate impacts on price growth from data and model

	$d \ln(P)/dr \times \Delta r =$	Implied ΔP (%)
A *Overall, 1996–2006*		
From model with $r = \rho + \pi$	$-5.3 \times -1.2\% =$	6.4
From model with $r \neq \rho + \pi$	$-1.0 \times -1.2\% =$	1.2
From data	$-6.8 \times -1.2\% =$	8.2
Actual price growth		42
B *Biggest change, 2000–2005*		
From model with $r = \rho + \pi$	$-5.3 \times -1.9\% =$	10
From model with $r \neq \rho + \pi$	$-1.0 \times -1.9\% =$	1.9
From data	$-6.8 \times -1.9\% =$	12.9
Actual price growth		29
C *Crash, 2006–2008*		
From model with $r = \rho + \pi$	$-5.3 \times -1.1\% =$	5.8
From model with $r \neq \rho + \pi$	$-1.0 \times -1.1\% =$	1.1
From data	$-6.8 \times -1.1\% =$	7.5
Actual price growth		-11

Notes: This table reports back-of-the-envelope calculations in which we attempt to explain observed house price growth using various estimates of the semielasticity of prices with respect to interest rates. Following Himmelberg, Mayer, and Sinai (2005), we examine a model where the interest rate is linked mechanically to the discount rate, by $r = \rho + \pi$. This generates the price semielasticity shown in row 1. Our more general model that allows r to vary without changing ρ is shown in row 2. Finally, row 3 takes the semielasticity estimated empirically on data from 1980 to 2008. Reported actual price growth is in log points.

one found a very strong link between interest rates and construction. As appendix C shows, that is not the case across a variety of specifications.

How much of the total increase in prices can be explained by lower interest rates? Our approach to answering this question is to compare the actual price change over a particular time period, with the change in price implied by the coefficients suggested by the regressions reported above and by the model. In the latter case, the predicted impact is determined by multiplying by the changes in the potential explanatory variables over the same time period. We consider three separate time periods: 1996 to 2006 (the total boom), 2006 to 2008 (the bust), and a variable-specific subset of the boom that corresponds to the period of the largest change in the relevant credit market variable.

The first panel of table 7.8 shows our results using real interest rates and prices in the entire United States. We use –6.8 as our estimate of the empirical semielasticity of prices with respect to interest rates (from column [l] of table 7.6). This figure is the raw ordinary least squares coefficient and it sits comfortably within the estimates from the model as well. Between 1996 and 2006, real prices using the FHFA index rose by 0.42 log points.[17] Over the same time period, real interest rates fell by 1.2 percentage points (or 120 basis points). As row three of the first panel indicates, this drop in real rates predicts a price increase of 8.2 percent, which is less than one-fifth of the total change over this period.

In order to compare these numbers with our model's ability to explain the boom, rows 1 and 2 show elasticities taken from the model. These elasticities come from computations where housing supply is somewhat elastic, the real rate is 0.04, and we allow for mobility and a 20 percent down payment requirement.[18] When prices are linked to interest rates, as in table 7.1, the model elasticity is comparable to the empirical result, at −5.3. Separating discounting from interest rates, we found a much smaller estimate of −1, which has even less ability to explain the boom than the ordinary least squares (OLS) coefficient. We find larger elasticities if we reduce the down payments, increase the growth rate, or assume a lower starting interest rate, but even so, we would be hard-pressed to find plausible parameters that generate an elasticity large enough to explain a substantial fraction of the price appreciation over this period.

The period in which interest rates predict the largest rise in prices is between 2000 and 2005, when real rates fell by 190 basis points (middle panel of table 7.8). Using our semielasticity estimate of −6.8, this change predicts a price rise of about 0.13 log points. Yet over this period, real prices actually rose by 0.29 log points, so even cherry-picking the time span, interest rate declines explain no more than 45 percent of the appreciation. Again, the results of our model—especially when $r \neq \rho + \pi$—predict smaller price increases than the OLS coefficient.

During the 2006 to 2008 bust, real interest rates continued to fall—by 110 basis points. Of course, that implies that prices should have risen—by 7.5 percent, given our elasticity estimate—as reported in the bottom panel of table 7.8. During this period prices actually fell by about 11 percent, so it is quite clear that interest rates cannot explain the bust. Because our model also predicts a negative relationship between house prices and interest rates, they also get the direction of price change wrong, but now the prediction error is smaller in magnitude.

Table 7.9 reports analogous results focusing on inelastically supplied metropolitan areas, defined as the lowest tercile according to Saiz's (2008) measure of supply elasticity. In this case, we again use the raw OLS estimated coefficient of −10.7 (from column [4] of table 7.7) as our empirical semielasticity. As the top panel shows, the 1.2 percentage point drop in interest rates

---

17. This is equivalent to the 53 percent change noted in the introduction. We work with log points here because that is the metric by which our model predictions are computed.

18. Except for allowing for a positive supply elasticity, the assumptions are the same as those in column (4) of tables 7.1 and 7.2.

Table 7.9   Predicted interest rate impact on price growth in supply-
                   constrained MSAs

	d ln(P)/dr × Δr =	Implied ΔP (%)
A *Overall, 1996–2006*		
From model with $r = \rho + \pi$	$-16 \times -1.2\% =$	19.2
From model with $r \neq \rho + \pi$	$-7.5 \times -1.2\% =$	9
From data	$-10.7 \times -1.2\% =$	12.8
Actual price growth		63
B *Biggest change, 2000–2005*		
From model with $r = \rho + \pi$	$-16 \times -1.9\% =$	30.4
From model with $r \neq \rho + \pi$	$-7.5 \times -1.9\% =$	14.2
From data	$-10.7 \times -1.9\% =$	20.3
Actual price growth		42
C *Crash, 2006–2008*		
From model with $r = \rho + \pi$	$-16 \times -1.1\% =$	17.6
From model with $r \neq \rho + \pi$	$-7.5 \times -1.1\% =$	8.3
From data	$-10.7 \times -1.1\% =$	11.8
Actual price growth		-16

Notes: This table reports back-of-the-envelope calculations in which we attempt to explain observed house price growth using various estimates of the semielasticity of prices with respect to interest rates. Following Himmelberg, Mayer, and Sinai (2005), we examine a model where the interest rate is linked mechanically to the discount rate, by $r = \rho + \pi$. This generates the price semielasticity shown in row 1. Our more general model that allows r to vary without changing ρ is shown in row 2. Finally, row 3 takes the semielasticity estimated empirically on data from 1980 to 2008. Reported actual price growth is in log points.

between 1996 and 2006 predicts about a 0.13 log point increase in housing prices, while actual house prices for this group of markets rose by a much larger 0.63 log points.

Our model can account for even less of the very high price appreciation experienced in inelastically supplied markets. Here we assume fixed supply and use the same parameter values as those for the calculations reported in column (1) of tables 7.1 and 7.2. These computations assume 1 percent annual real growth, a 20 percent down payment requirement, and 6 percent annual mobility. We take the elasticities computed at a real rate of 4 percent, both in the case of linked discount rates and a fixed, separate discount rate. In the former case the elasticity is −16, which predicts a 0.19 log point price increase, and in the latter case the elasticity of −7.5 predicts appreciation of only 0.09 log points (see the top panel of table 7.9).

The 190 basis interest rate drop between 2000 and 2005 predicts over a 0.2 log point price bump for this group, which again falls considerably short of the actual 0.42 log point increase in housing prices that was experienced by these inelastically supplied markets over these years (middle panel of table

7.9). During this specially chosen period, the predicted impact of interest rates on prices was considerable, but it still is not enough to explain more than half of the true price gain in these markets under our new assumptions. The traditional model with discount rates linked to interest rates does somewhat better here, predicting three-quarters of the true price growth, but this relies on an elasticity two-thirds larger than our empirical estimate. And as the bottom panel shows once again for the bust in prices between 2006 and 2008, interest rates have no ability to explain the price drop because their predicted impact is to raise prices during the period of the housing bust.

7.4   The Impact of Approval Rates on Housing Demand and Prices

Interest rates were not the only thing about credit markets that was changing, especially during the boom, so perhaps other factors were more important and can more fully account for what went on in housing markets. To investigate those possibilities, we now turn to our other credit market variables: approval rates and average loan-to-value ratios. In doing so, we can use variation across metropolitan areas by year, but we still face two principal problems. First, there is a major endogeneity concern because housing market conditions seem likely to influence bank policies. Second, empirical measures of credit availability are likely to be confounded by the changing characteristics of mortgage applicants. While we try to deal with each concern, they remain so considerable that we conclude that our results must be treated as being suggestive rather than definitive.

7.4.1   Mortgage Applications and Approval Rates

Let N_B denote the number of people who would like to buy a house if they could get credit, which in the model equals N_t/α or $K((1+g)^t/(\rho_t - g)/(\theta + ((1-\theta)(1-\varphi)r)/\rho_t + \tau/(\rho_t - g))P_t)^{1/\gamma}$. A fraction α of this group will be able to get credit and purchase a home. We assume that all people who want a home and can get a loan apply for the mortgage. We assume that there is some uncertainty about who can get a loan, so an additional share φ of the ineligible population wants to buy a home and applies for a loan. Thus an extra fraction $(1 - \alpha)\varphi$ of the entire population also applies for a loan, in addition to the α who will actually receive loans. The parameter φ might be interpreted as reflecting the level of optimism that high-risk buyers have about getting a loan.

The approval rate observed in real data (i.e., the proportion of applications that lead to a loan) does not equal α—the unconditional probability of getting a loan—but instead equals $\alpha/(\alpha + (1 - \alpha)\varphi)$, which is greater than α. If we compare approval rates over time, it is quite possible for α to rise and for the measured approval rate to decline if φ, which reflects optimism about getting a loan, also rises. For example, if α was initially 0.5 and φ was initially 0.25, then the measured approval rate would be 0.8. If α then rose to 0.6 and φ rose to 0.5, then the measured approval rate would decline to 0.75. A significant increase in approval would look like a decline in the actual approval rate if the share of high-risk individuals aggressively applying for loans also rose. Since a loosening of credit might well lead many marginal applicants to apply for loans, this problem could be quite severe.

Despite this, we will use the raw approval rate, and the approval rate correcting for individual characteristics, as our first measure of changes in the lending environment. We are essentially assuming that φ is fixed. In this case, the measured approval rate will show the correct direction of change, and if $\hat{a}$ denotes the measured approval rate then the real approval rate α will equal $\varphi\hat{a}/(1 - \hat{a}(1 - \varphi))$, which we report for a range of values of φ. While this provides a useful benchmark, we believe that it is still likely to substantially mismeasure the changes in the approval rate.

Our second approach is to assume that the value of φ increased over the boom. We make what we consider a reasonably extreme assumption; namely, that in 1996, φ equals 0.5 and that it increased by 0.025 per year for the next decade, reaching 0.75 by 2006. This would represent a 50 percent increase in the share of the people who will not get a loan, but who apply for a loan over this period.

Our third approach is to use the increase in the number of people who get loans, which should equal $\alpha'N'_B/\alpha N_B$, where α' and N'_B reflect the ex post values of these variables. Since the boom surely also led to an increase in the number of people who wanted to buy a home, we must have some means of correcting for N'_B/N_B. Unfortunately, we know of no good way of performing this correction. Our first approach is to assume that the growth rate of the number of buyers is three-quarters the growth rate of the number of accepted applications. Our second approach is to assume that the growth rate of interested buyers is one-half the growth rate in the number of accepted applications.

7.4.2   Measuring the Change in Approval Rates

In order to measure the availability of mortgages during the past two decades, we use data released by the Federal Financial Institutions Examination Council under the Home Mortgage Disclosure Act (HMDA). These data provide a relatively complete universe (203,511,952 observations) of all US mortgage applications between 1990 and 2008.[19]

---

19. We use the 298 metropolitan areas included in these files in our subsequent empirical analysis. Applicants are dropped if they have an explicit federal guarantee from the Federal Housing Authority (FHA), Veterans Affairs (VA), Farm Service Agency (FSA), or Rural Housing Services (RHS), if they withdrew the application (following Munnell et al. 1996), or if they have invalid geographic coding. In addition, we use data on all applications, whether for purchase or refinance. Restricting the analysis to purchases does not change our conclusions (reported later) in any material way. More specifically, there is no permutation of the data we could find that suggested this variable could account for the bulk of the boom in house prices.

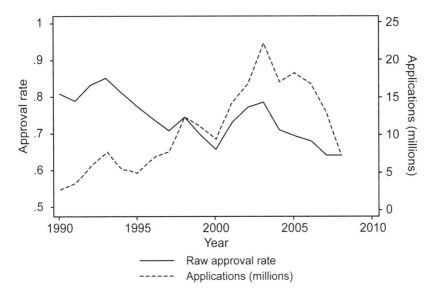

Fig. 7.2   Applications and approval rate
Source: HMDA data released by the Federal Financial Institutions Examination Council.

Figure 7.2 shows the number of applications in our HMDA sample in each year along with the raw approval rate. The number of applications skyrockets over the period from 1995 to 2005, nearly tripling over the decade. The approval rate, on the other hand, is reasonably constant, though declining slightly, over this period. It falls from 78 percent in 1995 to 66 percent in 2000, and then rapidly jumps back to 78 percent by 2002. It increases another percentage point in 2003 before falling back to 70 percent by 2005 and then declining to 65 percent in 2007 and 2008.[20]

The lack of an overall trend in approval rates as the housing boom intensified is somewhat surprising given that other work finds a substantial easing of credit for marginal borrowers during this period (Keys et al. 2010). On the other hand, Greenspan (2010) reports that issuances of adjustable-rate mortgages also peaked in 2004, and Bubb and Kaufman (2009) question whether increased mortgage securitization actually led underwriting standards to deteriorate.

The large expansion in the number of applications raises the possibility that there was a substantial shift in the composition of mortgage applicants: an increase in the parameter φ discussed earlier. A number of the individual characteristics included in the HMDA data do change during the sample period. For example, figure 7.3 shows the increasing share of applications

20. This time pattern of approval rates is consistent with that previously reported by Garriga (2009) using recent years' HMDA files.

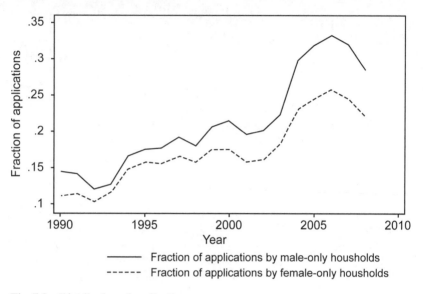

Fig. 7.3   Distribution of applications
Source: HMDA data released by the Federal Financial Institutions Examination Council.

made by single male and single female applicants, typically seen as riskier lending prospects than families. One important question is whether the rise in the number of applicants is itself a reflection of easier lending standards or whether it reflects a more general enthusiasm for the market on the part of potential buyers (or both). Figure 7.4 shows the changing approval rates for the three types of applications. The three series mirror each other, showing a decline until the year 2000, a rise between 2000 and 2004, and a decline after that period. This suggests that the 2000 to 2004 increase in applicants could be driven by increasing approval rates, but there is less evidence to support such a connection outside of those years.

In order to accurately measure credit availability, we aim to estimate the changing approval rate for a marginal buyer of constant attributes. We attempt to correct for differential selection of mortgage applicants by controlling for observable individual characteristics. In order to estimate the ease of a given person getting a loan in each metropolitan area in each year, we run the following regression for each year for which we have data:

$$(9) \qquad \text{Approval}_{i,j} = \zeta_1 \text{Individual Controls}_{i,j} + \zeta_2 \text{Metro Area-Year Fixed Effects}_j + u_{i,j}.$$

The dependent variable here, $\text{Approval}_{i,j}$, is a dummy indicating whether the application of individual i in metropolitan area j was approved (a value of 1 indicates approval; 0 indicates rejection). Appendix A reports the coefficients on applicant characteristics from one year's data, which include race, sex,

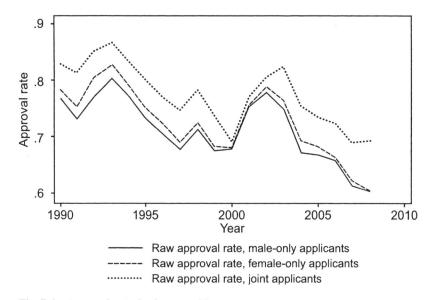

Fig. 7.4   Approval rates by demographic group
Source: HMDA data released by the Federal Financial Institutions Examination Council.

and a nonparametric specification of income. We also control for interactions between sex and income in this vector. We include metropolitan area fixed effects in each regression. They are the focus of this particular effort, as the year-by-metropolitan area-specific approval rates (controlling for applicant differences as best we can) are used to estimate the impact of changing approval rates over time on house prices. We estimate such rates for the nineteen years of HMDA data that are available, and for 298 metropolitan areas.

Our second approach is more nonparametric. We estimate an approval rate in each year and each metropolitan area for each population subgroup, denoted Approval$_{group,j,t}$, and then form a predicted approval rate using the population weights of applications as of 1996. This procedure is meant to hold the characteristics of potential borrowers fixed and let metropolitan area level approval rates change only because of changing approval rates within groups. The solid and plain dashed lines in figure 7.5 shows the time series pattern of national approval rates for the country as a whole, using these two methods of correcting the approval rate. There appears to be little upward trend in the demographics-corrected approval rates; however, we try to measure them.

Table 7.10 provides us with six different estimates of the changes in the approval rate. The first column shows how the raw approval rates change over time, which would be the actual approval rate if $\varphi = 1$. The second column shows the same pattern if $\varphi = 0.5$ throughout the period. This

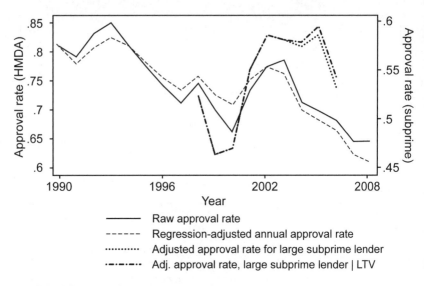

Fig. 7.5   Measures of mortgage approval rates

Sources: HMDA data released by the Federal Financial Institutions Examination Council and applications to a large subprime lender from Amit Seru.

correction does reduce the implied approval rate but it does not materially change the time-series pattern of approval rates.

The third column shows the implied approval rate if φ = 0.5 until 1996, then increases by 0.025 per year until 2006, and then declined by 0.025 per year after that. This change is relatively arbitrary, but it shows what a significant increase in applications by unqualified would-be buyers will do to the implied underlying approval rate. With this assumption, we estimate that the underlying approval rate increased by 14 percentage points from 63.5 percent in 1996 to 78.2 percent in 2004, and 10 percentage points from 1996 to 2006.

The fourth column infers the approval rates from the ratio of accepted mortgages in a given year to the ratio of accepted mortgages in 2005, the year of the largest number of accepted mortgage applications. Specifically, as $\text{Accepted}_t/\text{Accepted}_{2005} = \alpha_t/\alpha_{2005} \, N_{B,t}/N_{B,2005}$, we assume that the change in the number of buyers $N_{B,t}/N_{B,2005}$ equals $(\text{Accepted}_t/\text{Accepted}_{2005})^z$, where z is less than one, so $\alpha_t = (\text{Accepted}_t/\text{Accepted}_{2005})^{1-z} \, \alpha_{2005}$.[21] We show the results where $z = 0.75$ in column (4), which means that approximately three-fourths of the growth in accepted applications is due to growth in demand. Results for $z = 0.5$ are reported in column (5), which means that approximately one-half of the growth in accepted applications is due to growth in demand.

21. We think of this approach as partitioning the $\text{Log}(\text{Accepted}_t/\text{Accepted}_{2005})$ into $\text{Log}(\alpha_t/\alpha_{2005}) + \text{Log}(N_{B,t}/N_{B,2005})$, and assuming that $\text{Log}(N_{B,t}/N_{B,2005})$ is responsible for either three-quarters or one-half of the growth in acceptances.

Table 7.10   **Implied mortgage approval rates, 1990–2008**

Assumption on application growth	Raw approval rate (1)	Constant application rate (2)	Linear growth in applications (3)	Empirical application growth rate (4)	Empirical application growth rate (5)	Captured by observable risk score (6)
Model parameter	$\varphi = 1$ (%)	$\varphi = 0.5$ (%)	φ growing at 0.025 per year, 1996–2006, then declining (%)	Buyers growing at 3/4 growth rate of accepted applications relative to 2005 (%)	Buyers growing at 1/2 growth rate of accepted applications relative to 2005 (%)	n/a: Data from large subprime lender (%)
Year						
1990	84.4	73.0	73.0	54.6	36.7	
1991	80.4	67.2	67.2	55.1	37.4	
1992	83.8	72.2	72.2	57.1	40.2	
1993	84.9	73.7	73.7	60.5	45.1	
1994	84.7	73.5	73.5	63.0	49.0	
1995	81.7	69.0	69.0	62.6	48.4	
1996	77.7	63.5	63.5	65.2	52.4	
1997	75.8	61.0	62.1	66.0	53.7	
1998	76.3	61.6	63.9	69.4	59.5	77.3
1999	75.8	61.0	64.3	70.7	61.6	76.4
2000	76.5	61.9	66.1	70.9	62.0	77.1
2001	81.3	68.5	73.1	71.1	62.3	77.8
2002	83.8	72.1	77.1	72.4	64.7	78.3
2003	83.8	72.2	77.8	74.8	68.9	80.0
2004	83.7	71.9	78.2	78.1	75.2	82.6
2005	81.1	68.3	75.7	81.1	81.1	84.1
2006	78.9	65.1	73.7	79.5	78.0	84.9
2007	78.7	64.9	72.8	71.9	63.8	
2008	80.2	67.0	74.0	59.4	43.5	

Notes: Columns (1) through (5) report raw mortgage approval rates in the HMDA data, as well as adjusted approval rates under various assumptions about the growth rate in applications. The adjusted approval rates are calculated as $\varphi \hat{a}/(1 - \hat{a}(1 - \varphi))$, where $\hat{a}$ is the raw approval rate and φ is the fraction of high-risk individuals who apply for a loan. See text for details. Column (6) reports regression-adjusted approval rates from a large subprime lender, generously computed and shared by Amit Seru.

Column (4) shows a growth in the implied acceptance rate from 65.2 percent in 1996 to 79.5 percent in 2006. Column (5) shows a growth in the implied acceptance rate from 52.4 percent in 1996 to 78.0 percent. To our eyes, 52.4 percent seems like a low number given that the home ownership rate was 65 percent in that time period. Clearly more than 52.4 percent of the population was able to buy a home at some point in their lives.

Using richer data from a different market segment, namely subprime borrowers, reveals a somewhat clearer pattern. Approval rates for mortgage applications submitted to a large subprime lender, adjusted for a richer set of borrower characteristics, are shown in column (6), and in the remaining lines of figure 7.5.[22] The dashed-dotted lines show an increase of 13.3 percentage points in this lender's adjusted approval rate from 1999 to 2005, and that controlling for the application's loan-to-value ratio reduces the gain slightly to 12.5 percentage points.

While the time series of these approval rates look somewhat more promising as an explanation for the housing boom, the magnitudes of changes remain relatively modest. Even for the subprime population, the measured increase in credit availability is well within the range of the HMDA-derived estimates presented in table 7.10.

7.4.3   The Impact of Approval Rates on Price

The model predicted that a permanent change in approval rates influences prices according to the formula $\text{Log}(P'/P) = 1/(\varepsilon_P^I + \varepsilon_P^N)\text{Log}(\alpha'/\alpha)$. As dicussed earlier, this implies an elasticity of about 1/3, given standard supply and demand elasticities. While we may trust the theory more than the data, in this section we also estimate an elasticity of prices with respect to measured approval rates.

Using metropolitan area-level data pooled across years, we can now examine the impact of approval rates on the FHFA local house price index. In equation (10), we regress the log price index on our measures of adjusted approval rates taken from the ζ_2 vector and, hence, holding borrower characteristics constant.

$$(10) \qquad \text{Log(Index}_{j,t}) = \Omega_1 \text{Approval Rate}_{j,t} \\ + \Omega_2 \text{MSA}_j + \Omega_3 \text{Year}_t + \Omega_4 \text{Controls}_{j,t} + \varepsilon_{j,t}.$$

Approval Rate$_{j,t}$ is the estimated rate for metropolitan area j in year t, controlling for metropolitan area and year fixed effects. The other controls are interactions between a time trend and (a) mean January temperature and (b) the Wharton Residential Land Use Regulatory Index (WRLURI). The

---

22. We are deeply indebted to Amit Seru for computing and sharing these adjusted approval rates and adjusted loan-to-value ratios from his data on mortgage applications at a large subprime lender. These regressions control for borrower's sex, marital status, FICO score, presence of income documentation, self-employment status, and debt-to-income ratio.

latter measures the degree of supply restrictiveness in the area (Gyourko, Saiz, and Summers 2008).[23]

Results for different specifications of equation (10) are reported in table 7.11. The first regression finds that as raw approval rates increase by 1 percent, prices rise by 0.0018 log points, holding metropolitan area and year fixed. While the individual controls available are quite limited, the year effects help account for some important changes in applicant characteristics over the boom (see chapter 4). This coefficient is statistically significant and shows that prices and approval rates moved together positively. The second regression shows the regression-corrected approval rate, with standard errors corrected for estimation error in the approval rate by bootstrapping.[24] In this case, the impact of a 1 percent approval rate increase is to increase prices by 0.0021 log points. Our third regression uses approval rates based on 1999 applicant weights, as explained before. In this case, the coefficient falls to 0.14. In both cases, correcting for these group changes causes the estimated effect on prices to fall rather than rise. In regression (4), we control for state-year fixed effects so that all our identifying variation comes from differences across metropolitan areas within a given state for a given year. The estimated coefficient is stable at 0.20.

There are two potential problems with these coefficients. First, we are using measured approval rates, which do not reflect the relevant underlying approval rate unless φ, the rate of optimistic application, equals one. This mismeasurement will not be classical measurement error, and the problem will get more severe if φ differs from place to place and is correlated with the true underlying approval rate.[25] Second, the approval rate may be itself endogenous with respect to price.

If $\varphi = 1$, then these estimated effects are somewhat smaller than our theoretical predictions. The model predicted a semielasticity of $1/(3 \times$ Approval Rate). If the approval rate is 0.8, then this predicts a semielasticity of 0.42, which is somewhat higher than the effect estimated here, but still reasonably

---

23. There are few variables that are available on an annual basis at the metropolitan level, and those that are, such as employment rates, seem likely to be endogenous with respect to the housing market.

24. We use the estimated MSA fixed effects and their covariance matrix from the annual implementations of regression (9) to draw 100 realizations of the approval rates used in regression (10). Note that this ignores the covariance between annual fixed effects for a given MSA, but since we have 298 metropolitan areas and nineteen years of data, incorporating the cross-MSA covariances is more conservative. Furthermore, we cluster our standard errors in regression (10) by MSA. Following Mas and Moretti (2009, appendix), we add the estimated variance of $\widehat{\Omega}_1$ to the cross-equation variance of $\widehat{\Omega}_1$ to determine our composite bootstrap standard error.

25. To see the effect of mismeasurement, follow the model that tells us that the linear approximation for the logarithm of prices is that $\mathrm{Log}(P) = \mathrm{Log}(\bar{P}) + 1/(\varepsilon_P^I + \varepsilon_P^y)\alpha/\bar{\alpha}$ and the measured approval rate is equal to $\widehat{\mathrm{App}} + (\varphi(\alpha - \bar{\alpha})/(\bar{\alpha} + (1 - \bar{\alpha})\varphi)^2$, where $\bar{P}$, $\widehat{\mathrm{App}}$, and $\bar{\alpha}$ reflect the average values of price, measured approval, and true approval. The regression coefficient is therefore equal to $1/(\varepsilon_P^I + \varepsilon_P^y)$ divided by $\varphi/(\bar{\alpha} + (1 - \bar{\alpha})\varphi)^2$.

Table 7.11   Effect of credit availability on prices

Dependent variable	OLS log price (1)	OLS log price (2)	OLS log price (3)	OLS log price (4)	IV log price (5)	OLS log price (6)
Raw approval rate	0.18*** (0.037)			0.20*** (0.040)	1.32*** (0.25)	0.73*** (0.25)
Regression-adjusted approval rate		0.21*** (0.044)				
Approval rate corrected using 1996 weights			0.14** (0.040)			
Mean LTV						0.36*** (0.14)
Linear trend × January temperature/10	0.0022*** (0.00052)	0.0022*** (0.00052)	0.0022*** (0.00052)		0.0017*** (0.00053)	
Linear trend × Wharton regulation index	0.0058*** (0.00059)	0.0058*** (0.00059)	0.0058*** (0.00060)		0.0047*** (0.00063)	
Observations	5,646	5,646	5,645	5,608	5,646	924
Adjusted R^2	0.729	0.729	0.728	0.693		0.781
Fixed Effects	MSA	MSA	MSA	State–Year	MSA	MSA
MSAs	298	298	298	296	298	84
Years	1990–2008	1990–2008	1990–2008	1990–2008	1990–2008	1998–2008
First-stage F-statistic					8.71	

Notes: The dependent variable is the log metropolitan area FHFA price index. Standard errors, in parentheses, are clustered by MSA. All regressions include year fixed effects. Year dummies interacted with branch banking regulations and foreclosure speed instrument for approval rate.

***Significant at the 1 percent level.

**Significant at the 5 percent level.

*Significant at the 10 percent level.

similar in magnitude. Certainly, neither the theory nor evidence suggests elasticities of one or more.

While these estimated price impacts are modest, the observed positive relationship in these regressions could reflect reverse causality or omitted variables that drive both prices and approval rates. For example, if banks associate high prices today with even higher price appreciation in the future, that could lead them to approve riskier borrowers, which would cause the ordinary least squares relationship to be biased upwards. A second possibility is that higher prices lead to lower approval rates, because lenders recognize the longer-term mean reversion in housing markets (Glaeser and Gyourko 2006), which would cause the ordinary least squares coefficient to be biased downward.

This suggests that we should try to sign the direction of bias arising from possible reverse causality. We do so by using the January temperature and Wharton supply constraint index variables used before, which influence the demand and supply of local housing, respectively. Specifically, we interact these variables with year dummies to create instruments for housing prices. Using these instruments, we estimate the following regression of approval rates on prices, with both variables orthogonalized with respect to MSA and year fixed effects:

$$(11) \qquad \text{Approval Rate}_{j,t} = 0.097 \times \text{Log(Price)}_{j,t},$$
$$(0.018)$$

where the estimated coefficient's standard error is in parentheses.[26] Over these years, it seems that higher housing prices are associated with higher approval rates, suggesting that our OLS estimates from columns (1) and (3) of table 7.11 overestimate the causal impact of approval rates on prices. Appendix B provides a statistical model indicating that if this coefficient from equation (11) is accurately measured, the actual causal effect of approvals on prices is negative. While we do not believe that, the reverse linkage does raise serious doubt about whether approval rates are driving prices in a material way.

Our second approach is to use as instrumental variables (IV) the interaction between year dummies and fixed state-level regulatory characteristics toward branch banking and foreclosure. These estimates would be valid if these variables predict the underlying approval rates and do not influence the mistaken applications. These interactions are motivated by the calculations in appendix B, which suggest that approval rates will change more with global interest rates in places that have easier collection rules. But the calculation does not consider the potential correlation between these instruments and the share of people mistakenly applying for mortgages.

---

26. A higher coefficient results if we use only the interaction between January temperature and year dummies as instruments.

Our first state-level variable, taken from Pence (2006), is the average time it takes to obtain a foreclosure in a state. That variable certainly relates to the difficulties involved in collecting on a defaulting debtor, and—if the discussion and modeling in appendix B are correct—a higher value should dampen the interest rate sensitivity. Our second state-level variable is a measure of the restrictions on branch banking obtained from Rice and Strahan (2010). When branch banking was deregulated, some states kept restrictions on branch banking while others were more open. Presumably, places with fewer branch banks should have lower operating costs, and thus would have a stronger relationship between interest rates and approval rates.

These instruments have three potential problems. The first is that they may be correlated with other noncredit-related variables that could impact housing prices. The second is that they could influence the number of people who mistakenly try to get a mortgage. The third is that they could be correlated with other banking policies, such as lower down payment requirements that also affect housing demand. We are more troubled by the first two problems than by the third. While it is certainly true that the approval rate estimates using these instruments may be biased upwards because of correlation with other bank actions, our goal is not so much to estimate a pure approval rate effect as to gauge a total effect of credit market policies.

The fifth regression of table 7.11 reports the results when using these instruments. This regression is the IV analogue to the baseline OLS specification from column (1) discussed earlier. The coefficient on the metropolitan area-specific mortgage approval rate rises to 1.32. Even though this estimated price impact is not large enough to explain much of the housing boom, as we discuss later, the larger coefficient is surprising given that our earlier calculations suggested that the OLS estimates probably are biased up, not down. Moreover, this coefficient is larger than published estimates of the price elasticity of the demand for housing, which we have argued should set the upper bound for the impact of approval rates. However, the instruments themselves are weak, and if they are correlated with other banking-related actions that foster home purchases, then they will overstate the impact of approval rates. To the extent this is the case, this coefficient still has value since our ultimate interest is in the overall impact of credit factors on housing prices.

7.4.4   The Connection between Approval Rates and Price Growth

In table 7.12 we look at the price increases implied by our different approval rate series. The first panel looks at the 1996 to 2006 growth period; the second panel looks at the 2006 to 2008 decline in prices. The first four estimates use the theoretically predicted elasticity (1/3) rather than the empirical estimates to test the model. The predictions are based on four different approval rate figures. The first row shows the impact of changing approval rates if we just use the raw approval rate. Since the raw rate barely changes, it unsurprisingly has a trivial impact on prices.

Table 7.12   Predicted approval rate impact on price growth from data and model

	d ln(P)/dlog(α) $\times \Delta$log(α) =	Implied ΔP (%)
A *Overall, 1996–2006*		
Raw approval rate	$0.33 \times 0.015 =$	0.5
Approval rates assuming 0.025 annual growth in φ	$0.33 \times 0.149 =$	5.1
Approval rates assuming buyer growth is 3/4 growth in accepted applications	$0.33 \times 0.198 =$	6.8
Approval rates assuming buyer growth is 1/2 growth in accepted applications	$0.33 \times 0.398 =$	14.2
Raw approval rate and IV estimate (semielasticity)	$1.3 \times 0.012 =$	1.6
Actual price growth		42
B *Decline, 2006–2008*		
Raw approval rate	$0.33 \times 0.016 =$	0.5
Approval rates assuming 0.025 annual decline in φ	$0.33 \times 0.004 =$	0.1
Approval rates assuming buyer growth is 3/4 growth in accepted applications	$0.33 \times -0.29 =$	−9.3
Approval rates assuming buyer growth is 1/2 growth in accepted applications	$0.33 \times -0.58 =$	−18
Raw approval rate and IV estimate (semielasticity)	$1.3 \times 0.013 =$	1.7
Actual price growth		−10

Notes: This table reports back-of-the-envelope calculations in which we attempt to explain observed house price growth using various estimates of the elasticity of prices with respect to approval rates. Reported actual price growth is in log points. The estimated impacts of approval rates on prices come from theory, as discussed in the text, and from the regression reported in column (5) of table 7.11, relying on data from 1990 through 2008.

The second row shows the predicted impact of the approval rate if we assume that the underlying application rate for people who will not get a mortgage increases from 50 percent to 75 percent between 1996 and 2006. Using this assumption, the growth in the logarithm of the underlying approval rate is 0.149 (reflecting the roughly 15 percent increase in the implied approval rate), which predicts a 5 percent increase in prices. The third row measures the change in the approval rate from the change in the number of accepted applications. In this case, the logarithm of the approval rate rises by 0.198, which gives us a predicted price increase of nearly 7 percent.

The fourth row gives the best case for the change in approval rates, where we have estimated the change in approval rates based on the change in accepted applications, assuming that fully one-half of the rise in applications reflects a rise in the approval rates. In that case, the growth in the logarithm of the underlying approval rate is 0.398 and prices are predicted to rise by 14.2 percent. We consider this to be a true upper bound on the impact of rising approval rates, as we have assumed that America moved from allowing only 50 percent of interested buyers to get a mortgage to allowing over

80 percent of interested buyers to get a mortgage. Yet despite this massive increase in the share of possible buyers, standard housing market variables predict a price increase of only 14 percent, a quarter of the price increase that was actually observed over this time period. Since buyers should have reasonably expected the approval rate to mean revert, the price impact should surely have been lower than that amount.

The fifth row then uses our IV estimate and the actual change in approval rates. We are not comfortable using the IV estimate with our implied numbers because the IV estimate is based on a measured approval rate coefficient. Still, using these two variables again results in the implied price impact being small. These results are consistent with those of Mian and Sufi (2008), who find that expansion of credit availability at the zip code level can explain house price appreciation of only 4.3 percent from 2001 to 2005.

The second panel of table 7.12 looks at the ability of changes in the approval rate to explain the drop in prices after 2006. The first two rows show that neither the raw approval rate nor the approval rate corrected for a 2.5 percentage point decline per year in the share of unqualified people seeking mortgages can explain any of the drop. These measures of the approval rate continued to decline during the housing collapse.

The third row shows that when we estimate approvals by using the change in the number of applications, assuming that three-quarters of the drop reflects a drop in the number of interested buyers, the logarithm of the approval rate drops by 0.29. This implied drop can explain almost all of the fall in prices that we observe. The fourth row shows that when we assume that only one-half of the drop in successful applications comes from a decline in the number of interested buyers, we overpredict the drop in prices. The fifth row shows that even with the IV estimate of the impact of the raw approval rate, that variable cannot explain the decline.

Our ability to explain changes in prices with changes in the approval rates is quite limited. We lack either compelling time series information about the changes in the relevant approval rate and compelling empirical estimates of the connection between approval rates and prices. We attempt to compensate for these shortcomings by using theory to give us a predicted connection between prices and approval rates. Our theoretical predictions are in line with what we see in the data. We then try a number of different approaches to use measured approval rates and the rise in the number of applications to estimate the changing underlying true approval rate. Our procedures suggest that at most a third of the rise in prices can be explained with rising approval rates, and that figure requires extremely aggressive assumptions. Our best guess is that the impact of approval rates is substantially less than that. However, it is quite possible that a decline in the approval rate can explain much of the national price drop since 2006.

7.5   Impact of Leverage: Initial Loan-to-Value Ratios

We now turn to down payment requirements. To investigate the possible role of this factor, we must turn to another data source because the HMDA files do not report the purchase price, making it impossible to construct an initial loan-to-value ratio. One source that does collect both purchase price and initial mortgage amount is DataQuick, a well-known data provider in the housing industry.[27] This source purports to collect the universe of sales in the areas it tracks, but it does not cover the entire nation. DataQuick expanded its survey coverage in 1998, so that is the first year we can begin to put together a consistent data set across metropolitan areas.

We were able to construct initial LTVs at purchase for eighty-nine metropolitan areas across eighteen states and the District of Columbia from 1998 to 2008.[28] The number of transactions used to compute LTVs each year is listed in the first column of table 7.13. In any given year, our eighty-nine metropolitan areas comprise 35 to 40 percent of all home purchases in the nation.[29] The time series pattern of transactions closely parallels that for that nation, with the number of purchases in 2005 being 95 percent greater than that in 1998, and the number in 2008 being less than half (46 percent) than that in 2005.

The remaining columns of table 7.13 detail the distribution of loan-to-value ratios based on all observations in our eighty-nine metropolitan area sample. Because there still are outliers after cleaning the sample, we focus on the distribution of leverage between the tenth and ninetieth percentiles of data.[30] DataQuick provides information on up to three loans, and we report calculations based on the first or primary mortgage, as well as all loans. The leftmost panel of table 7.13 reports on the tenth, twenty-fifth, fiftieth, seventy-fifth, and ninetieth percentiles of the loan-to-value ratio,

27. We are grateful to Ferreira and Gyourko (2011) for providing summary statistics on these data.

28. The metropolitan areas are from across the United States, but it is not a random sample. For example, in the Northeast Census region, we have consistent data for areas in New Jersey and Pennsylvania only. New York state and the rest of New England either are not surveyed by DataQuick or do not have such data over the full 1998 to 2008 time period we are studying in this section. The Midwest and West regions of the country are better represented. States in the Midwest region with metropolitan areas consistently surveyed include Illinois, Michigan, Minnesota, Nebraska, Ohio, and Wisconsin. In the West, the states of Arizona, California, Colorado, Nevada, Oregon, and Washington are well covered. In the South region, metropolitan areas from Florida, Maryland, Oklahoma, and Tennessee are represented. A complete list is available upon request.

29. For example, we have 3.039 million sales observations in the peak year of 2005. This is about 37 percent of the combined 8.3 million sales of existing plus new home sales according to the National Association of Realtors and US Census.

30. For example, we only include observations that are coded as arms-length transactions by DataQuick. We also restrict the sample to homes with sales prices between $4,000 and $7,500,000. This largely eliminates a number of $0 trades, as well as a very few extremely expensive homes. We also winsorize the data so that the bottom and top 1 percent of observations are coded at the first and ninety-ninth percentile values in the distribution. Even after this cleaning, some very high loan-to-value ratios above one remain.

Table 7.13   Distribution of loan-to-value ratios in eighty-nine metropolitan areas over time

Year	Number of obs.	Distribution of LTVs using first mortgage only						Distribution of LTVs using up to three mortgages					
		10th (%)	25th (%)	50th (%)	75th (%)	90th (%)	Mean (%)	10th (%)	25th (%)	50th (%)	75th (%)	90th (%)	Mean (%)
1998	1,558,354	0	67	80	97	100	73	0	68	86	97	100	74
1999	1,749,790	0	68	80	97	100	74	0	69	87	98	100	75
2000	1,685,717	0	65	80	95	100	72	0	66	85	97	100	73
2001	1,794,506	0	68	80	95	99	73	0	69	88	97	100	75
2002	1,967,336	0	63	80	95	99	70	0	65	85	96	100	73
2003	2,127,516	0	60	80	94	99	69	0	63	82	96	100	72
2004	2,751,095	0	52	80	85	98	65	0	56	80	95	100	69
2005	3,039,726	0	60	80	80	95	65	0	64	86	99	100	71
2006	2,421,704	0	68	80	80	98	68	0	70	90	100	100	74
2007	1,777,035	0	63	80	95	100	69	0	66	90	100	100	73
2008	1,410,082	0	38	80	98	99	65	0	40	80	98	99	67

Source: Authors' calculations using eighty-nine metropolitan area sample from DataQuick microdata, 1998 to 2008. See the text for more detail on the sample and variable construction.

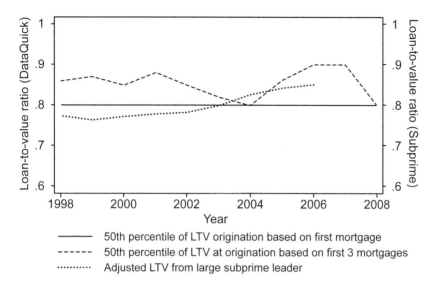

Fig. 7.6   Measures of loan-to-value ratios at origination

Sources: DataQuick data from eighty-nine metropolitan areas and applications to a large subprime lender from Amit Seru.

as well as the mean, for our full sample using only the first mortgage in the numerator. The right-most panel reports the analogous data using the sum of up to three mortgages in the numerator of the loan-to-value ratio.

There are a number of interesting features about these data. First, the results suggest that having a data source that includes junior liens could be important. Except for two years (2004 and 2008), there is a 5 to 10 percentage point difference in median LTVs, which implies that using only first mortgages will underestimate the typical home purchaser's degree of leverage. In our statistical analysis following, we use the LTV data based on all mortgage debt. Second, there has long been a large fraction of home buyers who purchase with little or no equity. At least 10 percent of purchasers in virtually every year are able to buy with no equity.[31] At least one-quarter have been able to buy their homes with no more than 5 percent equity (when one counts all the mortgages, not just the first lien). There has been remarkably little change in this fraction over time, too. Similarly, the median first mortgage has been for 80 percent of home value throughout the past 12 years, as shown in the solid line of figure 7.6. The median LTV using all mortgage debt was no higher in 2005 than it was in 1999. As shown in the dashed line of figure 7.6, it did peak in 2006 and 2007, before falling sharply in 2008, so

31. A closer look at the data showed that some borrowers clearly are able to finance more than 100 percent of their purchase price. In the San Francisco market for example, lenders record a purchase price and an internal appraisal value. Our LTVs are based on the purchase price. However, internal bank appraisals tend to be higher whenever the LTV is greater than one.

there is some interesting variation right around the housing market peak. Third, at least 10 percent of purchasers each year buy with all cash. And, there is relatively more variation in the fraction of buyers using substantial equity to purchase in their homes. In particular, there has been a sharp increase in the fraction putting down at least 60 percent equity between 2007 and 2008, as shown in the columns reporting LTVs for the twenty-fifth percentile of our sample distribution.

The results from our model already suggested that down payment changes are unlikely to have a major impact on house prices. The relative paucity of variation in LTVs over time suggests that home buyer leverage will not have much explanatory power empirically, either. While that is indeed the case, as we shall document, one needs to be cautious about making sweeping judgments about the role of changing down payment ratios with these data alone.

The distribution of loan-to-value ratios themselves is not changing very much over time, but we cannot control for changes in the sample of borrowers, including potentially important intertemporal differences in their credit quality, private discount rates, and so forth, because the DataQuick files contain no such information on the purchasers.[32] This could be important because we do know that the number of buyers changed substantially over time: it nearly doubled from 1998 to 2005, before falling by over half between 2005 and 2008. The dashed-dotted line in figure 7.6 shows the regression-adjusted leverage ratio from the large subprime lender mentioned earlier. This shows a modest increase of 8 percentage points from 1998 to 2006. These national trends also may mask important heterogeneity across regions, with credit loosening concentrated in certain cities or areas. In order to capture this phenomenon, and to empirically test the model's predictions about credit availability, we next consider metropolitan area-specific LTVs.

The MSA-level data used in our regression analysis turn out to be no more variable over time than shown in table 7.13.[33] The final column of table 7.11 reports the results of adding the mean metropolitan area-specific LTV to the MSA-adjusted approval rate regression. The sample size is smaller than for the approval rate regressions, as we only have LTV data beginning

---

32. DataQuick is one of the few sources that reports both purchase price and mortgage amount. Unfortunately, it does not report any demographic or income data on the buyers. Further progress on this issue will require the merging of data sources such as DataQuick and HMDA. It also would be useful to include some credit bureau information so that one could control for other borrowing, if one were going to use microdata. See Haughwout et al. (2011) for one promising effort in that direction. Their focus is on a better measure of speculators. In that regard, see also Chinco and Mayer (2011).

33. For example, every statement made about the aggregate data in table 7.10 applies to both Chicago (which did not experience a particularly large price boom) and Las Vegas (which did). Buyers in Las Vegas have long used higher leverage on average, with the median home buyer putting down no more than 11 percent equity in any year from 1998 to 2007 (and the equity share was 13 percent in 2008). Median LTVs are slightly lower in Chicago, but they are not appreciably more variable. In addition, at least 10 percent of buyers in both markets use all debt, and at least 25 percent use no more than 5 percent equity. The biggest difference is in the number of buyers over time. Between 1998 and 2005, the number of Chicago metropolitan area buyers expanded by 71 percent, versus 158 percent in Las Vegas (benchmarked against a

Table 7.14   **Predicted down payment impact on price growth from data and model**

	d ln(P)/d(1−θ) × Δ(1−θ) =	Implied ΔP (%)
Biggest change: 1998–2006 (median LTV)		
From calculation in text	0.36 × 4% =	1.4
From estimation	0.36 × 4% =	1.4
Actual price growth		37

Notes: This table reports back-of-the-envelope calculations in which we attempt to explain observed house price growth using predicted estimates of the semielasticity of prices with respect to down payment requirements. Reported actual price growth is in log points. Row 2 uses the estimated impact of down payments on prices from the regression reported in column (6) of table 7.11, relying on data from 1998 through 2008.

in 1998 and we can only cleanly match price, approval, and LTV data for eighty-four metropolitan areas. The 0.36 coefficient taken from the specification reported in column (4) of table 7.11 implies that as loan-to-value levels rise by 10 percent, prices rise by 3.6 percent. Note that the approval rate coefficient still is higher (0.76) in this OLS estimation, which uses a more restricted sample of metropolitan areas and years than the other regressions.

We also replicated table 7.11 using a measure of construction intensity, rather than prices, as the dependent variable. Those specifications are reported in table 7C.2, in the appendix. Once again we find that these credit market controls do not explain the bulk of the variation in single-family home construction, nor do they provide evidence that would invalidate the price impact results reported in this section.

Table 7.14 quantifies the potential impact of changing loan-to-value levels. Our estimated coefficient is 0.36 (from column [6] of table 7.11). Because the mean LTV did not change between 1998 and 2006 (when counting all loans, not just the first mortgage, as debt), it cannot explain the house price boom over this time span. Median LTVs are more volatile, rising from 86 percent in 1998 to 90 percent in 2006. The impact of this 4 percentage point change is depicted in the top part of table 7.14. Given our estimated coefficient, this predicts about a 2 percent rise in prices. The actual increase in prices during this period was 0.37 log points, so changes in leverage seem to have a very small ability to explain price growth over the full extent of the boom.

There is a 10 percentage point rise in median LTVs between 2004 and 2006, followed by a 10 point decline from 2006 to 2008. Given our model and regression results, this change would be associated with a 3 to 6 point change in house prices. Actual house values fell by about 0.1 log points during the 2006 to 2008 bust, so this variable could be responsible for an economically meaningful amount of the drop in prices. However, it cannot account for much of the boom.

---

95 percent increase across all our ninety metropolitan areas). This raises the possibility that the nature of buyers changed more in potentially important ways in Las Vegas. As noted earlier, we simply cannot control for this in our analysis.

7.6   Conclusion: So What Did Cause the Housing Bubble?

Interest rates do influence house prices, but they cannot provide any-thing close to a complete explanation of the great housing market gyrations between 1996 and 2010. Over the long 1996 to 2006 boom, they cannot account for more than one-fifth of the rise in house prices. Their biggest predictive influence is during the 2000 to 2005 period, when long rates fell by almost 200 basis points. That can account for about 45 percent of the run-up in home values nationally during that half-decade span. However, if one is going to cherry-pick time periods, it also must be noted that falling real rates during the 2006 to 2008 price bust simply cannot account for the 10 percent decline in FHFA indexes for those years.

There is no convincing evidence from the data that approval rates or down payment requirements can explain most or all of the movement in house prices either. The aggregate data on these variables show no trend increase in approval rates or trend decrease in down payment requirements during the long boom in prices from 1996 to 2006. However, the number of appli-cations and actual borrowers did trend up over this period (and fall sharply during the bust), which raises the possibility that the nature of the marginal buyer was changing over time. Carefully controlling for that requires better and different data, so our results need not be the final word on these two credit market traits.

This leaves us in the uncomfortable position of claiming that one plausible explanation for the house price boom and bust, the rise and fall of easy credit, cannot account for the majority of the price changes, without being able to offer a compelling alternative hypothesis. The work of Case and Shiller (2003) suggests that home buyers had wildly unrealistic expectations about future price appreciation during the boom. They report that 83 to 95 percent of purchasers in 2003 thought that prices would rise by an average of around 9 percent per year over the next decade. It is easy to imagine that such exuberance played a significant role in fueling the boom.

Yet, even if Case and Shiller are correct, and overoptimism was critical, this merely pushes the puzzle back a step. Why were buyers so overly opti-mistic about prices? Why did that optimism show up during the early years of the past decade and why did it show up in some markets but not others? Irrational expectations are clearly not exogenous, so what explains them? This seems like a pressing topic for future research.

Moreover, since we do not understand the process that creates and sus-tains irrational beliefs, we cannot be confident that a different interest rate policy would not have stopped the bubble at some earlier stage. It is certainly conceivable that a sharp rise in interest rates in 2004 would have let the air out of the bubble. But this is mere speculation that only highlights the need for further research focusing on the interplay between bubbles, beliefs, and credit market conditions.

Appendix A

Table 7A.1   **Mortgage approval coefficients**

Applicant sex[a]		Ethnicity[b]	
Joint application	0.021	Asian	−0.024
Female applicant	0.031	Black	−0.151
Unknown	0.009	Hispanic	−0.084
		Native American	−0.132
		Pacific Islander	−0.099
		Unknown	−0.172

Quantile of income[c]	
1	−0.224
2	−0.136
3	−0.098
4	−0.085
5	−0.054
6	−0.027
7	−0.039
8	−0.040
9	−0.008
10	−0.032
11	0.022
12	0.007
14	0.023
15	0.020
16	0.026
17	0.036
18	0.019
19	0.031
20	0.035
21	0.010
22	0.021
23	0.019
24	0.004
25	−0.018
Unknown	0.021

Notes: Coefficients are reported from a linear probability model in which mortgage approval is regressed on the covariates reported above, a full set of MSA dummies, and a full set of interactions between the income quantiles and applicant sex. The regression includes 13,920,695 mortgage applicants from the 2006 Home Mortgage Disclosure Act data. Applicants are dropped if they have an explicit federal guarantee from the FHA, VA, FSA, or RHS; if they withdrew the application (following Munnell et al., 1996); or if they have invalid geographic coding.

[a]Male applicant is omitted.

[b]White is omitted.

[c]Median quantile (13) is omitted.

Appendix B

Empirical Methods

One Instrument Estimation

We let $\tilde{P}_{jt}$ and $\tilde{A}_{jt}$ reflect the price and approval rates in area j at time t that have already been orthogonalized with respect to other variables such as the metropolitan area and year fixed effects. We then assume that $\tilde{P}_{jt} = \delta \tilde{A}_{jt} + \varepsilon_j$ and $\tilde{A}_{jt} = \gamma \tilde{P}_{jt} + \varepsilon_j$ or $\tilde{P}_{jt} = (\varepsilon_j + \delta\varepsilon_j)/(1 - \gamma\delta)$ and $\tilde{A}_{jt} = (\varepsilon_j + \gamma\varepsilon_j)/(1 - \delta\gamma)$. The OLS estimate, denoted $\hat{\beta}$, found by regressing price on approval yields:

$$\frac{\delta + \gamma \dfrac{\mathrm{Var}(\varepsilon_j)}{\mathrm{Var}(\varepsilon_j)}}{1 + \gamma^2 \dfrac{\mathrm{Var}(\varepsilon_j)}{\mathrm{Var}(\varepsilon_j)}},$$

which is greater than δ (for positive γ) whenever $1 > \delta\gamma$. If we let

$$R = \frac{\mathrm{Var}(\tilde{P}_{jt})}{\mathrm{Var}(\tilde{A}_{jt})} = \frac{\delta_2 + \dfrac{\mathrm{Var}(\varepsilon_j)}{\mathrm{Var}(\varepsilon_j)}}{1 + \gamma^2 \dfrac{\mathrm{Var}(\varepsilon_j)}{\mathrm{Var}(\varepsilon_j)}},$$

or $(R - \delta^2)/(1 - R\gamma^2) = (\mathrm{Var}(\varepsilon_j))/(\mathrm{Var}(\varepsilon_j))$, it follows that δ solves $\delta^2(\hat{\beta}\gamma^2 - \gamma) + \delta(1 - R\gamma^2) + \gamma R - \hat{\beta} = 0$. Thus $\delta = (R\gamma^2 - 1 \pm \sqrt{(R\gamma^2 - 1)^2 - 4(\hat{\beta}\gamma^2 - \gamma)(\gamma R - \hat{\beta})})/(2(\hat{\beta}\gamma^2 - \gamma))$. We have estimated $\hat{\beta}$ to be 0.26, and the estimated value of γ is 0.058. The ratio of the variance of prices (orthogonalized with respect to year and metropolitan area fixed effects) to the variance of approval rates (orthogonalized with respect to the same variables) is 6.7. These suggest that δ must either equal -0.13 or 17.2, and 17.2 is inadmissible since it would imply a negative value of $(\mathrm{Var}(\varepsilon_j))/(\mathrm{Var}(\varepsilon_j))$.

The Use of Regulations-Year Interactions as Instruments

The net present value of an infinite horizon loan of one dollar at interest rate R, which has a probability of defaulting equal to π_{Def} in each period, equals $\sum_{j=1}^{\infty}((1 - \pi_{\mathrm{Def}})/(1 + \rho_{\mathrm{Bank}}))^j (R + \pi_{\mathrm{Def}} \omega)/(1 - \pi_{\mathrm{Def}})$, where ρ_{Bank} is the bank's discount rate, and ω is the recovery rate for defaulted loans (beyond paying the last period's interest). The zero profit condition then implies that $(R - \rho_{\mathrm{Bank}})/(1 - \omega) = \overline{\pi}_{\mathrm{Def}}$, where $\overline{\pi}_{\mathrm{Def}}$ reflects the maximum default risk that the bank will take on, assuming that there is a maximum value of R (otherwise there would never be a maximum default risk).

Differentiating this expression with respect to the "global" interest rate tells us that $(\partial\overline{\pi}_{\mathrm{Def}})/(\partial\rho_{\mathrm{Global}}) = (\partial R)/(\partial\rho_{\mathrm{Global}}) - (\partial\rho_{\mathrm{Bank}})/(\partial\rho_{\mathrm{Global}})/(1 - \omega)$, which is negative as long as $\partial R/\partial\rho_{\mathrm{Global}} < \partial R/\partial\rho_{\mathrm{Bank}}/\partial\rho_{\mathrm{Global}}$, which we assume to be the case. Moreover, if the derivatives of R and ρ_{Bank} are independent of ω, the recovery rate, then $(\partial^2 \bar{\pi}_{Def})/(\partial \rho_{Global} \partial \omega) = (\partial R)/(\partial \rho_{Global}) - (\partial \rho_{Bank})/(\partial \rho_{Global})/(1 - \omega)^2 < 0$, so this effect will be stronger in places where the recovery rate is higher. If we think that larger banks are more globally connected, then $\partial \rho_{Bank}/\partial \rho_{Global}$ will be higher for those larger banks and so $\partial \bar{\pi}_{Def}/\partial \rho_{Global}$ will be larger in magnitude as well.

Appendix C
Interest Rates and Housing Construction

Table 7C.1 repeats the regressions of table 7.6 using construction, rather than housing, as the dependent variable. We use building permits as reported by the US Census Bureau in its Manufacturing, Mining and Construction Statistics data, with the log of the national number being the dependent variable in table 7C.1's specifications.[34] Not only is construction intrinsically interesting due to its impact on the larger economy, it also helps provide a check on our price results. Because construction statistics typically are better measured than house prices due to a permit being required for each home, finding an economically and statistically strong link between interest rates and building activity would at least raise the possibility that the relatively weak relationship between prices and rates is due to measurement in the former.[35]

Regressions (1) and (2) show the time series relationship between the ten-year rate and the logarithm of the number of single-family permits in the country as a whole.[36] The univariate coefficient is −8.27, with a standard error or 4.26. As with prices, the interest rate elasticity falls dramatically when a time trend is included, as shown in column (2). Construction levels, as well as housing prices, have been trending upwards over the past three decades. The results in columns (3) and (4) show no significant interest elasticities when we limit the sample to the period after 1985.

Regression (5) presents a changes-on-changes specification, yielding a coefficient of −4.82 that is not precisely estimated. Regression (6) reports

---

34. The data are available at http://censtats.census.gov/bldg/bldgprmt.shtml.

35. An independent impact is certainly possible, since builders may rely on financing for duration of their projects.

36. Not only is the interest rate impact on building activity interesting in its own right, but if one were willing to make a very specific assumption about the magnitude of the elasticity of housing supply (including that the elasticity is constant across areas), then the estimated elasticities reported in table 7C.1 provide an alternative means of evaluating the house price–interest rate relationship. For example, if we were to accept Topel and Rosen's (1988) national supply elasticity of two, we would expect the interest rate elasticity of construction to be approximately two times the price elasticities (under that admittedly strong assumption).

Table 7C.1 Semielasticity of national construction

Dependent variable	OLS log permits (1)	OLS log permits (2)	OLS log permits (3)	OLS log permits (4)	OLS permit growth (5)	OLS log permits (6)	OLS log permits (7)	OLS permit growth (8)
Real 10-year rate	−8.27*	−0.91	−6.94	0.11				
	(4.26)	(2.74)	(7.73)	(6.51)				
Change in real 10-year rate					−4.82			
					(2.85)			
Real 10-year rate, < 3.45%						−1.04	7.35	
						(12.7)	(10.2)	
Real 10-year rate, > 3.45%						−12.5**	−5.33	
						(4.51)	(5.05)	
Linear time trend		0.018**		0.012**			0.019***	
		(0.0080)		(0.0062)			(0.0063)	
Romer and Romer shock								6.30
								(6.03)
Constant	14.1***	13.5***	14.1***	13.6***	−0.0088	13.9***	13.3***	−0.018
	(0.19)	(0.22)	(0.29)	(0.26)	(0.042)	(0.40)	(0.22)	(0.047)
Observations	29	29	24	24	28	29	29	28
R^2	0.21	0.35	0.100	0.13	0.085	0.25	0.39	0.066
Years	1980–2008	1980–2008	1985–2008	1985–2008	1981–2008	1980–2008	1980–2008	1981–2008

Notes: Dependent variable: Log national single-family permits. The dependent variable is the log of total housing permits issued. Standard errors, in parentheses, are adjusted for heteroskedasticity and autocorrelation using the Newey–West method with 2 lags.

***Significant at the 1 percent level.

**Significant at the 5 percent level.

*Significant at the 10 percent level.

results when we estimate interest rate effects for low and high rate periods. Note that the results are the reverse of those for prices—there is a large effect of lowering interest rates from high levels, but not from low levels. Perhaps this has something to do with builders' capacity to fund themselves changing discretely when rates fall from high levels, but not from low ones. In any event, building activity goes up much more when rates fall a given amount from a high level rather than a low one.[37] Finally, in regression (8), we find that the Romer and Romer variable has a modest, but imprecisely estimated, correlation with new supply.

We have also estimated the analogues to table 7C.1 for high versus low supply elasticity markets, using our quantity measure as the dependent variable. We never find a statistically or economically significant relationship in any specification. Thus, there is no evidence that interest rate sensitivity of quantities in the housing markets differs appreciably across markets by their supply side fundamentals.

Appendix table 7C.2 reports the analogue to table 7.11, using the log of single-family permits, rather than the FHFA price index, as the dependent variable. The first regression shows that a 10 percent increase in the approval rate is associated with a 0.10 log point increase in the construction rate. As before, if we thought the price elasticity of housing supply was two, then we would divide these particular permit coefficients in half to obtain the implied price effects. The ratio of the elasticity of construction with respect to the approval rate divided by the price elasticity of housing with respect to the approval rate should equal the elasticity of housing supply. Comparing the relevant numbers from table 7.11 and table 7C.2 finds a ratio of 5.6, which is substantially higher than the elasticity of 2 reported in Topel and Rosen (1988).

When state–year fixed effects are controlled for (column [4]), the coefficient on approval rates becomes only marginally significant. The IV regression using the interest rate interactions (column [2]) yields a much higher coefficient of 2.37, which is relatively close to two times the 1.32 coefficient found in table 7.11. Regression (6) includes both the approval rate and the loan-to-value measure. The approval rate coefficient is substantially higher for this set of metropolitan areas, while the loan-to-value coefficient is positive but insignificant.

37. This change relative to prices does not appear to be due to construction activity growing all that much less than real prices during the boom. From 1996 to 2005 (when construction peaked), total housing permits in the United States increased by 40 percent (single-family permits rose by 48 percent over the same time period), compared to a 49 percent rise in the FHFA price index from 1996 to 2006.

Table 7C.2   Effect of credit availability on construction

Dependent variable	OLS log permits (1)	OLS log permits (2)	OLS log permits (3)	OLS log permits (4)	IV log permits (5)	OLS log permits (6)
Raw approval rate	1.00*** (0.16)			0.84** (0.47)	2.37*** (0.75)	4.75*** (0.52)
Regression-adjusted approval rate		0.97** (0.17)				
Approval rate corrected using 1996 weights			0.78*** (0.16)			
Mean LTV						0.25 (0.17)
Linear trend × January temperature/10	0.0053*** (0.0015)	0.0050*** (0.0016)	0.0053*** (0.0016)		0.0047*** (0.0016)	
Linear trend × Wharton regulation index	−0.012*** (0.0016)	−0.012*** (0.0016)	−0.012*** (0.0017)		−0.013*** (0.0018)	
Observations	5,645	5,645	5,644	5,607	5,644	924
Adjusted R^2	0.950	0.949	0.950	0.397		0.958
Fixed effects	MSA	MSA	MSA	State–year	MSA	MSA
MSAs	298	298	298	296	298	84
Years	1990–2008	1990–2008	1990–2008	1990–2008	1990–2008	1998–2008
First-stage F-statistic					8.71	

Notes: Dependent variable: Log single-family permits by MSA. The dependent variable is the log of housing permits issued in the metropolitan area. Standard errors, in parentheses, are clustered by MSA. All regressions include year fixed effects. Year dummies interacted with branch banking regulations and foreclosure speed instrument for approval rates.

***Significant at the 1 percent level.

**Significant at the 5 percent level.

*Significant at the 10 percent level.

References

Bubb, Ryan, and Alex Kaufman. 2009. "Securitization and Moral Hazard: Evidence from a Lender Cutoff Rule." Federal Reserve Bank of Boston Public Policy Discussion Paper no. 09-5, September.

Campbell, John Y., and Joao F. Cocco. 2011. "A Model of Mortgage Default." Unpublished Paper, Harvard University, October.

Case, Karl E., and Robert J. Shiller. 2003. "Is There a Bubble in the Housing Market?" *Brookings Papers on Economic Activity* 2:299–342.

Chinco, Alex, and Chris Mayer. 2011. "Noise Traders, Distant Speculators and Asset Bubbles in the Housing Market." Working Paper, NYU Stern School of Business, October 15.

Coleman, Major D., Michael LaCour-Little, and Kerry D. Vandell. 2008. "Subprime Lending and the Housing Bubble: Tail Wags Dog?" Working Paper, University of California, Irvine. Available at SSRN: http://papers.ssrn.com/sol3/papers.cfm?abstract_id=1262365.

Favilukis, Jack, Sydney Ludvigson, and Stijn Van Nieuwerburgh. 2010, "Macroeconomic Implications of Housing Wealth, Housing Finance, and Limited Risk-Sharing in General Equilibrium." Social Science Research Network Working Paper, May 7. Available at SSRN: http://ssrn.com/abstract=1602163.

Ferreira, Fernando, and Joseph Gyourko. 2011. "Anatomy of the Beginning of the Housing Boom: US Neighborhoods and Metropolitan Areas, 1993–2009." Working Paper, University of Pennsylvania. http://real.wharton.upenn.edu/~fferreir/documents/housing%20boom%20August%2018%202011.pdf.

Ferreira, Fernando, Joseph Gyourko, and Joseph Tracy. 2010. "Housing Busts and Household Mobility." *Journal of Urban Economics* 68 (1): 34–45.

Garriga, Carlos. 2009. "Lending Standards in Mortgage Markets." *Economic Synopses,* no. 23, Federal Reserve Bank of St. Louis. Posted May 6.

Glaeser, Edward L., Joshua D. Gottlieb, and Joseph Gyourko. 2010. "Can Cheap Credit Explain the Housing Boom?" NBER Working Paper no. 16230. Cambridge, MA: National Bureau of Economic Research.

Glaeser, Edward L., and Joseph Gyourko. 2006. "Housing Dynamics." NBER Working Paper no. 12787. Cambridge, MA: National Bureau of Economic Research.

———. 2008. "The Case against Housing Price Supports." *The Economists' Voice* 5 (6): Article 3.

Glaeser, Edward L., Joseph Gyourko, and Albert Saiz. 2008. "Housing Supply and Housing Bubbles." *Journal of Urban Economics* 64 (2): 198–217.

Greenspan, Alan. 2010. "The Crisis." *Brookings Papers on Economic Activity* 2010 (1): 201–46. Washington, DC: Brookings Institution.

Gyourko, Joseph, Albert Saiz, and Anita Summers. 2008. "A New Measure of the Local Regulatory Environment for Housing Markets." *Urban Studies* 45 (3): 693–729.

Haughwout, Andrew, Donghoon Lee, Joseph Tracy, and Wilbert van der Klaauw. 2011. "Real Estate Investors, the Leverage Cycle and the Housing Market Crisis." Federal Reserve Bank of New York Staff Report no. 514, September.

Haurin, Donald R., Susan M. Wachter, and Patric H. Hendershott. 1995. "Wealth Accumulation and Housing Choices of Young Households: An Exploratory Investigation." NBER Working Paper no. 5070. Cambridge, MA: National Bureau of Economic Research.

Himmelberg, Charles, Christopher Mayer, and Todd Sinai. 2005. "Assessing High House Prices: Bubbles, Fundamentals and Misperceptions." *Journal of Economic Perspectives* 19 (4): 67–92.

Keys, Benjamin J., Tanmoy Mukherjee, Amit Seru, and Vikrant Vig. 2009. "Financial Regulation and Securitization: Evidence from Subprime Mortgage Loans." *Journal of Monetary Economics* 56 (5): 700–20.

———. 2010. "Did Securitization Lead to Lax Screening? Evidence from Subprime Loans." *Quarterly Journal of Economics* 125 (1): 307–62.

Khandani, Amir, Andrew W. Lo, and Robert C. Merton. 2009. "Systemic Risk and the Refinancing Ratchet Effect." NBER Working Paper no. 15362. Cambridge, MA: National Bureau of Economic Research.

Mas, Alexandre, and Enrico Moretti. 2009. "Peers at Work." *American Economic Review* 99 (1): 112–45.

Mayer, Christopher J., and Gary V. Engelhardt. 1996. "Gifts, Down Payments, and Housing Affordability." *Journal of Housing Research* 7 (1): 59–77.

Mayer, Christopher J., and Todd Sinai. 2009. "US House Price Dynamics and Behavioral Finance." In *Policy Making Insights from Behavioral Economics,* edited by Christopher L. Foote, Lorenz Goette, and Stephan Meier, chapter 5. Boston: Federal Reserve Bank of Boston.

Mian, Atif, and Amir Sufi. 2008. "The Consequences of Mortgage Credit Expansion: Evidence from the US Mortgage Default Crisis." NBER Working Paper no. 13936. Cambridge, MA: National Bureau of Economic Research.

———. 2009. "The Consequences of Mortgage Credit Expansion: Evidence from the US Mortgage Default Crisis." *Quarterly Journal of Economics* 122 (4): 1449–96.

———. 2010. "Household Leverage and the Recession of 2007 to 2009." NBER Working Paper no. 15892. Cambridge, MA: National Bureau of Economic Research.

Mian, Atif, Amir Sufi, and Francisco Trebbi. 2008. "The Political Economy of the US Mortgage Default Crisis." NBER Working Paper no. 14468. Cambridge, MA: National Bureau of Economic Research.

Munnell, Alicia H., Geoffrey M. B. Tootell, Lynn E. Browne, and James McEneaney. 1996. "Mortgage Lending in Boston: Interpreting HMDA Data." *American Economic Review* 86 (1): 25–53.

Newey, Whitney K., and Kenneth D. West. 1987. "A Simple, Positive Semi-Definite, Heteroskedasticity and Autocorrelation Consistent Covariance Matrix." *Econometrica* 55 (3): 703–38.

Pence, Karen M. 2006. "Foreclosing on Opportunity: State Laws and Mortgage Credit." *Review of Economics and Statistics* 88 (1): 177–82.

Polinsky, A. Mitchell, and David T. Ellwood. 1979. "An Empirical Reconciliation of Micro and Grouped Estimates of the Demand for Housing." *Review of Economics and Statistics* 61 (2): 199–205.

Poterba, James. 1984. "Tax Subsidies to Owner-Occupied Housing: An Asset-Market Approach." *Quarterly Journal of Economics* 99 (4): 729–52.

Poterba, James, and Todd Sinai. 2008. "Tax Expenditures for Owner-Occupied Housing: Deductions for Property Taxes and Mortgage Interest and the Exclusion of Imputed Rental Income." *American Economic Review Papers and Proceedings* 96 (2): 84–89.

Rice, Tara, and Philip E. Strahan. 2010. "Does Credit Competition Affect Small-Firm Finance?" *Journal of Finance* 65 (3): 861–89.

Romer, Christina D., and David H. Romer. "A New Measure of Monetary Shocks: Derivation and Implications." *American Economic Review* 94 (4): 1055–84.

Saiz, Albert. 2003. "Room in the Kitchen for the Melting Pot: Immigration and Rental Prices." *Review of Economics and Statistics* 85 (3): 502–21.

———. 2007. "Immigration and Housing Rents in American Cities." *Journal of Urban Economics* 61 (2): 345–71.

———. 2008. "On Local Housing Supply Elasticity." Working Paper, The Wharton

School. Available at SSRN: http://papers.ssrn.com/sol3/papers.cfm?abstract _id=1193422.

Shiller, Robert J. 2005. *Irrational Exuberance,* 2nd ed. Princeton, NJ: Princeton University Press.

———. 2006. "Long-Term Perspectives on the Current Boom in Home Prices." *The Economists' Voice* 3 (4): 4.

Taylor, John B. 2009. *Getting off Track: How Government Actions and Interventions Caused, Prolonged, and Worsened the Financial Crisis.* Stanford: Hoover Institution Press.

Topel, Robert, and Sherwin Rosen. 1988. "Housing Investment in the United States." *Journal of Political Economy* 96 (4): 718–40.

The Future of the Government-Sponsored Enterprises
The Role for Government in the US Mortgage Market

Dwight Jaffee and John M. Quigley

8.1   Introduction

The two large government-sponsored housing enterprises (GSEs),[1] the Federal National Mortgage Association ("Fannie Mae") and the Federal Home Loan Mortgage Corporation ("Freddie Mac"), evolved over three-quarters of a century from a single small government agency, to a large and powerful duopoly, and ultimately to insolvent institutions protected from bankruptcy only by the full faith and credit of the US government. From the beginning of 2008 to the end of 2011, the two GSEs lost capital of $266 billion, requiring draws of $188 billion under the Treasured Preferred Stock Purchase Agreements to remain in operation; see Federal Housing Finance Agency (2011). This downfall of the two GSEs was primarily a question of "when," not "if," given that their structure as a public/private

Dwight Jaffee is the Willis Booth Professor of Banking, Finance, and Real Estate at the University of California, Berkeley. John M. Quigley was the I. Donald Terner Distinguished Professor and professor of economics at the University of California, Berkeley.

We are grateful to the Fisher Center for Real Estate and Urban Economics at the University of California, Berkeley, for financial support and to Sandley Chou for research assistance. We thank Stuart Gabriel of UCLA, Mark Willis of NYU, and Karen Dynan of the Brookings Institution, as well as the book editors, Ed Glaeser and Todd Sinai, together with all the participants in the two NBER conferences, for helpful comments. Dwight Jaffee adds, with great sadness, that John Quigley, friend, colleague, and coauthor, passed away on May 12, 2012. The chapter was essentially complete by that date, and the further changes are minor and made to prepare it for publication. For acknowledgments, sources of research support, and disclosure of the authors' material financial relationships, if any, please see http://www.nber.org/chapters /c12625.ack.

1. A third, much smaller, Government Sponsored Housing Enterprise is the Federal Home Loan Bank System (FHLBS). The issues for reforming the FHLBS are similar to many of the issues raised in this chapter for Fannie Mae and Freddie Mac, although we have not analyzed separately the FHLBS or other nonhousing government enterprises.

partnership provided a strong incentive for excessive risk taking. The failing mortgage market conditions in 2008 then determined the "when." This chapter traces the transformation of the GSEs from privately held institutions with powerful direction and political influence to their current status as vassals reporting to an administrative agency in the Department of Housing and Urban Development (the Federal Housing Finance Agency, FHFA).

Within the next few years, the GSEs will have to be restructured. Proposals for reform include recapitalizing them in some form as GSEs, reconstituting them as agencies of the federal government with more narrowly-specified missions, or privatizing the organizations. There are also proposals to replace the GSEs with a variety of new government mortgage guarantee/insurance programs. The GSE reform and mortgage guarantee proposals are both nested within the larger question of what are the likely consequences of alternative roles for government in the US housing and mortgage markets. This chapter is intended to help in the deliberations of "what to do" about these costly failures. We briefly review the history of the housing enterprises and their performance, including the recent housing crisis. We document the contributions of Freddie and Fannie to the operation of US housing markets, and we analyze the role of the agencies in the recent housing crisis. We search for evidence on the importance of Freddie and Fannie in achieving other important housing goals. We compare US policies with those adopted in other developed countries.

This is not the first time we have provided some analysis of the reform options in housing finance, either individually (Jaffee 2010a, 2010b, 2011; Quigley 2006) or jointly (Jaffee and Quigley 2007, 2010). However, it is our first attempt to relate the full history and to consider all of the options.

In section 8.2 we discuss the background and origin of the GSEs, the evolution of their structure as a public/private partnership, and the federal role in supplying housing credit. Section 8.3 provides a brief summary of home ownership and government policy. Section 8.4 describes the broader objectives and goals of the GSE institutions and analyzes the most recent failures of the credit market and the secondary housing market. Section 8.5 describes the likely consequences of a series of plans concerning the restructuring of the GSEs and alternative mechanisms for government support of the US mortgage market. It also provides a brief summary of the GSEs under their government conservatorship since September 2008.

8.2   Background

With the public sale of its stock and its conversion into a government-sponsored enterprise in 1968, the Federal National Mortgage Association (FNMA) emerged from obscurity as an agent in the market for home mortgage credit. The FNMA had been established in 1938, based on provisions in the 1934 National Housing Act, after the collapse of the housing market during the Great Depression. The 1934 act had established the Federal Housing Administration (FHA) to oversee a program of home mortgage insurance against default. Insurance was funded by the proceeds of a fixed-premium charged on unpaid loan balances. These revenues were deposited in Treasury securities and managed as a mutual insurance fund. Significantly, default insurance was offered on "economically sound" self-amortizing mortgages with terms as long as twenty years and with loan-to-value ratios up to 80 percent.

Diffusion of the new FHA product across the country required national standardization of underwriting procedures. Appraisals were required, and borrowers' credit histories and financial capacities were reported and evaluated systematically. The Mutual Mortgage Insurance Fund, established to manage the reserve of FHA premiums, was required to be actuarially sound. This was generally understood to allow very small redistributions from high income to low income FHA mortgagees. By its original design, the FHA was clearly intended to serve the vast majority of home owners.

In the 1934 act, Congress had also sought to encourage private establishment of National Mortgage Associations that would buy and sell the new and unfamiliar insured mortgages of the Federal Housing Administration. By creating a secondary market for these assets, the associations sought to increase the willingness of primary lenders to make these loans. No private associations were formed, however. When further liberalization of the terms under which associations could be organized was still unsuccessful, the Federal National Mortgage Association was chartered in 1938 by the Federal Housing Administrator following the request of the President of the United States. Federal action was precipitated particularly by concern over the acceptability of new FHA 90 percent twenty-five-year loans authorized that year.

At first, the association operated on a small scale, but its willingness to buy FHA mortgages encouraged lenders to make them. A 1948 authorization to purchase mortgages guaranteed by the Veterans Administration (VA) led the association to make purchases, commitments, loans, and investments that soon approached the congressionally authorized limit of $2.5 billion. Since the maximum interest rate on VA mortgages was below the market rate, FNMA's advance commitments to buy VA-guaranteed mortgages at par assured windfall gains to private borrowers or lenders. The 1954 Housing Act reorganized Fannie Mae as a mixed-ownership corporation with eligible shareholders being the federal government and lenders that sold mortgages to Fannie Mae. The FNMA was then able to finance its operations through sale of its preferred stock to the US Treasury, through sale of its common stock to lenders whose mortgages it bought, and by the sale of bonds to the public.

The Housing and Urban Development Act of 1968 transferred FNMA's special assistance program and the management and liquidation of part of its portfolio to the newly constituted Government National Mortgage Association. Its secondary market operations remained with FNMA, now owned entirely by private stockholders. Commercial banks were the primary beneficiaries of FNMA's secondary market activities in FHA and VA mortgages, since the banks specialized in originating the government-guaranteed mortgages. In contrast, the mortgages originated by Savings and Loan Associations (S&Ls) and Mutual Savings Banks were primarily "conventional" mortgages, meaning they received no government guarantee. The thrift institutions (covering savings and loan associations, mutual savings banks, and credit unions) lobbied for equal treatment, and were rewarded in 1970 with the establishment of the Federal Home Loan Mortgage Corporation ("Freddie Mac") under the regulatory control of the Federal Home Loan Bank System, the S&L regulator. Freddie Mac stock first became publicly available in 1989, although shares owned by Freddie Mac's financial partners had been traded on the New York Stock Exchange starting in 1984.

The structure of Fannie Mae and Freddie Mac as government-sponsored enterprises was established by the 1968 and 1970 legislation that created the two firms in their current form. They are private entities in the sense that they are shareholder owned with stock that traded on the New York Stock Exchange, were increasingly managed to maximize profits, and were not part of the federal government budget. They were also public entities in the sense that they were chartered by Congress (which could therefore change their charter), some members of the boards of directors are selected by the president, and they were regulated by the government to enhance a variety of public policy goals. They were aptly described as public/private partnerships.

This "partnership" left open the question whether the government would be liable for the debt instruments issued by the GSEs if the enterprises were to fail. While their charters indicated no formal guarantee, the GSEs immediately suggested there was an "implicit government guarantee," and market investors generally believed this was the case. Indeed, this expectation was fulfilled in 2008 when the government did guarantee all the GSE debt instruments as part of the Conservatorship. The implicit guarantee provided the GSEs with a strong incentive to carry out high yielding but risky investments, since the gains would go to the GSE shareholders, while serious losses would be the responsibility of the government. Starting in about 1990, it became increasingly clear that the GSEs were following this strategy, first by taking on significant amounts of interest rate risk, and later taking on significant amounts of credit risk in the midst of the subprime mortgage boom. Once the government acquiesced in allowing the concept of an implicit government guarantee to gain traction, it was inevitable that the combination of GSE risk taking and a market crash would cause the firms to fail.

8.3 Home Ownership and Government Policy

According to Tocqueville (1835), Americans have long been obsessed with owner-occupied housing. Richard Green (2011) sees this as a political issue, as societies are less disposed to make revolution when personal and real property is augmented and distributed among the population. Other recent work emphasizes the external benefits of owner-occupied housing, and a large social science literature has developed exploring the connection between higher levels of home ownership and the economic and social outcomes of households. Table 8A.1 in the appendix reports some of the findings linking home ownership to social outcomes. Two other papers (Dietz and Haurin 2003; Haurin, Dietz, and Weinberg 2002) provide an exhaustive comparison of the economic and social consequences for those living in owner-occupied and rental housing.

Most of the research supports the conclusion that home ownership has some positive effects upon the social outcomes for individuals and households. But the research does not conclude that the effect is very large. And even if the effect were large, nothing supports the conclusion that home ownership should be supported by the institution of the GSEs or their policy choices. In particular, the primary impact of instruments that focus on lowering the cost or expanding the availability of mortgages will be larger mortgages, which makes those instruments ineffective and costly relative to direct subsidies for home ownership. This is important since, as noted later, many of the popular arguments in support of subsidies for the GSEs are based upon the promotion of home ownership in the economy.

8.4 Policy Objectives for the GSEs

8.4.1 Primary Objectives

The GSE charters state the goals and responsibilities of the enterprises, and do so without direct reference to home ownership goals. Instead, they seek to:

1. Provide stability in the secondary market for residential mortgages.
2. Respond appropriately to the private capital market.
3. Provide ongoing assistance to the secondary market for residential mortgages (including activities relating to mortgages on housing for low- and moderate-income families involving a reasonable economic return that may be less than the return earned on other activities) by increasing the liquidity of mortgage investments and improving the distribution of investment capital available for residential mortgage financing.
4. Promote access to mortgage credit throughout the nation (including

central cities, rural areas, and underserved areas) by increasing the liquidity of mortgage investments and improving the distribution of investment capital available for residential mortgage financing.

5. Manage and liquidate federally owned mortgage portfolios in an orderly manner, with a minimum of adverse effect upon the residential mortgage market and minimum loss to the Federal Government.

This section reviews the key activities of the GSEs with respect to providing stability, assistance, and liquidity to the secondary market for residential mortgages. The specific objectives of the secondary market activities have varied over time, including operations to reinforce or offset fiscal and monetary policy, to increase residential construction, to make a market in federally underwritten mortgages, to reduce regional yield differentials, and to act as a mortgage lender of last resort. (See Guttentag [1963] for an extensive discussion of these key activities.)

Quantitative Impact of the GSEs on the US Home Mortgage Market

Table 8.1 reviews the quantitative role of the GSEs in the US mortgage market over the recent past. The top panel reports the outstanding amounts of whole home mortgages at the end of each decade from 1950 through 2010. Through 1960, all whole home mortgages were held directly in portfolios, and even by 1970 the only exception was $3 billion of whole mortgages backing the first mortgage-backed securities (MBS) issued by the newly established Government National Mortgage Association (GNMA). The largest portfolio investor has always been the depository institutions (commercial banks and thrift institutions). The "market investor" portfolio category includes capital market entities such as pension funds, mutual funds, and insurance companies. The GSE category covers the Fannie Mae on-balance-sheet portfolio through 1970 and the sum of the Fannie Mae and Freddie Mac portfolios thereafter.

Figure 8.1 shows the percentage of whole mortgages held directly in portfolios for each of the three investor classes. The depository institutions have always been the predominant holder of whole mortgages. At year-end 2010, for example, the depository institutions held 76 percent (= /$2,959/$3,918) of all whole mortgages that were directly held in portfolios, with the market investors and the GSEs each holding a 12 percent share. Starting in 1980, however, the portfolio holdings of whole home mortgages were increasingly transferred to MBS pools. The top panel of table 8.1 shows the three main categories of MBS pools: pools issued by the GSEs, by GNMA, and by private label securitizers (PLS).

The middle panel of table 8.1 shows each of the categories for whole home mortgage holdings as a percentage of the total amount outstanding. One major trend is that the portfolio holdings declined steadily from 100

Table 8.1   **Outstanding whole home mortgages**

				Year			
	1950	1960	1970	1980	1990	2000	2010
			A. Billions of dollars				
Portfolio holdings	$45	$141	$289	$851	$1,496	$2,297	$3,918
Depository institutions	27	95	207	642	1,066	1,669	2,959
Market investors	17	40	65	146	316	441	478
GSE portfolios	1	6	17	62	114	187	481
Mortgage pools	0	0	3	107	1,111	2,811	6,614
GSE pools	0	0	0	13	652	1814	4,311
GNMA pools	0	0	3	94	404	612	1,038
PLS pools	0	0	0	0	55	386	1,265
Total	$45	$141	$292	$958	$2,606	$5,108	$10,531
			B. Percentage of total				
Portfolio holdings	100%	100%	99%	89%	57%	45%	37%
Depository institutions	60	67	71	67	41	33	28
Market investors	38	29	22	15	12	5	5
GSE portfolios	2	4	6	7	4	8	5
Mortgage pools	0	0	1	11	43	55	63
GSE pools	0	0	0	1	25	36	41
GNMA pools	0	0	1	10	15	12	10
PLS pools	0	0	0	0	2	8	12
Total	100%	100%	100%	100%	100%	100%	100%
			C. GSE whole loans held + MBS issued				
	3%	4%	6%	8%	29%	44%	46%

Source: See data appendix.

percent of the total in 1960 to 37 percent of the total by 2010. Among the portfolio investors, both depository institution and market investor holdings declined steadily starting in 1970. The GSE portfolio holdings of whole home mortgages, 5 percent of the total in 2010, remained a small percentage of the total throughout the history, with fluctuations within the narrow band of 3 percent to 8 percent of the total.

The corresponding major trend reported in the middle panel of table 8.1 is the steady rise in mortgage pools as a percentage of the total, starting at 1 percent in 1970 and reaching 63 percent of the total by 2010. The GSE pools show the most rapid rise, reaching 41 percent of total outstanding home mortgages by 2010. The PLS pools also grew steadily, reaching 12 percent of the total by 2010. The GNMA pool share of total outstanding mortgages,

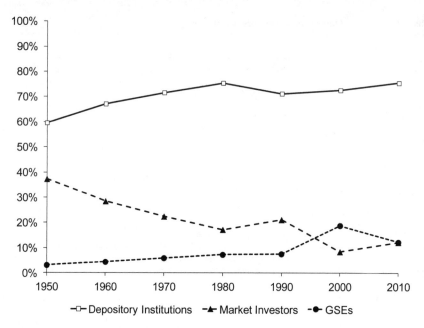

Fig. 8.1   Share of whole mortgages held directly, by holder class
Source: See data appendix.

10 percent at year-end 2010, fluctuated in a narrow range between 10 percent and 15 percent of the total from 1980 to the present.

The bottom panel of table 8.1 shows the direct GSE share of the home mortgage market, computed as the sum of whole mortgages held in the GSE portfolios and their outstanding MBS. While this GSE share rose steadily from 1950, the primary increase started in 1990, with the share reaching 46 percent of all outstanding home mortgages in 2010. This direct share does not include MBS from other issuers that were held in the GSE portfolios, a topic to which we turn later.[2]

While table 8.1 accounts for all outstanding home mortgages, it does not distinguish among the investor groups holding the MBS instruments created by the mortgage pools. This issue is addressed in table 8.2, in which ownership of the MBS pools has been allocated among the various investor classes. These values are then combined with the portfolio holdings of whole mortgages to determine the ownership structure of all home mortgages, whether held as whole mortgages or as investment in MBS pools.[3] It is apparent from

2. Quantitatively, including the GSE holdings of other MBS would raise the total GSE share to 47 percent and 48 percent for 2000 and 2010, respectively. This ratio actually peaked in 2003, reaching 50 percent.
3. As far as we are aware, this integration of whole mortgage portfolio holdings and MBS pools by investor has not been available previously.

Table 8.2   **Holdings of whole home mortgages and MBS by investor class**

	1950	1960	1970	1980	1990	2000	2010
			Billions of dollars				
Depository institutions							
Whole mortgages	$27	$95	$207	$642	$1,066	$1,669	$2,959
MBS	0	0	0	41	385	604	1,368
Total	27	95	207	683	1,450	2,272	4,326
Market investors							
Whole mortgages	17	40	65	146	316	195	478
MBS	0	0	3	66	714	1,446	4,444
Total	17	40	68	212	1,030	1,641	4,923
GSEs							
Whole mortgages	1	6	17	62	114	433	481
MBS	0	0	0	0	12	762	802
Total	1	6	17	62	126	1,195	1,283
Total home mortgages	$45	$141	$292	$958	$2,606	$5,107	$10,531

Source: See data appendix.

table 8.2 that, starting in 1980, market investors were expanding relative to the depository institutions and the GSEs, and that by 2010 the market investors were the largest investor class for the sum of whole mortgages and mortgage securities.

Figure 8.2 reports the percentage of outstanding MBS for the three holder classes.[4] It is apparent that the market investors have always been dominant in holding MBS positions. At year-end 2010, market investors were holding 67 percent (= $4,444/$6,614) of the outstanding MBS, with depository institutions holding 21 percent and the GSEs 12 percent.

Figure 8.3 combines the results for figures 8.1 and 8.2, reporting the share for each holder class of their combined positions in whole mortgages and MBS. By 2010, the market investors had the largest position, representing 47 percent of all home mortgages, with depository institutions in the second position, holding 41 percent of all home mortgages. At the same time, the GSEs were holding 12 percent of all home mortgages (as either whole mortgages or MBS) a share just below their average over the last three decades.

Figure 8.3 indicates that the GSE combined holdings of whole mortgages and MBS has always represented a relatively small share of total US home mortgages outstanding. In this sense, closing the GSEs now, in an orderly way, would have a minor impact on the US mortgage market. That is, the 12 percent GSE share could be readily replaced by a combination of market investors and depository institutions (who between them are already holding

4. The graphs start in 1970, since there were no outstanding MBS before that year.

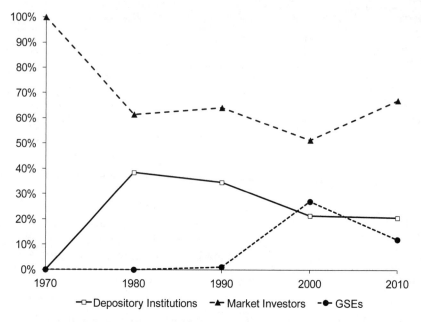

Fig. 8.2   Share of MBS outstanding, by holder class
Source: See data appendix.

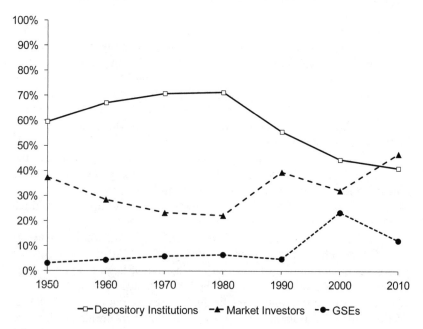

Fig. 8.3   Share of whole mortgages and MBS, by holder class
Source: See data appendix.

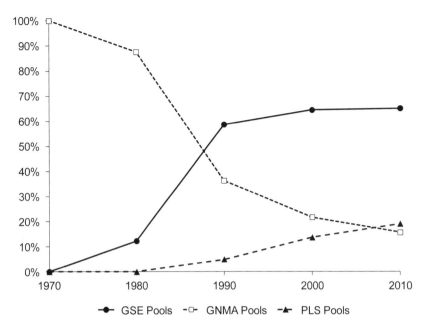

Fig. 8.4   Share of MBS outstanding, by MBS issuer
Source: See data appendix.

88 percent of US home mortgages). There are, however, two other measures of potential GSE benefits with regard to outstanding whole mortgages and MBS: (1) the contribution of MBS issued by the GSEs, and (2) stabilization of the US home mortgage market through countercyclical activities by the GSEs. We now consider these in turn.

The Role of GSE-Issued MBS

Figure 8.4 shows the relative shares of outstanding home mortgage MBS by issuer class. The GSE share has been dominant since 1990, representing 65 percent of all outstanding MBS in 2010. The share of private label securitizers (PLS) has been steadily rising, but still represented only 19 percent of outstanding MBS at year-end 2010. The GNMA share has been steadily declining, reaching a 16 percent market share by year-end 2010.

The dominant historical position of GSE MBS in the current US home mortgage is sometimes used to justify a future role for the GSEs in the market. But, at its core, the GSE dominance of the MBS market for home mortgages has been largely derived from the assumption of market investors—reinforced by GSE marketing—that the GSE MBS had an implicit government guarantee. In this sense, the dominant GSE MBS position is just an example of *crowding out,* whereby any asset with a low-cost government guarantee against loss will likely replace private activity in the same market. If the government guarantee were eliminated, there is every reason to expect that private market activity would simply replace the activity of the government entity.

A brief review of the history of US MBS development is valuable for understanding the limited contribution of the GSEs to MBS innovations.[5]

- 1968: GNMA creates first modern MBS by securitizing FHA/VA mortgages.
- 1970s: GSEs expand MBS market based on their implicit government guarantee.[6]
- 1980s: Salomon Bros. securitizes multiclass, nonguaranteed, MBS instruments.[7]
- 1990s: Multiclass (structured finance) mechanism is first applied to wide range. of asset-backed securities, including auto, credit card, and commercial mortgage loans.
- 2000s: Subprime lending rapidly expands by applying structured MBS methods.

Credit for the modern innovation of single-class MBS belongs to the government itself with the creation of the GNMA MBS. The GNMA was, and remains, an agency within the Department of Housing and Urban Development. Likewise, credit for the innovation of the multiclass MBS belongs to the private sector with the development of structured MBS by Salomon Bros. in the 1980s. In fact, the GSEs have always been followers, not innovators, in the MBS market. The success of the GSEs in establishing the market for their own MBS depended entirely on the perception of capital market investors as facing no credit risk as the result of the implicit federal guarantee. Absent this government guarantee, the single-class GSE MBS would have simply lost out in the marketplace to the multiclass, private-label, MBS.

The GSE proponents often argue that the GSEs reduced securitization costs and mortgage interest rates. Here, too, the reality is that the GSEs provide no benefit other than the implicit guarantee. A case in point is the TBA ("to be announced") forward market for GSE and GNMA MBS. While this market arguably expands the liquidity of the traded MBS, the

5. The US mortgage securitization probably actually began soon after the founding of the republic. Following the War of 1812, the US federal government was desperate for revenue and extended loans to homesteaders for property on the Western frontiers. Without the resources to make and hold these loans, the government pooled and sold these loans to investors. By the 1920s, securitization was already a well-accepted format for selling loans to investors. These mortgage-backed securities failed during the real estate crisis of the 1930s, and it was decades before US securitization was reactivated in 1968. See Quinn (2010) for a new history of US housing policy and the origins of securitization.

6. The GSEs could point to their $2.25 billion line of credit at the US Treasury as backing for their guarantee, a significant factor only in the early years when their scale of operations was relatively small. It also helped the GSE case that the US government never firmly and officially rejected the notion of an implicit guarantee.

7. The colorful development of private-label MBS under Lewis Ranieri at Salomon Brothers is wonderfully chronicled in *Liars Poker* by Lewis (1990).

benefit depends completely on the market's perception that the guarantees—explicit for GNMA and implicit for the GSE MBS—make credit risk irrelevant in the pricing and trading of the securities. It is equally noteworthy that the markets for *asset-backed securitization,* for the securitization of credit card, auto, and commercial mortgage loans, and other loan classes as well, expanded rapidly starting in the early 1990s without any contribution from the GSEs. Indeed, as with the original GNMA MBS, the GSEs benefited from the innovation by others, creating their own structured finance offerings once the market demand for such securities had been expanded through private market innovation.[8]

Finally, the claim is sometimes made that the GSE MBS activity is critical for the survival of the thirty-year, fixed-rate, residential mortgage. This claim is unwarranted. In fact, two features of the GSE MBS instrument directly deter the expansion of the long-term, fixed-rate, mortgage:

First, the GSE MBS transfer the entire interest rate risk imbedded in the fixed-rate mortgages to the market investors who purchased the instruments. The GSEs took no action to mitigate this risk.

Second, the GSE MBS generally disallowed prepayment penalties on all the mortgages they securitized. While borrowers may have felt they benefitted from this "free" call option, it greatly magnified the interest rate risk imposed on investors in the GSE MBS, and led to higher interest rates on the fixed-rate mortgages.

Finally, a number of Western European countries successfully use long-term, fixed rate mortgages, but have no entity comparable to the GSEs; Denmark is the most conspicuous example. The use of covered bonds also allows European banks to hold long-term mortgages on their balance sheets, while passing a substantial part of the interest-rate risk to capital market investors. We further discuss the experience of Western European countries in the section on mortgage markets without GSEs.

The Limited GSE Contributions to Mortgage Market Stability

The GSEs claim credit for taking actions to stabilize the US mortgage markets. The US Government Accountability Office (2009), however, finds little evidence of such benefits:

[T]he extent to which the enterprises have been able to support a stable and liquid secondary mortgage market during periods of economic stress, which are key charter and statutory obligations, is not clear. In 1996, we attempted to determine the extent to which the enterprises' activities would support mortgage finance during stressful economic periods by analyzing Fannie Mae's mortgage activities in some states, including oil producing states such as Texas and Louisiana, beginning in the 1980s.

---

8. See Downing, Jaffee, and Wallace (2009) for a discussion of how the GSEs profited by restructuring their simple pass-through MBS into more complex multitranche securitizations.

Specifically, we analyzed state-level data on Fannie Mae's market shares and housing price indexes for the years 1980–1994. We did not find sufficient evidence that Fannie Mae provided an economic cushion to mortgage markets in those states during the period analyzed.

Reports by the Congressional Budget Office (1996, 2010) come to similar conclusions. The academic literature also generally concludes that the GSE contribution to US mortgage market stability has been modest at best. This view is stated in early studies by Jaffee and Rosen (1978, 1979) and more recent studies by Frame and White (2005) and Lehnert, Passmore, and Sherlund (2008). In contrast, Naranjo and Toevs (2002), a study funded by Fannie Mae, found evidence of effective stabilization by the GSEs, as did other studies carried out internally by the GSEs. Unlike the previous studies, Peek and Wilcox (2003) focused on the flow of mortgage funds, and not on mortgage interest rates, and found the GSE contribution to be countercyclical. Of course, this research was all conducted before the subprime housing bubble and its collapse. As we now document, the GSE participation in the subprime housing bubble was decidedly destabilizing.

The GSE Role in the Subprime Mortgage Boom and Crash

The losses reported by the GSEs starting in 2008 leave no doubt that the GSEs acquired a significant volume of risky mortgages during the subprime boom. However, the extent, timing, and significance of these acquisitions is debated. For example, Jaffee (2010b) describes the GSE role as "expanding" the subprime boom, especially in 2007, whereas Wallison (2011, 2) concludes that GSE activity, based on their housing goals, was a primary "source" of the crisis. In this section, we evaluate the role played by the GSEs in the subprime mortgage boom and crash.

A quantitative evaluation of the GSE role in the subprime crisis faces a number of significant data issues:

1. Definitions for *subprime* and *Alt-A* mortgages differ across data sets, and certain high-risk mortgages are not included under either label.

2. Defining *high-risk mortgages* (including subprime and Alt-A instruments) is necessarily complex because mortgage default risk arises from numerous factors including borrower and property attributes (FICO scores, loan-to-value ratios, etc.), special amortization options (interest only, negative amortization, etc.), and fixed-rate versus adjustable-rate loans.

3. The GSEs could not acquire any mortgages with an initial loan amount above the conforming loan limit (so-called jumbo mortgages).

Our analysis starts by reviewing a newly compiled mortgage origination data set from the GSE regulator, the Federal Housing Finance Agency (2010a).[9] These data compare the risk characteristics of all mortgages

---

9. We thank Robin Seiler of the Federal Housing Finance Agency for providing us with a road map for the intricacies of these data.

acquired by the GSEs (whether securitized or held in retained portfolios) with the risk characteristics of all conforming, conventional, mortgages that were included in private label securitizations (PLS), tabulated by year of mortgage origination. Because the data set has nearly complete coverage and is restricted to conforming mortgages, it provides the best available direct—"apples to apples"—comparison of the GSE acquired mortgages relative to the comparable market. Nevertheless, there are two limitations. First, while the FHFA data include all the conforming mortgages that collateralized PLS MBS instruments, the GSE holdings of PLS tranches are not so identified. We do not expect a significant bias in the comparisons from this source, however, because the GSE PLS holdings were almost entirely AAA tranches with little ex ante credit risk.[10] Second, the FHFA data exclude conforming mortgages that were not securitized (i.e., they were retained in lender portfolios). To the extent that lenders did retain conforming mortgages with high-risk attributes, the FHFA data set will undercount the high-risk dimensions of the overall conforming origination pools, and will therefore overstate the GSE share of all high-risk originations. Here too, we do not expect a significant bias in our comparisons, because most subprime and Alt-A mortgages were securitized, and the securitization rate was even higher among those high-risk loans that were also conforming mortgages.[11]

Panel A of table 8.3 shows the dollar amount of the conforming mortgages by origination year and various risk attributes. Rows 1 to 3 report on loans with one of the identified high-risk factors: high loan-to-value (LTV) ratios, low FICO scores, and adjustable-rate mortgages (ARMs), respectively. However, there is some double counting since some loans have more than one of these attributes. The aggregate high-risk originations shown in row 4 nets out all double counting.[12] Row 6 shows the percentage of high-risk mortgages as a share of total conforming mortgages (in row 5). This

10. See Thomas and Van Order (2011) for further discussion. The PLS tranches as a share of total GSE acquisitions reached its high point at 22.9 percent in 2005, but had fallen to 7.4 percent by 2007. Furthermore, actual cash flow losses on GSE PLS positions have been modest to date, although the GSEs have recognized significant mark to market valuation losses on these positions.

11. For example, 2007 data from *Inside Mortgage Finance* indicate that only $33 billion (or 7 percent) of the subprime/Alt-A mortgages originated that year were not securitized. Even if these were all conforming mortgages, their share of total conforming originations that year would be less than 3 percent. Furthermore, *Inside Mortgage Finance* indicates that over 31 percent of subprime MBS and 9 percent of Alt-A MBS in 2007 were "GSE eligible"—that is, conforming mortgages eligible for GSE purchase—further reducing the incentive of portfolio lenders to hold these mortgages in unsecuritized form. It is also noteworthy that while there is no consensus conclusion from the expanding literature on whether securitization created lax underwriting standards—see, for example, the contrast between Bubb and Kaufman (2009) and Keys et al. (2010)—there is no finding that portfolio lenders were systematically retaining high-risk mortgages.

12. For example, for the fixed-rate mortgage originations in 2007, 2.2 percent had LTV > 90 percent and FICO score < 620. For adjustable rate mortgages in 2007, 19.2 percent had either LTV > 90 percent or FICO score < 620. Overall, in 2007 4.7 percent of the originated mortgages had more than one of the high-risk attributes.

Table 8.3   Conforming mortgage originations by origination year, characteristics, and GSE market share

	2001	2002	2003	2004	2005	2006	2007
A. Conforming originations, billions of dollars[a]							
(1) Loan-to-value ratio > 90%	108	121	154	130	112	115	169
(2) FICO score < 620	94	126	164	194	211	162	92
(3) ARMs	83	200	332	516	579	447	165
(4) High risk originations[b]	241	367	536	664	719	597	374
(5) Total conforming originations	1,064	1,451	2,074	1,331	1,454	1,307	1,117
(6) High risk as % of total conforming	22.6%	25.3%	25.9%	49.9%	49.5%	45.7%	33.5%
B. GSE Share of risk attributes							
(7) Loan-to-value ratio > 90%	92.2%	86.4%	76.0%	59.6%	58.4%	66.8%	93.1%
(8) FICO score < 620	63.9	56.7	47.0	25.1	22.4	32.5	76.8
(9) ARMs	50.7	60.5	56.5	36.8	29.0	33.1	62.6
(10) High risk originations	77.2	72.7	65.3	43.5	36.3	42.5	79.9
(11) GSE share total conforming loans	93.7	91.6	88.7	67.5	61.9	67.1	90.7
C. Relative Intensity (1.0 = "market portfolio")[c]							
(12) Loan-to-value ratio > 90%	0.98	0.94	0.86	0.88	0.94	1.00	1.03
(13) FICO score < 620	0.68	0.62	0.53	0.37	0.36	0.49	0.85
(14) ARMs	0.54	0.66	0.64	0.55	0.47	0.49	0.69
(15) High risk originations	0.82	0.79	0.74	0.64	0.59	0.63	0.88
(16) GSE total conforming loans	1.00	1.00	1.00	1.00	1.00	1.00	1.00

Source: All data are from Federal Housing Finance Agency (2010a).
[a]Conforming mortgage originations exclude originations retained in lender portfolios.
[b]Line (4) = (1) + (2) + (3) – adjustment for mortgages with multiple factors.
[c]Relative intensity = GSE share of risk attribute/GSE share conforming loans (row 11).

high-risk share of total conforming originations rose steadily through 2004 and then declined steadily thereafter.

Panel B of table 8.3 computes the share of the conforming mortgages acquired by the GSEs—whether as backing for their MBS or to hold on their balance sheets—for each risk attribute. For example, in 2001, the GSEs acquired about 92.2 percent of all conforming mortgages with LTV ratios above 90 percent. For all three of the risk attributes, the GSE share fell steadily through 2005 and then expanded rapidly through 2007. By 2007, the

GSEs were acquiring 79.9 percent of the high-risk, conforming mortgage originations. In interpreting these numbers, however, it must be recognized that, as shown in row 11, the GSEs represent a large share of the overall conforming mortgage market; as their overall conforming market share approaches 100 percent, their share of each risk attribute would necessarily do the same.

Panel C corrects for the large GSE share of the conforming market by computing a "relative intensity," dividing the GSE market share for each risk attribute in panel B by the overall GSE market share in row 11. A coefficient of 1 indicates the GSEs are holding the "market portfolio," whereas coefficients below 1 indicate they are avoiding risky mortgages, and coefficients above 1 indicate the GSEs are actively acquiring risky mortgages. The pattern for each of the three risk attributes shows the relative intensity rising steadily starting in 2005. In each case, the high point of the seven-year history was reached in 2007. Since the relative intensities over the full time span are generally less than one, it would appear the GSEs were not leading the market for high-risk lending as the subprime boom took off.[13] But the jump in relative intensity in 2007 for most of the indicators suggest that the GSEs then rapidly expanded their participation in the subprime boom. This is one key basis for our conclusion that the GSEs were a destabilizing influence on the conforming mortgage market as the subprime boom headed to its peak in 2007.

The analysis has so far focused on the GSE acquisition of high-risk mortgages as a share of the overall conforming mortgage market. We now consider the GSE acquisition of high-risk mortgages as a share of their total acquisitions. Table 8.4 reports the three attributes—high LTV ratios, low FICO scores, and ARMs—reported in table 8.3, as well as interest only, condo/coop, and investor loans. The time pattern is again distinctive, with the share of the GSEs' new business dedicated to mortgages with these high-risk attributes generally peaking in 2007, the only exceptions being the declining share of Fannie Mae ARM acquisitions and Freddie Mac interest-only loan acquisitions. These data thus present a second independent basis for our conclusion that the GSEs were a decidedly destabilizing influence on the conforming mortgage market as the subprime boom headed to its peak in 2007.

Mortgage Markets without GSEs

The abovementioned evidence indicates that the GSEs definitively expanded their share of high-risk US mortgages during the later stages of the subprime boom, but there is a further question of how the US mortgage markets would function without the GSEs. To help answer this, in this

13. Thomas and Van Order (2011), although using different data sets, come to the same conclusion.

Table 8.4   Conventional single-family business volume by attribute and year

	2001	2002	2003	2004	2005	2006	2007
Fannie Mae							
LTV > 90%	11%	8%	7%	10%	9%	10%	16%
FICO < 620	6	6	4	6	5	6	6
ARMs	6	9	10	22%	21	17	10
Interest only	n/a	1	1	5	10	15	16
Condo/coop	n/a	7	7	9	10	11	11
Investor	4	5	6	4	5	6	5
Freddie Mac							
LTV > 90%	11%	7%	5%	7%	6%	6%	11%
FICO < 620	4	3	3	4	4	5	6
ARMs	8	12	13	17	18	16	20
Interest only	n/a	n/a	n/a	3	1	0	0
Condo/coop	n/a	n/a	n/a	n/a	n/a	n/a	n/a
Investor	2	2	4	4	4	5	6

Source: Fannie Mae and Freddie Mac Annual Reports.
Note: Loans may have more than one of the characteristics. n/a = not available.

section we consider evidence from two sources: (a) how the US mortgage market performed without GSEs, and (b) the performance of the mortgage markets in Western European countries.

The evidence that private mortgage markets have operated effectively in the US economy can be summarized with three comments on the historical role of private markets within the US mortgage market. First, private markets have always originated 100 percent of US mortgages, and closing the GSEs would not affect this. Second, the GSEs have never held a significant share of the outstanding US home mortgages, this share being, for example, 12 percent at year-end 2010. Third, the GSE MBS share of total home mortgages first exceeded 30 percent only in 2007. This confirms that the private markets—depository institutions and capital market investors—are capable of holding or securitizing the large majority of US mortgages. It is also noteworthy that the market for jumbo mortgages—mortgages that exceed the conforming loan limit—has generally functioned quite satisfactorily.

Turning to the European evidence, the European economies and housing markets are sufficiently similar to the United States to provide a potentially interesting comparison, while they have the key distinction that government intervention in these housing and mortgage markets is far less than for the United States; in particular, none of these countries has entities with any significant resemblance to the US GSEs.[14] This conclusion is stated very clearly by Coles and Hardt (2000, 778):[15]

14. See European Central Bank (2009) for an extensive review of housing finance in the European Union countries.
15. Hardt was the Secretary General of the European Mortgage Federation at the time.

There is no national or European government agency to help lenders fund their loans. Mortgage loans have to be funded on the basis of the financial strength of banks or the intrinsic quality of the securities. EU Law (Article 87 and 88 of the EC treaty) outlaws state aid in the form of guarantees as there may be an element of competitive distortion.

Table 8.5 compares the US and Western European mortgage markets for a range of quantitative attributes from 1998 to 2010 based on a comprehensive database of housing and mortgage data for fifteen European countries from the European Mortgage Federation (2010). Column (1) compares the most recent owner occupancy rates for the United States and European countries. The US value is 66.9 percent, which is just below its peak subprime boom value. It is frequently suggested that the high rate of home ownership is the result of the large US government support of the mortgage market, including the GSEs. It is thus highly revealing that the US rate is just at the median—seven of the European countries have higher owner occupancy rates—and slightly below the average value for the European countries. Furthermore, the lower owner occupancy rates in some of the countries (Germany, for example) appear to be the result of cultural preferences rather than government inaction. A full analysis of the determinants of owner occupancy rates across countries should also control for the age distribution of the population, since younger households, and possibly the oldest households, may have lower ownership rates in all countries. Chiuri and Jappelli (2003) provide a start in this direction, showing that lower down payment rates are a significant factor encouraging owner occupancy after controlling for the population age structure in a sample of fourteen Organization for Economic Cooperation and Development (OCED) countries. The United States has also generally benefitted from very low down payment rates, but it still has an average ownership rate, reinforcing the conclusion that the government interventions have been largely ineffective in raising the US home ownership rate relative to its peers.

Column (2) measures the volatility of housing construction activity from 1998 to 2010 based on the coefficient of variation of housing starts as a measure of relative volatility. The US relative volatility is third highest out of the sixteen countries, implying that the government interventions have failed to reduce US housing cycles relative to those in Western Europe. Column (3) measures the volatility of house price changes based on the standard deviation of the annual house price appreciation from 1998 through 2010. Here the United States stands fifth, meaning the country has faced a relatively high rate of house price volatility. This negative result is all the more significant because the United States is far larger than any of the individual European countries, and thus the benefits of regional diversification should have lowered the observed US volatility.

Column (4) compares the level of mortgage interest rates in Western Europe and the United States, using "representative variable mortgage

Table 8.5 The performance of European mortgage markets in comparison with the United States

	Rate of owner occupancy latest year (1) (%)	Coefficient of covariation of housing starts[a] (2) (%)	Standard deviation of house price inflation (3) (%)	Mortgage adjustable rate average level (4) (%)	Mortgage interest rate average spread[b] (5) (%)	Mortgage To GDP ratio 2010 (6) (%)
Western Europe						
Austria	57.5	7.2	2.7	4.83	1.79	28.0
Belgium	78.0	15.2	7.4	5.61	2.58	46.3
Denmark	53.6	56.1	8.5	5.80	2.58	101.4
Finland	59.0	11.9	3.8	4.13	1.09	42.3
France	57.8	17.4	6.2	4.83	1.80	41.2
Germany	43.2	29.0	1.7	5.07	2.05	46.5
Ireland	74.5	99.2	14.2	4.32	1.15	87.1
Italy	80.0	25.7	3.4	4.70	1.56	22.7
Luxembourg	70.4	17.9	4.7	4.08	1.05	44.7
Netherlands	55.5	14.5	6.5	5.08	2.06	107.1
Norway	85.0	24.6	5.0	6.11	1.44	70.3
Portugal	74.6	35.5	2.9	4.43	1.35	66.3
Spain	85.0	93.0	8.1	4.16	1.08	64.0
Sweden	66.0	45.5	2.9	3.75	0.91	81.8
United Kingdom	66.4	25.0	6.8	5.12	0.93	85.0
EU average	67.1	34.5	5.6	4.80	1.56	62.3
US	66.9	45.5	7.3	5.07	2.26	76.5
US rank	8th of 16	3rd of 16	5th of 16	6th of 16	3rd of 16	6th of 16

Notes: Statistical measures computed with annual data by country for the years 1998 to 2010. Unless noted otherwise, the data are all from European Mortgage Federation (2010), an annual fact book that contains comprehensive mortgage and housing market data for the years 1998 to 2010 for fifteen Western European countries and the United States.

[a]Computations based on housing starts where available; all other countries use housing permits.

[b]The mortgage interest rate spread is based on the three-month Treasury Bill rate from the OECD Economic Outlook Database.

rates" for Europe and the Freddie Mac one-year ARM commitment rate for the United States. The column shows that the United States has the sixth highest average mortgage interest rate from 1998 to 2010, and exceeds the Western European average by 27 basis points. Since overall interest rates also vary across countries, as a further test, column (5) shows the average spread between the mortgage rate and the Treasury bill rate for each country. The United States ranks third highest based on the spread and exceeds the Western European average by 70 basis points. Of course, numerous factors determine these mortgage rates and spreads, including the precise terms of the variable rate mortgages, other contract features such as down payment requirements, and the generally greater credit risk of US mortgages. Nevertheless, the fact remains that despite the government subsidies and other interventions in the US residential mortgage markets, US mortgage rates have remained among the highest levels compared with the countries of Western Europe.

Finally, column (6) shows the 2010 ratio of home mortgages outstanding to each country's annual GDP, a standard measure of the depth of a country's mortgage market. The US ratio is 76.5 percent, which puts it sixth within this group of sixteen developed economies. A relatively high US result would be expected, given the large mortgage subsidies provided through the GSEs and other channels. It is noteworthy, therefore, that five Western European countries achieved even higher ratios without substantial government interventions in their mortgage markets.

The overall conclusion has to be that Western European mortgage and housing markets have outperformed the US markets over the full range of available measures. Although data are not provided here, a similar conclusion would hold for the Australian and Canadian mortgage markets (see Lea 2010). There are, of course, a wide range of possible explanations for the superior performance of the European mortgage markets.[16] The key point for present purposes is simply that the superior performance of the European mortgage markets is *not* explained by greater government intervention. In the absence of GSEs, almost all Western European mortgage lending is carried out privately by banks, primarily funded by bank deposits or covered bonds. Other indirect forms of government support, such as the tax deductibility of mortgage interest and property taxes, are also notably absent in most European countries.

8.4.2   Other Justifications for GSE Subsidies

The activities of the GSEs may be justified by the particular benefits accruing to specific classes of borrowers, or more specifically, to all home

---

16. As just one example, housing policies in some European countries—France seems a particular example—have had particularly adverse impacts on rental markets, thus providing an implicit incentive to home ownership; see Ellickson (2010).

purchasers and home owners from the activities supported by these institutions. As noted earlier, benefits in the stabilization of the mortgage supply and corresponding reductions in the volatility of housing construction and home sales seem not to be verified. But there are at least three other classes of potential benefits arising from the GSE:

1. Increases in the extent of mortgage credit accruing to income and demographic groups that policymakers appear to have deemed particularly deserving—credit that augments that supplied by the private marketplace.

2. Increases in the lending support provided to builders, owners, or residents of specific types of housing (e.g., multifamily rental housing) that would otherwise not be provided in the market.

3. Subsidies accruing more broadly to housing market participants; for example, to all home purchasers in the form of lower interest costs arising from the increased liquidity afforded by the GSEs and the implicit guarantee of repayment provided by those institutions.

This section reviews the evidence on the extent and distribution of these benefits.

Increased Credit to Targeted Groups and Geographical Areas

The original charter establishing Fannie Mae as a GSE in 1968 recognized a "national goal of providing adequate housing for low and moderate income households," and it authorized the Secretary of the Department of Housing and Urban Development (HUD) to require that a reasonable portion of Fannie Mae's purchases of home mortgages be related to this goal. Although regulations requiring the GSEs to allocate a fixed percentage of mortgage purchases to lower-income households were advanced in the 1970s, mandatory rules were not proposed in Congress until after the passage of the Financial Institutions Reform, Recovery, and Enforcement Act (FIRREA) of 1989. Ultimately, the Federal Housing Enterprises Financial Safety and Soundness Act of 1992 modified and made more explicit the "housing goals" to be promoted by the GSEs. The act directed the HUD secretary to establish quantitative goals for mortgages to "low- and moderate-income" households and for mortgages originated in "underserved areas." It also imposed a "special affordable housing goal" for mortgages for low-income housing in low-income areas. The 1992 legislation stipulated two-year transition goals, but after that period, the HUD secretary was empowered to promulgate more detailed regulations.

Under the HUD regulations, finalized in December 1995, the first goal ("low- and moderate-income housing") directs that a specified fraction of new loans purchased each year by the GSEs be originated by households with incomes below the area median. The second goal ("underserved areas") requires that a specified fraction of mortgages be originated in census tracts with median incomes less than 90 percent of the area median, or else in census tracts with a minority population of at least 30 percent and with a tract median income of less than 120 percent of area median income. The third goal ("special affordable housing") targets mortgages originated in tracts with family incomes less than 60 percent of the area median; or else mortgages in tracts with incomes less than 80 percent of area median and also located in specific low-income areas. Any single mortgage can "count" toward more than one of these goals. (For example, any loan that meets the "special affordable housing" goal also counts toward the "low- and moderate-income" goal.)

The numerical goals originally set by HUD for 1996 were modest—requiring, for example, that 40 percent of the GSEs' mortgage purchases be loans made to households with incomes below the area median. Over time, the goals for new business set by HUD have been increased.[17] The goal for mortgages to low- and moderate-income households has been increased from 40 percent in 1996 to 56 percent by 2008. Until 2007, mortgage originations by both Fannie Mae and Freddie Mac had reached their primary goals every year. The HUD goal for "underserved areas" was increased from 21 percent in 1996 to 39 percent in 2008. Originations by the larger GSE, Fannie Mae, exceeded this goal in every year; originations by Freddie Mac exceeded the goal in each year until 2008. The "special affordable" housing goal was increased by HUD from 12 percent in 1996 to 27 percent in 2008. Both GSEs surpassed this goal in loan originations each year until 2008.

Figures 8.5, 8.6, and 8.7 report the HUD goals and GSE progress in achieving those goals from their publication in 1995 to the federal takeover of the GSEs in 2008. In this view, it might appear the goals were successful in expanding the GSE lending.

Figures 8.8, 8.9, and 8.10, however, provide another perspective on the magnitude of the goals set by HUD for the GSEs. They report each of the three goals as well as an estimate of the share of all newly-issued mortgages in each of the categories. For example, in 2000 the HUD-specified "low- and moderate-income goal" was to reach 42 percent of new purchases for the GSEs. However, in 2000 low- and moderate-income mortgages, according to the same definition, constituted about 59 percent of all new mortgages. At that time, the "underserved areas" goal was 21 percent of GSE mortgages, while these mortgages constituted more than a 30 percent market share of new mortgages. In virtually all cases, the goals imposed were a good bit lower than the share of mortgage loans of that type originated in the economy. There is no evidence that the goals were set so that the GSEs would "lead the market" in servicing these groups of households.

17. Note, however, that at the time that the 1992 act was debated in Congress, only 36 percent of Fannie Mae's single-family deliveries were for housing whose value was below the area median. (See FHFA 2010b).

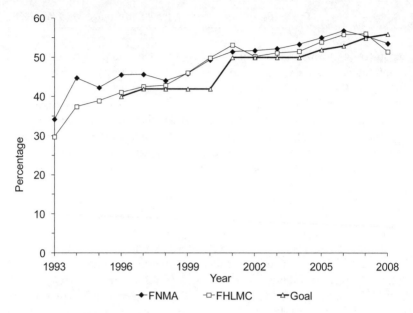

Fig. 8.5　GSE "low-moderate income" housing goal, 1993–2008 (percent of new loans to households with incomes below area median income)

Source: US Department of Housing and Urban Development, Office of Policy Development and Research, *Overview of the GSEs' Housing Goal Performance, 1993–2001, Overview of the GSEs' Housing Goal Performance, 2000–2007.*

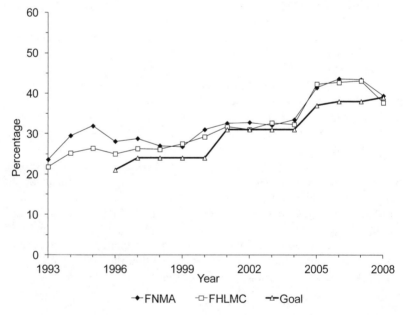

Fig. 8.6　GSE "underserved area" housing goal, 1993–2008 (percent of new loans credited toward goal)

Source: US Department of Housing and Urban Development, Office of Policy Development and Research, *Overview of the GSEs' Housing Goal Performance, 1993–2001, Overview of the GSEs' Housing Goal Performance, 2000–2007.*

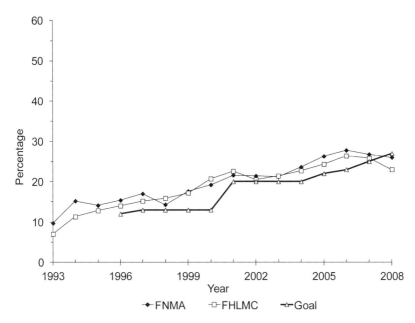

Fig. 8.7 GSE "special affordable" housing goal, 1993–2008 (percent of new loans credited toward goal)

Source: US Department of Housing and Urban Development, Office of Policy Development and Research, *Overview of the GSEs' Housing Goal Performance, 1993–2001, Overview of the GSEs' Housing Goal Performance, 2000–2007.*

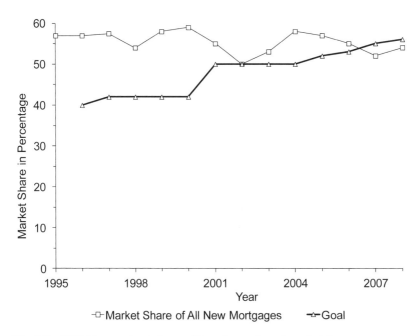

Fig. 8.8 GSE "low-moderate income" housing goals and market shares, 1993–2008

Source: Weicher (2010).

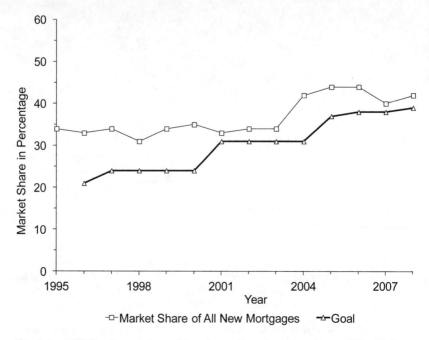

Fig. 8.9 GSE "underserved area" housing goals and market shares, 1993–2008
Source: Weicher (2010).

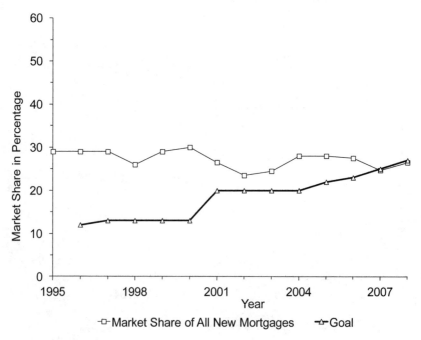

Fig. 8.10 GSE "special affordable" housing goals and market shares, 1993–2008
Source: Weicher (2010).

Increased Credit to Targeted Housing Types: Multifamily

Numerical goals for purchases of multifamily mortgages are not mentioned in the Financial Safety and Soundness Act of 1992, but there was considerable concern at the time that the GSEs were not financing their "fair share" of multifamily housing, especially small multifamily properties. For example, in 1991, small multifamily units accounted for less than 5 percent of Freddie Mac's multifamily unit purchases. At that time, small multifamily units constituted 39 percent of all recently-financed multifamily units (see Herbert 2001). Thus, the first rules for implementing the 1992 act put forward by HUD also included explicit goals for multifamily housing.

These goals have been in the form of dollar-based targets. Goals in 1996 to 2000 were approximately 0.8 percent of the mortgage purchases of Fannie Mae and Freddie Mac recorded in 1994; goals in 2001 to 2004 (2005 to 2007) were 1.0 percent of each GSE's estimated mortgage purchases in 1997 to 1999 (2000 to 2002). Beyond the achievement of these numerical goals, multifamily mortgage purchases also qualified for "bonus points" toward the achievement of the three goals specified in the 1992 law. It has been argued that these "bonus points" (discontinued in 2004) were a major inducement leading to an increase in participation by the GSEs in the multifamily housing market, particularly in their financing of small multifamily properties (see Manchester 2007).

Figure 8.11 reports the dollar goals for multifamily dwellings specified by HUD regulations and the performance of each of the GSEs. As shown in the figure, until quite recently purchases of multifamily dwellings exceeded the HUD goal by a substantial amount. Figure 8.12 also demonstrates that the GSEs' multifamily housing business was only a small fraction of the mortgage purchases of the GSEs in any year. It never amounted to even 7 percent of either GSEs' purchases. Finally, figure 8.13 reports the aggregate amount of commercial mortgage backed security (CMBS) and multifamily originations between 2003 and 2009 as reported by the Mortgage Bankers of America. Mortgage originations by Freddie Mac and Fannie Mae were small—less than $9 billion in any year. Until 2008, GSE originations were less than 20 percent of all such mortgage banker mortgage originations. Note, however that in 2008 and 2009, CMBS and commercial banks left the market entirely; originations by life insurers declined as well. Since the conservatorship in 2008, virtually all multifamily mortgages have been originated by the GSEs.

The Effectiveness of the GSE Goals in Directing Mortgage Credit:
Further Evidence

Of course, the finding that the GSEs have achieved the annual goals specified in regulations need not imply that Freddie and Fannie have been very effective in increasing mortgage credit to targeted groups. For example,

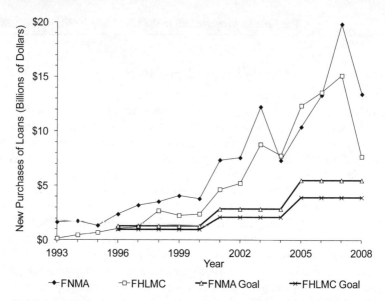

Fig. 8.11 GSE "special affordable multifamily" housing goals and GSE purchases, 1993–2008

Source: US Department of Housing and Urban Development, Office of Policy Development and Research, *Overview of the GSEs' Housing Goal Performance, 1993–2001, Overview of the GSEs' Housing Goal Performance, 2000–2007.*

Note: New loans to households residing in census tracts with incomes below the area median, in billions of dollars.

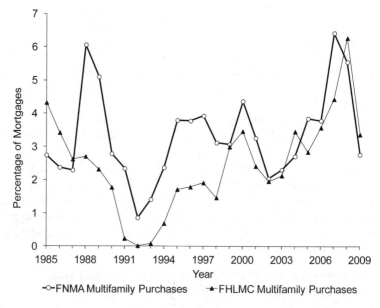

Fig. 8.12 GSE purchases of multifamily mortgages, 1985–2009 (as a percent of all mortgages)

Source: Federal Housing Finance Agency (2009, Historical Data Tables, 125, 142).

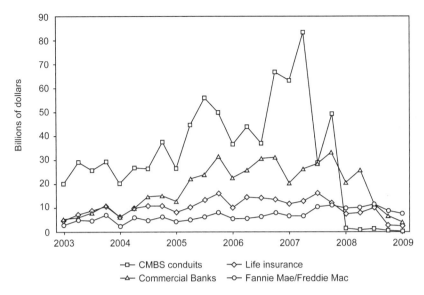

Fig. 8.13 Commercial and multifamily mortgage bankers' originations, 2004–2009
Source: Mortgage Bankers Association, September 2009.

many suggest that the numerical goals set for the GSEs have been far too low (e.g., Weicher 2010), and that as a result the GSEs have simply followed the market with a lag of a few years. Indeed, the data in figures 8.5, 8.6, and 8.7 provide no evidence that Freddie Mac or Fannie Mae purchased more than their "fair share" of mortgages in any of these areas of congressional concern. The GSE purchases of mortgages that satisfied any of these congressional goals—as a fraction of all new purchases—were consistently smaller than their "market share" in all newly-issued mortgages.

These simple comparisons suggest that any causal effect of the GSEs on lending to specific income classes, neighborhoods, and property types is not likely to be large—at least before 2008. Economic analysis of the potential impacts of the GSEs is also complicated by other public programs in effect. For example, in 1977, the Community Reinvestment Act (CRA) was passed to encourage banks to exert further efforts to meet the credit needs of their local communities, including lower-income areas. In identifying neighborhoods of special concern in administering the CRA, neighborhoods (census tracts) with median incomes below 80 percent of the area median income are targeted. As just noted, "underserved areas" of concern in GSE regulation are census tracts with median incomes below 90 percent of the area median income. In addition, many borrowers targeted under GSE criteria are also eligible for FHA loans or Veterans Administration (subsidized) loans.

The existence of parallel government programs under the CRA, FHA, and VA raises the possibility that the GSE purchases of qualifying mortgages simply displaced lenders who would have made the same mortgage under one of the other programs. To the extent that this has been the case, the GSE purchases would have had no noticeable impact on the mortgage market for the qualifying borrowers. Of course, it is a subtle empirical problem to determine whether the GSE purchases were simply displacing loans from the other programs. Nevertheless, a number of academic papers have sought to identify and quantify the effects of the GSE goals on local and neighborhood housing markets and on classes of borrowers.

Table 8.6 summarizes much of this research.

An early paper by Canner, Passmore, and Surette (1996) examined loans eligible for insurance under the FHA. The authors evaluated how the risk associated with these loans is distributed among government mortgage institutions, private mortgage insurers, the GSEs, and banks' in-house portfolios. The results indicated that the FHA bears the largest risk share associated with lending to lower-income and minority populations, with the GSEs lagging far behind. Bostic and Gabriel (2006) analyzed the effects of the GSE mortgage purchase goals upon home ownership and housing conditions in California. A careful comparison of neighborhoods just above the GSE cutoff for "low-moderate-income" and "special affordable" designation with nearby neighborhoods just below the cutoff found essentially no differences in the levels and differences in home ownership rates and housing conditions during the decade of the 1990s.

In a more sophisticated analysis using a similar comparison of neighborhoods "just above" and "just below" the GSE cutoff, An et al. (2007) focused on three indicators of local housing markets: the home ownership rate, the vacancy rate, and the median home value. The authors related (an instrument for) the intensity of GSE activity in a census tract to these outcomes, using a variety of control variables. The results indicated that increases in GSE purchase intensity were associated with significant but very small declines in neighborhood vacancy rates and increases in median house values. The authors conclude that the "results do not indicate much efficacy of the GSE affordable housing loan-purchase targets in improving housing market conditions" (235).

Two papers by Bhutta (2009b, 2010) adopted a regression discontinuity design to test the effects of the "underserved areas" goal upon the supply of credit to those areas. Rather than attempt to match similar neighborhoods for statistical analysis, Bhutta exploited the facts that census tracts qualified for CRA scrutiny if their median incomes were 80 percent of the local area, and they qualified for scrutiny under the HUD GSE goals if their median incomes were 90 percent of the area median design. Bhutta merged tract-level data on mortgages (from the Home Mortgage Disclosure Act) with neighborhood (census) data. Bhutta's results (2009a) do find a significant effect of the "underserved area" goal on GSE purchasing activity—but the effect is very small (2 to 3 percent during the 1997 to 2002 period).

Table 8.6   **Effects of GSE goals on housing market outcomes**

Author	Time period	Data	Effect of outcomes on GSE goals	Effect on other housing outcomes	Remarks
Wyly and Holloway (2002)	1997–2000	Loan applications from HMDA		Increase in subprime market share of 1 percent leads to a rise in nondisclosure (of race-ethnicity) of 0.6 percent in the refinance market. Nonreporting rates are the highest in the subprime refinance markets, especially in inner city and low-income areas.	An increasing number of HMDA loan applications contain no information on the applicant's race or ethnic identity. They also conducted a case study in Atlanta on the disappearance of race data.
Ambrose and Thibodeau (2004)	1995–1999	Dollar volume of purchase and refinance loans from HMDA, by MSA.	Lenders increased the supply of mortgage credit in areas with higher proportions of underserved borrowers. Increases in GSE purchases of seasoned loans in an MSA lead to increases in total mortgage origination volume in the MSA.	Volume of mortgages increased steadily between 1995 and 1998, declining slightly in 1999. There was a 27 percent increase in volume of purchase mortgages by 1998, and mortgage refinances increased 211 percent. In 1999, mortgage refinance volume fell 42 percent and purchase mortgage volume increased another 12 percent.	1998 appears to be an unusual year and significance of the coefficients might arise from the sudden increase in mortgage purchase and refinance volume that year.
Friedman and Squires (2005)	2000	Loan application and purchase data from 2000 HMDA, by MSA. Restricted to conventional loans originated to purchase one to four family homes.		Blacks and Latinos are more likely to purchase homes in predominantly white neighborhoods in MSAs where more loans are made by CRA lenders.	Based on census tract racial composition grouped into three descriptive categories: predominantly white, racially integrated, and predominantly minority.
Avery, Bostic, and Canner (2005)	2000	Total lending and lending experiences of institutions from the Survey of the Performance and Profitability of CRA-Related Lending, 2000		Almost 60 percent of institutions explicitly responded to CRA obligations; half engaged in community development activities, and 30 percent had home mortgage purchases and refinance activities.	Survey conducted by the Board of Governors of the Federal Reserve to measure responses of lending institutions to CRA.

(continued)

Table 8.6 continued

Author	Time period	Data	Effect of outcomes on GSE goals	Effect on other housing outcomes	Remarks
Bostic and Gabriel (2006)	1994, 1999	GSE loan purchase volume in California census tracts analyzed by MSA.	San Francisco MSA had a greater increase in home ownership rates in designated tracts. No significant differences observed elsewhere in California.	No significant differences in housing market performance between GSE-targeted census tracts and those just above and below the GSE target.	Model relates breaks from 80 to 90 percent and 90 to 100 percent of median income census tract effects to changes in housing market outcomes.
An and Bostic (2006)	1995–2001	Shares of HMDA loans sold on secondary market, by purchasing institution and census tract.	Increase in GSE market share of 1 percent leads to 0.27 percent reduction in submarket share.	Increases in GSE purchase activity are associated with declines in subprime mortgage activity, especially in neighborhoods with high minority populations.	Effect of FHA growth on submarket share is smaller.
An et al. (2007)	1995–2000	Annual GSE home loan-purchase, from HMDA, by census tract.	Increases in the percent of GSE purchases by tract are associated with declines in neighborhood vacancy rates and increases in median home values.	Significant deterioration in the credit quality of FHA-insured borrowers after 1996; GSEs may have given FHA borrowers in targeted tracts better access to less expensive, conventional, conforming loans.	Possible endogenity: GSE percent of purchase may be function of other housing market trends; GSE loan-purchase may be a function of housing market trends; GSEs might simply shift their purchase activity among neighborhoods.
Laderman and Reid (2008)	2004–2006	Loan application and origination information from HMDA, and loan performance data from Applied Analytics (LPS). Analysis is restricted to conventional, first-lien, owner-occupied loans originated in MSAs in California.		Loans made by a CRA lender within its assessment area in low-income neighborhoods were less likely (odds ratio .73) to be foreclosed than loans made by independent mortgage companies (IMCs) in the same neighborhoods. In moderate-income neighborhoods, CRA lenders were 1.7 times less likely to be foreclosed.	Analyzed CRA mortgage lending activities to measure effect on current crisis, but did not examine the impact that CRA investment or service components may have had on the current financial crisis.

Study	Years	Data and Method	Findings	Comments
An and Bostic (2008)	1996–2002	Home Mortgage Disclosure Act (HMDA) loan level application and origination information, matched to census tracts. Analysis is restricted to owner-occupied home purchase loans.	GSE market shares are lower in central city tracts and in tracts with high minority populations and high vacancy rates. GSE market shares are higher in more affluent census tracts (with higher home values and/or higher incomes).	FHA and GSE loan purchases represent a small share of the market of loans. Other factors (like subprime mortgages) could dominate the relationship the authors found. The first stage regression is problematic; it showed no relationship between targeted census tracts and GSE market shares.
An and Bostic (2009)	1995–2001	Shares of HMDA loans sold on secondary market, by purchasing institution and census tract.	Tracts with fewer total loans have less GSE penetration.	Negative and significant correlation between GSE and FHA market share, by census tract.
Bhutta (2009b)	1997–2004	Loan amounts, originations, and loans sold on secondary market, by purchasing institution and census tract, from HMDA. Analysis is restricted to census tracts in MSAs.	Goals increased GSE purchasing activity by 3 to 4 percent in targeted tracts and increased GSE-eligible originations by 2 to 3 percent on average.	GSEs do not purchase subprime loans; this study is based on two-stage least-squares (TSLS) regression.
			Negative relationship between annual GSE purchase growth and annual growth in subprime loan originations. A 1 percentage point increase in GSE share is associated with a 0.45 percentage point decline in subprime market share.	No evidence that underserved areas goal (UAG)-induced increases in GSE credit supply crowded out FHA and subprime lending. Regression discontinuity design. In contrast to the An and Bostic (2008) paper, Bhutta estimates the impact of the GSE Act separately on the number of GSE purchases, the total number of GSE-eligible originations, and the number of GSE-ineligible loans in targeted tracts.

(continued)

Table 8.6 continued

Author	Time period	Data	Effect of outcomes on GSE goals	Effect on other housing outcomes	Remarks
Bhutta (2010)	1994–2002, 1998–2005	Loan information by lender type, application status, loan purpose, secondary purchaser (if any) from HMDA, by census tract of the property and borrower income.	On lending, CRA had little impact, even during the 2000s when lending to lower income areas soared. Small increase in nonbank lending in CRA-targeted neighborhoods of large MSAs, particularly in areas with historically low home sales.	Increased bank lending does not crowd out lending by mortgage bank subsidiaries and independent mortgage companies.	Regression discontinuity (RD) design. Limitation of RD design is that it only measures the CRA's impact at the cutoff (80 percent of median income), so if there were a larger impact for borrowers and neighborhoods further below the cutoff, the RD would understate the CRA's true impact.
Bhutta (2010)	1997–2002	Mortgage originations and applications from HMDA, by census tracts in MSAs.	Small UAG effect on GSE purchases and mortgage originations GSEs purchase about 3.4 percent fewer loans in tracts below the eligibility cutoff.	No crowd out of FHA and subprime lending.	Regression discontinuity design. Analysis might understate UAG's effect because RD can only identify the goal's impact for tracts near the eligibility thresholds. Bhutta notes that the UAG mostly affects relatively stable tracts, indicating that GSEs respond where it is least costly.
Gabriel and Rosenthal (2010)	1994–2008	Loan purchases and originations from HMDA, by census tracts located within MSAs. Census tracts were adjusted to match the 2000 census.	The disappearance of GSE crowd out, with the 2007 financial crisis, suggests loans purchased by GSEs added substantively to the flow of mortgage credit.	From 1994 to 2003, GSE crowd out of private secondary market purchases was small. From 2004 to 2006, private loan purchases expanded and GSE crowd out estimates jumped to 50 percent. After 2007, GSE crowd out was small again.	Addressed GSE purchase endogeneity of instrumenting for applications using lagged tract home ownership rates. Increased local secondary market activity may result in some easing in local underwriting standards, causing local applications to increase. Thus OLS estimates would be biased upwards. With or without IVs, the trends were similar.

Avery and Brevoort (2010)	2001, 2004–2006	Loan origination and purchases from HMDA, by census tract, with three outcome variables: (1) Percentage of mortgage borrowers who were ninety or more days past due on at least one mortgage obligation, from Equifax. (2) Percentage of first-lien mortgage loans originated in a tract during 2004 to 2006 with estimated front-end debt-to-income ratios exceeding 30 percent, as a proxy for high-risk or subprime lending activity from HMDA. (3) House price changes between 2001 and 2006 and 2006 and 2008 calculated from HMDA.	No statistically significant relationship between loan sales to the GSEs and delinquency.	Found no evidence that CRA and GSE goals contributed to house price increases during the 2001 to 2006 buildup. CRA targeted census tracts show fewer loan delinquencies in 2008.	Regression discontinuity design. Believes loan quality and performance is important to measure for GSE and CRA goal success, in addition to loan volume. Loan performance data are missing; they measured loan quality by postbuildup delinquency rates and risk characteristics. Also, aggregation of analysis obscures the fact that subprime boom took on different forms in different geographic regions.
Moulton (2010)	1996–1997, 2006–2007	Loan originations and purchases, foreclosures, vacancies, high-priced loans, and other housing outcomes from HUD and HMDA, by census tract and also by loan applicant.	Special affordable goal (SAG) increased GSE purchases from very low-income borrowers by 4 percent but had no effect on mortgage lending. No evidence that the low- and moderate-income goal (LMIG) or UAG altered GSE purchase or mortgage lending decisions.	No relationship between GSE Act's affordable housing goals and increased foreclosures, vacancies, or other housing outcomes.	Regression discontinuity design. Diverges from Bhutta (2009) paper in a few ways. Bhutta uses data aggregated to the census tract level, while Moulton uses variation in loan applicant-level data to examine individual loan outcomes, allowing Moulton to examine the individual-level goals outlined in the LMIG and SAG.

A more recent paper by Moulton (2010), also using a regression discontinuity approach, finds no effect of the GSEs—on individual loans rather than aggregate credit allocations. Moulton uses micro data on mortgage loan applications to examine whether the GSEs' affordable housing goals altered the probability that a loan application was originated by a mortgage lending institution or that a loan was purchased by one of the GSEs. The analysis led to the conclusion that the GSE affordable housing goal had no effect at all on mortgage lending or on GSE purchases.

The consistent finding of little or no effect of the GSE goals on housing outcomes, mortgage applications, or mortgage finance could suggest that there is little effect of the GSE rules upon FHA lending as well. But several papers have reported that an increased market share of GSE mortgages in a census tract is associated with a decline in the FHA share of mortgages (An and Bostic 2008; Gabriel and Rosenthal 2010). These results may explain why the increases in lending mandated by the HUD regulations to achieve the congressional goals of the 1992 act have had very little net impact on housing and neighborhood outcomes. Small increases in GSE activity have been offset by roughly comparable declines in FHA activity.

The extent to which an expansion of GSE activity simply crowds out private mortgage purchases remains an open research question. For example, Gabriel and Rosenthal (2010) argue that increased GSE activity in the mortgage market involved little or no crowd-out until about 2005. After that, GSE activity crowded out private activity until the crash in mortgage markets in 2007.

But even if there were a complete crowd-out of private mortgage activity arising from GSE behavior, it is hard to attribute any of this to the goals set by the 1992 act—especially since the goals were substantially less than the share of these new mortgages in the market.

To summarize: the academic and scientific literature has generally found little effect from housing goals as they operated through the GSEs. The goals were low. Despite appearances, they provided no incentive for the GSEs to "lead the market" in providing credit to potentially riskier housing investments. They accomplished nothing in increasing credit for riskier loans.

But there is a view that the housing goals were actively harmful in facilitating the subprime housing crisis. This position has been put most forcefully by Peter Wallison (2011) in his rebuttal statement to the Financial Crisis Inquiry Commission. He argues that the requirement to meet the housing goals "forced" the GSEs to make substandard loans, which is why they ultimately acquired such large positions in subprime mortgages and subprime mortgage securities. Indeed, Wallison claims that the HUD goals actually "caused" the subprime crisis. Similarly, an impressive journalistic account of recent history in the mortgage market argues forcefully that the housing goals in the 1992 act led directly to the subprime mortgage debacle of 2008 (Morgenson and Rosner 2011).

Our earlier analysis of the empirical academic literature simply fails to support a claim that the GSE housing goals were a primary source of the subprime crisis. First, there are simple questions of timing. The GSE goals were enunciated in a law passed in 1992; it is implausible that their effect was not felt until a quarter century had elapsed. In addition, as we have noted, the GSE accumulation of subprime mortgages accelerated only in 2007, too late to have "caused" the subprime bubble (but certainly early enough to have accelerated it).

Second, as already noted, it appears that the GSE mortgage purchases in support of the housing goals were principally loans that would otherwise have been made by other lenders. Lastly, the subprime crisis has a long list of proximate causes (including US monetary policy, a global savings glut, the error of assuming a national housing pricing collapse was highly unlikely, etc.); see Jaffee (2009) for further discussion. The GSE housing goals just do not appear to have this level of significance.

Now it is certainly possible that the passionate rhetoric from the GSEs provided a convenient "cover" for the trend toward lower-quality, even toxic, mortgages by 2004 and 2005. Ironically (or perhaps diabolically), the rhetoric about "affordable housing" from the GSEs had little effect upon *their own mortgage purchases* until the subprime crisis was well under way.

8.4.3 Benefits to All Housing Market Participants

There has been active research seeking to establish the value of the enhanced liquidity and subsidy to home owners. In principle, the subsidy provided by the implicit guarantee can be calculated. Freddie Mac and Fannie Mae issue debt in the same market as other participants in the banking and finance industry participate. The yield difference ("spread") between the debt of the GSEs and that of other firms can be applied to the newly issued GSE debt to compute the funding advantage in any year arising from the GSE status. Of course, it is not quite straightforward to apply this principle and to produce credible estimates. The relevant benchmark estimate (i.e., the appropriate sector and bond rating) is not without controversy, and a comparison with broad aggregate indices combines bonds containing a variety of embedded options. Pearce and Miller (2001), among others, reported comparisons of GSE and AA-rated financial firms, suggesting that the agencies enjoyed a 37 basis point (bps) spread. More sophisticated comparisons by Nothaft, Pearce, and Stevanovic (2002) suggest that the relative spreads are about 27 bps (vis-à-vis AA-minus firms). Table 8.7 summarizes available comparisons. A careful analysis of yields at issue for GSE debt and the option-free debt issued by a selection of finance industry corporations (Ambrose and Warga 2002) concludes that the GSEs enjoy a spread of 25 to 29 bps over AA bank bonds and 37 to 46 over AA financials. Quigley (2006) provides a terse summary of available estimates.[18]

---

18. These estimates are in the range of the spreads that have been assumed (41 bps) by the Congressional Budget Office (CBO 2001) in estimating the annual federal subsidy to the GSEs. They are similar to the estimates of spreads (40 bps) used by Passmore (2005) in a more recent exercise.

Table 8.7   Estimates of GSE funding advantage

Author	Data	Comparison	Spread in basis points
US Treasury (1996)	Bloomberg	Agency vs. A Financials	53–55
Ambrose and Warga (1996)	Fixed Income Research Program	Fannie Mae vs. AA Financials	37–46
		AA Corporate	38–39
		A Financials	56–72
		A Corporate	55–65
Freddie Mac (1996)	Lehman Relative Value	Freddie vs. AA & A	39
		AAA	23
Toevs (2000)	Lehman Bond Indexes	Fannie Mae vs. AA-Indexes	37
Pearce and Miller (2001)	Bloomberg	Agency vs. AA Financials	37
Ambrose and Warga (2002)	Fixed Investment Securities Database	Freddie and Fannie vs. AA Banks	25–29
Nothaft, Pearce, and Stevanovic (2002)	Fixed Investment Securities Database	Freddie and Fannie vs. AA Debentures	30
		A Debentures	45
		AA MTNs	27
		A MTNs	34
Passmore, Sherlund, and Gillian (2005)	Bloomberg Lehman	Freddie and Fannie vs. AAA & AA Financials:	
		68 firms	41
		44 firms	38
		15 firms	38

Sources: Nothaft, Pearce, and Stevanovic (2002); Ambrose and Warga (2002); Passmore, Sherlund, and Gillian (2005). See Quigley (2006) for additional details. MTNs = medium term notes.

The substantial subsidies arising from the funding advantage of the GSEs means that mortgage rates for all home owners can be lower than they otherwise would be; that is, the subsidy can improve the well-being of home owners and home purchasers.

But of course, in the first instance the subsidy is provided directly to private profit-making firms with fiduciary duties to their shareholders. It is thus not obvious that all, or even most, of the funding advantage provided by the public subsidy is passed through to home owners. As documented by Hermalin and Jaffee (1996), the secondary market for mortgage securities (at least for those securities composed of loans comparable to the rules under which Fannie and Freddie operate) is hardly a textbook model of atomistic competition. The two GSEs are large, and each has a large market share of the conforming segment of the market. There are high barriers to entry, and the MBS product is more or less homogeneous. Moreover, mortgage originators have an inherent first-mover advantage in deciding which newly-issued mortgages to sell to Fannie and Freddie. This may force the GSEs to pay a premium for the mortgages they purchase in the market. These factors, duopoly and adverse selection, may mean that much of the subsidy accrues

Table 8.8   **Estimates of reduction in mortgage interest rates attributable to GSEs**

Author	Time period	Region	Reduction in basis points
Hendershott and Shilling (1989)	1986	California	24–39
ICF (1990)	1987	California	26
		7 states	23
Cotterman and Pearce (1996)	1989–1993	California	25–50
		11 states	24–60
Pearce (2000)	1992–1999	California	27
		11 states	24
Ambrose, Buttimer, and Thibodeau (2001)	1990–1999	Dallas	16–24
Naranjo and Toevs (2002)	1986–1998	US	8–43
Passmore, Sparks, and Ingpen (2002)	1992–1999	California	18–23
CBO (2001)	1995–2000	US	23
McKenzie (2002)	1986–2000	US	22
	1996–2000	US	19
Ambrose, La Cour-Little, and Saunders (2004)	1995–1997	US	6
Woodward 1996–2001 (2004a)	1996–2001	US	35–52
Passmore, Sherlund, and Burgess (2005)	1997–2003	US	15–18
Blinder, Flannery, and Lockhart (2006)	1997–2003	US	23–29

Sources: McKenzie (2002); Ambrose (2004), Blinder, Flannery, and Lockhart (2006); Passmore, Sherlund, and Burgess (2005); Woodward (2004b). See Quigley (2006) for details.

to the shareholders of the GSEs or to the owners of other financial institutions, not to home owners or home purchasers.

The effects of the GSEs upon mortgage rates can be approximated from the spread between the interest rates on mortgages that conform to the loan limits and underwriting guidelines of the GSEs and the rates on otherwise comparable mortgages. As in the analysis of funding advantages, it is not quite straightforward to apply this principle and to produce credible estimates. (For example, most research compares the rates paid by borrowers with loans one dollar below the conforming limit with rates paid by borrowers with loans one dollar above the limit. But the latter group of borrowers differs from the former group, or else they surely would have made an additional cash payment and taken a conforming loan.)[19]

Early analyses, for example, by Hendershott and Shilling (1989), comparing interest rates on Jumbo and conforming mortgages, indicated that this

19. Of course, other reasons besides the greater liquidity provided by the GSEs could explain some of an observed spread between Jumbo and conforming mortgages. Jumbo mortgages are generally prepaid more aggressively—borrowers have more at stake, if nothing else. This means that investors will require higher rates on Jumbos merely to compensate for the increased prepayment risk. On the other hand, borrowers with Jumbo mortgages have better credit, and they make larger down payments, which should create lower rates on Jumbo mortgages. See also, Ambrose, Buttimer, and Thibodeau (2001); Heuson, Passmore, and Sparks (2001); or Woodward (2004).

spread was 24 to 39 bps. More recent studies, for example, by Passmore, Sparks, and Ingpen (2002), by McKenzie (2002), and by the CBO (2001), conclude that the spread is 18 to 23 bps. These more recent studies differ mostly in their application of more complex screens to insure comparable data for conforming and nonconforming loans. Table 8.8 summarizes these comparisons. More recent work by Passmore, Sherlund, and Gillian (2005) suggests that this spread may be as low as 16 bps.

In summary, it appears that the GSEs' funding advantage is about 30 to 40 bps, and the effect of this is to reduce mortgage rates by 16 to 25 bps. Stated another way, on the order of half of the subsidy rate to the GSEs is transmitted to home owners in the form of reduced mortgage interest rates. Presumably, the remainder is transmitted to the managers of the GSEs, the shareholders of the enterprises, or to the owners of other financial institutions.[20]

8.5   Where Do We Go from Here?

As noted in the introduction, most commentators agree that the current structure of the housing finance system must be reformed in the very near term. A question of first-order importance is then the role of government in support of the US housing and mortgage markets, whether as a modification or replacement of the GSEs.

The research results reported in this chapter make it clear, we think, that the public benefits arising from the GSEs have been quite small. The establishment of Fannie Mae a half-century ago and the establishment of Freddie Mac forty years ago did stimulate a more stable national market for housing finance and did substantially improve the liquidity and access of the market. As reported earlier, however, the specific benefits arising from the GSE structure have been modest and were generally achieved by the 1980s. The GSEs have more often followed innovation in the secondary market than created it. In any event, there now exists a well-established national market for home mortgages.

There have been surprisingly few benefits to deserving households or neighborhoods that can be attributed to the GSEs. There has been political or partisan attention to the cause of home ownership among lower-income households as a result of powerful advocacy by the interests of GSEs, but there is little evidence that lower-income home ownership was stimulated at all, at least not until the run-up to the housing bubble.

It is true that the GSE structure has reduced interest rates on home mort-

---

20. Of course, the net effects of the GSEs upon public welfare and the economy has greatly exceeded the three effects upon housing market participants discussed here. Indeed, the evidence suggests that the macroeconomic effects of the structure and operation of the GSEs during the past half decade has been much more important for the economy than the direct housing-market effects of the institutions.

gages, by about a quarter percent or so. But this benefit to home owners has arisen from the federal guarantee for GSE debt. And the public cost of the subsidy has far exceeded the benefits of lower interest rates to home owners. About half of the overall subsidy has accrued to GSE employees, shareholders, and other market intermediaries. These large losses are directly attributable to the GSE structure, which was created in 1968. We believe it is fair to say that there is now a consensus among economists and legislators alike that the GSE structure of a public/private partnership must be considered a failed experiment. Similarly, as we discuss further later, the GSE structure has also made regulation of the housing market far less transparent and has extended some of the consequences of the housing bubble of the past half decade. The policy question is now how to replace the GSEs.

8.5.1   The Appropriate Role for Government in the US Residential Mortgage Market

If the GSEs in current form are to be closed, the fundamental policy question is to decide which government interventions, if any, should replace GSE functions and which should be performed by the private sector. Once that is decided, there is also the delicate issue of how to manage the transition from the current GSE conservatorship. Fortunately, there are two quite flexible instruments available to close down the GSEs in a smooth, safe, and dependable manner: (a) steadily reduce the conforming loan limit until it reaches zero; and (b) steadily raise the fee charged by the GSEs for guaranteeing MBS. Although we will return to questions of the dynamic transition later, the key question is to determine the appropriate role of government in the US mortgage market.

A large number of proposals have been offered for the reform of the US mortgage market, ranging from a mortgage market managed primarily by private sector entities to recreation of the GSEs as public/private hybrids (albeit with new controls). Summaries and analyses of the general approaches are available in US Government Accountability Office (2009), Congressional Budget Office (2010), and Bernanke (2008). The following is an annotated list of the three primary proposals scrutinized:

- *Reestablish GSEs with tighter controls and explicit guarantees.* The entities would continue their organization as public/private hybrids, but with tight government controls, sometimes described as a "public utility" model. In most plans, the government guarantees would apply to the underlying mortgages, not the newly created entities. A cooperative structure such as that of the current Federal Home Loan Banks is an alternative version. The number of entities to be chartered varies by proposal.
- *Restructure GSE functions explicitly within a government agency.* A simple version would create a government agency that would explicitly

insure mortgages up to some conforming limit and then securitize pools of these mortgages, very much as the current FHA and GNMA agencies operate for lower-income borrowers. The support for underserved borrowers and areas, including multifamily housing, currently covered under the GSE housing goals, would continue in a revised form as explicit government programs.

* *Privatization of the US mortgage market.* This proposal would create a fully privatized mortgage market, with no special federal backing for the secondary mortgage market, although this could include spinning out the GSEs as new private entities.

More recently, in February 2011, the US Treasury and Housing and Urban Development agency, US Treasury/HUD 2011), issued a white paper that offered a list of three policy options. The policy options were based on three principles (white paper, 11):

1. Pave the way for a robust private mortgage market by reducing government support for housing finance and closing down Fannie Mae and Freddie Mac on a responsible timeline.

2. Address fundamental flaws in the mortgage market to protect borrowers, to help ensure transparency for investors, and to increase the role of private capital.

3. Target the government's vital support for affordable housing in a "more effective and transparent manner."

In effect, these principles rule out the reestablishment of the GSEs as private/public hybrids.

The white paper offers three options for long-term mortgage market reform:

Option 1: A privatized system of housing finance with the government insurance role limited to FHA, USDA, and Department of Veterans Affairs assistance for narrowly targeted groups of borrowers.

Option 2: A privatized system of housing finance with assistance from FHA, USDA, and the VA for narrowly targeted groups of borrowers and a guarantee mechanism to scale up during times of crisis.

Option 3: A privatized system of housing finance with FHA, USDA, and the VA assistance for low- and moderate-income borrowers and catastrophic reinsurance behind significant private capital.

Since the publication of the white paper, most discussions of specific proposals among academics, public interest groups, and market participants have centered on versions of "Option 3." The alternative views expressed in these discussions mainly concern the extent and form in which the government's mortgage guarantees would be provided. Of course, if the government guarantee is sufficiently limited, "Option 3" is no different from

"Option 2." While these discussions have focused on the form of the government mortgage guarantee, most commentators agree that the abusive mortgage market practices that evolved during the subprime boom must be ended through regulation; see US Treasury/HUD (2011, 15–18). In fact, Federal Reserve (2008) actions to modify the Truth in Lending Act and a wide range of requirements in the Dodd–Frank Act have already gone a long way to eliminating any possible replay of such abusive practices in the US mortgage market. Most commentators also appear to agree that the GSE housing goals should be replaced with an explicit and transparent system of targeted support for access and affordability. An obvious solution, and one endorsed by the white paper, is to strengthen and expand the FHA for this purpose. The white paper also proposes a public commitment to affordable rental housing.

8.5.2   Government Insurance of US Mortgages

We now review the major issues and differences among the plans that are proposed as the mechanism to replace the GSEs with a program of federal government mortgage insurance. Specific versions are available from Acharya et al. (2011); the Center for American Progress (2010); Ellen, Tye, and Willis (2010); and Hancock and Passmore (2010). While the plans differ in details and specificity, a composite can be summarized:

1. The plans anticipate government regulations will set the underwriting standards to be met by all mortgages that underlie the qualifying MBS, roughly comparable to the standards historically applied by the GSEs. The plans also generally anticipate a size limit roughly equivalent to the conforming loan limit historically applied to the GSEs.

2. Investors in the qualifying MBS will be protected from all default risk by a combination of private capital and government guarantee. The government guarantee component is considered essential. The various plans differ primarily in the split between private capital and government guarantee.

3. Risk-based insurance premia will be paid to the private capital and the government as compensation for the risks they bear.

For simplicity, we refer to this structure as the "government insurance proposal." A key feature of the insurance proposal relative to any plan that would re-create the GSEs is that the government would set the underwriting standards and be compensated for the risk it bears.

The immediate question is whether the government can be effective and efficient in carrying out such a mortgage insurance program. Evidence is available from a variety of existing government insurance programs. Perhaps the most positive evidence is the FHA program itself. As noted earlier, this program has existed since 1934, sets its premiums on an actuarial basis, and has never required a government subsidy or bailout for its self-supporting programs. Most interestingly, as documented in Jaffee and Quigley (2010), the FHA effectively sat out the subprime boom, allowing its overall market share to fall from a peak share of 25 percent in 1970 to under 2 percent by 2006. Even more dramatically, its market share of loans to minority borrowers, which had been close to 50 percent of this market as recently as 2000, fell to well below 10 percent by 2006. In effect, the FHA took no action to deter its traditional clients from switching to private market lenders and the GSEs as the source of their mortgage loans. While this inaction could not protect the FHA from the rising loss rate that is now affecting most segments of the US mortgage market, it has certainly minimized the dollar amount of the losses that the FHA could still potentially impose on US taxpayers.

The FHA thus provides a model, or even a precise mechanism, for a broad government guarantee program, possibly covering the same market share—at times 50 percent of the overall market—that was traditionally served by the GSEs. Indeed, operating within its traditional programs, the FHA market share of total mortgage originations has already jumped dramatically from under 2 percent in 2006 to over 20 percent in 2010. The issue is whether the FHA mechanism, which has worked well serving a well-defined set of lower-income clients, can scale efficiently to serve what could be as much as three-quarters of the entire US mortgage market (summing a 50 percent GSE share with a traditional 25 percent FHA share). The major concern is whether the FHA—or any comparable government insurance plan—can resist the *political* pressures to reduce its underwriting standards and to subsidize its risk-based insurance premiums. The evidence here is not encouraging.

An interesting and comparable case is the National Flood Insurance Program (NFIP). The NFIP was created in 1968, following a series of disastrous midwestern floods that caused a large part of the private insurance industry to stop offering flood coverage. The NFIP legislation required premiums to be set on an actuarial basis, including risk-based premiums, to discourage the construction of new homes in flood zones. This noble goal floundered, however, when the owners of existing properties in dangerous flood plains successfully lobbied to obtain special "grandfathered" premium reductions. This all become evident when there were insufficient reserves to pay the losses created by Hurricane Katrina, thus requiring taxpayer bailout of the NFIP in an amount approaching $20 billion. For further discussion of the NFIP, see Michel-Kerjan and Kunreuther (2011), and of failed government insurance programs in general see Jaffee and Russell (2006).

The Terrorism Risk Insurance Act (TRIA) provides an alternative approach to government insurance and may provide a useful structure for a government mortgage insurance program. The TRIA was first passed by Congress in 2002, following the terrorism attack of September 2001. The issue was that, as a result of their World Trade Center losses, virtually all property insurers were refusing to renew policies on large commercial buildings unless there was a substantial government reinsurance program to cap their potential losses. The TRIA accomplished this goal with a structure in which the government provides the insurers protection against possible catastrophic losses while placing the insurers in the first-loss position with a series of deductibles and coinsurance requirements. Roughly speaking, TRIA 2002 required the industry itself to cover most of the losses that would have resulted from another event comparable to 9/11, but provided quite complete government protection against any losses above that level. The TRIA has now been renewed two times, and both times the deductible and coinsurance requirements have been raised, so a taxpayer loss would now occur only with truly extreme events.[21]

The specific proposals offered by Acharya et al. (2011) and Hancock and Passmore (2010) both reference "catastrophe insurance" as the coverage to be provided under their plans. A particular concern, however, is that MBS investors might not consider government catastrophe coverage to be a sufficient inducement for them to take the first-loss positions on portfolios of US mortgages. For example, while the property insurers may have been most concerned with the last 20 percent of the tail risk from terrorist attacks, investors in residential mortgage pools may be primarily concerned with the first 20 percent of the risk distribution. In that case, for a government mortgage insurance program to be effective, it may have to mimic the NFIP more than TRIA. In other words, even if the starting point were the principle of a backstop to catastrophe, the political process may create a plan that covers high-risk mortgages at subsidized rates; that is, GSEs with a different "cover."

This appears to be the conundrum for creating a feasible program for government insurance of US mortgages. While a true catastrophe government insurance plan appears feasible, investors and other market participants will, of course, have incentives to push as much of the first-loss risk as possible under the government's coverage. If the political process can stand firm on the issue, then it is quite possible that private incentives will create an efficient market for US mortgages. After all, it is hard to believe that only the countries of Western Europe have the ability to create effective mortgage markets while maintaining a low level of government intervention.

8.5.3   The Role of GSE Mortgage Market Activity under the Conservatorship

In concluding, it is relevant to comment on the role of GSE mortgage market activity since the two firms were placed under a government conservatorship in September 2008. Relevant data on the home mortgage acquisitions of the GSEs and for the total home mortgage market are shown in table 8.9 for 2009 and 2010. The raw numbers suggest a significant GSE and overall government role. For 2009 and 2010, annual GSE mortgage acquisitions

---

21. On the other hand, the government's TRIA coverage is provided without charge.

Table 8.9   Home mortgage activity, 2009 and 2010

Home mortgage activity in billions (US$)	2009	2010	Total
Fannie Mae mortgage acquisitions	700	608	1,308
Freddie Mac mortgage acquisitions	475	386	861
Total GSE mortgage acquisitions	1,175	994	2,169
Total Home mortgage originations	1,840	1,630	3,470
Share of total home mortgage originations			
GSE share of total originations	64%	61%	63%
FHA and VA share of total originations	24%	23%	24%
GSE, FHA, and VA share of total originations	88%	84%	87%
GSE refinanced acquisitions as share of their total	80%	79%	80%
Aggregate share of home mortgage refinancings	69%	67%	68%

Sources: Federal Housing Finance Agency (2010c) Annual Report to Congress, *Inside Mortgage Finance* (for total and refinanced mortgage originations), and Fannie Mae and Freddie Mac 2010 Annual Reports (for GSE refinancings).

as a percentage of total home originations was 63 percent. The FHA and VA activity averaged 24 percent of total home originations over the same period, so government programs participated in 87 percent of all mortgage originations for 2009 and 2010.

The high GSE market share under the conservatorship, however, can be misleading. First, 80 percent of all GSE mortgage acquisitions were refinanced loans, so only 20 percent of the GSE activity represented loans for home purchase. The GSE refinancing activity includes the refinancings that occurred under the Home Affordable Refinance Program (HARP). In comparison, for the overall mortgage market, home refinancings represented 68 percent of total mortgage originations, leaving 32 percent of the originations for home purchase activity. The conclusion is that while the GSEs dominated US mortgage market activity in 2009 and 2010, most of this activity was simply the refinancing of mortgage loans that had already been guaranteed by the GSEs. To be clear, refinancing activities are certainly beneficial to the borrowers, and generally so for the GSEs as well (since they reduce the likelihood of default on these loans for which the GSEs are already at risk). On the other hand, refinancing is a zero-sum game, since the investors who are holding the higher rate mortgages will have to reinvest their money at the now lower market rates. Indeed, the Federal Reserve, US Treasury, and GSEs are major holders of these GSE mortgage securities, so the HARP program is far from cost-free for the government itself.[22]

The GSEs also participate in the Home Affordable Modification Program (HAMP), along with servicers for non-GSE home mortgages. As of Septem-

22. See Remy, Lucas, and Moore (2011) for a Congressional Budget Office analysis of the most recent changes in the HARP program.

ber 2011, the GSE share of total HAMP modifications was 52 percent, only slightly above the GSE share of all outstanding home mortgages. This suggests that the participation rate in HAMP modifications was about the same for GSE and non-GSE mortgages. Perhaps more importantly, the HAMP program is widely considered to be a disappointment: as of September 2011, just over 800,000 loans had been modified, compared to the earlier hopes of 3 to 4 million loans.

The overall conclusion is that the primary mortgage market result of maintaining the GSEs under the government conservatorship through 2011 appears to have been their role as a catalyst for the refinancing of their existing mortgages. In terms of funding for home purchase loans, private market lenders have actually been more active than the GSEs, even without the benefit of a government guarantee.

Data Appendix

The Federal Reserve Flow of Funds (FoF) tables provide the longest (1945 to the present), consistent quantification of home mortgages outstanding.[23] The FoF data include a separation between mortgages held directly in investor portfolios and those held within mortgage pools for mortgage-backed securitization (MBS), including some detail on the holders of each category. For tables 8.1 and 8.2 and figures 8.1 and 8.2, we apply the FoF data for the aggregate outstanding home mortgages and the separation between loans held in portfolios and in mortgage pools.

For the separation of MBS outstanding among three issuer classes, the FoF data directly quantify MBS issued by private label securitizers (PLS, meaning MBS without government or GSE backing), and the sum of GNMA and GSE data. We obtain direct measures of GNMA MBS outstanding from the Historical Statistics of the United States (with the latest 2010 data from *Inside ABS*), and compute the GSE MBS outstanding as the residual, (which closely aligns with direct measures of GSE MBS from the company's own reports).[24]

For the separation of whole mortgages and MBS among three holder classes, the FoF data directly quantify the whole home mortgages and the securitized pools held by depository institutions (commercial banks, savings

23. The FoF (flow of funds) data are available at http://www.federalreserve.gov/releases/z1/Current/data.htm. Home mortgages are defined as mortgages on one to four family homes, thus excluding multifamily, farm, and commercial mortgages.

24. Both GSEs adopted an accounting change—integrating their outstanding MBS commitments onto their balance sheet—that makes their 2010 data inconsistent with all previous data. Our method avoids this accounting change, allowing us to maintain consistency throughout the sample period.

and loan associations, savings banks, and credit unions). Whole mortgages and MBS held in the retained portfolios of the GSE are obtained from the 2010 report to Congress by their regulator, Federal Housing Finance Agency (2010c), with the 2010 data obtained from the companies' Monthly Volume reports. Whole mortgages and MBS held by other investors are computed as the residual category.

Table 8A.1   Home ownership and social outcomes

Author	Time period	Data	Housing outcome observed	Comments
Rossi and Weber (1996)	1988–1995	General Social Survey and the National Survey of Families and Households, supplemented by data from the American National Election Studies, by individual	Home owners have slightly higher self-esteem, life satisfaction, and are more involved with community groups.	The effects of home ownership are not large and sometimes inconsistent. It is difficult to determine endogeneity.
Oswald (1996)	1960s–1990	Statistical Abstract and Eurostat, by country	Home ownership reduces workers' mobility, thus causing them to stay unemployed longer. A 10 percent increase in home ownership is associated with approximately a 2 percent increase in unemployment.	Small sample sizes makes the results unreliable.
Green and White (1997)	1980–1987	Panel Study of Income Dynamics (PSID), the Public Use Microsample of the 1980 Census of Population and Housing (PUMS), and High School and Beyond (HSB), by child	Adjusting for income and parental differences in the PSID data, children of owner-occupied homes have a predicted probability of completing high school of .91, compared to .82 for renters. The differential falls as income rises. In the PUMS, home owners' children had a .9 probability of being in school, compared to .83 for children of renters at the same age.	The HSB data comes from parents who completed high school. Probit models are used to account for selection bias due to differences between parents who own and rent. Also, using the lifetime earnings differential between a high school dropout and a high school graduate, the benefit of a government policy to encourage low income renters to own homes is estimated to be about $31,000.
DiPasquale and Glaeser (1999)	1972–1994	General Social Survey, German Socio-Economic Panel, by individual	Controlling for age, race, sex, marital status, children, income, education, residential structure type, and city size, homeowners are roughly 10 percent more likely to know their US representative, 9 percent more likely to know the identity of their school board head, 15 percent more likely to work to vote in local elections, and 6 percent more likely to work to solve local problems than renters. Home owners invest more in social capital and local amenities. Home owners are better citizens.	Authors use the average home ownership rate of the individual's income quartile as an instrument for home ownership. They could not measure the extent of the positive externalities. They also found home owners are less likely to move than renters. The cost of immobility is not calculated.

(continued)

Table 8A.1   continued

Author	Time period	Data	Housing outcome observed	Comments
Aaronson (2000)	1975–1993	Panel Study of Income Dynamics, children aged seven to sixteen	For the base case, where the child is white, male, lives in a household with married parents, two siblings, average income, and the head of household is a high school graduate, the probability of graduating from high school for children who live in owner-occupied housing is 1.5 percent higher than renters. Latent family stability factors explain as least 20 percent of the home ownership effect.	Response to the green and white paper. Argues that a child's school graduation does not depend on home ownership as much as it depends on the stability home ownership offers the child.
Green and Hendershott (2001)	1986–1992	Panel Survey of Income Dynamics, by individual	A 10-percentage point increase in home ownership increases unemployment by months (4 percent increase).	Response to Oswald paper. There are seasonal effects of unemployment and how quickly unemployed individuals find work. For example, in 1988, heads of households who became unemployed were reemployed significantly quicker in December than in other months.
Boyle (2002)	1983	Ontario Child Health Study, the National Longitudinal Study of Children and Youth, by child	The correlation between home ownership and child problem behavior was –0.18. The correlation between neighborhood home ownership rates and the incidence of child problems was not significant.	The study controlled for socioeconomic differences between owners and renters, but not for other parental characteristics like the physical, mental, and social health of the parents, which might have also affected the association between home ownership and child problem behavior.
Haurin, Parcel, and Haurin (2002)	1988, 1990, 1992, 1994	National Longitudinal Survey of Youth, children aged five to eight	The longer a parent owns a home, the greater the child's cognition skills and the fewer the child's behavior problems. The correlation between home ownership with "Behavior Problems Index" is –0.07.	The explanatory variables included both contemporaneous home ownership and duration of home ownership. (Controlling also for the mother's and father's characteristics separately—education, wage, and race, as well as socioeconomic variables—and for community factors like neighborhood characteristics.)

Conley and Gifford (2006)	1981–1994	Luxembourg Income Study, Comparative Welfare States Data Set, by country	Compared different countries and found that more widespread home ownership is positively associated with higher income inequality and negatively associated with welfare spending. A 1 percentage point increase in social insurance spending by the government results in 0.75 percentage point decrease in home ownership p.	This study does not measure the causal directionality of home ownership, social insurance, and welfare.
Munch, Rosholm, and Svarer (2008)	1993–2001	Statistics Denmark administrative registers, by individual	Home owners have a 29 percent lower unemployment risk than renters. Home owners have a wage premium 5.37 percent higher than renters, and owners set higher reservation wages for jobs outside the local labor market relative to renters.	Crude estimates.
Coulson and Li (2010)	1989, 1993	American Housing Survey, by cluster	Income increases with higher ownership rates, but the results are small and sometimes insignificant. The transition of a home from rental to ownership in a typical neighborhood creates $1,000–3,000 per year in positive externality value.	Measured the units of observation by neighborhood cluster, which typically had eleven houses.

References

Aaronson, D. 2000. "A Note on the Benefit of Homeownership." *Journal of Urban Economics* 47:356–69.

Acharya, Viral, Matthew Richardson, Stijn Van Nieuwerburgh, and Lawrence J. White. 2011. *Guaranteed to Fail.* Princeton, NJ: Princeton University Press.

Ambrose, B. W., Richard Buttimer, and Thomas Thibodeau. 2001. "A New Spin on the Jumbo/Conforming Loan Rate Differential." *Journal of Real Estate Finance and Economics* 23 (3): 309–35.

Ambrose, B. W., M. LaCour-Little, and A. B. Saunders. 2004. "The Effects of Conforming Loan Status on Mortgage Yield Spreads: A Loan Level Analysis." *Real Estate Economics* 32 (4): 541–69.

Ambrose, B. W., and T. G. Thibodeau. 2004. "Have the GSE Affordable Housing Goals Increased the Supply of Mortgage Credit?" *Regional Science and Urban Economics* 34:263–72.

Ambrose, B. W., and Arthur Warga. 1996. "Implications of Privatization: The Costs to Fannie Mae and Freddie Mac." In *Studies on Privatizing Fannie Mae and Freddie Mac.* Washington, DC: US Department of Housing and Urban Development, Office of Policy Development and Research.

———. 2002. "Measuring Potential GSE Funding Advantages. *Journal of Real Estate Finance and Economics* 25 (2/3): 129–50.

An, X., and R. W. Bostic. 2006. *Have the Affordable Housing Goals Been a Shield against Subprime? Regulatory Incentives and the Extension of Mortgage Credit.* April 28. Available at http://www.usc.edu/schools/sppd/lusk/research/pdf/wp _2006-1006.pdf.

———. 2008. "GSE Activity, FHA Feedback, and Implications for the Efficacy of the Affordable Housing Goals." *Journal of Real Estate Finance Economics* 36: 207–31.

———. 2009. "Policy Incentives and the Extension of Mortgage Credit: Increasing Market Discipline for Subprime Lending." *Journal of Policy Analysis and Management* 28 (3): 340–65.

An, X., R. W. Bostic, Y. Deng, S. A. Gabriel, R. K. Green, and J. Tracy. 2007. "GSE Loan Purchases, the FHA, and Housing Outcomes in Targeted, Low-Income Neighborhoods." *Brookings Institution Press:* 205–56. Washington, DC: Brookings Institution.

Avery, R., R. Bostic, and G. Canner. 2005. "Assessing the Necessity and Efficiency of the Community Reinvestment Act." *Housing Policy Debate* 16 (1): 143–72.

Avery, R. B., and K. P. Brevoort. 2010. *The Subprime Crisis: How Much Did Lender Regulation Matter?* August. Available at http://business.gwu.edu/creua/research-papers/files/subprime-crisis.pdf.

Bernanke, Ben. 2008. "The Future of Mortgage Finance in the United States." Speech at the UC Berkeley/UCLA Symposium: The Mortgage Meltdown, the Economy, and Public Policy. Berkeley, California, October 31. Available at http:// www.federalreserve.gov/newsevents/speech/bernanke20081031a.htm.

Bhutta, N. 2009a. *GSE Activity and Mortgage Supply in Lower-Income and Minority Neighborhoods: The Effect of the Affordable Housing Goals.* March. Available at http://www.federalreserve.gov/pubs/feds/2009/200903/revision/200903pap .pdf.

———. 2009b. *Regression Discontinuity Estimates of the Effects of the GSE Act of 1992.* March. Available at http://www.federalreserve.gov/pubs/feds/2009/200903 /200903pap.pdf.

————. 2010. *The Community Reinvestment Act and Mortgage Lending to Lower Income Borrowers and Neighborhoods.* February 5. Available at http://papers.ssrn .com/sol3/papers.cfm?abstract_id=1694762.

Blinder, A. S., M. J. Flannery, and B. G. Lockhart. 2006. "New Estimates of the Jumbo-Conforming Mortgage Spread." Unpublished Paper.

Bostic, R. W., and S. A. Gabriel. 2006. "Do the GSEs Matter to Low-Income Housing Markets? An Assessment of the Effects of the GSE Loan Purchase Goals on California Housing Outcomes." *Journal of Urban Economics* 59:458–75.

Boyle, M. H. 2002. "Home Ownership and the Emotional and Behavioral Problems of Children and Youth." *Child Development* 73 (3): 883–92.

Bubb, Ryan, and Alex Kaufman. 2009. "Securitization and Moral Hazard: Evidence from a Lender Cutoff Rule." Public Policy Discussion Paper no. 09-5. Boston: Federal Reserve Bank of Boston.

Canner, Glenn, Wayne Passmore, and Brian Surette. 1996. "Distribution of Credit Risk among Providers of Mortgages to Lower-Income and Minority Homebuyers." *Federal Reserve Bulletin,* 1996 (December): 1077–102.

Center for American Progress. 2010. "A Responsible Secondary Market System for Housing Finance." Available at http://www.americanprogress.org/issues/2010/09 /pdf/housing_finance_slides.pdf.

Chiuri, Maria Concetta, and Tullio Jappelli. 2003. "Financial Market Imperfections and Home Ownership: A Comparative Study." *European Economic Review* 47 (5): 857–75.

Coles, Adrian, and Judith Hardt. 2000. "Mortgage Markets: Why US and EU Markets Are So Different." *Housing Studies* 15 (5): 775–83.

Congressional Budget Office. 1996. *Assessing the Public Costs and Benefits of Fannie Mae and Freddie Mac.* Report, May. Washington, DC: GPO.

————. 2001. *Federal Subsidies and the Housing GSEs.* Washington, DC: GPO.

————. 2010. *Fannie Mae, Freddie Mac, and the Federal Role in the Secondary Mortgage Market.* Report, December. Washington, DC: GPO.

Conley, D., and B. Gifford. 2006. "Home Ownership, Social Insurance, and the Welfare State." *Springer* 21 (1): 55–82.

Cotterman, R. F., and J. E. Pearce. 1996. "The Effect of the Federal National Mortgage Association and the Federal Home Loan Mortgage Corporation on Conventional Fixed-Rate Mortgage Yields." In *Studies in Privatizing Fannie Mae and Freddie Mac.* Washington, DC: US Department of Housing and Urban Development, Office of Policy Development and Research.

Coulson, E., and H. Li. 2010. "Measuring the External Benefits of Homeownership." September. Available at http://erwan.marginalq.com/HULM11s/ec.pdf.

Dietz, R. D., and D. R. Haurin. 2003. "The Social and Private Micro-Level Consequences of Homeownership." *Journal of Urban Economics* 54:401–50.

DiPasquale, D., and E. L. Glaeser. 1999. "Incentives and Social Capital: Are Homeowners Better Citizens?" *Journal of Urban Economics* 45:354–84.

Downing, Chris, Dwight Jaffee, and Nancy Wallace. 2009. "Is the Market for Mortgage-Backed Securities a Market for Lemons?" *Review of Financial Studies* 22 (7): 2257–94.

Ellen, Ingrid Gould, John Napier Tye, and Mark A. Willis. 2010. "Improving US Housing Finance through Reform of Fannie and Freddie Mac." Furman Center for Real Estate and Urban Policy, New York University. Available at http://fur mancenter.org/files/publications/Improving_US_Housing_Finance_Fannie_Mae _Freddie_Mac_9_8_10.pdf.

Ellickson, Robert C. 2010. "Legal Constraints on Household Moves: Should Footloose Americans Envy the Rooted French." Paper presented at Symposium on Housing: Law and Policy at the University of Notre Dame Law School, September 17. Available at http://www.nd.edu/~ndlaw/conferences/lawecon/Ellickson.pdf.

European Central Bank. 2009. "Housing Finance in the Euro Area." Occasional Paper Series no. 101, March.

European Mortgage Federation. 2010. *Hypotstat 2010.* Available at http://www.hypo.org/Objects/6/Files/Hypostat%202008%20-%20light%20version.pdf.

Federal Home Loan Mortgage Corporation (Freddie Mac). 1996. *Financing America's Housing: The Vital Role of Freddie Mac.* McLean, VA.

Federal Housing Finance Agency. 2009. Retrieved from *Report to Congress 2009,* Historical Data Tables: http://www.fhfa.gov/webfiles/15784/FHFAReportToCongress52510.pdf.

———. 2010a. "Data on the Risk Characteristics of Single-Family Mortgages Originated from 2001 through 2008 and Financed in the Secondary Market." September 13. Available at http://www.fhfa.gov/webfiles/16711/RiskChars9132010.pdf.

———. 2010b. "The Housing Goals of Fannie Mae and Freddie Mac." FHFA Mortgage Market Note, February 1.

———. 2010c. *Report to Congress 2010.* June 13, 2011.

———. 2011. "Conservator's Report on the Enterprises' Financial Performance, Fourth Quarter 2011." Available at http://www.fhfa.gov/webfiles/23879/Conservator'sReport4Q201141212F.pdf.

Federal Reserve. 2008. "Highlights of Final Rule Amending Home Mortgage Provisions of Regulation Z (Truth in Lending)." Available at http://www.federalreserve.gov/newsevents/press/bcreg/regz20080714.htm.

Frame, Scott, and Lawrence White. 2005. "Fussing and Fuming over Fannie and Freddie: How Much Smoke, How Much Fire?" *Journal of Economic Perspectives* 19 (2): 159–84.

Friedman, S., and G. D. Squires. 2005. "Does the Community Reinvestment Act Help Minorities Access Traditionally Inaccessible Neighborhoods?" *University of California Press* 52 (2): 209–31.

Gabriel, S. A., and S. S. Rosenthal. 2010. "Do the GSEs Expand the Supply of Mortgage Credit? New Evidence of Crowd Out in the Secondary Mortgage Market." *Journal of Public Economics* 94:975–86.

Green, Richard. 2011. "Testimony." Senate Banking Committee. http://banking.senate.gov/public/index.cfm?FuseAction=Hearings.Hearing&Hearing_ID=a7b4b965-7291-4741-8507-fldbbb860ac0.

Green, R. K., and P. H. Hendershott. 2001. "Homeownership and Unemployment in the US." *Journal of Urban Studies* 38 (9): 1509–20.

Green, R. K., and M. J. White. 1997. "Measuring the Benefits of Homeowning: Effects on Children." *Journal of Urban Economics* 41:441–61.

Guttentag, J. 1963. *Federal National Mortgage Association,* Federal Credit Agencies. Washington, DC: Commission on Money and Credit, by Prentice Hall.

Hancock, Diana, and Wayne Passmore. 2010. "An Analysis of Government Guarantees and the Functioning of Asset-Backed Securities Markets." Finance and Economics Discussion Series no. 2010-46, Federal Reserve Board.

Haurin, D. R., R. D. Dietz, and B. A. Weinberg. 2002. "The Impact of Neighborhood Homeownership Rates: A Review of the Theoretical and Empirical Literature." March 6. Available at http://papers.ssrn.com/sol3/papers.cfm?abstract_id=303398.

Haurin, D. R., T. L. Parcel, and R. J. Huarin. 2002. "Does Homeownership Affect Child Outcomes?" *Real Estate Economics* 30 (4): 635–66.

Hendershott, Patrick H., and James Shilling. 1989. "The Impact of the Agencies on

Conventional Fixed-Rate Mortgage Yields." *Journal of Real Estate Finance and Economics* 2 (2): 101–15.

Herbert, C. E. 2001. *An Assessment of the Availability and Cost of Financing for Small Multifamily Properties.* August. Available at http://www.huduser.org/publications/pdf/smallmultifamily.pdf.

Hermalin, Benjamin, and Dwight Jaffee. 1996. "The Privatization of Fannie Mae and Freddie Mac: Implications for Mortgage Industry Structure." In *Studies on Privatizing Fannie Mae and Freddie Mac,* 225–302. Washington, DC: US Department of Housing and Urban Development (HUD).

Heuson, Andrea, Wayne Passmore, and Roger Sparks. 2001. "Credit Scoring and Mortgage Securitization: Implications for Mortgage Rates and Credit Availability." *Journal of Real Estate Finance and Economics* 23 (3): 337–64.

ICF Incorporated. 1990. *Effects of the Conforming Loan Limit on Mortgage Markets.* Report prepared for the US Department of Housing and Urban Development, Office of Policy Development and Research. Fairfax, VA.

Jaffee, Dwight. 2009. "The US Subprime Mortgage Crisis: Issues Raised and Lessons Learned." In *Urbanization and Growth,* edited by Michael Spence, Patricia Clarke Annez, and Robert M. Buckley, chapter 7. Washington, DC: The World Bank. Available at http://www.growthcommission.org/storage/cgdev/documents/ebook urbanization.pdf.

———. 2010a. "How to Privatize the Mortgage Market." *Wall Street Journal,* October 25.

———. 2010b. "The Role of the GSEs and Housing Policy in the Financial Crisis." Testimony before the Financial Crisis Inquiry Commission, February 25. Available at http://fcic.law.stanford.edu/hearings/testimony/forum-to-explore-the-causes-of-the-financial-crisis.

———. 2011. "Testimony." Senate Banking Committee. Available at http://banking.senate.gov/public/index.cfm?FuseAction=Hearings.Hearing&Hearing_ID=a7b4b965-7291-4741-8507-fldbbb860ac0.

Jaffee, Dwight, and John Quigley. 2007. "Housing Subsidies and Homeowners: What Role for Government-Sponsored Enterprises?" *Brookings-Wharton Papers on Urban Affairs:* 103–49. Washington, DC: Brookings Institution.

———. 2010. "Housing Policy, Mortgage Policy, and the Federal Housing Administration." In *Measuring and Managing Federal Financial Risk,* edited by Deborah Lucas, 97–130. Chicago: University of Chicago Press.

Jaffee, Dwight, and Kenneth Rosen. 1978. "Estimates of the Effectiveness of Stabilization Policies for the Mortgage and Housing Markets." *Journal of Finance* 33 (3): 933–46.

———. 1979. "Mortgage Credit Availability and Residential Construction." *Brookings Papers on Economic Activity* 1979 (2): 333–86. Washington, DC: Brookings Institution.

Jaffee, Dwight, and Thomas Russell. 2006. "Should Governments Provide Catastrophe Insurance?" *The Economists' Voice* 3 (5): Article 6. Available at http://www.bepress.com/ev/vol3/iss5/art6.

Keys, Benjamin J., Tanmoy Mukherjee, Amit Seru, and Vikrant Vig. 2010. "Did Securitization Lead to Lax Screening? Evidence from Subprime Loans." *The Quarterly Journal of Economics* 125 (1): 307–62.

Laderman, Elizabeth, and Carolina Reid. 2008. "Lending in Low- and Moderate-Income Neighborhoods in California: The Performance of CREA Lending during the Subprime Meltdown." Community Development Working Paper 2008-05, November.

Lea, Michael. 2010. "International Comparison of Mortgage Product Offerings." Research Institute for Housing America, September.

Lehnert, Andreas, Wayne Passmore, and Shane Sherlund. 2008. "GSEs, Mortgage Rates, and Secondary Market Activities." *The Journal of Real Estate Finance and Economics.* 36 (3): 343–63.

Lewis, Michael. 1990. *Liars Poker.* New York: Penguin.

Manchester, Paul. 2007. "Goal Performance and Characteristics of Mortgages Purchased by Fannie Mae and Freddie Mac, 2001–2005." HUD Housing Finance Working Paper HF-17.

McKenzie, Joseph A. 2002. "A Reconsideration of the Jumbo/Non-Jumbo Mortgage Rate Differential." *Journal of Real Estate Finance and Economics* 25 (2/3): 197–214.

Michel-Kerjan, Erwann, and Howard Kunreuther. 2011. "Redesigning Flood Insurance." *Science* 333:408–09.

Morgenson, Gretch, and Joshua Rosner. 2011. *Reckless Endangerment: How Outsized Ambition, Greed, and Corruption Led to Economic Armageddon.* New York: Henry Holt and Company.

Mortgage Bankers Association, Real Estate Finance Association. 2009. Various Figures. September. Available at http://www.gbreb.com/uploadedFiles/REFA /Education_and_Events/Content_Blocks/Freddie%20Fannie%20and%20FHA %20Presentation%20Final2%281%29.pdf?n=8957.

———. 2010. "Originating Lender Localness and Mortgage Sustainability." *Public Administration Review* 70 (3): 349–60.

Munch, J. R., M. Rosholm, and M. Svarer. 2008. "Home Ownership, Job Duration, and Wages." *Journal of Urban Economics* 68:130–45.

Naranjo, Andy, and Alden Toevs. 2002. "The Effects of Purchases of Mortgages and Securitizations by Government-Sponsored Enterprises on Mortgage Yield Spreads and Volatility." *Fannie Mae Papers* 1 (3): 1–14.

Nothaft, Frank E., James Pearce, and Steven Stevanovic. 2002. "Debt Spreads Between GSEs and Other Corporations." *Journal of Real Estate Finance and Economics* 25 (2/3): 151–72.

Oswald, A. 1996. "A Conjecture on the Explanation for High Unemployment in the Industrialized Nations: Part I." University of Warwick Working Paper no. 475.

Passmore, Wayne. 2005. "The GSE Implicit Subsidy and the Value of Government Ambiguity." *Real Estate Economics* 33 (3): 465–86.

Passmore, Wayne, Shane Sherlund, and Burgess Gillian. 2005. "The Effect of Housing Government-Sponsored Enterprises on Mortgage Rates." *Real Estate Economics* 33 (3): 427–63.

Passmore, Wayne, Roger Sparks, and Jamie Ingpen. 2002. "GSEs, Mortgage Rates, and the Long-Run Effects of Mortgage Securitization." *Journal of Real Estate Finance and Economics* 25 (2/3): 215–42.

Pearce, James E. 2000. *Conforming Loan Differentials: 1992–1999.* College Station, TX: Welch Consulting.

Pearce, James E., and James Miller. 2001. "Freddie Mac and Fannie Mae: Their Funding Advantages and Benefits to Consumers." *Proceedings, Federal Reserve Bank of Chicago* 2001 (May): 101–17.

Peek, Joe, and James A. Wilcox. 2003. "Secondary Mortgage Markets, GSEs, and the Changing Cyclicality of Mortgage Flows." *Research in Finance* 20:61–80.

Quigley, J. M. 2006. "Federal Credit and Insurance Programs: Housing." *Federal Reserve Bank of St. Louis Review:* 281–310.

Quinn, Sarah. 2010. "Government Policy, Housing, and the Origins of Securitization, 1780–1968." PhD diss., University of California, Berkeley. Forthcoming, Princeton University Press.

Remy, Mitchell, Deborah Lucas, and Damien Moore. 2011. "An Evaluation of

Large-Scale Mortgage Refinancing Programs." Congressional Budget Office Working Paper. Available at http://www.cbo.gov/publication/42752.

Rossi, P. H., and E. Weber. 1996. "The Social Benefits of Homeownership: Empirical Evidence from National Surveys." *Housing Policy Debate* 7 (1): 1–35.

Thomas, Jason, and Robert Van Order. 2011. "A Closer Look at Fannie Mae and Freddie Mac: What We Know, What We Think We Know and What We Don't Know." Available at http://business.gwu.edu/creua/research-papers/files/fannie-freddie.pdf.

Tocqueville, Alexis de. 1835. *Democracy in America.* London: Saunders and Otley.

Toevs, Alden L. 2000. *A Critique of the CBO's Sponsorship Benefit Analysis.* New York: First Manhattan Consulting Group.

United States Department of Housing and Urban Development, O. o. n.d. *Overview of the GSEs' Housing Goal Performance, 1993–2001.* Available at http://www.huduser.org/datasets/GSE/gse2001.pdf.

———. n.d. *Overview of the GSEs' Housing Performance, 2000–2007.* Available at http://www.huduser.org/datasets/GSE/gse2007.pdf.

US Department of the Treasury. 1996. *Government Sponsorship of the Federal National Mortgage Association and the Federal Home Loan Mortgage Corporation.* Washington, DC: GPO, July.

US Government Accountability Office. 2009. "Fannie Mae and Freddie Mac: Analysis of Options for Revising the Housing Enterprises' Long-Term Structures." GAO-09-782, September.

US Treasury and Housing and Urban Development. 2011. *Reforming America's Housing Finance Market, A Report to Congress.* White Paper, February. Washington, DC: GPO.

Wallison, Peter. 2011. *Dissent from the Majority Report of the Financial Crisis Inquiry Commission.* January 14. Available at http://www.aei.org/docLib/Wallisondissent.pdf.

Weicher, J. C. 2010. "The Affordable Housing Goals, Homeownership and Risk: Some Lessons from Past Efforts to Regulate the GSEs." In *The Past, Present, and Future of the Government-Sponsored Enterprises,* 1–28. St. Louis: Federal Reserve Bank of St. Louis.

Woodward, Susan E. 2004a. "Estimating the Jumbo Rate Premium with Clean and Rich Loan Level Data." Unpublished Manuscript, Sand Hill Econometrics.

Wyly, E. K., and S. R. Holloway. 2002. "The Disappearance of Race in Mortgage Lending." *Economic Geography* 78 (2): 129–69.

Contributors

Jack Favilukis
Department of Finance
London School of Economics
Houghton Street
London WC2A 2AE England

David Genesove
Department of Economics
Hebrew University of Jerusalem
Mount Scopus
Jerusalem, 91905 Israel

Edward L. Glaeser
Department of Economics
315A Littauer Center
Harvard University
Cambridge, MA 02138

Joshua D. Gottlieb
Department of Economics
University of British Columbia
#997–1873 East Mall
Vancouver, BC V6T 1Z1 Canada

Joseph Gyourko
The Wharton School of Business
University of Pennsylvania
3620 Locust Walk
1480 Steinberg-Dietrich Hall
Philadelphia, PA 19104-6302

Lu Han
Rotman School of Management
105 St. George Street
University of Toronto
Toronto, ON M5S 3E6 Canada

Andrew Haughwout
Microeconomic Studies Function
Federal Reserve Bank of New York
33 Liberty Street
New York, NY 10045

Dwight Jaffee
Walter A. Haas School of Business
University of California at Berkeley
Berkeley, CA 94720-1900

Benjamin J. Keys
Harris School of Public Policy
The University of Chicago
1155 East 60th Street
Chicago, IL 60637

David Kohn
Department of Economics
New York University
19 West 4th Street, 6th Floor
New York, NY10012

419

Donghoon Lee
Microeconomic Studies Function
Federal Reserve Bank of New York
33 Liberty Street
New York, NY 10045

Sydney C. Ludvigson
Department of Economics
New York University
19 West 4th Street, 6th Floor
New York, NY 10012

Christopher Mayer
Columbia Business School
3022 Broadway, Uris Hall #805
New York, NY 10027

Richard W. Peach
Macroeconomic and Monetary Studies
    Function
Federal Reserve Bank of New York
33 Liberty Street
New York, NY 10045

Tomasz Piskorski
Columbia Business School
3022 Broadway
Uris Hall 810
New York, NY 10027

John M. Quigley

Amit Seru
Booth School of Business
University of Chicago
5807 South Woodlawn Avenue
Chicago, IL 60637

Todd Sinai
The Wharton School
University of Pennsylvania
1465 Steinberg Hall-Dietrich Hall
3620 Locust Walk
Philadelphia, PA 19104-6302

John Sporn
Treasury Market Policy
Federal Reserve Bank of New York
33 Liberty Street
New York, NY 10045

Joseph Tracy
Federal Reserve Bank of New York
33 Liberty Street
New York, NY 10045

Stijn Van Nieuwerburgh
Stern School of Business
New York University
44 West 4th Street, Suite 9-120
New York, NY 10012

Vikrant Vig
London Business School
Regent's Park
London NW1 4SA England

Author Index

Acharya, V. V., 196n35, 248, 285, 403, 405
Adam, K., 240, 241
Adelino, M., 182
Agarwal, S., 144n1, 146n2, 147, 178, 182, 189, 190, 193
Aizenman, J., 241n3, 270
Alfaro, L., 237, 286
Ambrose, B. W., 181n23, 397, 398, 399, 399n19
Amromin, G., 147, 190, 193, 264
An, X., 390
Anas, A., 109
Ashcraft, A., 146, 175

Banerjee, A. V., 73
Barlevy, G., 19n1, 167n13, 264
Bayer, P., 19n1, 20, 33
Bedoll, D., 98n16
Belsky, E. S., 149
Ben-David, I., 168
Benmelech, E., 196n34
Bernanke, B. S., 239, 240, 241, 259, 261, 401
Bhutta, N., 185, 390
Blinder, A. S., 399
Bolton, P., 180
Bond, P., 168n16
Bostic, R. W., 390, 396
Boz, E., 239, 285
Brueckner, J., 108, 108n3
Brunnermeier, M., 33n9
Bubb, R., 173n18, 302, 333, 375n11
Bucks, B. K., 168

Buiter, W. H., 154
Buonaccorsi, 133
Burchfeld, M., 107, 108
Burnside, C., 20n1, 20n2, 23n3, 38, 57n20
Buttimer, R., 399n19

Caballero, R. J., 240, 241, 243n6, 254
Campbell, J. Y., 15, 19n1, 27n6, 46, 166n12, 180, 313
Canner, G., 390
Caplin, A., 224n13
Capozza, D., 128, 129, 131
Case, K. E., 19n1, 138, 306
Chen, C., 193n32
Chinco, A., 212n9, 348n32
Chomsisengphet, S., 150
Cocco, J. F., 164n9, 166n12, 313
Cohen-Cole, E., 231
Coleman, M. D., 313
Coles, A., 378
Cooley, T., 285
Corbae, D., 166n12
Cororaton, A., 224
Cotter, J., 45, 130, 131
Cutler, D., 6

Davidoff,, T., 23n3, 39n11
Davis, M. A., 96
DeCoster, G. P., 73
Demiroglu, C., 146
Demyanyk, Y., 149, 227n14
Deng, Y., 180n21

Diamond, D. W., 145, 196n35
Dietz, R. D., 365
Dinc, S., 189
DiPasquale, D., 24n4
Dlugosz, J., 196n34
Dokko, J., 185
Downing, C., 373n8
Driscoll, J. C., 274n15
Dunn, K. B., 166n11

Eichenbaum, M., 20n1, 20n2, 23n3, 38, 57n20
Ellen, I. G., 403
Ellickson, R. C., 381n16
Ellwood, D. T., 316
Elul, R., 223n12
Engelhardt, G. V., 309

Farhi, E., 240, 254
Favara, G., 265
Favilukis, J., 20n1, 167n14, 237, 238, 261, 302
Feldstein, M., 206
Ferreira, F., 20, 23n3, 39n10, 42n12, 57n20, 310n4, 345n27
Ferrero, A., 241, 242n4, 261, 270
Fisher, J. D., 19n1, 167n13, 264
Flannery, M. J., 399
Frame, S., 374
Frey, W., 206n3
Fuller, W., 133

Gabriel, S., 45, 130, 131, 390, 396
Gan, Y., 181n23
Geissler, C., 19n1, 20, 33
Geithner, T., 247
Gelpern, A., 188n22
Genesove, D., 126
Gerardi, K., 182
Gertler, M., 239
Gete, P., 241, 270
Ghent, A., 229, 229n16
Giglio, S., 15, 27n6, 180
Gillian, B., 398, 399, 400
Glaeser, E. L., 2, 6, 8, 19n1, 29n7, 29n8, 57n19, 71, 72, 106n1, 108, 117, 137, 138, 261, 302, 303, 304, 312, 312n6, 313, 325, 341
Goodman, L. S., 227
Gottlieb, J. D., 8, 19n1, 261, 304, 307, 312, 312n6, 313
Gourichas, P.-O., 240, 254

Green, R., 129, 130n10, 138, 365
Greenspan, A., 205, 212, 216, 302, 333
Guerrieri, V., 137
Guiso, L., 185, 187
Guttentag, J., 366
Gyourko, J., 2, 6, 19n1, 20, 23n3, 29n7, 29n8, 39n10, 42n12, 57n19, 57n20, 71, 72, 106n1, 117, 131, 137, 138, 224n13, 261, 302, 303, 304, 307, 310n4, 312, 312n6, 313, 325, 327n16, 339, 341, 345n27

Hancock, D., 405
Hardt, J., 378
Hartley, D., 137, 138
Hartman-Glaser, B., 194
Haughwout, A., 46n16, 98n16
Haurin, D. R., 309, 365
Heathcote, J., 96
Helsley, R., 128, 129, 131
Hendershott, P. H., 309, 399
Hermalin, B., 398
Heuson, A., 399n19
Himmelberg, C., 4, 19n1, 33n9, 46, 240, 241, 302, 303, 304, 309, 311, 321, 321n11, 322
Ho, C. T., 144n1
Holmstrom, B., 169n17
Hubbard, R. G., 218
Hurst, E., 137, 138

Imbs, J., 265
Ingpen, J., 400
Ivashina, V., 196n34

Jaffee, D., 362, 373n8, 374, 397, 398, 403, 404
Jagtiani, J., 208, 227
James, C. M., 146
Jiang, W., 146, 174
Jinjarak, Y., 241n3, 270
Julliard, C., 33n9

Kalemli-Ozcan, S., 237, 286
Kau, J. B., 180n21
Kaufman, A., 173n18, 302, 333, 375n11
Keenan, D. C., 180n21
Kennedy, J., 205, 212, 216
Keys, B. J., 145, 169, 172, 173, 173n18, 174n20, 196, 285, 302, 333, 375n11
Khan, J. A., 167n14
Khandani, A., 302
Kim, T., 180n21

Kiyotaki, N., 239
Kohn, D. L., 237, 256
Kole, L. S., 241
Kraay, A. C., 274n15
Krainer, J., 262n12
Krishnamurthy, A., 237, 240, 241, 243n6, 256
Kuang, P., 240, 241
Kudlyak, M., 229, 229n16
Kunreuther, H., 404

LaCour-Little, M., 313
Lai, R., 19n1
Laibson, D., 240, 241, 270
Landier, A., 168n15
Landvoigt, T., 138
Lang, W., 208, 227
Laufer, S., 263
Lehnert, A., 374
LeRoy, S. F., 262n12
Levitan, A. J., 181, 207
Lewis, M., 372n7
Linneman, P., 137
Lo, A. W., 302
Lockhart, B. G., 399
Loutskina, E., 146, 174
Lucas, D., 406n22
Lucca, D., 146n2, 178
Ludvigson, S., 20n1, 167n14, 237, 238, 261, 302

Makarov, I., 163n7
Malpezzi, S., 129, 130n10, 138
Manchester, P., 387
Mankiw, G. N., 9
Marcet, A., 240, 241
Martin, R. F., 241
Marynchenko, M., 138
Mas, A., 339
Mayer, C., 4, 19n1, 33n9, 46, 127, 129, 136, 138, 147, 151, 166, 181n22, 181n23, 188, 197, 207, 212n9, 218, 227n14, 232n18, 240, 241, 302, 303, 304, 309, 311, 321, 321n11, 322, 348n32
Mayo, S., 129, 130n10, 138
McCarthy, J., 46n15
McKenzie, J. A., 399, 400
Meese, R., 46n14
Mendoza, E. G., 239, 240, 285
Merton, R. C., 302
Mian, A., 7, 19n1, 33, 37, 57n20, 146, 174, 184, 238, 239, 265, 285, 302

Michel-Kerjan, E., 404
Milgrom, P., 169n17
Miller, J., 397
Mollerstrom, J., 240, 270, 2441
Molloy, R., 138
Moore, D., 406n22
Moore, J., 239
Moretti, E., 339
Morgenson, G., 396
Morrison, E., 181n22, 207
Morse, J., 231
Mukherjee, T., 173, 174n20
Munpyung, O., 262n12
Musto, D. K., 168n16

Nadauld, T. D., 146, 174
Naranjo, A., 374
Nathanson, C., 11
Nechayev, G., 19n1
Nelson, A. A., 146, 174
Newey, W. K., 322
Nichols, J., 261
Nothaft, F. E., 397, 398

Obstfeld, M., 249, 286
Orr, J., 98n16
Ortalgo-Magné, F., 46n14

Palumbo, M. G., 96
Passmore, W., 374, 390, 397n18, 398, 399, 399n19, 400, 405
Pathak, P., 15, 27n6, 180
Pavlov, A., 19n1, 33
Peach, R., 46n15
Pearce, J. E., 397, 398
Peek, J., 374
Pence, K. M., 151, 168, 182, 227n14, 342
Pennington-Cross, A., 150, 261
Piazzesi, M., 138
Piskorski, T., 145, 163, 164, 166, 180, 181, 181n22, 194, 197, 207, 285
Plantin, G., 163
Polinsky, A. M., 316
Poon, M. A., 285
Posner, E. A., 181n22
Poterba, J., 2, 6, 302, 303, 307, 309, 310, 324
Prat, A., 46
Purnanandam, A., 146, 174

Quadrini, V., 240
Quigley, J., 180n21, 362, 397, 399, 403
Quintin, E., 166n12

Rajan, R., 145, 196n35, 239, 265
Rajan, U., 146, 151, 173n19, 174
Ramcharan, R., 239, 265
Rebelo, S., 20n1, 20n2, 23n3, 38, 57n20
Reinhart, V. R., 261
Remy, M., 406n22
Rhee, H., 109
Rice, T., 239, 342
Richardson, M., 248, 285
Richardson, N., 149
Rios-Rull, J.-V., 240
Roberts, J., 19n1, 20, 33
Robinson, B., 19n1
Roll, R., 45, 130, 131
Romer, C. D., 325
Romer, D. H., 325
Rosen, K., 374
Rosen, S., 71, 316
Rosenthal, H., 180
Rosenthal, S. S., 71, 108, 108n3, 137, 396
Rosner, J., 396
Russell, T., 404

Sack, B. P., 261
Saiz, A., 2, 6, 29n7, 29n8, 57n19, 71, 72,
    106n1, 117, 131, 137, 138, 303, 316,
    316n8, 325, 327n16, 339
Sanders, A., 181n23
Sapienza, P., 185, 188
Schnabl, P., 196n35, 285
Schneider, M., 138
Schuermann, T., 146, 175
Seru, A., 145, 146, 151, 172, 173, 173n18,
    173n19, 174, 174n20, 180, 181, 197
Shan, H., 138, 185
Sherlund, S. M., 146, 151, 174, 374, 398,
    399, 400
Shiller, R. J., 19n1, 197, 302, 306, 321n11
Shilling, J., 399
Sinai, T., 4, 8, 19n1, 33n9, 46, 240, 241, 302,
    303, 304, 309, 310, 311, 321, 321n11,
    322
Smith, G., 46
Smith, M. H., 46
Somerville, T., 127, 129, 136
Souleles, N., 8
Sparks, R., 399n19, 400
Spatt, C. S., 166n1
Sraer, D., 168n15
Stein, J. C., 169, 173
Stevanovic, S., 397, 398
Stevens, D. H., 184n24

Strahan, P. E., 146, 174, 239, 342
Strange, W. C., 73
Streitfeld, D., 243n5
Suarez, G., 196, 285
Sufi, A., 7, 19n1, 33, 37, 57n20, 146, 174,
    184, 238, 239, 265, 285, 302
Summers, A., 131, 137, 327n16, 339
Summers, L., 6
Surette, B., 390

Taylor, J. B., 240, 241, 322
Tchistyi, A., 145, 163, 164, 166, 180, 194,
    197, 285
Thesmar, D., 168n15
Thibodeau, T., 399n19
Thomas, J., 375n10, 377n13
Tobio, K., 8
Tocqueville, A. de, 365
Todd, R., 19n1
Toevs, A., 374
Topel, R., 71, 316
Tracy, J., 224, 310n4
Trebbi, F., 184, 239, 285, 302
Tye, J. N., 403

Vandell, K. D., 313
Van Den Heuvel, S., 178
Van Hemert, O., 149, 227n14
Van Nieuwerburg, S., 20n1, 137, 167n14,
    237, 238, 261, 302
Van Order, R., 19n1, 180n21, 375n10,
    377n13
Vig, V., 145, 146, 151, 172, 173, 173n18,
    173n19, 174, 174n20, 180, 181, 197
Vissing-Jorgensen, A., 237, 256
Volosovych, V., 237, 286
Vytlacil, E., 146, 174

Wachter, S. M., 19n1, 33, 309
Wallace, N., 46n14, 373n8
Wallison, P., 374, 396
Ward, B., 108
Warga, A., 397, 398
Warnock, F. E., 248, 248n8, 256, 257, 261
Warnock, V. C., 248, 248n8, 256, 261
Weil, D. N., 9
Weill, P., 137
Weinberg, B. A., 365
Welch, I., 73
West, K. D., 322
Wheaton, W., 19n1, 24n4
White, A. M., 181n22

White, L., 374
White, M. J., 108
Wicher, J. C., 389
Wilcox, J. A., 374
Willen, P. S., 182
Willis, M. A., 403
Woodward, S. E., 399, 399n19

Yavas, A., 181n23
Yezer, A., 261
Yilmaz, B., 168n16

Zhang, Y., 182
Zingales, L., 181n22, 185, 188
Zwick, E., 11

Subject Index

Page numbers followed by the letter *f* or *t* refer to figures or tables, respectively.

Across market variation, of housing booms and busts. *See* Cross-market spatial variation of housing booms and busts

Agency bonds, defined, 248

Alt-A loans, 11, 156, 262, 264; defined, 156n5

American Dream, 143–44

Approval rates: house price growth and, 342–44; impact of, on house prices, 338–42; measuring change in, 332–38; mortgage applications and, 331–32; price impact of, 317–18

ARMs. *See* Hybrid adjustable-rate mortgages (ARMs)

Auto loans, 230–31

Auto loan securitization, 195

Boom and bust. *See* Housing market boom and bust of 2000s

Borrowers, 150–51; identifying eligible, for mortgage modification programs, 184–89

Builders, profits and, 100–101

Building industry, home, trends in, 86–96

Built-for-sale ("spec") housing, 91–92

Bureau of Economic Analysis (BEA), 248–49; holdings data, 248–49; transactions data, 249

CA. *See* Current account (CA)

Capital flows: FLVN model and, 244; theo-ries of linkage between house prices and, 240–47; trends in, 247–60. *See also* International capital flows

Car loans. *See* Auto loans

Case-Shiller repeat sales housing price index, 1

Catastrophe insurance, 405

CDOs. *See* Collateralized debt obligations (CDOs)

CDSs. *See* Credit default swaps (CDSs)

Closed-end second liens (CES), 12–13, 206; default performance of, 227–32; home equity lines of credit versus, 209; per-formance of, 210; performance of, rela-tive to other types of first liens, 224–27

Collateralized debt obligations (CDOs), gross flows across borders into, 259

Combined loan-to-value ratios (CLTVs), 262–63

Community Reinvestment Act (CRA), 389

Complex mortgages, 264

Conforming loan limit (CLL), 264–65

Consumption smoothing, house prices and, 241

Credit, increase in supply of, 13–14. *See also* Interest rates

Credit availability, measuring, 265–66. *See also* Financial market liberalization (FML)

Credit card loans, 231

Credit card securitization, 195
Credit default swaps (CDSs), gross flows
across borders into, 259
Credit market–based explanations, of housing market boom and bust of 2000s,
3–4
Credit standards (CS), 281–83; international
data, 292–93; US data, 289–91
Credit supply: exogenous changes in, and
financial market liberalization, 264–70;
movements in, 280–83
Cross-market spatial variation of housing
booms and busts, 105–6; in building
permits, 128–30, 136–37; data, 130–31;
in house prices, 128–30, 131–37
CS. *See* Credit standards (CS)
Current account (CA), 249–50; data, 287–89

DataQuick, 345
Department of Housing and Urban Development, housing goals of, 382–86
Diffusion index, 292
Down payment requirements: impact of, on
house prices, 313–14; role of, in housing boom-bust, 345–49

Easy credit, role of, in housing boom-bust,
302–3. *See also* Interest rates

Fannie Mae (Federal National Mortgage
Association), 2, 14, 361, 362–64, 382;
establishment of, as government-
sponsored enterprises, 364. *See also*
Government-sponsored enterprises
(GSEs)
Favilukis, Ludvigson, and Van Nieuwer-
burgh (FLVN) model of house prices,
237–40, 242–47
FDI (foreign direct investment), 248, 250
Federal Home Loan Mortgage Corpora-
tion. *See* Freddie Mac (Federal Home
Loan Mortgage Corporation)
Federal Housing Administration (FHA),
363, 403–4
Federal Housing Enterprises Financial
Safety and Soundness Act (1992), 382,
387
Federal Housing Finance Agency (FHFA)
price index, 318–21, 318n10
Federal National Mortgage Association
(FNMA). *See* Fannie Mae (Federal
National Mortgage Association)

FICO score point, 620, 12
Financial Institutions Reform, Recovery,
and Enforcement Act (FIRREA), 382
Financial intermediation: changing nature
of financing and, 168–69; evidence
from Keys, Mukherjee, Seru, and Vig,
169–73; market patterns and, 173–75;
market patterns and agency conflicts in
supply chain and, 175–77; regulation
and, 177–79
Financial market liberalization (FML):
defined, 236, 238; exogenous changes in
credit supply and, 264–70; house prices
and, 237–38, 261–70; increased availability of mortgage credit and, 263–64;
loan-to-value ratios and, 238, 261–63
FIRREA (Financial Institutions Reform,
Recovery, and Enforcement Act), 382
Fixed-rate mortgages (FRMs), 155
FLVN model. *See* Favilukis, Ludvigson, and
Van Nieuwerburgh (FLVN) model of
house prices
FML. *See* Financial market liberalization
(FML)
Foreclosure crisis, 12, 179–80; current status
of, 193–94; reasons federal govern-
ment intervened in, 191–93. *See also*
Renegotiation
Foreign direct investment (FDI), 248, 250
Foreign official holdings, 256–58
Foreign Official Institutions, 256
Freddie Mac (Federal Home Loan Mort-
gage Corporation), 2, 14, 361; establish-
ment of, 364. *See also* Government-
sponsored enterprises (GSEs)
FRMs (fixed-rate mortgages), 155

Global imbalances phenomenon, 247–48
Global savings glut hypothesis, of house
prices, 240–41, 302
Goals, housing, GSEs and, 382–86
Government insurance, of mortgages, 403–5
Government-sponsored enterprises (GSEs),
144; background, 362–64; benefits arising from activities of, 381–90; benefits
to all housing market participants and,
397–400; creation of mortgage-backed
securities by, 145; effects of, on mortgage rates, 399–400, 399t; effects of
goals of, on housing market outcomes,
391–95t, 396–97; future of, 361–62,
400–407; housing goals for, 382–86;

liability of government for debt instruments issued by, 364; mortgage market stability of, 373–74; mortgage markets without, 377–81; primary objectives of, 365–66; quantitative impact of, on US home mortgage market, 366–71; role of, in issuance of mortgage-backed securities, 371–73; role of, in subprime mortgage boom-bust, 374–77; securitization by, 195; securitization rates in, 149f. *See also* Fannie Mae (Federal National Mortgage Association); Freddie Mac (Federal Home Loan Mortgage Corporation)

HAMP. *See* Home Affordable Modification Program (HAMP)
Hard information, banks and, 196
HELOCs. *See* Home equity lines of credit (HELOCs)
Home Affordable Modification Program (HAMP), 147, 191–93, 206, 208, 406–7; closed-end second liens versus, 209
Home Affordable Refinance Program (HARP), 406
Home building industry, trends in, 86–96
Home equity lines of credit (HELOCs), 12–13, 206, 207; default performance of, 227–32; defined, 207n5; performance of, 210; performance of, relative to other types of first liens, 224–27
Home Mortgage Interest Deduction, 2
Home ownership, 365
House prices: annual growth of, 43–45; capital inflow–driven low interest rates theories, 241; consumption smoothing and, 241; controlling for demand fundamentals and, 46–56; cycles of, remaining after controlling for demand fundamentals, 46–56; data, 286–87, 288t; destruction of myths about, 2; empirical analysis of interest rates and, 318–31; endogenous housing supply, 314–17; financial market liberation and, 237–38, 261–70; FLVN model of, 237–40, 242–47; geographic clustering of, 40–43; global savings glut hypothesis, 240–41; growth in, and mortgage approval rates, 342–44; heterogeneity in timing of, by MSA, 38–40; heterogeneity in US, 24–33; higher domestic demand theories, 241; impact

of approval rates on, 338–42; impact of down payment requirements on, 313–14; and interest rates in areas with elastic and inelastic supply, 325–27; international capital flows and, 235–36; international evidence on fluctuations of, 270–83; literature on movements of, 137–38; measuring real, 318–21; national patterns of, 23–24; net capital flows and, 236–37; net foreign inflows and, 235; real growth and decline in (1990s–2000s, by MSA), 30–31f, 32f; regression analysis of, 272–83; rent ratio versus, 236f; similarities with 1980s, 33–38; theoretical link between interest rates and, 307–18; theories of linkage between capital flows and, 240–47; timing of, 21; troughs, 58–66t
Housing, trends in size, amenities, and quality of, 84–86
Housing and Urban Development Act (1968), 364
Housing bubble, conclusions on causes of, 350
Housing goals, GSEs and, 382–86, 396–97
Housing market boom and bust of 2000s, 19–22; anatomy of, 5–10; causes of, 10–14; data, 22–23; four questions about, 69–71; geographic clustering of, 40–43; growth in private label securitization and, 148–54; heterogeneity in amplitude of, 24–33; heterogeneity in timing of, 38–40; housing policy and, 2; impact of initial loan-to-value ratios and, 345–49; land markets during, 96–99; literature review of, 71–74; national patterns, 23–24; overbuilding and, 74–84; profits during, 100–101; public policy in wake of, 14–15; reasons why irrational expectations–based explanations have failed to garner support, 3–4; similarity with 1980s and, 33–38; supply questions about, 69–71. *See also* Cross-market spatial variation of housing booms and busts; Within-market spatial variation of housing booms and busts
Housing market crash, 1–2; housing policy and, 2; myths destroyed by, 2
Housing policy: after great housing market crash, 14–15; great housing market crash and, 2

Housing supply: endogenous, home prices and, 314–17; fixed, and fixed interest rates, 307–13
Housing supply elasticity, literature on, 137
Hybrid adjustable-rate mortgages (ARMs), 144; short-term, 155–57

Insurance, government, of mortgages, 403–5
Interest-only loans, 156, 157f
Interest rates: effects of GSEs on, 399–400, 399t; empirical analysis of housing prices and, 318–31; fixed, and fixed housing supply, 307–13; and house prices in areas with elastic and inelastic supply, 325–27; theoretical link between house prices and, 307–18; trends in US, 260–61; US, net foreign holdings and, 260–61. *See also* Credit
International capital flows, 235–40, 248–60; foreign official holdings and, 256–58; house prices and, 235–36; theories, 240–47; trends, 247–56. *See also* Capital flows
Investors, in mortgage-backed securities, 153–54
Irrational expectations–based explanations of housing market boom and bust of 2000s, 3–4

Jumbo nonagency securitized loans, 156

Land markets, during housing market boom and bust, 96–99
Land owners, profits and, 100
Land prices, during boom and bust, 96–99
Lenders, mortgage, 151–53
Loan-to-value (LTV) ratios: combined, 262–63; financial market liberalization and, 238, 261–63; impact of initial, on housing boom-bust, 345–49
Low documentation loans, 144
LTV ratios. *See* Loan-to-value (LTV) ratios

Mean values, 292
Moral hazard, importance of, 196–97
Mortgage applications, approval rates and, 331–32
Mortgage-backed securities: brief history of development of US, 372–73; gross flows across borders into, 259; investors in, 153–54; role of GSEs in issuance of, 371–73

Mortgage financing, 143–47
Mortgage lenders, 151–53
Mortgage markets: without GSEs, 377–81; performance of European versus US, 379–81, 380t
Mortgage pool, improving performance of, 194
Mortgage product development: alternative views, 167–68; efficiency view of, 163–67
Mortgage rates. *See* Interest rates
Mortgages: government insurance of, 403–5; nontraditional, growth in, 154–58; subsidized, 2. *See also* Subprime mortgages
Multifamily dwellings, GSEs and, 387
Mutual Mortgage Insurance Fund, 363

National Flood Insurance Program (NFIP), 404
National Mortgage Association, 363
Negative amortization contracts, 144
Negative amortization loans, 156; evolution of, 157f
Net capital flows, house prices and, 236–37
Net foreign asset holdings into United States, 236–37, 237n1, 249; longer-term trends in, 258–59; relative to US trend GDP, 258f; US interest rates and, 260–61
Net foreign holdings of US securities, 237, 237n1, 237n2
Net international investment position (NIIP), US, 249
Net percentage, 292
Nontraditional mortgages: growth in, 154–58; prepayment penalties and, 158; types of, 155. *See also* Subprime mortgages

"One size fits all" regulation, 197
Overbuilding, housing market boom and bust of 2000s and, 74–84
Owner-occupied housing, 365

Piggyback second liens, 209–10, 218, 230–31
Prepayment penalties, 158
Price growth, of housing, 7–8
Private label securitization, 144, 264; growth in, and housing boom and bust, 148–54; rise in share of, 371
Profits, of builders versus landowners, 100–101

Regulation, "one size fits all," 197
Renegotiation: challenges of effective, 179–80; identifying "eligible borrowers" and, 184–89; impact of securitization, 179–84; political pressure and, 189–90; role of servicer-specific factors, 190–91. *See also* Foreclosure crisis
Rental value of housing, determinants of, 46
Rent-housing price ratio, 236f
Rents, within-market spatial variations in, 124–26
Residential investment data, 289, 290t
Risk retention mechanisms, 194–95
Risky mortgage holdings, 259–60

Second liens, 205–10; aggregate lending patterns for, 212–17; correlation between delinquency of first mortgages and, 210; data, 210–12; default performance of, 224–27; default performance of matched first and, 227–32; delinquency puzzle of, 13; performance of, relative to other types of consumer credit, 223–32; piggyback, 209–10, 218, 230–31; rise in, 12–13; use of, to enhance leverage for home purchases, 218–23
Securities, mortgage-backed, investors in, 153–54
Securitization, 11–12; auto loan, 195; credit card, 195; future of, 194–95; GSE versus subprime, 195; impact of, on renegotiation of home mortgages, 179–84; private label, growth in, 144, 148–54
Securitization chain, redesign of, 197
Securitization process, 150, 150f
Senior Loan Officer Opinion Survey (SLOOS), 265–68; data, 93–96
620 FICO score point, 12
Soft information, banks and, 196
Spatial variations of housing booms and

busts, 105–7; cross-market, 105–6, 128–38; related literature on, 137–38; within-market, 105–6, 107–28
"Spec" (built-for-sale) housing, 91–92
Subprime lending, fall of, 158–63
Subprime market, development of modern, 148–49
Subprime mortgages, 11, 264; alternate view of development of, 167–68; effect of, on financial intermediation, 168–77; efficiency view of development of, 163–67; emergence and impact of, 163–79; increase in share of, 144; regulation and, 177–79; role of GSEs in, 374–77. *See also* Mortgages; Nontraditional mortgages
Subprime securitization, 195
Subsidized mortgages, 2

Terrorism Risk Insurance Act (TRIA), 404–5
Total assets, 248
Treasury International Capital (TIC) flows data, 248
Treasury International Capital (TIC) holdings data, 248
Treasury International Capital (TIC) reporting system, 248
Troughs, real house price, 58–66t

Variable CS, 292
Veterans Administration (VA), 363

Within-market spatial variation of housing booms and busts, 105–6, 107–8; in building permits, 126–28; data, 108–15; estimation equation for, 115–17; in rents, 124–26; results of estimation, 117–24. *See also* Cross-market spatial variation of housing booms and busts